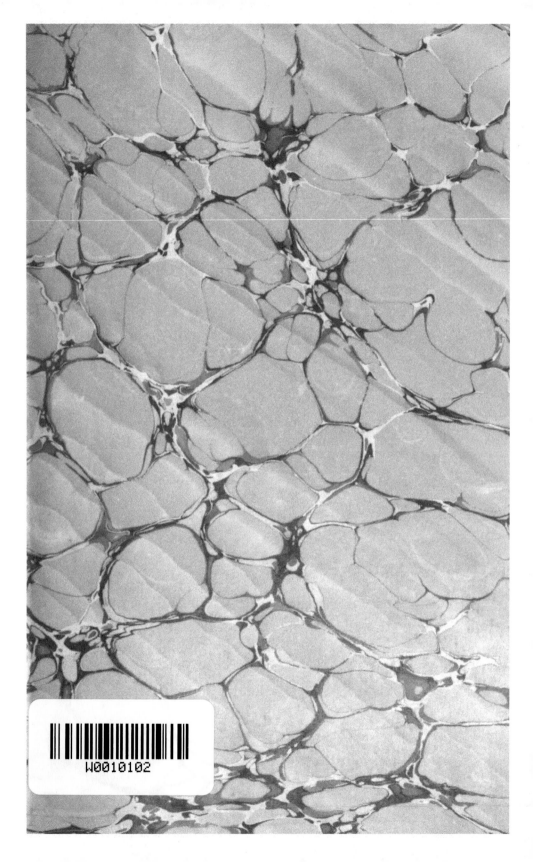

THE

Knickerbocker,

OR

60332

NEW-YORK MONTHLY MAGAZINE.

VOLUME XVIII.

NEW-YORK:

PUBLISHED BY JOHN BISCO, 121 FULTON-STREET.

1841.

INDEX.

THE KNICKERBOCKER.

Vol. XVIII.　　　　JULY, 1841.　　　　No. 1.

POPULAR POETRY OF MODERN GREECE.

FROM THE FRENCH OF M. FAURIEL.

LIKE all or nearly all the other nations of Europe, the Modern Greeks have two kinds, they might be called two grades, of poetry : one in all respects original and spontaneous, popular alike in substance and in form, traditional, and unwritten ; the other written, and into which labor and art, imitation and learning, enter more or less largely and more or less happily, according to times, places, and individuals.

The latter, springing up at about the same period with the modern literature of Europe, was at first, like that, the organ of the noblest thoughts and most refined feelings of the middle ages ; and if it has not since exhibited as lofty a flight and as complete a development, the two have never at all events been totally separated from each other, nor has it failed to attain for itself a striking degree of beauty and maturity. This portion of the vulgar* Greek poetry is, if not the most interesting, at least the most extensive and varied, and comprehends the most curious and the oldest productions, as well as the most ingenious and finished compositions.

But it is not of this portion that I propose to treat : such an undertaking would carry me far beyond the limits within which I am circumscribed. My design is simply to communicate, with considerable minuteness of detail, some idea of the other branch of Modern Greek poetry ; a poetry popular in every sense and in all the force of the term ; a direct and faithful reflection of the national character and spirit, known and felt by every Greek from the fact that *it* is Greek ; that it dwells on the soil and breathes the air of Greece ; a poetry in short, which lives not a factitious and often but apparent life in books, but in the people themselves, and in all the life of the people.

From the diversity of their subjects, the popular songs of the Greeks may all be arranged in three leading classes, domestic, historical, and romantic, or imaginative.

Under the title of *domestic* I include such as have been composed

---

* *Vulger* is here used as synonymous with *modern*, in opposition to *ancient* or *classic*.

expressly to be sung in the most solemn circumstances of the household and established festivals, and in compliance with social customs consecrated by immemorial usage. Of these there are several divisions, which I shall distinguish from each other as I advance, first speaking of those which appertain to social customs prevailing at particular yearly epochs, or festivals. An explanation of the mode in which two of the principal of these epochs, St. Basil's Day and the First of March, are observed, will furnish a sufficient illustration.

The feast of St. Basil is kept by the Greek church on the first of January, and that day is in Greece, as throughout Europe, a day of visits, compliments, and gifts, but with this difference, that in Greece every thing is conducted with more solemnity, with more amiability, and above all, more poetically than elsewhere. Companies of young people assemble and repair to the houses of their acquaintances to wish them a happy new year, and secure the customary presents. Now in every village, in every canton, this custom gives rise to a series of songs which belong to it exclusively, and it is to a certain national imprint of gracefulness, benevolence, and imagination, by which these songs are all more or less marked, that the festival in question is indebted for its character and interest.

The first of the series is in honor of the master of the house at which the young singers are visiting, and is addressed immediately to him. A second is sung in honor of the mistress, and is succeeded by as many others as there are persons to be complimented. If there be a son nearly grown, a separate song is devoted to him, and should he have sisters, they are not overlooked. The absent members of the family receive also their share of poetical remembrance and good wishes, some pretty verses of regret on their account being always recited to their friends who are present. In short, whatever can interest the family, whatever affords the opportunity of evincing sentiments of good will and esteem, becomes the theme of a particular song.

It may be added, that the youthful visiters, while passing into the dwelling, preface their complimentary songs by a special one in honor of the holiday and of St. Basil.

The First of March is as poetical a day in Greece as St. Basil's, and is celebrated very much as is the first of May in some other countries. Troops of young people and of children go from door to door singing the return of Spring, and collecting trifling presents, consisting commonly of eggs, cheese, or any product of the fields. Among several songs intended for this festival, there is one more remarkable than the rest, and peculiarly appropriate, on which, as I shall refer to it again, a few words only are here necessary. The song alluded to, which is a favorite through all Greece under the name of *Song of the Swallow*, is an artless outpouring of the indefinable delight imparted by the first breeze of Spring in a beautiful clime. It is sung by the children, bearing in their hands the figure of a swallow rudely carved in wood, and fitted to a species of mill, about which it is made to revolve rapidly by means of a string winding and unwinding on a small cylinder, to one end of which it is attached.

The other popular poems which I place, like the preceding, under the head of *domestic*, are those to which that denomination is more especially applicable, as they turn upon the most important incidents, the joys and sorrows of domestic life. I shall restrict myself to those which relate to departure for foreign countries, and to the solemnization of marriages and of funerals. [*]

The *funeral songs*, in which the death of relatives is deplored, have obtained the appellation of *Myriologia.* The myriologues are similar to the other domestic songs of the Greeks in this, that they are equally universal and equally dedicated to the specific purpose of each. But they present peculiarities which manifest their connection with some of the most prominent features of the national character and genius. I shall hereafter consider the kind and degree of poetic power which they require and imply, and now proceed with a rapid sketch of the funeral ceremonies of which they are a part, and with which they must always be looked upon as united.

A sick man has just breathed his last : his wife, mother, daughters, sisters, in a word, such of his nearest female relatives as are at hand, close his eyes and mouth, each giving free course to the grief inflicted by the calamity, according to her disposition and the strength of her attachment. This first duty discharged, they all withdraw to the house of some relation or friend in the vicinity, where they change their garments and array themselves in white, and as for the nuptial ceremony, except that their heads are uncovered and their hair unbound and pendant. While they are thus occupied, other women are attending to the corpse ; they clothe it from head to foot in the best apparel, and in this state lay it upon a very low bed, with the face uncovered and turned toward the east, and the arms crossed upon the breast.

These preparations being over, the relatives return in their mourning-dress to the house, leaving the doors open, so that all the women of the place, friends, neighbors, or strangers, may enter after them. A circle is formed around the corpse, and their grief breaks out anew and, as before, without measure or restraint, in tears, shrieks, or words. These irrepressible and simultaneous plaints are soon followed by lamentations of a different nature, that is to say, by myriologues. Ordinarily that of the nearest relative comes first ; after her, the remaining relatives, friends, or mere neighbors, in a word, all the women on the spot, who possess the ability, bestow this last tribute of affection one after another, and sometimes a number together. Not unfrequently there are found in the circle of assistants, women who have recently lost one of their own kindred, whose hearts are yet overflowing with sorrow, and who have some communication to make him. In the dead before them, they behold a messenger who will convey to the dead for whom they mourn, fresh testimony of their recollection and regret, and in consequence a myriologue destined for the latter is delivered to the former. Others content themselves with throwing on the deceased bouquets of flowers, or various light articles, which they implore him to be so good as to transmit to their friends in the other world.

The delivery of the myriologues is not interrupted until the arrival of the priests to accompany the corpse to the place of interment, and is still prolonged until the funeral procession has reached the church.

---

[*] These are omitted in this translation.

They cease while the priests are engaged in prayer and singing, but recommence as the body is about to be lowered into the grave. Nor do they end with the rites of sepulture, but are renewed on fixed occasions for an indefinite space of time. First, for a whole year from the day on which the death has taken place, the females of the family are permitted to sing myriologues only; every other song, however melancholy, however befitting the most serious impressions which the ideas of death, the grave, and a last farewell, can produce, would be reputed a diversion incompatible with the reverence due to the dead. Nor is this all: whenever they go to church, the women seldom omit, either before or after divine service, to meet at the tomb and reiterate the adieu of the burial-day.

When one of their relatives dies in a foreign land, an image of the person is laid upon the funeral bed, partially clad in the garments of the individual whom it represents, and is then addressed with the same lamentations as if it were a real body. These myriologues are still more full of sadness than others, as the inability to deposit and preserve in consecrated ground the remains of the beloved object is regarded as adding to the weight of the affliction.

Mothers also compose for their deceased infants myriologues which are often exquisitely pathetic. The child is bewailed under the emblem of a flower, a bird, or any thing in nature sufficiently beautiful for a mother's fancy to experience pleasure in conceiving a resemblance between it and her lost darling.

From what has been said, the reader must have inferred what I now explicitly state, that the myriologues are invariably composed and sung by women. The men bid _their_ final adieu at the moment when the corpse is committed to the earth : it is simple and laconic, being confined to a few familiar words, and kissing the lips of the deceased. They are or may be present while the women are singing their myriologues around the bed, but are always silent. I have never heard of a myriologue by a man, and if such cases have been known, they must have been exceptions to the existing practice. I say _existing practice_, because there are reasons for believing that at no very remote period, myriologues were, in some districts of Greece, repeated by the men. In Asiatic Greece and the Greek islands there are female myriologists by profession, whose services are procured for a regular compensation.

A myriologue is essentially distinguished from other popular poems by its being never prepared beforehand and at leisure, but always extemporized at the instant when it is uttered, and always adapted to the individual. It is, in the full signification of the word, a funeral poetical improvisation, inspired by sorrow.

Improvisations of this kind are always in verse, and the verse always in the usual metre of songs in general. They are likewise always _sung_, and to an air differing in different places, but which in any given place continues invariably employed in this department of poetry. The air is plaintive, as is suited to the subject, and slow enough to allow time for the words to make their way to the imagination, which is groping at random, uncertain whether, or how, it shall retain them. This air, unlike the majority of ordinary songs, terminates with very sharp notes. As to the length of myriologues, there is no prescribed and settled rule ; though sometimes very great, it commonly does not exceed that of other popular songs — that is to say, they are generally very short.

It is not, assuredly, without a violent effort of self-command, and an astonishing species of internal metamorphosis, that timid, ignorant, and uncultivated women accomplish the task which custom has imposed upon them. That task is indeed singularly difficult. They are obliged at a precise moment, a moment when grief has overwhelmed their ordinary faculties, to call up a power which they do not know to exist within them — the power of controlling, of subduing that grief in such a manner as to bring it out under the pleasing form of poetry and music, and that in sight of a crowd more or less numerous, which is concentrating on them its attention, and waiting to be kindled into emotion ! Frequently therefore, they are seen to fall, overcome by faintness in their exertion to rise, if I may so express myself, to the requisite elevation of tone.

But if the Grecian women are endowed with the poetic skill demanded and presumed in the improvisation of a myriologue, they are not all, as may well be supposed, on an equality in this respect. Some are eminently gifted, and their superiority operates as a title to consideration among their companions. These are specially invited to bid the farewells to the dead, and are expected to produce such as will awaken the sympathies of the hearers. A woman is noted in her village as a good myriologist, in nearly the same way as an accomplished improvisatore would attract observation in Italy.

It is perhaps with the view of acquiring this description of talent, perhaps from an instinctive thirst for lively and tender emotion, that the female villagers in some parts of Greece often exercise themselves in the open air, and amid the labors of the field, in composing fictitious myriologues, that is, myriologues which they have no occasion to use. They are sometimes founded upon events which have actually happened, but which do not directly affect the composer, such as the death of a neighbor or a stranger ; at other times they are based on occurrences purely hypothetical, or even fantastical, such as the wilting of a flower, the death of a lamb, a bird, or other animal.

It would appear from the foregoing remarks in relation to myriologues, that they constitute the most valuable portion of the popular Modern Greek Poetry, but from the nature of the case it is also that portion of which it is least easy to procure specimens wherewith to satisfy the reader's curiosity. A *bona fide* myriologue escapes from the mind without passing through the memory : the individual by whom it is pronounced is always in a state of unnatural excitement, in which she is incapable of watching her own actions and language, and that incapacity is as it were the condition on which alone she is enabled to perform the duty assigned her. Nothing is left in her mind but a confused consciousness of the temporary energy, the transient enthusiasm, with which she has spoken ; *what* she has spoken is unknown or unremembered. As to the assistants, and especially the men, who, taking no share in the myriologues, have only to listen, they are rendered by this very habit insensible either of curiosity or impatience ; they can recollect here and there some passages by which they have been more forcibly struck than by others, but that is all : in general, a myriologue is forgotten as soon as concluded.

Judging from the small number of fragments before me, their chief characteristic seems to be a passionate excitement, almost the delirium of grief. Here, doubtless, as every where, there are many common-place ideas and conventional phrases. But unquestionably also there are myriologues which are the offspring of a powerful inspiration, drawing forth the deepest secrets of the soul, and in which grief assumes an original and, if I may avail myself of the expression, entirely individual accent.

J. A.

A DEAD LANGUAGE.

Mute 'neath the shade of all the grove,
Mute in the faltering tones of love,
  Are the Cadmean letters old ;
Mute when the steed is urged to war,
Mute when the conqueror mounts his car,
  And when the beggar pleads for gold.

The boy with beauty on his brow,
The maiden when she plights her vow,
  Speak not Athena's music words ;
Nor to his dogs the shepherd bold,
When springs upon the parting fold
  The black wolf, feared of all the herds.

Nor from the oracle revered,
Nor round the Stadium where they cheered
  The victors in Olympia's games,
Nor from the gay or thoughtful throng,
Nor on Saphonian lips in song,
  Are heard her proud and princely names.

Ah! where has fled dear Hella's speech ?
Ionia's too no mothers teach,
  Nor lovely childhood prattles more :
Silent through all her bright domains,
They seem not native to her plains,
  Their voice is hushed upon her shore !

I see her hills, the clouds that kiss !
Upon her famed Acropolis,
  Of all her race, behold the shades !
Her Homer's lyre no hand can sweep,
And he who erst addressed the deep,
  And warriors with their gleaming blades.

The Grecian tongue is cold in death !
Yet ere expired its mighty breath,
  The temple's proudest niche had won ;
Above her marble's faultless mould,
Above her canvass' gorgeous fold,
  It bears her name eternal on !

Her structures all in ruins lie,
Her gods have left the heights to die —
  Her iron code no man obeys ;
Yet still her Plato's holy dreams,
And all that gave her poets themes,
  The plastic mind to beauty sways.

O! on the Words that man hath made,
The hues of youth can never fade,
  Nor Time's corroding fingers soil ;
The garments of the Soul are they,
And viewless else, would fleet away
  Her matchless and inspiring spoil !

B. F. P.

𝔇𝔲𝔰𝔱 𝔬𝔣 𝔗𝔯𝔞𝔟𝔢𝔩.

NUMBER ONE.

A BALL AT THE TUILLERIES.

LEANING one morning over the balcony of my hotel window in the Rue ——— , watching the living stream as it flowed toward the Boulevards, I observed a chasseur draw up at our porte-cochére.   He drew from his sabretache a large sealed paper, which he handed to our portress, who obligingly came out of her den to attend to him, then struck spurs into his horse, and cantered up the street.   I followed him with my eye as he dashed right and left among the omnibuses and backney coaches, till he turned the corner of the Rue de Provence, and was endeavoring to conjecture the object of so much despatch, when I heard a tap at my door, and a servant made his appearance. It was my obliging friend Baptiste, a cherry-cheeked Normand, who presented, with immense deference, a letter to my address, which he said was from the King, and had just been delivered.   It was stamped 'Maison du Roi, Service du Roi.'   So, curious to know what his Majesty might have to say to me, I broke the royal seal, and drew from the envelope a letter-sheet, twice-folded, containing pretty much as follows :

'MONSIEUR: ' Aux Tuilleries, ce 20 Fevrier, 183–.

  'J'ai l'honneur de vous apprendre qui vous etes invité au bal qui sera donné au Palais des Tuilleries, dans la soirée du vingt huit Fevrier courant. J'ai l'honneur, etc., etc.

                                                          'LE BARON A——,
  ' Les hommes en uniforme.'   'Aide de Camp du Roi.'

These invitations to the Tuilleries were at that time so profusely distributed, owing to the wish of the Citizen King to extend his popularity, that the Parisian wags called them 'Giboulées de Mars.'   But the honor was none the less to be prized because it was shared with several thousand persons.   More than one consultation did I hold with Staub, (the Parisian Stultz,) to settle the details of dress and decoration.

Behold us at length, on the evening of the ball, equipped in *habit de cour*, sword, chapeau, with an eagle in the cockade, to give what Webster calls the odor of nationality ; behold a couple of the sovereign people thus disguised, in a *voiture de remise* — no hackney coaches being admitted within the royal precincts — rolling down the Rue de la Paix, in the direction of the palace.   We were hardly half way across the Place Vendôme, when the carriage drew up close by the column.   On inquiring the cause, ' *Monsieur nous sommes à la queue*,' said the coachman.   This information being confirmed by our sable adherent behind, another of the sovereign people, we concluded that to unfold so prodigious a tail would probably require an hour or two ; so my companion composed himself in his corner for a snooze.   At a rate rather trying to mortal patience, the file dragged its slow length around the corner of the Rue Castiglione, from which point I could see that the train had grown prodigiously in our rear.

While crawling along the Rue de Rivoli, we had abundant leisure to contemplate the dingy old 'Chateau,' whose illuminated windows were throwing a blaze of light over the deserted gardens. Was ever edifice so ridiculous, for a palace, as the Palace of the Tuilleries? that is, as to its exterior? If it were not that the sanctifying influence of historical association consecrates every stone in the old-fashioned building, it would long ago have given place to a structure more in accordance with the refined and classical taste of the French people. The dusky front is loaded with niches and pannels, and busts, statues, vases, rosettes, and festoons; the peaked roof rises amid clusters of sprouting chimnies, in the semblance, as Geoffrey Crayon observes, of a gendarme's cocked hat; the quadriform cupola that surmounts the central tower reminds you of the cover of a potato-dish, and the pavillions at the wings are not unlike overgrown sentry-boxes.

At last we rumbled through the arched *guichet* of the Cour du Carrousel, which was guarded by a few municipal dragoons, radiant in helm and jack-boot, and followed across the court a line of lampions that led up to the principal entrance of the palace. The carriage doors were thrown open in a twinkling, and out we skipped, with more haste than dignity, while the vehicle was almost whisked from under us. We entered the vestibule, signing to our retinue to join the army of attendants drawn up on the left, while we turned to the right, and delivered our letters of invitation to a couple of ushers in black, who stood backed by a quantity of police and military. At the foot of the grand staircase was stationed a regimental band in full blast, who were making the walls ring with the overture to Norma. Though we ascended the noble flight with the reflection that the foot of Napoleon himself had often pressed that very marble, yet nothing portentous occurred on the occasion, and it seemed no such difficult matter after all to tread in the footsteps even of an Emperor.

The rooms where the ball was given were the principal suite, occupying the main building, from wing to wing exclusive, and looking on one side into the gardens, and upon the other into the court of the Carrousel. We first entered the Galerie de Diane, which might be as large as our city hotel assembly-room. The lighting up, that essential component, according to French notions, of a *joli bal*, was brilliant in the extreme. Only one set had been danced, and the floor was forming for a second. Along the walls, in graded rows, sat some of the loveliest women of the capital, with tints and toilettes yet fresh as the morning rose. The moment the music struck up, we pursued our devious route amid the crowds that surrounded the quadrilles, now dodging a 'cavalier seul,' now chassée-ing right and left. Passing through the Salle Louis Phillippe, crowded like the first with dancers, we gradually insinuated ourselves — my companion being familiar with the ground — into the Salle des Maréchaux, where the increased brilliancy of the uniforms, a greater density and diminished movement of the masses, who faced principally in one direction, indicated the presence of royalty.

This is a noble saloon, occupying the middle tower, (*Tour de l'Horo-loge,*) of equal dimensions on each side, with a vaulted ceiling, formed by the great central dome, and a narrow railed gallery, extending around the walls at a considerable height from the floor. It is hung with the full-length portraits — hence its name — of the living Marshals of France ; one of the frames being then vacant by the death of Marshal Mortier, Duke of Trevise, one of the victims of Fieschi's Infernal Machine. There was but one cotillion formed here ; this was directly in front of the King ; in it his daughters were dancing, and for their benefit Tolbecque's band in the gallery was giving the then novel and fashionable quadrilles of the Postillon de Lonjumeau, with percussion cap accompaniment, staccato. It was rather a tedious process to filter through the throng, but at length we gained a position tolerably near the front. The lookers-on formed a vast crescent enclosing the dancers, and facing the benches on which sat the Royal Family, backed by the dames d'honneur, wives of foreign ministers, and inmates of the Chateau. The King occupied the middle of the front bench. He was dressed in the simple uniform of a Colonel of the National Guard, with white pantaloons coming under the boot. He wore no star, cordon, or other sign of his rank. He is rather thick, and under the middling height, but as this is owing to the shortness of his legs, the defect is not remarked when he is seated. Though nearly sixty-five years of age, his brown wig curled into a graceful top-knot of the old school, and sparse gray whiskers, brushed jauntily forward, gave to his bronzed and furrowed features the look of a well-preserved gay campaigner of fifty. The narrowness of his forehead, and the breadth of the lower part of his face, though not unpleasing, but on the contrary rather giving dignity to his countenance, reminded one of a caricature of the royal physiognomy, under the semblance of a pear, just then very popular, on account of an unsuccessful prosecution of the artist, and the fruitless endeavors of the police to suppress its circulation. There was a stereotyped smile upon his features, and he occasionally half closed his eyes, as though he were near-sighted.

On his right was the Queen, Amelie, a thin, refined-looking woman, considerably past her prime. She wore a hat, and her very light hair, almost white, was créped and frizzed into vapory curls about her eyes, which were marked by the shadowy circle that Bulwer considers an ' indication of the mind or the heart overtasked.' She had a sad and tearful expression of countenance, owing, it was said, to her incessant anxiety for the safety of her husband, who was just about these times a favorite target for the bullets of the republicans. She looked the gentle and benevolent character the world gave her credit for. On the King's left sat his sister, Madame Adelaide, in a turban and dress of white and gold, a masculine-looking person, the very image of himself, with the same prominent weather-worn features. She must have seen a good deal of the world, but detraction has never breathed upon her name. She is said to be privately married to an aide-de-camp of the King. The fine hotel in the Rue de Varennes, occupied by our dashing fellow countryman, Colonel Thorn, is her property. The rest of the long bench was vacant on either side. The princesses, girls of eighteen or twenty, were dancing with great glee under their mamma's eye, with rather ineligible looking partners, for one was bald and the other corpulent. The elder of the two sisters, Marie, who afterward married the young Duke Alexander of Wurtemberg, and met with an untimely end, was a blonde like her mother, with an oval countenance and regular features. Clementine, the younger, had dark hair and eyes, but an aquiline nose almost too salient for beauty. They were both *en cheveux*, and wore simple white dresses of gauze over silk, gathered with a rose at the knee.

After a set or two had been danced, an onset of the waltzers broke through the thick array of our thronged legion, and we backed and sidled with the rest until we were enabled to retreat through a side door that led out upon the great balcony. A couple of vacated chairs invited us to contemplate at ease the fine view beneath us, of the gardens, and the river, and the long lines of light stretching through the Elysian Fields to the Triumphal Arch at the Barriére du Trône. From this window Louis le Grand no doubt often exhibited himself to the admiring gaze of his enthusiastic subjects, leaning perhaps his august elbows upon the very railing where we presumptuously rested the soles of our pumps.

The waltz over, we reëntered the room, and not to be singular, contrived each to extract a partner from the triple row of beauty that graced the walls, depositing sword and chapeau to guard the vacated seat; no idle precaution—for when, after sporting the fantastic toe, I reconducted the lady, I found her place so much encroached upon, that I thought myself lucky in detecting my sword-hilt under the elbow of a plump dowager, and in rescuing my oppressed chapeau from the folds of her satin dress.

Amid the assemblage of fine women, our own country was well represented. Boston and New-York would have felt proud of their daughters. Our Minister's lady and her youngest daughter sat in the row behind the royal family. Next to her was the Countess Le Hon. the Belgian Ambassadress, a celebrated beauty, blazing with diamonds, and very much *decollerée*. The world gave her credit for attracting the homage of the young heir apparent, the Duke of Orleans. But he was at the moment beyond the influence of her charms, being in the gallery, leaning with folded arms upon the balustrade, and engaged in a flirtation with a young lady that looked like an English girl. He was a remarkably handsome, fair-haired young man, with a bloom upon his cheeks, and an air of modest diffidence, unlike his flaxen-headed brother, the Duc de Nemours, whose insipid features are stamped with an expression of insufferable arrogance.

The military uniforms seemed to predominate over the plainer court dresses. There were English hussars, Austrian hulans, and Russian lancers, jostling the wearers of cracbats, grand cordons, and gold-bedizzened diplomatists. A conspicuous figure on the floor was a sandy-haired individual, in complete highland costume, with a lady on each arm. This proved to be a great Scotch duke, with his wife and daughter. He held by the sheath a claymore, with a golden basket-hilt, given to one of his ancestors by James the First. This worthy succeeded in attracting the attention of the King, and was presently conducted by an aide toward the royal seat. As Louis Philippe politely rose and held him in conversation, the ladies of the circle had an opportunity of admiring the highlandman's bony shanks, his golden sword-hilt, which he seemed to hold up to the King's nose, his kilt and plaid, philibeg, and other interesting nationalities.

The Greek ambassador brushed past us, in his national dress. He

was a hideous fellow, with a fiery, bulbous nose, embedded in a mous-
tache like a shoe-brush. To a poet he might suggest the morning
sun upon Olympus. He was no small favorite with the ladies, though
for the smiles and bows he received from them, as he went down the
line, he must have been mainly indebted to his scarlet scull-cap, and
gold-laced caftan, and snowy unmentionables, and embroidered leg-
gins.

The next room was devoted to refreshments. Behind a sort of
counter, extending across it, were lines of servants, who furnished from
tables behind them, to those visitors that presented themselves, such
simple restoratives as tea, ices, cake, groseille, and eau sucrée.
Profitting a moment by this royal attention to our wants, we went on
to the next saloon, occupied by card-players and betters, politicians
and diplomatists. At one of the écarté tables sat Count d'Appony,
the Austrian plenipotentiary, magnificently attired as a Hungarian
magnate. A sort of crimson *dolman*, lined with ermine, hung empty-
sleeved from one shoulder, but tied across his chest with a golden
cord ; his red morocco boots, reaching to the middle of the calf, were
seamed and bordered with gold, and seamed to make part of his pan-
taloon collant, which showed a pretty fair stage leg. A curved scime-
tar, in a golden-chased sheath, was suspended by chains in front, in the
oriental style, and around his neck was a jewelled collar of some
order. He seemed by his attitudinizing to be conscious of the admiration excited by his theatrical dress. Upon a bench near the same
table, sat our Minister, General CASS, in conversation with Lord
Granville, the British ambassador. The two men were not very unlike, except that the General's wig was brown, and the Earl's was
blonde. There was no mistaking their nationality, however, for all
the embroidery on the republican's simple *habit de cour* did not equal
the gold lace upon the Englishman's breast.

We strolled on into the deserted throne-room, at the farther end of
which, a door leading to the private apartments of the royal family,
was stationed an usher, ready to give a hint if necessary to any over-in-
quisitive guest. A throne has no terrors when there is no king upon it.
Napoleon once defined it to be merely ' *six planches de sapin et un
tapis de velours.*' So we insolently seated ourselves upon the steps,
by way of verifying the mighty emperor's definition.

On returning among the dancers, we found that his Majesty, with
half the ladies in his train, had disappeared in the direction of the
supper room, and that an invading army of hungry gentlemen, with
difficulty held in check by a few retainers, were besieging that important *place-forte*. It reminded one of the steam-boat scenes on the
Hudson, when the impatient travellers, with appetites sharpened by
the river breeze, congregate about the avenues to the dining cabin, in
momentary expectation of the dinner bell. We joined the formidable body of invaders, necessarily locking up a position near the rear.
Many of the ladies must have gone home supperless that night, for
after the first descent, the tables were given up to the tender mercies
of the men. But in what a style did we make our entrée ! Where
was that elegant courtesy, and mutual preference of each other's comfort, for which Frenchmen are so renowned ? There was not even
the affectation of the thing. Shade of Louis the Great ! how we dug

our elbows and hilts into each other's sides! But being all pretty well padded, there were probably no ribs broken, though there must have been some coats torn. A fellow countryman, whom we recognized at a distance in the crowd, held up his tattered sleeve by way of salutation, and made some observation in English about court manners, that must have been offensive if it had been understood by his neighbors ; but they only smiled.

We were borne along by the current through the corridors toward the Salle de Spectacle, in the northern wing, or Pavillon de Marsan, where the supper was given. We entered by folding doors opposite the stage, on the first tier of boxes. Upon the pit, which was floored over on a level with the stage, as well as in the first tier, which was dismantled for the purpose, were spread vast concentric tables, resplendent with candelabras, and loaded with delicacies. Behind the guests were rows of attendants in the boiled-lobster colored livery of the palace. In the upper boxes were ladies with plumed heads looking down upon the banquetters below. We passed to the left in the first tier, at a hint from an usher, and slid into the first vacant places. There was nothing peculiarly royal about the eatables, which were merely in good taste and great abundance. A claret jug of fine Bordeaux was placed at my elbow, and my champaigne glass kept constantly full by a fellow behind me. Bearing in mind the expectants to come after us, I lost no time in attacking a Mayonnaise and demolishing a pheasant; swallowed a few jellies, confitures de bar, and ices à la plombiéres, the most delicious kind of ice that is made, and was glad to withdraw, while yet able, from the annoying attentions of my solemn friend in the rear, with the inexhaustible champaigne bottle.

The King of the French had gone to bed, at least he had gone home ; but his renovated guests were in no such humor. Louder than ever rang through the saloons the quadrilles of Cosimo and the Huguenots, and Strauss' inspiriting waltzes. There is a limit, however, to the magic of Tolbacque's wand, and even to the saltatory powers of Parisian legs. Toward four o'clock, the refluent tide poured down the grand stair-case. The crush-room in the vestibule, screened from the fresh air by a glass partition, was now filled with muffled groups waiting for their carriages, whose successive arrival was announced by a gigantic porter, with a voice like an earthquake. There was some entertainment in observing the personages as they moved off in acknowledgment of their names. ' Les gens de Madame la Marquise de St. Betise !' Here a little lady with a tall moustached cavalier slipped out. 'Les gens de Monsieur le Comte de Boute-Jac !' Forth stepped a powdered antediluvian, wearing the cross of Saint Louis. ' Les gens de Monsieur Tonson !' roared the porter, at the top of his lungs. I observed through the scenes the opened countenance of our sable Ariel, and recognized the sonorous patronymic which I had desired him to give in for us. Several heads were turned inquiringly to see who might be the fortunate bearer of that historical name. But we were just then too busily engaged with a lady's shawl to satisfy the public curiosity, and suffered the carriage to be driven on, to give place to ' the Marquis of Carabas' people !'

To wait till our turn should come round again, in order to depart with dignity and safety, were intolerable, and to venture into the court on foot were at the risk of life and limb, owing to the furious cross-driving, to say nothing of a Scotch mist that was falling at the moment. But a bachelor's neck seems to be of no consequence to any body in particular; so ascertaining the whereabout of our coupé, which had cut out of the file, we made a desperate sortie, dashed across the court, escaped pulverization by a miracle, and rolled out of the royal pre-cincts, resolved to make up upon our morning pillow for the midnight hours of our BALL AT THE TUILLERIES.

NIGHT.

BY JOHN LOVE LAWRIE.

Upon the highest mountain's head
  Thou liest like some dark dream;
And in the vale thy hand is spread
  O'er rock, and tree, and stream ;
And solemn sounds thou utterest,
  For a mystic voice is thine,
And the mournful words thou mutterest
  Loud swell, or soft decline.

How beautiful art thou, O Night !
  Within thy pinions' shade
A thousand stars are twinkling bright,
  Upon the lonely glade;
And the dreaming wave is hush'd to rest,
  And the dew is on the flower,
And the zephyrs kiss the heaving breast
  Of many a perfumed bower.

How wonderful art thou, O Night !
  Thou liest dark and still,
And the sorrowing planets give no light
  Upon the darkened hill;
And the languid ocean throweth
  Its billows to the shore,
And the mountain streamlet goeth
  With a dull and solemn roar.

How terrible art thou, O Night !
  The winds are on the flood,
And the fiery planets in affright
  Along their temple scud :
And the Thunder's voice is talking,
  As he swoopeth o'er the tide,
And the sheeted rain is stalking
  Along the mountain side !

And the ragged clouds are driven
  Like smoke athwart the sky,
And far along the heaven
  The lightning's glances fly :
Night cometh with its mantling shroud,
  It cometh dark and lone ;
With the hollow wind, and the inky cloud,
  And the forest's swelling moan !

THE POLYGON PAPERS.

NUMBER ONE.

'OF making many books there is no end.' — SOLOMON.

——'Denique
Nullum est jam dictum, quod non dictum sit prius.'— TERENCE.

'Ridentur malè qui componunt carmina.'— HORACE.

OF the majority of deceased authors it may be said, (with due reverence,) 'They rest from their labors, and their *works* do follow them;' and of almost all the living professors of the 'black art,' the same peaceful termination to their toils may safely be predicted. Yet in spite of the inglorious fate of so many of my predecessors, and regardless of the chilling truths quoted at the head of this chapter, I have enlisted in the army of authors. It is not that I consider myself either a wit, a poet, or a philosopher. As for the first, I can laugh at a good joke; for the second, I can admire the poetry of others; and my philosophy enables me to bear misfortune without blaspheming, or even making a very frightful face. Although, in common with all who wield 'the mighty instrument of little men,' I possess my share of vanity, yet I rank among those who, in the words of GöETHE, listen to the song of another with more pleasure than to their own.

Why then do I mount the fame-bound vessel, which is already borne down by a crowd of argonauts to the very water's edge, and whose adventurous cruisers must pass through the 'blue Symplegades' of criticism, and gain, at best, but a meed of barren praise, with scarce a hope of winning the '*Golden* Fleece?' First, because every body writes; and, detesting an unfashionable character, I must 'follow the multitude to do evil.' I have been reading, studying, and observing, in my manner, for the best part of half a life, and have just discovered that I am far behind the spirit of the times; that the age of study has departed, and the period of universal authorship commenced. Reversing the laws of supply and demand, and trampling on every principle of literary economy, all men are now producers, and none are consumers, save of their own crops.

Secondly. I *may* be modest overmuch, and possess all the qualities of wit, poet, and philosopher, in the happiest union, and richest abundance. I never injured mother Nature, and see not why she should have been less liberal to me than to others of her children. I behold all over the world thousands of authors, whose ideas are either good, but stolen, or original, but worthless. I cannot be more shallow than some of these fellows; and if the all-patronizing and most clearsighted public read or endure them, perhaps they may read or endure me. No one knows his capabilities till the hour of trial. 'Full many a gem,' etc.

Thirdly. I am a predestinarian, and thinking myself fore-ordained to be an author, I should be loth to thwart the decrees of Providence. I have often, particularly when irritated, felt a preternatural sparkling dart from the eye, like a flash of ordnance from Parnassus, and have

frequently looked alternately on the sky and the earth, in a manner
corresponding to the Shakspearian description of ' the poet's eye, in a
fine frenzy rolling.'   I have observed, too, that whenever I wear a
collar, which is seldom, it is very troublesome, and looks *so* aristocra-
tic ; it has an invincible propensity to turn downward, à la Byron ;
clearly indicating a poetic temperament.   Yes ! I can hardly be mistaken in all these symptoms of Apollo's presence.   The Delian god
has forced his bridle in my mouth, and his goad in my side ; and like
those of the Cumæan sibyl,

> —— ' Et pectus anhelum,
> Et rabie fera corda tument.'

The inspiration grows strong within me, and I *must* write.   Therefore
I make the venture ; and as every one, were the disguise torn
away, would be found to think himself the first of mundane beings,
so, till I see proof to the contrary, I shall believe myself a capital
writer, and cradle my vanity in the sweet delusion that the friends of
the ' Old Knick.' look with almost as much avidity for the crudities of
POLYGON, as they do for the mellow maturity of the inimitable
CRAYON.

I have adopted my multangular title, to express the character of my
efforts, which will be exercised on matters connected with criticism,
morality, education, manners, poetry, and myself, together with a
plentiful sprinkling of nonsense, just to make the whole agreeable.   I
would write connected essays, or perhaps publish a book *in extenso,*
on some fresh and interesting topic, such as the anatomy of flies, or
the flood of Noah, had not a few little matters of my own shattered
the uniformity of my feelings, and a very diversified course of study
and of life, imparted to my mind something of an impulsive and
erratic movement.

' Something too much of this,' quoth Fastidiosus.   ' I hate egotism.'
So do I, Sir, I assure you.   It is always in my way.   So practise your
own sermon, stranger.   Forget yourself awhile, and listen to me.

POLYGON.

> —— ' Vos exemplaria *clara,*
> Nocturnâ versate manu, versate diurnâ.' — HORACE.

My library is small, but thanks to a love of reading, inspired in me
so early that I almost think it innate, I have read most of the worthies
in the lighter branches of literature ; I have read them, and however
unskilfully arranged, they are there — in my mind.   I have domesti-
cated their delightful images, and, like tropical birds caged in an un-
genial climate, their rich plumage and ever-ringing notes deceive me
of many a grief, and often transform the cheerlessness and silence of
winter into the varied hues and warbling melodies of spring.   Ah !
would they could always abide !   Would that the spirit, worn and
ruffled by bickerings and broils, might always fly to Shakspeare for
relief, and rest beneath the warm-colored wings of that bird of paradise !   But, all-potent as he was, his most ethereal fancies cannot
change the harsh nature of man into kindness, or purchase a remission
of our being's hard law, the primeval sentence, to procure by daily
labor our daily bread.   How happy would be the poor foragers in the

fields of poesy, could the recital of a gem from the 'Romeo' discharge a tavern-bill, or a stanza of Spenser sate the cravings of a cormorant tailor! And how reasonable would it be thus to pay for supplying the wants of the body, by a draught on the bank of souls! How abundantly then would 'poor Goldsmith' have fared! When, feet-weary and heart-sick, the penniless wanderer had reached a peasant-hamlet, or the chateau of some 'grand Seigneur,' the narration of some striking incident in the history of Rome, or the paraphrase of some splendid passage from Rome's great poet, would have procured him a kindlier greeting, a more savory supper, and a warmer bed.

This, however, may be deemed by practical men a mere Utopian dream; well enough, perhaps, for green Arcadia, and a pastoral age, but wholly unsuited to the flesh-and-blood substantialities of prosaic life. Well, I grant it. For I too have some common-sense princi-ples, and no more expect to see mankind regulate all their affairs by romantic moonshine, or poetic star-light, than any money-changer in the nation. Let money be now, as it has ever been, the necessary medium for the supply of our wants. Be it that the visions of bards have never been a present reality — possessing only an imaginary ex-istence, and that in the preterite tense. Still it remains as solid and useful a fact as any thing which can be seen and handled, that these sweet creations of unbridled fancy are of great and permanent advan-tage to mankind; as much so as the construction of canals, the inven-tion of steam, or any other improvement which these practical men stare at and glorify so much. Why? Because they contribute to ren-der life endurable; because they afford unspeakable delight to many when steeped to the very lips in poverty and decay; because, in short, they are like a firmament of stars, which, whether noticed and honored, or neglected and spurned, continually shed, directly or by reflection, a lovely light upon a race wandering in darkness and grovelling in the mire. I myself am one among the majority — that is to say, I am but poorly satisfied with myself, either in memory or in prospect. My little aspirations, whether wise or unwise, whether by my own fault or that of others, have successively sunk in disappointment. But I have become familiar with the heroes of the pen; their bright paintings are before my eyes; their immortal music is in my ears; their noble thoughts are with me in all my daily walks; and in such company I am happy. The 'Dii Majores' of Helicon are around me. I hear their golden words; they converse in different dialects; yet their language is all one — the language of the heart. I attempt not to class them. I know not which is Jupiter, or which Apollo, or which Mercury. The niceties of rank and precedence among them I leave for the cold rules of critics to determine; for me they are gods — all gods; and I thank them for administering to the pleasures of a feeble mortal.

Yes! blessed be ye, forever blessed, ye elect of our race, ye chosen of humanity, who have opened fountains of healing for the heart-sick, and the spirit-broken; fountains which will not, like the pool of Bethesda, renovate the exhausted frame, but will 'minis-ter to a mind diseased,' and reërect the prostrate energies of the soul! Blessed be ye, forever blessed, because when sudden darkness overshadowed the landscape of my youth, your tranquil light beamed through the cold clouds, and made my night more sweet and quiet than the day. Ye are worthy of all worship; and may he who would pluck one leaf from your laurels, find it clinging to his own forehead, like a burning-iron, imprinting there a brand of indelible disgrace! Blessed be ye, grave Historians, who have lifted the mists of time from the ocean of the past, and revealed it to our eyes, all covered with gallant sails, and strewed, alas! with many a noble wreck!—a scene replete with tenderest impulses and noblest sympathy. Blessed be ye, sententious Moralists, who have planted buoys along that dangerous coast, to warn us of the rocks and shoals near which our vessels glide. Blessed be ye, above all, sweet Poets, thrice blessed forever, who have thrown the sunshine of your fancies over the stormy waves, and from the fairy islands of enchanted song sent many a summer breeze, more fragrant than the spicy gales of Araby the blest, 'making old Ocean smile!'

The word *book* has for me an indescribable charm, a talismanic power. It comes to my ear and heart laden with associations of delight. If ever an unpleasing remembrance be awakened by the name, it is that I have so often forsaken an unfailing friend for the falsehood and folly of the world. Books are the long-sought, long-dreamed-of philosopher's stone. They have the quality of transmuting this iron world into gold. When properly used, they give health, youth, and beauty, to our better and abiding part. They are the grand apothecaries' shop for diseased souls. They contain medicaments for every affliction—balm for every wound. The long array of bodily ills, so pathetically recounted by Milton's angel to our weeping progenitor, has throughout its counterparts in the mind. And in the medicine-chest of literature there are cures for all. Has Disappointment cropped the flowers of Hope? Here is Seneca, with many a wholesome restorative whereby thy mind may recover at least its firmness if not its elasticity. Hast thou 'ingorged greedily and without restraint' of the world's unwholesome viands, till thy sated palate yearns for a plainer diet? I will show thee a more healthy regimen; fruits fresh-gathered from the gardens of Hesperus, and goblets crowned with choicest liquor from the sparkling Heliconian fount. Eat; they are delicious as the apples of love, mentioned in the 'Song of Songs which is Solomon's.' Drink; these waters will refresh thy soul, and after them thy sleep shall be 'airy light, from pure digestion bred.' They will be to thee, after thy long sensual trance, like 'hock and soda-water' to the lip of a waker from a night's debauch.

Ah! how sorrowfully was Byron—hapless lord of the lyre!—mistaken, when he penned the line:

'Man, being reasonable, must get drunk!'

Rather say, man, being reasonable, must drink the pure spirituous wine, the true Falernian, which has grown stronger, and clearer, and mellower, for ages. Champaigne is a bubble, a flash-vapidity, and an aching head. This strengthens while it exalts. The most copious libation produces no crapula, no heart-burn. Here are no lees. This cup will soothe like opium, exhilarate like ether, and purge like hellebore. Has Cupid waved his purple wings above thy couch, shedding sweet and subtle poison on thy slumbers? Here is

Ovid, with his ' Ars Amatoria,' to teach thee how to lead the coy nymph a willing captive; or should she prove inexpugnable, here is the ' Remedia Amoris,' which will enable thee to shake off the fetters which clog thy manhood, and enter into thy soul. Here also are Juvenal, with his sixth satire; and Pope, and Young, who will instruct thee to despise the whole sex — ' a consummation,' however, ' devoutly to be' shunned — at the bare mention whereof Anacreon shudders, Apollo drops his lyre, and the Muses utter an unmelodious scream. Art thou ' aweary of this great world,' tired of wearing forever the hypocritical mask, of humoring a fickle multitude, and torturing thyself? Here is Zimmerman, whose reflections will make thee affect the life of ' cloistered sage and thoughtful eremite.' Retire then awhile from the dusty arena, and the noisy rostrum; not to Bolingbroke's unphilosophic and fretful solitude, but to a quiet loneliness, there to talk awhile with thine own inmost heart, and hold wise communion with the sages of the earth. Art thou, in fine, the victim of ennui, the most fiendish of the demon tribe; sick of the homespun dullness, the ' never-ending, still-beginning' monotony of this daily life? What more sure and pleasant remedy than the dreams of Poetry, and the witcheries of young Romance? Here is Shakspeare, with the rainbow colors of his fancy changing and flashing forever around him. Here is Milton, who will bear thee on soaring wing to a world which himself created, and which will never perish, till the aspiring spirit returns to the God who gave it.

I have rarely been more affected than in reading a description, given by Heyne, I think, of his feelings on first entering a library, replete with the treasures amassed by the prime spirits of all ages. His emotions were almost as overpowering as those of the Jewish lawgiver, when he took off his shoes because he was on holy ground. He was, as it were, in the company of innumerable spirits; the purest essence of their ' essential' was around him. His was the true spirit of a scholar, who will never open a dusty tome, though rude the print and decayed the binding, without first doing inward homage to the mind which conceived and inhabits it. It seems a species of profanity, to look with irreverent and careless eye on that which cost many a patient vigil, was consecrated by exalted purpose, and bequeathed to posterity, accompanied with fervent hope. If, in the beautiful belief of the Greeks, a dryad was imagined to inhabit every verdant oak, and a nymph to haunt each moss-girt fountain, how much more might we suppose the genius of the author to reside in every book, watching over the destinies of his beloved temple, and regarding with placid or vengeful eye all who approach the consecrated precincts.

Ah! how deceived are you, who deem the book-worm an object of commiseration! Poor worldlings! I care not, though his researches be among the dusty schoolmen; he reaps more real pleasure from those dry and repulsive volumes, than all your fun and frolic, your gold and glitter, can ever bestow on you. Those quips and quiddities have for him a poetic charm; not like your raptures, fluttering and evanescent, but deep and abiding. The labyrinths of technical discussion may seem to you forbidding as the portals of the grave; but to him they are delicious as the Garden of the Sun. While you are torturing soul and body to gain the smiles of beauty, and the plaudits of the world, he, no matter how unwisely, is giving peaceful exercise to an immortal mind. I never see an old, patient, unremitting student, without a mixed feeling of wonder, envy, and esteem. He seems to be apart from his kind ; 'among them, but not of them.' He has turned his steps from the crowded walks of life. The din of business thunders not in his ears ; the glare of fashion blazes not in his eyes. He has 'renounced the world, the flesh, and the devil,' and lives only in a universe of his own ; an ideal creation — a residence of spirits. Think you he is unhappy ? Look through the windows of his study. 'T is morning. Do you see him bending over that ponderous folio — devouring its pages, his daily, almost his only, food ? Look again. 'T is high noon. See you not still the movements of the same thin severe lip, and the same eager, though faded eye ? Look yet again. 'T is midnight. The light of his lamp falls dimly on his meagre face ; he pauses, trims it, and again his eyes are attracted and his soul absorbed by that endless combination of letters. And what is their subject ? What matter, whether it be the musty lore of the Jewish Talmud, the splendid dreams of Plato, or the dull details of the Byzantine historians ? It is sufficient that his energies are all drawn forth, and his interest all awakened. The clock strikes one, strikes two, and 'waning nature warns him to repose.' He sleeps, and dreams that he is walking through whispering groves, conversing with the old philosophers ; Plato and Aristotle, Aquinas and Bacon. Or perhaps he fancies that he has shaken off the fetters of sense, and that his intellect has sprung from its supine inertness, to its unbowed, native stature. He wakes to a renewal of toil. But it is no toil to him. It is the one great pleasure of his existence.

It may be said that his enjoyments are selfish and his spirit miserly. I admit that he does not shape his life toward its great and appropriate end — the happiness of mankind in conjunction with his own. Yet he does not purposely pursue a cold-hearted, isolated existence. So far as he thinks of mankind at all, he wishes their welfare. He stands in no one's light. He slanders none for his own advantage. He makes no man the stepping-stone for his ambition. He removes no land-marks. He covets not his friend's wife, he seduces not his neighbor's daughter. His solitary pursuits are, at the worst, of but negative injury to society ; that is, by the subtraction of his own investment from the general stock of human interests and pleasures.

Leaving it, however, for casuists to decide how far this isolation is reprehensible, I may safely say that he who is resolved to live for himself alone, and enjoy the maximum of private happiness, should by all means pursue the literary walk. The groves of Academus are shaded by greener trees, enamelled with brighter flowers, and watered by purer streams, than any profane haunt in this varied world. If he be blest with the spirit of contentment and economy, here he may find a safe and pleasant refuge from the cares of life. The feverish anxieties, the tumultuous pulsations, the sickening disappointments, that agitate the hearts of others, are unknown to the quiet scholar. No bankruptcy stares him in the face. His countenance fluctuates not with the changes of the stocks. He lives continually on the principal and interest of his wealth ; and so far from diminishing, it increases daily. Each succeeding moment gives him a more sumptuous fare, a richer garniture, a more exhaustless store. Kingdoms may rise, empires may decay ; they lessen not the grandeur of his prospect — they take not from the breadth and richness of his dominions. His possessions are in the past ; they are locked up in the store-house of memory ; and there ' neither moth nor rust can corrupt, nor thieves break through and steal.' He may apply to himself, with double significance, those lines of Dryden, in which he has improved even upon the noble original :

> ' Be fair, or foul, or rain, or shine,
> The joys I *have* possessed, in spite of Fate, are mine :
> Not Jove himself upon the past has power,
> But what has been, *has been*, and I have had my hour.'

POLYGON.

SOUL-HYMN.

BY JAMES ALDRICH.

FEELING dim and seeing,
  Unmingled with alloy,
Of my higher being
  I sometimes do enjoy.

Vague longings for the true,
  The beautiful and good,
And aspirations new,
  But dimly understood :

These, in calm hours, tell me
  Of powers yet unemployed,
Of a capacity
  For joys yet unenjoyed.

On, fond Soul ! believing,
  Though long the sought thou miss,
Toiling and achieving
  Thy duty and thy bliss.

If in faith thou firmly
  Push forward thy design,
Not doubting, earnestly,
  The vict'ry shall be thine.

With all the Now in view,
  The Past no grief awakes ;
What Time imposes, do,
  Forgetting what it takes.

Onward, in improvement,
  Through Ænon's circling flow,
With progressive movement,
  The soul must ever go.

Through swift changes flowing,
  The end is never nearer,
But the way is growing
  Fairer still, and clearer.

Soon falls this house of clay,
  Should I therefore repine?
Myself cannot decay,
  For the I AM is mine.

Forth shall my spirit's light,
  When common fate I share,
Like the broad sun at night,
  To shed its beams elsewhere.

Strong within me liveth
  Through all my outward strife,
This deep faith, which giveth
  My quiet inner life.

KNEMIDOLOGY.

> 'Looking round,
> With honest speculation in mine eye,
> In quest of food for thought, ' By Jove! 't is here!'
> Quoth I; ' in yonder huge and gloomy pile
> Of dusty boots is inspiration hid.
> Come, bustle, honest Muse, and help me sing
> In fanciful disportings on this theme.''
>
>   'BOOTS: A SLIPSHODICAL LYRIC.'

'KNEMIDOLOGY!—what new thing under the sun is that?' asks the curious reader. Well, I do not know the precise location of the word in Carlyle or Coleridge; the definition is not found in Webster; but thus, were it there, I doubt not it would be given: 'KNEMIDOLOGY, *n.*, [*Greek* κνημις, ιδος, *and* λογος.] The Philosophy of Boots.'

This is often said to be an age of utilitarian philosophy, whose all-searching inquisition no power can resist, no particle evade. With equal ease it has analyzed an atom, or unfolded a universe. It has numbered the minutest animalcules in a drop of water, and laughed at their uncouth gambols in the little lake; and it has held glorious converse with myriads of solar systems, and thrilled with the voiceless melody of the morning stars. Surely, then, so broad a mantle may cover the philosophy of boots.

Through every age, the boot has enforced attention as a principal article of dress. The figured sandal found on the musty mummies of most-ancient Egypt; the red and purple *cothurnus*, in the brilliancy of whose jewels sparkled the wealth of the Roman wearer; the 'light fantastic toes' of our immediate ancestors, that tripped through the mazy minuet; or the exquisitely-finished opera-boot of the present day, whirling along the dizzy dance, or eddying in the wanton waltz, all have been prime-ministers of Vanity.

Chaucer, the first twilight star that sparkled in the constellation of English poets, thus discourseth to the ardent lover on the make and fit of boots:

> 'Of shoon and bootes new and fair,
> Look at the least thou have a pair;
> And that they fit so fetously
> That these rude men may utterly
> Marvel, sith that they sit so plain,
> How they come on and off again.'

Gay, in his humorous ' Trivia, or Walking the Streets of London,' thus adviseth as to their wear and fashion :

> ' When the black youth at chosen stands rejoice,
> And ' clean your shoes' resounds from every voice ;
> When late their miry sides stage-coaches show,
> And their stiff horses through the town move slow ;
> Then let the prudent walker shoes provide,
> Not of the Spanish or Morocco hide ;
> The wooden heel may raise the dancer's bound,
> And with the scalloped top his step be crowned ;
> Let firm, well-hammered soles protect thy feet,
> Through freezing snows, and rains, and soaking sleet.
> Should the big last extend the shoe too wide,
> Each stone will wrench the unwary step aside ;
> The sudden turn may stretch the swelling vein,
> Thy crackling joint unhinge, or ankle sprain ;
> And when too short the modish shoes are worn,
> You 'll judge the seasons by your shooting corn.'

And melancholy Philips thus bemoans their doleful exit :

> ' My galligaskins that have long withstood
> The winter's fury, and encroaching frosts,
> By time subdued, (what will not Time subdue !)
> An horrid chasm disclosed, with orifice
> Wide discontinuous ; at which the winds,
> Eurus and Auster, and the dreadful force
> Of Boreas, that congeals the Cronian waves,
> Tumultuous enter, with dire chilling blasts,
> Portending agues.'

These three have here written their life in short-hand. All English poetry, from Chaucer to Wordsworth, is but their memoirs. No description is perfect, till ' brave knight' and ' fair ladie' are booted and slippered to your eye.

What intellectuality appears in the boot, when we consider it as an index of the qualities of the mind ! A boot characterizes a man as surely as his countenance. From the light finished boot of the city exquisite, to the heavy brogue of the laborer ; from the uncinctured sandal of the wily Jew, to the clattering wooden clogs of the clumsy, stolid German ; from the moccasin of the free, acute, and light-heeled Indian, to the small whimsical shoe of the mentally-chained and childish Chinese ; how aptly each character is typified ! Who does not see in the elegant ladies'-slipper the sylphide step, and the exquisite form and beauty of the wearer ? In the loose, bony-looking, knotty boot, professional intellect, redolent of musty manuscripts, and ponderous, dusty black-letter tomes ? Does not the open shoe of the child, slightly run down in the heel, speak of the frank carelessness of merry youth ? — and the light pump, of the active roving tar ? Who could ever mistake the character of the courtly and fantastic ' long-toe' of the elegant and witty Cavalier, for that of the unpolished democratic ' jack-boot' of the severe and sullen Roundhead ? We might go on to say how the buckskin slipper tells of literary gentlemen, in loose morning-gowns : the stout shoe, innocent of blacking, of the pay-per-day mechanic ; the neatly blacked half-boot of the established merchant, who is rich enough to discard the fine boots of his younger and poorer days, and to wear half-boots and old clothes ; but verily, boot, shoe, pump, slipper, gaiter, moccasin, and every individual of every species, in the whole relationship, has a marked individuality. ' But what boots it ?' quoth the reader.

We find tongues in trees and sermons in stones : there is as surely a language in boots.   When, with venerable pomp and sesqui-pedalian circumstance of gown, the dear dignified old pastor soberly paces up the long aisle of the village church, what an inviting though circumspect squeak do his good old boots then utter of boundless benevolence to the infirm and poor, and good will to all mankind! Their familiar voice, in humble cottage or high hall, is welcome as a voice from heaven.   And when, through length of years or untimely blight, a friend is laid beneath the sod, and as he turns sadly away, the coarse clods tumble and thump upon the polished mahogany, for entrance to their kindred clay, with what doleful lamentations, bruis-ing the long grass, do they sigh their sole-felt sorrow!   Nor that boots have a language will he deny, who hath noted the merry, modest, inquisitive chirp of the little child's slipper, or the half-smothered but good-humored squeak of the shoes of the portly country dame, on a butter-peddling visit to the city.

It is granted then that boots have language.   What is language? The medium of thought.   The possession of language, then, implies the power of thinking; that is, rationality.   To 'make assurance doubly sure.'   All allow that boots have soles.   To rational beings only souls are given.   So we arrive again, by another course of rea-soning, at the same conclusion.

It was a lovely night in August, when the following things came to pass.   During the day, I had been almost roasted alive by the in-tense sweltering heat of the sun.   At night I went to bed near the window, from whence I had removed each sash.   After lying a few minutes, I threw off the clothes to enjoy the night air, which, reduced to the delicious lukewarmness of a vernal day, swept across my moist brow and cheeks.   The bright moon and stars marched in full array through the infinite and cloudless blue; and I raised my head upon my hand, to gaze through my window upon the dim soft landscape which slept before me in the mellow light.   In that calm, happy, half-dozing state, I was just likening the distant winding line of fog, which hung and curled over the sparkling river, to a procession of sister spirits, clad in white, in fairy land; when suddenly I was startled by a rustling and hopping noise, apparently in my old boot-closet.   I turned my head and listened.   Again it was repeated.   'A concealed robber!' thought I; and hastily half-dressing, I stepped lightly over and applied my eye to the latch-hole.   I leaped back immediately, as half-a-dozen ricketty, bare-boned old rats, that somehow gnawed a scanty sustenance around the old corners, flew like lightning out of the old rat-hole in the corner of the door, over my bare feet; and with their stumps of teeth chattering, and their glassy eyes popped half out with fright, they scrabbled and rolled, heels over head, the whole way down stairs.

Now this old closet had for years been a general depository for the cast-off boots and shoes of the family; and scattered over the place, all dusty, and some green and mouldy with age, lay in beautiful con-fusion the pedestals of several generations.

Again peering through the latch-hole, I could scarcely believe my eyes, when I saw one of the old musty rascals leisurely and stealthily hopping and shuffling himself toward the door where I stood. At one moment his big mule-ears were intently listening forward; at the next, he blew and shook off the accumulated dust of many an idle year. In a few minutes he was immediately beneath me, on the other side of the door, lying down, with his ear to the crack, listening as if to see whether the family were in bed and asleep. I stood perfectly still, and he could not see me. Except my heart, which, with the excitement, thumped a réveille upon my ribs, all was silent as the tomb. After a careful reconnoitering through the crack, he again stood up, took a long free breath, wiped the dust from his face, and fearlessly hopped over to the pile of boots on the other side. Immediately there was a raising of ears, then a stirring, and a peeping up of dusty faces. But there was now such a dust in the room, that I lost sight of them; only occasionally I could hear a stifled cough or a half-suppressed sneeze.

The dust was not long in settling. ‘ Oh! what a ghastly set met my eye! — and so strange-looking withal. The top of the backs of the boots appeared bent over, forward, and downward, so as to form a broad low forehead. Beneath, I was astonished to see two almost imperceptible slits in the leather dilate into a large pair of ash-colored eyes. They were without brows or lashes, and very often dryly and laboriously winked, with all the solemnity of an owl. The long inquisitive ears, enchanted into existence, incessantly wagged to and fro, like an elephant's, when the flies are troublesome. The whitish or dirty red edges of the boot-tops seemed like compressed lips, defining mouths of enormous capacity, whose cavernous recesses, like the horrible χασμ οδον' των of Anacreon's lion, occupied the lower halves of their countenances. The whole body appeared lean and empty with hunger. All were miserably dirty and musty. As the rays of the moon, disentangled from the dusty mass of spider-webs which festooned the little window, fell dimly like gray twilight upon this old and wrinkled assemblage, they resembled a brigade of sage apes, with no arms, and but one stumpy leg, met in solemn council.

When the dust had cleared off, the boots were ranged in regular order around an old box; the left-boots and children's-boots in front, the right-boots standing respectfully behind. All seemed disturbed and thoughtful. On the box, in the very act of making his bow, was a large venerable Wellington right-boot, of a rather more elegant demeanor than the others, that had belonged to an ancient doctor-cousin of mine, Physick Pippin, M. D. I looked with some curiosity for his mate. Her affectionate and nervous restlessness soon revealed her, close to him, and solitary in the crowd, gazing on him with solicitous regard. The twain seemed of an antique and courtly fashion, and were evidently the very ‘ prime’ of boot-respectability. Having swallowed a sob which was rising in his throat, his large eye being moistened with sorrow, he glanced over the queer assembly, opened that fearful mouth, and in a choked and husky voice, began:

‘ Gentleboots and bootesses: we have at length met together to accomplish our designs of revenge upon our common enemy.’ Here the speaker was seized with a violent fit of coughing, during which divers shreds of my missing linen, rags of all descriptions, and scraps of paper, were bountifully expelled. Presently he was relieved, by disgorging the last fragments of a rat's-nest, with four or five blind young ones. Having 'hemmed and hawed' several times, he at length proceeded : 'I feel my breath short and my lungs weak through inaction, so that I can only give you the essence of what I intended saying. We have endured scorn and insult, in silent patience, till forbearance is no longer a virtue. We have been shamefully cuffed and kicked, in the public service of our masters. At home, we have been cruelly neglected, and thrown into a gloomy dungeon, to starve almost to death, and to suffer pangs of the most intense thirst, only partly appeased occasionally by rain, dropping through our leaky roof. We have seen our loved companions dragged from our presence, and torn and hewed to pieces, to gratify the idle caprices of our cruel owners.

'What indignities have they not heaped upon us ! They have not granted us even brute existence. Of sex they have never dreamed. Strange ! that they should doubt it, while they acknowledge affection and companionship in almost all other existences ; when even the cold and inanimate vegetable, which comes and goes, and can only live in the breath of the summer wind, should have sex, and should love and be loved by a tender mate : when they see

> 'How sweetly in the evening breezes,
> Affianced roses bend and kiss.'

Ah ! little did the good and just of Greece and Rome, when they trimmed us out in every hue, and loaded us with jewels — when, with prophetic forecaste, they fixed forever in the heavens its brightest constellation, Bootes — little did they dream of our future mean estate !'

The poor fellow said all this with an incoherent fervor, that proved his sincerity. The tears that trickled down the dusty cheeks of his audience almost called up kindred drops in mine ; and in fact determined me at once to make known to the whole world their forlorn condition. I was exceedingly gratified, therefore, when, after seeming to be fixed in thought for a moment or two, he proceeded :

'Some of us, however, remonstrate against proceeding to extremities against all mankind, whatever be the matter and determination of our vengeance. My master, who was a professional man of reputation, often treated me with a kindness that gained my esteem. After walking through the streets, he always brushed off the choking dust, and restored me to my former glossiness. Ah me ! I remember too how often after the daily toil of his profession was ended, he used to seat himself by the brisk fire in his study, and pore over a volume of history or poetry till midnight. Then, while the snuff slowly mouldered from the end of the wick, which rose high above the flame, and threw a dusky shadow over the room ; while the hot tallow, like the molten lava from Ætna, streamed over the brim, and whitened the table around ; then I used to climb up the chair of the deep sleeper, and gazing over his shoulder, dimly ponder many a glorious page. And when the candles would burn down, and 'oily bubbles in the sockets dance,' how stealthily would I creep down, fearful and trembling lest he should awake ! It was thus I acquired a fund of information, which it is not often the luck of boots to possess. Indeed, my master's kindnesses and all those past enjoyments more than compensate his after negligence. Honestly, on more mature reflection' — and here the mellow thoughts of the past seemed to soften his former bitterness — 'do you not deem it best to first remonstrate with men, before we prosecute our design ? He could not but grant us justice. My goodness ! gentleboots, just let him consider, if some huge animal, as much larger than himself as he is larger than us, should take hold of him by the ears, throw his head back, and cram his foot down his throat ! — what a precious-looking ——'

'Bah ! bah !' exclaimed a conceited and effeminate voice, in the opposite corner, regardless of the deep solemnity of the occasion ; and up popped a foppish, fidgetty little fellow, with a small silken tassel swinging before him, who had belonged to a very fine gentleman, Lusyus Ladyfinger, Esq., a distant relation of ours. He had been able no longer to contain himself, and continued in rather a lofty pitch : 'Now I have been a boot long enough to know that what old Doctor Pippin says is all fudge. We intend to wring the tears from the villains, by griping their feet till every bone and nerve shall ache with the torture, and till every wrinkle and thread in their stockings shall be buried in the fiery, blistered skin !' Here he compressed his leathern lips, and looked stern. '*That's* the way we'll fix 'em ! If every boot would do that, and persist in not being stretched at all, we could all soon sit at our ease in the cobbler's window, or play what pranks we pleased in our old closets. And we must have revenge for our murdered companions. Bring forth the bodies !'

I was startled to see four blinking creatures solemnly carry forward on a shingle the ghastly remains of a pair of boots, from which I had cut the feet for slippers on that very morning.

In the meantime old Physic Pippin, M. D., frowned and shrugged his shoulders uneasily ; and when Ladyfinger had ended, coughed a little significantly. That dainty personage immediately sprang to his foot. 'I suppose, however,' said he, in a contemptuous and sarcastic tone, 'a few very strong-minded boots, and perhaps too the whole very honorable body of shoes, will reject any such spirited proposal.' Then winking very knowingly in the direction of the bootesses, and bobbing his head to the assembly, he dropped into his seat.

In a moment, the carcasses were dashed to the floor, all sprang to their feet, and groans, screams, stamping of feet, hisses, and female shrieks, were heard from every quarter. The tumult increased ; and it was not long before the whole infuriated body were biting, and yelling, and kicking, in deadly contest ; and a dust was raised which hid the combatants from my sight.

In the morning, when I awoke, I ran hastily to the old boot-closet. There were no signs of last night's battle. I rubbed my eyes, but still I could discover no traces. The dust slumbered upon the musty pile. The heavy cob-webs dangled down the dirty panes. Each boot lay as it had lain for years. I kicked one over, almost expecting a groan ; the dry dust only whirled up, like a cloud, in the straggling sunbeams. From that day to this I have never been able to solve the mystery, nor to catch any of those old boots at any of their mutinous frolics.

w. a.

SENSATIONS AND REFLECTIONS.

CAUSED BY THE EARTHQUAKE IN JANUARY LAST: BY FLACCUS.

'Some say the earth was fev'rous, and did shake.' — MACBETH.

I LAY at morn half-conscious of the dawn :
My pausing soul, touched by returning sense
Of duty, yet unwilling to forbear
Her rosy journey through the land of dreams,
Hung doubtful like a cloud 'twixt heaven and earth
Midway, or like a failing bird that long
Had beat the ether of sublimer spheres,
Reluctant downward drooped ; when suddenly
Shouted a mighty voice, and truant Reason
Leaped to her post : deep inward groans, as though
The uttered grief of Earth's capacious breast,
Came up, and her profound and solid frame
Shuddered beneath me, that my lifted couch
Quivered unsteady as a floating bark :
Wonder and awe oppressed me, and I felt
Held for the instant in the hand of GOD !·
I knew the frantic EARTHQUAKE in his car
Had rattled by, and laughed ; and visions swift
Trooped o'er my brain, of horrors manifold
That have befallen when this mighty orb
Cracked like a globe of glass, alarming nations
With the wild thunder ; whose deep-rung vibrations
Ran jarring from the tropic to the pole :
When cities shook, unseated ; and loose walls,
And staggering towers across the peopled streets,
Nodded and knocked their heads, in ponderous ruin
Deep-burying all below : wildest convulsion
Of all that agitate the frame of Nature !

How solemn 't is upon the rocking deep
To feel the mastery of the lawless waves !
Helpless, uncertain but their treacherous arms
That lift us up so high may part apace,
And down to dark and unimagined horrors
Leave us to sink : what double terror then
When sober Earth mimics the reeling sea !
And plains, upheaving into billows, yield
Unsolid to the foot of man and beast ;
When our sure dwelling, like a foundering bark,
Pitches and rolls, the plaything of those strange
Unnatural waves, while hideous underneath
Yawn greedier caves than deepest ocean hides,
Glutted with fragments of the shipwrecked earth,
Clashing and plunging down !   O ! let us kneel
And offer up the incense of our thanks
To Him that spared us blow so horrible,
And only laid his lightest finger touch
(Gently as though the frozen frame of Earth
Had barely shivered with the wintry chill,
Or as some wing of passing angel, bound
From sphere to sphere, had brushed the golden chain
That hangs our planet to the throne of God,)
To jog our sluggish memories that His hand
Upholds, commands us still.
                              Tremble, ye rich !
Where were your mansions now, had He, indignant,
Pushed from their firm foundations ?   Where your lands,
Had His unpitying hand, withdrawing, left
Their unsupported burthen to go down
To the strange bottom of some new-born sea?
Tremble, ye great ! ye puny apes of power,
That with mock-majesty misrule the earth,

Where were ye now, had His scorned sceptre
In earnest ire fell on your heads? Ye! whom
This lightest pulse of the almighty heart
Quails to your just dimensions! Yet wherefore
Bid warning to the rich, the great, alone,
When ALL should reverent bow : have we not all
A stake more priceless than command or gold —
His favor? Let our thousand hearts, that stirred
Like leaves at this hushed whisper of His might,
Pause, and with inward probing seek the cause
That drew the chiding of the sovereign down.
Are his commands forgot? — our solemn duties
Ill-done? or left, through folly's vain pursuit,
Untouched? Then let us wisely take new heart,
And from the couch that trembled at His touch
Rise up, resolved to bend us to our task
With manly zeal, that at the close of day
We may go up to meet our Master's face,
And claim the promised wages without shame !

Thus lulled to calm reliance in the fold
Of 'everlasting arms,' should lurking tempests
Spring sudden upon sleeping Nature; should
Rebellious fires, that in embowelled Earth
Lie prisoned, rise, and writhing to be free,
Burst her centripetal and iron bands —
Unhinging continents, uprooting mountains,
Until her ragged quarters all at large
Fly diverse into space, leaving a gap
Of yawning night, wherein our helpless form
Drops like a stone, piercing an unknown gulf,
Too deep for thought to sound — how would we smile
At baffled Fate! safe in the precious trust
That we had won us an Almighty friend,
And he would lend us wings to break our fall !

MODERATION vs. TEETOTALISM.

'Every *inordinate* cup is unblest.' — SHAKSPEARE.

THIS is the age of extremes. We said on a former occasion that all extremes are tyrannies. There is not one man in a thousand who keeps the prudent middle course, either in religion or politics; or indeed, in any thing that affects the social or moral tone of society. We exist in a constant fever of excitement; and those living on one side of an extreme, denounce with unmeasured severity all who dwell on the opposite. Because different men entertain different opinions, or do not worship by the same creed, is that a cause of quarrel? For that shall we call each other knaves, fools, or infidels? To do so, would argue against the good manners, nay, against the common sense, of the accuser. Every man should extend to his neighbor that courtesy which he claims for himself. This is the golden rule of good breeding. What courtesy, then, does he expect, who is ever ready to denounce all those who differ from him in opinion? Perhaps it never entered into his brain to ask such a question : he never thought of such a thing; or what is quite as likely, such a man never came honestly by a correct thought in all his life. The million get their thoughts from an intelligent friend, as they do their garments from a tailor, *ready made.* The garments are theirs by possession, if not by payment; and so the thoughts are theirs. Man is a sheep ;

as the bell-wether leads, the whole flock follows, whether it be to good pasturage or over a precipice. This truth, however, few are willing to confess : their self-esteem will not consent ; but it is not therefore the less true.

I am an advocate of MODERATION IN ALL THINGS. The inordinate use, the *general* use, of intoxicating draughts, I condemn, and should rejoice to see a custom so pernicious abandoned. Some who call themselves temperate, total abstinence people, simply because their drink is simple, are the most intemperate of men. They have indulged so long a time to surfeit in choice and high-seasoned dishes, that their appetites reject plain and wholesome food, with a feeling similar to that of the drunkard who rejects pure water. I have seen some give way to fierce and ungovernable passion, and heard them, with *intemperate* spleen, vilify and abuse their neighbors. I have seen men *thirst* for money as eagerly as the drunkard thirsts for liquor. I have seen others smoke cigars or chew tobacco till they became stupid or sick. And worse than all, I have seen reformed drunkards rush to opium. Yet they were called temperate, because they did not drink ! Because a man refuses the inebriate cup, does it follow that he is temperate ? By no means. Immoderate eating is as demoralizing to the body as intemperate drinking ; and, I might almost say, equally injurious are ungovernable passions. Walk in the thoroughfares : we may distinguish the plethoric glutton as easily as the bloated drunkard.

There is a class of ultras, some of whom I have seen eat most voraciously, who banish animal food, tea, coffee, and many most delicious et ceteras from their table, who use unbolted flour, and call it Graham bread ; who, in short, think it a virtue *not* to take the goods the gods provide. Such people confer no benefit on the public, but often inflict suffering on themselves. This Graham bread is as old as the hills, and was known for ages before the clan of Graham existed. To some constitutions it is most injurious, while to others it may be beneficial ; but, like Brandreth's pills, though much bepraised, it kills more than it cures.

Let us glance at the history of intemperance : it is a vice older than the records of man ; for in the oldest we find warnings addressed to the intemperate, and denunciations uttered against them. The annals of almost every tribe or people, savage or civilized, tell us that intemperance has prevailed, sometimes to a greater and sometimes to a less degree : yes, and in some regions and ages it was deemed a virtue. Man is ever prone to allege a plausible reason for the indulgence of his appetite. Among the heathen nations of old, feasts and festivals were introduced into their religious ceremonies. On some occasions the *drunkest* was often regarded as the most *pious.* He who drank the deepest, honored his gods the highest.

In the early ages of Christianity, certain customs crept into the church, so like those of the heathen, that we may venture to assert they were borrowed from them : they are not authorized in the gospels. During these ages, priests of various grades abased themselves by vile debaucheries ; the rich as well as the poor imitated their vices with more zeal than they emulated their virtues. Happily for the world, the teachers of religion are now most generally exem-

plary and temperate men; they labor to inculcate virtue with religion, and aim to prove that they are inseparable.   From the religious
ceremonies of man, eating and drinking have entered into nearly all
his secular customs.   Particular times and occasions had, and still
have, their own particular drink, or at least a drink known by a particular name.   Poets have sung loudly in praise of the convivial cup.
From the custom of honoring the birth day of saints by a festival,
we have learned to honor the birth days of distinguished men in a like
manner.   Almost every occasion of domestic felicity is celebrated by
a feast.   Politicians having control of public money, when they think
they have done the city some service, delight themselves and friends
by a luxurious dinner.   Benevolent men engaged in the works of
charity, reward their success by a sumptuous entertainment, too often
paid for by the funds that should feed the hungry.   It is a fact, and
one deeply to be lamented, that in all our social meetings, eating and
drinking are considered proofs of feeling and friendship.   ' If you
will not drink with me, you cannot esteem me.'   How often have we
all heard such a remark.   For my part, though I am but a *moderate*
man, I say with Cassio, ' I could well wish courtesy would invent
some other custom of entertainment.'   The drink of the ancients was
wines, sometimes spiced or drugged.   Alcohol was not discovered
till the thirteenth century; and many years elapsed before the secret
of its distillation was known.   In England it did not come into use
till some time in the seventeenth century.   Shakspeare, who frequently
mentions wine, ale, etc., makes no reference to alcohol, or *aqua-vitæ.*
But since the time that the people tasted it, its strides have been rapid
and fearful.

In our own country many good men are engaged in its importation
or manufacture, or in its sale.   Yes, pious citizens, who spare time
and spend money to convert the heathen, ship *rum* by the same vessel
that carries out the missionaries !   Are they temperate men ?   If the
thirst of gain did not drown their understandings, they would be convinced that Intemperance is the greatest enemy of Religion.   What !
send a missionary to the heathen with a Bible in one hand, and (to
speak metaphorically) a bottle of rum in the other !   Among a savage
people the consequences are inevitable : they will riot in excess; in
drunken madness the Bible will be trodden under foot, and blood will
stain its pages !

Good men too, contractors on public works, who necessarily employ a large number of hands, erect shantees at convenient points for
the accommodation of the laborers and their families.   Every such
establishment has a grocery, where, among articles of wholesome
food, liquor is sold.   The motive is sordid, and the eye is shut against
the evil consequences.   Even private manufactories, erected in the
country, have most generally dram shops in their vicinity.   These
offer temptations too strong to be resisted by the ignorant operative;
and the innocent country people around are enticed to dissipation.

Let us reform all these things ; let us frown upon every man in
office, no matter from what authority derived, who *invents* public
reasons to partake of public dinners : then may one bad practice be
abolished — one evil example removed.

If there be a single individual among the advocates of the temperance cause engaged in the traffic of ardent spirits, I must say that his profession is most inconsistent with his practice. Let him abandon either the society of which he is a member, or the trade in which he is engaged. While alcohol is distilled, purchasers will be found: the moment the demand ceases, distillation stops. How often is the miserable keeper of a grog-shop condemned for retailing three cents' worth of rum to the bloated wretch, while the millionaire who made the poison is caressed. We blame the ignorant agent, while the proud principal remains unscathed. If we were just, we should rather pity the poor retailer, and heap all our censure on the rich manufacturer. Truly the old adage is most correct: 'Money covers a multitude of sins.' Let the stern advocates of total abstinence direct part of their efforts to persuade distillers of the fearful consequences of their business; and if they cannot convince them, as indeed it is not to be expected they will, at least expel them from their society, and refuse to hold them in friendly intercourse. Let men be consistent in their actions, yet at the same time observe due *moderation*, and the world will be the happier.

Fanaticism is the enemy of truth, and heaven-born Charity holds no affinity with it. In all ages, heathen and Christian, it has wrought great evil in the world: the labors and teachings of the truly good scarcely resist its evil influence.

I have a friend, a warmer hearted or a better man than whom is rarely to be found. One December day he was bound up the East River in a steamer that plies along the Long Island shore. Soon after the boat had started from one of her landing places, the cry arose, 'A woman is overboard!' The passengers rushed to the gunwale, to look but not to help: the captain and crew, confused by the accident, were unable to take the speediest and surest means to save her. At this moment my friend rushed up from the cabin, and in an instant, accoutered as he was, he plunged into the river, and not without difficulty and danger, he saved the perishing woman. A thousand thanks and praises were lavished on him by the passengers, for what they termed his intrepidity, his humanity, and so forth. It happened, by the want of presence of mind of those on board, that my friend was nearly half an hour in the water, and he stood upon the deck chilled to the heart. In this disagreeable and dangerous condition, he asked for a glass of brandy-and-water; which receiving, he drank. Murmurs presently arose among those who stood around. One said, 'It is a sin to drink.' Another ejaculated, 'He is not a good man, after all;' while a third boldly declared: 'Drinking brandy has completely washed away all his humanity!' In one word, the temperance fanatics, and many chanced to be on board, would rather this worthy gentleman had contracted a fever, or had fallen into a consumption, or had lived rheumatic all his days, than that he should have tasted a drop of liquor. This was *their* reward, *their* charity for his act of daring humanity; one which *they* were too selfish, or too icy-hearted, even to attempt. My friend was right, perfectly right, to drink at such a time. It was good medicine, and most likely it saved him from a fit of sickness. Would any have blamed him on such an occasion except a fanatic? My friend felt hurt by these ungenerous exclamations, and I will warrant, if he keep his resolution,

the next time a ' tee-totaller' falls into the river, he may save himself.
My friend will never again peril his life in such a cause.

Alcoholic drinks are good at proper times and on proper occasions.
Cases occur where the materia medica affords no substitute.   We
cannot well do without alcohol.   Alcohol extracts the properties of
plants better than any liquid known : without it, many drugs are in-
soluble.   Perhaps for this declaration some may account us as one
of the wicked, who strive to spread false and pernicious doctrines.
We cannot help it : our consolation for this rebuke must be, that a
single truth will in its own proper time work more miracles than the
anathemas of a troop of fanatics.

Moderation is a blessing : Prejudice and Error walk hand in hand.
I desire to take a liberal view of my subject, and win the world to
moderation, by convincing the understanding, not by appealing to the
passions, of men.   I would not terrify people from vice by exposing
its awful consequences : I would rather entice them to virtue, by showing the heart-felt content it imparts, the respect it commands, and the
health it insures.

There is an old gentleman of my acquaintance, a man temperate
and virtuous, who for fifty years had drank regularly at his dinner a
glass of brandy and water.   He used, but never abused, heaven's
blessings.   Some time ago, having read an ultra total abstinence paper,
he was so affected by its sophistry, that he resolved instantly to give
up his accustomed habit.   He did so : in a very short time the result
was a fit of grievous sickness, that brought him to the very verge of
the grave.   Recovering health, the physician ordered him to resume
his brandy : he did so, and lives healthily.   The aged should never
abandon, and least of all abruptly, an old habit : there is much danger
in it.   But the young, by reason of their elasticity, may change, and
change again their way of life, with impunity.   They need however
no artificial excitement, no alcoholic drinks : youthful blood is warm
enough by nature.

By way of an episode, I shall here relate a true story.   An industrious young man was set up in ' the liquor trade' by his friends.   He
was told, and willingly believed, that the fumes of the spirits which
necessarily in the course of his business he would be obliged to pour
out, might injure his health, unless he tasted a little every morning.
Being very sober-minded, and desirous of getting on in the world, he
resolved that he should never, by any chance, fall into habits of intemperance.   To avoid even the bare possibility of such a calamity,
he bought a very small wine glass, and determined never to exceed
its limit daily.   All went on well for a time ; but, at last, lifting up his
glass one day to take his usual allowance, he looked at it very narrowly ; his face flushed, his passion arose, and he swore vehemently.

' Tom, Tom, you rascal ! where are you ?' calling his store-boy :
' where is my glass, you rogue ?'

' That is it in your hand, Sir,' said Tom.

' You lie, you villain ! it is not; my glass was twice as large, and
you have changed it for this thimble.'

' It is the very glass, Sir; I have made no change.'

' You have ; I am sure you have : this is not mine.   Go, Sir, instantly, and buy me a glass twice as large.'

It was done; and then for a short time all went on smoothly again. At length a scene similar to the first was acted, and a still larger glass was bought. This also in time proved too small. To remedy the evil, he resolved to drink its measure twice a day. The original limit, with his own knowledge, being once deliberately overstepped, he felt himself in danger, but had not the moral courage to resist his craving appetite. Day by day he sank deeper and deeper in dissipation, till at last he became a drunkard. Business, in consequence of his neglect, left him; friends forsook him; his affairs went wrong; poverty overtook him; and to close my story briefly, he died an outcast, unpitied, unlamented.

This tale may be seized upon by a certain class of temperance advocates to prove that all *moderate drinking* inevitably leads to *excess*. It makes me smile to hear teetotallers quote isolated instances to prove the truth of their creed; and then I sometimes think of the old woman's 'gin and sugar,' which she avowed was a panacea. It proves no such thing. One instance does not establish a truth, any more than one truth establishes a system. One atom will not make a mountain, nor one drop of water an ocean. To say that moderate drinkers are not safe, is to assert what the experience of every man proves untrue. There are few men, comparatively, in any age, who do not drink at some period or other of their lives. We have all of us drank in our day, unless debarred by constitutional inability. I have not a doubt that many members of the total abstinence societies were once moderate drinkers. Many live in the daily habit of taking a glass of brandy and water, or two glasses of wine, at dinner, and some at supper too. Yet of such men, hundreds of thousands are *temperate*, and live happily to a good old age, respected and honored.

Some men seem to have been *born* drunkards, as some are born thieves; others again cannot taste alcohol without being ill; and some would rather strike off their right hand, than touch unjustly one cent's worth of their neighbor's property. Unfortunately, too many men have physical failings, or propensities, which they cannot resist.

I for one have *drank moderately*, when it has suited my feelings or caprice, for twenty years. I feel in no danger; and to this hour, I account myself a *sober man*, in the usual acceptation of the phrase. I can drink or not, as it pleases me; but I will not taste a drop to please another man alive. Sometimes I feel that a glass of brandy or whiskey, properly mixed, does my health a positive benefit. 'Good wine is a good familiar creature, if it be well used.' Yet, at any moment I can entirely abstain, without the least discomfort. I have tried it, and sometimes for a month, sometimes for six months, at a time. A large portion of my acquaintances can say the same of themselves.

If I am asked to become a total abstinence man *for the sake of example to others*, that is another affair. On the broad principle of philanthropy, I am bound to show a good example to all my fellow creatures. There are few men, however, of philanthropy so boundless, who will deny themselves a pleasure or a benefit, to show an example to those whom they regard, not personally, but simply as fellow beings. I am perhaps one of them. If I moved the centre of a circle, and young, thoughtless men looked up to me for an example, and it was necessary to show that of total abstinence, I am ready at a moment to banish all intoxicating liquors from my house, and live, in the strictest sense, a temperate man. My position in society only requires me, at least I think so, to be simply a *moderate man.* Fire is an excellent slave, one with whom we would not willingly dispense, but he is a most tyrannical master. No man in his senses would kindle a fire in a hay-stack or in a pile of hemp; but who is afraid, on a cold night, to make a blazing one in his parlor grate? So it is with liquor; an excellent servant, but beware of him as a master! Some temperaments cannot control the appetite; all such should avoid temptation and danger in every shape. Any man may taste liquor occasionally, provided he possess one particle of self-control; but he, whether old or young, who cannot drink without rushing to extremes, is a madman, quite as mad as the man who could not kindle a fire except in a hay-stack or in a pile of hemp. All madmen should be well guarded, that they may neither trespass upon their neighbors nor injure themselves.

Alcoholic drinks are to the young superfluities, and were better avoided : the taste for them, like that for tobacco or opium, is acquired, not natural. Yet it is a question, whether if alcohol had never been distilled, the world would have been more temperate. History proves that people and nations whose customs or religion forbade the use of spirituous liquors, indulge in spices and drugs which are quite as debasing in their effects, both on the body and the mind.

Of late years, temperance societies have wrought much apparent if not real good. I remember the time well, when almost every merchant in the city went daily to the old Tontine, about noon, for his glass of brandy or beer. Not one respectable man in a hundred does such a thing now. It is unfashionable; it would injure his credit. Sit to-day at the ordinary of an hotel : there is scarcely a drop of brandy to be seen on the table : ten or fifteen years ago every body drank it, as regularly as he ate his dinner. Go to a private dinner, or an evening party: brandy is seldom offered there. A few years ago a sideboard was an indispensable article of parlor furniture, upon which various kinds of liquors were displayed, tempting the inmates and visitors. Now, sideboards are considered unfashionable, and clumsy lumber; and among the better classes of society, to offer drink, unless perhaps a glass of wine, is not held a refined custom. But although this salutary reform is apparent, are we sure that the world is more virtuous? Is crime lessened? How many still drink in secret, or how many, avoiding liquor, fly to other excesses quite as demoralizing?

While I applaud to the echo the efforts of temperance societies, and greatly rejoice in the reformation they have wrought, yet I cannot too readily admit that the world is more virtuous. I fear not to assert that the zealot who would instantly banish from the earth intoxicating drinks, and at the same time forbid mirthful indulgences, is a Quixotte, fighting against windmills. He may, it is true, effect apparent temporary good, but will not confer lasting benefits on mankind. Some in every age, from fashion, may abstain awhile; and some, without his assistance, will discover a new mode of indulgence, less baneful perhaps in its consequences on society, but not less injurious to the individual. Open some innocent and healthy vent for the excitability inherent in human nature, and the first real step to reform is taken — one that may lead to happy and lasting results.

What will total abstinence avail, if we do not teach lessons of truth and virtue ?   Men whose drink is water encourage the young to commit offences both against law and morals, whose example is demoralizing in the highest degree.   Parents teach their children to lie, to swear, to cheat, and even to steal ; and some who would shudder to be accused of inculcating crimes, yet by not punishing promptly and severely their first commission, indirectly sanction a second offence. Read the annals of crime, and we shall find numerous examples of persons incarcerated for life, or forfeiting life upon the gibbet, who never complained of liquor being the cause ; but who have declared that *temperate parents*, by example, or in express words, encouraged or applauded their *first* crime.   From that hour, they dated their moral degradation.

If we insist that all laxity of morals originates in the inebriate cup, then our sole attention should be directed to cure that fruitful source of crime.   But I presume the most zealous 'teetotaller' will not venture to avow such an opinion.   That we lessen poverty, degradation, and crime, arising from drunkenness, as we lessen intemperance, is a self-evident proposition.   That *moderate* drinking produces beggary, corrupts the morals, or induces to crime, I firmly deny.

If I correctly understand the object of temperance societies, and of the good men who support them, it is, NOT TO PREVENT DRINKING PER SE, BUT TO PREVENT ITS CONSEQUENCES, AS WELL TO THE INDIVIDUAL AS TO SOCIETY.   If alcohol were as innocent as water, all the world might ' drink like fish,' and not one single voice would exclaim against the practice.   If, therefore, my position be true, it is not enough to suppress the inordinate use of distilled liquors : we should provide wise means, that those we reform do not relapse into other habits quite as injurious to religion and to morals.   How shall this be done ?   He that would propose a perfect system of recreation, which, while innocent and invigorating, would give a peaceful vent to the excitability of our natures, would be a benefactor of his race.   Without such a system, how shall we proceed to real reform ?

The democratic creed is : No laws shall be enacted that restrict man in his natural rights, except in so far as may be necessary to protect him in his life, liberty, and property, and their peaceful enjoyment : hence it follows indirectly, that *every law is constitutional that promotes the general good.*

Now we all admit that intemperance is a fruitful source of crime. The law dares not revenge; it punishes justly : it is wiser to prevent the commission of crime than to punish offenders.   We all admit too that intemperance makes paupers, and pauperism creates a tax, which the industrious and sober citizen must pay.   Without thinking, for the moment only, of the private suffering and misery which intemperance produces, it is enough for our present purpose to ask, why should the community be taxed to suppress or punish crime, and to support paupers ?   It is an attack upon ' property,' which the social compact is bound to protect : hence any law that justly, mildly, and equably drives intemperance from the land, is constitutional.   I am aware that no law is obeyed which is contrary to the general feeling.

However wise or constitutional it may be, it lies dead upon the statute book. Has the time arrived when we may make enactments against intemperance ? I think it has, or at least is approaching fast.

We have long had municipal regulations against drunkenness ; but we must confess they have done little good. They are either imperfectly framed, or laxly enforced. Whatever might have been thought twenty years ago of a state law declaring intemperance a crime, I am persuaded that a judicious one would now be received with favor. All good people would lend their aid to enforce it. I verily believe that 'the good' constitute the majority. Such a law must be framed with consummate skill, else it will not be obeyed. Our citizens, our temperate citizens, even, will never submit to a law *persecuting* any class, or unnecessarily curtailing the natural liberty of any man. We have lately seen the effect of the ' fifteen gallon law' in a sister State. I apprehend the objections were not to the end proposed, but to the means adopted for obtaining that end. It was certainly most injudicious, in the present state of public feeling, to enact that no person should, under a severe penalty, buy or sell less than fifteen gallons of alcoholic liquor. In the first place, the opposition of drunkards is certain against all laws, the tendency of which is to suppress their particular vice, or pleasure, as they may please to term it : in the second place, that law enlisted many *moderate* drinkers against it ; men in reality, though perhaps not technically, as temperate as the most rigid ' teetotaller.'

I am not one of those who would attempt to cure the deep-rooted evil in a day, by condemning moderate drinkers ; or like the Emperor of China, seize and instantly destroy all the poison we could lay our hands on. I fear that would not avail. I would effect a gradual cure. Physicians inform us of maladies which they could easily eradicate in a day, but dare not, because a worse disease would certainly follow. As we daily see unhappy proofs that the law's punishment will not prevent crime, though it may deter many from the commission of it, so all the statutes that man could frame would not drive drunkenness from the land. Some natures will not be *compelled* even to do good ; compulsion would rather induce them to an opposite course ; while, if proper means be used, there are few indeed who may not be *enticed* to virtue.

In another article we may consider the effects of law and persuasion in the cause of temperance.

IMPLORA PACE: AN EPITAPH.

I.

Tired of life, its wisdom, folly,
  Of its hopes and of its fears,
Of its mirth and melancholy,
  Stranger ! I implore thy tears !

II.

Cold the grave my heart is pressing,
  Welcome, if emotion cease ;
Ask for me this only blessing,
  Peace profound — eternal peace !

WHERE ARE THE DEAD?

—— 'WHERE hath the spirit flown,
That, past the reach of human sight,
Ev'n as a breeze hath gone !'

O WHITHER are they fled,
  Those spirits kind and warm,
That, numbered with the dead,
  Have nobly braved the storm ?
And gained a port at last,
  A port of peace and rest,
Where, earthly perils past,
  Their happy souls are blest ?

In some bright-beaming star
  Do they weave the pencil'd rays,
That streaming from afar,
  Upon our vision blaze ?
Or is the flickering light
  That the varying twilight brings,
As it glimmers on our sight,
  The waving of their wings ?

Perchance along the sky,
  The far-off azure dome,
They wing them free and high,
  In their lofty spirit-home ;
And the cooling zephyr's wing,
  As it fans the brow of care,
In its voiceless whisperings
  May a message from them bear.

Perchance they lightly glide
  Where the friends of childhood dwell,
And linger by the side
  Of those they loved so well ;
Or in visions of the night,
  Come with their whispering tone,
And the dreamer's spirit light
  With a magic all their own.

I 've read a page that tells
  Of a home beyond the sky,
Where the ransomed spirit dwells
  With the God of love on high ;
Yet their crowns of living light
  They cast down at his feet,
To seek this lower night,
  And the child of sorrow greet.

Low, where dark shadows fall,
  On the heart, and on the brain,
Where earthly pleasures pall,
  And the bosom throbs with pain,
There, with kindly lingering stay,
  On their ministry of love,
They smooth the thorny way,
  And point to rest above !

E. E. e.

THE QUOD CORRESPONDENCE.

NUMBER TWO.

In my last communication, Mr. EDITOR, I mentioned that I occupied a house which had once been the scene of a fearful deed, and had since paid its penalty, by being shunned of all, and gradually acquiring an ill-omened character. With that strange zest for the fantastic, which seems to have clung to me from my birth, this very circumstance which prejudiced others against it, gave it favor in my eyes. The spectral and solitary chambers, the long and gloomy passages, the creaking stairs, the dark and sepulchral basements, all gave it an air of wild, yet to me fascinating mystery; and I have sat by the hour and listened to the wind as it wailed through the dark entries of the building, which seemed itself to moan like some old and decrepit human being. At such times a feeling of superstition comes over me. I people the house with images of those who lived here before me, of those who now are dead; and the voice of the sighing blast seems to me like the whispered sorrows of their troubled spirits. My mind gradually wanders on, until it rests upon the last bloody act which consigned the house to desolation. At times like these, I confess a strange weakness comes over me. I am obliged to throw open the window, and look upon the calm clear sky, and to listen to the hum of the living world about me, before I can divest myself of these dreary fancies. I have now become familiar with all the crannies and hiding places within its walls, and gradually begin to relish the solemn silence which reigns throughout its deserted rooms. The profound, and somewhat superstitious veneration with which I am regarded by the neighbors, begins to please my fancy; and I am often amused at the air of mysterious awe with which a group of small boys will collect on the opposite side of the street, and watch my motions, as I sit at the open window, in the fine spring afternoons.

Shortly after establishing myself here, I set to work to trace out the history of the house, and to learn the particulars of the transaction which has spread a gloom over it, and tarnished its fair name. During the whole time that I have been thus engaged, several persons have cordially volunteered their aid. In particular, I am much indebted to a small gentleman, with green spectacles and thin legs, who is a frequenter of the police office, and who heard the whole matter carefully detailed at second hand by a distinguished constable of this city; so that there can be no doubt as to its veracity. Others of the facts I gleaned from a fat lady who sells vegetables at a corner near me; and being a great gossip, she told me the whole story while I was purchasing a bunch of radishes. No sooner was it noised abroad that I was engaged in ferreting out the history of the murder, than information of all kinds came pouring in upon me; much that was useful, and some that I cared nothing about. In particular I remember one gentleman, in a snuff-colored suit, who stopped me in the street and inquired if I were Mr. Quod, and if I were engaged in writing the history of the haunted house. On my replying in the affirmative, he thrust his hand in his pocket, and produced a large red pocket-book, and taking from it a paper, which he placed in my hand, 'There, Sir,' said he, 'there!—you could never have got along without *that!* It's an epitaph which I wrote on the murderer. Say nothing about it; it's a present — altogether a present. You may use it as you please; though if the history is ever in print, I think it would not be amiss to put it in the title-page, then intersperse it once or twice in the course of the work, and finally bring it in with a grand flourish just over the 'Finis.' Gad! Sir, how it will make the thing sell! I'll buy ten copies myself.' As soon as he gave me an opportunity, I endeavored as delicately as possible to excuse myself, smoothing the refusal over as well as I could. He looked at me in blank amazement, and without saying another word, took the paper from my hand, replaced it in his pocket-book, which he carefully deposited in the bottom of his breeches pocket; and then giving me a compassionate glance, he tapped his forehead, and nodding to himself, as if to intimate that all was not right there with me, walked off.

From the several authentic sources just mentioned, I have become familiar with the whole transaction. It is a long story, and I have felt a strong interest in tracing out its tangled course. A short, abrupt detail of facts would be but a dull affair, so I have dressed it up, divided it into chapters, and present it as you find it below.

JOHN QUOD.

The Attorney.

CHAPTER I.

A few years since there stood within the neighborhood of the City Hall a huge wooden building, whose great height and dilapidation gave it rather a menacing appearance to passers-by. Its exterior was faded and bleached by time and storm; and from neglect and decay, the upper stories had settled and projected forward; so that in the dim nights, when its tall outline stood relieved against the sky, it looked like a gaunt giant, bent with age and decrepitude. High, narrow windows, in many places broken or begrimed with the dust of years, admitted a faint uncertain light into the unfurnished rooms, the walls of which were in many places dark and discolored, and hung with cobwebs. Occupants it once had; and the time had been when this old house had held up its head and lorded it over its more humble neighbors; but that time had gone by; and now it was the home only of the spider and the rat. There was however one exception. This was an attorney, who had a suite of offices at the end of a long dark passage on the second floor. He was the only human tenant of the house, and even he confined himself to his own portion of it. He never ventured in the upper stories; and except for the purpose of going in or coming out, visited no other part than his own rooms. There were dark rumors concerning him, and many shunned him as they did his house. It is with him however that we have to do; and the opening scene of our tale is in the two dim apartments in which he then sat.

His age must have been forty, though the deep furrows which ploughed his high, narrow forehead, and the haggard and wasted look of his face, might have added ten years to his appearance. His eyes were deep-set and glittering, of that jetty, opaque character which seems to emit their brilliancy from the surface; and appeared to peer into the secrets of every one, without reflecting any of their own. He was rather under the middle size, and of that disjointed, wiry make, which indicates great powers of endurance rather than positive bodily strength. Piles of loose papers were scattered carelessly on a table at his side, and several open law books, which appeared to have been in recent use, were lying on different chairs about him. In the recesses of the office were huge cases of pigeon holes, filled with the dust-covered papers of ancient, hopeless, and perhaps long-forgotten law suits. Book-cases of dingy volumes were ranged against the walls, and several massive folios were piled in corners of the room. A profusion of torn papers were scattered over the carpet, and added not a little to the disorder, which was already sufficiently apparent. Upon the table stood a solitary candle, whose faint light scarcely dispelled the gloom in its immediate vicinity, and gave a murky, spectral appearance to the tall book-cases and furniture, which were indistinctly visible beyond.

For some time the attorney sat with his thin fingers resting upon his knees, and his eyes fixed upon the fire. As he continued thus, his brow grew anxious, and he compressed his lips tightly, occasionally moving his head from side to side, and muttering to himself. At length he rose from his seat, and stepping cautiously to the door, locked it, trying the knob to see if it was secure. He then shaded the windows so as to prevent the light from being visible from without. This done, he took from a drawer a large brass key, and drew from an iron safe in the wall a bundle of papers, from which he selected one, and replacing the others, seated himself at the table. He then unfolded the paper, and held it up to the light, narrowly examining the hand-writing, and particularly the signature attached to it. Apparently not satisfied with this, he got up and searched among some other papers, until he found one bearing the same signature.

'Tis very like!' said he, after a careful comparison of the two; 'he'd swear to it himself; and if I could but find some fool whose conscience is not over-dainty, this would *make* me! I must find that man — I *must* find him; ay, though the devil himself bring him to me!'

A single sharp knock at the door, so suddenly upon the heels of his speech that it seemed a response to it, so startled him that he almost let the paper fall from his hands. The next moment he folded it hastily up, without attending to the summons, until he had replaced it in the safe, locked the door, and restored the key to its former place. The knock was repeated.

'Who's there?' he demanded.

'One who wants a lesson in deviltry,' replied a harsh voice from without; and the knocking was renewed with an energy that said but little for the patience of the person on the outside, and threatened soon to leave no obstacle to his entrance.

'It's *you*, Wilkins, is it?' said he, in an altered tone. At the same time he unlocked the door, and admitted a tall, powerful man, clad in an overcoat of coarse, shaggy cloth, and with his hat slouched low down over his eyes. His face was pale and haggard, his jaws large and prominent, and his eyes flashed from their dark caverns with sullen ferocity, like those of a hyena.

'You are the very man I wanted,' said the attorney, as he came in, at the same time shutting and locking the door.

His visiter, without paying the least regard to him, strode up to the fire, and drawing his coat, with a slight shiver, more tightly over his shoulders, extended his hands toward the flame.

'Put on more coal,' said he ; 'such a night might freeze one's soul ; and whatever I am now, you have made enough out of me, to keep me from dying of cold.'

The attorney was evidently accustomed to such language from his visiter; for he made no other reply to it than to request him to be seated, while he replenished the grate. Then, seating himself, and turning to him, he said :

'What 's on foot now ? Whenever you darken this door, I know there 's something to be done. What is it ?'

'The same that I spoke to you about before — that girl,' replied Wilkins, fixing his dark, scowling eyes on the pale, care-furrowed face of the other. 'Am I to live forever like a coupled hound ; or can the chain be broken ? Have you no remedy — no plan ? Cannot the devil, who is always at your right hand, help you to *something ?*'

The attorney slightly elevated his eye-brows, and muttered something about 'patience,' though he watched the countenance of the other like a cat.

'Patience !' exclaimed Wilkins, rising and speaking through his clenched teeth ; 'I *have* had patience ; and what has it brought ? It has reduced me from competence to what I am — a starving, wretched, and almost houseless beggar. It has worn me to the bone. It has destroyed my hopes, and now it is gnawing into my very soul. 'Patience !' Hark ye, Bolton, no more of patience ; if you cannot help me, I can help myself — and I *will*. But it 's hard to — to —— You know what.'

'To what ?' asked the attorney, looking at him, as if in doubt of his meaning.

'*That*,' said Wilkins, slightly opening his vest, and touching the handle of a concealed dirk.

'That !'

'Yes, THAT !' returned the visiter, savagely, setting his teeth, 'or shall I speak more plainly ? To cut her throat. Do you understand me *now ?*'

'Hush !' said Bolton, glancing suspiciously about the room, his thin features turning as rigid as if they had been cut from marble. 'Do n't speak so loud. No, no, you must not do *that*. That 's murder in the first degree ; the punishment is death. Do you hear that ? — *death !* I 'll have no hand in it.'

The brow of the bolder villain darkened, and his eyes flashed fire, as he half rose from his seat. Leaning forward and spreading out his fingers in the very face of the attorney, until they resembled the talons of a hawk, he slowly clenched them together, till they seemed buried in each other, and said in a voice which though but a whisper, was distinctly audible : 'If you dare to fail me *now*, Bolton, or betray me, or show by word or whisper, or even by look, I'll place you where you'll rot — ay, rot ! I'll —— '

'Hist, George !' said the attorney, starting up, and seizing him by the arm ; 'did you hear nothing ?'

Both listened attentively.

'Nothing but the wind howling through this old rookery,' said Wilkins : 'did you hear what I said when you interrupted me ?'

'Yes, I heard, and I'll not fail you. Why, George,' continued he, assuming an air of frankness that sat indifferently on him, 'are we not old friends — tried friends ? Have I not stood by you when none other would ? You have not forgotten the last time — the note for a thousand dollars.'

'No more of that,' interrupted the other, impatiently. 'We know each other *too well*,' continued he, laying an emphasis on the last words, which seemed to indicate that the acquaintance, though intimate, had not increased his confidence. 'But I did not come here to be reminded of old grievances ; I come to get a remedy for new ones. The only question is, will you help me or not ? This girl to whom I am married is in my way. I must be rid of her, and I have come to you for counsel. Will you give it ?'

Before Wilkins finished speaking, the attorney had recovered the habitual sneer that played about his thin lip, and replied quietly and with an appearance of decision that he felt sure would influence his companion :

'If you mean to murder, I will not. I have already risked much to help you, and will risk more, but I'll not risk my life. Beside, there are other means fully as good, and which do not lead to a halter.'

'Well ! what *are* they ? The safer the better. But listen to me. I *will* be rid of that girl ! by G – d I will ! — even though ——' He paused ; but the expression of demoniac hate and malice which shone in every feature, and from which the attorney, steeped as he was in wickedness, quailed as from the glance of an evil spirit, and the quick motion of his arm, as if in the act of stabbing, explained his purpose.

'It must not be — it must *not* !' was the reply, in a tone which had lost much of its former confidence. 'There are other ways, and they must be thought of. A divorce will leave you as free as you can desire. Do you wish to be rid only of *her*, or of the *knot* ?'

'Of both ! of both ! If ever man loathed woman, I loathe her. There is but one thought in life ; there is but one dream when my eyes are closed, and that is of hatred ; and there is but one person in that thought and dream, and that is *her* !'

'This is a sad affair indeed,' said the attorney.

'Sad !' said Wilkins, drawing his chair more closely to that of the lawyer, and speaking in a whisper ; '*sad?* — it's dreadful; it's wearing away my life. Bolton, if you could but look into this bosom and see its bitterness, hard, callous as you are, even *you* would shudder. There are moments when it seems as if all the devils in hell had taken possession of me. Yet I have strange fits of weakness too. I'll tell you what I did the other night. I had thought and thought on this one subject ; and it *would* keep running into my head, that if *she* were out of the way, how well I could get on. It was in my own room, at midnight, and there she lay, in a deep sleep, the bed clothes thrown partly down, and her throat bare. I know not how it was, but I found myself stealing to the bed with this dirk in my hand, and I held the point within an inch of her bosom. At that moment she turned in her sleep and said, ' Dear George, God bless you !' Curse me if I could strike ! I slunk back from the bed, and blubbered like a boy, for I felt strange feelings at work, which I have not had for many a day. I 'd rather not spill blood if any thing else can be done. Can 't we send her abroad ? You know if she is out of the way there 's nothing between me and the widow. Once let me get her fortune, and you shall not be the loser by it.'

' Can she prove the marriage ?'

' Beyond a doubt.'

' How long have you been married ?' inquired Bolton.

' Two years.'

' And is she true to you ? — true beyond suspicion ?' asked the lawyer, looking at him significantly.

' True as steel. Why, man will you believe it ? — in spite of all, she loves me !'

' Ah !' said the attorney, in a dissatisfied tone, that 's bad. If it were not so, and she had another lover, *and it could be proved* —— (he spoke slowly, and with great meaning in his looks,) the court of chancery would grant a divorce, and you would be free.' .

' Free ! free ! exclaimed Wilkins, springing from his seat, as one from whom a great weight had just been lifted ; ' Free ! Great God ! let me be free once again, and I 'll be a different man — an honest one.'

The attorney smiled, and although he said nothing, there was something in the calm, sarcastic curl of the lip, that stung Wilkins to the soul, and he turned fiercely upon him.

' Ay, I repeat it — ' an honest man.' What have you to say against it ?'

' Nothing,' said Bolton, drawing toward him a piece of paper, and writing something on it ; ' there 's what I must have, before I meddle in the matter.'

Wilkins took it and read : ' Two thousand dollars down, and five thousand more when you get the widow.'

' Bolton !' said he, in a choked voice, ' this is too bad. Two thousand dollars ! I have not ten dollars in the world. I do 'nt know what your drift is,' said he, suddenly stopping and looking steadily in the face of the lawyer, ' but you have a d — d suspicious look to-night; and there 's something in the wind more than you let out : beware how you trifle with me ! You should know me too well for *that*.'

Bolton attempted to smile, but only succeeded in producing a nervous contraction of the lip, at the same time turning deadly pale : at length he said, with some effort : ' You are right, I *have* something. Wait ! I hear a noise in the passage.'

Taking the light, he hastily unlocked the door, and traversed for some distance the dark entry which led to the lower floor. Nothing whatever was visible in the dim light, except the time-stained walls, and the broad chinks between the dilapidated planks. On re-entering the room, he went to each window and drew the shutters carefully together; after which, he made a total and general survey of the office.

'There's nobody; it was all fancy,' said he, replacing the light on the table. 'Now,' he added, 'I will speak plainly with you. I have that in my mind which you have on yours; a plan to mend my fortune. Assist me, and I will assist you, without fee or reward. Swear to keep my secret, and I will swear to keep yours.'

'What mischief's hatching now?' asked Wilkins, suspiciously.

'Swear first to keep the secret.'

'Well; here I swear —— '

'That will not do; I must have something more solemn.'

'Well, what do you want?' asked Wilkins, impatiently.

'Get on your knees, and with your hands raised to heaven, call down imprecations on your head, blight upon your prospects, and perdition to your soul, if you betray me. *Then* I'll believe.'

Without remark, and with a solemnity that struck awe even to the hardened heart of the man who incited him, Wilkins knelt down, and with uplifted hands, and eyes turned toward the throne of the great Omnipotent, called down upon himself maledictions that made the blood of his listener curdle, if he betrayed the confidence then to be reposed in him.

'Enough!' said Bolton, relieved by the conclusion of a ceremony so fearful. Drawing the key from the drawer, and once more unlocking the iron safe, he took from it the paper which had been so hastily deposited there, and spread it on the table.

'Here,' said he, hurriedly putting a pen in the hand of the other, as if afraid of his resolution giving way, 'just sign that; put your name there. I'll explain afterward.'

'What is it?' asked Wilkins, holding the pen exactly as it was placed in his hand, and looking at the attorney instead of the paper. 'Before a man puts his name to a thing like this, he likes to know what it is.'

'Merely a will,' said Bolton, nervously; 'only a will.'

'A will! Whose? — mine?'

'No; of an old friend of mine, John Crawford. I want you to put your name as a witness to its execution.'

'Ah! I see; you are helping him take care of his property, and you want me to witness it before he has even put his own name to it. I suppose I may read it, to make sure it isn't my own,' said he, running his eye over the paper: 'Natural daughter, Ellen Crawford; five thousand — all the rest, residue, and remainder;' umph! 'both real and personal — my valued friend Reuben Bolton — sole executor — subscribed, signed, sealed, declared, and published —— Bolton,' said he, quietly lowering the paper, 'you *are* a d—d scoundrel!'

'Perhaps so,' replied the attorney, shrugging his shoulders,' but what are *you*?'

'What want and suffering have made me. You have not even that excuse.'

'Perhaps not. You know the terms on which I will assist you. John Crawford was seized with apoplexy this morning; before to-morrow he will be in his coffin; and this will must be made and witnessed before then. I can imitate his signature so that he would swear to it himself. I will put it at the end of this, and you must witness it.

'Well, what then?' demanded Wilkins, suspiciously; 'suppose the old man dies: what is to be done next?'

'Little or nothing; merely swear that you saw him sign it — a few other trifling matters; few or no questions will be asked; a mere form. It will be completed in five minutes, and you will get the widow for nothing.'

'Nothing! Only a false oath, and risk of being entertained at public expense. Do you call that *nothing*? However, I'll do it,' said he, speaking in a clear, decided tone. 'But the girl — will she be quiet?'

'What can she do? Will she not be penniless?'

'Not exactly. There's a small legacy of five thousand, which will keep the life in a pretty long law-suit; and if she should happen to be litigious ——'

'Curse it! I never thought of that!' exclaimed Bolton, striking his hand forward, with an air of vexed impatience, and taking one or two hasty steps.

'Perhaps,' suggested Wilkins, 'the old gentleman intended to make a later will without the legacy.'

'Yes, yes, so he did,' said Bolton, laughing, catching eagerly at the suggestion. 'We'll do it for him, and you'll witness it?'

'Ay, if you'll unfetter me,' replied Wilkins.

'It's a bargain,' said the attorney, striking his hand into the open palm of the other; and thus was their iniquitous compact sealed.

As if by consent, both now seemed to think the conference concluded.

'Be here to-morrow evening at ten; and in the mean time gather up all that will throw suspicion on your wife. By-the-bye, the will requires two witnesses. Can you find another equally trusty with yourself? I have a clerk who will excel one of these days, but he is too young yet, and would be nervous."

Wilkins pondered a moment; at length he said: 'I know the very man; sharp, shrewd, without conscience, and with nerves like iron. But he is poor, and has no widow in his eye. You must pay *him* in ready money.'

'Leave that to me. And now I must spend the rest of the night in helping my old friend dispose of his property. . Ha! ha! ha!'

'Ha! ha! you are a deep one!' said Wilkins, taking up his hat. To-morrow night at ten. Good night!'

The attorney listened to his steps as they echoed along the passage, until they died away; then carefully locking the door, he lighted another candle, and seated himself to his work.

CHAPTER II.

IT was a cold night, and as Wilkins emerged from the building into the open street, he drew a long breath of pure air, as if it were refreshing once more to be free from the murky, stagnant atmosphere of that old house, and under the blue vault of the sky.

Thoughts and plans came crowding thickly upon him as he strode on, and hopes and fears, and with them was mingled a lurking dread of the poor girl against whom he was plotting; a half-acknowledged fear of what she might do, if driven to extremity; and above all, the whispering of his own conscience, which made a coward of him as he slunk through the dark streets. Skulking along like a felon, he made for one of the great thoroughfares, for he felt as if the crowd there would keep off his own thoughts.

It was still early in the evening, and the streets were thronged with that tide of population which during the first hours after twilight sets from the lower to the upper part of the town. None loitered, except the sick, the weary, and the homeless. Hundreds of those poor girls who spend the hours of daylight in the lower parts of the city in earning a pittance by tedious toil, were speeding like so many loosened birds to the homes where there were glad faces to welcome them, and kind hands to smoothe a pillow beneath their aching heads; or perhaps not a few craved but a place to cast down their work-worn frames to rest before another day of toil. Many a pale face and blighted form was among that crowd, and many a tottering limb and trembling hand; eyes that should have been bright, were dimmed with premature suffering, and features that should have worn the hue of health, and been radiant with gladness, were now wan and sunken, or illumined only by the sickly smile which flickers over the face of the invalid. Day after day they toiled on, but they felt that there was nothing in store for them; their childhood had had no joy, their youth no promise. Even hope was gone; and weary and heart-sick, they looked forward to but one place, where there was a calm and holy peace; where their toils would be ended forever — and that was the grave.

Mechanics and boys with their tin kettles, now that the labor of the day was past, in squads of five or six were hurrying on, some in silence, others with loud merriment, but all bound to that single sacred spot — home.

Wilkins mingled with the throng, and made his way among them, sometimes pausing to listen to the remarks of the passers-by, and sometimes brooding over his own plans.

The street through which he was passing was that great artery of the city called the Bowery; and just above where it empties itself into the triangular opening known as Chatham Square, he struck off into a by-street on the eastern side of it.

The dwellings in this neighborhood were of the meaner kind, built chiefly of wood, with patched and broken windows, here and there repaired by paper or by the introduction of an old hat or a pair of tattered inexpressibles. Throughout the whole there was an odd mixture of comfort and penury, and occasionally a faint effort at gentility in defiance of poverty; but in most cases, in the bitter struggle between human vanity and human want, stern necessity had got the upper hand.

A front room on a level with the street, in a mean house in the part of the city just described, was Wilkins' home. It was small and scantily furnished. A rag carpet, a small looking-glass, a common deal table, a bed, and a few rush-bottom chairs, were all; but with all its poverty there was an air of cheerfulness about it. A bright fire burnt merrily on the cleanly-swept hearth, and window-shades of painted paper, such as is used for walls, served to shut out the cold, and to impart an air of greater comfort. Every thing bespoke a great degree of poverty, combined with that rarest of all its accomplishments, cleanliness.

The only tenant of this room was a girl of scarcely more than nineteen, who sat at the table repairing some article of man's apparel. There was an expression of hopeful anxiety in the large dark eye, and a lighting-up of features which had once been beautiful, but were now rather thin and sharp in outline, with a nervous, restless motion of the body, and a hasty glance at the door, as each successive step approached, and a corresponding expression of disappointment as it receded.

How sure, yet how indefinable is the certainty with which we recognize a familiar footstep! For half an hour at least the girl had feverishly watched and listened. At last came a quick, firm step. She started to her feet, and had scarcely time to exclaim, ' That's him !' when the door opened, and admitted the tall form of Wilkins.

' I knew it was you !' exclaimed the girl, joyously, running up to him, and offering to take his hat.

' Well, what if you did ?' replied he, jerking the hat from her hand and throwing it on a chair. ' Let my coat alone will you ? I am able to take it off without help. Do you think I am as helpless as yourself, who can do nothing without being waited on ? Get me some supper, if you are not too lazy for that, and do 'nt trouble me; I 'm not in the humor.'

' I did not mean to offend you, George,' said she, shrinking from the angry yet irresolute glance that met hers ; ' indeed I did not. Are you ill, George ?'

' Get me some supper. Am I to stand starving here while you, who take care never to feel hungry yourself, pour your clatter in my ears ?'

The poor girl, who had not eaten since morning, lest there should not be sufficient left in the scanty larder to furnish a meal for her husband, for such was the relationship between them, shrank back and set about preparing the meal.

' Who 's been here since morning ?' demanded Wilkins, seating himself in front of the fire, and thrusting his feet in close proximity to the flame, that showed more desire of heat than consideration for shoe-leather. ' I suppose that Jack Phillips ; he 's here for ever.'

' No, only your friend Higgs ; he stopped but for a moment to inquire when I expected you, and did not even come in,' replied the girl, busying herself in arranging the table.

With a sulky growl, the import of which was lost in a contest between his voice and teeth, he sank back in his chair, and fixed his gaze in the fire, occasionally casting stealthy looks at his wife, eyeing her with a discontented yet irresolute glance. Several times he seemed on the point of saying something ; but just as it was crossing the threshold of his lips, the words shrank back, and he contented himself with poking the fire, and giving vent to a few indistinct mutterings.

'Curse it, Lucy!' he exclaimed at last, with a strong effort, as if anxious to break the silence; 'have you nothing to tell me? When did Higgs call here?

'About an hour ago.'

'Well, why could n't you say that at first? If it had been that fellow Jack Phillips, I should have heard it soon enough. He 's here too much.'

'Well, George,' said she, mildly, 'if you wish it, we can refuse to let him in. I thought he was a friend of yours, and for that reason I ——'

'Fell in love with him,' interrupted Wilkins, with a sneer; 'you see I know all about it.'

At this announcement Lucy turned short round, without saying a word, and fixed her dark eyes upon him with a look of surprise and incredulity that completely overmastered the dogged gaze it encountered.

'No, George,' said she, with a faint laugh, 'not *that;* but it 's ill jesting on such subjects: do n't say it again.

'But I *will* say it, and I *do!* 'Jesting!' By G——! I mean what I say — all of it.'

'No, no, George,' exclaimed she, with an hysterical laugh, and catching hold of his arm; 'you do not mean it — you *cannot*. I know it was only a joke; but you looked so very strange! It was *only* a joke — *was n't* it?'

'Was it?' muttered he, grinding his teeth, though without raising his eye to hers; 'we 'll see that! But give me my supper, for I must be out. Do n't keep me waiting.'

The girl made no reply, but releasing his arm, and turning her back toward him, hastily dashed her hand across her eyes, then went on with her preparations in silence. This lasted about five minutes, Wilkins gazing now at the floor, and now stealing a look at his wife.

'The supper is ready,' she said, at length. Wilkins rose hastily, and dragging the chair to the table, seated himself and began to eat voraciously, without noticing his wife, who sat at the opposite side, eyeing him with looks of suspicion and fear. Once or twice their eyes met, and Wilkins' dropped beneath hers.

'What are you staring at?' demanded he, angrily; can't a man eat without having every mouthful counted?'

The girl rose without reply, and taking a stool from the corner, drew it near the fire, and seated herself with her back to him.

'Did Higgs say what he wanted?' asked Wilkins.

'No; he only asked if you were in, and when I told him you were not, he went off.'

'I suppose he wanted money. I must see him. Do you know where he went?'

'He said he would wait at Rawley's, and that you would know where that was.'

Without farther words, Wilkins left the table, and put on his shaggy overcoat, jerking his hat on his head, and taking from the corner a stick, something between a cane and a bludgeon, he sallied out.

'Will you return soon, George?'

Wilkins slammed the door behind him, without any reply, and walked off.

His wife stood until the sound of his footsteps died away, her lip quivering, the large tears in her eyes, with her hand pressed painfully against her breast, and her breath coming short and with difficulty. The struggle was but for a moment. She threw herself in a chair, bent her head down upon the table, and wept long and bitterly.

WOMAN'S HEART.

Alas! That man should ever win
So sweet a shrine to shame and sin,
As woman's heart.

L. E. L.

I.

Say, what is woman's heart? — a thing
Where all the deepest feelings spring;
A harp, whose tender chords reply
Unto the touch, in harmony;
A world, whose fairy scenes are fraught
With all the colored dreams of thought;
A bark, that still will blindly move
Upon the treacherous seas of love.

II.

What is its love? — a ceaseless stream,
A changeless star, an endless dream;
A smiling flower, that will not die;
'A beauty — and a mystery!'
Its storms as light as April showers;
Its joys as bright as April flowers;
Its hopes as sweet as summer air,
And dark as winter its despair!

III.

What are its hopes? — rainbows, that throw
A radiant light where'er they go,
Smiling when heaven is overcast,
Yet melting into storms at last;
Bright cheats, that come with syren words,
Beguiling it, like summer birds;
That stay, while nature round them blooms,
But flee away when winter comes.

IV.

What is its hate? — a passing frown,
A single weed 'midst blossoms sown,
That cannot flourish there for long;
A harsh note in an angel's song;
A summer cloud, that all the while
Is lightened by a sunbeam's smile;
A passion, that scarce hath a part,
Amidst the gems of woman's heart.

V.

What then is woman's heart? — a thing
Where all the deeper feelings spring;
A harp, whose tender chords reply
Upon the touch, in harmony;
A world, whose fairy scenes are fraught
With all the colored dreams of thought;
A bark, that still would blindly move
Upon the treacherous seas of love.

A WORD ON ORIGINAL PAINTINGS.

It is always a marvel, frequently an annoyance, and, at times, a grief to me, to hear persons — to whose judgment on other topics I might willingly defer — speak of good *copies* of paintings, as in their estimation equal or 'almost equal to the originals themselves;' persons who have doubtless cherished with deep care the hand-writing of some friend; the Essay perhaps in which his opinions were developed and enforced; the Letter that spoke his impassioned Love; the lines of Poetry in which his spirit yet breathes and in the very characters of which his genius may perhaps be traced.

All these, now that the power that sketched them is mouldering in the dust, are resorted to like hid treasure, watched over, dwelt upon in solitude, spoken to, apostrophized, loved by the deep heart. Would they barter these relicks of delight against nicely-printed *copies* of the same productions? The copies to be curiously bound, and silver-gilt, the paper to be fresh and fair, the ink black, and the characters much clearer and more legible than in the original draft? Not for worlds! There is some latent, some mysterious yet undeniable connection between these lifeless manuscripts and the beings whose affections seem even yet to haunt and hover round them; and the pulse beats and the blood gushes through the loyal heart, as it vibrates again to the well-remembered words, and half listens for the voice that might have uttered them.

And now if this be the case with mere pen, ink, and paper — white paper and black ink — what becomes of it when the subject is a painting, in which the soul of the imperishable artist speaks its inmost graces of conception in the beau idéal of form? or in the varied wonders of expression? or blossoms forth its affections into colour? Colour! that deep, mute eloquence of Earth and Heaven! that one remaining beauty of Eden! That earliest sensation of joy that the mourner can admit into a broken heart! That choice of God when he would decorate the sky with a promise of His love! That poetry, surpassing words! The Soul's wealth, it's element, it's fountain of refreshment and joy!

Is all this to be accounted as nought? The long yearning, the deep earnestness of soul of the artist? The hallowed stillness of the studio in which the miracle of art has been achieved, is it no longer to be thought of? — and the half-planned, half-fortuitous movement of the brush, just short of sacred Inspiration, that transferred his Idea to the canvass, and clothed his spirit with gladness, and his name with lustre; making him familiar with the highest and purest imagination that has ever been accorded to man, a consciousness namely of the possession of creative power. Is it all — nothing?

Has my reader perchance frequently visited the studio of some true artist? I have myself no pretension whatever to art, but it has been my happiness more than once to have been, alone, in the studio of Thorwaldsen; and I have felt there, and elsewhere upon similar occasions, that the repose that pervaded it was occupied; the quiet that reigned there was a living quiet; it was a silence in which sensation lingered ; a rich capacity of existence ; an intense atmosphere of life waiting to be appropriated. I have been in that of one of our American artists, distinguished for his calm yet precious colouring, watching his efforts with rapt attention, when suddenly his pencil has shed the hue that relieved, at the same instant, his heart and my own ; and Joy has enveloped us, begirt us both at the same moment as with a sun-beam. There was a spiritual light around us, and although the silence was unbroken, I felt as if his soul had spoke to mine. If it had been the habit of our country, I could not but have embraced him as he stood, pallet, pencil, linen-jacket, and all !

Now this spirit, or, if you will, this *character* of hallowed stillness and this solemn effusion of the soul of the artist ; the hopes, the fears, the affections, the rapturous delight with which he has at last found his pencil give utterance and visible existence to some long-cherished combination of his fancy ; all this, which forms his life, is bestowed upon the offspring of his genius, and for century after century shall live and breathe and haunt and dwell around the noiseless unobtrusive canvass of the original painting, that hangs, mellowing its tints from year to year, in intermingling beauty and immeasurable grace ; the admiration, the solace, the joy, the reward, the refinement of thousands who flock to it from distant passages of Earth :

> ' Thither,
> As to their fountain, other stars repair,
> And in their urns draw golden light.'

And are the works of the mere operatives who infest the galleries of Europe — and frequently by their numbers almost exclude the visiter, or confine his view with their sheets of canvass to an occasional or partial glimpse of the object of his far pilgrimage — are these mechanical copies to satisfy our longings for the art, while the immortal production itself is to be seen merely by crossing the Atlantic and the Simplon ?

Are they to occupy, with their leaden outlines, and muddy tints, and wooden limbs, and abortive expressions, that sanctuary in the young American heart, where the first aspirations after excellence are nurtured and bred ; and where and at the moment when the taste is formed and the soul expands and is refined, or is repressed and fades, or perishes, as images are denied or are accorded to it, to exalt, extend or vivify its capacities, to show GOD in the beautiful, and HIS presence in the sublime alike of nature and of art ?

Ought these copies in justice even to be permitted to take place of that image in the memory, which calls around it, from the grave of the past, the emotions that possessed us at the first view of some original inspiration ? When we stood in front of it ? near it ? within its presence ? within the nimbus of it's existence communing with the spirit of its author ? I think not : I think the copy obscures the recollection of the original, and blinds the imaginative eye ; deadens the memory of sensations that have formed our happiness ; and destroys that bewilderment of joy which it is so delightful to remember ; that tumultuous movement when we could only say to each other, after a long breath : ' And this is Raffaelle !' Oh moment, beyond the reach or future measurement of Time !

No! these imported academic copies of the great paintings of Europe, which are so fast increasing in number upon us, are often worse than valueless in the effects they produce alike upon the inexperienced, the young, and the travelled amateur. They still the inquiries and 'satisfy the sentiment' of the first; they injure the imaginative powers of the second; and outrage the memory of the last.

A few well-chosen engravings are, for every purpose of usefulness or of true pleasure, worth all that have ever been brought to America; and a whole wilderness of copies were well-bartered for one of ALLSTON's deeply-imaginative female heads; one of his exquisite visions of the moral and intellectual beauty of Woman; revelations of the Heaven of her interior spirit : or for one of those Skies which our own WEIR, in his quiet way, stretches abroad in full aërial perspective, above some ruined tower, or solitary mountain-lake,

> 'Where GOD alone is to be seen in Heaven.'
>
> JOHN WATERS.

'LIFE'S A MOMENT.'

> ' Das Leben ist
> Nur ein moment, der Tod ist auch nur einer.' — SCHILLER

I.

THE dew-drop on the blooming flower
  Reflecting rainbow tints at morn,
May sparkle brightly for an hour,
  The golden cup awhile adorn :
'T will vanish in the sun-ray's gleam
Like the dim phantom of a dream !

II.

The mist that gathers on the hill,
  As light and transient as the air,
Its sombre hues the distance fill,
  And seem to hold a dwelling there;
But like a thought, a glance, 't is past,
Its essence in oblivion cast.

III.

The waves that seek some distant shore
  Are borne along the sounding sea,
And joyful in their stormy roar,
  To far-off lands in mountains flee ;
But ere they reach the sought-for bourne
They sink, and others rise in turn.

IV.

And like the dew-drop's fleeting hour,
  Or like the vapor's transient stay,
Or like the wave's ephemeral power,
  Man's life and death are but a day ;
At morn, the revel and the crowd,
At eve, the death-knell and the shroud !

THE BATTLE OF NEW-ORLEANS.

'IMPIGER, iracundus, inexorabilis, acer,
Jura neget sibi nata.'

THE American is grandiloquent to excess. It would seem as if every man, woman, and child among us felt all the magnitude and importance of the problem that we are solving in history, and made use of terms and tropes to match. With the title of '*La Grande Nation*' we should never be contented. Nothing but 'the greatest nation on the face of the earth' will satisfy us. In the United States the 'wingéd word' soars on pinions as extended as those of the condor.

On the list of blessings which the American thanks God for, the military glory of his country stands first. How any one could so mistake the spirit of democratic institutions as to look for their triumph through war, would be wonderful, did not that reverence for physical power which leads us to admire the strong man, make every one desire to claim might, if not for himself, at least for his nation. This war feeling would not be so likely to originate now-a-days. It has come down to us from of old, but has taken strong root, and will flourish many years yet. Indeed one can easily imagine that Englishmen or Frenchmen should exult in the prowess which their stout heroes have shown throughout past centuries. The names, places, and traditions which surround them, tell of iron warriors and hard-fought conflicts. They have good cause for exultation. Our greatest glory is not to be found in war records, and can never be gained in battle. We have indeed had our skirmishes, like other people, and are even now carrying on in Florida what we are pleased to call a war, but which might more properly be termed a hunt, and that too very bunglingly; but to hear our orators, one would imagine that Julius Cæsar had campaigned against the Five Nations, Marlborough marched and countermarched on the lakes, and Napoleon commanded an expedition against the Rocky Mountains.

Panegyrists begin at the revolution and summon the great shades of Greece and Rome to stand up and be measured with the heroes of seventy-six. Valiant men, no doubt; but we cannot help thinking that the ancients thus rudely apostrophized might feel somewhat vexed, as did the prophet Samuel when her ladyship of Endor evoked him at the foolish request of Saul : Why hast thou disquieted us ? What did they more than other brave men fighting for their homes ? Than the Saxons, Goths, Swiss, Dutch, Russians, Germans, Spaniards ? They did well, but they could not be men and do otherwise. The revolutionary struggle is assuredly matter of great congratulation, but scarcely of excessive boasting. The Americans fought manfully ; but with such a cause and with such a leader, an army of Chinese would cover themselves with glory. Of the use they made of victory we may well be proud ; the honor of the victory they must share with Frenchmen. Nevertheless, this war had a result. Something was gained ; that is something to boast of. But when we see the frontier land operations of 1812, '13, '14, cited as pretences for self-uplifting, we cannot help thinking of the long hour by Shrewsbury clock, and exclaim as we read, '*Nil cum est, nil defit tamen.*'

Mournful to us are the records of our military deeds in this quarter. No nation ever plunged herself more recklessly into a war, or behaved more foolishly when engaged in it. Without any adequate preparation, unarmed and empty-handed, the United States rushed into conflict with England. The avowed object of this government, on the declaration of hostilities, was to overrun Canada, and few on either border doubted of the complete success of an invasion. The American certainly did not, if we may judge by General Hull's proclamation. 'Had I any doubt of eventual success,' says our Leonidas, 'I might ask your assistance, but I do not. I come prepared for every contingency. I have a force which will look down all opposition.' And if common sense had guided in the slightest degree the plans of the Cabinet, the General, weak, vacillating, and superannuated as he was, might have made good the words of his play-bill. An energetic push for Quebec and Montreal, at this period of the war, would have decided the fate of Canada. But instead of ordering such a march, Mr. Secretary sent this old man on a round-about journey through an almost unexplored waste ; and this to occupy a trifling fort which must necessarily have fallen with all its dependencies after the taking of the capital. The General, as we all know, after innumerable delays, and attempts to 'look down opposition,' surrendered without striking a blow. This was the first of a series of disgraceful and ludicrous reverses. The same scene was enacted over and over again. Gasconading generals issued their play-bills ; advanced and retreated like the French king whom the well-known couplet has immortalized ; and sent off despatches to Washington of battles with buckram foes. Military stores of all kinds were shamefully wanting. Officers disobeyed orders with impunity, and men deserted in companies. In some instances the delinquents were fined twelve and a half cents for the misdemeanor.* Such severity, we suppose, was necessary as an example. General Smyth publishes an address which Sir John Falstaff himself might have penned. 'The horses drawing the light artillery of the enemy are wanted for the service of the United States ;' and again : 'You will share the eternal infamy that awaits the man who having come within sight of the enemy basely shrinks in the moment of trial.' The thrilling proclamation is terminated by the encouraging cry : 'Come on, my heroes ! and when you attack the enemy's batteries, let your rallying word be, ' The cannon lost at Detroit, or Death !'† The troops were awaiting the order to march, when Hero Smyth called a council of war, 'that furnisher of excuses for doing nothing,' and sounded a retreat. Perhaps he imagined that he escaped from 'eternal infamy' by his clause, for he never came 'within sight of the enemy,' and was too happy to ask permission to visit his wife and children. He hies on the paternal errand, never again to appear. General Dearborn commands his attack from the deck of a ship ; Perry, not yet *the* Perry, hurries about to learn the plan of debarkation. No one knows, and least of all the commander.‡

'Nul d'eux n'en savait rien, tous criaient cependant.

---

* See BRANNAN's Military and Naval Letters. †CHRYSTIE. ‡ MACKENZIE's Life of PERRY.

The wind of De Salaberry's bugles blows Hampton's corps away. O that the general had carried one half of the lead that he had in his scull, in the soles of his shoes, like the gossamer Greek! Then he might perhaps have stood his ground by mere *vis inertiæ*, and not have ruined the campaign by disobeying the orders of his chief, General Wilkinson. Trusty affidavits convict this officer of drunkenness at a time when if ever a man should be sober. For being *vino gravis*, Wilkinson might find some jolly precedents among heroes ancient and modern, but where could he find one for his favorite maxim, 'A commanding officer ought never to expose his person?'[*]

Whatever these gentlemen may have been in the field, on paper they were certainly Orlandos and Rinaldos. Their despatches may serve as models to future generals of their stamp. The Cabinet, we suppose, listened to these rather than to facts, for we do not hear that Smyth, Hampton, or Wilkinson ever met with any punishment. Indeed, throughout the war, merit of all kinds, real and imaginary, was sure to find its way to Washington on foolscap. Colonel Campbell, who commanded in some Indian skirmish, took care to inform the department that Sergeant Strother I. Hawkins loaded and discharged his pistol at the enemy several times![†] May not America be proud that she numbered among her defenders so valiant a Hawkins, and a Campbell in whose noble bosom such exalted heroism could not excite a feeling of envy?

There is little here to console us, save the knowledge that the enemy was quite as inefficient as ourselves. The greater part of the struggle resembled a fight between two drunken men, both falling at each blow. Proctor and Prevost were worthy antagonists for Hull and Hampton.

Why were Americans so languid on the land, when on the sea, the boasted home of the Briton, they were winning honor? On the 17th of August William Hull surrendered at Malden; on the 19th, Isaac Hull captured the Guerriere; and the sound of the victorious cannon of Perry and M'Donough might almost be heard on the spot where Hull, Smyth, and Hampton brought shame on their flag, and infamy on themselves. How shall we account for so great a contrast? Both sailors and soldiers were Americans — both mostly recruits. Blame cannot be thrown on the militia, for Harrison, Brown, and Jackson managed to make them effective. The fault lay wholly with the commanding officers, and with the department, for giving such men commissions. Here and no where else is it to be sought for. Soldiers have no constitutional scruples, no timid scruples of any kind, with a man to lead on, a man like Perry or Barney; then they stand by their guns until struck down by the bayonet. An army without a chief has often been compared to a body without a head. The comparison is too favorable. The headless army does not even possess the vis inertia of the dead body, but melts away before fire like wax. At some future day, when Time shall have extirpated all the actors and hearsay performers in these skirmishes, perhaps another IRVING will give a history of this frontier war, surpassing in droll and ludicrous adven-

---

[*] ARMSTRONG.   [†] BRANNAN's Military and Naval Letters.

ture the famous campaign of the New-Amsterdamers.   At least there will be material enough.

Of the South we can tell a different story.   The English had determined at an early period to obtain possession of New-Orleans, and their Danish descents in the Chesapeake were merely feints to divert attention from the main object.   The plan was excellent.   A defenceless coast, an unfortified town ; a total want of munitions of all kinds ; disaffected negro slaves ; a population half French, half Spanish ; every circumstance seemed favorable ; and they already exulted, when considering the value of the prize which was to be obtained so easily.   The great market of the Mississippi and Ohio valleys was within their reach ; and animated by their success at Washington, they regarded the expedition rather as a *promenade militaire*, in quest of ' beauty and booty,' than as an invasion in which plunder was to be bought with blood.   Rumors of their intentions had already reached Louisiana, and excited much alarm and a shiftless desire to do something for defence.   Lafitte, the smuggler, whom the British attempted to buy over, warned the authorities repeatedly of the approaching danger; and though a foreigner, a pirate, and an outlaw, offered to serve with all his band against the enemies of America.   Yet little was accomplished : the government, as remiss here as elsewhere, had provided neither arms nor ammunition.   Even a frigate of small draft, destined to the defence of the lake, remained unfinished, despite the earnest solicitations of Commodore Patterson.   Nothing was ready except the General — ANDREW JACKSON.   His military talents were fully equal to the occasion.   In various expeditions against the Creeks, he had already evinced that iron energy, indomitable perseverance, and ceaseless activity, so necessary to a commanding officer.   He was the general for an emergency.   Not one of the wavering, but a man who would keep his object as steadily before him as the mariner his port, and trample down and crush without remorse whoever barred the path.   A character indispensable in a chief, for in war especially success is the only thing worth consideration.

On the 2d of December, 1814, General JACKSON arrived in New-Orleans, on his return from Pensacola.   The city was in great confusion.   Committees of all kinds were disputing, quarrelling, and more desirous to fight each other than the enemy.   His appearance restored tranquillity, for he had that strength about him on which men in danger willingly rely.   The General lost no time in tardy deliberations.   Martial law was proclaimed ; the writ of habeas corpus suspended ; free men of color and prisoners enrolled ; the Baratarians welcomed to the ranks ; and every point which he thought menaced by the attack, visited and fortified.   On the 14th, news came of the capture of the six gun-boats on Lake Borgue, the only protection of the coast in the absence of the unfinished frigate.   The invaders were at the door, and men knew that the hour of trial had arrived.

Some ragged fishermen, who earned a miserable livelihood on the shores of the lake, went over to the British and advised them to land at the Bayou Cataline, one of the thousand creeks which intersect the swamps of Louisiana.   The Bayou was well chosen, for the Mississippi at this point was not more than six miles distant from the lake.   On the 16th of December the army was conveyed in boats to

Pine Island, 'a miserable swamp, not only devoid of all human habitations, but bare even of trees and shrubs.'* On this waste they remained five days, suffering all the hardships of an exposure to cold and rain. Many of the black troops, unaccustomed to a change of climate, fell asleep beside their fires, and expired. On the 22d the avant-garde, consisting of sixteen hundred men, under the command of General Keane, was reëmbarked, and rowed to the Bayou, a distance of sixty miles, without even an awning to protect them against the showers which fell during the night. Bodily discomfort was forgotten in the certainty of success; and when the boats took the ground under the high reed-covered banks of the Bayou, the troops leaped ashore with alacrity, and pushed forward through the swamp, where the cypress and the conqueror's laurel grew side by side in boundless profusion, to Villere's plantation, on the left bank of the Mississippi.

Thus far every thing had gone well. A quick march of ten miles over a level road would have placed the prize within their grasp. Colonel Thornton, the second in command, earnestly pressed an immediate advance : sixteen hundred men, he maintained, were fully adequate to the task of surprising an unfortified city; and no time was to be lost in delays, for the escape of several prisoners would soon announce their arrival to the Americans, and prepare them for defence. General Keane, however, thought it safer to wait for the second detachment, and to reserve the advance for the next day. Consequently the order was passed to bivouac. The troops, in high spirits, piled their arms, lighted their fires, and dispersed in search of provisions, fully impressed that 'as the Americans had never yet dared to attack, there was no great probability of their doing so on the present occasion.'† The following proclamation was posted in different places along the high road :

'Louisianians ! — remain quiet in your houses ; your slaves shall be preserved to you, and your property respected. We make war only against Americans.'

All other hostile demonstrations were reserved for the morrow.

One Rey, who had contrived to escape from the English, arrived in New-Orleans at noon of the same day, and announced the disembarkation of the troops. General JACKSON immediately despatched a party to reconnoitre the enemy. Before two hours had elapsed, the scouts came in, a night attack was planned, and orders issued to the corps who were to take part in it. The armed schooner Carolina was directed to drop down the river, and to take up a position abreast of the enemy's camp. About seven o'clock the Carolina came leisurely to an anchor before the levee. So great was the security of the British that they were gathered in crowds upon the bank, watching with an idle curiosity the manœuvres of the vessel, which they took for an ordinary coaster. Suddenly the trumpet was heard from her decks : 'Give them this, for the honor of America!' and the darkness of the winter evening was lighted up by the flash of her broadside, as she poured a shower of grape and round-shot among

---

the astonished Englishmen.　More than one hundred were killed before they recovered from their panic.　The survivors crouched behind the levee for protection ; and here they lay an hour, listening in silence ' to the pattering of grape-shot among their huts, and to the shrieks and groans of those who lay wounded beside them.'*

A discharge from the picquets on the right summoned them from their shelter.　Two thousand Americans, led on by General JACKSON in person, had forced their way into the camp, and were bearing all before them.　In the obscurity of the night the ranks were broken ; Americans and English mingled together, *legit que virum vir.*　Every man fought for himself alone, as in the old Homeric conflicts.　Musket and pistol were laid aside for sword and bayonet, and the western rifle, wielded with both hands like a war-club.　After two hours of hard fighting, the English were reinforced by the second detachment from the ships, and succeeded in beating off the attack.　General JACKSON withdrew his men, and the enemy retreated once more to the welcome shelter of the levee.　In this affair the British lost four hundred in killed, wounded, and taken ; the Americans two hundred and fifty.　The prisoners captured by Keane consisted almost entirely of lawyers.　The members of the bar of New-Orleans had enrolled themselves in a volunteer corps, and accompanied General JACKSON in this expedition.　They were entrapped by the English, and seized to a man.

JACKSON's measures were as well planned as prompt ; and the employment of the schooner in particular merits all praise.　This vessel alone kept the enemy chained to their position for three days.　During this all-precious interval, the famous embankment of cotton bales on Rodriguez Canal was commenced, which was destined twice to foil every effort of the invaders, and to give the death blow to all their hopes of conquest.

The whole of the next day the British remained beneath the bank, suffering the extremes of cold and hunger : as soon however as it was dark, the army filed off and took up a position on the right, out of reach of the Carolina's guns.　By giving her broadside a great elevation, the schooner succeeded in throwing shot among them, causing great annoyance though little execution.

On the 25th Sir Edward Packenham arrived in camp, and assumed the command.　The next day a battery of ten guns was erected on the bank, and a fire of hot shot opened on the Carolina.　The second ball took effect, and in fifteen minutes she was abandoned by her crew, with the loss of only one killed and six wounded.

On the 28th, the British army, under the command of Generals Gibbs and Keane, advanced in two columns about three miles, when they came in sight of the American troops posted behind the unfinished breast-work.　The left column on the river was instantly greeted with a tremendous fire from the guns of the frigate Louisiana and those already mounted on the lines.　'Scarce a bullet passed over or fell short of its mark, but all striking full in the midst of our ranks, occasioned terrible havoc.'*　The column was soon forced by the carnage to deploy into lines of battalions, and finally to halt and

---

* British Officer.

lie down in the ditches which intersected the plantation. On the right, the attack might have succeeded, had it been energetically directed, for the works were unfinished, and only a few guns mounted ; but the loss suffered by the left division was so great as to induce the commanding officer to order a halt. In the ditches they remained until late in the afternoon, when the different regiments filed off, man by man, amid shouts and showers of balls from the American lines. A few guns which had been directed against the Louisiana were carried off by hand, by a party of sailors. The loss which the enemy suffered in this affair is astonishing ; the more so when compared with the trifling injury they caused their antagonists. Only ten men were killed within the lines, and but one wounded on board of the frigate, whose guns fired eight hundred balls during the engagement. The same disproportion is remarkable throughout the invasion. Many a gallant Briton laid his bones beneath the cypresses of Louisiana.

General Packenham did not return to his old position, but encamped on the battle-ground of the 23d of December ; his outposts extending in some places to within three hundred yards of the American lines. Finding the works so well defended, he determined to consider them as a regular fortification, and to breach them. The 28th, 29th, 30th, and 31st were employed in bringing up heavy guns from the fleet. The labor and hardships incurred in the transportation of twenty-four pounders by hand through a quaking morass, can scarcely be conceived. Throughout this period the position of the British was any thing but enviable. The scarcity of provisions had reduced them to half allowance, and driven them to still their hunger with the sugar they found on the plantations. As they had no tents, they were forced to sleep upon the ground ; and Louisiana in December is not exactly the spot one would select for passing the night *al fresco.* Even the enjoyment of the damp earth was denied them. The Americans did not grant them a moment's repose. From the day of their landing they had been engaged in one continued battle. Beside the shot that were constantly thrown among them from guns greatly elevated on the lines, the American artillerymen would advance with a few field-pieces within range, fire half a dozen rounds, and retreat so rapidly as to baffle pursuit, while bands of riflemen lurked about the picquets and shot down the sentinels. The English had a great dread of the Tennesseeans, whom they denominated ' Dirty Shirts,' from the color of their hunting-frocks. These night excursions were very popular among the ' Dirty Shirts ;' they termed them hunting parties. One of these worthies is said to have killed and stripped three sentinels on the same spot in one evening, and to have made his escape into camp with the booty.* This system of warfare, although much inveighed against by English writers, we think both justifiable and wise. When armies meet on foreign ground to decide some state question, about which they may be supposed to know little and to care less, we can understand that a kind of chivalric understanding should exist between combatants. Such wars are but duels on a large scale, and the courtesy which directs antagonists in affairs of honor ought certainly to be exercised. The case is far otherwise with invaders.

* Major Latour's War.

Then a man fights for his native soil; for his family and friends; for his possessions, which would be plundered; for his home, which would be ransacked and destroyed. He considers his foes in the light of house-breakers, and every man slain one enemy less, and very justly. This system too succeeded admirably in a military point of view, by harassing and discouraging the English. The repulses they had met with, the incessant labor and constant excitement in which they were kept by the ever-recurring attacks, had disheartened the troops, and made them heartily sick of the expedition.

On the night of the 31st of December, Packenham's men were employed in erecting batteries for thirty heavy guns. The work was accomplished before dawn. The sun rose behind clouds, and for some time the mist was so thick that the American lines could not be distinguished. At eight o'clock the white tents of the camp became visible, and the cannonade commenced. The fire was principally directed against M°Carty's château, which was occupied by JACKSON as his head-quarters. Although the house was pierced through and through repeatedly, the staff escaped without a wound. The American batteries responded feebly at first, but gradually grew brisker, and at length surpassed the British both in rapidity and precision. The enemy had rolled hogsheads of sugar into the parapet of his battery, under the impression that it would be as effectual as sand in deadening the force of balls; but it proved otherwise, for the shot crashed through the casks as if they had been empty, dismounting the guns and killing the gunners. Cotton bales, on the contrary, proved a much better defence; and although some of them were rather rudely knocked about by the twenty-four pound shot, but little execution was done among the Louisianians. At three o'clock the fire of the English had slackened very much; and while the Americans, reserving a few guns to return their feeble salutes, directed the remainder against the infantry, who consequently retired in precipitation, leaving many dead on the field. Soon after, the enemy ceased firing altogether, and abandoned his guns. JACKSON's loss did not exceed fifty, in killed and wounded.

The Americans had good reason to be elated by their success. That thirty pieces of cannon should be silenced by fifteen, only five of which were of equal calibre, was far more encouraging to the invaded than any advantage they had yet obtained. Satisfied with the result of the affair, they made no attempt to carry off the guns, which were accordingly removed by the English, with much labor, on the ensuing night. Five however were ultimately left behind.

Once more frustrated in his hopes, Sir Edward Packenham changed his plan of attack. It was now determined that a body of troops should cross the river, and that an advance should be made on both banks at once. A canal two miles in length by six feet in breadth was commenced, in order to convey the boats from the Bayou to the river. It would seem never to have occurred to the general that ships' boats could be pushed on rollers over land in half the time it would take to dig such a canal. Meantime the work was continued, and completed on the evening of the seventh.

JACKSON had not been idle during these five days. The Rodriguez

breast-work was now raised to the ordinary altitude, covered by a
ditch, and fifteen guns placed at proper distances along the line; and
moreover a battery mounting eighteen guns had been erected on the
other side of the river, so as completely to enfilade the English bivouac.   No precaution was omitted nor labor spared to strengthen
the position and to harass the enemy.   Major General Lambert's arrival with two regiments had increased the British army to nine thousand effective men.   The Americans, although rated at twenty-five
thousand by the ' British Officer,' mustered but four thousand men on
the lines.   Fascines and scaling-ladders had been prepared by the invaders for the troops on the left bank, who were to advance at the
sound of Thornton's guns on the opposite side.   The Louisianians
were fully apprized of the approaching attack by the activity and turmoil they had remarked in the enemy's camp, and were ready at all
points to encounter it.   Affairs stood thus on the evening of the
seventh.

BATTLE OF NEW-ORLEANS.

PLAN OF THE BATTLE OF THE EIGHTH OF JANUARY: REDUCED FROM MAJOR LATOUR'S CHART.

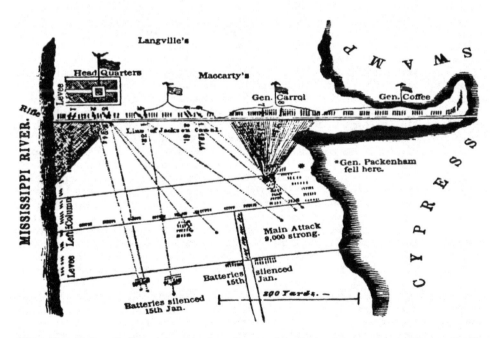

On the 8th of January took place the last desperate effort of the
British to obtain possession of the prize they had been taught to deem
so easy.   A reference to the plan will show the respective positions
of the combatants.

General Keane with twelve hundred men was to make a sham attack on the river bank, while General Gibbs, with the main body, was
to storm the works on the right, in the direction of batteries six and

seven. Fascines and scaling-ladders were entrusted to the Forty-Fourth regiment, and success was considered certain. JACKSON, on the other hand, lay snugly entrenched behind his embankment of mud and cotton bales, his left *appuyé* on the swamp, his right on the Mississippi. General Coffee and the Tennesseeans occupied the extreme left of the line, and the batteries were served by the United States' artillerists and militiamen, except No. 2, which was entrusted to the crew of the late Carolina, and No. 3, commanded by privateer captains, and served by Lafitte's men.

The attack was to have taken place before sunrise, but owing to the caving-in of the canal, the army did not arrive within musket range until dawn. They were received by a well-directed volley, which threw them into disorder; but they soon rallied, and were advancing steadily to the assault, when Packenham discovered that the Forty-Fourth regiment had come into the field without the fascines and ladders. Colonel Mullens was ordered to return for them, but losing all command of himself, forsook his men. Packenham immediately despatched an aid to bring them up. This officer found them in the greatest confusion. The General, upon hearing this, placed himself at their head, and ordered the column to press on at double quick time. Twice they charged, exposed to a murderous fire of musketry and cannon, which mowed them down by ranks. The deeds of the thirty-two pounders are especially commemorated : 'One single discharge,' says the Subaltern, 'served to sweep the centre of the attacking force into eternity.' The officers exerted themselves to the utmost to rally their men, but all efforts were useless. Two or three hundred gained the ditch, and endeavored to climb the parapet, but the soft earth gave way beneath their feet, and only seventy succeeded in the attempt, all of whom were captured. The death of Sir Edward Packenham, who fell like a brave man at the head of the Forty-Fourth, and the mortal wound received by General Gibbs, completed the universal dismay. The column turned and fled. On the river the advance of General Keane's detachment stormed an unfinished battery occupied by a rifle corps : instead of supporting his men, and entering the lines at that point, General Keane marched with his column across the plain to the aid of the main body. Such a movement only served to increase the confusion. His troops caught the general panic, and Keane himself was borne, desperately wounded, from the field. Meantime the brave band that had taken the battery, unsupported by their friends, and unable to retreat, perished to a man by the rifles of the Louisianians. On the right bank, Colonel Thornton carried all before him ; drove the Americans from two entrenched positions ; and was in full pursuit, when a messenger brought the news of the disaster of the main army, and the order for an immediate retreat, which he effected without opposition. It appears evident, from all statements of this affair, and from JACKSON's address, that the conduct of the militia on the right bank formed a striking contrast to the bravery of the troops on Rodriguez Canal.

Here the carnage had been awful. 'A space of ground extending from the ditch of the American lines to that on which the enemy drew up his troops, two hundred and fifty yards in length by about two hundred in breadth, was literally covered with men, either dead or severely wounded.' At least three thousand brave fellows lay stretched upon the plain, and all wearing the British uniform; for the American loss did not exceed twenty-five men in killed and wounded.

General Lambert, on whom the command had devolved, abandoned all hopes of taking New-Orleans. A quick and safe retreat was the only object aimed at. During his preparations, he was harassed as before by the Americans, but nothing serious was attempted. The British were still too powerful to be driven to despair. Matters remained thus until the 17th, when the prisoners were exchanged on both sides: on the 19th, every Englishman had vanished.

The war was now virtually ended. The details of Lambert's skilful retreat; the nine days' bombardment of the fort at Plâquemines; the taking of Fort Bowyer; the disputes concerning negro slaves; the triumphal entry of General JACKSON, and the usual addresses and illuminations; and finally, the ratification of peace, followed hard upon each other, and have little bearing on the great feat of arms we wished to commemorate. On the 23d of December, nine thousand English soldiers, who had served with success in Europe, landed on the territory of the Union. One month after, the survivors, worn out, baffled, disheartened, their two commanders slain, were reëmbarking at the same place, leaving three thousand gallant comrades to moulder beneath the cypresses of Louisiana. There is scarcely an instance in modern history, perhaps none, in which men, unaided by contagion, have repelled an attack with so little injury to themselves, and such fearful slaughter to their opponents.

To JACKSON belongs the honor of the victory. The promptitude with which he planned the attack of the 23d, the skill displayed in his dispositions, and the energy with which they were carried out on that eventful night, saved New-Orleans from destruction. The next morning the British would have blown his force to the winds, and have seized the city as easily as they had anticipated. But awed by the boldness of a foe they had hitherto despised, and held in check by the guns of the Carolina, they gave the Americans time to complete the famous breast-work, before which, as before an altar of Liberty, England's bravest and best were sacrificed.

We owe ANDREW JACKSON a long debt of gratitude, not only for having repelled an invasion the results of which might have been most disastrous, but also for having proved to Great Britain, (what hitherto she had maintained to be problematical,) that the American militia could and would fight, if skilfully commanded.

Years after, the General finds himself at the head of the nation he defended, and makes more enemies by a word than he had ever beaten off with his sword. Perhaps he possessed too little of the pliability of his emblematic tree for a statesman, and would better have left the China closet of politics to one who had less of the headstrong and headlong bull in his nature. But posterity will decide on this also. Our business with him was as commanding officer at New-Orleans on the 8th of January, 1815; a day on which he earned his title to a seat at WASHINGTON's right hand.

FR. FLÁNEUR.

LINES

TO A GREEK GIRL, MET IN THE ISLAND OF METELIN.

WHAT spirit of the dell is here,
  That, as the sunset lights decay,
Alone, but without sign of fear,
  Trips past me, like a woodland fay :
Till, stopping as she spies me, see !
  With looks that more of mirth express
Than bashfulness, yet gently free,
  She gazes mute and motionless.

The summer sun has touched her brow
  And brightly sparkles in her eye,
But lets the snow, that lurks below
  Her dimpled cheek, unmelted lie :
And smooth, as pebble of the rill,
  The forehead by her dark locks 'twined,
Light, sportive ringlets, ready still
  To dance when piped to by the wind.

A spirit of the wood or stream,
  A thing of airy substance wrought,
She seems — the creature of a dream,
  Whose image haunts the waking thought :
A moment, as the stars of night
  Whose gloom the streaks of twilight sever,
Beam faintly, greets my startled sight —
  A moment seen, then gone forever !

G. HILL.

OUR SCHOOL AT STOKEVILLE.

A STRAY CHAPTER.

AMONG my early recollections of the primitive days of Stokeville, the Village School is the most vivid. It was buried in a walnut grove that skirted the western border of the town, and was an old brown building, carved and slashed from end to end. In the spring of the year the whole grove was sweet with bursting buds, and vocal with the songs of birds. In midsummer we used to find shelter in it from the rays of heat that steeped its canopy. In autumn, its long shadows pointed far eastward into the village, while its western border was kindled into a living flame. I see the old school-house now, as it was when I trudged to it a boy. But it is swept away !

Such was our school-house — the only one within three miles. It was to this spot that all Stokeville was driven for knowledge and power — for 'knowledge is power.' We hired our school-masters then ; *nine* dollars a month, and boarded ; and such specimens of intellectual humanity as fell upon us were never before nor since paralleled.

Mr. EPHRAIM MILLS, from Connecticut *'strait,'* was the first gentleman who took the urchins of Stokeville in hand, 'for better or for worse.' I am not about to inflict upon the reader a minute account of Mr. Mills' inauguration, nor of the ' gang' over which he had been called upon to preside.   We had Bill Jones, a red-headed, freckled-faced boy, who swore he would whip the master before the week was out ; Jack Janes, a tall, loose-jointed, long-limbed fellow, who ' did n't care *how* many rules the master made — *he* should n't obey 'em ;' Pete Pierce, who prided himself upon his tricks never being found out ; and Bob Boles, and Ned Hawkes, and a score of ' Hanks' and ' Dicks' and ' Johns ;' all together as wicked and perverse a generation as ever tried the temper of man.

Monday morning, bright and early, the school was to ' begin.'   All the children in Stokeville had white collars and clean aprons on that morning at least.   There was a great strife among mothers, and greater pride among their offspring.

I well recollect the day on which Ephraim Mills took the boys of Stokeville in hand.   I was at my post at nine o'clock precisely.   The ' master' made his appearance at half past nine.   He was a short, pot-bellied little man, with a full, red face, and a head as big and green as a pumpkin.   His little round eyes stared to the right and left, as wild as an owl's, as he waddled along in to take his throne.   He wore a white hat upon a head which was covered with a profusion of red hair ; a bandanna handkerchief was about his neck ; and he sported a checked vest, and a pair of corduroy pantaloons.

Mr. Mills hung his hat upon a peg.   He then turned slowly around, and calmly surveyed the field before him.   The school sank at once into profound silence.   He walked across the floor and back again, and after taking a second survey, addressed us as follows :

' Boys, I have come here to teach school.   Nëow, every one on you has got to behave yourselves.   I have taught school 'afore, now I tell you ; and if you behave yourselves, all will go well ; but if you *do n't*, there will be trouble !   I whip terribly when I *do* whip ; but I am a good master when *you* behave.   Now mind what I tell you ; you must all on you behave yourselves.'

There was a subdued ' snicker" from one end of the school-room to the other, when Ephraim concluded.

' The next thing I shall do,' continued Mills, ' is to divide all on you into classes.   There is nothing like system in schools.   And first, I must have your names.'

Mr. Mills then began at one end of the school room and asked the name of every scholar in order ; in the course of which duty a laughable colloquy occurred.

' What 's your name ?' said he, to a lank Yankee boy.

' Aaron.'

' Spell it, if you please,' said Ephraim.

' Great A, little A, r-o-n,' answered the pupil, promptly.

' Dutch Honnes,' as he was called, a thick-headed urchin, came next.

' Well, what 's *your* name ?' inquired Mr. Mills.

' My name 's Honnes,' he answered.

' Well, how do you spell it ?   See nëow if you can do it as slick as Aaron did.'

'*Great Honnes, little Honnes, r-o-n !*'

The laugh was decidedly against the ' master.'

' Now,' said Mr. Mills, when the confusion had a little subsided, ' as I said before, I 'll divide all on you into classes.   All on you who study the grammar, go together ; all on you who cypher, go together ; all on you who are l'arning to read, go together.'

The school wheeled into divisions as suddenly as a military company ; and the ' master' seemed to look upon us with as intense an air of self-superiority as Bonaparte would have done upon an army of new-recruited soldiers.

' Very well, very well,' said Ephraim. Now all on the grammar class take the high benches on the east ; all on the geography class, the high benches on the west ; and all o' the reading scholars take the low benches. SCHOOL 'S COMMENCED !'

' School 's commenced !' was uttered by Ephraim with infinite authority, accompanied by a stamp of the foot, and a whirling of the ruler, which was absolutely terrific. It had the desired effect. Every boy was as whist and silent as though he had suddenly been changed to stone.

An hour passed, when the voice of Ephraim was again heard. ' Third class, that is reading-class, come up to read. Bring your books ; form in a line ; stand up strait, and speak plain.'

The class straggled along up, some coughing, some blowing their noses, some grinning, and some leering.

' Fine healthy-looking lot of boys,' said Ephraim, as he surveyed them. ' Turn to your places.'

Every boy wet his thumb and turned to the place selected in the ' English Reader,' which chanced to be that beautiful paraphrase of the one hundred and nineteenth Psalm, commencing, ' The Lord my pasture shall prepare.'

' Now begin,' said Ephraim.

The boy at the head commenced in a whining tone, taking care not to make a pause, or catch a breath, until he had reached the end of the verse, when he drew one that might have been heard far out in the grove, looking up at the same time for a word of praise.

' You do well,' said Ephraim ; ' you read quick and smart, and that 's what I like to see. Now the next thing I want to know,' said he, ' is, do you *understand* what you read ? Every thing depends on that. I have commenced this school with a determination of making all my boys understand. Now,' he added, abstractedly, ' what is understood by the first line you have read, ' The Lord my pasture shall prepare ?' Can you tell me, Jack Janes ?'

Jack looked on the floor, and seemed sadly puzzled. Hesitating for some time in this position, he at length broke out :

' *I* do n't know, Sir.'

' Do n't know, Sir !' repeated Ephraim ; why, I am thunder-struck at your ignorance ! Why, it is as old as Greece and Rome, and used to be spoken by Cicero and Demosthenes. Can't *you* tell, Bill Jones, what that line means ?'

Bill Jones was about as much troubled as Jack Janes. *He* could n't tell, and so it went to the foot of the class.

' Well neow every boy pay attention, while I explain, and do n't none on you forget what I say. This sentence, as I said before, has reference to the Greeks and Romans, who were a great people, living in Africa, about four thousand years ago ; but I do n't recollect the exact period. They were a roving race of people, and lived pretty much as many folks in New-England do, by their pasture land, and the manufacture of butter, cheese, and such like ; and as they were all believers in the Christian religion, and somewhat superstitious, they used to sing this hymn at the beginning of each year; ' The Lord my *pasture* shall prepare.' That 's it. Will you all recollect ?'

Every child nodded his head, and muttered ' Umph.'

' Now,' said Ephraim, ' you can all take your seats ; and be sure to *understand* your reading lesson next time.'

The bustle of the reading-class returning to their seats had not subsided, before the master's voice was again heard :

' Class in astronomy and geography ! Re-*cite*.'

The astronomy and geography class formed with more dignity than the junior class which had preceded it. Mr. Mills seemed to look upon its members also with an increased degree of respect. After they were collected in order, Ephraim told them that geography was a great study ; that ' he himself did n't know nothing of the world only what he got from this ;' that his grandfather had studied a great deal of it, and once visited Lake Erie in person. He said he hoped we would all meet his expectations in this sublimest of all sciences. He would now proceed to ask some questions :

' William Dobbs, how is the state of Maine bounded ?'

' On the north by the Gulf of Mexico, east by Arkansas, south by the Potomac, and west by Massachusetts.'

' Very well, Sir. The next — Nicholas Rice : What is the principal river in Maine ?'

' The Sabine.'

' Very well. The next — Joseph Mills : What is its capital ?'

' St. Augustine.'

' That 's right. The next — Henry Dobbin : What is its produce ?'

' Hemp and beeswax.'

' Right. The next — Israel Booth : How many parts of the earth are covered with water ?'

' Europe and Asia.'

' How many with land ?'

' Africa and North America.'

' What is the shape of the world, Nicholas Rice ?'

' Partly round and partly flat.'

' Which part is flat ?'

' That part near the equator.'

' Very well said, indeed : The next — Joseph Mills : What is an equator ?'

' An equator is a large brass ring put around the earth, which holds it together, while it turns upon its axles.

' Answered well. The next : What are the poles ?'

' The poles are large irons run through the world, on which it turns round a thousand miles a minute.'

' Or rather,' said Ephraim, ' nine hundred and ninety miles a minute. The next : How many miles is the sun from the earth ?'

' A hundred millions.'

' It is *supposed* to be that,' said Ephraim, ' but we have no certain means of knowing. The next : Is the sun inhabited ?'

' No, Sir — but the moon is.'

' Who inhabits the moon ?'

' The man in the moon.'

' That is very well — *very* well. We can all *see* the man in the moon,' said Ephraim, 'and therefore we know the moon is inhabited.' You all pass good examinations in astronomy. Let us put a few more questions in geography. ' Which is the largest city in the world ?'

' China.'

' Which is the largest river ?'

' The Mississippi.'

' The largest island ?'

' Long-Island.'

' Very well. Now take your seats, and go on with your lessons.'

This is a brief sketch of Ephraim Mills, and his class in its first recitation in what he called astronomy and geography. There was quite a pause after this searching examination. Nothing was heard but the murmur of boys conning their books. Ephraim retired to a chair, where he stretched back in a state of exhaustion, fanning himself, and brushing the big flies from his flaming face.

In the other departments of his school, Ephraim exhibited the same kind and degree of talent as in the instances just mentioned. Yet he was a school-master, and taught Stokeville school, and received therefor the sum of *nine dollars per month*, and ' boarded round !'

I am not going to inflict upon the reader the history of Ephraim's entire administration as ' Knight of the Ferule.' The history of one day is the history of another. In his *capacity* there was ' neither variation nor shadow of turning.' All Stokeville was pleased with him, because they were ignorant of him, and all the children were compelled to submit to his authority. It must be borne in mind that the Inspectors of Common Schools in Stokeville, at this period, were about as competent for *their* office as our school-master was for his. They were well matched ; and take them altogether, the way in which education, literature, and the fine arts thrived, was truly astonishing. Every scholar, of course, was soon on the high road to distinction.

For the first five years of my boyhood, during the early days of Stokeville, such were my instructors. The good people thought that so long as they had a ' master,' and the ' school' went on, all was well. Whether he was capable or incapable, was of no sort of consequence. They thought it a duty to send children to school, but it mattered little whether they learned or not. Learning in fact was decidedly unpopular. The old people reasoned thus : ' *They* had never had but three months schooling, yet they were well off in the world, and as capable of carrying on business as some of their neighbors who had been to college.' This argument, strengthened by what they called ' practical illustration,' was of course invincible. How many Stokevilles, Stokeville schools, and Stokeville school-masters, there are in existence yet !

THE WIDOW-MATCH.

In but *one* thing the twain agree,
And mutual discord waive ;
He Julia joins to wet with tears
Her former husband's grave !

THE BIRD OF ARABY.

' THERE is a superstition among the Arabians, that a Bird called *Manah* issues from the brain of every dead person, and haunts his sepulchre, uttering lamentable screams, and divulging to the ears of the initiated all the secrets and crimes of the deceased.'

I.

BIRD of the hollow tomb!
Born of the brain, where once rich dreams could play,
　　Of luxury and bloom ;
Where passed the spirit hence from Death away,
When on the unconscious breast the pall funereal lay ?

II.

Speak ! — Thou in darkness born :
Thou, nursed of Silence, midst the faded dead,
　　From friends lamenting, torn ;
Thou on whose fabled wing no ray is shed —
Prattler of sins long past — of deeds remembered !

III.

Thine is a mournful voice,
Thou trumpeter of by-gone acts of shame ;
　　It bids no heart rejoice —
It breathes of Pride with its pervading flame —
Of Lust and Power that ruled, till the Destroyer came.

IV.

Dark Bird ! — it is not thine
In the blue chambers of the air to soar ;
　　Amidst the gay sunshine,
And Araby's aroma-gales, to pour
Sweet songs, that melt in air the Groves of Spices o'er.

V.

But by the wasting form
Of erring Sinner 't is thy lot to be,
　　Thou compeer of the worm !
Tattling to stranger's ear that bends to thee,
Of crimes in secret done, when that still heart was free!

VI.

Yet in the wakeful breast
Of living Man, a mightier than thou
　　Hath a stern voice impressed :
'T is CONSCIENCE, whispering, till the shadowed brow
Grows thoughtful in remorse, that shone in pride but now!

VII.

He is not lost, whose soul
Leans to the lessons of that hidden Guide,
　　And bows to their control ;
They check the purpose wrong — unholy Pride —
Soothing the heart with peace to heavenly scenes allied.

VIII.

And he is doubly blest
Who woos that calmness in his breast to dwell :
　　Night hath for him sweet rest —
Day uttereth speech to day — and visions tell
His self-approving heart that all within is well!

Philadelphia.　　　　　　　　　　　　　　　　　　　　　　　　　c.

LITERARY NOTICES.

INCIDENTS OF TRAVEL in Central America, Chiapas, and Yucatan. By JOHN L. STEPHENS, Author of 'Incidents of Travel in Egypt, Arabia Petræa, and the Holy Land.' In two volumes. pp. 898. New-York: HARPER AND BROTHERS.

WE take some credit to ourselves that the KNICKERBOCKER was among the first, if not *the* first of the American journals, to awaken a general interest among us in the wonderful antiquities of Central America; and we incline to believe that the impulse of travel, of which the volumes before us are the noble fruits, was derived originally from the original papers and drawings in this Magazine. But be this as it may: certain it is, that though the HARPERS have published many grand books in their day, yet we doubt whether any of their issues have ever come up, in all respects, to the interest and elegance of these superb octavos; we say 'in all respects;' having reference thereby to the novelty of the scenes and objects with which Mr. STEPHENS makes us acquainted, to the never-tiring charm of his narrative and descriptions, and to the really magnificent engravings, with nearly a hundred of which the volumes are illustrated and embellished. These engravings, it must be observed, are mostly from steel plates, executed by skilful artists, from drawings made on the spot by Mr. CATHERWOOD, who accompanied Mr. STEPHENS in his 'travel,' and who superintended the engraving through all its stages, so as to insure perfect accuracy: moreover the subjects are eminently curious as well as beautiful, being the mysterious remains of aboriginal architecture and sculpture which alone now indicate the sites of great cities once existing in Central America and Mexico; cities whose inhabitants must have been far advanced in mechanical skill at least, and which must have teemed with rich, ingenious, and industrious populations; but of whose origin, history, and fate, even of whose names, no record is preserved, and of which little is known, tradition itself being silent respecting them. Six of these ruined cities — these desolate relics of a people long since passed away — were visited by Mr. STEPHENS; Copan, Quirigua, Tecpan-Guatimala, Palenque, Ocosingo, and Uxmal; the ruins of each were thoroughly explored, and faithful drawings were made of the singular edifices, bas-reliefs, statues, and hieroglyphics with which they abound, and the like of which has been discovered no where else, either in Europe, Africa, or Asia. They are equally remarkable for their elaborate beauty and their perfectly unique character.

But the engravings, or their subjects, or the descriptions of them given by Mr. STEPHENS, although a prominent feature of attraction in the work, do by no means constitute its only or its principle attraction. The countries visited by him in the extended journey of which these volumes are the rich result, abound with curious and highly interesting objects for the study of the moralist, the historian, the naturalist, and the statesman. Their social and political condition is almost as unique as their ruined cities, and at every page we have details most striking in novelty, variety, absurdity, pathos, terror or wonder. Then there is the personal adventure, the narrative of which is given with such inimitable graphic effect, such an air of unquestionable reality, and with such perfect and humorous *bon-hommie*, as few travellers exhibit in their writings, but which, as they constitute the principal charm of Mr. STEPHENS's former volumes, will be looked for and most abundantly found in these. We know that public expectation has been greatly awakened in relation to this work; that people are prepared to find it wonderfully curious, entertaining, and instructive: such was our own anticipation; and we cannot praise it more highly than by saying that the anticipation was realized and satisfied to its full extent. The time that will have elapsed between the issuing of these volumes and the publication of the present number, makes us fear to occupy our pages with any of the numerous passages which are every where pencilled in our sadly bedog's-eared copy; for such is the popularity of 'Incidents of Travel' bearing our author's brand, that a second edition would be likely to accompany our extracts from the first. We content ourselves with the modest preface:

'The author is indebted to Mr. VAN BUREN, late President of the United States, for the opportunity of presenting to the public the following pages. He considers it proper to say, that his diplomatic appointment was for a specific purpose, not requiring a residence at the capital, and the object of his mission being fulfilled or failing, he was at liberty to travel. At the time of his arrival in Central America, that country was distracted by a sanguinary civil war, which resulted, during his sojourn there, in the entire prostration of the Federal Goverment. By the protection and facilities afforded by his official character, he was enabled to accomplish what otherwise would have been impossible. His work embraces a journey of nearly three thousand miles in the interior of Central America, Chiapas, and Yucatan, including visits to eight ruined cities, with full illustrations from drawings taken on the spot by Mr. Catherwood. Its publication has been delayed on account of the engravings; but on one consideration the author does not regret the delay. Late intelligence from Central America enables him to express the belief that the state of anarchy in which he has represented that beautiful country no longer exists; the dark clouds which hung over it have passed away, civil war has ceased, and Central America may be welcomed back among republics.'

BIOGRAPHY AND POETICAL REMAINS of the late MARGARET MILLER DAVIDSON. By WASHINGTON IRVING. In one volume. pp. 359. Philadelphia: LEA AND BLANCHARD.

OUR readers are familiar with the name of the young and gifted LUCRETIA DAVIDSON, whose wonderful poetical powers and gentle character were set forth in a volume which was noticed in an early number of this Magazine. The present work is a memoir of a younger sister, who possessed the same moral and physical constitution, and was, until she died, prone to the same feverish excitement of the mind and kindling of the imagination, which had acted so powerfully on the fragile form of the early-called LUCRETIA. We know of nothing more touching than the record of her brief career; her precocity of talent, her vivid imagination, and above all, the sweetness of her disposition, which shone through all her lingering and painful illness, and the intermingled ties between the fond parent and the affectionate child. A correspondent has laid before us some brief recollections of the family of LUCRETIA MARIA and MARGARET MILLER DAVIDSON, which we take the liberty of introducing in this connection. Alluding to the volume under notice, he observes: 'It is well that the writings of such an uncommon genius have fallen into the hands of an editor like Mr. IRVING. This publication, together with the memoir and remains of LUCRETIA MARIA DAVIDSON, edited some time since by Professor MORSE, of the New-York University — which was reviewed in the London Quarterly Review, and pronounced to be an exhibition of early talent, to which no age or nation had produced a superior — deserve to go down to posterity in intimate association, and to receive a wide circulation. The latter work has not received in this country the attention which it merits. It ought to be republished in the inviting form of the later work, that these gifted and lovely sisters may together occupy the centre-table of every lady, and ornament the library of every scholar, in the country. While light works of foreign literature, which have little or no moral purpose to recommend them, are circulated through the nation, it is due to the American character that such bright and pure gems of native genius as these 'Remains' should not be overlooked nor neglected. The writer of these pages has been intimately acquainted with the family to which these young women belonged, and it is always recollected with deep interest.

Often has he experienced their hospitality in Plattsburgh, though the youngest sister must have been an infant when his intercourse with it ceased. He well recollects LUCRETIA MARIA, when a child, as an amiable and thoughtful little girl. He had no idea, however, of the genius that slumbered within her. As she grew up, she was as much distinguished by the elegance of her form, the simplicity and neatness of her dress, and the brilliancy of her countenance, as by her intellectual endowments. He well recollects the general notice which herself and an elder sister attracted by their very interesting appearance on the occasion of the 'commencement' of the University of Vermont at Burlington, when she might have been fifteen years of age. The mother, a very amiable woman, has been through the greater part of her years afflicted with severe ill-health; but though her hold on life has been feeble, she has lived to mourn over the early departure of three lovely daughters, the eldest of whom became the wife of the Rev. Mr. TOWNSEND, an Episcopal clergyman in Canada. The mother, undoubtedly beautiful in her youth, possessed a gifted mind; though too much devoted to her family, and too severely borne down by illness, to be extensively addicted to literature. A peculiarly kind and affectionate disposition was her prominent characteristic. There was, however, a great deal of poetry in her structure of mind, though her simple and affectionate disposition was at the farthest possible remove from display. Whenever an extraordinary genius arises, one always looks to find something uncommon in the intellectual character of the mother. The part which she has borne in the recent memoir of her daughter must cause her to be held in high estimation. The writer well recollects her once 'telling a story,' in his social intercourse with the family, which was said to have been founded on facts that occurred in the early history of New-Jersey, which for interest of incident and fascination of coloring was equal to any tale he ever read; yet it was related in the most simple manner, and was the mere overflowing of an elegant mind and a feeling heart. That story would assuredly prove most effective in print, could it be recorded precisely as it fell from her lips. A quarter of a century has not effaced the recollection of some of the leading incidents: The eldest son of a nobleman in England, having fallen under the displeasure of his father, fled to America and came to New-Jersey. Being destitute of any means of support, he resorted to school-keeping. Among his scholars was a lovely girl, the daughter of a plain farmer in the neighborhood. She attracted his attention, for he saw that she was a young woman of rare endowments. His own character and parentage were unknown, but he was regarded as an amiable and accomplished young gentleman. After a season of courtship, he married her, still continuing the profession of school-keeping. Not long after this his father died, and news came to him that he was heir to the title and estate. This information, to their astonishment, he conveyed to his wife and her parents. She perhaps trembled at the idea of an elevation to a station which her education so little prepared her to fill; and her parents, lest this exaltation should cause their beloved daughter to despise and forget them. But the fears of neither were realized. Her husband sent her to a school to receive a finished education; and when removed to her new situation, she shone with brilliancy among the noble ladies, her companions; and what is best of all, she cherished the kindest regard for her humble parents, and often cheered them with the most affectionate messages and valuable presents. . . . When the Remains of LUCRETIA MARIA DAVIDSON appeared, one of the first things for which the writer looked, was to see if this tale had not been wrought by her into poetry.'

In cordially commending these 'Remains' to the reader, we say with our correspondent: 'Let not Americans be chargeable with neglecting native genius. It may be hoped that the recent publication will revive an interest in the work of the elder sister, and that they will both have a circulation in some degree commensurate with their extraordinary merits. It would cheer the hearts of the bereaved parents to find the rare qualities of their lovely daughters duly estimated; and the profits of an extensive sale of these works would probably not be disregarded by a family eminently deserving, but not wealthy.'

EDITOR'S TABLE.

'DISCE MORI.' — Learn to die, is the solemn and all-important lesson taught in a volume by CHRISTOPHER SUTTON, D. D., Prebend of Westminster, London, in 1600, a new edition of which, from the press of the Messrs. APPLETON, is before us. 'Man,' says the quaint author, 'has here only a course to finish, which being finished, he must away;' and he entreats the living to remember that the 'healthiest, where or when we know not, all must down, when DEATH cometh; which Death is like the serpent Regulus — no charming can charm him.' Of all lessons or learnings, he adds, than a lesson of learning to die, 'what more weighty, what more divine? What is it to have the force of Demosthenes, the persuasive art of Tully? What is it by arithmetical account to divide fractions, and never to think of numbering the time we have yet to live? What is it, by geometrical practice, to take the longitude of the most spacious prospects, and not to measure that which the prophet calleth only 'a span long?' What is it to set the diapason in a musical concert, and for want of good government, to lead a life all out of tune? What is it with the astronomer to observe the motions of the heavens, and to have his heart buried in the earth? With the naturalist, to search out the cause of many effects, and let pass the consideration of his own frailty? With the historian, to know what others have done, and to neglect the true knowledge of himself? With the lawyer, to prescribe many laws in particular, and not to remember the common law of nature, a law general? Surely all is nothing worth!' The style of this little volume is remarkable for its terseness, and for its redundance of forcible and felicitous metaphor. We perceive here the source of every striking thought with which the author of 'Lacon' has transfused his well-known passage upon death. Indeed, the entire work is saturate with profound thought and solemn admonition. It is a book well calculated to make us 'meditate of our final end, at our lying down, which doth resemble the grave, and at our rising up, which may mind us of a joyful resurrection,' and to make this remembrance the key to open in the day and to shut in the night. How truthful and sententious are the lessons which ensue: 'O world, most unworthy to be affected of us, where are the riches that poverty hath not decayed! Where is the beauty that age hath not withered! Where is the strength that sickness hath not weakened! Where is the pomp that time hath not ruined! We are but tenants at will in this clay form. The foundation of all the building is a small substance, always kept cold by an intercourse of air: the pillar whereupon the whole frame stays is only the passage of a little breath; the strength, some few bones tied together with dry strings or sinews: howsoever we piece and patch this poor cottage, it will at last fall; and we must give surrender, when Death shall say, 'This or that man's time hath come.' First, we mourn for others; a little after, others mourn for us. Now we supply the places and offices and heritages of them that were before; and ere long be, others shall come afresh in our rooms, and rule where we rule, sway where we sway, and possess all which we have gathered together with care, kept with fear, and at last left with sorrow.'

Willis Gaylord Clark.

—

'Our brother is no more!' DEATH, the pale messenger, has beckoned him silently away; and the spirit which kindled with so many elevated thoughts; which explored the chambers of human affection, and awakened so many warm sympathies; which rejoiced with the glad, and grieved with the sorrowing, has ascended to mansions of eternal repose. And there is *one*, reader, who above all others feels how much gentleness of soul, how much fraternal affection and sincere friendship; how much joyous hilarity, goodness, poetry, have gone out of the world; and he will be pardoned for dwelling in these pages, so often enriched by the genius of the Departed, upon the closing scenes of his earthly career. Since nearly a twelve-month, the deceased has 'died daily' in the eyes of the writer of this feeble tribute. He saw that Disease sat at his heart, and was gnawing at its cruel leisure; that in the maturity of every power, in the earthly perfection of every faculty; 'when experience had given facility to action and success to endeavor,' he was fast going down to darkness and the worm. Thenceforth were treasured up every soul-fraught epistle and the recollection of each recurring interview, growing more and more frequent, until at length Life like a spent steed 'panted to its goal,' and Death sealed up the glazing eye and stilled the faltering tongue. Precious seasons! — sacred scenes! Would it were in our power *now* to transfer them from our cherished records: but the hand wavers and the heart overflows. Leaving these therefore, with many other treasured remains and biographical facts for future reference and preservation in this Magazine, we pass to the following passages of a letter recently received from a late but true friend of the lamented deceased, Rev. Dr. DUCACHET, Rector of St. Stephen's Church, Philadelphia; premising merely, that the reverend gentleman had previously called upon him at his special instance, in the last note he ever penned; that 'his religious faith was manifested in a manner so solemn, so frank, and so cordial,' as to convince the affectionate pastor that the failing invalid, aware that he must die of the illness under which he was suffering, had long been seeking divine assistance to prepare him for the issue so near at hand:

'AT four o'clock on Friday P. M., the day before his death, I saw him again, he himself having selected the time, thinking that he was strongest in the afternoon. But there was an evident change for the worse; and he was laboring under fever. His religious feelings were however even more satisfactory, and his views more clear, than the day before. He assured me that he enjoyed a sweet peace in his mind, and that he had no apprehension about death. He was 'ready to depart' at any moment. I was unwilling to disturb him by much talking, or a very long visit, and made several attempts to leave him; but in the most affectionate and pressing manner, not to be resisted, he urged me to remain. His heart seemed full of joy and peace; overflowing with gratitude to GOD for his goodness, and with kindness to me. Leaving him, after an hour's interview, I promised to return on Saturday A. M., at ten o'clock, and to administer baptism to him then. This was done accordingly, in the presence of his father-in-law, and three or four other friends and connexions, whom he had summoned to his bed, as he told me, for the express purpose of letting them see his determination to profess the faith of the gospel which in life he had so long neglected. It was a solemn, moving sight; one of the most interesting and affecting I ever saw. More devotion, humility, and placid confidence in GOD, I never saw in any sick man. I mentioned to him that as his strength was evidently declining, it would be well for him to say every thing he desired to say to me then, as his voice and his faculties might fail. He then affectionately placed his arms around my neck; gently drew my ear near to his lips, that I might hear his whispers; and after thanking me over and over again for my small attentions to him, which his gratitude magnified into very high services, he proceeded to tell me what he wished done with his 'poor body.' He expressed very great anxiety to see *you*, and he very much feared that he should die before your expected arrival at midnight. But he said he left that matter and every other to God's disposal. As I was leaving him, he said, 'Call again to-day,' which I promised to do in the evening. He told me he felt a happy persuasion that when he passed from this miserable world and that enfeebled body, he should enter upon 'the inheritance incorruptible, undefiled, and that fadeth not away.' He asked: 'Do you observe how these words labor to convey the idea of Heaven's blessedness to our feeble minds? The 'inheritance *incorruptible!*' Beautiful thought! '*Undefiled*' — more beautiful still! '*That fadeth not away*' — most beautiful of all! I think I understand something of the peace and glory these redoubled words were designed to express.' And then, raising his wasted hand, with great emphasis he said, 'I shall soon know all about it, I trust!'

'In the evening, about seven o'clock, I received a message from him to come immediately to him. I was there by eight. I was surprised to find that he had rallied so much. There was a strength I had not seen before; and his fine open features were lighted up with unusual brilliancy. In every way he seemed better; and I flattered myself that he would live to see you, and even hold out for a day or two more. I had much charming conversation with him about his state of feeling, his views of himself as a sinner, and of God, and of Jesus Christ as a precious Saviour, and of heaven, etc. He then handed me a prayer-book, adding, 'That was my ANNE's,' meaning his wife's. 'Now read me the office for the sick in this book. I want the whole of it. I have read it myself over and over, since you pointed it out to me, and it is delightful.' He then repeated the sentence, 'I know that my Redeemer liveth, and that he shall stand in the latter day upon the earth,' and asked if that was not a part of it. I told him that that belonged to the *burial service.* 'Then,' said he, 'it is quite suitable for me, for it will soon be read by you over my grave.' I sat by his bed, and found the place. Waiting in silence to receive his signal to begin, I thought he was engaged in secret prayer, and was unwilling to interrupt him. But he remained silent so long, seeming to take no notice of me, that I spoke to him. I found that his mind was wandering, and that speech had failed. He muttered indistinctly only. From that moment, he sank gradually away. His emaciated limbs were retracted and cold; his pulse failed; the shadow of death gathered fast and dark upon his countenance; his respiration became feebler and feebler; and at last, at precisely five minutes past ten, he died. So imperceptibly and gently did his happy spirit flee away, that it was some time before we could ascertain that he had gone. I never saw a gentler death. There was no pain, no distress, no shuddering, no violent disruption of the ties of life. Both as to the mind's peace and the body's composure, it was a beautiful instance of ευθανασια. The change which indicated the approach of his last moment, took place about half an hour only before he died. Such, my dear Sir, are all the chief particulars I can remember, and which I have thought you would desire to know.' —

A few summary 'Reflections' upon the character of the lamented deceased succeed, which, although intended, as was the foregoing, only for a brother's eye, we cannot resist the desire to cite in this connexion:

'He was, so far as his character revealed itself to me, a man of a most noble, frank, and generous nature. He was as humble as a little child. He exhibited throughout most remarkable patience. He never complained. But once, while I was on bended knees, praying with him for patience to be given him, and acknowledging that all he had suffered was for the best, he clasped his hands together, and exclaimed, 'Yes! right, right — all right!' · · · He was one of the most affectionate-hearted men I ever saw. Every moment I spent with him, he was doing or saying something to express to me his attachment. He would take my hand, or put his arm around my neck, or say something tender, to tell me that he loved me. He showed the same kind feeling to his attendants, his faithful nurse, REBECCA, and to the humblest of the servants. · · · He was of course, with such a heart, grateful for the smallest attentions. He received the most trifling offices with thanks. I observed this most remarkably on the evening of his death. I had taken my son with me, that he might sit up with him on Saturday night, if occasion should require. When I mentioned that the youth was in the room, he called for him; welcomed him most kindly, thanked him over and over for his friendly intentions; and in fact, broke out into the warmest expressions of gratitude for what his sensitive and generous heart took to be a high act of favor. All this was within an hour and a half of his death. · · · Finally, I believe he was a truly religious man. I have no doubt that he was fully prepared for his end; and that through the sacrifice of the cross, and the Saviour who died there for sinners, he was pardoned and accepted. He has gone, I feel persuaded, to the abodes of peace, where the souls of those who sleep in the LORD JESUS enjoy perpetual felicity and rest.'

———

SURELY all who peruse the foregoing affecting record, may exclaim with the poet whom we lament :

> ' It were not sad, to feel the heart
>   Grow passionless and cold —
> To feel those longings to depart,
>   That cheered the saints of old ;
> To clasp the faith which looks on high,
> Which fires the Christian's dying eye,
>   And makes the curtain-fold
> That falls upon his wasting breast
> The door that leads to endless rest.
>
> It were not lonely, thus to lie
>   On that triumphant bed,
> Till the free spirit mounts on high,
>   By white-winged seraphs led ;
> Where glories earth may never know,
> O'er ' many mansions' lingering, glow,
>   In peerless lustre shed ;
> It were not lonely, thus to soar
> Where sin and grief can sting no more !'

One of the Philadelphia journals, in announcing the demise of the dear Departed, observes : 'Mr. CLARK was a scholar, a poet, and a gentleman. 'None knew him but to love him.' His health had for a long time been failing. The death of his accomplished and lovely wife, a few years ago, upon whom he doated with a passionate and rapturous fondness, had shaken his constitution and eaten his strength. None but intimate friends knew the influence of that sad affliction upon his physical frame. To the last his heart yearned over the dust of that lovely woman. In his death-chamber, her portrait stood always before him on his table, and his loving eye turned to it even in extremest pain, as though it were his living and only friend.' This is literally true. Beyond question, moreover, the seeds of the disease which finally removed him from the world, were ' sown in sorrow' for the death of the cherished companion of his bosom. His letters, his gradually-declining health, his daily life, his published writings, all evince this. The rose on the cheek and the canker at the heart do not flourish at the same time. The MS. of the '*Dirge in Autumn*' came to us literally *sprinkled* with spreading tear-drops ; and the familiar correspondence of the writer is replete with kindred emotion. To the last moment of his life, he kept a collection of 'his ANNE's' letters under his pillow, which he as regularly perused every morning as his Bible and prayer-book. Her portrait, draped in black, crossed the angle of the apartment, above his table, where it might gaze ever upon him with its 'large, bright, spiritual eyes.' Never shall we forget his apostrophe to that beautiful picture, when his ' flesh and his heart failed him,' and he knew that he must soon go hence, to be here no more : ' Sleep on, my love!' said he, in the beautiful and touching words of the Bishop of Chichester's 'Exequy on the Death of a Beloved Wife,' and in a voice scarcely audible through his frequent sobs:

'Sleep on, my love, in thy cold bed,
   Never to be disquieted:
My last 'good night'!—thou wilt not wake
   Till I thy fate shall overtake:
Till age, or grief, or sickness, must
   Marry my body to that dust
It so much loves; and fill the room
   My heart keeps empty in thy tomb.

'Stay for me there; I will not fail
   To meet thee in that hollow vale;
And think not much of my delay,
   I am already on the way;
And follow thee with all the speed
   Desire can make, or sorrows breed.
Each minute is a short degree,
   And every hour a step toward thee;
At night, when I betake to rest,
   Next morn I rise nearer my West
Of life, almost by eight hours' sail,
   Than when Sleep breathed his drowsy gale.'

Most just the tribute we have seen paid to the affection and patience and grateful spirit of the deceased. To the last, his heart was full-fraught with all tender reminiscences and associations. In the first stages of his illness, when as yet it was scarcely known to affect his general routine of life, he thus replies to a remonstrance from the writer against the growing infrequency of his familiar letters: 'In these spring days, L———, all my old feelings come freshly up, and assure me that I am unchanged. I shall be the same always; so do you be. 'Twinn'd, both at a birth,' the only pledges of our parents' union, we should be all the world to each other:

'We are but two—a little band—
   Be faithful till we die;
Shoulder to shoulder let us stand,
   Till side by side we lie!'

As he gradually grew weaker and weaker, the 'childhood of the soul' seemed to be renewed; the intellectual light to burn brighter and brighter, and the chastened fancy to become more vivid and refined. May it be vouchsafed to us hereafter so to set forth the examples we have preserved of these excellencies, that if the eye that is dim were instinct with mortal vision, it might approve, and the heart that is cold might respond with renewed affection! WILLIS was for some months aware that he had not long to live. 'I shall die,' said he, a few weeks since, 'in the leafy month of June; beautiful season!' And turning his head to gaze upon the trees in the adjoining cemetery-grove, whose heavy foliage was swaying in the summer wind, he murmured to himself the touching lines of BRYANT:

'I know, I know I shall not see
   The season's glorious show,
Nor will its brightness shine for me,
   Nor its wild music flow;
But if around my place of sleep
The friends I love shall come to weep,
   They may not haste to go:
Soft airs, and song, and light, and bloom,
Will keep them lingering by my tomb:
These to their softened hearts will bear
   The thought of what has been,
And speak of one who cannot share
   The gladness of the scene.'

How forcibly were the recollections of this scene borne in upon the mind, as the long procession, following the friend for whom they mourned, defiled into the gates of St. Peter's, on that brightest morning of the month of his heart; the officiating divine from whom we have quoted chaunting eloquently the while the touching and beautiful service for the dead! Upon the soft velvet green-sward and the white marble vault-slabs shimmered down through venerable trees the warm sunlight, flecking all the expanse below; but where was *he*, to whose eye every phase of nature was a delight; whose 'silent voice, speaking in forms and colors,' was ever in his ear; the divinity whom he worshipped with fervent, poetical devotion — looking ever through nature up to nature's GOD! Yet we buried not there our friend, our brother, but only the frail tenement in which he dwelt complainingly for awhile, as in a home. 'It was the *material* mould only that earth claimed; it was *dust* alone that descended to dust.'

But he has gone! leaving behind him a name to live, as we trust, in the heart of the nation. As a moral poet, we know not a 'line which dying he could have wished to blot. He was an AMERICAN, in all his heart, and loved to dwell upon the future destiny of his beloved country. He was a sincere, unvarying, unflinching FRIEND; and although in his long career as editor of an influential daily journal, and in his enlarged intercourse in society, it were not strange were it otherwise, yet it has been truly remarked by one of his contemporaries — *all* of whom, let us gratefully add, have borne the warmest testimony to his genius and his worth — that 'it may be said Mr. CLARK had no enemy, and only encountered attacks from one or two coarse and unworthy sources, against which no character, however gentle and deserving, could have immunity.' Another observes, that 'it was in the character of an editor that he won upon the feelings and affections of so many, and entitled himself to the regard of his brethren of the press, toward whom he always acted with courtesy; positive, when invited by kindred propriety; negative, when he believed unkindness or inability to appreciate courtesy existed.' So to live among his fellow men as did the deceased, and at last, 'with heart-felt confidence in GOD, and the sacramental seal almost fresh upon his brow, gently to fall asleep in JESUS, looking with a Christian's hope for a Christian's reward,'* — surely, *thus* 'to die is gain!' And in view of such a hope and such an end, well may we who, left behind to drag a maimed life, exclaim with the poet:

> 'O Death! thy freezing kiss
> Emancipates — the rest is bliss —
> I would I were away!'

THE LATE MISS LANDON. — We welcome with cordial pleasure two volumes from the press of Messrs. LEA AND BLANCHARD, Philadelphia, containing the 'Life and Literary Remains of 'L. E. L.', by LAMAN BLANCHARD. We receive the work at too late a period, and under circumstances too painful, to attempt a review of it in detail for the present issue. We had the pleasure to number Mrs. L. E. L. MACLEAN among our private correspondents; and shall take occasion hereafter, in an adequate notice of the volumes before us, to quote a few striking and characteristic passages from some of her later letters. We hope these volumes will find a wide sale in this country. Miss LANDON was proud of the approbation of her American readers. 'If any thing on earth,' she writes us, in one of her cherished epistles, 'can realize that glory which is to a poet its own 'exceeding great reward,' it is the fame that comes from afar, when song has gone over the waters like the dove, and like that dove brought home its own sign of life and beauty.' The first volume comprises a sketch of the literary and personal life of its subject, and is interspersed with numerous letters. A large portion of the writings of the author, here given to the public, are entirely new, including a tragedy which does honor to her reputation.

---

* Obituary in the Episcopal 'Banner of the Church.'

Our Foreign Budget. — By the latest steam-packets we have received from attentive correspondents in London and Paris sundry entertaining communications, with
the magazines and periodicals for the month, and other fresh publications from the
English, French, and Scottish capitals. With the following gossipping letter from
Paris — which, how light soever it may seem, is yet not without its fruitful lessons to
our anti-American copyists — and a glance at the new publications, we are compelled
to content ourselves for the present.

THE GRAND OPERA, PARIS.

'The fame of the Grand Opera was the main cause of my coming to Europe. I am
quite willing to confess it ; and I shall hope to pay Paris another visit from your side, for
the same reason. My arrival was on a Sunday, and that very evening there was to be
a performance. What was I to do ? 'Do as they do in Rome ?' I was not cynic,
or at least Parisian enough, to violate my well-trained conscience, although it became
much easier after a few weeks' wear in the capital. I yielded with reluctance to Conscience, not without first proceeding to take a view of the exterior of the edifice, which
was surrounded by a dense crowd. I continued to gaze, until the performance commenced, when I slowly loitered away. On the morrow, remembering the crowd before
the door, I determined to be on the spot at an early hour ; but notwithstanding my
arrival more than an hour and a half before the time, I found at least an hundred and
fifty persons, as enthusiastic and anxious as myself, crowded around the door. 'Crowded'
did I say ? No, I belie the gentlemanlike nation. There was no crowding. They were
entering as orderly as we enter a place of public worship. This fine order, however,
must not be altogether attributed to the phrenological bump or organ of that name. There
were plenty of bayonets walking about the passages, to prick the refractory into sub-
jection to ' Heaven's first law.' · · · The accommodations for the *wait-ers* are excellent. One is neither exposed to the weather nor to annoyance from standing indiscriminately in a vast assembly. A series of stalls are constructed, which traverse the front
from side to side, through which you range, two by two, without having one's elbows
in your ribs, or the brim of his hat clipping your eyes. And should you unfortunately
arrive late, it matters little, for the best positions, or those nearest the door, are usually
retained by some gentlemen, (as they seemed by their air and dress,) who will exchange
with you, 'for a consideration.' After waiting an hour or more, not without amusement, an opportunity of seizing which a Frenchman never suffers to escape, the clock
struck seven. Instantly the door flew open, and the column advanced ; not hurricane
fashion, sweeping all before ; but cool, *too* cool for my excited nerves. Paying little
more for a ticket than at the Park Theatre, I betook myself to the choicest part of the
house, the *pit ;* devoted to dilettanti, connoisseurs, etc. How nice the arrangement !
No cut-asunder seats, but all nicely cushioned, with stuffed backs, and rests for the
elbows ; a seat entirely to one's self, which you retain during the whole evening, provided that on going out you deposit any article upon it. · · · Thus seated to my satisfaction, I proceeded to reconnoitre my whereabout. It was truly the Grand Opera,
if grandeur and magnificence are intended by the term. The paintings of goddesses,
graces, and cupids on the dome and before the boxes ; the extensive use of gilding ;
the chandeliers, the glittering lights, admirably disposed ; the array of fine ladies, radiant with flowers, plumes, and jewelry ; the dark streak formed by the moustaches of
lords, dandies, etc., in the first tier, contrasted with the ivory teeth of the laughing belles ;
the vast mirrors in the boxes, and the rich, tasteful curtains of blue and other civilized colors ; tier on tier five or six deep, equally with the first resplendent with grace and beauty ;
and fops with lighter purses, and ornaments of paste ; retaining soul and body together by
a few bowls of *soup-maigre* and a half bottle of *vin ordinaire,* that they may obtain means
to visit this place of enchantment ; all these are but parts of the great scene. · · · In
a few minutes a buzz ran through the audience. Casting my eyes to the vent beneath

the stage, I beheld the little commander, HABENECK, enter, spectacles on nose, smiling graciously, and followed by his *corps d'armée* of an hundred or more. His position is more elevated than the rest ; and being seated, he reviewed the troops ; now observing the right wing, or the wind instruments, then the left. All right. *Tap-tap!* and waving his magic bow, slowly and majestically moved off the overture of *Robert le Diable*, for the one hundredth time, like a vast steam-ship, amid the perfect silence instead of the plaudits of the audience. It was amusing to watch his movements. Now he slowly waves his bow, for the air is pathetic ; anon he waxes hot ; his arm begins to acquire force ; he directs rapidly his eye toward each column, as he would have it fall in, or retreat, until at length he lashes himself into a perfect rage ; he rises to his feet, and dashes his bow across his instrument, but without touching it. Presently, all subsides, gradually as it began. The utmost order prevails during the performance. There is no 'clapping' until the air or part, though never so long, is finished. The slightest whisper brings down the instant '*Pish!*' of the whole house. A few heads may be marking time, with eyes in a fine frenzy rolling, as if possessed with a spirit ; or an admiring elbow may be seen nudging the ribs of a friend ; but all is perfectly noiseless, until at length a burst of applause, like the explosion of long-generated and pent-up steam, announces the general enthusiasm, in howls of delight and 'bravos' and 'bravissimos' innumerable. · · · The first and second tiers are divided into private boxes. One of these, directly in front of the stage, is reserved for the King and Queen. It is seldom occupied, and is only distinguished from the rest by two highly-gilded chairs. There is no 'third tier' or brothel ; and if any disreputable females *are* present, they are indiscriminately disseminated over the house. There are latticed boxes, where one, unobserved, can yet observe the audience. These, if adopted in our country, would prove convenient and profitable ; for there are many among us who, fearful of their example on others, absent themselves from these operatic entertainments. The latticed boxes, I am informed, are more patronized than any other portions of the house. I must not forget the vast Saloon, some two hundred feet in length, filled to repletion with exquisites, etc., who seldom enter the interior, on account of 'the horrible wind-instruments and big bass-viols !'

'Great attention is paid to the scenery, decorations, and dresses, even down to the silk stockings of the vast and well-drilled chorus. Between the acts of the opera comes the *ballet ;* consisting of some fifty perfectly-drilled dancers, and among them three or four of the first file — a TAGLIONI, an ELLSLER, or a CERITO. Here they cut such fantastic tricks before high heaven as might make the angels weep. Here, on account of the scantiness of the drapery, artists, painters, poets, philosophers, wits, assemble, to observe nature undisguised ; and here the young doctor receives the first rudiments of anatomy. Is this the reason, think you, why the Parisian doctor excels all the rest of the world ? I groan over my own morals, when I find myself affecting the ballet ; but am greatly consoled when I see the most delicate and refined ladies looking on unabashed. A greater display of garb would be disgusting, even to the vile ; for it is a well known Parisian fact, that a slight attempt at dress, or what we should term modesty, is far more enticing than perfect nudity. · · · The passion of the French for dancing is intense. In 'Robert the Devil,' though a German opera, some fifty young witches rise from the dead in their winding-sheets, but soon shuffle off their mortal coil, to a condition the next remove from nudity, and in this state commence dancing after a most diabolical pattern ; making night hideous, and 'we fools of reason most terribly to shake,' lest they should really catch their little deaths of cold. · · · Notwithstanding the annual grant by the government of about one hundred and thirty thousand dollars, and a pension of thirty thousand for decayed actors, and the free use of the theatre, it will not clear its expenses. The principal singers are taught expressly by the government ; the scenery is painted by an academy instituted for that purpose ; and every thing is on the most liberal scale. Yet, though the French doat on it as 'their mother,' they would overturn the government, 'for a frisk,' and with the gain of anarchy, 'acquire a loss,' (so important to them) of every place of public amusement, now supported by the state. Boobies !' —

THE MAGAZINES strike us as unusally rich and various in their contents. BLACKWOOD has several capital papers. '*Ten Thousand a Year*' exhibits, in the present number, no attempts at the ultra pathetic, which sometimes in the writer's hands degenerate into mere melodramatic situations and sheer mawkishness. It is in pictures of men, in expositions of subtle points of human character and action, that this author excels. We have been much impressed with the article entitled '*Russia as it was in the Summer and Winter of* 1812,' a spirited delineation, resting on a direct personal experience. The annexed passage, descriptive of the gathering of the Russian army toward Smolensko, is graphic exceedingly :

'But now began to swarm and thicken about us, even more and more, that vast equipage of war, stretching to the frontiers of Poland from the central depths of Asia, which connected itself with the events of this ever memorable year. Carriages, by thousands, in a line, loaded with the food of armies; oxen, by tens of thousands, moving westward to the general shambles; tumbrils, artillery, officers' equipages in never-ending succession. Often, for half a day together, we were brought to a dead halt, from the mere impossibility of making way against this heady current of Asia and Europe militant. What served to embroil the moving masses still more, was the long line of prisoners, many political prisoners, some already prisoners of war, escorted by swarms of Cossacks and Hulans, who were transferring them to the inland depths of Russia. Then at night, what new aspects of this vast moving, breathing, fluctuating panorama! If the night happened to be cloudy and dark, then myriads of watch-fires gleamed over the sea-like expanses of level ground; soldiers, prisoners, herdsmen, wagons, recruits, women, officers, commissaries, all dancing, singing, or, at times, drinking together; here, for miles in succession, scattered to a quarter of a mile's distance on each side of the road, you would pass whole divisions of the army, thirty thousand strong, all in their shirt sleeves, roasting, frying, broiling, boiling, their main luxurious meal, after the fatigues of the day were over; farther on, if the night were starlight or moonlight, you would come suddenly upon white, snowy tents, raising themselves in ghostly silence from among the blooming heaths; and farther still, you would pass multitudes who, having no such luxuries as tents, were adopting the far wholesomer plan for all weather (but especially for hot summer nights) of *bivouacking*, and might be seen stretched at their length by whole pulks and regiments, sleeping under the canopy of the heavenly host, and scarcely observing the ceremonies of sentries or outposts in this region of wild sylvan nature — as yet so far from the enemy.'

Equally vivid and striking is the following sketch of a scene at Smolensko, the very heart and centre of strategic movements, and the rallying point for the armies gathering from all the capital routes through Russia, to withstand the four hundred and fifty thousand fighting men whom NAPOLEON had brought across the Niemen :

'Continually in this week at Smolensko, streaming through the streets, but to more advantage as approaching along the roads from Moscow or St. Petersburg, one would see the pompous array of armies under every variety and modification that Europe or Asia can furnish. Now came, for hours together, the sea-like tread of infantry, the main masses of modern warfare, the marching regiments of the Czar's armies. Then, after an interval of ten minutes, would be heard the thunder of cavalry approaching; and immediately began to fly past us, like a hurricane, squadrons after squadrons of those whose horses had drunk from the Wolga or the Caspian; many with Siberian fur barrets, who lived near the icy ocean; fine races of Tartars from the Kabarda and the Crimea; men from three different sides of the Euxine, and both sides of the Ural Mountains; stately Cossacks from the Don; Kalmucks, with flat noses, and bodies square, and armed, even in this era of civilization, [hear it, Captain Dalgetty!] with bows, and sounding arrow-sheafs rattling on their backs. But perhaps the most interesting (certainly the most beautiful) interlude in this prodigious mask of martial life was, whenever a squadron of Circassian cavalry cantered past; all of them in glittering steel shirts of mail, all carrying floating plumes of the most beautiful description in their helmets, all superbly mounted, men and horses alike presenting the same tall, graceful, slender figures and features, contrasting so powerfully with the quadrangular massy bodies and sidelong leer of the ugly Kalmucks and Bashkirs.'

The antagonist thought was natural to the writer, which presented the utter stillness, the inaudible tread, of that final grave which was so surely stealing onward to swallow up, in one common abyss of darkness, the horse and his rider, the master and the slave, the mover of this mighty uproar, and the poor suttler that dogged his heels for bread. 'Five-and-twenty or thirty years hence, thought I, say in the year 1840, what will have become of these innumerable captains, marshals, plumed cavaliers so stately and exulting, beneath whose sounding tread the earth shakes on this day of August, 1812!' Let the following picture of the fate which befel the adversaries of these martial masses, on their retreat from Moscow, assist the reader's imagination in solving this query :

"Through the whole extent of the wide region between Pleskow and Wilna, the eye beheld no signs almost of life; every where roofless houses, with not so much as a cat mewing among the ruins; shapeless wrecks where there had been villages or churches; heaps of forlorn chimnies, stone window-frames or mullions, rafters scorched and blackened; oftentimes piles of nondescript rubbish, from which rose up through melting snow smouldering flames, vapors, and a hideous odour, that too often bespoke the secret crimes lurking below — bodies decaying and slowly burning, probably those of unoffending peasants. · · · On the second, third, and fourth days of our journey, we began to meet the long files of prisoners. What a spectacle! Literally a succession of lazar-houses and hospitals turned out into the open air. Meagre wretches, crawling along with difficulty, not always in a human posture, but on their knees, blood-soaked rags hanging about them, their faces blue, or even livid purple, and endeavoring to draw warmth as well as nutriment from pieces of loathsome raw horse-flesh. Many died before our eyes, as we slowly moved along, and in crowds at the posting-stations. That part of the sick for whom sledges had at last been found, were packed in layers, one over the other, with straw between them. Which would die first, it had been impossible to judge, in these hurried packings of human creatures. Which *had* died, it became difficult to know; the straw perhaps, or the man above him, preventing any clear examination of the face; and the dreadful effects from decomposition being now slow to express themselves decisively under this iron rigor of frost. And thus at the posting-houses, where piles of these victims were accumulated, for want of horses, the groans of suffering, shrieks of anguish from festering wounds, the parting spasm or farewell sigh of the departing, might all be heard (sometimes all at one moment) from the same sledge; while from others, the silence, total or comparative, would announce that the last struggle was past. As often as this event was discovered — an event desirable in all eyes, when so many were waiting for any protection from the icy wind or the exposure of the road — the corpse or corpses would be hastily removed; in doing which, as the death or deaths might have occurred indifferently in any layer, upper or lower, a disturbance more agonizing than their wounds was often given to such as might remain alive. But what was done with the corpses extracted from these freights of misery? Were they buried? Not at all. That would have been a work of toil in the frozen state of the groun. · · · Through the whole route to Wilna, dead men had been hung up on the branches of trees, with marks of ignominy on their persons — brands impressed on their ghastly foreheads — stakes driven through their hearts. Sometimes where the snow lay too heavily on these boughs, or the furious north-easter, with the weight of the dead men, had weakened them too much, the whole mass, broken bough and corpse, would all come down together, and lie across the narrow road. Oftentimes in the middle of the night, when all was dark in the wild 'tormented' air, and only the ground was illuminated by the snow, suddenly our eight horses would all fall back upon their haunches, snort, rear, plunge; and when we alighted with our torches to examine the cause of this tumult, we generally found a litter of wood disbranched from some tree that overshadowed the road, but in the centre a human body, and perhaps a face half withered by frost, half eaten by a wolf, yet still, among mouldering and ruins, not improbably presenting a faded expression of horrid human passions. · · · From the river Duenna to Wilna, however many were the cross roads, or however expansive might be the heath or the forest through which the traveller was left to choose a track, no stranger could ever have needed a guide, but might, through these hundreds of miles, have guided himself by the unburied corpses."

It needs some such horridly forcible limning from nature as this, to enable one fully to appreciate the appropriateness of the design which CRUIKSHANK sent to Paris for a monument to NAPOLEON; a pyramid of skulls, rising high in air from a wide and shadowy base, and on the top the skeleton of the Great Captain, standing in his military boots, with his bony arms folded upon his fleshless ribs. The article we have been considering, in connection with another entitled ' *When I was in the Legion,*' which describes the processes of recruiting, drilling, punishing, etc., in the British army, one would think must subdue in all English readers any strong predilection for military life, or the 'honors of war' A description of the success of a wily, wheedling sergeant, in raising recruits in Ireland, is followed by the subjoined group of pictures, which is scarcely excelled by CARLYLE's memorable sketch of the French and English 'Dumdrudge :'

'You have often turned to look, no doubt, at a squad of recruits, shepherded by a sergeant or a corporal, straggling through the streets, lame as dogs with their march of probably some hundred miles from the country, and have smiled, maybe, to hear their rude remarks upon the new world of town, through which they are hurried like a herd of bullocks, on their way to Chatham, Woolrich, or some other of those military warehouses, where great quantities of this sort of cattle are wanted for exportation. You have often seen them, no doubt; but did your thoughts ever revert to the peaceful scenes they came from, and the parents, friends, and, it may be, sweethearts they have left behind, or to the little world of wo that troubles the humble sphere they have left for ever? On looking forward, did you ever reflect on the fate through future years of these poor young men, going through life in the dull unvaried routine of the mechanical duties of that, to the private man — most mechanical of all professions; carrying a musket under the broiling heat of a tropical sun — wearing out life under the walls of a garrison town — and if they finally escape, through singular good luck or strength of constitution, the many casualties of disease or accident, that in the course of five-and-twenty years' service, kill the regiment they belong to thrice over, in what condition do they return to their native country? See a ship load of the poor fellows land at Chatham, lantern-jawed, hollow-eyed, saffron-skinned, bent almost double, eaten up with disease, and all but dead men ;

and to think that these are the same fellows that went abroad full of life, hope, and expectation, and return thus to find death their only promotion, and the grave their most comfortable quarters.'

A sketch is given of a poor culprit, who, attended by a corporal and two rank and file with drawn bayonets, is brought to the surgeon's quarters to be inspected for a punishment certificate. A fine young fellow in rude health is often thus stripped and examined, to see if he is in condition for the lash : fingered and pawed like a bullock by a butcher; and dismissed with a diploma qualifying him to be scourged till his backbone and his flesh part company. In the present instance, however, the humanity of the doctor saves the pale and trembling victim, and in a manner sufficiently amusing. A laughable scene is also here recorded, wherein a certain surly, ill-tempered officer, whose wife and sister were in the habit of visiting him at the barracks, gives orders, out of spite to subordinate officers, whose families had hitherto enjoyed the same privilege, that 'no females are to be allowed in barracks after tattoo, under any pretence whatever :'

'It so happened that, on the morning after this announcement appeared in the order book, an old lieutenant, who might have been the major's grandfather, with a few years to spare, and whom we used to call 'the General,' on account of his age and gray hairs, was the officer on duty. To the sergeant of the guard the General gave the necessary orders, with strict injunctions to take care that the order of exclusion should be obeyed to the letter; and the sergeant was too old a soldier not to have learned the doctrine of passive obedience.

Shortly after tattoo, sundry ladies as usual presented themselves at the barrack gate, and were of course refused admission; when, to the surprise of the sentinel on duty, the major's lady and sister-in-law made their appearance, and walked boldly to the wicket, with the intention of entering as usual. To their astonishment, the sentry refused them permission to pass : the sergeant was called, but that worthy was quite as much of a precisian as the ladies, and his conscience would not permit him to let them in.

'Do you know who we are, Sir?' inquired the major's lady, with much asperity of voice and manner.

'Oh! certainly,' said the sergeant. 'I knows your ladyships very well.'

'And pray, what do you mean, Sir, by this insolence?'

'I means no insolence whatsomedever, marm : but my orders is partickler to let no female ladies into this here barrack after tattoo, upon no account whatever, and I means to obey my orders without no mistake.'

'Then you have the effrontery to refuse admittance to the lady of your commanding-officer! screamed the Honorable Mrs. Snooks.

'And her sister!' shrieked the second lady.

'Most sartinly, marm,' replied the non-commissioned officer, with profound gravity; 'I knows my duty.'

'Good gracious, what assurance!'

'No insurance at all, marm; if your ladyships was princesses you could n't come in after tattoo; my orders is partickler.'

'Do n't you know, sirrah, that these orders cannot be intended to apply to us?'

'I does n't know nuffin about that, my lady; but orders is orders, and must be obeyed.'

'Impudence!'

'Imperance or no imperance, I must do my duty; and, I can tell your ladyships, if my superior officer was for to give me orders not to let in the major himself, I would be obligated to keep his honor out at the pint of the baggonet!'

The officer of the guard was sent for, and the officer of the guard sent for the orderly book, which by the light of the guard-room lantern was exhibited to the ladies, with much courtesy, by the General, in justification of his apparent rudeness.'

The '*Hints to Authors*' treat of 'The Biographical;' and the same redundant satire pervades the present number that has rendered all its predecessors so entertaining. The 'specimen' which the writer gives us, illustrates the modern mode of elevating the subject of a memoir, by glossing over his faults, or rather converting them into virtues. Mr. JOHN GUBBINS, a low personage, addicted to theft and other small peccadilloes, is the hero. The merely cursory reader would scarcely discover that he was a villain. He is a drunkard, moreover, and the founder of a unique society for his order, the antipodes of teetotalism, which is thus described in a letter quoted by the biographer :

'Despising from the bottom of his heart the miserable milksops who cheat the revenue and reduce themselves to the level of the beasts, whose only drink is water, he has resolved to found a great institution, to which any person shall be admitted on payment to him of twopence, and taking what he calls the 'Toxication pledge. But far from following the example of the aforesaid hypocrites in limiting his association to those only who take the 'Total' pledge, he has resolved to divide the association into two classes, to either of which a proselyte shall have the privilege of belonging ; one to be composed of those who take the Total Drunkenness pledge ; and the other, of those who take the Occasionally Sober Pledge. In taking the total drunkenness pledge, it is to be understood that the person binds himself at some one hour or other of each lawful day, and twice every Sunday, to produce in himself, by means of one or more of the following liquors, viz: Beer, Ale, Flip, Eggbot, Purl (early or otherwise,) Gin, Brandy, Whiskey, Rum, Wine, Shrub, Hollands, Swizzle, Toddy, Punch, Stingo — alone or mixed, according to his own taste — such a degree of philosophical equanimity as not to be aware of whether he stands on his head or his heels — not to be able to speak so as to be understood by his nearest friend — nor to be able to maintain what philosophers have absurdly call'd the centre of gravity; and, in short, to be in that truly elevated condition, when the floor begins to be rebellious, and the room swings round in imitation of a windmill. The Occasionally Sober Pledge does not mean that any one day is to be wholly spent without contributing one's share to the increase of the revenue; but simply, that occasionally it shall be lawful to stop short of the extreme point to which the others are bound to proceed, and indeed to leave off at that happy stage when a man feels it his bounden duty as a Christian, and a man of honor, to thrash a policeman, or wrench off a knocker, or frighten an unprotected woman, in the manner practised already by some amateur members of the highest rank. The Occasionally Sober Pledge does not in the least preclude a man from being as totally drunk as he pleases, while, on the other hand, the т. p. p. binds a person to abjure the o. s. p. as insufficient and unsatisfactory.

The end of such a reformer may be anticipated. He keeps his ''Toxication pledge' to the letter, until his friends tell him that he is killing himself by inches; to which he replies, that 'in such a cause, he did n't care if he died by the square yard.' *Delirium Tremens* at length carries him off, and we are treated to his portrait, in the same vein :

'Mr. Gubbins was considerably below the middle height, being little more than five feet high; but, as if to compensate for the deficiency, he was considerably beyond the average width. His hair was of a deep red hue, his countenance full of dignity and sweetness, with a very short and very flat nose; while his face was saved from too feminine an expression by a remarkable projection of his two front teeth, and extremely protuberant lips. His legs were what are usually called bandy, and he had splay feet of peculiar size. With these personal advantages, his success in life is not a matter of much surprise.'

Frazer's Magazine has two or three very clever articles, the best of which are, the '*Report of the Meeting of the Scientific Ass-sociates,*' (a satire upon the useless topics so often elevated into temporary notoriety by small scientific societies,) and 'Specimens of the *Table-Talk of the late John Boyle.*' We quote a passage from the speech of a remarkably scientific professor, upon one of his 'various important matters connected with every-day life.' The learned gentleman observed : 'The mode of shaving differed in different individuals. Some were very close shavers; and others were greater adepts at cutting unpleasant acquaintances than themselves. It was however most important that the art of shaving should be reduced to a nicety, so that a man could cut his beard with the same facility as he could cut his stick. It was also of consequence that an accurate calculation should be made of the number of shaving-brushes and the number of half-pounds of soap used in the course of the year by respectable shavers; for he had observed that some of them were very badly off for soap. There was also a great variation in the price of labor. Some barbers undertook to shave well for three-halfpence; others charged a much higher sum. This was probably the effect of free competition; and he must say that the government deserved well of the country for not encouraging any monopoly. At the same time there was a looseness in the details of the profession, which he should like to see corrected. An accurate register ought to be kept of the number of individuals who shaved themselves; and of those who shaved daily, every other day, and once a-week only. He could hardly contemplate the immense benefits which science would reap if such matters as these were properly attended to. · · · Again, it was important to know the number of hairs generally found on the head of a person in good health at a given time of life, and whether the number differed much in individuals; and if a person who had a thick head was likely to have more or less hair than one whose head was not quite so thick.' As next in importance, the learned professor submitted the results of some calculations 'as to the number of individuals who wore spectacles during the year 1839 in the United Kingdom.'

'The late John Boyle,' whoever he may have been, was evidently a scholar and a gentleman, and familiar with the highest society, literary and other, in Great Britain. His table-talk is rich and various. We have space but for one or two extracts :

Reading Authors.—'The most ferocious monsters in existence are authors who insist on reading their mss. to you. I really believe the greater part of them are descended from the Hyrcanian tigers.

They are cannibals, beyond the pale of society. I speak strongly, because I have suffered much from fellows of this sort. Often have I blessed the memory of Byron, who, at the close of one of his letters (inviting a friend to Newstead), and after he had enumerated all the pleasures they should enjoy, 'books, baths, wines, bright eyes,' etc., thus writes: ' *Nil recitabo tibi.*' Never was a more agreeable promise to a visitor of a literary man.'

AN AFFECTIONATE SCHOOLMISTRESS. — 'I once read the following P. S. to a letter: it was written by a schoolmistress to the mother of a child of her 'establishment:' ' *Will dearest Mrs.* —— *allow her affectionate friend, Mrs.* —— (the schoolmistress) *to get interesting Eliza a stays ?*'! By the way, that is not a bad idea of my friend Coleridge, who calls those strings of boys and girls who parade the metropolis in regimental rank and file, '*walking advertisements.*'

' FIRST AND SECOND REASON. — 'A very acute man used to say, ' Tell me your *second* reason ; I do not want your first. The second is the true motive of your actions.'

Mr. BOYLE accuses MOORE of being a plagiarist of the most unblushing order — a 'pigmy who has decked himself with the trappings of many a Colossus,' and who deserves to be 'driven from the field, denuded and disgraced.' He says :

'MOORE's plagiarisms are intolerable. The man is an indefatigable thief. He has laid under contribution every imaginable book, from the biography of his namesake, Tom Thumb, to the portly folios of the fathers of the church. Perfectly unscrupulous in his marauding expeditions, and impartial in his attacks, he is found at one moment rifling a saint, and in the next pillaging a sinner. Every outpouring from the wells of literature has brought grist to his mill. You have asked me for some specimens of his most open and barefaced plagiarisms. You shall have them. They are selected at random from a large mass of thefts which I have silently noted from time to time, and which, after my demise, shall see the light. MOORE knows of the existence of these documents; I have shown them to him myself; and be assured that while I live he will never have the courage to republish one of his writings ; for I have informed him often that immediately he issues a new edition of any of those stolen goods, I shall expose his frauds to the world. And he knows me too well to doubt my word.'

The 'exposition' follows, beginning with 'Plagiarism the First' and ending with 'Plagiarism the Sixteenth,' in which the writer, by parallel quotations, traces near a score of MOORE's most celebrated metaphors, sentiments, and similes, directly to Suckling, Massinger, Addison, Shirley, Dryden, Heywood, Kirk White, and others. The proofs of the charges are irrefragable.

—

THE DUBLIN UNIVERSITY MAGAZINE is the Blackwood of Ireland. Indeed very many of its papers have no superiors in the Scottish monthly. The crowning attraction is '*Charles O'Malley,*' by the author of 'Harry Lorrequer.' This is one of the most delightful novels we have read in a dozen years. It is full of various incident, and nothing can exceed the beauty of its descriptions, the flow of its rich humor, and the charming ease of its style throughout. The writer has just now no rival — not even DICKENS, fruitful and gifted as he is. We are glad to perceive that the publisher of the '*New World*' literary journal, the best of our mammoth sheets, and not inferior to the '*Boston Notion,*' has made arrangements with the author to receive the proofs of each number in advance of the publication in Great-Britain ; and has also reprinted the entire back numbers, which are *given* to each new subscriber of the 'New-World.' With such liberality, it is not surprising that this journal has a circulation of upward of twenty-five thousand copies. —

'GEORGE CRUIKSHANK'S OMNIBUS' is a monthly publication, the entertaining character of which is sufficiently defined by its title ; for every reader is familiar with this artist's irresistibly comic powers. The cover represents an omnibus under full headway, with a view into the multifaced interior, and of two personages seated with the driver, whose commingled expression would make his team break out into an unanimous 'horse-laugh,' if the animals were capable of appreciating pictorial humor. The title-page is a complete picture-gallery, and might provoke a day's study ; and indeed all the numerous drawings, in the two numbers before us, are such as only CRUIKSHANK could have sketched. He is assisted by rare pens in the literary department, who sustain the spirit of his motto: ' *De Omnibus rebus et quibusdam aliis.*' The character of the *vehicle* is never lost sight of. In the notice to correspondents, a female contributor, whose 'fare' was crowded out of the first number, is thus informed by the driver that she is also too late for the second : 'I say, Tom, here's that there elderly lady a-coming as wanted to go with us at our first start;' to which the cad replies: 'Ay; well, it's no use, Bill — she's too late ag'in. Ve're all full. All right — go on l'

AMONG the foreign issues at hand, we acknowledge from a friend at Brussels specimen numbers of the 'Universal Atlas of Geography,' physical, political, statistical, and mineralogical. By PH. VANDERMAELEN. It must be a popular work abroad, since we observe the names of half the crowned heads of Europe among its subscribers, not to speak of nobles, and distinguished scientific and literary men without number ; including, moreover, our friends, Baron VAN TUYLLVANSSROOSKERKEN, of Eindhoven; DE STOETWEGEN UTTERWAL, Receiver-General at Zwolle; VAN DER OYE SCHIMENELPENNINCK, at Leyden; NATHUSIUS DE HUNDISBURG GOTTLOB, at Magdeburgh; and Count BEZBONEDKO KONCHELOW, at St. Petersburgh. May their names never be less! The '*établissement géographique*' at Brussels has our best wishes for its continued success.

THE FINE ARTS.

NATIONAL ACADEMY OF DESIGN. — We have taken up our marked Catalogue; but on looking over it, find that the gossipping comment running through it in pencil would, if written out, so impinge upon this department as to exclude much matter already in type. We select almost at random a few of the more prominent pictures, leaving however many unnoticed which perhaps, on revisiting the exhibition, we may remember with regret, as not being included among the subjoined.

NUMBER 1. 'The Happy Valley,' from Rasselas. JESSE TALBOT. There are many things to praise in the execution of this picture; but is there much *originality* about it? Is it not mainly made up from the works of others? Especially, has not the artist levied largely upon COLE? 'Imitation — *large.*'

NUMBER 8. Portrait of a Gentleman. H. P. GRAY. This is a very fine picture, and fully justifies the praise which has heretofore been awarded in these pages to this young and promising artist. No. 218, also, by the same, is in a similar category.

NUMBER 9. 'View on the Hudson.' W. J. JEWITT. We understand Mr. JEWITT to be a young artist : he is certainly one of talent. *Macte virtute*, Mr. JEWITT.

NUMBER 10. 'Group of Children.' H. INMAN. With many of our artist's beauties, this group is not without its defects, as it strikes us; one of which is, that it is rather too green in color.

NUMBER 11. This is a picture of great merit; well and poetically conceived, and of great breadth of chiar' oscuro. The artist is a young man of decided promise, and only needs encouragement, to accomplish great things. There is a little feebleness in the execution of the picture, which would be overcome by more practice and study from nature.

NUMBER 21. Portrait of a lady. W. PAGE, N. A. Fine, when seen at a great distance; but the rough and lumpy manner in which it is painted renders a near view of it disagreeable. Mr. PAGE really deserves censure for such affectation in the execution of his pictures. He ought to have more judgment than to waste his time in such frivolities. He has great talent.

NUMBER 22. 'Columbus before the Council of Salamanca.' R. W. WEIR, N. A. An elaborate and highly-finished picture. Some of the figures are beautifully painted; the two on the right, especially, are well conceived and finely executed. The accessories also are in admirable keeping. The only defect, in our judgment, is the figure of Columbus, which seems too old, and to lack dignity. No. 147 is a landscape by the same artist; and an admirable painting it is. The river in the distance has the dim, cool hue of nature, and the mountains are solemn and imposing. Nos. 285 and 306 show Mr. WEIR's versatility of talent. These are female portraits, of the small cabinet size, faultless in the drawing and draperies, and in the life-tints natural and pleasing.

NUMBER 27. 'Mercy's Dream.' D. HUNTINGTON, N. A. We have already adverted to this picture, and now find the promise of its commencement fully redeemed. It possesses very great beauty, and goes far to counteract the impressions of the low character of the exhibition, which arise from a general view of it. The main effect is very pleasing. The back-ground is grand. The figure of Mercy, too, is exceedingly lovely, and seems as if it were just waking from a sweet sleep. The right arm seems to us to be rather feebly drawn, and inferior to the rest of the figure. The Angel is less felicitously conceived and executed : the head is not beautiful, and the hair is indifferently managed. As a whole, however, this picture reflects great credit upon Mr. HUNTINGTON, and we hope it will not be the last subject of the kind which his pencil shall illustrate.

NUMBER 28. 'Landscape view in Sullivan County.' H. INMAN. We spake of this landscape while it was yet upon the artist's easel. Our first impressions are confirmed, save that the color, in the strong light of the new apartments, seems something too green. The figures are fine.

NUMBER 32. 'Death's First Visitation.' T. HICKS. This, we learn, is by a young artist. It has much of promise in it. The painter has evidently a fine feeling for color. The flesh tints in particular are very true.

NUMBER 46. 'Fourth of July.' J. G. CLONNEY. There is very decided merit in this effort. The negroes are painted with great truth. There are other figures as well executed; and the composition, though crowded, is well arranged. There is something too much of the vulgar, however, in the subject, as here portrayed. We hope to see a pencil so capable, employed upon details more interesting to a pure and refined mind.

NUMBER 53. 'Cider Making.' W. S. MOUNT, N. A. We see here much of Mr. MOUNT's peculiar graphic talent. This picture is better than any which the artist has produced for several years. It *tells* upon the beholder at once. The groups are felicitously chosen and well depicted; but the color is rather harsh and disagreeable.

NUMBER 80. Portrait of a Lady. C. G. THOMPSON. Mr. THOMPSON is not well represented this season. He is an artist however of too much talent and reputation to suffer from the exhibition by others of his more hasty and less elaborate efforts. We like the face and hair of this portrait; but the sky is less to our taste.

NUMBER 91. 'The boyish Reverie.' W. H. POWELL. There are charming *points* in this picture, and some defects, which latter however we cannot now indicate. Mr. POWELL is fast fulfilling the rich promise of his spring. Look at Nos. 85 and 223. These are honorable evidences of his improvement and of his talent.

NUMBER 110. 'The Vesper Hymn : an Italian Twilight.' T. COLE, N. A. This picture will sustain a close study. The fore-ground is bold and rich; the water, in light and shadow, very beautiful; the 'addittaments' well chosen, and the distance soft and aërial. No. 189, by the same artist, will not find so many admirers; yet we can testify that it is a most forcible transcript from nature — save only, that the mist from the falls, floating and dissolving airily away, along the sides of the mountain gorge, is hardly *watery* enough in hue. The *blue* tint is too perceptible.

NUMBER 111. Portrait of a Lady. F. ALEXANDER. Simple and easy; a picture of great beauty.

NUMBER 117. The landscape of this picture has merit. The effect especially of moonlight over the scene is well managed. No. 254, by the same artist, is simply ridiculous. It would be a rich treat to hear ALCOTT, the transcendental seer of Boston, lecture in the Orphic way upon this huge fœtus of an idea.

NUMBER 122. 'Hudson River Scenery.' J. P. BEAUMONT. Is the *natural* clean banished from the Hudson ? — or are such fantastic details as these *real* transcripts from nature ? Guess not.

NUMBER 135. Portrait of a Lady. W. PAGE. This is *almost* a fine picture; but the pale and dough-like color of the flesh, the cold blue back-ground and faded purple of the dress, deprive us of the power of looking at the otherwise beautiful execution with satisfaction. Mr. PAGE lacks 'the better part of valor.'

NUMBER 141. Cabinet Picture. L. P. CLOVER, Jr. A very pretty sketch. There is a humble fire-side coziness in the general effect, as well as a moral lesson. Mr. CLOVER excels in this class of paintings.

NUMBER 156. 'Summer Evening.' C. VERBRUYCK. A very pleasing little landscape.

NUMBER 157. Portrait of A Lady. C. C. INGHAM, N. A. An extraordinary picture, and perhaps the best our artist ever executed. The subject is a beautiful one, and must have been painted *con amore*. MIERIS or GERARD DOW might have been proud of the work. The head and neck are exceedingly beautiful; the flesh has less than usual of Mr. INGHAM's ivory-like texture; the hair is reality, and the drapery almost an illusion. The disposition of the figure and of the hands and arms might we think have been more happily chosen. 'But that's not much.'

NUMBER 197. CHRIST, the Good Samaritan.' F. S. AGATE, N. A. There is a pleasing effect of color and chiar' oscuro in this picture; *but*, the subject is very obscurely treated.

NUMBER 219. 'The Mother and Child.' WASHINGTON ALLSTON. We have here deep tone and brilliant effect of color; and moreover that purity of style which belongs to the works of this distinguished artist. The back-ground and accessories are in his finest manner; but the face of the mother, as well as the hands, seems badly drawn; and the child, to our eye, appears cramped. The white drapery is exquisite : the carnations, though beautiful, are perhaps too pallid. The great defect of the painting is, that it seems like an imitation of old works that have been injured by Time and the hand of the picture-cleaner.

Number 252. Frame of Pencil-drawings. By an Amateur. Beautiful. No. 256, by the same, deserve the like praise.

Numbers 260, 264, 5; 275, 6, 9 : Oriental Views. J. Allom. All the drawings by this gentleman, who is an English artist, are executed with great taste and freedom. They are the originals whence were taken the superb engravings which embellish Miss Pardoe's 'Turkey.'

Now, adopting of necessity that modern style of criticism which gives a 'curtailed abbreviation, compressing the particulars,' we must ask our city readers to justify or condemn the following 'lump,' by personal examination : No. 263, 'Design for a Villa,' by A. J. Davis; pleasing. 270, Portrait of the late Gen. Harrison; bad. 294. 'Blow Hot, blow Cold;' by Purcell; good. 297. 'Italian Composition,' by Lieut. Flagg, U. S. N. 'Shocking — positively shocking!' 328. Family Group, by C. Weindell; very beautiful. This gentleman's *Miniatures* are *good*; so too are those of Fanshaw, Shumway, Miss Hall, (see No. 312,) and Mad. Guillet. Of the *Busts*, those by Coffee should not have been exhibited, nor the one by Gallagher. Launitz has a very fine marble bust of the late Gouverneur Morris, and a beautiful one of a little girl, in the same material. Ives' bust of Ithiel Town is a very fine thing; those of Noah Webster and Mr. Benjamin are also good. The one of Dr. Wainwright is not at all like the original. Kneeland's 'Bust of a Gentleman,' though disfigured by a tasteless fancy-color, is worthy of his rising reputation. It is a *speaking* likeness of the original. Even the hair, which might seem to the observer to be too elaborately curled, is literally ' to the life.' The whole has freedom and boldness, and a Roman dignity. Though roughly finished, it is not the less striking. Brackett's works appear to less advantage in the exhibition than at his rooms. His bust of Mr. Stetson is a capital likeness, and much superior, as a work of art, to his 'Bust of a Lady.' Mr. Brackett is steadily prosecuting his noble art, and with a success most satisfactory to himself.

THE CONTRAST.

I.

Do you see that proud, overbearing man, riding in his gilded carriage? Look! he stops before a magnificent mansion, and liveried lacquies, obedient to his nod, assist him to descend.

Do you see that poor, miserable boy, whose tattered clothes scarcely shield him from the inclemency of the weather? Mark! with a beseeching look he solicits the rich man to purchase a pencil or a card of pens; and behold, how contemptuously he is spurned!

Twenty-five years ago that pompous man was as poor, as friendless, and as wretched as the urchin he despises.

II.

Twenty-five years have passed since that day. The same parties meet: lo! the contrast.

The once poor boy stands in the pride of manhood, active, intelligent, rich. A lovely woman, his wife, leans upon his arm, and three blooming girls are by his side. Grace in every action, benevolence in every expression, and affluence smiles in his unostentatious adornments.

An old man approaches. The tottering step, the thread-bare garments, and the painful expression that frets in every feature, too plainly denote a man of want and wo. Better dead, than thus to drag on a miserable existence!

This may at the first blush appear to some an improbable romance. It is a truth.

III.

In a country like ours, there is no man, however poor, if aided by industry, economy, and virtue, but may rise from the lowest ranks of society to the highest. The knowledge of this fact is a blessed incitement to the young, and cheers them on to struggle nobly in the paths which lead to honor and independence, despite the thousand obstacles that oppose their course.

IV.

There is no man, however affluent, but by extravagance, and morals lax, may fall from his high estate, and close his days in penury and wo.

V.

Let none despise the poor because of their poverty; let none flatter the rich because of their wealth. We may conquer poverty; wealth may subdue us. All men of equal virtue are equals. If one man possess more intelligence than his fellows, though that of itself may not elevate him in the ranks of the good, yet it brings him added respect, and wins a willing admiration from all men:

' The good alone are great.'

J. L.

PATENT CHEMICAL-OIL LAMPS. — Those who are 'wanting light' will exclaim 'Eureka!' when they sit down under the exceeding brightness of the chemical-oil lamps, found in all varieties at the establishment of Mr. HOOKER, 466, Broadway. We have never encountered any thing half so effective, and so excellent in all respects. They are peculiarly constructed; the light being regulated by the draft, with a button which plays over the flame. The great beauty of these lamps consists in their simplicity. They are made of brass, and are very plain and '·genteel' in appearance. The oil which is burned in them is a chemical preparation, very clean in its properties, insomuch that it will neither soil nor stain, and is free, moreover, from all smoke or smell. The lamps will burn twelve hours without trimming. They may be seen in use at the Astor and Franklin houses, and indeed in the dwellings of all those of our citizens who have once seen them.

The 'BURNING FLUID' is a portable light, calculated more especially for family use. It is perfectly clean, and free from all smoke, smell, or grease. Common lamps may be altered at a trifling expense, for the employment of the fluid. There is no danger of explosion in either one of these articles; and the expense of burning is from one third to one half cheaper than that of oil.

LITERARY RECORD.

BARTLETT AND WELFORD'S NEW CATALOGUE OF BOOKS: — We have here a catalogue of books on a new plan in this country, though it has long been pursued in London and on the continent. We are glad to see it attempted among us, and trust it may remunerate the publishers. It embraces nearly four thousand different works, in every department of literature and science, and numbers more than twelve thousand volumes. The advantage is, that the full title of every book is given, the edition, date, style of binding, and the *price*. By this plan, people at a distance have an equal advantage with those on the spot in selecting books adapted to their tastes. Another excellent plan in this catalogue is the criticisms, or bibliographical notes, appended to many of the better class of books. These criticisms are selected from well known authorities, and must have great weight in recommending the works to which they apply, to notice. They are perspicuous, and seem to be selected with much care from Hallam, Hazlitt, Doctor Johnson, Dibdin, Chancellor Kent, Horne, Chalmers, Bishop Nicholson, and others. Among the magazines and reviews referred to, or quoted, are Blackwood, the London Quarterly, Edinburgh, British Critic, Athæneum, Retrospective Review, Gentleman's Magazine, North-American Review, etc. These critical notes render the catalogue quite a readable book to one fond of bibliography, and are excellent guides for any one collecting a library, without bibliographical works at his hand.

DOWNING'S LANDSCAPE GARDENING. — Messrs. WILEY AND PUTNAM have recently published a 'Treatise on the theory and practice of Landscape Gardening, adapted to North America; with a view to the improvement of country residences, comprising historical notices and general principles of the art, directions for laying out grounds and arranging plantations, the description and cultivation of hardy trees, decorative accompaniments to the house and grounds, the formation of pieces of artificial water, flower gardens, etc., with remarks on rural architecture.' The author is Mr. A. J. DOWNING, of Newburgh, well known as an accomplished landscape gardener; and it is but justice to say, that his work is a timely and well-digested treatise upon all the various matters designated in its title. It is eminently *practical* in its teachings, and is embellished with several good wood engravings, illustrating rural architecture. Of these, however that of Mr. IRVING's country residence, since copied into the 'New-York Mirror,' is the least faithful to its picturesque original.

'THE COMMERCIAL EMPORIUM' is the title of a quarterly pamphlet, published by the Messrs. YOUNGS, Clinton-House, and designed to serve as a 'Strangers' Guide to the most fashionable hotels, theatres, museums, public gardens, saloons, exhibitions, amusements, excursions, refectories, shops, stores, and the most interesting localities and establishments in the city of New-York and its environs.' It touches upon almost all the places of familiar resort about town; and does not omit, we are glad to perceive, to record among other matters a word in praise of PATTINSON's excellent and popular *café*, corner of Nassau and Ann-streets, where the first 'dish of ripe strawberries, smothered in cream' was seen the present season, and where the rarities of *all* seasons are to be first encountered.

GOSSIP WITH READERS AND CORRESPONDENTS. — Among the articles in preparation for the KNICK-ERBOCKER, are many unedited manuscripts, *Ollapodiana*, poetry, etc., of the lamented WILLIS GAYLORD CLARK. Some of these will appear in our next. · · · We agree entirely with '*Anti-Humbug*' that the practice of appending, without their consent, the names of respectable and benevolent citizens to the charity calls of hackneyed '*Theatrical Benefits*' is a species of gross deception, which deserves castigation; the more, that in nine cases out of ten, many of the gentlemen selected are too averse to publicity to expose the cheat. · · · The reader will recognize, in the excellent article in preceding pages entitled '*A Ball at the Tuilleries*,' a practised and distinguished pen; and he must needs rejoice with us, that the writer will frequently shake off his '*Dust of Travel*' in our pages. · · · We foresee some discussion of the article entitled '*Moderation vs. Teetotalism*,' in the present number; but it must be admitted that the advocates of *Total Abstinence* will here find some of their strongest arguments ably enforced, even by an adversary; who, it is proper to say, is a gentleman of the most exemplary character, and warmly esteemed and respected by all who know him. Speaking of curing intemperance, reminds us of the following pleasant anecdote of Lord PEMBROKE, which we find in our note-book:

'Of all the Mede-and-Persian laws established in his house, the most peremptory was, that any servant who once got drunk should be instantly discharged — no pardon granted, no excuse listened to. Yet an old footman, who had lived with him many years, would sometimes indulge in a pot of ale extraordinary, trusting to the wilful blindness which he saw assumed when convenient. One fatal day, even this could not avail. As my lord crossed the hall, John appeared in full view; not rather tipsy, or a little disguised, but dead drunk, and unable to stand. Lord Pembroke went up to him, 'My poor fellow, what ails you? you seem dreadfully ill; let me feel your pulse. God bless us! he is in a raging fever! get him to bed directly, and send for the apothecary!' The apothecary came, not to be consulted, for his lordship was physician-general in his own family; but to obey orders; to bleed the patient copiously, clap a huge blister on his back, and give him a powerful dose of physic. After a few days of this treatment, when the fellow emerged weak and wan as the severest illness could have left him, 'Hah, honest John,' I am truly glad to see you alive; you have had a wonderful escape though, and ought to be thankful — very thankful indeed. Why, man, if I had not passed by and spied the plight you were in, you would have been dead before now. But, John,' lifting up his finger, 'No MORE OF THESE FEVERS!'

If any AMERICAN reader can peruse '*The Battle of New-Orleans*,' from a favorite correspondent, and not feel a thrill of natural exultation and pride, he has no feelings in common with us. It is a masterly picture of a *masterly* event. · · · '*The Ellsler Mania*,' by our theatrical correspondent, came too late for timely insertion. Let it suffice to say, that this charming *artiste* maintains her popularity unabated. Her name alone would crowd the Park Theatre to the dome, though her appearance were but to aid the 'complimentary benefit' of the 'supe'-actor who disseminates daily its small bills. · · · We had intended to say a word touching the clever '*Contrast*,' by an esteemed friend, on another page; but the mechanical '*fitness* of things' there has prevented. It is the first of a series of brief *Nouvelettes*, which will have more moral and less words than the majority of modern novels. · · · The following papers, with those heretofore alluded to, are placed on file for insertion: 'Reflections on Humphrey's Life of Putnam; 'The Quod Correspondence,' Number Three; 'The Country Doctor,' Chapter Sixth; 'The Sentiment of Antiquity;' 'The Polygon Papers,' Number Two; 'Old Dutch Houses and their Associations;' 'Dar su Vida por sa Dama,' from the Spanish; 'The Wakullah,' a Sketch. The annexed articles await consideration: 'La Nouvelle Heloise,' from the Note-Book of a Student; 'Marriage;' 'The Stobhall Regiment;' 'On the Decay of Drinking in New-England;' 'Naming the Day,' a Hint to Lovers; 'A Fox Story. · · · Notices, at much length, of the following publications, intended for the present number, are in type for our next: 'Collections of the New-York Historical Society;' 'Taste and Morals;' Mr. BARNARD's Common School Report; TURNER's 'Companion to Genesis;' The 'American Repertory;' ROOSEVELT's 'Science of Government;' 'Le Lis Blanc;' Popular London Dictionaries; CATLIN's Indian Gallery.

THE KNICKERBOCKER.

VOL. XVIII.   AUGUST, 1841.   No. 2.

'OLD PUT.' AT THE BAR:

OR SOME REFLECTIONS ON HUMPHREYS' LIFE OF MAJOR-GENERAL PUTNAM.*

BY JOHN FELLOWS.

VOLTAIRE opens the preface to his history of Charles Twelfth, king of Sweden, as follows : ' INCREDULITY, says Aristotle, is the source of all wisdom ;' and adds : ' This maxim is exceedingly proper for all who read history, and ancient history in particular. How many absurd stories ! How many fables shocking to common sense ! What then ? *Do not believe a word of them.*'

How applicable the foregoing caution may be to the reader of the essay before us, he must judge. At any rate it is a well known fact, that writers of biography, particularly of military men, are much addicted to exaggerations in relating the exploits of their hero ; with a view, it would seem, not only of exalting his fame, but also of rendering their history the more entertaining.

This work of Colonel Humphreys certainly contains relations of chivalrous deeds of valor, and hair-breadth escapes, seldom met with in *modern* history, and which are perhaps without a parallel. It is to be regretted, however, that many statements here made in regard to our revolutionary war have by late writers, conversant with the facts, been shown to be palpable mistakes. These errors, nevertheless, had remained uncontradicted for many years ; and from the imposing manner in which the narrative was presented to the public, by a companion in arms of the General, and being, it is believed, the first regular work published in relation to the war, it must have had, it may readily be conceived, a powerful influence on succeeding historians of that event, and which is visible in their productions.

Colonel Humphreys was a poet, and is reported to have been a flippant, gentlemanlike person, of good address, full of vanity, but not distinguished for sound judgment. And the subject of his memoir is well known to have been a rough, uneducated man, and extremely

---

* 'AN Essay on the Life of the Hon. Major-General ISRAEL PUTNAM. Addressed to the State Society of the Cincinnati of Connecticut, and first published by their order. By Colonel DAVID HUMPHREYS. With Notes and Additions.' Boston : 1818. First edition, 1788.

garrulous and egotistical in advanced age. The former, by his own showing, derived his information mainly from the latter; the work therefore might with propriety be denominated an autobiography, and the Colonel the amanuensis of the General. He was indeed, at one period of the war, his aid, and in that capacity had a fair opportunity to listen to the recital of the General's achievements.

It is not proposed to enter into a general review of this work, but merely to select some of the most striking passages, and to apply such observations as the subjects seem to justify. The author, in his prefatory remarks, observes :

> 'The numerous errors and falsehoods relative to the birth and achievements of Major-General Putnam, which have at a former period been circulated with assiduity on both sides of the Atlantic, and the uncertainty which appeared to prevail with respect to his *real character*, first produced the resolution of writing this essay on his life, and induced the editor to obtain *materials from that hero himself*. And he seizes with eagerness an opportunity of acknowledging his obligations to Doctor Albigence Waldo, who was so obliging as to commit to writing many anecdotes, *communicated to him by General Putnam* in the course of the present year. A multitude of proofs might be produced to demonstrate that military facts cannot always be accurately known but by the commander-in-chief and his confidential officers.
> 'Should this essay have any influence in correcting mistakes, or rescuing from oblivion the actions of that distinguished veteran, it will be an ample compensation for the trouble, and excite a consolatory reflection through every vicissitude of life.'

It is passing strange, that the achievements of a Major-General in our revolutionary war, if he performed any worthy of notice, should so soon after its close have sunk into oblivion, and that it required the hero himself to trumpet his own fame. The remarks of the biographer might perhaps apply to a subaltern officer, who may have performed heroic actions not recorded in history, and which justice required should be brought into notice. Military operations intended, may be known only to the commander-in-chief, but when put in execution, become notorious. It is in vain, however, that we search for any notable action of the subject of this memoir, in the revolutionary war. He was nearly sixty years old at its commencement; was evidently placed in a station which nature and his education had not qualified him to fill; and was therefore kept in the *reserve* during nearly the whole period of his service, where no action was expected, and consequently no generalship required. The biographer proceeds :

> 'Israel Putnam, who, through a *regular gradation* of promotion, became the senior Major-General in the army of the United States, and next in rank to General WASHINGTON, was born at Salem, in the province, now State, of Massachusetts, January 7, 1718. · - - To compensate partially for the deficiency of education, though nothing can remove or counterbalance the inconveniences experienced from it in public life, he derived from his parents the source of innumerable advantages in the stamina of a vigorous constitution. Nature, liberal in bestowing on him bodily strength, hardiness, and activity, was by no means parsimonious in mental endowments.
> 'In the year 1739, he removed from Salem to Pomfret, an inland fertile town in Connecticut: having here purchased a considerable tract of land, he applied himself successfully to agriculture. The first years on a *new farm* are not, however, exempt from disasters and disappointments, which can only be remedied by stubborn and patient industry. Our farmer, sufficiently occupied in building a house and barn, felling woods, making fences, sowing grain, planting orchards, and taking care of his stock, had to encounter the calamities occasioned by drought in summer, blast in harvest loss of cattle in winter, and the desolation of his sheep-fold by wolves. In one night he had *seventy* fine sheep and goats killed, beside many lambs and kids wounded. This havoc was committed by a she-wolf, which with her annual whelps had for several years infested the vicinity. The young were commonly destroyed by the vigilance of the hunters, but the old one, on being closely pursued, would generally fly to the western woods, and return the next winter with another litter of whelps.'

This is an awful account of calamities, indeed ! The most wonderful part of it is, that a single she-wolf should in one night have killed seventy sheep and goats ; and that after having caught a tender lamb, she should suffer it to escape with only a wound. She perhaps adopted the maxim that it is as well to die for an old sheep as a lamb; or possibly she preferred mutton to lamb : on this point we are left entirely to conjecture. Few goats are raised in New-England, sheep being much more profitable ; the bulk, therefore, of Mr. Putnam's loss upon this occasion must have consisted of the latter. Now the average number of sheep kept by old farmers in Connecticut, at the period alluded to, may I believe fairly be set down at between thirty and forty ; each family keeping no more than were necessary to furnish a sufficiency of wool for its own consumption. That Mr. Putnam, therefore, who had just commenced clearing new land for the purpose of cultivation, should have possessed such a number of sheep as it appears he did, is truly surprising ; for, from the manner the story is told, it would seem that the loss he sustained was a mere thinning of his flock.

As the rencontre of Mr. Putnam with the wolf in question is the first of his heroic acts on record ; as it has excited great wonderment both in Europe and America ; and as it seems to have laid the foundation of his future fame and fortune, I will transcribe the story entire, as related by Colonel Humphreys :

'This wolf at length became such an intolerable nuisance, that Mr. Putnam entered into a combination with five of his neighbors to hunt alternately until they could destroy her. Two by rotation were to be constantly in pursuit. It was known that having lost the toes from one foot by a steel trap, she made one track shorter than the other. By this vestige the pursuers recognized, in a light snow, the route of this pernicious animal. Having followed her to Connecticut river, and found she had turned back in a direct course toward Pomfret, they immediately returned, and by ten o'clock the next morning the blood-hounds had driven her into a den, about three miles distant from the house of Mr. Putnam. The people soon collected with dogs, guns, straw, fire, and sulphur, to attack the common enemy. With this apparatus several unsuccessful efforts were made to force her from the den. The hounds came back badly wounded, and refused to return. The smoke of blazing straw had no effect ; nor did the fumes of burnt brimstone, with which the cavern was filled, compel her to quit the retirement. Wearied with such fruitless attempts, (which had brought the time to ten o'clock at night,) Mr. Putnam tried once more to make his dog enter, but in vain ; he proposed to his negro man to go down into the cavern and shoot the wolf: the negro declined the hazardous service. Then it was that the master, angry at the disappointment, and declaring that he was ashamed to have a coward in his family, resolved himself to destroy the ferocious beast, lest she should escape through some unknown fissure of the rock. His neighbors strongly remonstrated against the perilous enterprise: but he, knowing that wild animals were intimidated by fire, and having provided several strips of birch-bark, the only combustible material which he could obtain, that would afford light in this deep and darksome cave, prepared for his descent. Having accordingly divested himself of his coat and waistcoat, and having a long rope fastened round his legs, by which he might be pulled back, at a concerted signal, he entered head foremost, with the blazing torch in his hand.

'The aperture of the den, on the east side of a very high ledge of rocks, is about two feet square ; from thence it descends obliquely fifteen feet, then running horizontally about ten more, it ascends gradually sixteen feet toward its termination. The sides of this subterraneous cavity are composed of smooth and solid rocks, which seem to have been divided from each other by some former earthquake. The top and bottom are also of stone, and the entrance, in winter, being covered with ice, is exceedingly slippery. It is in no place high enough for a man to raise himself upright, nor in any part more than three feet in width.

'Having groped his passage to the horizontal part of the den, the most terrifying darkness appeared in front of the dim circle of light afforded by his torch. It was silent as the house of death. None but monsters of the desert had ever before explored this solitary mansion of horror. He, cautiously proceeding onward, came to the ascent ; which he slowly mounted on his hands and knees until he discovered the glaring eye-balls of the wolf, who was sitting at the extremity of the cavern. Started at the sight of fire, she gnashed her teeth and gave a sullen growl. As soon as he had made the necessary discovery, he kicked the rope as a signal for pulling him out. The people, at the mouth of the den, who had listened with painful anxiety, hearing the growling of the wolf, and supposing their friend to be in the most imminent danger, drew him forth with such celerity that his shirt was stripped over his head and his skin severely lacerated. After he had adjusted his clothes, and loaded his gun with nine buck-shot, holding a torch in one hand and the musket in the other, he descended the second time. When he drew nearer than before, the wolf, assuming a still more fierce and terrible appearance, howling, rolling her eyes, snapping her teeth, and dropping her head between her legs, was evidently in the attitude, and on the point of springing at him. At the critical instant he levelled and fired at her head. Stunned with the shock, and suffocated with the smoke, he immediately found himself drawn out of the cave: but having refreshed himself, and permitted the smoke to dissipate, he went down the third time. Once more he came within sight of the wolf, who appearing very passive, he applied the torch to her nose, and perceiving her dead, he took hold of her ears, and then kicking the rope (still tied round his legs) the people above, with no small exultation, dragged them both out together.

'I have offered these facts in greater detail, because they contain a display of character ; and

because they have been erroneously related in several European publications, and very much mutilated in the history of Connecticut, a work as replete with falsehood as destitute of genius, lately
printed in London.' — p. 20.

The history here alluded to was written by the Rev. Mr. Peters,
a tory refugee, who fled from Connecticut to England on the breaking out of the war of independence. The work was quite in the
Munchausen style, and intended to ridicule the people among whom
he had officiated as a gospel minister. I have not the book before
me, but I recollect one of his anecdotes stated that a company of
bull-frogs removing in the night from a pond nearly dried up, in quest
of one better supplied with water, and passing near a village, keeping up their usual croaking, so frightened the inhabitants that many
sought security by flight. They were taken, says the author, for a
body of English soldiers. This queer writer found the foregoing
wolf-story ready manufactured to his hand, and deeming it appropriate to his purpose, he incorporated it in his book, with perhaps a
little ' extra trimmings.'

The relation of such an extraordinary feat would naturally be
seized upon by an author like Mr. Peters, with the view of turning
it into ridicule. And in fact there are strong objections to its credibility. The difficulty of drawing a man out, feet-foremost, from such
a winding cavern, seems insurmountable. The mention of blood-
hounds, in a country where, it is believed, no such species of dog
ever existed, is also liable to criticism. Beside, a gentleman who has
visited the place assures me that the chasm in the rock is by no means
extensive, and that the representation of it here given is entirely
groundless. An affair like this, to establish its title to belief, required
a *procès-verbal,* signed by the witnesses present, under oath.

After the enumeration of the foregoing grievances, the writer observes :

'Prosperity at length began to attend the agricultural affairs of Mr. Putnam. He was acknowledged to be a skilful and indefatigable manager.' · · · 'But the time had now arrived which was to
turn the instruments of husbandry into weapons of hostility, and to exchange the hunting of wolves
that had ravaged the sheep-folds, for the pursuit after savages, who had desolated the frontiers.
Putnam was about thirty-seven years old, when the war between England and France broke out in
America. His reputation must have been favorably known to the government, since among the first
troops that were levied by Connecticut, in 1755, he was appointed to the command of a company in
Lyman's regiment of Provincials.'

It was no doubt urged that a man who had exhibited such undaunted courage, as above reported, in a rencontre with a wild beast,
would be a proper person to contend with a savage foe. The author
having got his hero into the army, where he had an opportunity to
display his adventurous propensities, details his wonderful achievements in a manner which, however pleasing in romance, is offensive
to history, as requiring too severe a tax on human credulity : that
is, although possible to have taken place, yet carrying such an air of
romance as to lessen, if not totally to destroy, their credibility.
Whether this arises from the poetic turn of the reporter, or from the
exaggerated accounts given him by the actor himself in the surprising
events narrated, I will not pretend to decide. I will transcribe a
few of them. The first that occurs, was on an occasion of Captain
Rogers and Captain Putnam being detached with a party of light
troops for the purpose of obtaining accurate knowledge of the position and state of the works at Crown-Point.

'It was impracticable to approach with their party near enough for this purpose, without being discovered. Alone, the undertaking was sufficiently hazardous, on account of the swarms of hostile Indians who infested the woods. Our two partizans, however, left all their men at a convenient distance, with strict orders to continue concealed until their return. Having thus cautiously taken their arrangements, they advanced with the profoundest silence in the evening; and lay, during the night, contiguous to the fortress. Early in the morning they approached so close as to be able to give satisfactory information to the General who had sent them, on the points to which their attention had been directed : but Captain Rogers being at a little distance from Putnam, fortuitously met a stout Frenchman, who instantly seized his fuzee with one hand, and with the other attempted to stab him, while he called to an adjacent guard for assistance. The guard answered. Putnam perceiving the imminent danger of his friend, and that no time was to be lost, or farther alarm given by firing, ran rapidly to them, while they were yet struggling, and with the butt-end of his piece laid the Frenchman dead at his feet. The partizans, to elude pursuit, precipitated their flight, joined the party, and returned without loss to the encampment.' — p. 26.

'Few are so ignorant of war as not to know that military adventures in the night are always extremely liable to accidents. Captain Putnam, having been commanded to reconnoitre the enemy's camp at *the Ovens* near *Ticonderoga*, took the brave Lieutenant Robert Durkee as his companion. In attempting to execute these orders, he narrowly missed being taken himself in the first instance, and killing his friend in the second. It was customary for the British and Provincial troops to place their fires round their camp, which frequently exposed them to the enemy's scouts and patroles. A contrary practice, then unknown in the English army, prevailed among the French and Indians. The plan was much more rational; they kept their fires in the centre, lodged their men circularly at a distance, and posted their centinels in the surrounding darkness. Our partizans approached the camp, and supposing the centries were within the circle of fires, crept upon their hands and knees with the greatest possible caution, until to their utter astonishment, they found themselves in the thickest of the enemy. The centinels, discovering them, fired and slightly wounded Durkee in the thigh. He and Putnam had no alternative. They fled. The latter, being foremost, and scarcely able to see his band before him, soon plunged into a clay-pit. Durkee, almost at the identical moment, came tumbling after. Putnam, by no means pleased at finding a companion, and believing him to be one of the enemy, lifted his tomahawk to give the deadly blow, when Durkee, (who had followed so closely as to know him) inquired whether he had escaped unhurt. Captain Putnam instantly recognizing the voice, dropped his weapon ; and both, springing from the pit, made good their retreat to the neighboring ledges, amidst a shower of random shot. There they betook themselves to a large log, by the side of which they lodged the remainder of the night. Before they lay down, Captain Putnam said he had a little rum in his canteen, which could never be more acceptable or necessary ; but on examining the canteen, which hung under his arm, he found the enemy had pierced it with their balls, and that there was not a drop of liquor left. The next day he found fourteen bullet-holes in his blanket.' — p. 28.

It appears that the Captain and Lieutenant started together, and, in the manner of Jack and Gill, almost at the identical moment tumbled into a pit : and is it possible that the brave Captain Putnam, under these circumstances, was so frightened as to take his companion for an enemy ? His canteen was pierced with balls ; one would have sufficed to discharge its contents. He found his blanket had *fourteen bullet-holes*. Here it is evidently intended to intimate that this had been caused by fourteen separate balls. But the blanket must of course have been rolled up and slung on his back ; one ball, therefore, might have committed all the damage sustained. This explanation, however, would lessen the imminent danger in which the Captain wished to represent himself upon this occasion.

Captain Putnam was promoted to a Majority by the legislature of Connecticut, in 1757.

'As one day Major Putnam chanced to lie with a batteau and five men on the eastern shore of the Hudson, near the Rapids, contiguous to which Fort Miller stood, his men on the opposite bank had given him to understand that a large body of savages were in his rear, and would be upon him in a moment. To stay and be sacrificed, to attempt crossing and be shot, or to go down to the falls, with an almost absolute certainty of being drowned, were the sole alternatives that presented themselves to his choice. So instantaneously was the latter adopted. that one man who had rambled a little from the party, was, of necessity, left, and fell a miserable victim to savage barbarity. The Indians arrived on the shore soon enough to fire many balls on the batteau before it could be got under way. No sooner had our batteau-men escaped, by favor of the rapidity of the current, beyond the reach of musket-shot, than death seemed only to have been avoided in one form to be encountered in another not less terrible. Prominent rocks, latent shelves, absorbing eddies, and abrupt descents, for a quarter of a mile, afforded scarcely the smallest chance of escaping without a miracle. Putnam, trusting himself to a good providence, whose kindness he had often experienced, rather than to men, whose tenderest mercies are cruelty, was now seen to place himself sedately at the helm, and afford an astonishing spectacle of serenity. His companions, with a mixture of terror, admiration and wonder, saw him incessantly changing the course, to avoid the jaws of ruin, that seemed expanded to swallow the whirling boat. Twice he turned it fairly round to shun the rifts of rocks. Amidst these eddies, in which there was the greatest danger of its foundering, at one moment the sides were exposed to the fury of the waves; then the stern, and next the bow glanced obliquely onward, with inconceivable velocity. With not less amazement the savages beheld him sometimes mounting the billows, then plunging abruptly down, at other times skilfully veering from the rocks, and shooting through the only narrow passage ; until at last they viewed the boat safely gliding on the smooth surface of the stream below. At this sight, it is asserted that these rude sons of nature were affected with the same kind of superstitious veneration which the Europeans in the dark ages entertained for some of their most valorous champions. They deemed the man invulnerable, whom their balls on his pushing from shore could not touch ; and whom they had seen steering in safety down the rapids that had never before been passed. They conceived it would be an affront against the *Great Spirit* to attempt to kill this favored mortal with powder and ball, if they should ever see and know him again.' — p. 54.

The author was a graduate of Yale College, and being a poet by profession, had doubtless thoroughly studied Homer and Virgil ; and he has evidently endeavored to imitate their graphic powers of delineation ; and it must be confessed has succeeded to admiration. But he should have recollected that in this case he was writing prose, and not poetry — history, not fiction ; and he should have curbed the ardor of his muse, and confined himself to sober matter-of-fact narrative.

As to the 'superstitious veneration' in which this hero is here said to have been held by the aborigines of this country, '*do not believe a word of it.*' Be assured they at this time were not so readily imposed upon : they had seen, fought, and killed too many white men, to entertain such an exalted opinion of any of them. As they are good marksmen, the Major must have been far enough out of the reach of their musketry when they fired at him ; although from the perturbed state in which he was, he may have supposed himself providentially preserved. All the time wanted to start a batteau is that which is required for the men to seize and ply the oars ; it is then immediately under way. This, it appears, Major Putnam ordered done, the moment he was informed there was a body of Indians in the vicinity, leaving, perhaps without necessity, one poor fellow to be sacrificed.

The Indians at any rate soon found that Putnam, if invulnerable, was not invincible, for in a rencontre he had with them a little after this affair, he was obliged to surrender himself a prisoner :

'Major Putnam had discharged his fuzee several times, but at length it missed fire, while the muzzle was pressed against the breast of a *large and well-proportioned savage*. The warrior, availing himself of the indefensible attitude of his adversary, with a tremendous war-whoop, sprang forward, with his lifted hatchet, and compelled him to surrender ; and having disarmed and bound him fast to a tree, returned to the battle.' A change of position of the combatants ' occasioned the tree to which Putnam was tied to be directly between the fire of the two parties. Human imagination can hardly figure to itself a more deplorable situation. The balls flew incessantly from each side, many struck the tree, while some passed through the sleeves and skirts of his coat. In this state of jeopardy, unable to move his body, to stir his limbs, or even to incline his head, he remained more than an hour. So equally balanced, and so obstinate was the fight ! At one moment, while the battle swerved in favor of the enemy, a young savage chose an odd way of discovering his humor. He found Putnam bound. He might have despatched him at a blow. But he loved better to excite the terrors of the prisoner, by hurling a tomahawk at his head, or rather it should seem his object was to see how near he could throw it without touching him : the weapon struck in the tree a number of times at a hair's breadth distance from the mark.'

The Indians finally drew off, taking Major Putnam with them ; and when they had encamped for the night, ' it was determined to roast him alive !' An awful account of the preparations made for the purpose, is given by the biographer. He was however saved by the interference of a French officer, and taken to Montreal. Here he met with Colonel Peter Schuyler, also a prisoner, but on parole, who generously furnished him with clothing and money ; and not long after procured him to be exchanged with himself.

To form the character of a complete hero, it is imperious that he perform some signal acts of gallantry toward the fair; and an opportunity now occurred for the Major to distinguish himself in this respect, which he did in true Quixotic style :

‘At the house of Colonel Schuyler, Major Putnam became acquainted with Mrs. Howe, a fair captive, whose history would not be read without emotion, if it could be written in the same affecting manner in which I have often heard it told. She was still young and handsome herself, though she had two daughters of marriageable age. Distress, which had taken somewhat from the original redundancy of her bloom, and added a softening paleness to her cheeks, rendered her appearance the more engaging. Her face, that seemed to have been formed for the assemblage of dimples and smiles, was clouded with care. The natural sweetness was not, however, soured by despondency and petulance, but chasteued by humility and resignation. This mild daughter of sorrow looked as if she had known the day of prosperity, when serenity and gladness of soul were the inmates of her bosom. That day was past, and the once lively features now assumed a tender melancholy, which witnessed her irreparable loss. She needed not the customary weeds of mourning, or the fallacious pageantry of wo, to prove her widowed state. She was in that stage of affliction when the excess is so far abated as to permit the subject to be drawn into conversation, without opening the wound afresh. It is then rather a source of pleasure than pain to dwell upon the circumstances in narration. Every thing conspired to make her story interesting. Her first husband had been killed and scalped by the Indians some years before. By an unexpected assault, in 1756, upon Fort Dummer, where she then happened to be present with Mr. Howe, her second husband, the savages carried the fort, murdered the greater part of the garrison, mangled in death her husband, and led her away with seven children into captivity.’

But it appears, that ‘a young French officer’ had conceived a violent passion for her. ‘He pursued her whersoever she went, and although he could make no advances in her affections, he seemed resolved by perseverance to carry his point. Mrs. Howe, terrified by his treatment, was obliged to keep constantly near Major Putnam, who informed the young officer that he would protect that lady at the risk of his life.’ It is added in a note, that ‘two or three incidents respecting Mrs. Howe, which were received by the author from General Putnam, and inserted in the former editions, are omitted in this, as they appeared, on farther information, to be mistakes.’ Who discovered these mistakes? General Putnam or Colonel Humphreys? The probability is, that the incredibility of some of the reports had been suggested to the latter, which induced him to suppress them. But if they were corrected by the General himself, the circumstance showed his liability to error, which ought to have cautioned the biographer against continuing many of the extravagant relations in the foregoing detail.

‘Colonel Putnam, (Putnam had been raised to this rank previous to the close of the war,) at the expiration of ten years from his first receiving a commission, after having seen as much service, endured as many hardships, encountered as many dangers, and acquired as many laurels as any officer of his rank, with great satisfaction laid aside his uniform, and returned to his plough.’

Hostilities between Great Britain and her American colonies commenced on the 18th of April, 1775, at Lexington, Massachusetts :

‘Putnam, who was ploughing when he heard the news, left his plough in the middle of the field, unyoked his team, and without waiting to change his clothes, set off for the theatre of action. But finding the British retreated to Boston, and invested by a sufficient force to watch their movements, he came back to Connecticut, levied a regiment, under authority of the legislature, and speedily returned to Cambridge. He was now promoted to be a Major-General on the Provincial staff, by his colony; and, in a little time, confirmed by Congress, in the same rank on the Continental establishment. General Ward of Massachusetts, by common consent, commanded the whole; and the celebrated Doctor Warren was made a Major-General.

‘Not long after this period, the British commander-in-chief found the means to convey a proposal privately to General Putnam, that if he would relinquish the rebel party, he might rely upon being made a Major-General on the British establishment, and receiving a great pecuniary compensation for his services. General Putnam spurned at the offer; which however *he thought prudent at that time to conceal from public notice.*’

Mr. Sweet, in his ‘Sketch of Bunker-Hill Battle,’ says : ‘On the first news of the battle of Lexington, Putnam mounted his horse, rode in a single day one hundred miles, arrived at Cambridge, and attended a council of war on the 21st of April.' He must have been full of fight, or have supposed his presence at the scene of action very essential to the country. Mr. Sweet, I find, obtained his information from the same source as Colonel Humphreys — at second hand from the family of General Putnam. Is it possible that Colonel Putnam would not pay the general officers and other gentlemen he was going to meet in council so much respect as to put on his military, or at least his Sunday coat, which every Connecticut farmer is always supplied with? Respect for himself, it would be thought, would have induced him to have done this. I am therefore inclined to believe this to be a *mistake.* I suspect also that the General was hoaxed in regard to his being offered a bribe by General Gage. For, however well qualified he might formerly have been, as a partisan officer, his age at this time in some measure, but more particularly his want of education, and rough manners, rendered him unfit to fulfil the duties of Major-General.

The ridiculous story, however, respecting the intercourse said to have taken place between Gage and Putnam, appears, according to the editor, to have been fabricated in England. He says :

'An article, void of foundation, mentioning an interview between General Gage and General Putnam, appeared in the English gazettes in these words : ' General Gage, viewing the American army with his telescope, saw General Putnam in it, which surprised him ; and he contrived to get a message delivered to him, that he wanted to speak to him. Putnam without any hesitation waited upon him. General Gage showed him his fortifications, and advised him to lay down his arms. General Putnam replied, he could force his fortifications in half an hour, and advised General Gage to go on board the ships with his troops.'

Colonel Humphreys, in speaking of the battle of Bunker-Hill, says : ' In this battle, the presence and example of General Putnam, who arrived with the reinforcement, were not less conspicuous than useful. He did every thing that an intrepid and experienced officer could accomplish. The enemy pursued to Winter-Hill ; Putnam made a stand, and drove them back under cover of their ships.' The editor says : ' Such was the statement made in some American newspapers of that day, but without any foundation in fact. There was no pursuit of the British beyond Bunker-Hill.' Had the aid-de-camp of General Putnam need to apply to vague newspaper reports for correct information of this battle ? How often did the General reiterate to him his achievements on the memorable day of that contest ! At any rate, this biography was published some years before the decease of the subject of it, who might have had any mistakes he thought proper corrected ; but it seems he chose to pocket the affront of the misstatements. The author has also committed another error in his account of this affair. He says, the troops sent on this service were 'under the orders of General Warren.' Whereas Warren acted as a volunteer, and refused the command of the redoubt offered to him by Colonel Prescott, but fought valiantly with his musket.

But I shall show, in the sequel, that General Putnam is justly entitled to no laurels for his conduct on this occasion ; that he was an inactive spectator, in a secure position, during the whole time of the engagement ; that he appeared only in the retreat, carrying off, it is said, some camp equipage upon his horse. Indeed the above statement in respect to him amounts to nothing, except that part of it which found to be erroneous.   ' He did every thing,' etc., but no specification is given, because there was no tangible act to admit of it :

'In the beginning of July, General WASHINGTON, who had been constituted by Congress Commander-in-Chief of the American forces, arrived at Cambridge to take the command. Having formed the army into three grand divisions, consisting of about twelve regiments each, he appointed Major-General Ward to command the right wing, Major-General Lee the left wing, and Major-General Putnam the reserve. General Putnam's alertness in accelerating the construction of the necessary defences was particularly noticed and highly approved by the Commander-in-Chief.'

On the foregoing the editor remarks, in a note : ' It was not in Putnam's nature to be idle : inured to habits of industry himself, no man was better calculated to make others so ; and WASHINGTON, observing the great progress that had been made in a short time, and with but few men, in raising a work of defence, said to him : ' You seem to have the faculty, General Putnam, of infusing your own industrious spirit into all the workmen you employ.''

General WASHINGTON saw at once what sort of employment General Putnam was calculated for ; and he was accordingly engaged in superintending the erection of fortifications, or placed in reserve in the interior, for the most part, during the time he remained in service, which was till December, 1779 ; when ill health caused him to retire.

'In order to cover the country adjoining to the Sound, and to support the garrison of West Point, in case of an attack, Major-General Putnam was stationed for the winter of 1778–9, at Reading, in Connecticut. He had under his orders the brigade of New-Hampshire, the two brigades of Connecticut, the corps of infantry commanded by Hazen, and that of cavalry by Sheldon.
'The troops, who had been badly fed, badly clothed, and worse paid, by brooding over their grievances in the leisure and inactivity of winter quarters, began to think them intolerable. The Connecticut brigades formed the design of marching to Hartford, where the General Assembly was then in session, and of demanding redress at the point of the bayonet. Word having been brought to General Putnam, that the second brigade was under arms for this purpose, he mounted his horse, gallopped to the cantonment, and thus addressed them : ' My brave lads, whither are you going? Do you intend to desert your officers, and to invite the enemy to follow you into the country ? Whose cause have you been fighting and suffering so long in? Is it not your own ? Have you no property, no parents, wives or children ? You have behaved like men so far; all the world is full of your praises; and posterity will stand astonished at your deeds; but not if you spoil all at last. Don't you consider how much the country is distressed by the war, and that your officers have not been any better paid than yourselves ? But we all expect better times, and that the country will do us ample justice. Let us all stand by one another, then, and fight it out like brave soldiers. Think what a shame it would be for Connecticut men to run away from their officers.' After the several regiments had received the General as he rode along the line with drums beating, and presented arms, the sergeants who had then the command, brought the men to an order, in which position they continued while he was speaking. When he had done, he directed the acting Major of Brigade to give the word for them to shoulder, march to their regimental parades, and lodge arms; all which they executed with promptitude and apparent good humor. One soldier only, who had been the most active, was confined in the quarter-guard; from whence, at night, he attempted to make his escape. But the sentinel, who had also been in the mutiny, shot him dead on the spot, and thus the affair subsided.
'About the middle of winter, while General Putnam was on a visit to his out-post at Horse-Neck, he found Governor Tryon advancing upon that town with a corps of fifteen hundred men. To oppose these General Putnam had only a picquet of one hundred and fifty men, and two iron field-pieces, without horses or drag-ropes. He, however, planted his cannon on the high ground, by the meeting-house, and retarded their approach by firing several times, until, perceiving the horse (supported by the infantry) about to charge, he ordered the picquet to provide for their safety, by retiring to a swamp inaccessible to horse, and secured his own, by plunging down the steep precipice at the church upon a full trot. This precipice is so steep, where he descended, as to have artificial stairs, composed of nearly one hundred stone steps, for the accommodation of foot passengers. There the dragoons, who were but a sword's length from him, stopped short; for the declivity was so abrupt, that they ventured not to follow; and, before they could gain the valley, by going round the brow of the hill in the ordinary road, he was far enough beyond their reach.'

I am induced to believe that General Putnam here, as in the case of Lieutenant Durkee's following him into the clay-pit, labored under a false apprehension. I have descended this famous hill, at the place where Putnam is said to have bolted from the main road, leading my horse. The dragoons surely would not hesitate to have done the same, to secure the old General ; who, I am confident, could not have gained much, if any, by being on horseback. The road is of course made winding, for the purpose of rendering the ascent more gradual, and consequently an object a short distance ahead would be out of sight of persons in the rear; which was, no doubt, the case with Putnam when he made his escape, as above related.

Colonel Humphreys' life of Putnam was first published in 1788. The General had been attacked with paralysis, in December, 1779, which deprived him of the use of his limbs on the right side. 'In that situation,' says his biographer, 'he has constantly remained, favored with such a portion of bodily activity as enables him to walk and ride moderately; and retaining unimpaired his relish for enjoyment, his love of pleasantry, his strength of memory, and all the faculties of his mind. As a proof that his powers of memory are not weakened, it ought to be observed, that he has lately repeated from recollection all the adventures of his life, which are here recorded, and which had formerly been communicated to the compiler in detached conversations.' In the edition of the work which I use, published in 1818, it is added, that General Putnam was attacked with an inflammatory disease on the 17th of May, 1790, and died on the 19th of the same month.

General Putnam, it appears, was of a convivial disposition; and wishing to amuse his neighbors on winter evenings, was doubtless in the habit of detailing his adventures, and occasionally ornamenting them with a spice of the wonderful, to render them more acceptable and entertaining to his company; till by frequent repetition these addenda escaped the notice even of the narrator himself. There is no other way of accounting for his not contradicting many of the absurdities and errors contained in this memoir, which he must frequently have read.

It is unfortunate for the truth of history, that this publication ever appeared, as it has had great influence with succeeding historians, sanctioned as it was by the Connecticut Society of Cincinnati, composed of revolutionary general and field officers. It is probable, however, that none of the members of this society read the manuscripts; and if they had, although they had heard of the wolf affair, and of the miraculous escape of the General, at Horseneck Hill, they must have been utterly ignorant of his exploits with the Indians in the French war, as these were known to no living soul but himself.

If the characters of our revolutionary officers of the highest grade can be sustained only by incredible Munchausen stories, the sooner they fall into oblivion the better for the honor of the country.

I will take a brief notice of a 'Sketch of the Battle of Bunker Hill, by S. Sweet;' published in 1818, and here appended to the work of Colonel Humphreys. The author says:

'With the advice of the council of war, General Ward issued orders to Colonel William Prescott, to the commander of Colonel Frye's regiment, and Colonel Bridge, to be prepared for an expedition, with all their men fit for service, and one day's provisions. The same order issued for one hundred and twenty of General Putnam's regiment, and one company of artillery with two field pieces.

'With these troops Colonel Prescott was ordered to proceed to Charlestown, *in the evening,* take possession of Bunker Hill, and erect the requisite fortifications to defend it.' — p. 208.

'General Putnam having the general superintendence of the expedition, and the chief, Colonel Gridley, accompanied the troops.' — p. 210.

'At *daybreak,* General Putnam ordered Lieutenant Clark to send and request of General Ward a horse for him to ride to Bunker Hill. The Lieutenant went himself, but the General's impatience could not await an answer. On his return he found him mounted and departing.' — p. 117.

These two contradictory accounts are doubtless derived from the same source ; the narrator through lack of memory forgetting, when relating one story, that he had told a different one respecting the same transactions upon another occasion.   That Mr. Sweet communicated with the family of General Putnam, and received his information from it, he expressly states.

Our author says : ' The drums beat to arms.   Putnam left his works, commenced on Bunker Hill, and led his troops into action.' — p. 227. It will hereafter appear that this statement is a *mistake ;* that he commenced no works on Bunker Hill ; that he calculated on the defeat of the Americans, and made no effort to prevent it.   His whole care seems to have been bestowed on saving the entrenching tools.   His opinion of the issue of the combat, at the time, is thus related by Mr. Sweet: ' As General Warren passed on to the scene of action, he met with General Putnam, who observed, that ' From long experience, he perfectly comprehended the character of the British army ; they would ultimately succeed and drive us from the works, but from the mode of attack they had chosen, it was in our power to do them infinite mischief, though we must be prepared for a brave and orderly retreat, when we could maintain our ground no longer.' — p. 220.

This must have been a private conversation, if it ever occurred, between these two generals ; for certainly General Putnam would not have been so imprudent as to advance such an opinion publicly.   The relation of it, therefore, must be derived from him ; but whether the opinion were expressed before or after the fact, may be doubtful.   At any rate, his want of faith in the success of the American arms upon this occasion is apparent ; and this seems to have paralyzed his exertions toward its accomplishment.   He remained on horseback at a distance from the battle-ground, prepared for a speedy retreat whenever his own safety might require it.   Notwithstanding these forebodings of Putnam, Mr. Sweet says, ' The Americans were impatient to be led against the enemy.   General Putnam, Colonel Prescott, and other veterans, demanded that advantage should be taken of this disposition of the men, and their wishes gratified.'   What glaring inconsistency ! *'Do not believe a word of it.'*   This is an instance of poetical history ; trimmings are required to make a complete hero.   Putnam is here made to advise an action which he was convinced would end in defeat !

A pamphlet of thirty-six pages, published at Portland in 1835, has fallen into my hands, which puts an end to all farther doubt respecting the conduct of General Putnam on the occasion in question.   It is entitled, ' History of the Battle of Breed's Hill : by Major-Generals WILLIAM HEATH, HENRY LEE, JAMES WILKINSON, and HENRY DEARBORN.   Compiled by CHARLES COFFIN.'

Mr. Coffin has added the testimony of other very respectable witnesses, who were engaged in the action, and is deserving of great praise for the trouble he has taken in placing the history of the important event treated of, on its true basis, and beyond the reach of cavil. He has prefaced the pamphlet with the following notice :

' Having for years been satisfied that the accounts of Breed's Hill Battle, as given by Gordon, Warren, Ramsey, and Marshall, are defective and imperfect, I have been induced to publish the transaction of that memorable event, as given by four American Major-Generals, who were either in the action, or had the best possible opportunities of being fully acquainted with the details of it, and who from their profession were better qualified to give a full and fair narrative, than any others who have undertaken it; to which are added, the deposition of a number of highly respectable gentlemen who were eye witnesses and partakers of the glory of that proud day. The following sheets, it is believed, will give a more full and accurate view of the troops engaged, by whom commanded, and all the transactions of the day, than any narrative extant. My objects are truth and justice to the living and the dead.'

I shall select a few passages only from this pamphlet, respecting the immediate matter at issue, without regard to the details connected therewith, which are not essential to my purpose.

BATTLE OF BREED'S HILL. — The following is from the ' Memoirs of Major-General WILLIAM HEATH, published in 1798.'

'Perhaps there never was a better fought battle than this, all things considered; and too much praise can never be bestowed on the conduct of Colonel William Prescott, who, notwithstanding any thing that may have been said, *was the proper commanding officer* at the redoubt, and nobly acted his part as such, during the whole action.

' Just before the action began, General Putnam came to the redoubt, and told Colonel Prescott that the entrenching tools must be sent off, or they would be lost; the Colonel replied, that if he sent any of the men away with the tools, not one of them would return; to this the General answered, ' They shall every man return.' A large party was then sent off with the tools, and not one of them returned: in this instance the Colonel was the best judge of human nature. In the time of action, Colonel Prescott observed that the brave General Warren was near the works; he immediately stepped up to him, and asked him if he had any orders to give him. The General replied that he had none, that he exercised no command there: ' The command,' said the General, ' is yours.'

Our next extract is from Major-General HENRY LEE's ' Memoirs of the War in the Southern Department,' published in 1812. General Lee merely glances at the battle of Bunker Hill. He says :

'Warren, who fell nobly supporting the action, was the favorite of the day, and has engrossed the fame due to Prescott. No man reveres the character of Warren more than the writer ; and he considers himself not only, by his obedience to truth, doing justice to Colonel Prescott, but performing an acceptable service to the memory of the illustrious Warren, who being a really great man, would disdain to wear laurels not his own. · · · The military annals of the world rarely furnish an achievement which equals the firmness and courage displayed on that proud day by the gallant band of Americans; and it certainly stands first in the brilliant events of our war. When future generations shall inquire where are the men who gained the highest prize of glory in the arduous contest which ushered in our nation's birth, upon Prescott and his companions in arms will the eye of history beam.'

From ' A Sketch of the Battle of Breed's Hill, by Major-General JAMES WILKINSON,' published in 1816, we take the following :

' If General Putnam had moved up with Colonel Gerrish and the men who remained stationary within six hundred yards of the combat, which lasted an hour and a half, the triumph of the provincials would have been decisive, and those of the British corps who were not killed must have surrendered, which would probably have terminated the contest, and prevented the disseverment of the British empire; but I understand from high authority, that it was in vain Colonel Prescott sent messenger after messenger to entreat General Putnam to come to his succor ; he rode about Bunker's Hill, while the battle raged under his eye, with a number of entrenching tools slung across his horse, but did not advance a step, and was passed, with Colonel Gerrish at his side, by Stark and Dearborn, as they retreated, near the spot where they saw him when they advanced ; and for this conduct Colonel Prescott never ceased to condemn the General.' . . . . ' All the reinforcements which arrived at Bunker Hill, after Colonel Stark had passed, halted and kept company with General Putnam and Colonel Gerrish.'

Account of the Battle, by Major-General HENRY DEARBORN, published in 1818 :

' When the troops arrived at the summit of Bunker's Hill, we found General Putnam with nearly as many men as had been engaged in the battle; notwithstanding which, no measure had been taken for reinforcing us, nor was there a shot fired over our retreat, or any movement made to check the advance of the enemy to this height ; but on the contrary, General Putnam rode off with a number of *spades and pick-axes in his hands,* and the troops that had remained with him *inactive* during the whole of the action, although within a few hundred yards of the battle-ground, and no obstacle to impede their movement but musket balls.'

' The total loss of the British was about twelve hundred, upward of five hundred killed and between six and seven hundred wounded. The Welsh fusileers suffered most severely ; they came into action five hundred strong, and all were killed or wounded but eighty-three.

'I will mention an extraordinary circumstance to show how far the temporary reputation of a man may affect the minds of all classes of society.

'General Putnam had entered our army at the commencement of the revolutionary war, with such a universal popularity as can scarcely now be conceived, even by those who then felt the whole force of it, and no one can at this time offer any satisfactory reasons why he was held in such high estimation.

'In the battle of Bunker's Hill he took post on the declivity toward Charlestown neck; where I saw him on horseback as we passed on to Breed's Hill, with Colonel Gerrish by his side. I heard the gallant Colonel Prescott (who commanded in the redoubt) observe after the war, at the table of his Excellency, James Boudoin, then Governor of this Commonwealth, 'that he sent three messengers during the battle to General Putnam, requesting him to come forward and take the command, there being no general officer present, and the relative rank of the Colonel not having been settled; but that he received no answer, and his whole conduct was such, both during the action and the retreat, that he ought to have been shot.' He remained at or near the top of Bunker Hill until the retreat with Colonel Gerrish by his side; I saw them together when we retreated. He not only continued at that distance himself during the whole of the action, but had a force with him nearly as large as that engaged. No reinforcement of men or ammunition was sent to our assistance; and, instead of attempting to cover the retreat of those who had expended their last shot in the face of the enemy, he retreated in company with Colonel Gerrish, and his whole force, without discharging a single musket; but what is still more astonishing, Colonel Gerrish was arrested for cowardice, tried, cashiered, and universally execrated; while not a word was said against the conduct of General Putnam, whose extraordinary popularity alone saved him, not only from trial, but even from censure. Colonel Gerrish commanded a regiment, and should have been at its head. His regiment was not in action although ordered; but as he was in the suite of the General, and appeared to be in the situation of Adjutant General, why was he not directed by Putnam to join it, or the regiment sent into action under the senior officer present with it?

'When General Putnam's ephemeral and unaccountable popularity subsided or faded away, and the minds of the people were released from the shackles of a delusive trance, the circumstances relating to Bunker-Hill were viewed and talked of in a very different light, and the selection of the unfortunate Colonel Gerrish as a scape-goat considered as a mysterious and inexplicable event.

'I have no private feeling to gratify by making this statement in relation to General Putnam, as I never had any intercourse with him, and was only in the army where he was present, for a few months; but at this late period, I conceive it a duty to give a fair and impartial account of one of the most important battles during the war of independence, and all the circumstances connected with it, so far as I had the means of being correctly informed. It is a duty I owe to posterity, and the character of those brave officers who bore a share in the hardships of the revolution.'

I will take a short notice of the other interesting and satisfactory documents adduced by Mr. Coffin; commencing with the 'Statement of the Honorable ABEL PARKER, Judge of Probate':

'As I was in the battle on Breed's Hill, on the 17th June, 1775, and there received one ball through my leg, another having passed through my clothes, all accounts of that battle are to me extremely interesting. But I had not seen an account which I considered in any degree correct, until the one published by General Dearborn. But notwithstanding the correctness of his description of the battle, some persons seem to be much exasperated by it, in particular as to what he asserts in regard to General Putnam. As long as they confined themselves to mere declamation, without bringing forward any evidence to disprove General Dearborn's statement, I deemed it unnecessary for me to appear in vindication of it. But, on perusing a letter from Colonel Trumbull to Colonel Putnam, (son of the general,) wherein mention is made of a conversation with Col. Small, in London, I concluded that to remain longer silent, would be absolutely criminal. I shall therefore, in as concise a manner as possible, state what I know relating to that memorable battle.'

It is not necessary to follow the Judge in the whole of his detail. He was attached to Captain John Nutting's company, in Prescott's regiment:

'The company,' he says, 'left the town, and marched to join the regiment on the hill. When we arrived there, the fort was in considerable forwardness, and the troops commenced throwing up the breast-work mentioned by General Dearborn. We had not been long in that work, before the cannon-shot from a hill in Boston, and the vessels lying in the river, were poured in upon us in great profusion. Some time before this there were brought to the fort several brass field-pieces, one of which was actually fired toward Boston, but the ball did not reach the town. In the time of this heavy fire, I, for the first time that day, saw General Putnam. standing with others, under cover of the north wall of the fort, where I believe he remained until the British troops made their appearance in their boats. At this time the artillery was withdrawn from the fort, by whose orders I know not, and General Putnam, at or near the same time, left the fort.

'When the British first made their attack with small arms, I was at the breast-work, where I remained until I received my wound from the party who flanked it: I then went to the fort, where I remained until the order to retreat was given by Colonel Prescott. After my arrival at the fort I had a perfect opportunity of viewing the operations of the day, and noticed Colonel P. as the only person who took upon him any command. He frequently ordered the men from one side to the other, in order to defend that part which was pressed hardest by the enemy; and I was within a few yards of him, when the order to retreat was given; and I affirm, that at that time *General Putnam was not in the fort*, neither had he been there at any time after my entering the same; and I have no hesitation in declaring, that the story told by Colonel Small to Colonel Trumbull, concerning General Putnam's saving him from the fire of our men at that time, is altogether unfounded.'

Colonel . Trumbull, it appears, was completely hoaxed by this Colonel Small, of the British army, who induced him to alter the first draught of his picture of the battle, in order to give ‘ his friend,’ as he called him, General Putnam, and himself conspicuous positions in the action ; thereby rendering his picture, as an historical portrait, worthless, in fact offensive to the view, in exhibiting a representation contrary to what actually took place. The testimony of several others who were present and took part in the contest, is given in the pamphlet, fully confirming the statement of Judge Parker in regard to Colonel Small.

Rev. Dr. WILLIAM BENTLEY, in his Statement published in Salem in 1818, says :

‘ I was with General Stark, on the 31st of May, 1810. Among the maps, prints, and papers I carried him, were some portraits, and among them was one of General Putnam. I recollect that, upon the sight of the head of General Putnam, he said, ‘ My *chaplain*,’ as he called me, ‘ you know my opinion of that man. Had he done his duty, he would have decided the fate of his country in the first action.’ He then proceeded to describe to me the scene of action, and told me where he saw General Putnam, and what was done on the occasion. His remarks were as severe as his genius and the sentiments of ardent patriotism could make them. As General Stark always used the same language on the subject, it will be recollected by many of his friends.’

The following are certificates of the Rev. DANIEL CHAPLIN, D. D., of Groton, and the Rev. JOHN BULLARD, of Pepperell : ‘ This may certify to the public, that we whose names are here given, were in habits of intimacy with Colonel W. Prescott, of Pepperell, a man of the strictest integrity, during most of the period after he left the revolutionary army until his death.’ Here they state his remarks respecting General Warren, of his refusing to take any command, etc., and add :

‘ Colonel Prescott further informed us repeatedly, that when a retreat was ordered and commenced, as he was descending the hill, he met with General Putnam, and said to him, ‘ Why did you not support me, General, with your men, as I had reason to expect, according to agreement?’ Putnam answered, ‘ I could not *drive* the dogs up.’ Prescott pointedly said to him, ‘ If you could not *drive* them up, you might have *led* them up.’ We have good reason to believe further, from declarations of some of our parishioners, men of respectability, whose veracity cannot be doubted, who belonged to Colonel Prescott’s regiment, and were present through the whole service, that General Putnam was not on Breed’s Hill the night preceding, or on that day, except that just before the attack was made, he might have gone to the fort and ordered the tools to be carried off, that they might not fall into the hands of the enemy in the event of his carrying the works, and holding the ground, and that he and his men, with Colonel Gerrish, remained on the side of Bunker Hill toward the neck during the whole action.’

Thus it appears that General Putnam, at the battle of Bunker Hill, regardless of the lives of the brave men who fell on that glorious day, vindicating the cause of their country, was solely occupied in removing the camp equipage and brass field-pieces ; taking away the very means that might have produced a different result to the contest.

How has it happened that the conduct of this man upon this occasion has not met with the universal reprobation of the country ? His unbounded popularity on his entering the revolutionary army, is the reply. ‘ And,’ says General Dearborn, ‘ no one can at this time offer any satisfactory reasons why he was held in such high estimation.’

Mankind are fond of the marvellous, and listen with intense avidity to relations of surprising acts of heroism and hair-breadth escapes. The country had been filled with the wonderful achievements of this hero in the French war, as detailed by himself, and afterward recorded by Colonel Humphreys ; and his memorable victory over the she wolf, like the feats of the fabled Perseus, paved the way for the favorable reception of other acts equally valorous. Here is the solu-

tion of the mystery.   General Putnam was looked upon as the Hercules of America, of unequalled prowess and skill in war.   But the
greatest boasters are not always the bravest in action ; and this principle was tested at the battle of Bunker Hill.

In regard to the conduct of Colonel Gerrish, there is the greatest
reason to believe that he was induced by Putnam to remain with his
regiment, with him, as a *corps de reserve ;* which, however, was not
intended by the latter to be brought into action.   And being under
the protection, and perhaps as he thought under the command, of a
Major-General, he presumed himself excusable for disobedience of
the order of the commander-in-chief.   'The Colonel,' says General
Wilkins, 'was cashiered, but the General, being distinguished for his
popularity, served as third in command at the termination of the
American revolution.'   General Dearborn observes, that after this
battle General Putnam was viewed in a very different light from
what he had been before, and that 'the selection of the unfortunate
Colonel Gerrish as a scape-goat was considered as a mysterious and
inexplicable event.'

Now it appears to me that this difficulty admits of an easy explanation.   General Putnam was not ordered to Bunker Hill ; if he had
been, he must have had the command as the superior officer.   He
was therefore not amenable for a dereliction of duty, none having
been imposed upon him.   He appears to have gone near the scene
of action, with what view does not expressly appear, except that of
securing the entrenching tools ; although his biographers endeavor to
place upon his brows the laurels nobly won by others.   Mr. Sweet
contradicts his own previous statement, when he says, 'General Putnam, having the general superintendence of the expedition, accompanied the troops.'   He had before declared that Putnam sent a
request to General Ward for a horse to ride to Bunker Hill, and of
course without orders from that officer.   There is no record in history, it is presumed, where a superior officer is ordered on an expedition as a mere *superintendent,* and the command at the same time
given to an officer of inferior grade.   What duty, in such case, de-
volves upon a superintendent ?   To take care of the camp equipage ?
Nonsense ! The commander is the superintendent.   The creation of
this awkward office is entirely gratuitous; got up to account for
General Putnam's being at or near the battle-ground, and as an
apology for his looking on and taking no part in the action.

It is time the public should be disabused in respect to the character
and services of General Putnam.   Nearly all the accounts of the
American revolutionary war, all encyclopedias and biographical works
published in the United States, in treating of him, falsify history in the
most shameful manner.   As a sample, take the following from a late
biography by the Rev. J. L. BLAKE, D. D.   He says :

'Israel Putnam, Major-General in the American revolutionary war,
was a native of Massachusetts.   He settled in Connecticut, and early
discovered that energy and decision of character which distinguished
him through life ; and the remarkable instance he gave of it in the
destruction of a wolf will always go with his name.   He was engaged
in the French war, and a detail of his adventures and distresses
border on romance.   He was one of the first to take up arms at the

occurrence at Lexington, and performed a distinguished part at Bunker Hill. He had an important command during the whole war.'

Farther comment is unnecessary. The reader, from the proofs we have cited, must be convinced that the entire life of General Putnam, as given by his biographers, not only 'borders on,' but actually is, '*romance.*'

FALLS OF THE STAUBBACH:

BERNESE ALPS.

AMID the Laterbrunnen fire
  The rapid Staubbach takes it leap,
And with its Alpine music stirs
  The pines that fringe the misty steep ;
Where, piled against the summer sky,
The massy blocks of granite lie.

Far, far below, in peaceful shade,
  The bright roofs shine with mosses green,
And many a graceful Bernese maid
  With low-slouched peasant hat is seen ;
And brooks and leaves in sweetest tune,
And children like the birds of June.

There, when amid the stooping firs
  The wild sweet winds of autumn blow,
Shaken from boughs, the opening burrs
  Patter upon the roofs below ;
Nine hundred feet they journey down,
Before they reach that mountain-town.

And ripened berries, large and red,
  Dropping amid the cascade's spray
From the wet bushes overhead,
  Whirl in the pools, and swim away ;
And sweetly there at eve is heard
Love-note of maid and mountain bird.

But when the piercing night-wind sings
  O'er those old rocks so high and brown,
Far down below the lightning springs,
  And blazes through that little town ;
While hoarsely GOD's deep thunder calls
To Jungfrau through the granite halls.

It is a glorious thing to stand
  Upon those crags, when smoky haze
Hangs o'er the bloomy mountain-land,
  In the long golden summer days,
With the bright cliffs on each side green,
And the deep chasms scooped between.

For there, by fetters undefiled,
  And fearless of the tyrant's rod,
'Mid nature's temples vast and wild,
  Earth's noblest men have worshipped GOD ;
Freely, among the gorges bare,
Breathing the sweet, brisk mountain-air.

And well may the rough Oberland
  Make the wild Bernese strong and free,
For who can dwell where GOD's own hand
  Hath traced the lines of Liberty,
Nor inly feel that bolt and chain
For his free limbs are forged in vain !   H. W. R.

THE COUNTRY DOCTOR:

AN AUTOBIOGRAPHY: WRITTEN AT THE REQUEST OF GLAUBER SAULTZ, M. D.

CHAPTER SIXTH.

IF the mere familiarity with scenes of disease and wretchedness be sufficient to blunt the sensibilities, then must the hearts of men in our profession be like so many nether mill-stones; indurated, without life, and never throbbing at the calls of humanity. So far from this being the case, I believe it to be quite the contrary; for if the liberal man by following the dictates of his heart becomes confirmed in an habit-ual benevolence, and a delight in deeds of charity, it is improbable that he whose whole business and duty it is to alleviate bodily pains and suffering, should become gradually obdurate and insensible. This is scarcely according to the analogy of things. One may seem to be that which he is not; and it is in general true that those of the acutest feelings are the most averse to showing them; but keep them rigor-ously down, and never suffer so much as a tear to bear witness to the warmest of sympathies. For such conduct in the medical man there is the most cogent reason and necessity. He can scarce sub-scribe to the precept, to 'weep with those who weep.' In the dark-ened chamber where Solicitude walks upon tip-toe, and the gaunt form of Death stands near, unwilling to be deprived of his victim, a calm judgment and a tearless eye must keep watch over the destiny which may be trembling at its exact crisis, and which the slightest wavering, a look, a token, an unguarded word, may decide forever. Hence the physician, whatever be his natural ardor, learns early to place a check upon himself; rarely yielding to impulse, and gazing on death itself with apparent indifference. But whoever will consult the annals of the medical profession, will find among it some of the most perfect models of all that is kindly and humane; nor will I admit that the practice of so noble an art tends to harden the heart; at least, I speak according to the multiform experience, and from the unsophisticated mind, of a Country Doctor.

In the course of many years of unremitting devotion, it has been my lot to witness some scenes of a melancholy nature, as may appear from these memoirs. The events related in the last chapter, though not occurring in the ordinary routine of practice, were such as fell natu-rally in my way; and they have brought up the recollection of the following incidents, which may perhaps be deemed worthy of record; and I will insert them in this place, as I find them mentioned in the copy of a letter to a friend.

———

' THE summer has set in gloriously, and nature is full of charms for her votaries. How still and sacred is this retirement! Nothing but the temple-music of groves, and the murmuring of brooks, and the distant roar of the sea. I participate daily in that kind of feeling expressed by Pliny, in one of his letters written from his agreeable retreat: '*O mare! O littus! verum et secretum* μουσειον *! quam multa* *invenitis, quam multa dictatis !'* But alas ! whither can we go to escape the melancholy casualties of life ? Not long since an interesting family came here for the purpose of residing during the summer. It consisted of four children with their parents, the eldest scarce having attained the age of fourteen years, all musicians of distinguished ability, performing skilfully on various instruments, and masters of the harp. It was impossible to hear them without admitting that they possessed great talents, early developed, assiduously cultivated, and brought to a rare perfection for such a tender age. Wherever they had been, they were upheld by their own merits, eliciting the praises and astonishment of all the lovers of art. Few could ever hear them perform together, and forget the strains told with such true feeling and expression, that they irresistibly affected the heart.

' But what shone preëminent in these children, even above the rare possession of musical skill, was an innocence and amiability of character, which gained the affections of all to whom they were known. With them music was a passion, a heaven-born gift, loved for its own sake, and cultivated among themselves emulously, yet without envy. For they possessed different degrees of talent, though all highly endowed by nature ; but unlike musicians of a riper age, they suffered no evil passions or root of bitterness to spring from the practice of their sweet art. In appearance they were interesting. They had soft, blue eyes, light hair, yet soft and flowing, fair complexions, and a speaking intelligence of face. It is not wonderful that they were harpists ; they came from the mountains of WALES.

' Not many days since, these happy children went out to take recreation in the fields. At some distance from this, is a beautiful deep lake, embosomed in hills, and surrounded on all sides by charming scenery. It is a spot where those who love nature in her most pleasing variety might be contented to pass their lives. The day had been somewhat warm and sultry — in other respects beautiful. Scarcely a ripple was on the lake. The willow trees with their pendent limbs drooped motionless in its tide, which imaged every leaf and blossom, with every fleecy speck upon the sky above ; and the sky itself was as serenely pure as if it were the resemblance of some higher heaven. It was a holiday among children, and many of them, happy-faced and innocent, were gathering wild-fruits and flowers, or disporting under the old trees which overshadowed the turf on the hill-side down to the very margin of the wave. As the wild-roses in the water, so the children's laughter was clearly reflected from the hills, calling to mind the poet's beautiful thought, *vocis imago.*

' The young minstrels, roving about unconstrained, and seeing a small boat moored, took possession, and launched out, making music to the sound of the oars. At first they kept near the shores, visiting each cool recess and grotto formed by the impending banks ; afterward spreading sail to catch the faint breeze, they venturously bore away into the middle of the lake. Very suddenly, while all parties enjoyed themselves, a change came over the scene. Black and surcharged clouds drifted rapidly overhead, and at last from horizon to horizon filled up all the firmament. The light of the sun was nearly eclipsed, and solemn darkness, like that of night, heralded a great storm. The little children in the groves, unable to reach a distant shelter, crouched tremblingly down, as if to court protection, under the giant trunks of the old oaks. They huddled close together, whispering to each other, scarcely daring to speak aloud from a sense of awe. All things were still and expectant. The buzzing of insects was no more heard. The birds ceased singing in the branches or in mid-air, and rested silently on their nests. The surface of the lake seemed like molten lead, reflecting only dead images. The pause continued a little time, and a few big, plashing drops were shaken from the skirts of the clouds. Then a wind-storm arose, so violent that it seemed the bursting of a tornado. The mountain pines rocked to their very base, the trees groaned and creaked, and their high tops were bent and twisted, like the slender and elastic sapling which defies the storm.

' The air was full of leaves, already become sere and yellow, and blossoms and the petals of flowers, and every volatile thing which floats on the breeze. Multitudes of dry and crisped leaves, the remnants of last year's glory, were borne eddying high in air, and away. Whenever the wind lulled, the muttering of thunder was heard, and the sound of distant, steadily-advancing rain. Oh! how glorious are the storms which summer heats engender, and darkness in the daytime, which makes the soul feel solemn; when the setting sun in ghastly contrast shineth yet from the windows of his palled chambers, and cannot scatter the surrounding gloom. God draweth near in his pavilion of darkness, not less than in his resplendent light. Oh! it is glorious to watch the clouds rolled as by unseen spirits into airy battlements, and the light flash, and to hear heaven's grand artillery; to follow the viewless and mysterious winds in their pathway of destruction; to revel and exult in the war of elements, to trust in God and feel a sense of safety!

' I was passing along the high hill-top, and saw the storm advancing. I looked down over the agitated surface of the lake on the little sail-boat afar from the shore, and trembled for it. In another direction my eye roamed over the expansive prospect to where the dark horizon was bounded by the distant sea. The horses were galloping affrighted over their pasture-grounds, and every living thing sought shelter. I saw the trees of the plain with their heads bowed, and the wheat crops with their long, silvery stems bent down, and the immense corn-fields, agitated and beaten down to the ground. Presently it commenced to rain violently, with thunder and sharp lightning, which seemed almost overhead. The skies were lighted by a sudden and fantastic brilliance, revealing fiery chasms and zig-zag fissures of the black clouds, and serpentine forms writhing in the electric air. Thus while I stood still or moved slowly on, uncertain what to do, whether to seek the dangerous covert of the woods, or stand the violence of the rain, which already gorged every rill, and branched off in many torrents to the lake, a ghastly flash coming at the same instant with a stunning report leaped down from the skies into the tops of the very trees where the little children had fled for safety.

' I marked the bolt where it fell, and waited a moment in suspense; and presently I saw the bands of children rush out of the grove, flying distracted down the mountain-side, screaming, and stretching out their hands for aid. I sprang from the vehicle, left the miserable beast unable to make headway in the place where he stood, and ran breathless to the spot. It was on an opposite cone or eminence of the ridge of hills, arrived at by crossing a little valley. Dashing through the pools of water which had there collected, and the wet grass and bushes, and beckoning back the scared fugitives, I arrived in full time to contemplate the ruin which had been done. The lightning had smitten and shivered a gnarled oak to its very base, and struck the queen-child. She lay dead on the grass, crowned with flowers, and with flowery trophies scattered all around. I raised her up. Her beautiful eyes were closed forever, and her red lips were never more to give birth to merry laughter. Her companions had woven for her a rosy diadem which she was to continue to wear in the grave. God had smitten her, not in vengeance but in compassion, and she was blasted like a tender flower, before the canker worms of grief or guilt could prey upon her heart, and having lived a short time on earth, she was transferred at once to a better clime, forever there to bloom in youth and beauty.

'This is not all the sad scene; nor let it be supposed that I am dealing wholly in the creations of romance. A gust coming down the mountain-side upset the frail boat, and the young minstrels struggled in the waves. Three clung to the keel; the other, who was the eldest born, sank down apart. Thrice he rose up, and on the last time, as he might have directed toward his younger brothers a look for aid, one of them was enabled to seize an oar and shoot it toward him with a direct and steady aim over the waves. It passed by him, he touched it lightly with his fingers, it moved away, and he sank down and disappeared. The other brothers were rescued from the waves.

'An hour passed away, and the storm abated, and then the body of the young minstrel after a short search was drawn up on the shores of the lake. I saw him stretched on the green grass, in his tunic and morocco girdle, with all his gold and silver medals which he bore about him, the trophies of many triumphs in his art. And just then, the sun, as if in mockery, shone out again gloriously over all the landscape; on the glossy leaves, and on the big, brilliant drops which glistened like gems on the grass and foliage; and the clouds rolled away, and all the elements were calmed. There were his young brothers, scarce recovered from their exhaustion, weeping about him, and a gazing crowd looking on and scarcely appreciating the grief of their young hearts. For the sweetest harp among them had been silenced, even while its echoes still lingered, and they could literally hang their own upon the willows which overshadowed the lake where their brother had died. I am certain that it will be many months ere those gifted children can again make melody in their hearts, or on their strings, and when those harps are once more strung, like that of INNISFAIL, they shall tell a tale of 'more prevailing sadness.' It must be a mournful dirge, commencing with the moaning of winds, and the noise of thunder, and the flash of lightning, and the fall of rain, during which a little barque may be fancied on a troubled lake, and the listeners may be constrained to shed tears. And they must go home and rehearse it to their native mountains, which will mournfully prolong the echoes, that the young bard has perished :

> Ye nightingales that mourn amid thick leaves,
> Tell the Sicilian streams of Arethuse
> That Bion the young herdsman is no more,
> And with him the sweet Doric muse is dead.   Moschus.

' I know not whether it be a common superstition among mankind, but am more inclined to think that it is truly founded on observation, that the young whose talents too early expand, cannot live long on the earth. The child of brilliant intellect, the young minstrel, the poet lisping in numbers of unearthly sweetness, how seldom do they survive to redeem the promise of their childhood, and the hopes of those who tremblingly watch them as they approach their prime ! The transient journeyings of such can scarcely be measured by days or hours, or by our modes of computing time. They pass through a vivid existence, fulfil their destiny, and then in all their purity are gathered home. Every church-yard is filled with the memorials of these ; and methinks that the words of the Greek are true, that ' *Whom the gods love die young.*' Often now do I pass by the grave of the young minstrel, and amidst the stillness of the place remember the sweet, obsolete music of his harp, and how his very soul spake out of his passionate eyes when he threw his fingers over the strings. Yet here amidst every influence which is most soothing in nature, here where the brooks murmur, and the birds sing, and the winds scatter the petals of the wild rose over the grassy mound, he has found a fitting sepulchre. And while we lament his young genius so quickly quenched, perhaps he has been taken away from much ' evil to come.' For in that he died young, he died happily ; and it may be safely presumed that the strings which were so skilfully attuned on earth, have been exchanged for a triumphant harp in heaven.'

MY MOUNTAIN HOME.

'Home is *home*, though never so homely.'

I.

I 've a sweet little home amid the green mountains,
    Which I fly to at night as a bird to its nest ;
Where the rustling of leaves and the gush of fresh fountains
    Are like songs of bright spirits to lull me to rest.

II.

And there in the bosom of peaceful seclusion
    Dwells my own mountain-dove, the dear mate of my heart !
Unscared by the noise of the world's rude confusion —
    Undeceived by its glitter, unallured by its art.

III.

And still, to add smiles to our sunny contentment,
    A *dovelet* of late to the soft nest has come ;
Thus *filled* is our wine-cup, of God's own presentment,
    In the peace and the bliss of my sweet mountain home !

THE SENTIMENT OF ANTIQUITY.

BY A NEW CONTRIBUTOR.

THE passion which controls the antiquarian in the investigation of ancient things, is in this country, from the character of our population and the genius of our institutions, in a great measure suppressed ; and to give the thought prompted by that passion a place among the sentiments in this age of *new* things, will by many be considered unphilosophical and improper. Among the nations of the old world it has always taken this rank, and has there exerted a powerful and controlling influence. If this be the result of education, it has by a long course of usage become a second nature ; and having for ages been woven into the habits and manners of the people, and in many cases made the ground of religious faith, has at length identified itself with their existence. This sentiment, for such we shall call it, looks not into the dark, uncertain future, and takes but little interest in the present, but delights to dwell on the past ; to read and revive stories almost forgotten, and to give a permanent and sacred character to deeds of other days. Through the operation of this principle, the old feudal castles, once the seat of a tyrant surrounded by serfs, the place of oppression and bloodshed, now deserted and dilapidated, tell us not of the wrongs but of the magnificence of their former lordly occupants. The monasteries, fantastic monuments of superstition, by their antiquity impress us with awe and devotion. Time

> ' Has moulded into beauty many a tower,
> Which, when it frowned with all its battlements,
> Was only terrible.'

Sallust, who still lives in his works, and is admired for his genius, has a reputation not marred by the profligacy of his life, nor by having plundered the unfortunate Numidians. The works of Ovid and Horace, school books in the hands of our children, and universally read and admired, contain sentiments, which if advanced by a modern writer, would consign the author and his production to disgrace. The common law, or *lex non scriptæ*, of England, consists of customs which are considered as binding, when they have been so long used ' that the memory of man runneth not to the contrary.' And Professor Christian and Lord Coke maintain ' that precedents and rules must be followed, even when they are flatly absurd and unjust, if they are agreeable to ancient principles.' It is evident from the history, the stories, and the tragedies of the Greek and Roman nations, that they had a strong and religious regard for every thing ancient. Horace, when speaking of the hero Munarius, says that he

> ' With greedy joy inquires of various things,
> Of acts and monuments of ancient kings.'

And again :

> ' Munarius boasting of his blood that springs
> From a long loyal race of Latian Kings.'

The patriarchs acknowledged the power of this sentiment. The last and dying request of Israel was, 'that at death he should be carried back again to Canaan and be laid in the burying-place of his fathers.' The same feeling was manifested in a different but equally striking manner by his descendants, who gloried in their parentage, and considered it the highest honor to be called an ' Israelite indeed.' It was through the operation of this sentiment that the Romans were called Quirites, and that the Grecians established their system of Polytheism. Their θεοι, or gods, were heroes who by some act of bravery or deed of virtue had identified themselves with their country, and thus their names were handed down by tradition, until time divested their nature of its humanity, and ripened their virtues into acts of divinity. This is evident from these lines of Medea :

> ' Εϱεχθειδαι το παλαιον ολ σι οι
> Και Θεον παιδες μαχαϱων.'

During the fourteenth century this sentiment exerted an unbounded influence for good. Europe during the thirteenth century was fast verging into barbarism. The manners of the people were coarse, their ideas confused, their morals degraded, and their habits abandoned. Their situation was rendered more deplorable and hopeless by the melancholy fact that they were indifferent toward all improvement, and rested in contentment and ease amid scenes of ignorance, crime and misery. At this time Dante, Petrarch, and Bocaccio arose. They looked upon the field of desolation, and mourned over the ruins of their race. Having learned by experience that all attempts at reformation by combatting the existing prejudices would be fruitless, and would engulf them in public indignation, they remained long in doubt how they could better the condition of their countrymen. Being scholars and men of great research, they had learned that the society of ancient Greece and Rome was far superior to that of their own age, and that if it could be brought back to its former standard their object would be effected.

This was done in a most extraordinary manner by means of the sentiment of antiquity. They excited the curiosity of the people in relation to things ancient, caused diligent search to be made for old manuscripts, and established a school to preserve and spread each new discovery. Admiration was kindled in every breast for Greek and Latin learning, for their institutions, their opinions, their politics, their philosophy, and their literature. Old manuscripts became of great value, and those who possessed them were ambitious to show that they were covered with the dust of centuries. Every new discovery was hailed with joy ; the history of its preservation was written and made the subject of public recital. The writings of Homer, Virgil, Socrates, and Plato, were read more as a matter of curiosity, than from any desire for improvement. The thoughts and opinions of the ancient authors by these means acquired importance, and obtained a silent but powerful influence over their manners and habits, and prepared the way for that bold race of independent thinkers, of prelates and scholars, who then came forward and elevated Europe from the darkness and desolation of the middle ages, and led on the glorious reformation of the sixteenth century.

This phenomena of mind exerts to this day a powerful influence, even among the most enlightened nations of Europe. Antiquarians it is true have mourned over the decline of heraldic taste, and that the privilege of wearing the '*coot annoris*' is no longer confined to persons of noble birth and of great distinction, but may be enjoyed as the reward of enterprise and honest industry. Engravers in England have recently ventured to advertise in their shop windows, 'arms found here.' This sentiment is however still cherished; and some of the nobility and many private families in that kingdom retain with devotional feelings the old ensigns of their early ancestors. In their halls are hung trophies of the chase and of battle; their rooms contain the old family furniture; in their wardrobes are hung the equipage, and about their grounds are placed the evidences of ancestral pride and distinction. The heraldic office is still kept, the family records preserved, and the birth and name of every child is placed on the 'family tree,' as fruit upon a parent stock whose roots are grounded in antiquity. By referring to these registers of the past, many houses, as the Howards, the Gows, the Seymours, and the De Cliffords, can trace their pedigree back to the time of the Norman invasion.

Most of the European nations frame their laws so as to encourage and perpetuate this feeling. In this country the honors and emoluments of government are open to the attainment of every citizen. There, they generally descend from father to son. Here the estate of the parent is divided equally among all his children, and at death often passes out of the hands of the family. The auctioneer follows the undertaker; the property is sold, the family is scattered, and all the associations of the place are broken up. There the estate descends to the oldest son, who enters into possession of the old castle halls, points to the improvements on the surrounding lawns, gardens, parks and other pleasure grounds, and calls them his own. He retains the family records, the tokens of friendship, and all the trophies of past achievements which are hung around the halls, and these are considered as so many mirrors reflecting glory upon his name and state. He is stimulated to add to these mementoes of the past and to carry out the improvements already commenced, and thus make himself worthy of remembrance — a connecting link between generations that were and are thereafter to exist. He looks upon these works and remains of his ancestors not only with pride, but with those cherished emotions which the man advanced in age feels when he reflects on the isolated scenes of childhood; on the fields, the woods, the streams, which memory for some mysterious reason has selected from the general forgetfulness of the past and preserved for calm reflection during riper years. It is sweet to remember the parting words of kindness and love; to listen to strains of music dying away in the distance; but infinitely more sweet is it to stand upon a point of time in the house of our ancestors, and turn over the family records; to decipher the initials on the family tree; to wear their ornaments and arms, and to look upon their portraits and hold communion with their spirits.

Sir Walter Scott wrote to please the fancy and captivate the imagination, not merely by elegance of expression and beauty of diction, but also by the selection of subjects calculated to awaken sympathy and interest the heart. And when we observe how indefatigable he was in his research after old customs, ballads, legends, and other reminiscences, and perceive how deeply interesting and exceedingly beautiful he has by these means made his prose and poetical writings, we may realize the power of this sentiment, and also that time is not always marked by decay, but often preserves events and things, to make them more desirable by the mellow tint of age. In a letter to Wm. Clark, our antiquarian says : 'I dined a few days ago *tête-à-tête* with Lord Buchan, and heard a history of all his ancestors, which he has hung around his chimney-piece.' When he was writing the Minstrelsy of the Scottish Border, he was in the habit of riding annually for several years into Liddesdale, exploring every ruin, from foundation to battlement. He traversed the valley of the Yarrow and Ettrick, visiting every scene of history, romance, and tradition, gathering ballads, legends, trophies of magnificence, and

> ' Old rude tales, that suited well
> The ruins wild and hoary.'

Not satisfied with his own researches, he employed a Mr. Train to collect old ballads and ancient lore, who, with one Newton Stewart, engaged in the same business, traversed the border country, and became so notorious that they were sought after by beggars and pilgrims, who came to recite old songs and relate old stories.

We have already intimated that this sentiment has but little influence in this country. We are comparative strangers on the soil, and having neither personal nor ancestral interest in the Indian legends, they soon pass into oblivion. The changing character of our population tends to break up associations as soon as they are formed. The heroes of the revolution, and the early settlers of the country who are living, tell of their exploits, their perils, and their sufferings, and the generation which succeeds them listen to their recitals with interest; but as they reflect neither honor nor profit upon their descendants, and can elevate them to no place in society or government, they and their stories are soon forgotten. Many of the nobility of England derive their wealth, their respectability, and their office, from ancestors not as great in battle, nor as patriotic and virtuous, as the fathers of the American revolution; and yet the sons of the latter are born without a patrimony or a place. It is not to be expected that the sentiment of antiquity can have a controlling influence over the minds of a people who will cut down an ornamental tree for fire-wood, erect work-shops over the dead, and turn a grave-yard into pleasure grounds. The tomb of WASHINGTON is to this day neglected, and most of the old forts of revolutionary times are fast falling into decay. Murray, in his travels in America, was struck with our indifference in regard to sepulchral relics or monuments of antiquity. Speaking of Jamestown, where the fathers of America first established themselves, he says : 'Nothing now remains of that parent settlement, except the ruins of the church, which mark the place whence the tidings of christianity were first preached in the western world. Instead of showing any reverence for this classic and holy ground, the church has been allowed to fall to pieces, the grave-stones have been rudely torn from their places, nor is there the slightest barrier remaining to protect this their earliest religious and ancestral monument from the invasion of the pigs and cattle.'

This want of regard for things ancient, results from the original, re-cent, and peculiar origin of our government. The character of nations, as of individuals, is moulded and formed in infancy. England was settled by a tribe of Celtæ, or Gauls, who were fishermen and traders; and she is now distinguished for her navy, and her commercial relations :

> 'She roams upon the mountain wave,
> Her home is on the deep.'

America was settled by persons who were dissatisfied with, and who wished to overthrow, the old forms of society and government, and establish a new order of things. Consequently, we are an experiment-ing nation, and pride ourselves more on new organizations and laws, than in perpetuating those heretofore established. Children glory not in following in the footsteps of their parents; they prefer to strike out into some path discovered by themselves. The politician, the moralist, the christian, ask not for the standards of their fathers; they throw themselves upon their own minds, and rely upon their own private judg-ment, enlightened by divine truth, for right direction. They look not upon the nations who lived in the first days of the world as *ancients*, nor do they pay more respect to a people because they claim an existence extending back many thousand years. Our own government is consid-ered as having been formed in the era of *true antiquity*, when the world was ancient, and not in the inexperience of its youth. The public mind has long been tending toward the present modes of thinking. By the reformation, man was released from the thraldom of human forms and ceremonies, rendered almost sacred by long usage, and was directed by the inward spirit from the mystic light of former times, to a bright futurity of hope and promise. Men were then urged onward to duty, and became bold thinkers and actors in the drama of life : and two parties have ever since been on the public arena, the one defending, and the other attacking antiquity; the one acts upon the belief that hu-manity is to be perfected by bringing society back to its primitive con-dition, and the other, that it is in its progressive state, and is marching on to a destiny more glorious than the world has ever known. The latter and prevailing class in our land are looking for a new heaven and a new earth, and are endeavoring to sweep away every form and ceremony founded on artificial distinctions, and which tend to retard the free and aspiring spirit from advancement. Burke was the first to attack court ceremonies, founded, as he says, upon 'manners and cus-toms long since expired.' Maria Antoinette, acting upon his precepts, held the old rules of etiquette of the French court in disdain, and suf-fered obloquy, and even death on the scaffold, rather than conform to the ridiculous usages of feudal times. Her sacrifice brought about a reformation; and now, in the language of a modern writer, 'The ad-vancing tide of public opinion is making sad havoc on the old intrench-ments of dignity.' In religion, in morals, in every thing, reason is summoned to separate time-consecrated errors from truths of the deep-est moment. The forms and fashions of the world's absurd laws and habits, offices with quaint and pompous titles, are passing away, and even the battles of the conqueror are only remembered as the dread visions of a dismal night. Antiquarians, sentimentalists, and titled dig-nitaries, may mourn over the change; and indeed, 'many precious rites and customs of our ancient ancestry' may be swept away; but he who looks forward to the individuality and perfectibility of our race, will, it is true, see much to cause lamentation in the contest now going on; in the collision of mind with mind, and mind with power and usage; but he will also see shadowed forth the final glorious destiny of man. And when he views the wreck of worldly pride, he will find consolation in the words of the Psalmist, when addressing his Creator: 'Thy years are throughout all generations. Of old hast thou laid the foundations of the world, and the heavens are the work of thy hands. They shall perish, but thou shalt endure; yea, all of them shall wax old like a garment; as a vesture shalt thou change them, and they shall be changed. But Thou art the same, and thy years shall have no end. The children of thy servants shall continue, and their seed shall be established before thee.' Yes, there is encouragement in the thought, that the names and deeds of the truly great and good shall remain, amid the general wreck of matter, and will have a bright existence with Him who is the Ancient of Days: that they shall rise,

> ' As stars of hope, beaming from brighter skies,
> To teach the soul oppressed by tyranny
> Its noble birthright and its destiny.'

EVENING.

> "Εσπερε πάντα φέρεις
> Φέρεις οίον
> Φέρεις αίγα
> Φέρεις μαλερι παίδα. — SAPPHUS FRAG.

Oh! holy evening hour!
   Thou bringest all that's best —
Dew to the thirsty flower,
   And to the weary, rest.
The bee forgets to roam,
   The bird hies to her nest,
And the little child comes home
   To his fond mother's breast.

Sweetly thou drawest near,
   Humming a low, faint song;
Thy bright eye flashing clear,
   The silver streams along.
All earth and heaven hush
   To hear thy mystic hymn,
Charming the clouds that flush
   Above the world's dark rim.

Spirit of reveries,
   And vague, romantic dreams!
The very rocks and trees
   Love well thy dewy gleams:

Long let thy mantle lie
   Upon the purple lea,
While 'neath the golden sky
   Thou tarriest with me.

For ever, blessed eve!
   Could I sit here alone,
And idle fancies weave,
   To harmonize thine own.
With what a gentle sigh,
   And smile of chastened light,
Thou biddest day good-bye,
   And welcomest the night!

But ah! like life's fair dream,
   Thy transient glories fade—
Blue mist and golden gleam.
   Blending in one deep shade.
My soul grows dark, alas!
   Dark as thy shadows are,
Upon the pools that glass
   Thine own beloved star.

Richmond, (Va.,) 1840.   Bon Roski.

THE QUOD CORRESPONDENCE.

The Attorney.

CHAPTER III.

On leaving the house, Wilkins directed his steps down the Bowery to Chatham street, crossing which, he struck through that portion of the town lying between Chatham and Centre streets, and notorious as the abode of crime and infamy.   Every thing about him bore the mark of corruption and decay.   Houses with unglazed sashes, unhinged doors, roofless and crumbling away beneath the hand of time, were leaning against each other to support themselves amid the universal ruin.   Unlike the rest of the city, there was no life, no bustle; all was stagnant: its inhabitants seemed buried in a living grave.   Crowds of miserable objects, the wrecks of human beings, were loitering about the dismal holes which they called their homes; some shivering on the side-walks, nestling together to steal warmth from each other's carcasses; some, bloated and half stupified with hard drinking, went muttering along, or stopped to brawl with others like themselves.   Young females, too, with hollow cheeks and hungry eyes, were loitering among the herd. Many of them had been born to nothing better; but there were those among them who once had friends who loved them, and had looked forward to a future without a shadow: but they had come to this; they had broken the hearts of those who would have cherished them, and had drunk of crime and wo to the dregs.

Hardened as Wilkins was, he shuddered and grasped his bludgeon more tightly, as he hurried through this gloomy spot.   Stifled screams and groans, and sounds of anger and blasphemy, burst upon his ear, mingled with shouts of mirth; and he observed figures shrinking in the obscure corners of the buildings as he passed, and watching him with the cautious yet savage eye of mingled suspicion and fear; for he was in the very heart of the region where thieves and cut-throats were skulking, to avoid the vigilance of the police, and had common lot with the penniless and homeless who came there only to die.   With a feeling of relief he emerged from this doomed spot, and came to a quiet street.   It was growing late in the night, and it was nearly deserted, and so silent, that his footsteps echoed on the pavement as he walked along. As he turned a corner, a solitary female, squalid and in rags, endeavored to stop him, and spoke a few words, half in jest, half in supplication.   Utter destitution had driven her forth, to seek in sin the means of satisfying her craving hunger.   Wilkins shook her off with a curse, and walked steadily on.   The girl uttered a faint laugh, and looked after him until he turned a corner.   ' He does not know what hunger is,' muttered she.   Drawing her scanty clothing more closely about her, and crouching on the stone step of a large house, she leaned her head against a door-post, and wept.

Traversing several narrow alleys, and turning at one time to the right and at another to the left, Wilkins at last came to a mean looking

·house, having a small sign over the door, indicating that it was a tavern, and with a number of illuminated placards in the windows, intimating that lodgings were to be had, and that various liquors might be purchased at the moderate sum of three cents a glass. In addition to these, a number of more modest notices were placed in the same window, for the benefit of the smoking community as well as for the drinking.

Wilkins pushed roughly past two or three persons, and entered a dingy room, strongly impregnated with the fumes of tobacco and spirits, and enveloped in a cloud of smoke. It was filled with persons who looked as if they would not hesitate to ease a pocket, or if it were necessary, to extend their civility so far as cutting your throat. Some were savage, silent, and sullen; others, under the influence of what they had drank, were humorous and loquacious : some, steeped in intoxication, were lying at full length upon wooden benches, others were leaning back in their chairs against the wall, saying nothing, but blowing out clouds of tobacco smoke. The only one of the whole group who aspired to any thing like sobriety, was a small man in a shabby suit of black, who sat in a corner endeavoring to expound some knotty point of politics to a gentleman near him, who was blinking at him with an air of deep conviction, arising either from his being thoroughly impressed by the force of the argument, or profoundly involved in liquor.

In the midst of this disorderly throng, sat Mr. Rawley, keeping guard over a row of shelves, occupied by a small congregation of glass decanters, each one being decorated with a small medal, which silently hinted to the by-standers the kind of liquor to be found in the bowels of the vessel. Mr. Rawley looked gravely around on his set of ' reg'lars,' as he termed his steady customers, and smiled approvingly at each successive drain upon the vitals of his bottles. He showed in his own person that he approved of enjoying the blessings of life, for he was a stout man, with a face wide at the bottom, and tapering up like an extinguisher, and in the midst of it was a solemn bulbous nose, somewhat red at the end, owing to Mr. Rawley's being afflicted with a propensity of smelling at the stoppers of his own decanters. At his right hand stood a large white bull-dog, who seemed to have been squeezed into a skin which was too small for his body, by reason of which his eyes were forced out like those of a lobster. He had the square head and chest of a dog of the first magnitude ; but probably to accommodate the rest of his body to the scanty dimensions of his skin, he suddenly tapered off from thence to the other extremity, which terminated in a tail not much thicker than a stout wire. He was, as Mr. Rawley observed, a ' reg'lar thorough-bred bull,' and acted as under bar-keeper to his master ; and when Wilkins entered, was standing with his eyes fixed in the corner occupied by the argumentative gentlemen before mentioned, as if he felt that he could take a very effective part in the discussion, but had some doubt as to the propriety of the step.

As soon as Wilkins entered, the dog walked up to him, and very deliberately applying his nose to his knee, smelt from thence downward to the instep, around the ankle, and up the calf to the place of beginning.

' Come away, Wommut !' exclaimed Rawley; ' let the gentleman alone — will you ?'

Wommut looked up at Wilkins, to satisfy himself that there was no mistake as to his character, and then walked back as stiffly as an old gentleman in tight small-clothes — but made no remark.

Wilkins took no notice either of the dog or his master, but looked around the room.

'I do n't see Higgs. Is he *there ?*' asked he, abruptly, nodding his head toward an inner chamber.

'No, he 's up stairs,' said Mr. Rawley.

'Alone ?'

'I believe so. He wanted paper, and took that and a candle, and went off.'

'Does he stop here to-night ?'

'If he *forks* first ; but,' continued he, tapping his pocket, 'I think his disease *here* is of an aggravated natur'.'

Wilkins left the room, and ascending a narrow staircase, which creaked under his weight, came to a dark passage. A light shining from beneath a door at the farther end of it, guided him to the room he sought, which he entered without ceremony. Seated at a table, engaged in writing, was a man of about forty, dressed in a shabby suit, buttoned closely up to the throat, to conceal either the want of a shirt, or the want of cleanliness in that article of apparel ; and a high stock encasing his neck, probably for the same purpose. He was rather below the middle height, with a full, broad forehead, sharp gray eyes, and features rather delicate than the reverse, with the exception of the jaw, which was closed and compressed with a force as if the bone of it were made of iron. The face altogether was sly and commonplace ; but the jaw bespoke nerve, resolution, and energy, yet all concealed under a careless exterior, and an affectation of extreme levity. On the table near him stood his hat, in which was a dirty cotton handkerchief, a newspaper, two cigars, and part of a hard apple, with which last article he occasionally regaled himself, to fill up those intervals of time when his writing had got the start of his ideas.

As Wilkins entered, he looked up for an instant, then pushing back his chair, and dropping his pen, with some show of alacrity, came forward and extended his hand.

'How are you, my old 'un' ?'

'Well,' replied Wilkins, laconically ; 'what brings you here ? What are you writing ?'

'A billy-dux,' said Higgs, gravely, 'to one as wirtuous as fair. But it 's a secret which I can't reveal.'

'I do n't want you to. I came to see you about a matter of business : one of importance to — to many persons, and one in which you must take a part.'

'Ah ! what is it ?'

'Who 's in the next room ?'

'I do n't know. It 's empty, I believe.'

'Go and see ; and look in all the rooms, and be quiet as you do so.'

Higgs, taking the light, went out, and Wilkins took occasion to open a long closet and look in, to see that no listeners were there, and then seated himself at the table.

'All empty, except the farthest one. Tipps is there, dead drunk,' said Higgs, reëntering the room, and closing and locking the door after him.   He then drew a chair directly in front of Wilkins, and placing a hand on each knee, looked up in his face.

'Can you keep a secret?' he asked, after a close scrutiny of his features, and looking full into two eyes that never blenched.

'Can't you tell?   You ought to be able to.'

'Will you swear?'

'What's the use?   It don't bind any stronger than a promise.   Out with it.   I'll keep a close mouth.'

'Well, then,' continued Wilkins, watching him sharply, to see the effect produced by his communication, and at the same time drawing his chair closer, and speaking in a whisper, 'suppose you knew of a murder, and there was a reward of a thousand dollars offered, and you knew the man who did it, and could give him up, and could get the money, all without risk to yourself?   Would you do it?'

'No.   I'll have no man's blood on my head,' replied the other; and pushing back his chair, he took up the light and held it full in Wilkins' face.   'Is that so?'

'No,' returned Wilkins, apparently relieved.

'Well, what have you got to tell?'

'Suppose,' continued the other, 'the crime was a forgery, and the reward the same; what would you do?'

'That's only imprisonment.   I'd give him up.'

'But what if you were paid *not* to do so?' said Wilkins, eagerly.

'Then I wouldn't,' said Higgs, quietly.

'What if you were paid to have a hand in it? — would you do it?'

'What is the pay?' demanded the other, instantly catching his meaning.

'A thousand dollars.'

'I'll do it.'

'And will not let it out?'

'No.'

'Nor turn state's evidence?'

'No.'

'But suppose the person to be wronged is a girl, young, handsome, and unprotected?'

'Mr. Wilkins,' said Higgs, assuming an air of decision, and thrusting one hand in his breeches pocket, while he extended the other toward him, 'I'd cheat her all the same.   For a thousand dollars, I'd cheat my own mother!'

'Enough! that's settled, you are engaged.   And now for another.   Suppose you had a friend who is in trouble, and wants your assistance?'

'Well ——'

'And relies on you, and must go to hell without you?'   Wilkins paused, and scrutinized the hard, stony face that almost touched his own.   'And suppose that friend,' continued he, slowly, and with apparent effort, 'had a wife who stood in his way, who prevented him from rising in the world, and who took advantage of his absence from home to welcome another; and suppose, if that could be proved, he could get a divorce, and marry a fortune, and make you a present of a thousand or two? — do you think you could prove that first wife's crime?'

'Lucy?' said Higgs, inquiringly.

Wilkins nodded.

' I suppose so.   It 's been a long time coming to a head.   I expected it, months ago.'

' You will prove what I told you ? '

' It ar'nt true, though ? ' asked Higgs, peering very anxiously in the face of his friend.

' No.   But what of that ? '

' Nothing — only I wanted to know.'

' Then you will prove it ? ' reiterated Wilkins.

' Of course I will.   But George,' said Higgs, slowly, ' I always liked Lucy ; there 's not her like on earth.'

' Hell and furies ! ' exclaimed Wilkins, starting to his feet, and clenching his fists, ' if I do not get the divorce, if I cannot shake her off by the law, I will by — something else ! '   As he spoke, he dashed his heavy hand against the table, as if it clutched a knife.   ' Will you help me ? '

' I will.   Better *that* than murder ; but you 'll be the loser.   Mark my words.'

' I'll risk it,' said Wilkins ; ' and now my business is ended ; so good night, and do not fail to be at my house to-morrow morning at sunrise, and I 'll tell you more.'

' I will,' was the reply, and Wilkins slammed the door after him.

When Mr. Higgs heard him fairly descending the stairs, he took the apple from his hat and carefully wiped it with the sleeve of his coat, and after turning it round several times, with his eye fixed on it as if searching for a spot to begin, he took a large bite, and resumed his pen and his labors.   Wilkins left the room, and strode rapidly down stairs into the bar-room, and was quitting the house, when he found his path obstructed by Wommut, who being in doubt whether he had settled his reckoning, with an amiable smile which displayed a row of remarkably strong teeth, evinced an inclination to remonstrate against his leaving the premises.

' Call off your dog, Rawley,' said Wilkins, angrily, ' or I 'll dash his brains out.'   As he spoke, he raised his heavy bludgeon.   The eyes of the dog glowed like living coals, as the club rose in the air ; but farther hostilities were arrested by the voice of the bar-keeper, who called the animal away.   After giving Wilkins a look, such as champions in the days of yore were in the habit of bestowing on each other, when they pleasantly intimated the hope that they might meet at some future day, where there would be none to interfere with their pastime, Wommut walked stiffly off, as if laboring under a severe attack of rheumatism.

Wilkins paused no longer than to allow the dog to get out of his path, and then hurried off toward his own home.

CHAPTER IV.

TEARS to many bring relief, but to the broken heart they only widen the wound : and when Lucy, after the departure of her husband, gave full vent to the bitter gush of grief, her tears did not lessen it.   She thought of times past, never to return ; of the happy hours of her childhood, and of those who had loved her then ; of the mild face of her mother, who had watched her in sickness ; of her little brothers, who had clustered about her; of the bright fireside, and of the light-hearted group that assembled around it in the cold winter evenings. Yet she had quitted them all. She looked round the dimly-lighted room, with its scanty furniture, and the still more scanty repast, which remained as Wilkins had left it. She had quitted all that her young heart had loved, to follow *him*, to live thus — and to have that heart trampled on. 'Well, no matter!' thought she; 'perhaps he was ill, and when he returns, a few kind words will make up for all.' Even this thought brought a ray of comfort with it; and dashing the tears from her eyes, she rose to remove the things from the table, when a step, which she at once recognized as her husband's, sounded in the passage, and he entered the room.

His greeting was a rough one. Dashing his hat to the floor, and muttering something, the import of which was lost between his clenched teeth, he dragged a chair to the centre of the room, stamped it heavily on the floor, and sat down opposite Lucy.

'Has any one been here? Holla! what are you snivelling about?' said he, taking her by the arm, and holding the candle full in her face.

'I am not well, George, indeed I am not,' said she, bending down, and resting her forehead on his shoulder, to conceal the tears that would gush out in spite of her.

'Thunder!' exclaimed he, starting to his feet with a violence that nearly threw her down; 'am I never to come home without being greeted in this way? You women must think red eyes are very attractive. Will you have done with this, I say?'

'There, there, George,' said she, in a choked voice; 'it's all over now. I'll not do so again.' There was a slight quivering of the lip, to conceal which she busied herself with the table: and Wilkins threw himself back in his chair, and watched her with moody looks, as she removed the things, and placed them in a cupboard in a corner of the room: Then, throwing a knot of wood on the fire, she drew a chair beside her husband, and seating herself in it, took his hand.

I verily believe that the devil sometimes takes up his abode in the heart of man; and that night he had made his quarters in that of Wilkins, or else the gentle, half timid half confiding glance with which his wife looked up in his face, and the affectionate manner in which she wound her soft fingers around his hard, bony hand, would have softened his mood; but it did not. Griping the hand that rested in his, until the girl cried out from pain, he flung it from him.

'Damnation! Can't a man sit a moment in peace, without being whimpered or worried to death! I wish to God you were where I got you from!'

The girl made no reply, but drew off to a far corner of the room, and seated herself; but the evil spirit of Wilkins was now fully roused, and he followed her up.

'I repeat it,' said he, shaking his clenched fist over her head; 'I wish you were where I got you from!'

His wife cowered down in her seat, and kept her eyes fixed on the floor, without making any reply.

'Are you dumb?' shouted the miscreant, shaking her violently, 'or are you deaf? Do you hear what I say?'

'Yes, George,' was the scarcely articulate reply.

'Hav'n't you got an answer, then?' demanded he, in a hoarse voice.

Lucy shook her head, and buried her face in her hands; but Wilkins caught her by both wrists, and by main strength held her up in front of him, face to face.

'What answer have you to make?' demanded he, fiercely; 'answer me, I say.'

'Indeed, George, I have none,' replied his wife, trembling so that she shook in his grasp; for in all his paroxysms he had never been like this; 'indeed, I do n't know what answer to make. I am sorry you want to be rid of me; my mother is in her grave; and I have now only you. I have few friends, and none to love me but you; the others are far off.'

'Does Jack Phillips live so *very* far off?' said Wilkins, with a sneer.

'What do you mean?' demanded his wife, extricating her wrists from his gripe, and standing erect, and confronting him; 'what do you mean?'

'Oh! you do n't *know*, do n't you?'

'No, I do *not* know; but I suspect much — *all!*' said she, with an energy that surprised though it did not shake the purpose of her husband; 'and this I will say, that whoever attacks my name, be he foe or friend, or even husband, or dares to cast, by word or sign, a shade upon me, is a foul slanderer! A woman's fame is a thing that will not bear tampering with; and he is a villain who would throw the weight of a feather against it, and doubly so, if he be one who should protect it!'

Wilkins' features fairly writhed with wrath. Seizing the girl by the arm, he dragged her to the table, and striking his fist upon it with a force that made the candlesticks rattle, he asked: 'Do you dare deny it? — that you have met *him* in my absence — false-hearted as you are! that you have seized occasions when I was away, to dishonor me — to make yourself — I will not say what. Speak! speak, I say; do you dare deny it?'

'I *do!*' replied the girl, confronting him, and returning his look without blenching; 'I *dare* deny it, and I *do;* and whoever invented this tale, is a false-hearted liar, be it man or woman — *I* say so. Who is it? Bring me to him; place me face to face with him, and then let him dare to speak it. Who is it?'

'You 'll find out soon enough,' said Wilkins, savagely; and he jerked her arm from him; 'sooner than you want to.'

'No! not sooner than *that*,' replied Lucy, again approaching him; 'it never can be too soon. Now — here! I am ready.'

'Keep off! she-devil!' exclaimed Wilkins, in turn terrified by her wild eye and phrenzied actions: 'keep off; you had better.'

'I *will not*, until you tell me the name of the slanderer. Tell me, will you?'

'Keep off, I say,' said Wilkins, retreating.

'I will not! Tell me! tell me!' repeated she, looking up in his face in supplication. Wilkins clenched his fist and struck her to the floor.

If ever there was a felon stroke it was *that:* and he felt it so; for his arms fell paralysed to his side, and he trembled at the outburst which he thought would follow; but it did not. Without cry or word, Lucy rose from the floor, and holding her hair from her temples, looked him full in the eyes. Every drop of blood had deserted her face and was gathered about her heart. Her breath came thick and hard, like the struggle of the dying, and there was something terrible in the dark dilating eye, as she paused for an instant and fixed it upon the wretched man who now stood before her, cowering and conscience-smitten. She walked across the room and took her bonnet and shawl from a peg on which they were hanging.

'Where are you going?' at length asked her husband. Lucy made no reply, but proceeded to tie the strings of her bonnet, and turned toward the door.

'Where are you going at this hour?' again asked Wilkins, walking toward her; but she waved him back.

'God only knows! — but this is no longer a home for me.' As she spoke, she rushed out. With disordered steps she ran along the dark streets. She did not heed the direction she took, nor did she notice that persons, attracted by her appearance and excited manner, turned to gaze at her. There was that in her heart that deadened all external sense. Several times she was spoken to by those who, attracted by her beauty, argued ill of her character, by seeing her alone and unprotected at such an hour of the night; but she heeded them not; she rushed on until they left her, guided only by the fierce impulses of a broken heart. She traversed the damp streets until they grew more and more lonely: the busy stir of evening had gradually subsided; the weary and the wicked, the happy and the wretched, had long since gone to their beds, and the only sound that broke through the night-stillness, was the melancholy clink of the watchman's club upon the pavement, or the drowsy song of some midnight bacchanal, as he staggered home to sleep off his potations in nightmare dreams. To the poor girl there was no home; and after wandering about nearly the whole night, nature gave way; and leaning on the steps of a large house, she fell into a swoon.

THE UNREQUITED.

A TRUE LIMNING.

The face was young; but its once happy look
Was gone: the cheek had lost its color, and
The lip its smile: the light that once had played
Like sunshine in those eyes, was quenched and dim,
For tears had washed it; her long dark hair
Floated upon her forehead in loose waves
Unbraided, and upon her pale thin hand
Her head was bent, as if in pain: no trace
Was left of that sweet gayety which once
Seemed as grief could not darken it — as care
Would pass, and leave behind no memory.

       Oh! there are some
Can trifle, in cold vanity, with all
The warm soul's precious throbs; to whom it is
A triumph, that a fond devoted heart
Is breaking for them; who can bear to call
Young, fresh flowers into beauty — and then crush them

THE BACHELOUR'S LAMENTE.

THE dew from off the flower is shed,
  The morn of Life is o'er;
Its roseate hue for aye hath fled —
  And I may love no more, Ladye,
      And I may love no more.

The brow is bright that woman charms,
  But mine is wrinkled o'er;
And young the heart that fancy warms;
  And mine is young no more, Ladye,
      And I may love no more.

The time hath been, these locks were brown
  That now are frosted o'er;
My lightsome eye all dull hath grown
  And speaks of love no more, Ladye,
      And I may love no more.

And cold and wintry is the heart
  Ardent and bright of yore;
It could not play the lover's part,
  And I may love no more, Ladye,
      And I may love no more.

The Bark is on the ocean lost,
  And ne'er shall reach the shore;
The Autumn leaf floats tempest-tost —
  And I may love no more, Ladye,
      And I may love no more.

No Wife these arms is born to bless,
  No child will climb my knee;
The fond, the frank, the true caress —
  'Tis all deny'd to me, Ladye,
      'Tis all deny'd to me.

The mutual hope; the mingling prayer;
  The consciousness, that she
My cares, my griefs, doth more than share —
  'Tis all deny'd to me, Ladye,
      'Tis all deny'd to me.

The glance inspiring Joy; the thought
  Her hope, her Stay to be;
Her trust, her Confidence unsought —
  'Tis all deny'd to me, Ladye,
      'Tis all deny'd to me:

For, off the flower, the dew is shed
  The morn of life is o'er;
Its roseate hue for aye hath fled
  And I may love no more, Ladye,
      And I may love no more.

—

'When I said I would die a Bachelour, I did not think I should live 'till I
were marryed.'

JOHN WATERS.

THE POLYGON PAPERS.

NUMBER TWO.

THE men of this day are continually boasting of the immense additions they have made to the empire of knowledge. And, in truth, if we compare her present possessions with her former narrow limits, we have some reason for exultation at the conquests we have won, and for amazement at the indefinite expansibility of the human mind. The sciences, which were formerly necessary to the reputation of a *savant*, are now the mere alphabet of him who aspires to the name of scholar, and the ' seven humanities ' are but the stepping-stone to a score of loftier grades in the staircase which leads to the pinnacle of fame. The branches which anciently earned a doctorship in the schools would now scarce qualify one to stand behind a druggist's counter; and a freshman of a mushroom college must have pursued more divisions of learning than, three centuries since, would have won him a cardinal's cap. It is getting to be a very desperate undertaking, that of being a learned man ; for now-a-days all mankind know every thing. Those who devote their whole attention to keeping pace with the literature and science of the day, are amazed to see their contemporaries shooting past them with portentous velocity. While they are attempting to grasp the discoveries of last year, every body else is inventing something new and important. While they are plodding on in their old-time vehicle of studious application, the whole world beside seem to have mounted a steam-car, and to be clattering forward with dizzy speed into the realms of unknown and unimaginable splendor, which stretch far away to the westward of what was sunset and darkness to our blear-eyed fathers. Or, rather, while they, poor leaden-minded witlings ! are picking up and examining the sulphureous fragments of some exploded meteor, the daring intellect of man, bestriding the tail of a new-created comet, is frisking in bewildered triumph through the spaces of an ' untravelled separation.' The discharges from the electric battery of science have flashed in so rapid and dazzling repetition, that Skepticism, on her insulating stool, is the recipient of one ceaseless shock, and the *nil admirari* spirit of Philosophy, charged at every point, finds her hair bristling with an accumulating thrill of astonishment and terror.

A finite man, whose faculties are not commensurate with the universe, and a modest man, who cannot talk loudest where he knows least, begins to find himself sadly out of place in this omniscient world. He must be an apparent ignoramus or a real hypocrite. He who has learned only what seemed to him worth learning, and read only what appeared worthy of perusal, is subject to hourly grief and humiliation. A common farmer will ' swamp him ' by remarks on argillaceous sand-stone and conglomerated rock ; and a boarding-school miss bring confusion to his face, in a discussion on the parallax of Jupiter, and the prolate spheroidicity of the earth. The ostler will hardly water his horse, without talking of oxygen and hydrogen, and all the gaseous brotherhood ; and the ferryman will rest upon his oars to enlighten him on the pressure of fluids and the theory of the tides. He cannot drink his wine without being involved in difficulties on the process of fermentation, and the chemical affinities of alcohol, nor can he speak of a change in the weather, without discovering his ignorance of the composition of air, and the miraculous revelations of the compound blow-pipe. Electricity and magnetism, phrenology and hieroglyphics, free trade and the banking system, Malthusian economy and the steam-engine, are familiar as tops and marbles to the very children in the streets; and he is compelled to hold his peace, or appear like a man surrounded by Cimmerian darkness in the very blaze of noon. It passes his comprehension that he should acquire less by unwearied application than his neighbors gain without reflection and without care. Yet it must be so; for surely men could not talk so learnedly without knowledge, and he concludes they are born with an instinct to know every thing.

In the good old days of Erasmus, it was a sufficient outfit for polite society to have read the classics, and run lightly over the infant sciences of astronomy and the mathematics. A thorough knowledge of Greek and Latin, increased by an acquaintance with the Fathers, and one or two shallow plunges into Hebrew, produced a perfect prodigy. The time now expended on geography was then enough to master Cicero and Cæsar, and the years employed in the mysteries of interest, and the wilderness of fractions, sufficed to bury Homer and Virgil full length in the caverns of memory. The wonders of algebra, and the labyrinth of fluxions, had not then been invented to craze the brain and dim the eyes. The magnetic needle had not yet conducted the mariner to the 'isles of the ocean,' and compelled the would-be scholar to plume his wings, and stretch them over the same breathless flight. Our continent still slumbered in the embraces of the vast unknown. Central and southern Africa, and northern and eastern Asia were a non-existence. Now, all these countries are brought to light, and the man of general information must be acquainted with the topography, history, and productions of them all. In the age of Chaucer, it was enough to read of India in Strabo, that it was a country where wool grew on trees, and in Arrian, that the 'Macedonian madman' lost many of his braves in his aimless wanderings through the land of the Gadrosians, and the deserts of the Indus. Now, one must superadd a knowledge of Hyder Ally, Warren Hastings, and Juggernaut. Anciently it would do to read Livy, Tacitus, and some compilers of the Brazen Age; now one must not only peruse those *aboriginal* authors, but bebecome minutely versed in the affairs of modern Italy — Popes and Doges, Guelphs and Ghibelines. Previous to the discovery of printing, the learned were content to be familiar with Cecrops and Codrus, the Amphictyons and the Areopagites. Who in the nineteenth century knows any thing of Greece, if he be ignorant of Bozzaris, Missolonghi, and Lord G. G. N. Byron? In those days of scribes and parchment, one might start forth on a literary cruise, if he knew that 'all Gaul is divided into three parts, the Belgians, Aquitanians and Celts.' Now, we must travel downward through a long series of '*grands monarques,*' King Pepin and Charlemagne, Hugh Capet, Napoleon, and the Citizen King.

Of the British Islands, '*toto divisos orbe Britannos,*' the scholar was satisfied to know that the Phœnicians used to sail to the Cassiterides for tin, and that the Druids delivered their oracles and performed their worship under the primeval oaks. This will not do now. He must open the ponderous folio, and skim the light abridgment; he must become expert in the doings of wise King Alfred, and the dissensions of Saxon chiefs; the mysteries of feudal tenure, and the glories of the Virgin (?) Queen; the quarrels of Cavaliers and Roundheads; and the long, breathless struggle of an unyielding race with the towering Demon, whose shadow darkened the world.

Are you out of breath? So am I. Yet these are but *specimens* of the new historical burdens imposed on our shoulders. And none of the former burdens are withdrawn, in consideration of fresh impositions. *Hei mihi!* We are fallen upon evil days. It is necessary to know all our fathers knew, and learn all that has been done or discovered since.

Let us glance at the fine arts, and see how imperiously the universal connoisseurship of the times has bidden every man fill his mind with artistic knowledge, and his mouth with technical phrases. That musty being, starched, thin, and rectangular, a pedant, is no longer to be found. The lawyer is now not merely a lawyer, nor the merchant a simple merchant, nor the parson a parson only. They have all graduated in a polytechnic school; their acquirements are multifarious, many-sided. The fences which of old enclosed the sciences, and scared off poachers by a quick-set hedge of thorny terms, are broken down, and the domains of art have become one mighty manor, possessed in fee-simple, and grazed over in unlimited freedom by the entire community of men. Instead of being single-minded votaries of particular pursuits, all have turned *dilettanti* at every thing. The professor of Greek can handle the palette and the pencil, and the dauber of canvass can scan the choruses of Æschylus. Have not penny magazines and octodecimo cyclopedias imparted to the very barbers a delicate and infallible *virtù?* Cannot all men 'talk like a book' about the Laöcoon, and Apollo di Belvidere, Rembrandt, and Correggio, chiar'-oscuro, and fore-shortening? Is there an ambitious tradesman in England or America who will not enact the *virtuoso* on pediments and entablatures, the composite order, basso-relievo, and intercolumniations? Do not the ears of an amateur public elongate with intelligent ecstasy at the performance of an intricate composition from Mozart, or in listening to a fashionable *cantatrice*, as she agonizes through an Italian song, scaling the steeps and leaping the precipices of discordant concord? What taste! What acumen! What men! What an age! Alas! alas! dear reader, what shall *you* and *I* do among these capacious, omnivorous, all-digesting minds? Oh! for the shoulders of Hercules, 'humeros Deo similis,' to sustain the Atlantean burden! Yet up! — bestir yourself! Will you be the lowest of the *oi polloi* — a mere earth-worm, ranking among the '*numerus fruges consumere nati*'? Oh, foul dishonor! 'Awake, arise, or be forever fallen!' If you cannot *equal* your fellow-mortals, at least *resemble them.* Borrow their garments; assume their manners, and adopt their tone. Buy abridgments, study dictionaries, and if you cannot learn the things themselves, yet fail not to acquire their *signs.* Send forth your faculties after words, in the fire-track of the lightning, and gather in the knowledge of terms on the wings of the whirlwind. Then, whatever may be your secret humiliation, you may move before an 'enlightened public' with courageous eye, and forehead unabashed.

To give, however, the last finishing touch and crowning horror to this picture of despair, let us turn a moment to the department of light literature; for here the grievance is still heavier, and is fast growing intolerably galling to narrow shoulders. The amount of literary productions which are not merely readable, but which *must* be read, or citizenship in the republic of letters forfeited, has become absolutely immense. None can pass muster except Milton and Shakspeare are his own. Dryden, Pope, Addison, Young, Thompson, Johnson, Cowper, and Goldsmith, must all be read. Fielding, Smollet, Richardson, Junius, Burke, Sheridan, and Fox, are all to be digested. Who is even with the march of mind that is not perfectly acquainted with Scott, Bulwer, Mackenzie, Wordsworth, Coleridge, Southey, Rogers, Campbell? — and every body else, for these are not a tithe. And this is only the English division of the flowery garden. But must not the scholar be familiar with all the great names and productions in the other modern nations and languages? Is a man any thing, does he know what all mankind know, if he be ignorant of a single circumstance in the life, or a single line in the writings, of Racine and Molière, Voltaire and Victor Hugo? Is n't he the veriest schoolboy who cannot quote by memory from the soaring Dante, the gentle Tasso, the flighty Ariosto, and the tender Petrarch? Who has the impudence to declare that he has not read Cervantes and Le Sage, Alfieri, Lessing, and Schiller? And then all the other authors, somewhat inferior to these, yet world-renowned. Father Jove! I am weary.

Oh, ye third-rate and fourth-rate miracles; ye geniuses of five-feet-eight, and five-feet-ten; ye towering mediocrities — torture of my life! I execrate your names! Why did you indulge the 'longing after immortality?' Why did you approach so nearly to the heroic stature and the tragic tread, as to deceive mankind into the toil of reading you? Did you not reflect that you would have posterity? Or did you suppose that, as you had swallowed your pigmy fathers, in like manner your yet more gigantic descendants could devour and *chylify* both you and them? And so they can; for they are all Goliaths, save a few poor mannikins of dwarfish stature and slender frame, whose shrunken proportions are crushed to the earth by the load of your writings. May the avenging furies of your murdered children pursue you to the Limbo of Vanity, your present residence; may they haunt you, as your memories haunt us; nightmares to scare away the spirit of repose by night, and spectres to still the pulse of joy by day!

'What!' cries the modest reader, for whom alone I write, with a stare of ludicrous amazement, 'must I really learn all this?' 'All this!' — yes, Sir, and all beside, or you cannot rank among our modern *literati.* 'But is it not impracticable for one individual to traverse all these fields of light or heavy erudition?' 'Impracticable!' — not at all! What has been done may be done again; and still more, what is done daily by all, *you* can do. Have you none of the excursive, all-embracing spirit of the age? Have you no money at all? If you possess fifty dollars to lay out in epitomes, and reside near a circulating library, and can lay a thin *lamina* of brass over your face, the business is done. You are a universal scholar, a thousand-sided genius; at home all over the hill-tops of Aonia; acquainted with the note of all the bull-frogs that ever croaked from the fountains of Helicon; and familiar with each *cabbage*-leaf that has fattened the asses of Parnassus.

In former days there was no royal road to knowledge. Each pilgrim to her shrine had to hew his pathway with the axe of application through tangled forests, or burst it over rugged Alps with the vinegar of self-denial. But now, a king's highway has been opened to her temple, direct and spacious, and accessible to all; graded and railed, and whizzed over by countless cars, laden with eager nations, and propelled by labor-saving machinery, at incredible speed and with unprecedented cheapness. To become a fluent professor, or a faultless artist in the most difficult and delicate of manual sciences, there is no longer occasion to study their fundamental principles, or dwell for earnest years upon the works of masters. What folly were it for you, in whose minds the rules of art are an instinct, and perfection a spontaneous growth, to visit the magazines of pictorial or statuary wealth! Saunter not through the apartments of the Louvre, nor linger in the gallery of the Medici. Glance at copies of the paintings, quiz re-casts of the statues, and ' go ahead!!' Create or criticise; pile coloring on the canvass, or shed ink upon the paper; 't is immaterial which. Fear not; you cannot fail, for chance shall be the guide of your genius, and conjecture the god of your inspiration. I forbear to tell how easy it is to pass sentence, 'like one who knows,' on all the productions of poetry, eloquence, history, and philosophy, and with what marvellous facility one may ' complete to order ' beautiful specimens of unstudied, original imitation, in all these departments.

' But, is it not impossible for one man really to master all these things?' '*Master* them?' Of course it is. We were talking of lip-wisdom, technological learning, and parrot criticism. If you are not rushing in with the mass for the renown of uncircumscribed acquirements, I answer freely, that it is impossible for me, and will be so for you, I doubt not, and for all who prefer the centre of things to the surface, the kernel to the shell. Impossible! — it is the square of impossibility multiplied by the cube of insuperable toil ; and this involved into itself till the processes of common arithmetic are exhausted, and logarithms have lent their *ne plus ultra* of assistance. I have been bursting for the last half hour behind my mask of simulation ; bursting with bitter spleen at the foolish absurdity of the aim.

What! thou silly Œdipus! wilt thou stop to unravel every senseless riddle propounded by the Sphinx of Time? Be a man ; hold yourself equal with your fellow-men, and you will then perceive, that if your thoughts and actions would be mostly insignificant and idle in their eyes, so should theirs be unworthy of a glance from you. It is not indispensably requisite for the inquirer after truth to ascertain all the deviations from falsehood to be found in each philosophical system of ethics or physics, that has been broached from the days of Pythagoras and Plato, to those of Adam Smith and Baron Cuvier, since nearly all have started forth like diverging *radii* from one common centre of ignorance and presumption. Nor is it an insurmountable obstacle to the acquisition of a poet's spirit and a critic's eye, to have neglected drinking of some few of the myriad streams which have flowed from the fountain heads of Moses and of Homer, through the cerebral conduits of three thousand years. The works of the few great masters stand stereotyped in brass, and the pages of the thousands who have been immortalized by thievish blockheads like themselves, are but languid re-impressions from faded copies of those splendid archetypes. Dim not your eyes, therefore, in gazing at these showy fowls, who sport the borrowed plumage and trill the stolen music of the birds of paradise, whose wings first glittered through the heaven of fancy.

Nor, lastly, is it absolutely essential to enlargement of the intellect, to know all that has been done or said by all the great hunters of the earth, from Nimrod to Mehemet Ali; for most of their actions were the offspring of madness or of chance; and history in general is but one long and confused recital of mutual aggression and mutual revenge. It is highly profitable, no doubt, to be familiar with the chief incidents and actors in the enactment of life's great drama; but it adds not to the instructiveness of the spectacle, to watch the entrance and exit of each minor character. If, according to Aristotle, the soul is purged by the passions of pity and terror, in witnessing the trials of injured innocence, or the downfall of triumphant guilt, yet an endless, serio-farcical motley, where the successive scenes are so many reäppearances of folly, cupidity, and crime, overwhelms it with horror, and sickens it with disgust. It contributes little to purify the feelings, to see the tragic demons of superstition and tyranny forever stalking across the tessellated stage; and it awakens only the ghost of mirth in the feeling heart, to behold the comic spirits of mimicry, credulity, and pride, burlesquing humanity, and

> ' Playing such fantastic tricks before high Heaven,
> As make the angels weep.'

To the inquiry, what is it necessary to know and what to read, the answers would be as various as are the minds of those who might propound it. The food which is good for some would be death to others. And happily, the characters and needs of men are so variously constituted, that every species of literary agriculturists can find a market for their products, and the fickle palates of consumers may all be gratified. The departments of science and solid learning I leave to the management of abler hands. That field is too extensive and too difficult, as well for the writer as for the occasion. I would remark, however, that while one may learn any thing and every thing, according as his taste, his age, his means, or his time, may permit, yet in each particular branch he should study a *few* authors, and study them *well*. My present thoughts aim only at polite literature, and especially poetry. To him, therefore, who has the eye to see and the soul to feel the beautiful, in its forms of loveliest loveliness, and who would wish to be *intimate* only with the preëminently great, while his every-day acquaintances should be chosen somewhat at hazard, I will address myself in an ensuing number.

POLYGON.

'GUARD THY YOUTH.'

THAT promise Autumn pays which Spring began,
And what the schoolboy was, such is the man;
The sap and tender bud in childhood shoot,
And youth the blossom gives, but age the fruit.

DISAPPOINTMENT.

I know a maiden fair to see,
Take care!
She can both false and friendly be,
Beware! — beware!
Trust her not — she 's fooling thee! — LONGFELLOW.

I.

I BREATHE no sigh, I shed no tear — in peace I seem to dwell;
None hear my heart's deep throbbings, each a sad and painful knell:
My brow is calm, and though perchance my cheeks look thin and pale,
The ready smile refutes at once the idle gossip's tale.

II.

So unto all I will appear, a reveller of the world,
Sailing upon a summer sea, with banner bright unfurled;
They shall not guess the dismal freight my doomed barque groans beneath,
Nor that the helmsman is Despair — the wished-for haven, Death!

III.

And if I mourn my baffled hope, too high to be fulfilled,
My dream o'erpast — the dearest pulse of feeling harshly stilled;
I would not turn upon my heel thy favor to regain —
Thy truth was but a painted thing — thy love a gilded chain!

IV.

I blush to own the folly that confided all in thee,
And scorn myself, when I recall my past idolatry :
Yet oh! the spirit of my shrine did seem so fair to view,
That for perfection's sake on earth, it should have been as true!

V.

But yet I blame not, since the fault was Nature's, not thine own,
And for the rest, 't is meet that I unto myself atone :
In vain I lightly count my loss as but a moment's dream,
'T was all the light and beauty of my life's o'ershadowed stream!

VI.

The current still must onward flow, in darkness and in dread,
Above the wreck of treasured things that shows its channelled bed;
While Memory, fond naiad, there will garner for her cave
The fragments which thy careless hand hath cast into the wave.

VII.

But hold! — am I not dreaming? Let me never dream again!
My bliss hath been a transient gush — thus passing be the pain;
Avaunt Remorse! I should rejoice, with smiles upon my brow,
Since not another shaft of Fate can ever wound me now.

VIII.

The world is all before me, and my path leads far away —
No flowers to lure my footsteps, and no friends to bid me stay;
I turn to look my latest, ere I hurry to my doom,
Upon the lone, the lovely star, that sets in evening's gloom.

Richmond, (Va.)   BON ROSNI.

WEBSTER.

BY MRS. MARY E. HEWITT.

THE lofty pine that tops thy native hills,
And boldly rears its column to the sky ;
That when the vale the loud-voiced tempest fills,
Lifting the stately cedars from on high,
Doth with a giant's heart its rage defy ;
Graspeth with vigorous root the kindred soil,
And with the storm doth battle mightily ;
That, all unbowed amid the wild turmoil,
Stands where the angry cloud hath spent its wrath,
All crowned with sunbeams 'neath the bright'ning sky ;
And high above the swollen torrent's path
Still towers erect in unscathed majesty ;
The mountain pine, the brave and hardy tree,
Oh, patriot heart ! doth fitly emblem thee.

THE WAKULLA.

A SKETCH FROM THE NOTE-BOOK OF A CLERGYMAN.

AN editor is supposed to know every thing, and therefore *you*, my dear Mr. KNICKERBOCKER, of course need not be informed that THE WAKULLA is one of the lions in Middle Florida; but as the same omniscience is not accorded to all who twelve times a year listen to your wide-spreading instructions, I hope it may not be amiss to say something about it for *their* benefit. So great a lion is it, in the estimation of the few who have seen it, that I confidently believe it will attract many visiters into the country, so soon as we shall be rid of certain other wild animals, who at present are rather anxious not to be caught, and who show a great aptitude in catching. The pursuit of the picturesque in the enemy's country is accompanied generally with too much danger to be entirely agreeable; and therefore, until the Seminoles are safely shut up in the great menagerie on the other side of the Mississippi, I can hardly hope that many of your readers will be induced to seek for even so great a curiosity at the hazard of their lives.

Having heard much in its praise, I sallied out one fine September morning, in company with some officers of the army, and made use of the Tallahassee railroad to get ten miles nearer to the spot. At the ' Steam Mill,' or rather at the place where the steam mill had been, and where, until it was consumed, it used to utter such measured and sonorous tones to the listening pines, we met by appointment the commander of a neighboring post, who had some fine horses waiting for us, and a waggon and a guard tarrying for the specie which my companions had in charge.

Leaving the specie and the escort to come on at their leisure, we mounted our horses, and confiding in their spirit, and the pistols of our leader, we struck across the country for Fort Stansbury, the place appointed for our rendezvous. This we found to be a more desirable residence than we could have expected. It was a large log-house, erected by some unfortunate proprietor, whom the Indians had long ago expelled; and under the hands of the officers it had acquired an appearance of refinement, in addition to its original air of substantial comfort. Of course I am speaking comparatively. I do not wish to have it understood that in winter or in rainy weather one would find much protection under a roof so open to the skyey influences, or from logs which lie so invitingly agape for the wind to enter: but on the day we approached it, we hailed it as ' the shadow of a great rock in a weary land.' There was a fine breeze stirring the branches of the lofty pines, and yet a fiery sun beaming down from the heavens; and I do not remember when I have been more comfortable than when I was fairly seated in that rough old house, with hat and coat off, and nothing to do but to get cool.

By the time we had effected this desirable object, and had inspected all the improvements of our host, the specie had arrived, and the men were mustered for payment. This was a proceeding which I had never witnessed, and therefore, beside the privilege it afforded of looking at gold and silver, which is not much enjoyed now-a-days, I was interested in watching the countenances of the soldiers as they were called up to the table to receive their pay. With the exception of a very few, who looked as if they could keep what they got, they seemed to me to care very little about it, and to gather the shining dross into their fists with as little unconcern as we Floridians would scoop up sand or shells. This having been accomplished to the satisfaction of all concerned, we again took up our line of march; our leader mounted on a noble steed with an eye of fire; Major W—— bestriding a smaller horse, called ' Bu'ster,' who had a most peculiarly busy look when he was in motion; Mr. C—— riding rather a hard-trotting animal, and I bringing up the rear upon a ci-devant race-horse of the Georgia turf. We had two mounted men with muskets in our company, and eight soldiers had been sent ahead to make their way on foot to the Wakulla.

On our way, we crossed one of the *wet hammocks* with which this country abounds. Although it was mid-day above, the thick trees and clustering vines made it twilight for us; and it was impossible to avoid casting an anxious look around upon every side, as our horses stumbled and splashed along through a semi-fluid mass, partly roots and decayed logs, and partly the blackest of mud and the dirtiest of water. For about a mile, however, we were more fortunate, and ' Jackson's trail ' being in our way, we had the pleasure of following ' in the footsteps of an illustrious predecessor.' From this, however, unlike Mr. Van Buren, we were compelled by necessity to diverge; and having overtaken our van-guard, we proceeded more leisurely with them on our way, until we reached the river.

Arrived upon the bank, we found the water so high that the boat was at least twenty yards from the natural shore, and such a thick grove of cypress and juniper intervening, that it could not possibly be brought nearer. As the mountain would not come to us, like Mahomet we concluded to go to it; so after much curvetting on the part of the horses, and much coaxing on our part, we succeeded in getting them near enough to leap into the boat, and leaving the soldiers to hold them, we launched out into the deep.

Here I must pause to remark how singularly the mind of an orderly man will act. When I wrote above, THE WAKULLA, I intended to commence my description precisely at the time and place where and when we left the horses for the boat; but then it occurred to me how unnatural it would appear for us to be mounted and in the woods, without first telling where we came from, and for what. Every reader would inquire : 'Who are you ?'—'what were you doing there ?' etc. Some writers can commence ' *in medias res,*' and make their heroes act as if they were not upstarts, and make their story flow as if it were not broken into cataracts, and all sorts of irregularities. But I have no such talent. I must have my antecedents ; I must begin with the beginning ; and I am free to confess that I have not felt comfortable since I commenced this narrative, because I failed to mention that I was waked up at five o'clock by a sleepy servant, and cut my face by shaving in too great a hurry ; to say nothing of scalding my mouth with hot coffee, and after all, being barely in time for the railroad car.

If in any case I could be induced to vary from my regular habits, and venture upon abruptness, it surely would be the present ; for a more irregular, unreasonable, and unaccountable theme no writer ever happened upon before. Picture to yourself a RIVER leaping out of the earth at a single bound, and running off like mad in a current a quarter of a mile wide, and at the rate of four knots an hour ! And although your imaginary painting will come far short of the real scene, yet it will excite in you something of the wonder with which one actually beholds THE WAKULLA.

Our first sensations, when we shot out from the reeds and bushes which skirt the margin, were those of great dizziness. The water is so pure and clear, that we felt suspended in the air, and clung to the boat very much as we may suppose an aëronaut finds himself clinging when in his sublimest flights. The air above you is scarcely more transparent than the water below : the thin shadows of the clouds are thrown a hundred feet below you, and spread out at the bottom of the spring ; and the image of your boat is carried down with perfect fidelity, and with its oars and rudder looks like some huge animal crawling with outstretched legs along the ground. The modest fishes have no sort of privacy ; and what is worse for them, though better for the fishermen, they have no safety. You can watch the hook as it sinks, and can accurately place the tempting bait within an inch of the abstracted and innocent nose. The smallest silver coin is perceptible at the very bottom, and some say that the date of the coin is discernible — but that *I did not see.*

The aperture through which the river rises is about fifty feet in diameter, the sides being formed of rough and jagged edges of limestone. It is supposed that the water comes in under these rocks from the north, and some think that it is the outlet of Lake Jackson, a large body of water that lies about twenty miles to the north. Nothing was certainly to be determined by an examination so superficial as was ours. The shadows cast by the rocks were too deep to be pierced by the eye, and all that we could make of it was a well about fifty feet in diameter, and a hundred and twenty feet in depth, pouring forth a flood of the purest water that ever blessed my eyes.

We spent so much time in our devotion to the river-god, that we were obliged to make great haste in our return; and a wilder and more harem-scarem ride it has never been my fortune to achieve. We dined at the camp with as much expedition as the cook (who insisted upon serving three courses, though he had but one half-dozen of blue ware) would allow; then we mounted again, and put our horses to their greatest speed, that we might not be too late for the cars. We accomplished our purpose; and bidding the gallant young soldier adieu, we rattled back to town in the peculiarly unromantic fashion which railroad travellers are compelled to adopt. And so much for 'THE WAKULLA.'   L.

DREAMS OF THE PAST.

'GATHERING Memory's wasted flowers,
My soul goes back to youth again.'

Oh! the verdant turf is the softest bed
On which to pillow the weary head;
The green Earth welcomes us to rest,
Like an infant on its mother's breast.
No fairer roof has princes' hall,
Than here is thrown o'er each and all;
And the moon looks down that hath watched our life
From its earliest joy to its latest strife,
And seen us change with the world's rough wear,
Heartsick with folly and sad with care;
Hoping or drooping, or sad or gay,
While *she* moves on, the same alway:
Passing by coldly the ruined wall,
And the brilliant and beautiful festival;
The winds still stir with a home-like sound,
Sweeping and whistling the trees around,
With the same loud whoop and the same low call
As when they came to our father's hall,
And we lay awake to list to their din,
As if angel-anthems were mingling in.

We have been since then in sorrow, I ween,
And days of trouble have stretched between;
And yet as I lie on the turf to-night,
And look above, as Chaldean might,
Watching the stars I have loved so long,
And bending my ear to the winds' shrill song,
The voices of loved and lost come by;
And whenever I close my weary eye,
I stand in the halls of my old domain,
And rest in my vacant place again,
With the friends of my youth who have gone to rest,
And left me lone on the world's cold breast.
Oh, would that this dream could forever stay!
I would lay me down on this couch alway:
But the morning light breaketh still on earth,
With more care for the sad, for the gay more mirth,
And sendeth me forth alone again,
To war with a world of sorrow and pain.

A. RIVERS.

SKETCHES OF THE COUNTRY.

NUMBER FOUR.

THIRTY miles north of Lake Winnepisiogee — a wretched misnomer, by the way, of the old Indian Winneepissaukee — is the nice little village of Conway. From here the views of the White Hills are exceedingly grand, their huge bodies embracing the whole horizon from the west around to the northeast, and their tops wreathed in clouds and snow. As you advance north, they fill up more of the space on every side, until at last you find yourself completely begirt with them, their rough sides hemming you in every where. As you approach them, population becomes more sparse, the land more rough and sterile, and every thing begins to assume an appearance of unformed, chaotic matter. We went on our way very cheerfully, over glade, and brook, and dingle, now threading the thickening forest, and now slowly passing the frail and tremulous bridges. 'Speak well of the bridge that carries you safe over,' says the adage, and I am sure that I never felt so much disposition to do a series of bridges justice; for while they always discharged their duty, they always left one wondering how they were able to do it. Here and there a log-house appeared in the midst of a clearing, its wood chimney, and mud-plastered sides, and windowless holes, looking cheerless enough. Generally speaking, there is too little neatness around log-houses to give the picturesque cottage air, so attractive to the traveller; and the squalid children crowding out of the door to gaze at the passer-by, or rolling with the pigs in the mud and sand, make the *tout ensemble* of a new settler's habitation very repulsive.

The valley which is traversed by all travellers visiting the White Hills is intersected by the Saco river. A most delicious valley it is, shut in all around by mountains, fertile in the greenest grasses, and the loftiest trees, and most lovely, because it is the only level spot the eye rests upon in its reach over the huge elevations around. In the midst of this valley is the house of the elder Crawford. His sons, whom we shall have occasion to mention hereafter, all of them mountain men, descendants, in height and strength of limb, from Anak, live farther on. They pass a strange life of it, these Crawfords — three months in the year receiving and entertaining visiters from all parts of the world, and the other nine living in utter solitude. Still they are well content with their lot; hale, hearty, jovial fellows, all; ready to oblige the visiters to the hills in every possible way, and intimately associated in the traveller's mind with the curiosities of the place. It is here that you begin first to take in the greatness of these mountains. All around you, overtopping each other, they rise, and their immense size contrasts strangely with the house, the trees, every thing indeed near you. Your ideas are enlarged by taking in objects so much greater than you have ever seen before; and for a time there is a painful sensation in bringing the mind up to all this greatness and grandeur. As you get accustomed to them, the gratification is increased, and you are never tired of looking at the variety of prospects presented to you as you pass along. Now there is the deep and scarred indentation which the avalanche has left; then the dense, dark forest, into which no intruder has ever been, and on the trees of which no axe has ever fallen. *Here* is the deep precipice, and over it leaps the silvery streamlet; while *there* is some narrow and winding pathway, past rock and moor and hillock. Sometimes you find the solid body rock torn all in fragments, and the huge boulders scattered in thick profusion over the ground, making whole miles the very 'abomination of desolation.' Farther on, the dwarf-oak and clustered hazles cover acres of ground, contrasting strangely with the high towering forests around. The summits of the mountains are generally bare of all vegetation, and except for one summer month, are covered with snow. The hot days of the last of July and the first of August usually melt away most of the old snow, although many of the crevices hold it unmelted from year to year, while the first of September, and oftentimes before that, the morning breaks upon the snow-covered tops.

The younger Crawford, who has been the guide up the hills for many years, tells a great many laughable stories of the pertinacity of travellers in making the ascent after the season has past. He gives his advice only as to the practicability of ascending, or the probability of a clear sky from the top, leaving the traveller to decide as to whether he will attempt it. A South Carolinian came here a few years since, on the last of September, which is a month later than the ascent is ever made. Mr. Crawford gave him his advice; told him of the difficulties of ascent so late in the year, and urged him against it. All would not do. He had travelled hundreds of miles to stand on the highest land in the States, and he was not to be diverted from his purpose. He was accordingly furnished with horses, provisions, blankets, and all necessary comforts, and by early light, on the first clear morning, he set off with his guide on the perilous undertaking. After reaching the foot of the hill, they dismounted, secured their horses, and commenced the ascent. Before half of the labor had been accomplished, the clouds covered the heavens, and a thick fall of snow set in upon them. Still our traveller was undismayed, and encouraged and urged forward his guide. The snow fell so fast that the difficulty of moving onward increased every moment; and worse than all, the usual landmarks were buried from sight, so that the guide declared he was uncertain of the way. The stranger, however, was resolute; and through snow mid-leg deep, and the howling of a furious storm, he urged on the fainting courage of his guide. Late at night the top of the mountain was reached, through difficulties that none but those who have been to the top of Mount Washington can imagine. When the guide proclaimed that the point had been gained, and that they stood on the very top, our traveller doubted, fearing that the guide, finding all persuasions to return fruitless, had determined to deceive him. 'Is this positively the top of the hill?' 'Yes, Sir, positively.' 'Will you swear to it?' 'Yes, Sir.' 'Hold up your right hand.' The guide held it up. 'You solemnly swear, that to your knowledge this place on which we stand is commonly called the top of Mount Washington, and is the spot to which you conduct all travellers who come to ascend the mountain. So help you God!' The guide took the oath, and added, 'This, Sir, is the pile of stones which the travellers who come up here have heaped up.'

The gentleman put his hand upon the pile, and exclaimed, 'I am satisfied; now let us return.' The descent was accomplished with great difficulty, and at imminent peril, for the snow had so covered the path that it could not be seen at all, and it was not until noon of the next day that they arrived safely back at Crawford's.

We reached the Notch just after noon. The entrance of the chasm is formed by two rocks standing perpendicularly at the distance of twenty-two feet from each other; one about twenty, the other twelve feet in height. This opens you into a narrow defile, extending two miles in length, between two huge cliffs, apparently rent asunder by some great convulsion of Nature. This convulsion Dr. Dwight thinks was that of the Deluge, since there are no proofs of volcanic action any where in this region. Half the space is occupied by the Saco river, and the other half by the road. As you proceed in this pass, the huge mountains of bare cliffs and rocks tower above you on either side, and the view behind you is completely shut in, while that before opens upon bluffs and precipices of granite. Trees spring out from the rough projections, and wrench themselves from the narrow crevices, giving an air of caprice to the scene. The river winds along, bubbling over a rocky bed in some places, running in a deep channel in others, turning this moment round in its mimic whirlpool, and the next starting rapidly off in its deep-worn channel. And then the cascades, up to the very skies, leaping in white foam down precipice after precipice, looking like some pure white riband floating in the air! How the waters sparkle in the sunshine, and tremble in the breeze, and bend downward a thousand ways, in their rapid course! The fine basin of solid rock, too, in which they lie, so still, and pure, and cool:

'A place itself so sweet and lonely,
Seems fit for lovers, and lovers only.'

The deep, dark forest is in keeping with the whole; its low, sea-like music lulling your whole spirit into symphony with the beauty and grandeur of rock, water, and scaur. More than half-way through this valley stands the house occupied by the Wileys, the unfortunate family who were buried in an avalanche of the mountains in 1824. The story is a sad one, and every one who remembers the interest to which the tale was listened, after the event happened, visits the place with melancholy associations.*

After you emerge from the Notch, the mountains begin speedily to open with increased majesty, and often rise to a perpendicular height little less than a mile. The bosom of both ranges on each side of you is overspread by a mixture of evergreens with the large forest trees. The conical firs and spruces cover the tops of the smaller hills, and give an eastern air to the scenery. Farther up, vegetation seems stinted, and a forest of trees, scarce higher than one's head, shows the region of sterility and cold. Farther still, the smooth gray rocks, or the scanty earth, enveloped in a shroud of dark-colored moss, point out the region of perpetual winter.

A few hours' ride from the Notch brings one to the house of ETHAN

* See a former volume of the KNICKERBOCKER.

A. CRAWFORD, *par eminence* the Man of the Hills.   No person who has visited the White Hills, will ever forget the good nature, directness, honesty, and mirthfulness, of mine host of the mountains.   In personal appearance he is a most imposing man, standing six feet seven inches in his stockings, and exceedingly stout and well-proportioned.   As a runner and wrestler, he is well known at all the village gatherings, while in leaping he would easily outdo the famous juvenile feat of old Christopher North; nor would he fear to encounter 'the flying tailor o' Ettrick, auld Hirplin Hurcheon, wha at hap-stap and loup, bate Christopher a' till sticks.'   He is very strong, too, having oftentimes carried a lady in his arms half-way up Mount Washington.   Imagine such a man, with a rough, brown face, well tanned by exposure to sun and wind, but smiling benevolence upon you, putting on a fur hat, over which brush has never been drawn, with a coarse homespun coat and pantaloons, a shirt-collar open at the neck, and stout cowhide shoes, and you have a glimpse of our host and friend, Ethan A. Crawford.   Go up to him and ask him whatever question you please, so it be but civilly put, and mark the good nature streaming out from his eyes as he answers you.   Request from him a favor to yourself or your friends, and see how readily and cheerfully he moves to do it.   Follow up your questions and demands; ask things which you know he cannot obtain for you without great inconvenience to himself or household; nay more, worry his dogs, over-ride his horses, leave open his garden gate, dirty his parlor, and still he is the same imperturbably good-natured Ethan A. Crawford.

The family are of Scotch descent, and have lived for three generations among the mountains.   I was told the following anecdote some years ago, respecting the manner in which the property now belonging to the Crawfords was obtained from old Governor Wentworth.

The governor, who was fond of seeing human nature under every form and in the absence of all ceremony and constraint — a taste which the dignity of his station prevented from being gratified at his own house — was in the habit, while he resided at Wolfborough, of making excursions, without ceremony, and often unattended, into the various parts of the State.   In one of these tours, he came upon the new log-house of the Scotch squatter, and finding the good man away at his work, he endeavored to render himself very agreeable to the buxom wife at home.   Ignorant of the high station of her guest, the lady stoutly opposed his proffered gallantries, and on the return of her husband from the woods, complained to him of the incivility of the stranger.   Crawford who, like his descendants of this day, was a man of great good nature, rather fancying the appearance of the governor, and tired of his long solitude among the mountains, passed off the complaint as a good joke upon an old man, and invited him to stay all night.   The governor assented, and Crawford, adjusting his out-of-doors work, returned to the house, his tongue loaded with inquiries, and his heart full of glee.   The governor was pleasant and facetious; the host became free-hearted and jovial, till at last, with a friendly and most familiar salutation betwixt the guest's shoulders, and a hearty and protracted shake of the hand, the gude-man declared he was the 'best fellow he had met wi' sin the days o' the bailie o' Glasgow, wha was aye fou' six days out o' the seven, and ended his life at last ae drifty night amang the snaw.'

As the night passed away, the ale flowed more freely, and the song resounded from the old rafters : the governor's wit enraptured the host, and the lady even, overcoming her first dislike, grew gracious to so merry-hearted a guest. Early in the morning the stranger departed, not however without insisting upon a visit from his kind-hearted and hospitable landlord, at his house in Wolfborough, where, under the name of ' old Wentworth,' he was, as he alledged, sufficiently well known. The visit in the course of time was paid, and the attendants, being apprised of the jest, had Crawford introduced, very much to his surprise and confusion, into the governor's presence. Here he was banqueted and feasted for some days, in a most princely manner, and dismissed at last with a deed of a thousand acres of the land where he had settled.

The evening view of the scenery from Crawford's house was exceedingly fine. The afternoon had threatened rain, but as night came on, the last lingerer among the dark clouds moved off, leaving only those high masses of white vapor, which among the mountains are the surest indications of fair weather. The pale moon rode high among them, pillowed as they were upon the deep blue of the sky, forming towers, and palaces, and islets, so changeful and fleeting that they seemed like the creations of fairy land. Some lofty pine trees near the house, in the greenness of their new foliage, sighed gently in the soft breeze that had sprung up in the west, and the uneven, dark outline of the mountains loomed out in the faint moonlight, with a mysterious depth of shadow, well suited to the solemnity and stillness of the hour. Wearied with the journey and the intense excitement we had felt all the day, our party bade each other good night, and retired to rest, assured by our host that the morning would bring us a bright sky for our projected ascent of Mount Washington.

AUGUST.

How still the air ! The yellow harvest-fields
No breezes bend in smooth and graceful waves,
While with their motion, dim and bright by turns,
The sunshine seems to move ; nor e'en a breath
Brushes along the surface with a shade
Fleeting and thin, like that of flying smoke.
O'er all the woods the top-most leaves are still.
Even the wild poplar leaves that, pendent hung
By stems elastic, quiver at a breath,
Rest in the general calm. The thistle-down,
Seen high and thick, by gazing up beside
Some shading object, in a silver shower
Plumb down, and slower than the slowest snow,
Through all the sleepy atmosphere descends ;
And where it lights, though on the steepest roof,
Or smallest spire of grass, remains unmoved.
Whiter than wool, a single fleecy cloud
On the soft bosom of the air becalmed,
Drops a lone shadow, gray, distinct and still,
On the bare plain, or sunny mountain's side,
Or polished mirror of the upland lake.

THE LITTLE KITTEN.

NOT BY WORDSWORTH.

—— A harmless kit,
　That merely nips its tail,
And gives a munch at every fly —
　Why should its spirits fail?

I met a little pussy-cat,
　She was 'four weeks old,' she purred,
And two of her paws were dapper gray,
　And two with white were furred.

'Hither and thither, little puss,
　How far may you be going?'
'How far? — 'tis seventy miles,' she said,
　'By the fever in me glowing!'

'And what's the place? I pray you name;'
　She answered, 'Lola's pond;
And twelve of us, since Friday night,
　Were in the bottom drowned!'

'Three shining black, and three Maltese,
　Three white, and two like me,
And we are soaking in the pond
　Beneath the willow tree.'

'You say that three were shining black,
　Three white, and three Maltese;
Yet ye are *twelve* within the pond —
　I pray you, how is this?

'You skip about, my little kit,
　Your life it is not cleft;
If nine and two are in the pond,
　Then you're the one that's left.'

'Our tails are loose and out of use,'
　The little kit replied;
'You'll find us well with a diving bell,
　And we are side by side.

'And often when they come to fish
　We cannot choose but dread,
Lest for one thing that is alive,
　They'd hook a dozen dead.

'The three that first went in the pond
　Were black as ravens are;
Then three Maltese, and two like me,
　And three as lilies fair.'

'Then you're the one that's left,' said I,
　If eleven are in the sea?'
'Why Sir,' the kitten did reply,
　'How obstinate you be!'

'But they are deep within the sea,
　While you on earth are found;'—
'Twas blowing breath against the wind:
The kitten thus would speak her mind,
　'I say we all are drowned!'

THE ROYAL PLAGIARIST,

OR HISTORY OF 'DAR SU VIDA FOR SA DAMA' OF CALDERON.

———

TRANSLATED FROM THE SPANISH.

———

'Dar su Vida por sa Dama' is the title of a Spanish drama, which was played for the first time in 1627, and is still extant in an anonymous collection, now somewhat scarce, published at Madrid about the same period. The composition and representation of this piece were attended by circumstances which may be said to form a striking and romantic chapter in the history of literary labors.

It was in the beginning of February, of the year above mentioned, that two men were seated in a small chamber of the palace of Madrid. The one might have been thirty years of age, and was habited in a costume of cloth of gold; the other, a well-formed and handsome cavalier, of five-and-twenty, wore the uniform of a lieutenant of artillery. The elder, with his head resting on one hand, with the other played carelessly with the tassel of pearls attached to his belt; while the younger, with his small, quick eyes fixed upon a manuscript which lay unrolled before him, read aloud with an impressive voice to his companion. The manuscript was a play, and the reader had arrived at the last scene.

'Very good! excellent!' frequently exclaimed his auditor; and the young man, excited by these laconic eulogies, redoubled the enthusiasm of his declamation, and ventured to improvise occasionally a touching and sublime sentence. As he approached the conclusion, he interrupted himself, to explain respectfully some uncertainty between two modes of terminating the piece. The subject was that of a young cavalier enamored of a beautiful damsel, who was constantly putting his love to severe and trying tests, and who finally enjoined upon him a task which could only be accomplished at the imminent hazard of his life. The author had some doubt whether the exaction of this last proof of affection from her lover would be consistent with the character of an attached woman: he was inclined, however, to represent his hero as perilling his life to prove his devotion. His auditor was of a contrary opinion.

'A woman never desires the death of a man who loves her,' said he, in a self-sufficient tone. 'The hero has already given ample proofs of his love, and the heroine should at length be satisfied. Beside,' continued he, coldly, 'his compliance with a command so palpably cruel, would argue a degree of infatuation altogether incredible.'

The first objection had some weight with the *militaire*. The second was so revolting to his generosity, and excited him to maintain with so much spirit and feeling the possibility of a lover sacrificing his existence to attest his devotion, that his antagonist involuntarily exclaimed, while regarding the dramatist with admiration :

'Proceed, then, to the last proof, young man. This conviction will inspire you to add another noble scene.'

'And the play shall be called 'Dar su Vida por sa Dama,'' said the officer, chivalrously ; and he commenced reciting the final scene, as he had conceived it.

'Charming! charming!' exclaimed his auditor, delighted with the improvisation. 'I am much pleased with you, young man,' he added, taking at the same time possession of the manuscript; 'and I promise you that this piece shall be played within a month in the private theatre of the palace.'

Blushing with joy and pride at this assurance, the officer rose to express his gratitude, but the other interrupted him :

'I annex one condition to this favor, however,' said he, 'which is, that no one — you understand me, *no one* — shall know that you are the author.'

Confused and disappointed at these words, the young man was about to remonstrate, when a look from the other prevented him. Awkwardly assenting, he withdrew without hearing, or if he heard, certainly not comprehending, a promise made to him by his patron as he retired, of a gratuity from the treasury of the king.

It is proper here to inform the reader that this young aspirant to literary fame was Don Calderon de Barca, then a simple lieutenant of artillery, but subsequently the author of one hundred and twenty masterpieces of dramatic composition, to which the one in question was the prelude. His joy at learning that his play was to be enacted at the theatre of the palace, and his mortification at the hard conditions attached to the favor, will both be perfectly understood, when the name of the personage with whom he had been closeted is mentioned. The gracious patron and flattering critic was no other than Philip IV., king of Spain, and dramatic author by the process just described, after the fashion of his illustrious contemporary, the Cardinal Richelieu. In comparing Philip to Richelieu, however, the advantage is on the side of the cardinal; for the emulator of Corneille contented himself at least with giving them his plays to correct, while the patron of Calderon coolly fathered those composed by others, having merely suggested to them the subjects. The celebrated Don Lope de Vega had for a long time furnished the monarch with the materials of dramatic fame, but growing tired of the degrading service, he had latterly been desirous of finding a substitute ; and Calderon having confided to him his intention of writing dramas, he presented the young officer to the king as a genius of great promise ; and thus the officer of artillery, encouraged by wise counsel, had arrived at the honor of writing a play for the king of Spain.

The condition imposed by the king afflicted Calderon the more, that a romantic project was connected with the representation of the first drama. Having conceived a *grande passion* for one of the most beautiful women of the court, the Countess Antonia D'Avalos, he proposed to declare his passion for the lady on the day when she should discover, by the play, his definition of love. He had thrown his whole soul into the work, and in its most impassioned scenes had aimed at picturing his own devotion. The sublimity of the dénouement and the chivalrous character of the title had no other origin or end. And now it was all lost for poor Calderon ; the king would reap the benefit, and his Majesty thought that *money* would atone for the sacrifice ! The first impulse of the young man was to resist such tyranny ; but Don Lope declared that by so doing he would ruin himself, and that even his love should prompt him to be silent. The play was cast immediately, as the king had promised. The rehearsals were directed by De Vega, and attended by the monarch. The author, it was said, wished to remain unknown. But an august name was already whispered at court in connexion with the new drama. Such was the usage on these occasions; for Philip was reserved and dissimulating, even in his plagiarisms. He never *said* that a piece was his, but amused himself by permitting others to say it. This time, however, whether in obedience to the royal wish, or from some other cause, the usual surmises in regard to all *anonymous* dramas produced at court were hazarded by few, and in a very low tone ; so that the day of representation arrived without a suspicion on the part of the majority as to who was the author.

Calderon received in the morning, to strengthen his fortitude, the title to an annual pension from the private purse of the king, and in the evening had the honor to be placed in the back part of the alcove set apart for his Majesty. Was this distinction the result of gratitude or of distrust on the part of Philip ? The young officer was too much occupied to reflect on the subject ; for directly before him, so placed that he could distinctly observe the varying expression of her countenance, sat the Countess Antonia d' Avalos, and by her side the king. The sensations of Calderon were a curious compound of happiness and misery, which it would have been difficult to analyze. He saw reflected in her beautiful face his own sentiments, as expressed in the play. He marked her admiration of the best scenes, especially of those of a passionate character. More than once he saw her ready to applaud, had the *modesty* of the king permitted him to give the signal. He saw the tears trembling in her eyes, as she awaited the last proof of love ; he saw them fall thick and fast on her palpitating breast, as the dénouement approached. Philip at length laid aside etiquette, under pretence of encouraging a young actor, and then the beautiful hands of the countess were vocal with transport. For a time Calderon revelled in the pride of successful authorship, forgetful that he was forbidden to profit by it ; and recovered not from the ecstacy into which the praise of Antonia had thrown him, until the principal actor advanced to name the author of the drama. He listened with shame and rage to the following address :

'Thus ends,' said the actor, bowing, 'Dar su Vida por sa Dama !' The author is a writer of this city. He hopes your kindness will excuse any errors he may have had the misfortune to commit.'

If Antonia could but have recognized in Don Calderon the cause of her emotion ! But how, alas ! should she distinguish him, a poor star, eclipsed by the sun of royalty ? Would she but turn toward him by accident, and behold him trembling behind her chair !

Heaven accorded to the lover the boon he asked. More than once already, (by the power which ladies possess of detecting the presence of an admirer, and by another power not less exquisite, of seeing every thing which passes around them while appearing to observe nothing,) more than once during the representation, had she remarked the young officer of artillery, and noted the varying expression of his agitated countenance. She saw that he was under the influence of powerful emotions, and fancied from his manner that they were in some way connected with herself and with the play. The expression of his eyes when he turned them toward her could not be mistaken. They seemed actually to blaze with rapture when she applauded the play, but in a moment after they were cast down in despondency. The countess was aware of the literary usages of the king, and knew Calderon to be a man of talent. Had she then a presentiment of the truth ? It would almost seem so; for as she rose to withdraw from the theatre, she turned toward him, and fixing her eyes on his, said in a soft expressive voice :

'This piece does honor to the intellect of the author, and I would give a great deal to know the '*writer of this city.*''

Calderon in his heart interpreted her words, 'I should love the author,' and replied by a look full of gratitude. But an accident which threw him back upon his *rôle*, prevented him from assuring her that she was understood. The king as well as Calderon had been struck by the remark of the countess, and had approached her quickly. In the conversation which ensued between them, Calderon saw his laurels unscrupulously gathered by another, and the homage due to his own genius bestowed upon the king.

'Oh, it is too much !' thought he; and he laid his hand on his sword, as if calling on it for vengeance : 'one may sacrifice to one's king, glory and a name; but *love !* — that is impossible !'

As she passed him, escorted by Philip, Antonia observed that Calderon regarded her as before, and found herself, oddly enough, situated between him and the king; both loving her, and both resting their claims to her notice on the same grounds; Philip seeming to demand eulogy as a right, and Calderon tacitly to claim it. Free, from her position, and *galante* by character, Antonia amused herself by coqueting with each of her admirers, resolved however, at all hazards, to make Calderon explain himself, on the very first opportunity. With the secret disposition of the young officer, we may imagine that it required an effort of resolution on his part to resist an attack from such a quarter, and to keep his promise to the king. He had resisted, however, for nearly a week, when a romantic circumstance developed the mystery.

Philip gave a grand hunt in the environs of Madrid, and the Countess d' Avalos and Don Calderon, together with most of the gentlemen of the court, were of the royal party. Soon after reaching the hunting-ground, a vast and beautiful forest about ten miles from the city, the king, who had followed Antonia with admiring eyes as she rode among the cavaliers in attendance, succeeded at length in detaching her from the *cortége;* he profited by this occasion to render himself agreeable, intermingling his gallantries with long poetical tirades; when a fearful incident disturbed the conversation. An immense wild boar, which had been roused from its covert by the hunters, burst through the brush-wood a few yards in advance of the king and his companion, and dashed furiously toward them. At sight of the enraged animal, with bristles erect, and the foam flying from his tusks, the horses took fright, and the palfrey of the countess suddenly leaping aside, threw her with violence to the earth.

The first impulse of the king was to fly to the assistance of the lady ; but the terrible aspect of the maddened beast, as he swerved aside to charge upon his prostrate victim, put his Majesty's chivalry to flight, and he recoiled involuntarily, from surprise and terror. This, for a man who recited verses in praise of heroic devotion to the sex, was without doubt a flagrant inconsistency; but Philip was more politic than brave, and loved better to talk of generosity than to practise it. Shouting for aid, he raised his carbine, fired, and lodged a ball in the body of the boar. The beast reeled on receiving the shot, and the king congratulated himself for a moment on having saved the countess. He was mistaken, however: the career of the animal was arrested but for an instant, and he again rushed to the attack. The young lady would now inevitably have fallen a sacrifice to his fury, had not a deliverer suddenly appeared in the person of a young cavalier, who, rushing from a by-path which there intersected the main road through the forest, before the king could recognize him, had precipitated himself sword in hand upon the monster, at the very instant when he was about to bury his tusks in the side of his victim.

The attack was made with such frantic and desperate energy, that the blade of the cavalier passed completely through the body of the boar, the hilt striking against his shoulder, and notwithstanding his enormous weight, driving him back half a spear's length; while the assailant, driven forward by the same impulse, fell upon the expiring brute, and before he could recover himself, received a severe wound. He soon regained his feet, however, and having finished his work with another thrust of his good steel, turned his attention to the countess. She soon recovered, and recognizing Calderon in her deliverer, poured forth her gratitude with all the fervor of an enthusiastic Spanish maiden's nature.

The opportune appearance of Calderon was soon accounted for. The jealous officer had followed the countess and the king from the moment they became separated from the *cortége*, and was spurring along a by-path, with the intention of meeting them at the angle of the road, and interrupting their *tête-à-tête* at all hazards, when he heard the screams of the countess, and urging his horse to its utmost speed, arrived on the spot in time to perform the gallant exploit already recorded.

'Seignor Pedro,' said Antonia, 'how have I merited such heroic devotion from you?'

'It is thus that I love!' replied the poet, with enthusiasm.

'*Dar su Vida por sa Dama*,' said the young lady; 'you join example to precept, and I know *now* the ' writer of this city.' '

'Hush!' said Calderon, blushing, and looking round to see if the king was near.

'Give yourself no uneasiness; your secret shall be well kept,' said Antonia, at the same time laying one hand on her heart, while she gave the other to the poet, who kissed it with rapture.

Thus it was that Calderon commenced his dramatic career; and thus love instead of glory rewarded his first effort as an author.   B.

EPIGRAM

ON A VERY PLEASANT BUT VERY UGLY WOMAN.

WHILE in the dark on thy soft hand I hung,
And heard the tempting siren in thy tongue,
What ardent flames, what anguish I endured!
But when the candle entered — I was cured!

ART THOU NOT CHANGED?

BY FREDERICK COLTON.

——'Never more, my heart,
Canst thou be my sole world, my universe.'—BYRON.

BRIGHT are thy days, O Childhood! sunny days!
　The morning light to dark existence given,
When life's young sun rises in its own rays,
　And in those rays creates itself a heaven.
Ah! there 's a light o'er early being flung,
That fades from earth when we no more are young!

Oh! how our hearts, how all things earthly, change,
　As forth we go into the blighting world;
Where all we meet, in our wild, feverish range,
　Seem on a sea of sin and passion whirled:
How soon the sunlight of the soul is flown,
Which played around us e'er 'the world' was known!

Art *thou* not changed? Do the same feelings now
　Come fresh and joyous, that were once thine own?
When clustering locks lay on thy childish brow,
　And life was new, and almost all unknown?
Clingest thou still, in days of sterner truth,
To the gay visions of thy dreaming youth?

Does the green earth still seem the same bright thing
　It ever seemed when childhood's days were fleeing?
When thy young soul was in the merry spring
　Of its new-wakened but eternal being;
And saw whate'er was to its vision given
In the pure light of its own native heaven?

Dost thou still feel the same rich gush of thought,
　Guileless and pure, spring upward from thy soul?
Thou, on whose brow the wearing world has wrought,
　Thou, who art struggling for Ambition's goal?
Ah! the clear waters of the mountain spring
Grow dark and turbid in their wandering!

The voice of life grows sadder with our years;
　We see at length our early shrines deserted —
We kneel in worship, but we kneel in tears,
　Devoted still, though worn and broken-hearted:
While the bright forms of other days arise,
With heaven still sleeping in their faded eyes!

Ah! thus we change — and yet we know not how:
　There is a mystery in this life of ours;
A wizard spell, on heart, and soul, and brow,
　Working with strange and darkly-hidden powers,
That leaves but little for life's sunless even,
Save tears for earth's past joy, and hopes of heaven.

Hartford, (Conn.,) July, 1841.

OLD DUTCH HOUSES AND THEIR ASSOCIATIONS.

BY T. B. THORP.

I HAVE a great tenacity of early recollections. I thought much in my first breeches. The ancient city in which were passed the years which impress themselves most strongly on my imagination and memory, was well calculated to afford speculation for youthful minds formed like mine. There were tangible inconsistences in society and in architecture, that struck the dullest fancy at once. My discernment of contrasts was not above that of those around me, but only in speculating on the reasons of them. My first essay in public life, that I particularly recollect, was going from house to house, wishing the inmates a 'happy new year.' The custom was a noble one, for the blessings of children must have an incense about them as they ascend to heaven. My little companions often crossed my path in these labors of love. I wrought as hard as they, but always with less profit; and it set me to speculating on the cause. I ascended the steps of the most wealthy modern mansions; but my 'happy new year' met with a cold rebuff from a grinning servant, and a door perhaps was slammed in my face. At length some unpretending house, by its low step and fanciful knocker, would tempt me to try my fortune. An old dame, as neat as a maiden quakeress, would answer my summons, greet me with 'God bless the child!' fill my hat with cakes, and send me on my way rejoicing. This oft-repeated good luck made me at last cautious of the imposing mansions of modern date; and so ancient did I at last become, that I would stop at no door unless I could see the date over it, with magnificent stairs, as I thought, leading up to the weathercock that invariably surmounted these hospitable dwellings. Thus I early learned a lesson, confirmed by the experience of after-life, that modern pretension and display sink into insignificance when compared with the honest hospitality of the olden time.

Thus early were my predilections formed for old Dutch houses and their associations; and my passion increased with every new year. I became acquainted with all the ancient dwellings extant in the city in one day. I looked upon them as sacred. The dark figures, indicating their age to be more than an hundred years, grew into an unbounded antiquity in my childish imagination.

Among the many buildings that attracted my youthful fancy, was one opposite my grandfather's house. It was small, with a very peaked roof, half hidden by decayed trees and other marks of time. This little house looked oddly enough, surrounded as it was by glaring brick buildings, of the latest 'approved construction.' It seemed to court the shade, like some excellent old country dame who finds herself suddenly among the gay society of a city; and like the country dame, too, it was far more comfortable and useful for being out of fashion. In this cosy nook lived the relic of one Baltus Van Zant; a little woman, clad in a short-gown of deep blue, with a dark petticoat. Her feet peeped out plainly from under her dress, and gave indications of having once been small and well-proportioned. I never remarked, for years, that she did not live entirely alone. Not a neighbor visited her house. She seemed to have no sympathies with the generation around her, but went her own way, like a horse in a mill. This made me set her down as a witch, and I shunned her accordingly. But much as her manner of life once surprised me, now that I reflect upon it, I see something exalted in her solitude in the midst of a bustling city; a tenacity of old habits and opinions, that has in it something of the sublime; a contempt of innovation, which though it may retard the building of balloons and rail-roads, detracts nothing from the total amount of human happiness.

There was but one window in the little mansion I have alluded to, which faced the street, and was invariably thrown open on Mondays. There dangled from its sill much parlor furniture that needed 'an airing;' and the widow could be seen all day flourishing a mop, a broom, and a dusting-rag, alternately. About three o'clock this bustle would cease. One article after another would disappear; the old lady would gather a bunch of lilac leaves from the garden, carry them into the house, close the window, and not open it again until the following Monday. Independent of this work, which my old grandmother called 'cleaning the parlor,' the widow seemed to be constantly busy in fighting the dust that rose from the street, and in scouring the front door and stoop of her dwelling. How well I remember that clean front door to this day, and the milk-whiteness of the benches ranged on either side! There were no 'washes' nor paint here, such as now make so many 'whited sepulchres.' It was the virgin purity of the wood, sinking into little hollows around the heads of the nails, so searching had been the sand in pursuit of dirt.

In the latter part of September of every year, late in the day, a country waggon, loaded with stockings and woollen yarn, invariably stopped at widow Van Zant's. The horses attached to it were fat and sleek-looking; and although on their gray noses age was impressed, still they thought themselves young, having never for twenty years had the least occasion to try their speed. The owner was an old-fashioned Dutchman, who struck me as being connected in some way with the little house he was visiting. There was the same ancient look about him, the same indications of comfort. The lady accompanying him was a duplicate of widow Van Zant, only a little more gay and prepossessing to a youngster like me. This worthy couple would walk up the stoop, and after the most scrupulous scraping of the feet and dusting of clothes, enter the house. Then the parlor window would fly open, and an ardent excitement within soon succeeded. For a day or two, the pair of old ladies would be seen in the street together, with small bundles in their hands, such as are done up in dry-goods stores. Late in the afternoon, however, they sat silently employed in knitting on one of the benches of the 'stoop,' while the male visiter was smoking a long pipe opposite to them. At sun-down they would vanish into the house. On the first Saturday succeeding this visit, the waggon again drew up at the door, and the party drove off. Widow Van Zant resumed her cleaning with renewed vigor, the yearly interruption in her routine of life having passed away.

In —— street, I recollect, when a boy, in company with my playmates, trying to get into any of the fifteen rooms in an old deserted

Dutch house, without going through the parlor! We never could do it. In these latter times, after seeing much of the fashionable architecture which enables a private family to occupy a ' temple,' with pillars all around, and makes churches without pillars, and no temples at all, I cannot recall the plan of that old Dutch house. Tradition avers that the owner was a bachelor, and when somewhat old, he rented it out to a numerous family that had just pioneered its way from Cape Cod, and settled upon the unwieldy and fat society of an originally Dutch city with all the voracity of a nest of carbuncles fastened upon a whale. The poor Dutchman, who loved comfort and quiet, reserved the parlor for his own use; but no sooner had the family taken possession of the premises, than they were constantly spinning through his room, in a manner perfectly astounding. No one could stir without coming into his presence. He swore that it was a plot to kill him, and offered the family a large sum if they would leave the house; but they made more noise than ever. Confounded with the constant clamor, Mynheer took to his bed, and after a short illness, died. His last hallucination was, that he had lain ill for an hundred years in the public road, opposite the Staadt-Huys in Amsterdam.

The school-house where I whiled away many a year grew dark at evening sunset in the forked shadow of the old ' VANDERHEYDEN PALACE.' That venerable building was as romantic as any castle ever built on the rolling Zuyder-Zee. It was a noble specimen of the classic Dutch. Nothing could be finer than its imposing front, sending up its sharp points far into the sky, towering over the surrounding buildings like pyramidal monuments. The boat weathercock on one of these, how it used to box about in the wind, screaming at every turn with the accumulated rust of a century! The rampart horse on the other was always flying round, and kicking about like mad. Then the little round holes just below the weathercocks; the small iron cranes just below the holes; and the little windows just below the iron cranes; all perfectly useless, perfectly Dutch, and perfectly beautiful! I loved that old house, for the descendants of Vanderheyden occupied it in my day; and between school hours I used to romp through its old halls, and climb into its dusty garrets, with sensations little short of those which Galileo felt, when he swept his telescope for the first time across the heavens. How I used to wonder that such a tall building could be erected! How I used to pore over some brass-clasped, corpulent little volume, that would turn up among the neglected rubbish of some out-of-the-way corner! How we boys used to besmear our faces with cob-webs, and imagine the makers of them down our backs, while we were attempting to climb up and look out of the little hole under the horse weathercock!

It was in truth a glorious old house. The rooms were airy, and a coach-and-six could have galloped through the halls. The old fire-places looked in summer like comfortable bedrooms opening into the parlors, their large door-ways ornamented with pictures on china, and ' goose's wings.' Then the tall china jar of asparagus in the centre of these little rooms! Oftentimes have I, with a dozen other little folk, ' played baby-house ' in them, and gazed with delight at the sky-blue ceilings, in search of stars in the day-time. And little Marie Vander-heyden, too, with her mixture of old Dutch looks and modern accomplishments; the cap for her head changed from the little quilt of her ancestors to a simple net, that concealed not her sweet auburn hair, nor detained the clustering curls that shaded her forehead and neck; her little waist yet exhibiting above and below it lines strangely resembling those discernible in her grandmother's picture, taken at seventeen. Sweet Marie! — all Dutch, yet mingling every modern improvement in her person and in her mind so divinely, that she shed a loveliness over the past, and gave a sanctity to the present. I *loved* old ' Vanderheyden Palace !'

As a sort of reverse to the 'palace,' I always looked with pleasure upon old BOCLE SPEIGELS' HOUSE. It was an anomaly in architecture. Nothing like it was any where else to be met with in the wide world. Bocle, so tradition reports, waited two long years for yellow bricks from Holland, to build him a house, that he might consummate his marriage with the prettiest girl among his acquaintance. The third year commenced, and his sweetheart began to show dissatisfaction; when suddenly he began with commendable zeal to build a cage for his bird, of wood;· and when he had nearly completed it to the eaves, the bricks arrived. Unwilling to have them wasted, he finished the second story of brick : and very puzzling was this new style to the old burghers. They one and all averred that there was something *wrong* about Speigels' house; but what it was they could not tell. Some wag remarked, that Speigels had put the foundation of his house where the top should be. To this joke Speigels invariably replied, that ' de tamned yankees were turning the city upside-down, and his house would come right in time.' This remark was bandied about; and as innovaticn increased, and good old Dutch manners, as well as houses, fell into disrepute, Bocle rose in esteem among all the ancient families, for his penetration and forecaste, as being the only man among them fully prepared to come right end up, in the confusion around them. On the strength of this character for foresight, he was elected to represent the Dutch interest as an alderman; and it is worthy of remark, that all his public acts were solid at the top, but totally destitute of proper foundation, and calculated only to be useful when the present order of things are entirely reversed. Singular as it may appear, Bocle has been extensively followed by legislators of the present day; for thousands of laws are now annually made, which are apparently of brick or stone, but which are really built upon the weakest of wooden foundations.

The cleanliness of the KNICKERBOCKERS about their houses is proverbial. The habits of the widow Baltus Van Zant in this respect is no fable. I have seen this passion carried beyond all reason; and singular as it may appear, I have actually wept over its desolating effects. On the suburbs of —— may still be seen the ancient residence of Mynheer VANDERSCHUVEN. It is a house that IRVING would delight to honor. Although situated on a public road, the thick tressel-work of an hundred Lombardy poplars screened it from the profane gaze of the passerby. I have often fancied that they clung to it and grew up around it, as if aware that there was danger of its being removed from their grateful shade. It is a perfect house of its kind; and I would sooner be its owner by inheritance, than the heir of twenty 'shingle palaces' of modern date. It has remained in the possession of the Vanderschuvens until the present day; and the last representative of that once numerous family is widowed and childless. She lives exclusively within her little domain, talks Dutch to a superannuated old negro servant, eats suppaan-and-milk, kool-slaa, and sour-krout, 'to encourage,' as she says, 'old family feelings.' But of her neatness, which even excelled that of the widow Van Zant, I would more particularly speak.

Old Vanderschuven, when he first settled the place, started with what was in our early times considered a fortune. He brought with him from Holland not only bricks to build himself a house, but many luxuries beside, in the way of furniture. Among these latter, were three pictures by TENIERS, which his father had purchased from the painter himself. In fact, it was a matter of some pride with the old man to boast of his father's intimacy with the great artist; and he used to sit, in his old age, and point out the houses on them, call over the names of the churches and steeples, and call the scene 'home.' One of these pictures represented a 'skating scene' on the Hague; and he once had it carried in great state down to the edge of the Hudson river, to examine whether the skaters on that noble stream at all resembled those on the Hague. The old man surveyed the living and pictured actors before him for a long time, but at length concluded that the *real* skaters did very well, but that they lacked the gracefulness of the jolly little figures before him, which the painter's art had so wonderfully preserved. These paintings descended with the house to the old man's children, and so on from one generation to another, until they fell into the hands of the present representative of the family.

Melancholy to relate, a taste for the fine arts did not increase with the descendants of Vanderschuven. The beauties of the pencil had little charm even for Vanderschuven's children; and *their* children only called them valuable, because their grandfather had loved them. Occasionally, the old carved oak frames had been wiped off, and an obtruding speck had been removed from the paintings; but it remained for the present owner to clean off the dirt. It is said that grief has many outlets; and it would seem that the widow, the present owner of the pictures, took to cleaning them to assuage her sorrows. Scandal even affirms that she consoled herself on the death of her husband with the idea that all obstacles were now removed; that 'clean *now* she could and would;' and when I first saw these noble pictures, they *were* clean, heaven help the mark! I contemplated them as they really were, beautiful in ruins, and almost wept over the propensity, proper though it was, which thus destroyed them. There they hung, the copper on which they were painted showing through in glistening spots among the trees, in the clear blue sky, and among groups of trunk-breeched Dutchmen. The whole had for a long time, at stated periods, passed under the ordeal of soap and sand! The delicate penciling of TENIERS could be plainly traced in spots, and grew doubly valuable as it disappeared in the general dimness. How often have I rubbed my eyes to see if the defects of the picture were not in my own vision; and how have I left them, (the venerable form of the excellent widow at the moment being in my eye,) more in sorrow than in anger, that they were thus despoiled — a sacrifice, worthy of the gods, to the spirit of Dutch cleanliness!

But let me finish my recollections with a memorial of 'the church,' whose sweet influences ever sanctify the social pictures of the past. I once wandered into the settlement of the KNICKERBOCKERS, in hopes of seeing the great historian. The 'gentleman that took me' was in search of an estray cow. Journeying on through the lovely valley of Schaghticoke, it was not difficult to be pleased; and although I did not find the great man for whom I was looking, yet I saw his relatives, and that was a satisfaction, at least. I saw, moreover, the village church in which I presumed he was christened; and I was blessed by the worthy dominie, who 'wagged his pou' in the pulpit of the same. It was a sweet little church, with a straight-forward congregation, a straight-forward choir, and a straight-forward dominie. Every thing was perpendicular about it, save the steeple, which had the miraculous power of sustaining itself comparatively upright, with the centre of gravity far without the base. The builder might have had some new-fangled notions of religion, contrary to the synod of Dort. Steeples, it is said, like ministers, point direct to heaven, and the architect of this spire may have fancied he had discovered a new road at an angle of forty-five degrees. Happy indeed are the people that worship in that church, so solitary and so obscure that it has thus far escaped the desolating hand of 'Improvement!' An isolated spot, breathing nothing but pure Dutch; the only uncontaminated foothold of that great people who built the noble houses cherished in our recollections; a people born in the 'Golden Age,' who lived and died under the impression that this world was a very good one, and that they had not lived in vain.

E R O T I C .

' Des Mahlers Pinsel und des Dichters Lippe
Die sussesate, die je von frubem Honig
Genahrt war, wunscht, ich mir.'

GOETHE'S 'TORQUATO TASSO.'

I.

A PENCIL give me, dipped in hues
  The rainbow's glitt'ring arch hath shed;
And let its magic art suffuse
Those colors o'er, like morning dews
  Upon the painted flow'ret's bed;
Till Fancy's plastic hand imbues
My canvass thus divinely fair,
In sweet illusion, thou art there.

II.

Give me the lip, as sweet as e'er
  By nectar nourish'd in the bower
Where fairies through the myrtles peer,
And radiant forms within appear;
  And tones imbibed of magic power,
That ravished each deep list'ning ear:
Then will I tell a tale, shall hold
Thy heart in love's enchanting fold.

H. N. B.

LINES TO A LADY.

BY GEORGE D. PRENTICE.

I.

LADY — I love, at eventide,
  When stars, as now, are on the wave,
To stray in loneliness, and muse
  Upon the one dear form that gave
Its sunlight to my boyhood: oft
That same sweet look sinks still and soft
Upon my spirit, and appears
As lovely as in by-gone years.

II.

Eve's low, faint wind is breathing now,
  With deep and soul-like murmuring,
Through the far pines — and thy sweet words
  Seem borne on its mysterious wing;
And oft, mid musings sad and lone,
At night's deep noon, that thrilling tone
Swells in the wind, low, wild, and clear,
Like music in the dreaming ear.

III.

When Sleep's calm wing is on my brow,
  And dreams of peace my spirit lull,
Before me, like a misty star,
  That form floats dim and beautiful;
And when the holy moonbeam smiles
On the blue streams and crimson isles,
In every gush poured down the sky,
That same light form seems stealing by.

IV.

It is a blessed picture, shrined
  In memory's urn; the wing of years
Can change it not, for there it glows
  Undimmed by 'weaknesses and tears;'
Deep-hidden in its still recess,
It beams with love and holiness,
O'er hours of being, dark and dull,
Till life seems almost beautiful.

V.

The vision cannot fade away;
  'T is in the stillness of my heart,
And o'er its brightness I have mused
  In solitude: it is a part
Of my existence; a dear flower
Breathed on by Heaven: Morn's earliest hour
That flower bedews, and its blue eye
At eve still rests upon the sky.

VI.

Lady — like thine, my visions cling
    To the dear shrine of buried years;
The past, the past! it is too bright,
    Too deeply beautiful, for tears;
We have been blest: though life is made
A tear, a silence, and a shade,
And years have left the vacant breast
To loneliness — we have been blest!

VII.

Those still, those soft, those summer eves,
    When by our favorite stream we stood,
And watched our mingling shadows there,
    Soft-pictured in the deep blue flood,
Seemed one enchantment. Oh! we felt,
As there at Love's pure shrine we knelt,
That life was sweet, and all its hours
A glorious dream of Love and flowers.

VIII.

And still 'tis sweet. Our hopes went by,
    Like sounds upon the unbroken sea,
Yet memory wins the spirit back
    To deep, undying melody;
And still around her early shrine
Fresh flowers their dewy chaplets twine,
Young Love his brightest garland wreathes,
And Eden's richest incense breathes.

IX.

Our hopes are flown — yet parted hours
    Still in the depths of memory lie,
Like night-gems in the silent blue
    Of Summer's deep and brilliant sky;
And Love's bright flashes seem again
To fall upon the glowing chain
Of our existence. Can it be
That all is but a mockery!

X.

Lady, adieu! — to other climes
    I go from joy, and hope, and thee;
A weed on time's dark waters thrown,
    A wreck on life's wild-heaving sea;
I go; but oh, the past! the past!
Its spell is o'er my being cast —
And still to Love's remembered eves,
With all but hope, my spirit cleaves.

XI.

Adieu — adieu! My farewell words
    Are on my lyre, and their wild flow
Is faintly dying on the chords,
    Broken and tuneless. Be it so!
Thy name — oh it may never swell
My strain again — yet long 't will dwell
Shrined in my heart — unbreathed, unspoken —
A treasured word — a cherished token.

LITERARY NOTICES.

NEW SANCTUARY OF PROGRESSIVE THOUGHT AND SCIENCE. By a STUDENT IN REALITIES. In one volume. pp. 296. London : JOHN BROOKS, Oxford-street.

THIS remarkable volume reaches us through our London publishers, addressed to the editor, 'with the regards of the author.' Who the author is, however, is not mentioned ; but his portrait, prefixed to the work, affords us an inkling of his identity. The huge volume of forehead, the calm smile upon the lips, and the whiskers of sable silver, strike us as belonging to a sometime correspondent of this Magazine, who several years since attracted general attention to its pages, by a series of papers on 'Life,' in which he advocated the theory that caloric or electricity was the true source and principle of human existence. The general title of the volume under notice is, 'Serious Thoughts generated by perusing Lord BROUGHAM's Discourse on Natural Theology ;' but its several subsections compose separate pamphlets, containing 'Broad Hints on Education and Politics,' 'Physics vs. Metaphysics,' 'Phrenology vs. Pschychology,' the 'Identity of Intellectual Education with Progressive Civilization,' etc. To enable our readers to judge of the peculiar character of opinions said to be spreading abroad, of which something has already been heard in the deprecations of religious journals on this side the Atlantic, and which, were they to become in any wise general, could not fail to subvert the faith and influences now held sacred throughout Christendom, we proceed to set forth some of the prominent theorems of the book before us.

Human nature, the author contends, is nothing more than a sensitive substance, of the first order, so organized as to manifest a progressive developement through successive periods of time, and to admit, at all periods, of numberless modifications, through the variety of surrounding circumstances. Our physical organs, he argues, when at work, *generate thought*. The faculty of thinking is the power of producing thought ; and thought is but an elaboration of the nervous centre, the brain, just as the liver elaborates bile, and the male organs elaborate fecundity ; for these elaborations, when carried to excess, are equally detrimental to the substance that produced them. Thought and meditation fatigue and wear out the organs peculiar to their actions, just as much as any excessive muscular exertion tires and strains other glands : and here 'the spiritual,' as it is called, is identified with the material, precisely in the same manner as matter has been identified with mind. Before he can admit that the soul is *not* the result of organization, our author requires proof equal to demonstration, that the body, with all its parts, cannot of *itself* manifest the thinking phenomena. He traces the vital principle to the nervous energy, and the nervous energy to electrical action. Religions are with him systems of moral and physical science, which, under circumstances the most unfavorable to mental progress, have yet satisfied, for the time being, the organic want of mankind, to pursue and explain things unknown : in other words, the first natural cravings for *real* convictions.

What is now called *superstition*, he says, is but the religion, laws, worship, and ceremonies of our forefathers, no longer in harmony with our present better feelings; what is now called *religion*, is but the mystic laws, worship, and ceremonies *of the day*, assented to by large majorities, kept in ignorance of the natural sciences; and what is now called *infidelity* and *heresy*, is but the increasing symptoms of innovation in matters of faith, and the manifest influence of a *new mediation*, expressed as yet but by a small minority, whose feelings being changed by a progressive knowledge in harmony with mind, cannot sympathize with old and stationary dogmas of faith, but who nevertheless religiously pursue all the *real* knowledge to be attained. All these, however, it is contended, are but one and the same feeling — a natural instinctive *want;* only that it is expressed by one or the other of these words, as touching the past, the present, or the future : and the reason why this is so, is, that the progressiveness of human intellect has always had the power to modify human instincts, just as civilization has always subdued barbarism. There are no wants, no feelings, no thoughts, no actions, that are not at once, in the series of changes, the effect of former impressions, and the antecedent facts to every subsequent one. We need only ask the attention of the reader to the following extract, to insure precisely that regard for the 'great truths' of our author, which their character would seem to require :

"It is our impression, that he who devotes his life to '*seeking after God*,' as it is curiously termed, acts precisely like a madman, who supposing himself lost, would set off to look for himself, over the earth and through space : for all the while, *he is actually the self-generator of the idea which he pursues.* It is merely attempting to realize or to personify a natural feeling, which feeling or impression is nothing more than a *quality*, an *instinct*, *a product*, of some organized matter, performing certain functions according to a series of laws, constituting what is called human life : an organized sensitive substance seeking for positive science, before sufficient culture, time and observation could manifest upon earth the superior intelligence of knowledge in reality.

"We must also protest against the mystic theory of life and death. The functions of life are such in man and woman, as well as in other animals, that a certain period of time, or a too sudden modification of the substance from one state to another, (as for instance a sudden loss or gain, very bad or very good news abruptly made known,) may suspend them forever in an instant : the organized matter, or the human substance, then ceases all functions, which, according to the laws of life, had produced *sensitive intelligence, reason, thought, instinct.* Organic matter is then submitted to a series of other laws, which, while they manifest and constitute what is called *dissolution, death*, originate a fresh series of lives ; a transformation, a transmutation ; a supply to someother organizing process. Thus it is, that through chemical agency, *all is in all.*

"Intelligence to perform such natural transformations is therefore ever present in all matter, and may consequently be justly called a *quality of matter*, or one of its qualities among many others ; but because, forsooth, it escapes our notice ; because the manifestation of intelligence, or mind, soul, spirit, call it what you will, is not so evident to our senses in the act of the morbid dissolution of all organized substances as it is in the act of sensitive life ; the ignorance of former times assumed, and interested motives still perpetuate the error, that, when the faculty of assimilation ceases in any *human substance* so as to cause death, a certain spirit or soul has actually departed from it.

"It had also been invented and assumed as fact, that such spirit or soul had been blown into matter by a '*God, Creator* and *Governor*' of the universe, and assumed beside, to complete a mystic system for the credulity of ignorance, that death was caused by the said Creator actually calling back to him that spirit or soul, in order to reward or punish it, according to certain laws made by him. Why then in the name of truth and common sense, not admit the same for all other animals, plants, crystals and metals, where and within which intelligence, soul, or spirit, is manifested, though in a different and lesser degree, and with which, the power of growth and developement ceasing, decomposition or death ensues, on the very same principles ? ' The powers of the magnet,' says WHALEY, ' and other electrical phenomena, are no less wonderful to our mind than human intelligence. The action of chlorine gas upon the metals, so as to produce, spontaneously, heat and light ; the definite multiple and proportional combination of the atoms ; their powers of choosing and refusing, as if each atom could see, and select one shape of atoms in preference to another, and count the exact number with which it can unite ; are all powers, qualities, properties, no less astonishing than the actions of the beings called intelligent.''

"In the name of this advanced age, then, what useful knowledge can we derive from the ancient doctrine respecting ' soul or mind ?' Is not the very word '*doctrine*' become offensive to all rational hearers ? And beside, have WE lost all power of ratiocination ? Is there no instinct left in the organic world for us to listen to ? Can we not, on the contrary, investigate, examine, and question ourselves with far greater facilities of observation, with far more positive knowledge of man's organization, and with far greater variety of improved means to direct the sagacity of our inquiries, than could possibly have been available by any of the philosophers of antiquity ? — however worthy of our praise and admiration their ' doctrines ' may be, considering the age in which those doctrines were conceived ?''

"That those ' ancient doctrines ' and the dogmas of faith erected upon them, have done much good, no one denies ; but only as temporary and consolatory notions, well adapted in their day to ignorance. But now, that human intelligence has taught mankind how to manage and coerce the physical world ; how to direct all the elements and the inexhaustible forces of Nature ; how to make them labor FOR him, upon all the substances within his reach ; now that moral unions, guided by positive knowledge, could make of this earth a sensitive ' paradise ; ' the human species has in reality little to learn, because it has little to care about your mystifying immortality, or ' eternal bliss,' in a supposed or even in a ' real ' future state of individual existence after death.''

' Physics,' says our author, ' are preparing to throw metaphysics overboard.' It is in the earth, the waters, and the visible heavens, in the organic world, in the elements of Nature's secret powers, and above all, in the human brain, that the research which is to develope the *true soul* is to be prosecuted by our new philosophers. And when man shall have subdued, controlled, and directed the electric fluid and magnetism, as he now does fire and water, then will the power of human thought and science be understood !

La Déesse: an Elssler-atic Romance.　By the Author of 'Straws.'　pp. 44. New-York : Carvills and Company.

Mr. Field may certainly plume himself upon two admirable qualities in a good poet — variety and copiousness. Moreover, he is evidently a lover of nature, and lays its minuter beauties, ' caviare to the general,' to an appreciating, an admiring heart. Withal, he can infuse a caustic but not ill-natured satire into his verse, which is not the less effective that it is not in all cases ' open to the meanest capacity ;' yet the coat will always be found to fit those who wear it. We cannot say we greatly affect the *nucleus* which Mr. Field has chosen, around which to weave his playful and sarcastic verse, it being just now something of the tritest, considered as a theme. But this does not interfere with the *execution* of the poem, an example of which we annex ; a picture of the scene rendered immortal by ' Sam Jones, the Fisherman,' and his solemn almanac-oath :

" Convenient to a certain highland
　　Called ' Noversink,' and nigh an Island
Not very famous yet in song,
Yet famous too, and known as ' Long,'
There spreads a low enchanted bar,
　　Where pilgrim eyes delight to look,
There mermaids and a light-house are —
　　The ' Hook ! '

" The Hook ! the ocean waters bound it,
　　And ah ! 't is full of witchery,
Seen from your bark, when coming round it,
　　With moonlight on the moved sea.
It shines as every grain of sand
　　Were starry atoms sleeping there ;
　　The light-house, a huge guardian were
Of the enchanted strand !
And fairy sails are skimming by,
　　And sometimes music softly floats
Upon the air — for frequently
　　They *sing out* from the pilot boats ;
And softened by some half a mile,
　　' Sam Jones' becomes a pleasing strain ;
His ' solemn oath' begets a smile,
　　And ears are lent to list again.''

" Ah ! gaze afar, upon the deep,
　　Where sea and sky in silver meet ;
A stilly yet a radiant sleep,
　　As of reposing angels sweet !
All, all is one wide flood of light,
Or sea, or air ! the baffled sight
(And surely it may be forgiven,)
Confounds the brightened earth with heaven

" Gaze ye with a bewilder'd eye !
　　Seemeth it not a revelation

> Of that far, glorious land on high,
>   Which saints behold in meditation?
> And look! there is a something there—
> An object—is 't of earth or air?
> 'T is shining, but or bird or boat,
> Whether designed to fly or float,
> Seems just about an equal guess;
> Distant, uncertain, bright no less;
> And on it comes—what can it be?
>   As we have said, the night is calm;
> Such airs as live, come fanningly
>   From *off* the land, in sighs of balm."

Now that which our bard saw in the distance, was a veritable steamer, and in that vessel was FANNY ELSSLER, whom he accompanies to town, traces her reception, public and private, and describes the various personages who seek her favor, and sue for her attention. But are not all these things written, and well written, in the book? Verily: therefore, reader, possess yourself of the same, and as you peruse its fair and well-printed pages, thank your stars that we had not space to anticipate your enjoyment by more copious extracts.

COLLECTIONS OF THE NEW-YORK HISTORICAL SOCIETY. Second Series. pp. 485. New York: Printed for the Society.

THIS is the most important volume yet published by the New-York Historical Society, and reflects great credit on the gentleman, (GEORGE FOLSOM, Esq.,) under whose editorial care it is brought out. The papers contained in it are chiefly early accounts of the discovery and settlement of New-York. The first is Chancellor KENT's Historical Discourse; VERRAZZANO's letter to the king of France, giving an account of his voyage to America, in the year 1524, when he entered the harbors of New-York and Newport, and traced the coast upward of four hundred leagues; third, Indian tradition of the first arrival of the Dutch in Manhattan Island; fourth, LAMBRECHTSEN's History of New Netherlands; fifth, VANDER DONCK's description of New Netherlands, from the Amsterdam edition of 1656; sixth, extracts from the voyage of DE VRIES, translated from an early Dutch MS. These voyages took place between 1630 and 1640, and contain much curious matter relative to New Amsterdam; seventh, extracts from DE LAET's New World; eighth, JUET's Journal of Hudson's voyages; ninth, Captain ARGALL's Expedition to the French settlements in Acadia and Manhattan Island in 1613; tenth, DERMER's Letter, containing an account of his voyage through Long-Island Sound in 1619; eleventh, Correspondence between New Netherlands and New Plymouth, in 1627; twelfth, Charter of Liberties and other documents; thirteenth, a catalogue of the members of the Dutch Church, with the names of the streets in the city of New-York, in 1686; from the MS. of Rev. HENRY SELWYNS, with an introductory note by Doctor DELBITT; fourteenth, New Sweden, or the Swedish settlements on the Delaware, by the Rev. ISRAEL AURELIUS, translated from the Swedish; fifteenth, some accounts of the Dutch Governors, etc. etc. The illustrations are, a map of New Netherlands and a view of New Amsterdam, in 1656; a portrait of Governor STUYVESANT, and a view of Government House, New-York, 1795. From the foregoing, it will be seen that the Historical Society is awakening from the lethargy in which it has been reposing many years; and from the success which has already attended the publication of this volume, we hope it may be induced to continue its exertions, by collecting together all the valuable relations of the early history of the colonization of our great State, which are now becoming exceedingly rare. The volume is on sale at Messrs. BARTLETT AND WELFORD's, Broadway.

EDITOR'S TABLE.

PHOSPHORESCENCE OF THE OCEAN. — We are indebted to a friend who sailed from this country not long since for England — and from whom, on behalf of our readers, we hope frequently to hear during his residence in the British capital — for the following facts in relation to the causes which produce the phosphorescent light of the ocean. Numerous theories have been advanced, to account for this wonderful and beautiful phenomena ; but it has been left, if we mistake not, for our correspondent, by patient and persevering experiment, to 'pluck out the heart of the mystery,' beyond all gainsaying.

—

'ON the third or fourth day from Sandy-Hook, we found ourselves tossing about in the uncertain navigation of the Gulf Stream. Fearing to encounter the dreadful accumulations of ice and snow on the Banks of Newfoundland, the Captain had pushed on at once in a due east course, which I believe is not the usual route, and thus we were brought more speedily within the baffling influence of squalls, sunshine, calms, gales, and storms, always attendant upon the course of the stream. In one of these calms, hanging listlessly over the bulwarks of the ship, looking vacantly into the deep blue waters beneath, my attention was arrested by a number of fantastical forms, which seemed to have the power of motion like that of snakes, only slower. I inquired its name, and what they were, but in vain. At length, urged by curiosity, I seized one of the ship's buckets, fastened the end of a rope to the handle, plunged it overboard, and pulled it up full of water. I looked into it, but seeing nothing save water, I immediately threw it back. I again and again essayed, without discovering the object which I sought. I now looked over the side of the vessel, and still saw objects floating in great quantities, and every now and then sending forth a lingering flash of prismatic light, resembling an opal. By this time the water in the pail had become quiet; and on looking more intently into its very midst, I discovered the object of my search; and gently putting the hollow of my hand under one of them, I brought it out of its element; and wonderful to behold, found its lengthened form was composed of some scores of perfect living animals, each distinct in a living individuality, transparent and colorless, of the fashion and form of crystals, possessing two horns, projecting above its mouth, by which they were enabled to string themselves together, and become, to the common observer, one animal. A slight touch separated them, and a violent dashing of the water would also break the continuity. No one on board had ever observed them before. Elevating one upon the end of my finger, and placing it in relief against the bright sky, I found it to possess violent muscular motion, like the breathing of an animal after great exertion, but which I believe to be only muscular power. The annexed sketch will convey some idea of the animal in its isolated and connected state.

'The first one is of the longest size I saw. It was angular, like cut glass, and consisted of a thin jelly-like substance, which soon dissolved and ran down my finger like water, leaving behind the membraneous covering, scarcely discernible. In the centre of each was an assemblage of very thin blue veins, two or three of which radiated until lost to the eye in their minuteness.

'I now found myself animated by the spirit of a naturalist. The languor and ennui of an idle voyager left me : I was ever after looking out for new objects of interest. A few days after, when we had made some ten or twelve degrees more of east longitude, I noticed, as we swept through the water, a round jelly-like substance, of a sponge-color, floating at various depths. For one of these I fished a long time in vain; at last I induced the mate to try his luck, promising him a bottle of wine if he obtained me one. It was not long before he caught one in a pail, and emptying it with the water into a white wash-basin, I kept it for three days in my state-room, changing the water twice every day. During this time I watched and noted down its habits. As it was a very curious animal, I made two colored drawings of it, in two positions, in my sketch-book. It resembles in form a mushroom before it has reached its full growth. It is perfectly transparent, and the body part colorless; but the great number of brown specks which are sprinkled over it give it the sponge-like color, when seen at a short distance. On the under part of the rim are thirty-two points, or to express myself more properly, the periphery separates into thirty-two points, half an inch long, which contract and expand together. Inside of these are eight round pipe-like feelers, about the thickness of a fine straw, but of a bright pink color. These last have the most astonishing power of extension, reaching even to ten inches or more, and of suddenly drawing themselves within the compass of half an inch in length. They are thrown out in fine lines in every direction, in search of food; and when they seize hold of their prey, it is hurried to their common mouth, situated in the same position as the stem of the mushroom, and of about the same size. At an inch in length, it divides into four speckled brown tapering tubes, opening in their entire length, but kept closed by a membrane of the same brown color, and which is very similar to a shirt-frill. Into and within these folds the food is huddled. These four tubes and their frills serve also as a tail to steer the animal by, and are indued with great sensitiveness in every part. We here see the anomalous union of mouth and tail.

'It seems to have but two senses — feeling and taste. During the time I kept it, I fed it upon small pieces of beef and pork. In six hours a piece of beef three fourths of an inch long and one fourth of an inch thick was digested. The animal being perfectly transparent, I could plainly watch the wasting process of digestion. The pork it first swallowed, but in the course of the night it had ejected it into the membraneous folds of its tail. In the night, my state-room being perfectly dark, I touched it with my finger, *when instantly every one of the thirty-two points flashed forth a luminous phosphorescent light!* I waited a short time, when placing my hand under it, I lifted it up, and the whole mass became luminous. Letting it drop, I found that it had transmitted some to my fingers, which shone brightly for a few seconds after. I have hence inferred that the animal is endowed with this wonderful property, to terrify 'the larger fry' that would otherwise prey upon it. In this case, the light is not attended with a shock like that of the electric eel. I now regret that I did not examine the first species by night, for it is my firm belief that they have equally the power of emitting phosphorescent light. If this be true, it will account for the opal-like irradiance noticed in the day-time. I have thus satisfied myself as to the cause of the luminous appearance of the sea. It does not proceed from putrescent matter held in solution, as formerly thought, but is unquestionably derived from these and other kinds of living jelly-fish, which are found of every size, from mere animalcuæ to a foot or more in length. In fact they are a creation as multitudinous in variety as quadrupeds, birds, etc. In warm calms and other periods, they rise near the surface, when the agitation of the water causes them to flash forth their light; and when this is done in the midst of foam, every globe of air (foam being composed of air-bubbles) becomes a lens to reflect light, varying in strength according to its proximity; and thus are the millions of lenses scattering and multiplying light, until the whole whitened mass appears a sheet of fire.

'One morning, upon the striking of eight bells, or four o'clock, I got up, knowing that the crew at that hour pumped up water to wash the decks. Under the flow of water from this pump, I stretched out a cambric handkerchief, to intercept the animalculæ; and by this means I gathered in the small compass of a tumbler thousands upon thousands! One kind resembled a flea, (and was as nimble,) save that it was white and transparent, and not quite so large: it jumped, however, to as great a distance in the liquid, and with as much velocity, as do the red vermin so well known in the thinner medium of air in which they dwell.'

THE PUNSTER-KING. — Of all bores in the infinite regions of boredom, defend us from the infatuated individual who holds himself bound to nose you out a pun like a pointer-dog, in every conversation into which he may hope to obtrude his far-fetched abortions! Not that we dislike a natural pun, which springs fresh from the mind and the occasion, and is produced without effort: and precisely of this class are the puns of THOMAS HOOD, by acclamation punster-king over all realms. There is a quaintness, an oddity of humor, pervading his efforts in this kind, which have never been excelled, and seldom approached. He is equally successful in weaving these playful characteristics into prose or verse. Who can ever forget, having once read it, his brave Bow-Ben, who 'sailed with old BENBOW,' and who fought until

> —— 'a cannon-ball took off his legs,
> When he laid down his arms?''

But the valiant sailor left a name behind him, and honors were paid to his manes:

> 'His death, which happened in his berth,
> At forty odd befel;
> They went and told the sexton, and
> The sexton toll'd the bell!''

Among HOOD's recent productions is a 'Tale of a Trumpet,' which is replete with sly puns and felicitous turns of expression. It is a story of dame Eleanor Spearing, who had two flaps on her head for a pair of gold ear-rings to go through:

> 'But for any purpose of ears, in a parley,
> They *heard* no more than ears of barley.'

As 'extempore racks for an idle pen,' or ears to stick a blister behind, they were well enough; but as for hearing, they 'might as well have been buttered, done brown, and laid in a dish.' Dame Eleanor did n't know the pur of her own sleek tabby from the sound of a *boatswain's* 'cat;' and although she had a clock, she could only ' give it *credit* for ticking,' for she could not hear it. She had employed all the approved nostrums for her infirmity :

> ' Almond oil she had faithfully tried,
> And fifty infallible things beside ;
> Hot and cold, and thick and thin,
> Dabbed and dribbled, and squirted in ;'

but all to no purpose. At length a pedler comes to her door with a patent trumpet, for affording the deaf, at a trifling cost, ' the sense of hearing, and the hearing of sense.' Dame Eleanor, however, is startled at the price, which she deems ruinously dear; but the pedler makes answer :

> ' Dear ! — O dear, to call it dear !
> Why it is n't a horn you buy, but an ear :
> Only think, and you 'll find, on reflection,
> You 're bargaining, Ma'am, for the voice of affection ;
> For the language of wisdom, and virtue, and truth,
> And the sweet little innocent prattle of youth :
> Not to mention the striking of clocks,
> Cackle of hens, and crowing of cocks :
>
> And zounds ! to call such a concert dear !
> But I must n't swear, with my horn in your ear.'

The dame listens eagerly to the faithful picture which the pedler draws of her want of such an instrument, but still higgles about the price. It was ' rather more than she had expected to pay.' But the vender is inexorable :

> ' Eighteen shillings ! it 's worth the price :
> Supposing you 're delicate-minded, and rather nice
> To have the medical man of your choice,
> Instead of the one with the strongest voice ;
> Who comes and asks you how 's your liver,
> And where you ache, and where you shiver ,
> And as to your nerves, so apt to quiver,
> As if he was hailing a boat on the river !
> And then with a shout, like Pat in a riot,
> Tells you to keep yourself perfectly quiet !
>
> Or a tradesman comes, as tradesmen will,
> Short and crusty about his bill,
>   Of patience, indeed, a perfect scorner ;
> And because you are deaf, and unable to pay,
> Shouts whatever he has to say,
> In a vulgar voice that goes over the way,
>   Down the street, and round the corner ! '

> ' I warrant you often wake up in the night,
> Ready to shake to a jelly with fright,
> And up you must get to strike a light,
> And down you go, in you know not what,
> Whether the weather is chilly or not,
> (That 's the way a cold is got,)
> To see if you heard a noise or not ! '

A hint from the dame that other trumpets of equal excellence had been afforded at a more reasonable rate, is without avail; for the pedler replies :

> ' It 's not the thing for me, I know it,
> To crack my own trumpet up, and blow it;
> But it is *the best*, and time will show it.
>   There was Mrs. F.,
>   So very deaf,
> That she might have worn a percussion cap,
> And been knock'd on the head without hearing it snap :
> Well, I sold her a horn, and the very next day
> She heard from her husband at Botany Bay ! '

HOOD requires no sharpening of the ' perceptive faculties,' on the part of his readers, by means of frequently-recurring Italic characters. His equivoques are sufficiently apparent without his saying in so many words, with his inferior imitators, ' Here is the place to laugh; here we intend to be funny.'

REMEMBRANCES OF THE DEAD. — 'There are departed beings,' says an eloquent native writer, 'whom I have loved as I never again shall love in this world; that have loved me as I never again shall be loved. If such beings ever retain in their blessed spheres the attachment which they felt in this; if they take an interest in the poor concerns of transient mortality, and are permitted to hold communion with those whom they have loved on earth, I feel as if now, at this deep hour of the night, in this silence and solitude, I could receive their visitation with the most solemn but unalloyed delight.' To arrive at sensations of such 'sweet sorrow' as this, the Afflicted must be made *familiar* with his bereavement. He must first *realize* that the loss of the Departed is no dream; like the visions of the event, perchance, from which he has often awakened in the troubled watches of sleep, rejoicing with exceeding joy that they were but vapors of the night. He must walk the peopled streets, and yet *alone*, while each echo of his footstep sounds hollow from below, as from the 'narrow house' of the loved and lost. He must have associated all changes of Nature and of the Seasons with that last resting-place. *There* alone the pale moonbeams repose, like a shroud of spirit-light; there falls the soft summer rain; there will the painted leaf tremble in the autumnal wind, and rustle on the faded sward; and there, over the stark walls, in the creaking trees, and curled around the cold monumental stones, the howling storm will carve the 'frolic architecture of the snow.' The voices of the dead will ever call to him; and

> ' When the clear stars are burning high in heaven,
>   When the low night-winds kiss the flowering tree,
> And thoughts are deepening in the hush of even,
>   How soft those voices on the heart will be!'

But hear him whom we mourn, in another passage of his dying thoughts, penned but a short time before he went hence, to be here no more:

THE LOVE OF THE DEAD.

BY WILLIS GAYLORD CLARK.

NOTHING but limited and erroneous views of the life present and to come, we conceive, can prevent reflecting intelligences from taking that true observation which merges both into one. Intervals there are indeed between separation and reünion, but how brief at the longest — how checkered at the best! That is a beautiful sentiment of GOETHE, where he compares our little round of being to a summer residence at a watering place: ' When we first arrive, we form friendships with those who have already spent some time there, and must soon be gone. The loss is painful; but we connect ourselves with the second generation of visiters, with whom we spend some time, and become dearly intimate; but these also depart, and we are left alone with a third set, who arrive just as we are preparing for our departure.' In this view of human life there is nothing to displace the idea of earthly communion with those who are absent. It is a curious truth, that when two friends part, they are as it were dead to each other, until they meet again. Letters may be interchanged, but the PRESENT of the one is not the PRESENT of the other; and what gloomy events may happen between! So that in this respect to be out of sight, in the estimation of affection, is as it were to be out of the world. How little real difference then is there between absence in a world of peril or transitory continuance, and death indeed! — save only that absence is probation, and death is not. It is a trite simile, perhaps, that in this world we are like ships on the ocean, each steering alone, amid the strife of elements; and in the far forward distance shadowed before us are the dim outlines of the land of death. Some reach it soonest; but thither ALL are bound; and their state is fixed, immutable, eternal. No change comes there, to the dwellers in that Land of the Blest, with its waters of crystal, BEYOND the shadow, ' where the bright islands of refreshment lie.'

> ' No darkness there divides the sway
> 'Twixt startling dawn and dazzling day;
>   But gloriously serene
> Are the interminable plains;
> One fixed, eternal sunset reigns
>   O'er the wide, silent scene.'

These two emblems of the progress to that gate where, ere they pass, all who enter must 'pay down their symbol of mortality,' express the source and goal of life, sublunarily considered. Slowly, one after another, the race of mankind are passing away. There are sad partings and sweet remembrances. Let the first be viewed as merely separations for a season; a friendly severance of the holiest ties, in hope of quick renewal. Above all, O thou that readest, if thou art a mourner, BE FAITHFUL TO THE INJUNCTIONS OF THE DEAD! In that diversified book of SOUTHEY'S, 'The Doctor,' he describes the tranquil pleasures of a bereaved husband. They were 'to keep every thing in the same state as when the wife was living. Nothing was to be neglected that she used to do, or that she would have done. The flowers were tended as carefully as as if she were still to enjoy their fragrance and their beauty; and the birds who came in Winter for crumbs were fed as duly for her sake, as they formerly were by her hands.' This calm communion of the present and the absent becomes religion, hope, fidelity; enduring tenderness beyond the stern frigidity of time; and well may each one of that retrospective brotherhood, large always in the world, who have loved and lost the lovely, and have, with theirs, to meet the world's encounters, thus greet adoptedly the dear departed:

> 'The love where death has set his seal
> Nor age can chill, nor rival steal,
>   Nor falsehood disavow;
> And what were worse, thou canst not see
> The wrongs that fall on thine or me.'

'For me,' says the eloquent Sir THOMAS BROWNE, 'I count this world, not as an inn, but as an hospital; where our fathers find their graves in our short memories, and sadly tell us how soon we shall be buried in our survivors.' How comfortable a thing is it then to remember the dead, knowing that it is but for a season, and then union will come! Thus, with him who mourns the absence of a consort or sister,

> 'The idea of her life shall sweetly creep
> Into his study of imagination;
> And every lovely organ of her life
> Shall come apparelled in more precious habit,
> More moving delicate, and full of life,
> Than when she lived indeed.'

THE 'MAMMON OF UNRIGHTEOUSNESS.' — The subjoined advertisement, one of hundreds of a similar character addressed from time to time 'To the Clergy' of England, has been copied from the *London Times* into some of the American journals: 'An incumbent would resign directly, with patron's consent, to one not under forty-six years of age, a beautiful living, a perfect gem, one of the prettiest things in England, with excellent new free-stone front house, in good repair, facing a park, in the county of Somerset, at the skirts of a small market town, with every necessary of life cheap; productive garden, lawn, pleasure-ground, wall-fruit; six acres of pasture adjoining; coach-house, and stabling for six horses; out-houses! No trouble as to income; *duty easy*, spot healthy, roads and society good; the whole worth £280 a year. *Terms:* Incoming incumbent to pay down £1,900 to indemnify present incumbent's outlay on the spot, and for his fixtures, and his old wine, worth £180; also for live stock, including three cows, horses, and pony carriage; piano-forte, by Stoddart, cost eighty-five guineas; hand-organ, by Flight, cost thirty-eight pounds; plate and linen, and a few pictures.' A Boston journal, in allusion to this comfortable picture of ministerial 'labors,' asks this pungent question: 'Who can wonder at the total absence of religion in this benighted western region, where we have no sleek voluptuaries to teach us the way we should go, with their 'perfect gems,' 'pleasure-grounds,' 'wall-fruit,' 'easy duty,' 'old wine,' 'pony carriages,' and 'hand-organ!' But satire aside: let the reader contrast the condition of these laborers in the 'primrose-paths' of the LORD's vineyard with that of Saint PAUL, who in labors more abundant was chargeable to no man, but taught the people publicly, and from house to house, his own hands meantime 'ministering to his necessities, and to them which were with him!' It is inconceivable the harm which such announcements as the above cause to the professors of the simple religion of CHRIST and his apostles. To the many who preach or profess what they do not practice, in this regard, we commend the following anonymous passage, which we find in our note-book : ' Of all the indications of a worldly spirit, none is so distinctly and emphatically denounced in Scripture as a love of riches. Of all the 'things of life' against which the Gospel warns mankind, on account of its dangerous and demoralizing influence, none is so conspicuous as wealth. This influence is described in every variety of expression that language can supply. It is depicted by every striking representation that inspired wisdom could suggest. We are not left to deduce it from the general spirit of Scripture, nor to demonstrate it from the tenor of any particular text. It is the theme of constant, undisguised, and intelligible reprobation. It is exposed in a multitude of maxims, and illustrated by a series of parables, that defy the meanest apprehension to misinterpret, or the most crafty to pervert. Yet whom do these passages deter from the pursuit or enjoyment of wealth? Do they serve to alarm that class of christians who remonstrate with such morbid piety against popular amusements? — or to check, under a sense of spiritual danger, their desire to increase their worldly means? Do the serious deny themselves the use of riches, on account of their tendency to corrupt the human heart? We apprehend not. As far as we are enabled to discover, they testify no reluctance whatever to follow the footsteps of the ' worldly ' in the road to wealth. We look in vain for any distinguishing mark in this respect between the two classes of society — that which is ' of *the world*,' and that which is ' *not of the world*.' All appear to be actuated by the common impulse — to push their fortunes in life. All exhibit the same ardent, active, enterprising zeal in their respective pursuits. ' The mammon of unrighteousness' seems to inspire none of the serious either with terror or aversion.'

NOMENCLATURES AND SO FORTH. — DEAN SWIFT is reported to have been fond of a species of composition which consisted all of Latin words, but by allowing for false spelling, and running the words into each other, the sentences would contain good sense in English. We remember an example or two of this, in his laughable consultation of four physicians upon a lord who was dying. ' *Is his honor sic?*' one inquires : ' *Præ lætus felis pulse. It is very hei.*' Another, alarmed at the case, is wholly unable to prescribe or consult : ' *Iambicum as mutas a statu!*' he exclaims. A third cites a doubtful medical authority, and on appealing to one of his brethren, is answered : ' *Nono, Doctor, I ne ver quo te aqua casu do :*' ' I never quote a quack, as you do.' At length they all become involved in a squabble, and one wiser than the rest proposes that the disputants shall vacate the premises : ' *Lætus paco fitis time ;*' which is rather obscure Latin-English for, ' Let us pack off, it is time.' Now why would not this method serve a good purpose as a substitute for the various nomenclatures which have been handed down to our times, and which, with constant additions, must eventually result in inextricable confusion to the general reader, if not to the student? We have often amused ourselves at the solemn pomp with which some trivial matter has been mystified by means of the terms of a Latin nomenclature. A pleasant instance is now before us, in the last number of SILLIMAN's ' Journal of Science,' in the report of a Mr. DANA, who sailed in a United-States' ship-of-war in 1833, ' to make personal exploration for the Hessian Fly,' an insect so named from having been found among the straw brought by the Hessians into New Jersey during the Revolution, but *better* known, perhaps, as belonging to the genus *Lasioptera,* or *Cecidomyia,* or more specifically, the *Destructor* of SAY. Our explorer's examinations ' were rewarded with the most gratifying success; for they proved that the Hessian Fly was also an inhabitant of Europe!' He actually collected at Minorca, Toulon, and Naples, several *larvæ* and *pupæ*, from which were evolved on the 16th of March, (do n't forget the date!) 'two individuals,' which his recollections, 'aided by a drawing of the Hessian Fly, with which he was provided,' enabled him at once to 'pronounce to be the *Cecidomyia Destructor*, or if *not*, an animal very closely allied to it!' Then ensues a description of the *habits* of the real animal. It appears that he 'deposits a cylindrical translucent egg on the *ligula* of the leaf, about the fiftieth of an inch long, and four hundredths of an inch in diameter.' After a while, 'the *larvæ* assumes a brownish tinge, and its outer skin becomes the *puparium* of the *pupæ*; when the pressure of the *larvæ* and *pupæ* upon the *culm* of the wheat-plant destroys it.' To the *pupæ* the insect is traced with great distinctness; beyond that, however, 'its evolutions are wrapped in obscurity.' We are glad to find that there are *parasites* of the *Cecidomyia Destructor*, which attack its eggs and *pupæ*; and of these, we rather affect the *Ceraphon Destructor* and the *Platygastor*, with the two active fellows of the tribes of *Chalcidiæ* and *Oxyuri*. These are minute but very spirited *Hymenoptera*; and we should like to see them individually introduced *by name* to our American farmers! — for they are great friends to the crops.

Seriously, however: we wish some one of our correspondents, who has felt the ridiculousness of much of the useless display of learned *names*, in this age of ostentation, would take up this theme and discuss it thoroughly; and we should be pleased also to see another somewhat kindred subject appropriately handled; we mean that class of piddling, arithmetical bores, 'by courtesy called 'statistical Fellows,'

> 'A prying, spying, inquisitive clan,
> Who jot down the laboring class's riches,
> And after poking in pot and pan,
> And routing garments in want of stitches,
> Have ascertained that a working man
> Wears a pair and a half of average breeches!'

Men who estimate elaborately the amount of money which might be saved to the country by going without the conveniences and comforts of life, and the benefits generally which would accrue to the citizen, if he would but consent to make himself miserable.

'EVERY BODY'S BOOK, OR SOMETHING FOR ALL.' — This neat little volume, from the press of Messrs. WILEY AND PUTNAM, may be pronounced the *very* book for the season; and we predict, from its merit and cheapness, that it will soon be in the hands of hundreds of railroad and steamboat travellers, and a favorite at all watering places and scenes of fashionable resort; in short, in all places, whether in town or country, where occasional leisure may be enjoyed. The preface speaks confidently, but truly, of the character of the book:

''EVERY BODY'S BOOK?'—Yes: *Every Body's Book*; by which we mean a book that *every body* may take up, if it be for only fifteen minutes, and find in it *something* to interest and instruct—to entertain or amuse.

'Suppose you have taken your seat in a rail-road car? You are to have an easy, rolling ride, and plenty of leisure on your hands. What most do you want? Something entertaining or amusing to read; something *short*, and a good *variety*. In the book before you, you have *the very volume you need.*

'But you are in a steamboat, perhaps, and a long sail is before you? Very well: day or night, it must prove at times a little tedious, and you will need diversion. There is nothing in the way of your positive enjoyment of the various matter in this book.

'In a rail-car or steamboat, or in the parlor of an evening, this volume is capable of amusing, instructing, diverting, or entertaining *any* reader.

''Here is assurance!' (says one, possibly,) '*any* way!'

'No assurance at all, Mr. Reader. The book is the first of a series. It has been prepared with care, printed with care, and the writers for it have no superiors in the country. It is *intended* to be popular, and it *will* be, 'in spite of fate,' or opposition; and it is *cheap* enough for any body.

''Why, what are its great attractions?' some one may ask.

' *Read it, and see.* Read the delightful essay of IANTHA; the thrilling story by LEGGETT; and let your heart, if you are an AMERICAN, glow with the fires of love and patriotism over the bright picture of *Our Own Country*; then turn to the revolting scenes of cruelty in Russia; to the awful sketch of a *Battle-Field by Moonlight*; and contrast these with the simple story of *The Lamb*, the laughable scenes of *Life in New York*, and the stirring ' *Records* ' of the ' Old Man,' who writes so eloquently of ' long time ago.' Read these, and the other articles in the book, and you won't ask ' What there is *attractive* about it ? ' You will find that it is *all* attractive. READ IT, AND JUDGE. That 's the best way.'

EDITOR'S DRAWER. — We had arranged for a copious ' drawer' in the present number; but the two following papers are all for which we can find space :

THE HORSE AND HIS RIDER.

BY LAWRIE TODD.

' THE horse knoweth his owner,' and he knows much more. I verily believe he knows more than many of the two-legged animals who ride on his back; and I am quite sure there is more of the spirit of christianity in his practice, than is to be found in many of the bipeds aforesaid; for the horse, especially the carman's, rests on the Sabbath, whereas his rider often works harder for the devil on that day than he does for food to keep soul and body together on any other day in the week. Beside, the horse will caress the hand that feeds him; but thousands of his riders thank not GOD, in whom they live, and move, and have their being. To illustrate my position, let me give you a few anecdotes of this beautiful and friendly animal. Of a two-horse team, belonging to the Earl of ——, near Oxford, one was very vicious, the other quite the reverse. In the stall next to the gentle horse, stood one that was blind. In the morning, when the horses, about twenty of them, were turned out to pasture, this good-tempered creature constantly took his blind friend under his protection. When he strayed from his companions, his kind friend would run neighing after, and smell round him, and when recognized, they would walk side by side, until the blind friend was led to the best grass in the field. This horse was so exceedingly gentle that he had incurred the character of being a coward, when only himself was concerned; but if any of them made an attack upon his blind friend, he would fly to the rescue with such fury, that not a horse in the field could stand against him. This singular instance of sagacity, I had almost said of *disinterested humanity*, may well put the whole fraternity of horse-jockeys to the blush. They, to be sure, will fight for a brother jockey, whether he is right or wrong; yet they expect him to fight for *them* on the first similar occasion; but this kind-hearted animal could anticipate no such reciprocity.

Some years ago, the servant of THOMAS WALKER, of Manchester, (Eng.,) going to water the carriage-horses at a stone trough which stood at one end of the Exchange, a dog that was accustomed to lie in the stall with one of them, followed the horses as usual. On the way he was attacked by a large mastiff, and was in danger of being killed. The dog's favorite horse, seeing the critical situation of his friend, suddenly broke loose from the servant; ran to the spot where the dogs were fighting, and with a violent kick threw the mastiff from the other dog into a cooper's cellar opposite; and having thus rescued his friendly companion, returned quietly with him to drink at the fountain.

GOD, speaking to Job, asks him : ' Hast thou given the horse strength? Hast thou clothed his neck with thunder? He mocketh at fear, and is not affrighted; neither turneth he back from the sword.' Shortly after that mighty battle which closed the career of BONAPARTE, and stayed his wholesale murders, and at the disbanding of part of the British army, the remains of a troop of horse, belonging to the Scotch Grays were brought to the hammer. The captain being rich, and a man of feeling, was loth to see these noble fellows turned into butcher, baker, or beer-house drags, after helping to drive the French from Spain, and to turn the flank of the *Invincibles* at Waterloo. He therefore bought the whole lot, and set them loose in one of his fine grass parks, to wear away their old age in peace. One warm Summer evening, when it was just dark enough to render lightning visible, a vivid flash was instantly followed by a loud report of thunder. At this moment the horses were grazing leisurely, and apart from one another; but seeing the blaze, and hearing the report, they thought a battle had begun. In a minute they were in the centre of the field, all drawn up in line, their beautiful ears quivering with anxiety, like the leaf of a poplar trembling in the breeze, listening for the word of the rider to lead them to the charge. My informant, who was an eye-witness of this wonderful scene, told me he had often seen these horses. Many of them bore honorable scars on their faces, necks, and shoulders, but none on the rump. A Scotch gray never ' turns tail.'

Some few years ago, a baker in London purchased an old horse at public sale. He placed on his sides a pair of panniers, or large baskets, suspended by a strong leathern strap across the back, where he himself sat, while his feet rested on a block of wood attached to the sides. Thus accoutred, he sallied forth to supply his customers with hot rolls, etc. One day he happened to be passing the gate of Hyde-Park at the moment the trumpet was sounding for the regiment of Life-Guards to fall in. No sooner had the sound assailed the animal's ears, than he dashed like lightning through the Park, with the baker on his back, into the midst of the squadron! The poor man, confounded at being placed in military line in the front rank of the Life-Guards, began to whip, kick, spur, and swear; but all to no purpose. His old charger was so aroused at the sound of the trumpet, that to move him from his station was impossible. The soldiers were exceedingly amused at the grotesque appearance of the baker and the deportment of his steed, and were expressing their surprise at the apparition, when an old comrade recognized the animal, and informed the corps that the horse once belonged to the regiment, but had been sold, on account of some infirmity, a few years before. Several of the officers kindly greeted their old companion; and the colonel, delighted at the circumstance, gave the signal to advance in line; when the baker, finding all resistance useless, calmly resigned himself to his situation. The trumpet then sounded the charge, and the rider was instantly carried, between his two panniers, with the rapidity of the wind, to a great distance. Various evolutions were then performed, in which the animal displayed sundry equestrian feats. At length the sound of retreat was proclaimed, when off went the sagacious creature with his rider. After having performed his duty in the field, he was content to resign himself to the guidance of the bridle in a more humble walk of life.

Now, friend KNICKERBOCKER, is it not a burning shame to see how these useful animals are tortured and abused in your city, in clam, oyster, and apple-carts? — compelled to drag loads beyond their strength, while their ribs may be counted at a hundred yards distance, and their rump-bones stand up like the stone ornaments round the spire of St. Thomas' Church? Many people seem to have philanthropy, sympathy, and feeling to spare for every one — wives, children, and horses excepted.

G. T.

THE following 'straw' will show which way the wind blows with the writer. We hope that reasoning, satire, and ridicule, united, may awaken our countrymen at length to a sense of the necessity of an international copy-right law.

INTERNATIONAL COPY-RIGHT.

BY J. M. FIELD.

AUTHORS is a distressed set!
  Of singular constitution;
The everlastin' cry is but
  Of suffering, persecution!
And now another kink; ideas
  Is 'property,' it seems,
And poets' sons must fatten on
  Their sires' bequeathed dreams!

They buys a quire of paper; next
  A poem on 't they builds;
Eternal its foundation — fame
  Wall, roof, and turret gilds!
A brainy palace! life and means,
  And all derived from thence;
Curs'd if they sees 'tween it and bricks
  The slightest difference!

'Twixt brains and bricks! — they think that if
  A man leaves bricks alone,
To do, the fool! what left undone,
  Blocks of brick he might own;
They think this work well done, his wealth,
  And see in — nonsense quite —
Editions multiplied through years,
  But his rewarding 'Right!'

They think that what is called the race
  Of Nature's noblemen —
The mental lords who honors win,
  Have right to fence them then;
That as the 'rise of property'
  Oft makes grandees of sots;
Copy-rights should 'recorded' be,
  Like deeds of corner-lots.

Then for the English authors, they 've
  A mighty fellow-feeling ;
And 'cause we helps ourselves, they says,
  Confound 'em ! that it 's stealing ;
That we should apples raise ourselves,
  Be rather wise than 'cute,
And go and help to build a wall
  Around our neighbor's fruit !

They say that some of 'em have laid
  Out orchards of their own ;
But that their fruit unpurchased rots,
  Or else aside is thrown ;
As if we should be pleased to pay
  To enter their enclosures,
Rather than the *free* pippins pick
  From sunnier exposures !

Seventeen millions of us ! Tax
  Their intellectual feed?
To fat the *few* of us who write,
  Stint the vast all who read ?
What is a ' native lit'rature ! '
  We read — and books is books ;
Heaven sends the meat, let England or
  The devil send the cooks !

Author and Actor ! Here 's a case ;
  They thinks it very hard
That KNOWLES a dollar nightly here
  Can't claim as his reward ;
While stiltified MACREADY shall
  As ' *William Tell* ' delight,
'Cause acting can't be stereotyped,
  At fifty pounds per night !

Humbug ! It 's KNOWLES' misfortune — and
  The manager so saves
The trifle which at times, perhaps,
  Had saved some from sad graves.
We all *live* by misfortune, and
  All benefiting by —
MACREADY count your income — KNOWLES
  Unbenefited die !

Now these immortal ' Straws' — why we
  Just gives 'em to the wind ;
And that they fly at all, we are
  Too satisfied to find :
Contented well to lie on straw,
  As other poets do ;
And thrice content, could we but learn
  To *live* upon it too !

' LE LIS BLANC.' — The first number of a ' Monthly Journal of the Astoria Institute for the Education of Young Ladies,' thus entitled, lies before us. It is well
' edited by the Tutoress of the establishment, with the advice and assistance of the
Rector,' and is admirably executed, upon fine white paper. We do not much affect
the taste which suggested the French headings to the various departments of the
' White Lily.' It smacks slightly of the ridiculous ; but yet may possibly serve
some useful purpose which is not apparent to the uninitiated. The contents of
the publication are various and appropriate. We remark in ' *The Righteous Never
Forsaken*,' the source whence our friend and correspondent, STACY G. POTTS, Esq.,
now in the old world, derived his story of ' *The Last Herring*.' He must have
filched it from the ' *Bureau des Elèves*' of ' *Le Lis Blanc ;*' a fact which ought to be
announced in a notice of his ' Village Tales ' in the department of ' *La Bibliotheque ;*'
or dwelt upon in the inculcations of ' *Le Moniteur ;*' or preserved briefly in the
' *Calendrier de l' Ecole*.' Vive la bagatelle !

RECOLLECTIONS OF THE LATE WILLIS GAYLORD CLARK. — Interspersed among the recent passages of our note-book, are many alloquial records of 'our departed brother, taken hence by the will of GOD.' A few of these, just as they were jotted down at the time, or shortly subsequent, we propose occasionally to transfer to these pages. —

'I HAD returned from a garden near at hand, with a handful of flowers. It was a beautiful morning; so *very* beautiful, that it was difficult to realize, while enjoying it out of doors, that one who loved so well the delicious season, *could* be stretched on a bed of languishing, (from which he was never to rise alive,) on such a day. The early dew glistened in the odorous cups, as the feeble invalid took the flowers in his hand. Pointing to a bouquet which had been sent in to him the day before by a near neighbor — a lady whose kind attentions during long months of illness had been unremitting — he said: 'Bring flowers!

> 'They have tales of the joyous woods to tell;
> Of the free blue streams and the sunny sky,
> And the bright world shut from the languid eye!'

'His thoughts here naturally turned upon the kind almoner of Nature's bounties to whom he had so often been indebted; and he spoke of Woman with exalted fervor. His eulogy was essentially in terms that he had before employed, in remarking upon the same theme. It was no sudden, grateful remembrance of those

> ——'whose kindness long ago,
> And still unworn away by years,
> Had made his weary eyelids flow
> With grateful and admiring tears:'

it was an in-dwelling conviction, a heart-felt tribute to affectionate, devoted WOMAN. 'She delights,' said he, 'to minister to our comfort, to invest our path with the roses of delicate enjoyment. I love to see her by the couch of sickness; sustaining the fainting head, offering to the parched lip its cordial — to the craving palate its simple nourishment; treading with noiseless assiduity around the solemn curtains, and complying with the wish of the invalid, when he says:

> 'Let me not have this gloomy view
> About my room, about my bed;
> But blooming roses wet with dew,
> To cool my burning brow, instead:'

disposing the sunlight upon the pale forehead, bathing the hair with ointments, and letting in upon it from the summer casement the sweet breath of heaven! In her all that is sacred and lovely seems to meet, as in its natural centre. Last at the cross and earliest at the grave of the SAVIOUR, she teaches to those who have lived since his sufferings, the inestimable virtue of constant affection. And when she is wronged, she is forgiving; when destroyed, she still turns with an eye of earnest regret to that paradise of innocence from which her passions have driven her; and in solitude, by day or at evening, 'she waters her cheek in tears without measure.' —

'WILLIS awakened me at three o'clock one stormy morning toward the last of March, that I might hear the driving sleet sift against the window-shutters, and the bleak wind *sough* in the branches of the leafless trees, in an adjoining square; a scene in which, in his eyes, there was always something of the sublime. 'I've been thinking, L——,' said he, 'of an old ballad, which I want to repeat to you. I have been saving it for an *Ollapodiana*, and in the very next one I write I mean to introduce it. On such a night as this it always comes creeping into my mind. I have no idea who wrote it, nor where I got it. It has been with me from childhood, I suppose; yet until lately I hardly knew it. I could give the KNICKERBOCKER an analysis of it, and a picture of its first full impression upon my mind, which I think would be more effective than any one of OLLAPOD's subsections hitherto.' He then repeated the following:

POLYDORE.

A BALLAD.

On Rimside Moor, a tempest-cloud
　Its lonely shadows cast,
At midnight — and the desert flat
　Reëchoed to the blast:

When a poor child of guilt came there,
　With frantic step to range,
For blood was sprinkled on the garb
　He dared not stay to change.

' My God! oh, whither shall I turn!
　The horsemen press behind!
Their halloo, and their horses' tramp
　Come louder on the wind.

' Why did I seek these hated haunts,
　Long shunned so fearfully?
Was there not room on other hills
　To hide and shelter me?

' Here 's blood on every stone I meet —
　Bones in each glen so dim;
And comrade Gregory, that 's dead —
　But I 'll not think of him!

' I 'll seek that spot where I was wont
　To dwell, on a former day;
Nor terrors vain, nor scenes long past,
　Shall scare me thence away.'

Through wellknown paths, though long untrod,
　The robber took his way,
Until before his eyes the cave
　All dark and desert lay.

There he, when safe beneath its roof,
　Began to think the crowd
Had left pursuit, so wild the paths —
　The tempest was so loud.

The bolts had still retained their place —
　He barred the massy door,
And laid him down, and heard the blast
　Careering o'er the moor.

Terror and Guilt, united, strove
　To chase sweet Sleep away;
But sleep with toil prevailed at last,
　And seized him where he lay.

A knock comes thundering to the door —
　The robber's heart leaps high:
' Now open quick! Rememberest not
　Thy comrade Gregory?'

' Whoe'er thou art, with smothered voice
　Strive not to cheat mine ear;
My comrade Gregory is dead —
　His bones are hanging near.'

'Now ope thy door, nor parley more,
  For sure I 'm Gregory ;
And 't were not for the gibbet's rope,
  My voice were clear and free.

'The wind is high — the wind is loud —
  It bends the old elm tree :
The blast has tossed my bones about
  This night, most wearily.

'But come thou forth ; we 'll visit now
  The elm o' the withered rind ;
For though thy door is barred to me,
  Yet I will be more kind :

'There is my home ; the raven there
  Is all my company ;
And he and I will both rejoice
  At such a guest as thee !'

          .   .   .

Some words he muttered o'er the latch —
  They were no words of good ;
Then by the embers of the hearth
  In all his shackles stood !

A wreath of rusted iron bound
  His grim unhallowed head,
A demon's spark was in his eye —
  Its mortal light was fled.

Few words are said : he drags him forth —
  Through forest paths to the elm they wind,
Where a halter, with a ready noose,
  Hung dancing in the wind.

And straightway to that dreadful noose
  He lifts sad Polydore ;
The storm's dark thunders, breaking loose,
  Roam loud the welkin o'er.

The rope is tied ! Then from his lips
  A cry of anguish broke,
Too powerful for the bands of sleep,
  And Polydore awoke.

Now vanished all — the accursed elm,
  His dead companion gone !
With troubled joy, he finds himself
  In darkness and alone.

But still the wind, with hollow gusts,
  Fought ravening o'er the moor ;
These checked his transports, while they shook
  The barricaded door.

WE cannot describe the thrilling manner in which this fine ballad was delivered. The solemn, lonely hour ; the wind howling without, now swelling to a momentary tempest, and now dying away in fitful gusts ; the flapping of blinds near and far along the street ; the pattering of rain, hail, and sleet against the window-panes ; the invalid speaker's imagination evidently kindling as he went on, until his voice and strength were wellnigh exhausted ; all together formed a scene which we can never forget. We have done the theme but scant justice, and feel how feeble is this record compared with the masterly analysis and vivid sketch of personal impression which would have accompanied the presentation of the poem by the lamented 'OLLAPOD.'

GOSSIP WITH READERS AND CORRESPONDENTS. — The leading paper in the present number will startle many of our readers. The facts which it discloses, on what seems to us unimpeachable authority, can scarcely fail to effect a great change in public opinion, touching the exploits and military renown of Gen. PUTNAM. 'Where ignorance is bliss, 't is folly to be wise,' however; and we have made up our mind still to place implicit belief in the *wolf story*. Its incidents were drilled into our memory in early school exercises, and we cannot 'bate a jot of our boyish credulity. For the rest, the facts must make their own comment. We begin to see now why it was that WASHINGTON, in one of his letters to Gen. GATES, soliciting him to take command of the forces for the defence and security of the Highland posts, after mentioning several officers, said 'he need not name Gen. PUTNAM.', The State of New-York, he added, 'disliked him, and had no confidence in him.' Two or three errors in this article escaped the vigilance of the proof-reader. Page 100, fifth line from the bottom, read 'engineer' after 'chief;' page 102, eighth line from the bottom, for 'over' read 'to cover;' and for 'Wilkins' read 'Wilkinson,' on page 105, toward the top. . . . *Apropos* to this: A Buffalo journal, the name of which our 'exscissorized' slip does not enable us to mention, has taken our correspondent 'FLANEUR' to task for his lack of *amor patriæ*, in not lauding more vehemently the military deeds of our forefathers. In reply to the remark of our correspondent, that 'they were valiant men no doubt,' that 'they did well, but could not have been *men*, and done otherwise,' the editor observes:

"'Valiant men no doubt!' 'What did they more than other brave men fighting for their country!' Are these the words of an American? We will answer what they did. Unarmed, undisciplined, unpaid, unclothed, unfed, they beat the best troops in the world, with the best appointments in the world; troops who endeavored, when arms did not avail them, to *bribe* the poor soldier of freedom, but were foiled too, in that. Show us one instance where the ancients fought under such circumstances, with such determination, with such unshaken valor, through such a period of suffering, or against such apparently hopeless odds. Did not all Europe consider the struggle preposterous? How many nations at that time would have advanced money in abundance, had they entertained a hope that the country would have become independent, that the legions of England would have been foiled! America has the military glory of unsullied arms, of unsullied humanity; of having worn freedom without excess, even though her opponents were guilty of constant barbarities, of repeated excesses, and of disgraceful cruelty. Look too at the difference. The English were fighting under officers of recognized authority; men of education: they had no wants unprovided for, no hardships to endure, save those that must always follow the soldier. No fears of a halter if they were beaten; no fears of ill treatment if they were made captives. The Americans were fighting under governments that were but half formed, and half recognized. Their officers were taken from the forest and the furrow: difficulty and distress were their companions, and yet they did not give way to despair. Your Roman might have died upon his sword, and there an end; but the American lived to see his oppressor driven from the land; his bright arms stained with blood, with cruelty, with injustice; and the American saw the oppressor depart from his shores without insult or excess.

Fitly spoken, Sir Journalist, and like a true American: yet the writer whom you condemn loves our common country as well as yourself; nor would he pluck a leaf from her well-earned bays. . . . '*The Rich and Poor of America*,' a well-written paper, comes, we cannot doubt, from one who really desires what he professes to hope for, 'with all the ardor of one who has himself suffered the pangs of poverty,' the 'amelioration of the condition of the poorer classes in our country, and especially our cities.' With due deference, however, to the benevolent promptings of our correspondent's heart, he hopes for too much, in his prospective picture. 'The poor ye have with you always,' said the SAVIOUR; and every age has verified the inspired truth:

'When God built up the dome of blue,
And portioned earth's prolific floor,
The measure of his wisdom drew
A line between the rich and poor;
And till that vault of glory fall,
Or beauteous earth be scarred with flame,
Or saving love be all in all,
That rule of life will rest the same.

'We know not why, we know not how,
Mankind are framed for weal or woe;
But to th' Eternal law we bow —
If such things are, they must be so.
Yet let no cloudy dreams destroy
One truth outshining bright and clear,
That wealth is only hope and joy,
And poverty but pain and fear.

'Behold our children, as they play;
Blest creatures, fresh from Nature's hand,
The peasant boy as great and gay
As the young heir to gold and land:
Their various toys of equal worth,
Their little needs of equal care;
And balls of marble, huts of earth,
All homes alike endeared and fair.

'They know no better! Would that we
Could keep our knowledge safe from worse!
So power should find and leave us free,
So pride be but its owner's curse;
So without marking which was which,
Our hearts would tell by instinct sure,
What paupers are th' ambitious rich!
How wealthy the contented poor!'

Should we, on a more careful examination, decline the article in question, it will be left to the writer's address at the publication office within the time specified. . . . GARRICK'S '*Beauties of the Modern Drama*' we should hope to find a place for, but for the formidable chirography of the writer. We have encountered some 'cramped pieces of penmanship' in our day, but never before saw any MS. which so completely realized the old idea of a spider escaping from a bath in an inkstand, and trailing his saturated legs over a sheet of paper. The writing master who should exhibit the characters in contrast with a decently legible script, as a specimen of 'improvement in *sixty* lessons,' would be set down as a charlatan at once. We have gathered, however, from the communication, (though that, under the circumstances, is scarcely an appropriate term,) that the writer is justly severe upon the *horse-drama*, with which some of our theatres have frequently regaled the public, and especially upon the ' taste which can crowd a house nightly, to witness the contemptible exhibition of a man playing the part of a *baboon* and a *blue-bottle fly!*' He seems to think that such things are not done elsewhere, but he is in error. BUNN, the well-known London manager, speaking lately of a poorly-written horse-spectacle, observed that the scenic pageant was very effective. ' It would save any play,' said he. ' Egad, I do n't believe but what it would *make Shakspeare go down!*' But all this is nothing new. In the days of ADDISON, animals divided the honors with, if they did not bear away the palm from, the biped histrions, insomuch that it became necessary for rival establishments who had not the real ' lions,' to *make* them, out of such materials as they possessed. A sketch of two of these manufactured actors is amusing enough. The first lion, at one play-house, was a candle-snuffer, who, being a choleric fellow, overdid his part, and would n't suffer himself to be killed without too violent a tussle for his life : beside, he grew more surly every time he came out of the lion, being vexed that he had not fought his best, and that he had suffered himself to be thrown on his back in the scuffle ; and hinting significantly that he would fight his antagonist, *out of* his lion's skin, for what he pleased. He was considered a dangerous animal, and was discharged, on the plea that he reared himself so high upon his hinder paws, and walked in so erect a posture, that he looked more like an old man than a lion. The second lion was a tailor by trade, who belonged to the theatre, and was a mild and peaceable man in his profession. He was too sheepish altogether. After a short, modest walk upon the stage, he would fall at the first touch of his two-legged adversary, without grappling him, and enabling him to make his melo-dramatic points. This lion was in the practice also of giving him a rip in his flesh-colored ' tights,' to make work for himself in his private capacity of tailor ; and these defects, we are told, occasioned his dismissal. . . . ' Mr. AUGUSTUS MINNS's' flattering paper on ' *The True Gentleman*,' we *incline* to print, but for obvious reasons must omit. He says he saw in our ' Table,' in an old number of the KNICKERBOCKER at Saratoga Springs, ' some very beautiful comments ' upon his theme ; and he considers himself a living example of their truth. He tells us that his friends give him credit for something altogether beyond the tailor's art ; and he contrasts the successful attraction of his manner with that of another ' gentleman ' from town, whom he describes as being externally quite the thing. ' JONES,' says he, ' accomplished his coat, and it is really a love of a garment ; CHASTELLEUX, bre-vet d' invention of the square-toed Paris boot, is his *cordonnier ;* SPENCER achieved his glossy chapeau ; his teeth are white, and his hands, without speckle or freck, are the miracles of WRIGHT's French Medicated Soap. In fact,' he adds, ' till you had heard him speak, or saw him move, you would really take him for a gentleman-like man of the world — you would indeed ; but his manner is *so* quick, he gives way to his feelings *so* readily, and praises matters which please him, with *such* ardor, that one sees at once he is really rather *gauche ;* that he has never travelled, nor acquired the *nil admirari* mode, so characteristic, indeed so distinctive, of our circles.' . . . The admirable *Poem* by GEO. D. PREN-TICE, Esq., in preceding pages, is placed in type from his MS. found among the papers of one whom he loved while living, and whose death he has feelingly lamented. It was sent to the late WILLIS GAYLORD CLARK, to be forwarded for publication in an English annual ; but it must either have come too late for that purpose, or have been accidentally mislaid among a miscellaneous collection of man-uscripts. . . . With due deference to ' P. G.' and his ' *Remonstrance*,' we must say he is altogether in errors. A mob may *think* right, perhaps, but it always *acts* wrong ; and that great referee, the Public, is not always open to the *right* ' appeal.' What Lady MORGAN or her husband says about that many headed monster, is ' pretty much so.' It is, forsooth, a humane public, a charitable public, a *discriminating* public, (Heaven bless the mark !) Yet the word is but the representative of a congre-gation including all the fools and knaves of the community ; a large dilution of the few persons whose opinions a man of sense would take on the boiling of a potato. . . . ' *Boarding Houses*,' by a ' Bach-elor,' is something too long for our pages. Beside, ' is there no offence ? '— nothing personal ? ' Some of his ' benevolent annoyances ' are not unlike those recorded of STEELE, when he first went up to London to reside. He was forced to quit his first lodgings by reason of an officious landlady, who would be asking him every morning how he had slept. He then fell into an honest family, and lived very happily for above a week ; when his landlord, who was a jolly, good-natured fellow, took it into his head that he wanted company, and would therefore frequently come into his chamber to keep him from being alone. This the victim bore for two or three days ; but the intruder telling him one morn-ing that ' he was afraid he was *melancholy*,' he thought it was high time for him to be gone, and at once took new lodgings. About a week afterward, he found that his jolly landlord, who was an honest, hearty man, had put him into an advertisement in the daily papers, something in this wise : ' Whereas a melancholy man left his lodgings on Thursday last, in the afternoon, and was afterward seen going towards Islington, if any one can give notice of him to E. B., fishmonger, in the Strand, he shall be well rewarded for his pains !' . . . ' *Salamandrines in Alexandrines*' dragged their slow length along too tardily for insertion in the present number ; and it will be quite too cool for them in September. . . . Our contributors must exercise *the* cardinal virtue — ~~patience~~. Several favors, recently at hand, shall have early attention.

LITERARY RECORD, ETC.

'The Northern Light' is the title of a monthly journal recently commenced at Albany, which promises to become a valuable addition to our periodical literature. It is neatly printed, in the convenient and tasteful form of the ' *Quarto New World*,' upon fine paper, and its internal excellence is not less creditable to its proprietors and editors than its external appearance. We remark among its contributors many writers whose names are a guaranty for the quality of their communications; including Mr. John A. Dix, Prof. Alonzo Potter, Edwin Croswell, Esq., Willis Gaylord, Esq., James Taylor, and our own esteemed correspondent, Alfred B. Street, Esq. 'A Forest Nook,' by the last-named gentleman, is one of those beautiful pictures of still-life, for which the writer is so remarkable. For example: after a minute transfer to paper of the various trees which compose the ' nook,' we have the following exquisite daguerreotype view of the interior:

'The scorching glare
Without, makes this green nest a grateful haunt
For Summer's radiant things: The butterfly,
Fluttering within and resting on some flower,
Fans his rich velvet form: the toiling bee
Shoots by, with sounding hum and mist-like wings:
The robin perches on the bending spray
With shrill quick chirp; and like a flake of fire
The red-bird seeks the shelter of the leaves.
And now and then a flutter overhead
In the thick green betrays some wandering wing
Coming and going, yet concealed from sight.
A shrill loud outcry — on yon highest bough
Sits the gray squirrel, in his burlesque wrath
Stamping and chattering fiercely: now he drops
A hoarded nut, then at my smiling gaze
Buries himself within the foliage.
The insect-tribes are here: the ant toils on
With his grain-burden; in his netted web
Gray glistening o'er the bush, the spider lurks,
A close-crouched ball, out darting as a hum
Tells his trapped prey, and looping quick his threads,
Chains into helplessness the buzzing wings.
The wood-tick taps his tiny muffled drum
To the shrill cricket fife, and swelling loud,
The grasshopper his grating bugle winds.
Those breaths of Nature, the light fluttering airs,
Like gentle respirations, come and go,
Lift on its crimson stem the maple leaf,
Displaying its white lining underneath,
And sprinkle from the tree-tops golden rain
Of sunshine on the velvet sward below.'

'The Gordon Miscellany,' a sheet of 'Miscellaneous Poems by Alanson Wilkins,' which has been sent us by the writer from Dartmouth College, is unworthy to contribute a feather's weight to the mail-bag of 'Uncle Samuel.' Had the young man no friends to dissuade him from deliberately printing mere *rhymes* like these? — *bad* rhymes, moreover, at the best — in which ambitious dulness seems struggling to rise to mediocrity, but never reaches it? A favorable specimen of the writer's poetical powers, re-punctuated, ensues. It is a part of the long lament of a damsel that her lover does n't come, as he said he would:

'Ah! whither, whither does he roam,
  Away from me, away from home!
What makes my Edward linger so?
  'T is strange; I 'm sure I do not know.

'That he should soon return, he said,
  And yet three long, *long* days have fled;
Ah! me, what can the matter be?
  'T is strange; I 'm sure I do not see.

'If he but knew my bosom's woe,
  Would he stay longer? — oh! no, no:
My fearful heart begins to burn;
  'T is strange that he does not return.

'I 've decked our lovely garden bower
  With many a gay and tinted flower:
Come, Edward, come, this seat to share!
  'T is strange; where can he be? — oh! where?''

It is a rich example of the small burlesque, to hear such a poetaster as this prate of ' *criticism*,' with as much self-complacency as if his ' writings' were not out of soundings beneath it.

'LIFE AND TIMES OF RED-JACKET.'— A delay somewhat beyond the first of the month, (which, we may add, will not occur again,) enables us to announce the publication, by WILEY AND PUTNAM, of one of the most beautiful volumes we remember ever to have seen from the American press; the 'Life and Times of RED-JACKET, or SA-GO-YE-WAT-HA; a Sequel to the History of the Six Nations. By WILLIAM L. STONE.' The volume is as full and as perfect as the materials which the author could collect would allow. It is the first complete record of the forensic efforts of the great orator of the Six Nations. Neither diligence nor expense has been spared to make the collection perfect of all the chieftain's speeches and notes of speeches, that have been preserved; the whole arranged according to the dates of their delivery, and in connexion with the history of the occasions and the events which called them forth. It is, in short, a very entertaining book, as we shall aim to show more at large hereafter. It is illustrated with a superb engraving by DANFORTH of WEIR's celebrated painting of the illustrious chief, a view of his residence, and an admirable engraved title page, which reflects scarcely less credit upon the artist, than does the beautiful typographical execution upon the care and skill of Mr. OSBORN.

THE REVIEWS.— We have the NEW-YORK and NORTH-AMERICAN Reviews for the July quarter; but our examination of their contents has been less thorough than we could have wished. One of the most useful articles in our own Quarterly, is that upon PLITTS' Report on the Post Office. We commend it to our readers, in the absence of ability to transfer extracts to our pages, as replete with important views and suggestions by one who comprehends and clearly treats his subject. There is a just and excoriating review of 'Ten Thousand a Year,' an excellent article on our Navy, and another upon Texas, with notices of current works. The only papers in the 'North-American' which we have found leisure to peruse, are the review of MACKENZIE's Life of PERRY, the works of GEORGE SAND, ARMSTRONG's 'Notices of the Last War,' and ROBERTSON's 'Travels in Palestine and Arabia.' All these are interesting papers; and even were the others of a different character, which we are not prepared to say, they would amply redeem the Number from any suspicion of dulness. We trust both these Reviews are well sustained, for each is an honor to the country.

THE 'AMERICAN REPERTORY.'— We have heretofore adverted in terms of praise to this useful and well-conducted Magazine; and each succeeding number has served to confirm our first favorable impressions. Beside being beautifully printed, it is all that it claims to be in the more essential qualities of internal excellence. Its editor, JAMES J. MAPES, Esq., is a Professor of Chemistry and Natural Philosophy in the National Academy of Design; Honorary Member of the Scientific Institute of Brussells, of the Royal Society of St. Petersburgh, and of the Geographical Society of Paris; Member of the Lyceum of Natural History of New-York: Honorary Member of the National Academy; and Corresponding Secretary of the Mechanics' Institute: and his journal is a repository of arts and manufactures; embracing records of American and other patent inventions; accounts of manufactures, arts; observations on natural history and mechanical science; philosophical and literary essays; and a summary of public documents connected with these subjects. It contains also the transactions of the Mechanics' Institute of the city of New-York; the General Society of Mechanics and Tradesmen; Lyceum of Natural History of the city of New-York; National Academy of Design; the Jersey-City Lyceum; and many other scientific institutions.

'THE NEW-YORKER.' — We have spoken so often of the merits of this excellent weekly news and literary journal, that we could only repeat our high opinion of its plan and general execution, were we to devote a half page to the purpose. Its judicious literary selections; its well-digested political, foreign, and domestic intelligence; and withal, its neat and tasteful appearance and convenient form, make it among the best of our popular weekly journals. It is to be regretted, perhaps, that Mr. GREELEY's devotion to his widely-circulated daily, ' *The Tribune,*' leaves him but little leisure to supply the original literary department, which is evidently committed to a less healthful and discriminating taste, and to a more ambitious but less practised and influential pen. Yet there are even here perceptible industry, and a commendable desire to succeed, which must needs accomplish their end, in the end.

'THE MUSICAL CABINET.'—We argue well for the progress which the science of music is making in this country, from the increase of sterling periodicals devoted to this delightful art, the only one which has nothing sensual about it. The ' Musical Cabinet,' edited by Messrs. WEBB and HAYWARD, and published by Messrs. BRADBURY AND SODEN, Boston, the first number of which is before us, is a very superior publication of this class. Its externals of printing and embellishments are in admirable taste ; and its design — which is ' to send forth monthly a choice collection of music, sacred, secular, vocal, and instrumental, together with useful and instructive articles of musical literature, the whole to be derived from the best sources ' — if carried out in the spirit of the opening number, will leave nothing to be desired in a periodical of its character. Mr. VAILL, No. 91, Nassau street, is the New-York agent.

ARISTOPHANES. — Prof. FELTON, of Harvard University, has just given to the public ARISTOPHANES' comedy of ' *The Clouds,*' one of the most interesting remains of the theatrical literature of Athens. ' Though, like every other comedy,' says the Professor, ' its wit turns upon local and temporary relations, yet it has what is not common to every other comedy, a moral import, of permanent value.' Such a work, from the pen of a man of the most profound acquaintance with the political institutions of his age, possessing an extraordinary creative genius, and altogether the master-mind of the Attic drama, cannot fail to have an influence in promoting the study of the literature of Greece among us; to which end, let us add, the copious notes of the American editor will in no small degree contribute. Cambridge : JOHN OWEN.

SERMONS BY REV. JOHN M. KREBBS. — We are indebted to the author for copies of two sermons, one entitled ' The Leader Fallen,' delivered on the occasion of the death of the late President, and the other ' Merciful Rebukes,' a discourse on the late national Fast. Of both these sermons we had previously heard good report from a friend who had the pleasure to hear them delivered at the Presbyterian church in Rutgers-street, and a perusal has more than confirmed our anticipations of their character. The writer has used ' all plainness of speech ' in setting forth the evils of party spirit, and the consequences of sin in a nation ; while his discourse upon the death of Gen. HARRISON is among the very best to which that melancholy dispensation of Providence has given rise. Messrs. HARPER AND BROTHERS, and Mr. JONATHAN LEAVITT, are the publishers.

TURNER's ' COMPANION TO THE BOOK OF GENESIS.' — This work is intended as a companion to the first part of the Pentateuch. It is designed to accompany the inspired record as a servant and attendant, and not to lessen its importance, or supersede its use. Both the analysis and notes of the author illustrate the book of Genesis by a constant reference to the original text, to other portions of Scripture, and to the best sources and aids of interpretation. Satisfied that an affectation of knowledge only displays ignorance, and that an attempt to shroud in mystery what is clear, or to explain what is to us intelligible, necessarily tends either to superstition or infidelity, Mr. TURNER has wisely left the data which he adduces to establish the true and necessary sense, without obtruding his mere opinions upon the reader. Messrs. WILEY AND PUTNAM are the publishers of this excellent and useful volume.

TASTE AND MORALS. — We have but space to thank a correspondent for a copy of a neat pamphlet, containing two lectures on the ' Connexion between Taste and Morals,' by MARK HOPKINS, D. D., President of Williams College, (Mass.) The writer attempts to prove that the prevalence of a cultivated taste is favorable to morals, and that there is an intimate connexion, both in individuals and communities, between good taste and good morals. The positions of the lecturer are sustained with signal ability, and in a style so attractive, and with examples so apposite, that it may well be believed the author's pen and life naturally illustrate the truth of both branches of his essay. We have laid these lectures by for future reference, should our limits admit.

THE ' LADY'S BOOK.' — This Philadelphia monthly is decidedly the first of its class in this country, whether we regard its numerous superb engravings, or the quality, extent, and variety of its literary attractions. We know of no publisher in the country who more faithfully and promptly discharges his whole duty to his readers, than Mr. GODEY. We observe, among recent accessions to his unequalled list of distinguished lady-contributors, the names of Miss MITFORD, Hon. Mrs. NORTON, and Mrs. S. C. HALL, all secured by Mrs. SIGOURNEY, as regular correspondents, in her recent travels abroad. We need not invoke continued success for a publication so effectively sustained as the Philadelphia ' Lady's Book.'

CATLIN'S INDIAN GALLERY. — Our town readers are not unacquainted with the character and extent of CATLIN's Indian Gallery, now exhibiting at the Egyptian Hall, London. He proposes to publish, in two royal octavo volumes, a work entitled ' The Manners, Customs, and Condition of the North-American Indians,' with four hundred illustrations, etched and outlined from his original paintings. This will be truly a superb work. It will be issued in England under the distinguished patronage of Her Majesty, QUEEN VICTORIA, PRINCE ALBERT, the Queen Dowager, the Duchess of Kent, and many of the English nobility, who are subscribers to the work. It will be ready for delivery in New-York on or before the first of August, by Messrs. WILEY AND PUTNAM, where subscriptions may be registered.

COMMON SCHOOLS OF CONNECTICUT. — If our readers in different quarters of the Union desire to note the influence and count the value of general education, we would refer them to the recent Report of the Secretary of the Connecticut Board of Commissioners of Common Schools, HENRY BARNARD, Jr., Esq., a clear and well-written pamphlet lying before us, and which we cannot but hope may be widely circulated, in parts at least, throughout the country. The plans for the improvement and better organization of common schools, and for the erection and furnishing of school-houses, might be emulated with advantage by every State in the republic.

PHYSIOLOGY AND ANIMAL MECHANISM. — This is the first of a series of First Books on Natural History, published under the direction of the 'Royal Council of Public Instruction of France,' and written by men eminent in science, and which have acquired great popularity abroad, hundreds of thousands having already been sold. Should the present volume be favorably received, others of the series, upon zoology, ornithology, botany, geology, etc., will follow. The translator is Dr. RUSCHENBERGER, author of 'Three Years in the Pacific,' and other works. TURNER AND FISHER, Philadelphia.'

PUBLIC GALLERY OF THE FINE ARTS. — We are well pleased to learn that active exertions are making in this city to establish a Gallery for the exhibition of the best paintings and statuary which can be obtained, and which is to be open at all times to the public, free of expense, after the manner of the Louvre at Paris, and similar collections in other cities of the Continent. We hope the plan, with the details of which we are not familiar, may be carried into successful operation.

NEW MUSIC. — We are indebted to Mr. ATWILL, of Broadway, near Fulton-street, for three new and very handsomely executed pieces of music, 'The Gambler's Wife,' the words by Dr. COATES, the music rendered memorable by RUSSELL; 'Old King Time,' the music by the same; and 'Will Nobody Marry Me?' the words by GEORGE P. MORRIS, Esq., and the music also by Mr. RUSSELL. We see, in such embellished and clearly printed music-sheets as these, what great improvements have been effected in this species of engraving.

MR. HAVELL'S COLORED VIEWS. — We have heretofore adverted, in terms of cordial praise, to Mr. HAVELL's colored engraving of New York. We are glad to perceive that it has been followed by two others, in the fine 'Series of Views of the Cities of America,' Boston, and Hartford, (Conn.) Both are excellent engravings, and faithful representations of their originals. The coloring is well managed. The left of the last-named print, especially, has a Claude-like richness and mellowness of hue, altogether unusual in kindred specimens of the art.

'VOICES OF THE NIGHT.' — Not a word need be added to the eminently *practical* fact, that the tasteful and beautiful volume before us, from the press of Mr. JOHN OWEN, of Cambridge, (Mass.,) is a copy from the *fifth edition* of LONGFELLOW's 'Voices of the Night.' A sale so extensive, in the short space of six months, literally 'speaks volumes' in praise of one of the most thoughtful and gifted poets and accomplished scholars of our day. Messrs. APPLETON AND COMPANY are the New-York publishers.

ROOSEVELT'S 'SCIENCE OF GOVERNMENT.' — 'The Science of Government, founded on Natural Law,' a small volume by CLINTON ROOSEVELT, Esq., is a work, to settle the great principles of which, and to give them form and substance, has 'cost the author the best ten years of his life.' Of such a book we would not speak without first giving its arguments and deductions the most thorough examination. As yet, however, we have not even found leisure to award it a hasty perusal. It is accompanied by two maps, intended to illustrate the writer's theory.

WRITINGS OF THE LATE WILLIS G. CLARK. — Choice selections from the prose and poetical writings of the late WILLIS G. CLARK, including the 'Ollapodiana,' with all his best printed and several original poems, as well as prose sketches, are in preparation for the press. The work will be accompanied by a memoir and portrait. It will be issued by the BROTHERS HARPER.

THE KNICKERBOCKER.

| Vol. XVIII. | SEPTEMBER, 1841. | No. 3. |

POPULAR MISNOMERS.

GRAVE AND LUDICROUS ERRORS PERPETUATED IN WEBSTER'S DICTIONARY.

A CANDID CRITICISM.

BEFORE proceeding with the remarks which I propose to make on NOAH WEBSTER's definitions of sundry words, I would observe that his dictionary, in my opinion, is superior to any other English dictionary that has fallen under my observation. Perhaps no other lexicographer ever paid equal attention to a work of the kind, or was better qualified for the task. He has spent the greater portion of a long life in scholastic pursuits ; in writing school-books, in which he has made great improvements on the works of others of a kindred class ; in making himself master of the languages from which the English is derived, and by that means acquiring an accurate understanding of it. And he has produced a work that does honor to literature and to his country. It has been re-published in England, and adopted by some of the universities of that country as a standard work.

It is probable that Webster's Dictionary is a greater improvement on Johnson's than that of the latter on Bayley's. Bayley, by the way, was a man of consummate learning. The authorities adduced by Johnson in support of his definitions, and which are generally supposed to have been searched out by him, were chiefly prepared to his hand by Bayley, and published in the folio edition of his dictionary. Johnson would not have undertaken that drudgery. Although there might have been an apology for this display of learning when Bayley published, as the language was not then perhaps permanently fixed, there could be little need of its continuance by his successor. What is wanted in a dictionary is only the established meanings of words, without regard to the authors who first made use of them in the sense given.

It is evident that Dr. Johnson could have paid but little attention to the compilation of his dictionary. 'From 1747 to 1755,' says Davenport, in his ' Dictionary of Biography,' ' he was engaged in his English Dictionary. In the interval, however, he gave to the world the ' Vanity of Human Wishes,' ' The Rambler,' and the tragedy of ' Irene.' These labors, however, were more productive of fame than of profit.

He was still obliged to toil to provide for the passing day, and thus necessity called into existence the ' Idler,' ' Rasselas,' and various productions of less consequence. At length, in 1762, a pension of three hundred pounds was granted to him by the Crown.'

When the avocations of the doctor at the time he was concocting his dictionary are taken into consideration, it is clear he could not devote much labor to that work. Indeed, he seems to despise the occupation, for he defines a lexicographer : ' A writer of dictionaries ; a harmless drudge, that busies himself in tracing the original, and detailing the signification of words :' saying in effect that the employment was beneath the attention of the ' leviathan of literature,' Dr. Johnson. This from almost any other man would be pronounced pedantic affectation. At any rate, the light manner in which he treats the subject is *prima facia* evidence that he would not pay that assiduous attention to it which its importance required.

Although a person may not be qualified to take a full view of the whole ground of a survey, he may be so well acquainted with its minute parts as to point out defects. ' *Humanum est errare ;* ' and it would be strange that no error should occur in the formation of a dictionary, particularly of a language deriving its origin from so many sources as that of the English.

After these introductory observations, as an apology for my undertaking, I proceed to examine the etymologies and definition of certain words, as given by Mr. Webster.

' YANKEE. — A corrupt pronunciation of the word *English*, by the native Indians of America. HECKWELDER : edition of 1839.' It was suggested to Mr Webster that the vast difference in the sounds of the words Yankee and English rendered it morally impossible that the former could be a corrupt pronunciation of the latter ; and the obvious origin of the word was pointed out to him. In his last edition, (1841,) he adds to the foregoing, ' or more probably of the French word Anglois ;' retaining the obsolete spelling of the word, which renders it to an American ear nearly as foreign to the sound of Yankee as the word English. In fact, he leaves the origin of the word involved in darkness and uncertainty. The *oi*, in the above and the like words, is said to have been changed, by Voltaire, into *ai*. The origin of the term evidently arose thus : The Canadian French of course called the first settlers of New England *L' Anglais*, ' the English,' pronounced *Angla*, which with the Indians might easily slide into Yanka, or Yankee ; the French sounding *e* as we do *a*. The authority adduced by Webster, Mr. Heckwelder, was a missionary among the American Indians, who appear to have given *him* substantially the true origin of the word Yankee ; but by a misunderstanding in one of the reporters, Webster or Heckwelder, the word *English* has been substituted for *Anglais*.

' CAUCUS. — A word used in America to denote a meeting of citizens to agree upon candidates to be proposed for election to office, or to concert measures for supporting a party. The origin of the term is not ascertained.' This word, as used in New-York, and probably in most places in the Union, denotes a meeting of a few influential men of a party, to concert measures to be acted upon at a general meeting ; but in Boston, where the term originated, I am informed that it signifies a general meeting of a party. Daniel Webster, in an address reported as delivered by him at a public meeting, noticed sundry measures which he said had been acted upon ' at a previous *caucus*,' evidently meaning at a meeting similar to that then held. This distinction is somewhat important in relation to the origin of the word, which arose as follows :

On the 2d of March, 1770, a quarrel took place at the premises of John Gray, a rope-maker, between a soldier and a man in the employ of Gray, and the former was severely beaten. He soon returned, accompanied by some of his comrades. An affray ensued between the soldiers and the rope-makers, in which the latter were overpowered. The people became greatly exasperated, and opportunities were sought for retaliation; and on the fifth of the same month, in a similar affray, the soldiers fired upon the people of the town, three of whom were killed, and five wounded. The anniversary of this tragical event, usually called the ' Boston Massacre,' was kept for a long time afterward with great solemnity.

These occurrences induced the rope-makers and caulkers, whose occupations brought them in contact, to form a society, which doubtless was joined by those of other trades. At the meetings of this society, patriotic and inflammatory addresses were delivered, and the most violent resolutions passed against the British government and its agents and instruments in America. The tories, in derision, denominated these assemblies of the members of this society, *caulker*-meetings; and the word in time became corrupted to *caucus*, which, as before observed, is the term still used in Boston to denote a general meeting of a party.

This fact, although not generally known, has been handed down in oral tradition by many inhabitants of Boston, as I was assured by the late John Ferguson, formerly surveyor of the port of New-York, who obtained the information of the Rev. Dr. Freeman, the first Unitarian clergyman of the town of Boston. The adoption by the people of Boston of the term caulker, or caucus, to designate their public meetings, which was intended as a slur by the tories, is similar to what happened afterward in France, where the republicans assumed the name of *Sansculottes*, given them by their enemies in contempt.

It has required considerable circumlocution to explain fully the subject in question; but as caucus, as well as Yankee, is a term peculiar to America, it appeared to me especially important to ascertain its origin beyond controversy.

DEMOCRACY : REPUBLIC. — These words are in constant requisition in the United States; they are as familiar as household gods; and here at least ought to be well understood. But if their interpretations by Drs. Johnson and Webster be correct, that is far from being the case. Bayley defines democracy thus : ' *Demos*, the people, and *crateo*, to exercise power : *Greek*. A form of government where the supreme or legislative power is lodged in the common people, *or persons chosen out from them.*' This it seems was the understanding of the word in Bayley's time ; and it is believed that it has been constantly used in the same sense ever since the fall of the small democracies or republics of

Greece, where all the people assembled together to make their laws. But Dr. Johnson will not allow the people to entertain a democracy, except upon the old Grecian plan, which in the present state of civilized nations he knew to be impracticable. He defines the word : ' Sovereign power lodged in the *collective* body of the people.' That is, ' gathered into one mass.' His definition of republic is : ' Commonwealth ; state in which the power *is lodged in more than one*. Common interest ; the public.' According to this definition, all the governments of Europe are republics, with the exception of the autocracy of Russia, where the power resides in a single individual.

This in fact is perhaps as much as can fairly be made of the term republic, in reference to its original acceptation, and the practice under it, by the Romans, from whom it is derived. It bears no intrinsic meaning in regard to the form of government, signifying simply *public affairs*, without designating the agents for their management. It has however a conventional meaning, equivalent to that of democracy ; that is, according to Bayley's definition of the latter.

Dr. Webster agrees with Dr. Johnson in respect to democracy, but differs from him in regard to republic. He defines these words as follows : ' DEMOCRACY. — Government by the people ; a form of government in which the supreme power is lodged in the hands of the people *collectively*, or in which the people exercise the powers of legislation. Such was the government of Athens.' ' REPUBLIC. — *Res* and *publica ;* public affairs ; a commonwealth ; a state in which the exercise of the sovereign power is lodged in representatives elected by the people. In modern usage it differs from a democracy or democratic state, in which the people exercise the powers of sovereignty *in person*. Yet the democracies of Greece are often called republics.'

Where does Dr. Webster find the ' modern usage ' to justify the distinction he makes ? Wherever the power of legislation rests with the body of the people, whether they choose to assemble in mass to make laws, or to appoint agents, as in the United States, to act in behalf of the whole, the government is to all intents and purposes a democracy, a government of the people. The power of delegation covers the whole ground ; and no lexicographer, whatever objections he may have to the term democracy, can change its established and inherent signification.

Since writing the above, I have examined a London copy of Dr. Johnson's Dictionary, published in 1799, said to be the eleventh edition, ' revised and corrected.' In this, the editor, in the definition of democracy, has very judiciously rejected the word ' collective,' thereby rendering the congregating of the people in mass for the purpose of legislation a non-essential attribute of democracy. This omission was made after the death of the author, which occurred in 1784. In some of the American editions of the work I observe the word is retained, and in others omitted, depending doubtless on the editions from which the copies are taken. Among the former, I notice the Philadelphia edition of Todd's Johnson.

The London editor of course disagrees with Dr. Webster as to the ' modern usage,' in relation to the acceptation of the words democracy and republic. And that Dr. Webster's opinion on the subject is contrary to the general acceptation of the term democracy in America, is evident from the contest now carried on between the two political parties into which the country is divided, each claiming the honor of possessing a superior right to the appellation of democrats.

'SANSCULOTTES. — *French:* without breeches; 'ragged fellows.'' Words often differ materially, in their practical application, from the original meaning of the constituent parts of which they are compounded. This word was coined in the time of the French revolution, and applied by the royalists, in contempt, to those who rose against oppression in vindication of their rights; as the Americans had done before, and whose example they followed. The men whom this term was intended to stigmatize immediately adopted the title, and every friend of freedom was denominated a *Sansculotte.* LAFAYETTE, CONDORCET, BRISSOT, were Sansculottes. Nothing was more common in the addresses of the revolutionary party than the following: 'It is expected that every *good Sansculotte* will perform his duty to his country and the sacred cause of liberty.' These calls were made to all the friends of the revolution indiscriminately; and surely they were not all 'ragged fellows!' So popular was the name, that when the government changed the calendar, dividing the year into twelve equal months, the five intercalary days remaining were called '*Sans Culottides,*' and were consecrated; the first to the 'Festival of Genius,' the second to that of 'Labor,' the third to that of 'Deeds,' the fourth to that of 'Rewards,' and the fifth to that of 'Opinion.'

That the meaning of words depends upon the uses to which they are applied, and not always in conformity to their derivations, may be seen by the following examples: WHIG literally signifies *whey,* or *butter-milk;* and it became the name of a party, according to Bayley, in the following singular manner: 'It was first applied to those in Scotland who held their meetings in the fields, their common food being sour milk; a nickname given to those who were against the court interest in the times of King Charles and James II., and to such as were for it in the succeeding reigns.' So of 'Locofoco,' a name given to a political party in the United States, which bears no kind of relation to the professions and principles of those it designates; like that of *Sansculottes,* which, as we have seen, in the time of the French revolution indicated the republican party. The word has become obsolete in France, and it is hardly worth while to revive it, or any of its class, in America.

'SANSCULOTTISM. — A ragged state of men.' *Without-breechesism* would probably be the best English translation of this word, if it were French; but it probably can be found in no other dictionary extant, of any language. If any English writer has introduced the term, he probably intended it to have a political bearing, and not to be understood in the sense here given. Be that as it may, Dr. Webster's dictionary would meet with no great loss if this and the preceding word were 'expunged.'

As the following remarks on the English language, by Sir JAMES MACKINTOSH in his History of England, are not irrelevant to the subject in hand, I will close this article with them: 'From the Anglo-Saxons we derive our language; of which the structure and a majority of its words, much greater than those who have not thought on the subject would at first easily believe, are Saxon. In seventy-nine words of Addison, whose perfect taste preserved him from a pedantic or constrained preference for any portion of our language, we find only fifteen Latin. In later times the language has rebelled against the bad taste of those otherwise vigorous writers, who instead of ennobling their style, like Milton, by the position and combination of words, have tried to raise it by unusual and far-fetched expressions. Dr. Johnson himself, from whose corruptions English style is only now recovering, in eighty-seven words of his fine parallel between Dryden and Pope, has found means to introduce no more than twenty-one of Latin derivation. In all cases where we have preserved a family of words, the superior significancy of a Saxon over a Latin term is most remarkable. ' Well-being arises from well-doing,' is a Saxon phrase, which may be thus rendered into the Latin part of the language : ' Felicity attends virtue ;' but how inferior in force is the latter ! In the Saxon phrase, the parts or roots of words, being significant in our language, and familiar to our eyes and ears, throw their whole meaning into the compounds and derivations ; while the Latin words of the same import, having their roots and elements in a foreign language, carry only a cold and conventional signification to an English ear.'

THE PRAIRIE LAKE.

' With the sunbeams dancing upon its fair bosom, it glittered in the border of the prairie like a pure gem upon the forehead of beauty.'

NOTES OF A TRAVELLER.

I.

Thou 'glorious mirror !' on whose shore
Silence for centuries hath slept,
Save when the rolling thunder's roar
Over thy peaceful bosom swept ;
Or broken by the war-whoop shrill,
Or Indian maiden's song, or plaintive whip-poor-will.

II.

Can thy clear waters mirror back
No trace of ages buried there ?
Left ancient centuries no track
Upon thy sands, to tell us where
Their first lone visits dawned on thee,
Or last they fled thy shores, back to eternity ?

III.

Ah, no ! — thou *need'st* no record keep
To tell the world what thou hast been ;
For ever in thy calm, sweet sleep,
Thou wert what even now thou art seen :
A beauty, blessed with changeless youth,
A mirror of the skies — a lovely type of Truth.

E. H. B.

THE VOICE OF OCEAN.

'THE SOUND OF MANY WATERS.'

THE voice of OCEAN sounding o'er
The face of level wastes; or backward flung
From rocks precipitous, lone, rugged, wild;
Or rolling up the far-receding slopes
Of mountains; or making cities tremble,
My bosom fills with pleasurable awe!
It is a voice peculiar, having type
In nothing shadowing its solemn depth,
Low underneath factitious gravity
Of venerable instruments, that swell
In hoary minsters; type in nothing meet,
Of its complaining sweetness, gentle crash
Of tones harmonious in dissonance,
Which entering in the soul, engender there
A melancholy musing, prone to tears.

All sounds of nature, or of earth or sky,
To men familiar, are to me not strange;
The hum of busy marts; the measured tread,
The acclamations, and the sullen roar
Of multitudes; the booming of fall-blasts
Through naked forests, and the grave rebound
Of thunder on the hills, when summer-storms
In clouded majesty through ether move,
To minister rebuke to thoughtless men;
Explosions, too, from mouth of cannon, charged
With artful combination, fraught with fire:
And not oblivious of a wondrous thing,
The rush of frantic waters to the verge
Of dizzy height, and plunge in yawning gulf,
Which shuddering received them to its depths!

All these and similar as oft as heard,
To mute attention fixed, have won my ear:
With sweeter melody of purling streams;
Of winds in dalliance with vernal leaves,
Or sobbing o'er their vernal beauty fled;
Of tribes vociferous in tiny song
Emerging scarce from silence; and of copse
With warbled bliss vibrating, when the morn,
With blushes mantled, entered at the east:
But still, in all this audible report
Of sound magnificent, sonorous, soft,
From choral minstrelsy, I have not heard
Expressive symbol of that peerless voice!
It hath a soul, a fulness, power replete
With tenderness, that fills, but never sates
The hungry, earnest auditory sense.

Full oft I've sallied forth, when moonlight pale
A silver tissue lay, spread o'er the world:
When tacit stars looked out intelligent
From heavenly windows, listening each
To mortal thoughts, and seating me alone,
In spot secluded and yet elevate,
Drank in the music of the heaving flood —
The diapason of the mighty Deep!

THE QUOD CORRESPONDENCE.

NUMBER FOUR.

WHAT a dreary thing it is, Mr. EDITOR, to walk through the crowded street, and see smiles wreathing around bright faces, when they meet faces as bright as themselves; glad eyes lighting up at the sight of those whom they love; friend meeting friend, taking him by the hand, with kind wishes and inquiries; and then to look in upon your own lonely heart, and feel that none of these are for you. It has made *my* heart ache many a day. None in that crowd knew, as I lingered near them, how much a single word of kindness would have cheered the threadbare old man at their elbow; and that I was loitering there only to hear a tone from the heart, although addressed to a stranger. But that is past; and although at the commencement of my 'Correspondence' my friends were limited to a small boy, and a dog of no great respectability, and my acquaintances to a testy gentleman with thin legs and green spectacles, and a woman who sells vegetables near me, yet I have suddenly grown into importance. I am looked up to by the neighbors as a great historian. The fame of my house is noised abroad. I see strange people stopping in front of it, eyeing it mysteriously; and a small man, with a ragged coat and a dirty face, sat the whole of yesterday on the curb-stone opposite, making a sketch of it.

I have also received several written inquiries respecting my habits and history; and my correspondence has so much increased, that the postman claims me as an acquaintance, nods familiarly when we meet, and sometimes holds up a letter half a block off. There is something exceedingly pleasant and cheering in the expressions of good-will which run through the most of these letters. I make it a rule, as far as I can, to answer them punctually; but the following having been sent without an address, before continuing my tale I trust that you will insert them with my reply.

'OH! MY DEAR MR. QUOD!

'Do n't be frightened, though I am. You 've mortally offended our lodger, Mr. Hotchkins, the gentleman in a snuff-colored suit, whose epitaph you refused. He vows he 'll be the death of you. He 's bought a bundle of quills, a bottle of ink, and a whole ream of paper — but no pistol; and he swears he 'll review you. I do n't know what that means, but I suspect it 's some kind of murder; and Mr. Hotchkins is a dreadful man. All the children are afraid of him, and he *does* hate cats so! Ever since that piece of yours came out in print, he looks so very dreadful, that whenever the door of his room unlocks, I run up in my own, and shut myself in, until I hear him go out of the street door. And I dare n't ask him for his board; and he owes me for two weeks, making four dollars; and for washing an odd stocking, a cotton handkerchief, and one shirt — one shilling; which is very cheap. And if you 'd like it, Mr. Quod, I 'll do all your washing on the same terms; and if you ever think of changing your lodgings, I 've a nice little room which will just suit you; and a dog, just like the one you have; and he sha' n't trouble you at meal times; and your boy may come to see you whenever you like — I 'm *so* fond of children! I would n't dare to write this letter if Mr. Hotchkins had n't gone out, for fear he 'd find it out; he 's so knowing, and I 'm so dreadful afraid of him. If I was in your place, I 'd go straight to the police office and swear the peace ag'in him: that would bring him to his senses, if any thing would. Do n't neglect my warning, and believe me,

'Yours lovingly, ELIZA SMITH.

'P. S. I do n't know the number of your house, and if you 'll give it to me, I 'll send Polly to bring your dirty clothes to the wash once a week. Mending is extra.   E. S.'

The next letter is from a gentleman who appears to belong to that respectable fraternity ycleped 'the fancy:'

'Mr. JOHN QUOD, ESQ.: DEAR SIR:

'Just inform me, will you, where that fellow Rawley lives. I know that dog of his 'n, that Wommut. He 's my dog Slaughter, and that fellow must have stole him, and changed his name. There 's no mistake about it: there never was another so like Slaughter as that Wommut, except Slaughter's own self; and if ever I lay my eyes on him, (Rawley, I mean,) I 'll set my ten commandments on that red nose of his 'n, which you say *smells* at the necks of decanters, though I think it *drinks* at 'em too! (Pretty good, is n't it?)

'That Slaughter is come of a first-rate stock. He 's out of Sleeping Beauty, and his sire was the celebrated bull-dog Murder, who was game to the very teeth — to the teeth, Sir; and you 'll believe it, when I tell you how he died. They set him at a bull, and he took him just by the nose, and there he hung. No let go to *him!* They pounded and beat him, but 't wan't no use: so at last those infatuated individuals determined to sacrifice that promising dog, merely for obeying the impulses of his natur'. First, they chopped off his tail, then his legs, then his body: but his head hung on until they forced open his jaws: but will you believe it, Sir? — there was so much game in that animal, that his very *teeth* would n't give up; and when the head fell off, all them grinders remained sticking in the bull's nose: 's a fact! — and they was obliged to send for a celebrated dentist, and have 'em all extracted, at a dollar a tooth. So you see, Mr. Quod, what a famous stock he 's from: and if you 'll only tell me where that Rawley is, you 'll eternally oblige me; and I 'll thrash Rawley, and send you a pup of the same breed.   'Yours to the very marrow, ISAAC SNAGG.'

In reply to the letter of Mr. Snagg, I can only say that I cannot now inform him where Mr. Rawley resides. The events narrated in that number of the 'Correspondence' took place several years since. Mr. Rawley has moved away, and Wommut, who was then well stricken in years, is probably gathered to his fathers.

From the bottom of my heart I thank Mrs. Smith for the friendly caution against the machinations of her bloody-minded lodger. She may depend on it I will keep an eye on him, and in pursuance of her advice will consult my friend with green spectacles and thin legs, who being, as I have mentioned before, a frequenter of the police office, is conversant with such matters, and no doubt can give me many salutary hints on the subject. As regards the latter part of Mrs. Smith's letter, I would mention, that my washing is under the superintendence of an elderly colored lady, from whom I am reluctant to take it at present: nor have I any intention of changing my quarters; but should I do so, Mrs. Smith may be assured that I will not forget the kindly feelings which dictated her letter; and if Mr. Hotchkins were out of the way, that I could no where feel happier than under the roof of one who, with the characteristic benevolence of her sex, has extended her arm to shelter from injury a stranger who had no other claim upon her than that given by age and sorrow.   JOHN QUOD.

The Attorney.

CHAPTER V.

FOR more than an hour after the departure of his wife, Wilkins sat listening to every footstep that passed, in the expectation that she would return; but by degrees the tread of the passers-by grew less and less frequent, and presently the deep solemn tones of a neighboring church, tolling the hour of midnight, came sounding in the stillness of the night like a knell. Wilkins sat still in his chair and counted the strokes. 'One, two, three, four — five, six, seven, eight — nine, ten, eleven, twelve! — midnight!' said he, drawing a long breath, and looking stealthily around the room, 'and not home yet!' He went to the window and raising the paper curtain looked out in the street. The night, which was clear at first, had become damp and misty, and the pavement was covered with a slimy mud. No one was stirring. The shops were all shut, and the street was pitchy dark, except in the immediate vicinity of a lamp, which diffused a sickly yellow light. He turned from the window, and going to the bed, threw himself upon it, and endeavored to sleep; but the last look of his wife haunted him. He thought of *her*, wandering alone, helpless and unprotected, through the dark streets; he thought of her first greeting that evening; of the kind and ever bright heart which had cheered him in the early days of his marriage, when his prospects were better, and had clung to him the more closely as they darkened. When he closed his eyes, the lids seemed to scorch his eye-balls; and after tossing about for hours, he sprang up with a deep curse. He now walked rapidly up and down the room, in the vain hope of ridding himself of the fever of his own thoughts. He attempted to strike up a jovial song; but the sound of his own voice startled him into silence. Now the idea occurred to him that it must be near morning, and he went to the window and looked toward the east, in hopes of seeing the daylight glimmering in the sky : but all was dark.   He listened for the striking of the clock. Never did time move so sluggishly ; but at length it came : 'One, two, three — three o'clock !   Three good hours to daylight !   I can't sleep !' he muttered, looking at the bed : 'no, d—n it !   I 'll not lie there and be haunted by her : *Her !*   I wonder where she is ?   Where ! — what do I care ?   Have I not got what I wanted ?   Has n't she, of her own free will, deserted me ?   Ha ! ha ! ha ! I 'm in luck !   How light my heart feels at its riddance !'

He paused, for he knew that he lied.   He felt that he was a villain. He took up the light, went to a small glass, and perused his face to see if it were not branded there.   He gazed and gazed, until he fancied that he could trace the impress of every evil passion, stamped as with a fiery seal, in characters which none could mistake.   In a savage humor with himself and all the world, he clenched his teeth, and muttered : 'Well, it is written there ; my every look says it ; and by G—d I 'll not belie my own face !   And now,' said he, tossing himself on the bed, 'I 'll try to sleep once more.'

This time he was more successful, for soon his deep, heavy breathing, and his motionless position, showed that his feverish frame for a time at least was at rest.

The repose of the guilty is ever broken ; and when the glad light of morning stole in his chamber, Wilkins rose unrefreshed.   His eyes were bloodshot, his mouth parched, and his head throbbed violently. He stood for a while staring about the room, before he could collect himself sufficiently to recall what had happened ; then dragging a chair to the black chimney-place, he seated himself with his elbows resting on his knees, his head between his hands, and twisting his fingers in his matted hair.   He sat thus, neither moving nor speaking, until aroused by a knock at the door.   'Come in !' said he, without altering his position.   The door opened gently, and but partially.   'Come in, I say !' repeated he, looking over his shoulder ; 'no one will bite you.'

The person thus addressed opened the door widely, walked in, stared around inquiringly, then stopped short, and looked at Wilkins as if to seek an explanation.

'You see, Higgs, *she's off !*' said Wilkins, in reply to the look ; 'cleared out last night.   I expected it long ago.'

'Humph !' replied Higgs, clearing his throat, and remaining exactly in the same position ; 'I expected it myself.   I thought you 'd drive her to it at last.   Women ar' n't iron, nor brutes.'

'I know *all* women are not,' replied Wilkins, averting his face with a feeling of shame which he could not shake off ; 'but *some* are.'

'And so are some *men*,' replied Higgs, with the same imperturbable composure.

'Holla, there !' exclaimed Wilkins, turning his chair about so that he faced his friend, and sitting bolt upright, while he stared with all his eyes ; 'what 's in the wind now ?   Was it a sermon you were writing last night, and have you come here to preach it ?'

'George,' said Higgs with some solemnity, 'I have not pressed a bed since the night before last ; nor, excepting a hard apple, have I tasted any thing but water since then. Under this accumulation of evils, I feel moral.'

'The devil you do!' said Wilkins, rising and going to the cupboard, from which he drew a bottle and a tin cup, and handed them to Higgs; 'then the sooner you get rid of your morality the better. Drink deep,' said he; 'it will clear your ideas.'

'I think so myself,' replied Higgs, tossing off about a gill of pure brandy, and again pouring into the cup the same quantity, which he disposed of with equal alacrity. 'That will do for the present,' said he, returning the bottle to Wilkins, and carefully wiping his mouth with the back of his hand.

Wilkins took it, poured out some of the liquor, drank it off at a swallow, replaced the bottle and cup, and motioned Higgs to draw a chair to the table.

For some moments these two worthies sat face to face, on opposite sides of the table, each intently scrutinizing the countenance of the other.

'Well,' said Higgs, wearied with this long examination of lineaments which, to confess the truth, were not the most prepossessing in the world, and whose natural deficiences were not at all diminished by the lack of a very recent application of either water or a razor; 'I'm a beauty, aint I?'

'What did you mean by your speech to me, when you came in?' demanded Wilkins distrustfully, without heeding the remark, and without moving his eyes from the face of his visiter.

'I meant poverty and thirst!' replied Higgs, leaning back in his chair, and returning, without quailing, the stern inquiring glance of his comrade.

'And you will abide by the agreement of last night?' demanded Wilkins, without any abatement of the harshness of his voice.

'That's what I came for,' replied Higgs, quietly.

'You'll give every aid you can?'

'I will.'

'And will never blab?'

'No.'

'Higgs,' said Wilkins, 'I have known you many a long year, and I believe you; but remember this: if we succeed, you shall have your pay in full — down to the very cent; but your mouth must be as close as the grave; for if you let out on us, there will be one man murdered whose name I could mention.'

'Well, I'll agree to it. And now about Lucy — your wife.'

'You'll swear strong *there?*' said Wilkins, mastering an evident disinclination to speak of her. 'Last night's freak, cunningly worked up, will tell strongly against her. If that fails, you must not want other evidence. When we have once commenced, we must not be foiled.'

'Trust to me,' replied Higgs, with a look of wonderful self-complacency. 'If swearing will carry the matter, you may consider it settled. I feel a strong personal interest in the affair.'

'Ah! ha!' said Wilkins, assuming a jocular tone; 'the thousand touches you nearly.'

'No,' returned his companion, with a sentimental shake of the head, at the same time pulling up his stock ; ' it 's not that. The cash is not amiss ; but *all* my feelings are not mercenary.'

Wilkins was touched at the disinterested feeling of his comrade, and extending his hand to him said : ' I was wrong, Bill, to doubt you ; you *are* a good fellow — you are a *friend.*'

' So I am,' returned the other ; ' but it was n't *that* that I meant.'

' Well then,' said Wilkins, with some abatement in the fervor of his gratitude, ' what *did* you mean ?

' Why,' replied his friend, ' I have been thinking that when you had obtained this divorce, and you and Lucy were cut adrift, that *I* would marry Lucy myself. I always had a liking for that woman.'

Had a bullet pierced Wilkins to the heart, the pang could not have been greater. His arms fell powerless. Every fibre of his sinewy frame relaxed ; his face grew wan and ghastly ; and he sank back in his chair as if smitten with death ; his jaw hanging down, and his eyes staring with a hideous glare upon Higgs.

' God ! George! what 's the matter ? ' exclaimed that gentleman, springing up, and instinctively rushing to the cupboard for the liquor ; ' here, swallow this,' said he, extending a cup-full ; ' here, it will do you good. What ails you ? '

' Nothing, nothing, ' returned Wilkins, putting aside the cup ; ' 't is past now. I have these turns sometimes. But Higgs, I think you had better not marry Lucy. You do n't know her : you 'll repent it.'

' I 'll risk it,' replied the other, replacing the bottle. ' As soon as the divorce is granted, I 'll make the attempt.'

Again Wilkins felt that sensation of deadly sickness ; but he bore up against it.

' I 'm not too well-to-do in the world at present,' continued Higgs ; ' but when I 've touched the thousand you promised, we 'll go to the country, and be quite snug and comfortable.'

Never, since the early days of their marriage, had the love of Lucy appeared so enviable as when he heard the coarse-minded man at his side speaking of her as his own. ' A thousand ! ' If he but had it, he would give up the widow, *all*, to have *her* with him ; to see her happy face looking up in his, and to know that there was one who would cling to him to the last. In the midst of these thoughts, the recollection of the preceding night came gloomily over him. Fearful, however, of exhibiting his emotions, he turned to Higgs, and said with a sneer : ' Well, success to your suit ! I wish you joy of your wife with a tainted fame.'

' But wo' n't I know how little she deserves it ? ' exclaimed Higgs, with more animation than was usual in him ; ' wo' n't *I* know that her like does n't live, and that all attacks upon her are false ? I ought to ! '

Wilkins felt that he was caught in his own snare. Now was the time for his fate to be decided ; to go on, or to stop at the threshold of crime. For a moment, he hesitated. The struggle was short, but it was fearful. The decision was made, and by it he marked out for himself a course of crime and misery that, had he known its full bitterness, would have sickened his very soul. He was in no mood to continue his conference; and making a plea of not feeling well, he proposed that they should walk out, and defer the discussion of their plans to some more convenient occasion.

'Just as you like,' replied Mr. Higgs, making the only change that his means afforded him, preparatory to going into the cold air, by buttoning the lower buttons of his coat, and thrusting his hands in his breeches pockets.

Wilkins dragged rather than put on his shaggy over-coat, and shutting the door after them, and depositing the key in his pocket, the two sallied out into the street.

CHAPTER VI.

In a by-street which staggered to its destination with all the devious windings of a drunken man, was a small eating-shop, down six steps in a cellar, and with glass doors shaded by scanty curtains of red moreen. From time immemorial it had been an eating-house, and had been distinguished by a sign over the entrance, representing an elderly gentleman with a large stomach, a fat face, and a fiery nose, who was seated at a table, griping in his hand a fork stuck to the handle in a sirloin of beef, and looking venomously at a lean little fellow with mazarine blue eyes and dimity small-clothes, who occupied a small corner of the same picture. The old gentleman was typical of the larder below, and was meant to be illustrative of the state to which hard eating and hard drinking, backed by a good digestion, would bring a man; but if he was intended as a bait for the passers-by, he was certainly a most untempting one; for a more uncomfortable, ill-looking, irascible, red-nosed old gentleman one would scarcely wish to see. The thin man was a pale, half-starved devil, with a hungry eye, who looked as if he had sucked his last meal out of the spout of a bellows, and was none the better for it. The whole picture was a fable, and the small eating-house below, with its six steps and red curtains was the moral to it.

But Time had had a word to say in the matter. The sign-board had hung there year in and year out. The school boys who had pelted it with stones and snow-balls had grown into men, and others had taken their places; but there the old sign still hung. Its typical character, however, was changed; for although the old gentleman retained his rotundity of abdomen, he had acquired a thread-bare look; his face had subsided into a pale, unhealthy brick color; his eyes were fixed intently on nothing, which he seemed to see at the far end of the street; and as the penalty of his former high living, he appeared to be going off in a severe dropsy. As for the pale man, he had gradually withdrawn himself from the public gaze; and a pair of sickly blue eyes, looking mournfully out of the sign-board, alone told where he once had been.

Whatever may have taken place in the sign-board, the small eating-house still held its ground. It was none of your new-fangled establishments which aspire to French cookery and clean table-covers. It was a solemn place; dark, damp and smoky, with dingy table-cloths, broken castors, and the regular number of dead flies reposing at the bottom of the oil-cruet.

In the middle of the room was a small stove, near which a sleepy bar-keeper dozed in his chair, and between his naps kept watch with a restless, uneasy glance over one customer, who sat at a small table, with his hat on, his coat buttoned up to the chin, and his legs resting on a chair. There was something in the calm composure of the man not to be mistaken. It was Mr. Higgs. He had long since finished his meal, as an empty dish and plate testified, and was deeply immersed in a newspaper. Occasionally he raised to his lips a small mug which had contained beer, but which had been empty more than an hour; and then plunged into the paper more deeply than ever. At every rustle of the paper the bar-keeper opened his eyes heavily, concentrated them with a dull leaden stare on Mr. Higgs; wondered what there could be in that paper to take up so much of his attention; why he did not pay for his dinner and go; and then, in the midst of these reflections, nodded off into another slumber. Still Mr. Higgs read on, up one column and down another; he turned the paper over and over, and over again. It grew dusky, then dark. He ordered the candles which stood in the bar to be lighted, and slowly and deliberately read on. Every thing, editorial, statistical, geographical; shipwrecks, accidents, melancholies; horribles, outrages, marriages and deaths; and then with a coolness that was perfectly astounding, he commenced upon the advertisements. Three mortal hours had he been there! The bar-keeper stood bolt upright and walked three times across the room, coughed violently, and poked the fire. The fire was getting low, which made the dozing uncomfortable; so he went for wood. No sooner was he out of the room than Mr. Higgs rose, sauntered leisurely to the door, sprang up the steps, and scampered off at full speed; fogetting in his hurry to pay his little bill. He darted up one street, down another, across a third, around corners, and altogether showed a knowledge of blind alleys and dark passages that was perfectly wonderful, until he turned into a wide street, at some distance from where he started. Here he subdued his pace to a rapid walk.

He had agreed to meet Wilkins at a particular hour, and as it was near the time, he made directly for the place where he expected to find him. It was a cold, damp night: the sky was filled with murky clouds, drifting across the black heavens like an army of spectres hurrying forward on some ill-omened errand. The streets were wet and sloppy; the shop windows covered with a dense moisture, which trickled down them like tears; and the lamps inside emitted a glimmering light, just enough to show how dismal the streets were, without cheering them.

Higgs, however, wended his way, impenetrable to cold and damp. He met a few people muffled to the throat, with their heads bent down, to keep the mist out of their faces. In one street he passed a shivering woman, crouching in a dark door-way, and in another an old shed, under which a beggar-boy was sleeping soundly on the damp ground, with a rough, wiry dog keeping watch at his side. He did not stop until he came in front of a small house, in a dark cross-street, with a lamp before it, on which was written in red letters, 'QUAGLEY'S RETREAT.' Without knocking, he opened the door, and found himself in a room brilliantly lighted with gas, and having a billiard-table in the centre of it. One or two rough-looking men were lolling on wooden settees: two others were engaged in playing at the table; and a stunted boy, with a square mouth, officiated as marker, and kept the score of the game. In one corner Mr. Quagley was reposing on a wooden bench, laboring to get through a profound slumber into which he had been forced by the united efforts of six tumblers of water, liberally diluted with gin, and casually imbibed by him in the course of the last hour.

Higgs paused as he entered, took off his hat and knocked it against the wall, to shake off the moisture; unbuttoned his coat, and taking it by the collar, shook it violently, stamped on the floor as if he intended to kick a hole through it, then replaced his hat, buttoned his coat, seated himself on a bench near the table, and looked at the stunted marker, who returned his stare without flinching. Higgs nodded to the stunted marker, and the stunted marker nodded back again.

'Holla!' said Higgs, addressing him.

'Holla yerself!' replied the boy, without moving.

'Hav n't you got legs?' demanded Mr. Higgs.

'Yes, I have,' said the boy, looking complacently down at two slim supporters, which were comforting themselves with the mistaken idea that they filled a large pair of inexpressibles.

'Well, cant you use them?' demanded Mr. Higgs.

'Yes, I can,' said the lad, without stirring, except to count up the scores of the two players.

'Well, why do n't you?'

'I are a-usin' 'em,' said he, straightening himself up, to show fully what a weight those two slim legs were supporting.

'You *are* a nice boy,' said Higgs, looking at him with a very supercilious eye.

'I know I are,' replied the boy, returning his stare with interest.

'Of course you are. Who's your mother?'

'Who's your 'n?' said the stunted marker, giving his square mouth an agonized twist, by which he was in the habit of deceiving himself into the belief that he was laughing, and concluding the performance by thrusting his tongue in his cheek, pulling down the corner of his eye, applying the end of his thumb to the tip of his nose, and at the same time indulging the rest of his fingers in a few aërial gyrations. Having got through these and several other lucid gesticulations, by which small boys are in the habit of testifying their sense of keen enjoyment, he settled down into a subdued gravity, and went on scoring the game as if nothing had happened.

'Now that you 've got through that pleasant performance,' said Mr. Higgs, 'perhaps you can answer a plain question.'

'Perhaps I can,' said the boy, standing bolt upright, and shouldering his stick.

'Has Wilkins been here to-night?'

'No he has n't,' he replied; 'nor I do n't care if he do n't come,' he added gratuitously, 'that 's more.' As he said this, he instantly set about repeating the performance which he had just concluded, with corrections and emendations.

'Holla there!' shouted Mr. Quagley, awakening in the midst of the exhibition, and rising from his recumbent position and looking full at the boy, who became grave instantly. 'A cussed nice sort of baby you are; a sweet 'un! 'Tend to what you've got to do, will you? None of them shines here — mind that. They wo'n't go down.' And Mr. Quagley shook his head at the boy, in a manner which intimated that if what he had said did not operate, he might be induced to administer a more powerful medicine, that would.

As he spoke, Mr. Quagley rose, and still keeping an eye on the stunted marker, and giving his head one or two additional shakes, partly to settle his brains in their right place, and partly to let the boy know that he was in earnest, walked across the room, and seated himself at the side of Higgs.

'Mr. Higgs,' said he, solemnly, 'you are a gentleman, and can appreciate a gentleman's feelings.' And Mr. Quagley paused for a reply.

'I hope I can,' replied the person thus addressed.

'Well then,' continued Mr. Quagley, after having settled that point to his satisfaction, 'you see that there boy;' and he nodded toward the stunted marker.

Higgs replied that he believed he did.

'Well Sir, I keep that boy on his poor mother's account. Now that's honorable, aint it?'

Mr. Higgs replied that it was — very.

'I knew you could appreciate a gentleman's feelings,' said Mr. Quagley. 'What'll you drink?'

'Rum cocktail,' said Higgs, without an instant's hesitation.

'Gin slings is healthier for the liver,' said Mr. Quagley; 'shall it be slings?'

'No, a rum cocktail,' replied Higgs, resolutely; 'it can't hurt *my* liver; I aint got one.'

Mr. Quagley pondered for some time as to the possibility of that fact; but after having made several desperate efforts to corner an idea which was running loose in his head, he said it was no matter, and went off to prepare the drinks, with which he soon returned. Seating himself by the side of Mr. Higgs, he pleasantly introduced his elbow between that gentleman's two lowest ribs, and winking at the stunted marker, whose back was toward him, said: 'He's one of the tallest kind, that boy.'

'He does n't look so,' said Mr. Higgs, removing with the end of his little finger a small speck which was floating in his tumbler.

'I know he do n't, but he *is*. I mean in character, you know.'

'Oh!' said Mr. Higgs, 'that's it.'

'Yes, that's it. He's a boy of the tallest kidney.'

'I should think he was, and then he has so many pleasant little ways with him,' replied Mr. Higgs.

'Do you think so?' said Mr. Quagley, earnestly. 'Well, I think so myself; but then you know it would n't do to let him *know* it, you know. It 'ud spile him.'

'Of course it would,' said Mr. Higgs, gently shaking his glass to stir up the sugar in the bottom of it; 'of course it would.'

'Do n't be a-lookin' here!' shouted Mr. Quagley to the boy, in pursuance of his system. 'You'm to look at the table, and you'm to mark the game; and if you do n't, you'm to be wollopped.'

'That's the way to larn 'em,' said Mr. Quagley, in a low tone, in continuation of his observation. 'Good evening, Sir; a stormy night.' This last remark was addressed to Wilkins, who had just then entered, and was standing a few feet inside of the door, with his hand shading his eyes from the strong light, and looking about him to see who were in the room.

'Oh! you are here, are you?' said he, coming up to Higgs. 'It's time we were on the move. Come.'

Higgs rose, and bidding Mr. Quagley 'good night,' followed his comrade into the street.

'What o'clock is it?' asked Wilkins, who seemed in one of his most sullen moods.

'I do n't know; 'most ten, I s'pose.'

Without making any remark, with his teeth set, and a scowl on his face, Wilkins led the way until he came to the house in which the attorney had his office.

'There's where he keeps,' said he, pointing to the old building, towering far above them in the darkness, and apparently stretching out its arms to beckon them on. 'It will tumble down some day, and I wish it was down now, for I never go into it without feeling as if I were entering the gate to hell.'

Higgs stood in front of the house, and as well as the darkness would permit, surveyed it from top to bottom. 'Quite an elderly mansion. I do n't half like it. D—d if I believe a man who lives in such a house can pay; and d—d if I work without it — that's plump!' As he said this, he thrust his hands to the very bottom of his pockets, and planted his feet on the ground, with an expression that seemed to say to them, 'Stir at your peril.'

'Come along, will you?' said Wilkins, impatiently; '*you* have nothing to fear. You need n't do any thing till you're paid. You can hear what he's got to say, and if you do n't choose to take a part in it, you need n't. You'd better, though.'

'Well, go on,' said Higgs, apparently satisfied; 'lead the way, for it's bloody dark, and smells as damp and close as a church-yard.'

Fumbling and groping their way into the dilapidated doorway, they came to the foot of the stairs.

'Here we are,' said Wilking, pausing. 'Up that stairs, and we are at his room. Now mind me, Higgs; if the pay's good, no quaking, no qualms; not a muscle must move. He's got an eye like an eagle, and it won't escape him.'

Higgs uttered a low, significant laugh, and pulling down his coat, and up his cravat, by way of giving additional respectability to his appearance, said: 'Pshaw! go on, won't you?'

'Wilkins, reässured by the indifferent manner of his comrade, ascended the narrow stairs, and feeling his way along a dark passage, knocked at the door of the office.

To this there was no reply.

'He's not in,' said Higgs.

'Yes he is.   He 's hiding his papers.   He 's not sure who are standing on this side of the door.   Click, slam; there goes the door of his
iron safe; they are under lock and key.   Now I 'll knock again.'

'As he spoke, Wilkins again applied the head of his stick to the door.
The next moment a cautious step was heard, the key was noiselessly
turned, to induce the supposition that the door had not been locked,
and a moment afterward they were told to come in.

On entering, they found the attorney sitting at a table strewed with
papers, one of which he was apparently engaged in perusing.   His hair
was disordered; his face pale and wan, as if he had lately undergone
much fatigue; and his whole person in disarray.   He did not look up
until they were nearly at the table, and then quietly, as if he scarcely
noticed their entrance.   No sooner, however, did he see who they were,
than he threw the paper aside, rose and said:

'So you 've come.   I am glad of it.'

'I thought you 'd be,' said Wilkins.   'This is the man I told you
about,' he added, jerking his head sideways toward Higgs, who stood
eyeing the attorney from head to foot.   'He knows all about it; so you
are saved that trouble.'

Without replying, Bolton opened the door and looked down the passage.   He then locked it, and led his friend into the back office, and
closed the door.   After this, he took one of the lights from the table,
and held it up in Higgs' face.   Never perhaps had two pairs of more
unflinching eyes met.   Every line, every feature, every muscle, was
examined and reëxamined.   At last Bolton replaced the light, and said
he was satisfied; to which Higgs replied that he was glad of it, for he
thought he never would be.

Bolton took the reply in good part, and after a few remarks, proposed
to proceed at once to business, for which the two worthies expressed
themselves perfectly ready.

Opening the iron safe, he took out of it a paper, on which was endorsed in large letters, '*The last Will and Testament of John Crawford.*'

'Is that the new one?' asked Wilkins, as he brought the paper to the
light.

'That 's it.'

'And without the legacy?'

'Yes; he has altered his mind since I saw you,' said the attorney,
laughing, 'and I drew the paper to suit him.'

'I supposed he would,' said Higgs; 'how *is* the old fellow?'

'He holds out yet, but they say he wo' n't long.'

'And the girl, his daughter, his *natural* daughter, as you call her in
the paper — but that 's a lie, you know — how will she take his
death?'

Bolton made no reply to the last part of the remark.   'She do' n't
know about it yet.   When she finds it out, it will be a perfect hurricane
at first, but it will soon blow over.'

Wilkins replied that he supposed so; and Higgs, not feeling any particular interest in the conversation, amused himself by smelling at the

mouth of a bottle on the mantel-piece. On ascertaining that it contained ink, he comforted himself with a very moderate draught of cold water from the pitcher, and seating himself near the fire, set about heating a poker red hot.

After some farther conversation, Bolton inquired of Higgs if he was ready to witness the paper, to which he replied that he was — almost.

'Are you acquainted with its nature and contents?' asked the attorney.

'I know it's old John Crawford's will; but I don't know what's in it.'

'That's not necessary,' replied Bolton : ' you are to swear that you saw him execute it ; that he acknowledged it to you to be his last will and testament, and asked you to become a witness to it ; and that you did so in his presence. You must swear to this.'

'Hadn't I better read it?'

'No; you are not expected to know the contents. It would be suspicious if you did. He wouldn't read his will to a stranger, although he might use him as a witness.'

The force of this remark seemed to strike Mr. Higgs, who made no reply, but returned to the fire, and again introduced the poker between the bars of the grate.

A pen was now carefully nibbed, and handed to Wilkins, who in a rough bold hand wrote his name and place of residence.

'Now, Mr. Higgs,' said Bolton, turning to him, ' will you sign?'

'I was told,' said Higgs, pausing in his occupation at the grate, and looking up at the attorney, ' that the old gentleman had requested you to hand me over a thousand, when I became a witness to his final wind-up.'

'A check is filled out for half that amount, and ready for you,' said Bolton, opening a drawer in the table, and producing the check. 'The other five hundred will be yours when the will is proved. It will be a fortnight or so after his death.'

Higgs looked at the check. Placing it in his pocket, he took up the pen and scrawled his name and place of abode beneath that of Wilkins.

'That will do,' said Bolton. He then folded the will up, placed it in the safe, locked it up, and laid the key on the table.

'That's done,' said he. 'No doubt the old gentleman feels easier, now that his property is cared for.'

'I suppose he does; he ought to,' replied Higgs. 'Every body hasn't such kind friends. What a pity! It would save them *so* much trouble !'

Bolton laughed, and said : 'Mr. Higgs, you know the risk of this matter. We sink or swim together. You 've got part of your pay. If we succeed, you 'll get the rest — you and Wilkins; and we *must* succeed, if you perform your part well, and keep your own counsel. If you *don't*, look out ! — that 's all.'

'I will,' said Higgs, quietly. 'If I intend to let out on you, I 'll murder you first; so you may be certain your secret 's safe, unless you should happen to wake up some pleasant morning, and find your throat cut.'

Higgs did not alter his voice as he spoke.   Its tone was even particularly soft; but the attorney drew back as from a snake; for there was *that* in the sharp gray eye, as it looked in his own, and in the sudden but momentary change of feature, that sent the blood to his heart in torrents.   Before he recovered himself, Higgs got up, and taking his hat, said: 'I must be off now.   When you want me, you can let me know, and tell me beforehand what's to be done.   Good night.'

No sooner was he gone, than Bolton turned to Wilkins and asked: 'Do you know this man well?   We are both in his power; and if he should prove false, he may put us where neither of us would care to go.'

'I have known him for years.   I've explained all to him, thoroughly. He knows the risk,' was the reply; 'and if you perform your part as well as he'll do his, all will end as you wish it.'

'If it had n't been for that last look of his,' said Bolton, 'I should have doubted it.   D — n it!   I did n't half like the expression of his eye when he talked so pleasantly of 'cutting my throat.'   Eh? Did you notice that?'

'Do n't tempt him to do it, then, that's all,' said Wilkins.

The attorney paced up and down the office, in deep thought; sometimes stopping short and looking in the fire, and then walking on, as if he never intended to give up.   At last he paused.

'That girl you were talking about,' said he, addressing Wilkins; 'what have you done there?'

Wilkins was crouching rather than sitting in his chair, his hat drawn over his eyes, and his knees gathered up as if for a spring.   He did not reply until his companion repeated the question.

'She's gone,' he said, at last.

'Left you!' exclaimed Bolton; 'you do n't mean eloped?'

'She's gone,' replied Wilkins, 'for good, I suspect.   She went last night at ten, and I have n't seen her since.'

'Has she any relatives, or any female friend, to whom she might go at that hour?'

'No.'

'Where do you suppose she went to?'

'God only knows!' replied Wilkins; '*I* do n't.'

'She did n't go for nothing, I suppose?' said Bolton, looking him full in the face.   'What was it?'

'Well,' said Wilkins, 'I'll tell you.   When I went home, I was full of what we had talked of.   I was half mad; and when I got to the house, I cursed her, and did all I could to get her up to what we wanted.'

'Well?'

'And so when I found nothing else would do, I struck her — down to the very floor.   There!' said he, starting from his chair, and dashing his hand across his face, 'that's all!   She could 'nt stand *that*, and she went.   And now,' continued he, beating his hand violently against his forehead, 'it sticks here — here!   This d — d head of mine is filled with all sorts of strange fancies and images of *her*.   Do what I will, there they stick.   I have been drinking too, but I can't drink them away. I went to the widow's, but I could n't make up my mind to go in; and I was afraid to go to my own home; it seemed as if it was no longer a home without *her :* so I have wandered the streets since morning. I have eaten nothing, and am weary and foot-sore.'

As he spoke, the wretched man placed his arms on the table, and leaned his head heavily upon them. He remained so but a moment, before he started up and stood erect in front of the lawyer. 'Bolton,' said he, 'you must carry this matter through without flinching: you *must*, by G — d ! — for you have made me what I am. I was an honest man till I fell in with you; and you know what came then.'

'What?' demanded the attorney, sharply.

'What comes to every man that falls in your clutches,' said he, speaking thick and fast. 'I had money — that went : I had business — that went ; I had friends, a fair name, bright hopes, and prospects — and *they* went ! All — every one of them ; nothing left; not one single soul ! And you,' said he, shaking his clenched fist in his face, 'you were the d — d cringing, skulking thief that stole them away, one by one, so that before I knew it I became what I am ! You said last night you 'd have nothing to do with a murder,' exclaimed he, with a wild fierce laugh, that made the room ring. 'I do n't know *that*. You might be mistaken there. Do you know,' said he, suddenly sinking his voice, and going up to the attorney, and leaning his elbow heavily on his shoulder, while he looked over in his face, 'do you know I often wonder that I do n't cut your throat at once, and have done with it ? I swear I *do !* It must come to that at last. What have you got to say to that ?'

'That you 'd be a fool for your pains,' said Bolton, with an appearance of indifference which he was far from feeling. 'If I got you into difficulties, I 'm the only man who can get you out, and you know it. But you are too much excited to-night. Come here some other time, and we 'll talk over your matters. You are worn out now.'

'So I am,' said Wilkins, whose momentary passion was over. 'Hand me that pitcher.'

The attorney complied, and Wilkins raised it to his lips, and took a long draught.

'This law plays the devil with one's nerves. I 'll talk it over to-morrow. I scarcely slept last night; and to-day every thing has been like a dream. I wonder if I 'll sleep to-night. I 'll try, any how. Good night.' As he spoke, he took his hat, and before the attorney was aware of his intention, had quitted the room.

Bolton listened, as step after step echoed through the deserted building; but long after Wilkins had left him and had sought his guilty home, did the lawyer walk up and down that room. The fire went out without his knowing it : one candle burnt to the socket, and at last flickered out; but he did not notice it. It was not till a neighboring clock struck three, with a tone so solemn and clear that it seemed at his very elbow, that he was aware it was far in the night. Extinguishing the remaining light, he locked his office and sought his own abode.

PASSAIC:

A GROUP OF POEMS TOUCHING THAT RIVER.

—

BY FLACCUS.

—

> 'Oh could I flow like thee, and make thy stream
> My great example as it is my theme;
> Though deep, yet clear, though gentle yet not dull,
> Strong without rage, without o'erflowing, full.'
>
> DENHAM's COOPER's HILL.

———

TALE FIFTH.

THE MARTYR: A REVOLUTIONARY BALLAD.

I.

When on the field of battle the soldier sinks to death,
And to his suffering country's cause devotes his latest breath,
His country, ever grateful, rewards him with a name
On everlasting marble carved, and hands him down to fame.

II.

But in our early struggle, o'errun by cruel foes,
Full many a nameless martyr sank, weighed down by bitter woes:
Who suffers like the soldier, should reap renown as well —
Oh! sure he should not be forgot, whose trials now I tell.

III.

'Twas night in deep mid-winter, when fields were choked with snow,
And widest streams were bridged with ice, and keenest blasts did blow;
A heavy muffled tramp through the village streets went by:
All shuddered in their beds, for they knew the foe was nigh.

IV.

Soon from that fearful silence alarming clamors peal,
And rising gleams along the snow the dreadful truth reveal;
'Rouse! rouse ye all! the town is fired!' — cries friend to friend — 'and lo!
The triple ranks! the flashing steel! — we're mastered by the foe!'

V.

Wide flames, with showers of dropping stars, that quench the stars on high,
Now flapping loud their mighty wings, rush flying up the sky:
Now mothers clasp their children, and wail aloud their woes,
And gathering, hide their little store from savage plundering foes.

VI.

For oft the rude marauders had plied their cruel trade,
And Hedden, with a few bold hearts, had oft the robbers stayed:
But now with stealthy step, at the hour of midnight dead,
They come! — they burst the doors — they drag the old man from his bed.

VII.

'Renounce thy faith! yield up thy mates! or, by King George, we 'll cast
Thy rebel limbs on yonder snows to stiffen in the blast!'
'My limbs are little worth,' he cried; 'their strength is nearly gone;
My tongue shall ne'er belie my heart, nor shame my cause: lead on!'

VIII.

Then furious all, they throttle him; when 'Hold!' their leader cries,
'Despatch him not! we 'll try his pith, before the rebel dies:
Let him with us unclad return! and though unmoved by steel,
Perchance a march along the snows will cool his patriot zeal!'

IX.

Loud yells applaud the sentence!—then, frantic with despair,
Wife, children kneel for mercy, but they find no mercy there:
For they rudely thrust them by, and they drag the old man forth,
And crouching quake his bare limbs, as they feel the cutting North.

X.

Then rings the shouldered musket, then taps the rattling drum,
And with rapid step they tramp, for the freezing winds benumb:
By the savage light of flames on their dreary march they go,
That shoot their shadows far before, along the glaring snow.

XI.

No pity for their victim would move their hearts of stone,
But still his bare feet tread the snows that chill him to the bone:
And many an icy splinter would gash them with its blade —
The blood that stains his every step their brutal march betrayed.

XII.

And when his stiffened limbs would lag, by age and sickness lamed,
With bayonet-thrust they urge him on, till cruelty is shamed:
God bless the soldier's heart! who cried, 'This sight I cannot see!'
And round him threw his blanket warm, that clothed him to the knee.

XIII.

Now hard as marble pavement, black Passaic stops the way:
Like serpent stiff in winter sleep, her torpid volume lay;
And in the midnight hush not a sound she gave the ear,
Save the long peal of parting ice, like thunder crackling near.

XIV.

But still the word is 'March!' and they tramp the icy floor:
But the old man's feet are numb, and they feel the cold no more.
Full many a weary mile he drags, but ere the break of morn,
In prison thrust, he drops at once, exhausted and forlorn.

XV.

Why linger in my story? His heavy trials past
Broke down the feeble strength of age — he drooped and sank at last:
But God the martyr's cruel death has well avenged, for see!
His murderers beaten from the soil — his land, his children free!

THOUGHTS ON ACTING AND ACTORS.

'ALL THE WORLD'S A STAGE.'

THE infatuation that possesses many persons to go upon the stage is the most natural feeling in the world. The thought of such a step, we venture to assert, crosses many a mind, young and ambitious, in its early struggles for distinction. The easy notoriety there gained; the showiness, the freedom, the off-hand kind of life, such a profession confers, have charms for the mind yet uninstructed in the knowledge that peace is happiness. The contrary character is the wonder. That a growing, excitable being should be willing to buckle himself to tasks, like law, medicine, and divinity; live for years in obscurity, in the hope of some distant success, is the marvel. It is what many are forced to and led to by parental authority, and stronger custom; but it is what few, with all their hearts, and with any plan of their own, contrive of their own free will. As the waters of the hills find the ocean by running in the channels already scooped out, so many men arrive at comfort and competence, and even celebrity, by following the channels of custom. To few can be awarded the palm of entirely self-wrought success. Indeed, for a young mind to spurn custom is dangerous in the extreme; as fruitless as for waters to attempt to gain the ocean by a new path: they would meet with falls and precipices, hills and rocks, which they could not foresee. The old paths are the safe ones.

A love for distinction is a better feeling than it at first seems to be. It is a desire for sympathy, for communication, for action. But it must be an honorable distinction. It is not notoriety that men seek; for this might be obtained by any one, by wearing strange attire, or assuming an unusual manner; a thing which some *do*, though rarely. The mind craves notice, that it may not feel alone. It asks not so much for superiority, as not to pass life in utter silence and insignificance. ' *Omnis homines*,' says SALLUST, ' *qui sese student præstau uteris animalibus, summa ope niti decet vitam silentio ne transeunt.*' He is already great and immortal, who can be content to live supported by a conscious dignity: who is so absorbed by a sense of beauty and a love for virtue; who is so lifted up and so entranced by his contemplations of God and nature and eternity, that he has no time to think of himself, and to calculate his worth. He is never great who is ever thinking of his greatness; as he is never rich, as far as riches confer happiness, who is always counting his treasures. The graspings of the ambitious, like the cravings of the miser, poison the fountains of peace. The world finds out the really great. No flower is born to blush unseen. There is no wasted sweetness. The violet that unfolds its rich and velvet leaves in the grove untrod by mortal foot, may delight the birds and dumb creatures; nay, it may delight the observation of God himself, and have a deep meaning for the gaze of spiritual beings. The man of noble soul sacrificing himself, unconsciously great and good, unconsciously teaches and moulds the minds about him ; and, if made for no other end, he too may be made for the admiration of those higher beings, whose gaze is wide and universal ; who must delight in flowers, and beauty, and virtue. But these are not common men. Few can be content with so simple a life ; few are willing to seek first the kingdom of heaven, for they do not believe that all these things, honor, competence, peace, will be added unto them.

Those persons who dress themselves up for show by candle-light, and wear mock jewels and paper crowns, are the actors *proper*. They proclaim their object. They ask applause, which they love better than bread. They have not entered upon this life merely for the sake of getting food and shelter. No ; these low motives disgrace few creatures in any calling. They love your sympathy ; they ask your favor and countenance. As they utter the sentiments of a Shakspeare or an Otway, think you they do it for so much a night only ? — for mere money ? We believe they have higher aims ; and though the life of an actor, apparently from circumstances unavoidably connected with it, may tend to weaken a regard for those rules that hold society so strictly ; though a half-starved life, as a theatrical one often is, is not a very nice school for the calmness and serenity that are almost necessary to virtue ; yet to the lowest actor there are aspirations for fame and hopes of advancement. Even the men who take on and off the chairs and tables would excel in expertness in their parts, as any one may observe. At the better class of theatres they are neatly dressed, and generally have elaborate heads of hair. It is difficult to avoid a feeling of pity for these humble aspirants for renown, as with blushing cheeks they play these dumb services. Equally difficult is it to restrain one's disgust for those brazen-faced rascals who push themselves forward in the choruses, and with half-drunken eyes leer up to the galleries. Such fellows, did they but know it, are infinitely below the chair-movers and table-setters.

A man may be so circumstanced in his bodily economy that he can never make a good actor, and still have a fine conception of character, and be an excellent critic of others' performances. Shakspeare, it is notorious, was no actor. It must be no pleasant task to a man whose soul is wrestling with the passions and ambition of a hero, to fill the subordinate places in a play ; to feel one part and to say another ; to hear and know a thing to be mangled, and yet not have the physical power to better the utterance of it. And yet in the wise division of gifts by Nature it is questionable if she does not refuse to the highest order of mind and taste the best physical endowments. Your *very* well-made, handsome man is rarely a poet or a scholar. There is (who will deny it ?) a certain awkwardness about the body of a man who has a great mind at work. Whether a good frame does not make one feel independent of mental cultivation, or whether the very act of thought does not tend to a contempt and neglect of the outward, as a cause for this, let who that can, say. So it is almost universally. The only great man we ever heard of who made dress a successful object of study was Lawyer Pinckney, who used to wear a buff vest, or waistcoast, as it was called in his day, and a blue coat with metal buttons. He was nice to a hair in the adjustment of every article of his apparel, and still was a great jurist and sound political economist. Goldsmith's passion for dress only made him ridiculous; the revenge his intellect took upon his body.

Was there ever a very great actor who was a remarkably elegant man in his person? Look at KEAN and BOOTH. By 'great actor' we mean not successful actor. FORREST is a very successful actor, but every one that sees him is as much taken with his fine muscular form as with his reading. There was not when I last saw him a deep intellect stamped upon him. A man of excellent sense he undoubtedly is, as his letters show, and far from being destitute of taste; but we flatly deny to FORREST the possession of a refined style of acting or any appearance of nice scholarship. There are some actors in our country who never will be great; and yet it is impossible to see them and not feel that they are gentlemen in their feelings and scholars in their minds. MURDOCK, a name perhaps almost unknown to the majority of our readers, formerly of the Boston stage, is of this class. Now any judge will say at a glance that he had rather hear Murdock read a play in private than Forrest. This may appear extravagant; but we are expressing our own opinions, and not those of other people. GARRICK, the most successful actor the world has ever seen, was a miser and niggard; and no one feels any deep respect for his memory. The life of the man detracts from the actor; and we can better bear with the self-destroying vagaries of COOKE, the riots of KEAN, and the thousand follies which disgrace the biography of the drama, than we can feel admiration for the 'genius,' as it is called, of Garrick, joined as it is with so much meanness and paltry selfishness. The truth is, we feel that he was *not* a genius; for it is next to impossible for a mean man to have genius.

The reputation of female performers, and the degree of interest and applause which they excite, is very dependent upon our personal feelings for them, independently of any judgment of their success in their art. An interesting woman, such as ELLEN TREE or MISS CLIFTON, might make a thousand blunders, and yet come off with applause, provided she exhibited an enticing person, well-rounded legs, and an exuberant bust, to advantage. There is a charm about the countenance of Madame CELESTE, in some of her parts, as fine as any thing I ever saw in woman; and it is a simplicity which enables her to do a thousand things that would disgust us in any other woman. She is a woman, and yet a child. How different the impression made by Madame VESTRIS! And yet this last actress probably excels all those whom we have mentioned. Her '*I love Peter!*' was sung as sweetly as ever song was uttered. Madame Vestris is not a charming woman, and hence was not in this country a successful actress. There is something wanting. Perhaps we suspect she is rather old. At any rate, her case proves our position, that the success of an actor is an accidental matter in part. Mrs. DUFF, where art thou, 'all cold and all serene?' — frost-work and fire; ice reflecting the setting sun! Stately Mrs. POWELL, where art thou, with thy impersonations of Lady Macbeth? Every actor has one part, he must have, in which he surpasses all other of his parts; and the Lady Macbeth of Mrs. Powell was said to be second only to that of the SIDDONS. COOPER shone in Virginius, as WALLACK does or did in Rolla.

But to go a little back to what we were talking about. One great cause of the low estimate good people form of the stage and actors is the low estimate they *practically* make of themselves. As a class they are not simple and quiet in their private lives. They do not make themselves scholars in their profession and study for a view of their own, but take their cue from the stage-manager. As their clothes indicate, they seek the showy, the gaudy, the superficial, rather than the neat, the useful, and the true. This may be rather a habit than any thing else. They become accustomed to producing effects in all things which are illegitimate. If they wear paper crowns and tin tinsels at night, they are easier content to wear paste and pinchbeck in the day-time. False collars, false hair, and false eye-brows must have had their origin in the art of representation. Only think of representing a clean shirt by a false bosom, collar, and wrist-bands! The legs and shoulders which have gained applause on the boards will be very apt to be seen in the public streets, though far from being other than stuffing. Those painted cheeks and cork eye-brows which cause sighs and sonnets; those luxuriant tresses, and even those quite as false though winning smiles, which often make actresses the divinities of the youth of our cities, will be very apt to try to keep up the illusions of the night in the day-time.

If it be possible, let actors be men and women, fathers and mothers, brothers and sisters, and not *actors*, off the stage. Let them not be so often frequenters of public places, and stand to be gaped at by a crowd. Show us a young actor who studies not only the words of his part, but who devotes his time to a general improvement of his mind; who aims to be a scholar, and believes his profession to be a moral engine to help reform the vices of the times, and we will show you a man who will rise first to self-respect and then to public favor. We care not what may be his voice or his legs. He *will rise*, and better still, he will do good. No profession gives dignity to a man. It is the man that must give dignity to the profession. There are some boot-blacks and servants in our city who absolutely command more respect than some lawyers and merchants; whose standing is better in the community; whose credit is better. And why should it *not* be so? The stage never degraded any man; and the wonder is, as we before said, that so few men of education try it.

To turn to acting *improper*, which belongs to our subject. It is amusing to see the acting of the street, the church, and the drawing-room. The affected walk, from the turgid strut down to the indifferent, indolent lounge. That mincing Miss and that brazen stalker are acting upon a wide stage. Those waving plumes and that velvet cloak; those ribands, laces, flounces — all are the world's stage-dresses, and the wearers are the actors. Sir Consequence plays his part not meanly. He impresses servants and chambermaids. The bar-keeper keeps a sober countenance as he looks him in the face, while he unfolds his well-stuffed wallet. He walks away pleased with his success, and does not see the sneer of his humble servants. They pay respect only to his money; and, poor fool! he thinks it is his personal merit that has secured the homage. Mr. Modesty talks in a confidential whisper to the shopman, and makes all his inquiries with an 'If you please, Sir,' and 'May I ask?' etc. He oppresses you with his humility; and his presence is worse than a dog-day. Nobody is at ease with him, half through pity and half from contempt for his puppyism. Mr. Bold blusters, talks and laughs loud in the bar-rooms, and winks at the by-standers. He takes the world by storm. He interlaces his remarks with oaths, and looks fierce if run against in a crowd.

But Sunday is the great play-day of the world. Everybody assumes a part; appears something which he is not. My lady's maid looks finer than her mistress, and the footman cleaner than his master. Apprentices and clerks mount on horse-back, and try to look easy as they 'gulp their weekly air.' All would look demure in church and decent in the street. It is a dangerous day to pick up a chance acquaintance, or to form a chance opinion of a person's character and piety. By common consent, as by law, no *process*, unless a criminal one, can be served on that day. People are allowed to go at large in any guise that suits their fancy, so it does not endanger the state. People up to the elbows in filth during the week, and not necessarily either, on Sunday wear gloves; and those who are steeped in vice for the six days, repent on Sunday. Even the poor omnibus-horses enjoy a kind of exemption from labor, so privileged is the day.

We have no space to notice the acting of the drawing-room, ball-room, and dinner-party; the match-making, the toadyism, the flattery, the gossip, the quackery, that offer so much room for remark. There seems to be an universal taste for acting of some sort; but of all acting, we prefer that of the theatre, and believe that *a well-conducted stage* may be made a means of refining the manners and sentiments of the age: and therefore we wish actors *proper* all success.

J. N. B.

SONNET.

TO THE ALTAR AT THE COSA DE PIEDRAS AT PALENQUE.

THOU standest yet, a sacred monument
Of th' unknown past; a scroll of sculptured stone,
Whose mystic language, from old forests sent,
'Mid all the living can be read by none :
Yet those strange characters were proudly meant
To blazon forth to all succeeding time
The memory of some name or deed sublime,
With hues to be with all the future blent.
How vainly hopeth man, when on the sand
Of Time's still changing shore he trusteth Fame shall stand !

STRIFE OF THE OCEAN-SPIRITS.

BY S. D. DAKIN.

'Questi non hanno speranzi di morte ;
E la lor cieca vita è tanto bassa,
Che 'nvidiosi son d 'ogni altra sorte.'   DANTE: 'INFERNO.'

A SHIP is on the angry deep,
  Where the mysterious stream
From Mexic gulf, with widening sweep,
  Warm with the torrid beam,
    Like summer rain,

Lashes the iceberg's lofty dome,
  And melts its bulwarks old,
Its emerald pillars wreathes with foam,
  And casts its towers of gold
    Prone on the sea.

The Ocean-spirits burn for strife
  With the proud ship, and dare assail
Its frame of oak instinct with life,
  Its heart that throbs in iron mail,
    And breath of fire !

Ages their victories have known,
  And in full many a darksome cave
Imperishable wrecks are strown,
  That chronicle the fate they brave,
    Mid ocean's tombs.

Shall human spirits pent in clay,
  And doomed to struggle there
With fiends of hell still worse than they,
  And demons of despair,
    A fearful brood !

Presume to wage th' unequal strife
  With spirits of the air and sea ?
Claim elements where these are rife,
  Their servitors to be —
    A vast domain !

Oh ! wild from fleshless lips the shriek
  Went up the creaking mast,
And hideous forms clomb up the peak
  Of cresting waves, aghast,
    And scowled their rage !

And from the far-down caverns dark,
  And slimy quicksand plains,
Uprose a host, uncouth and stark,
  Whom th' upper air disdains
    To bless with breath :

And heavenly light withholds its sheen,
From denizens so fierce and grim,
Of depths so foul; and black clouds screen
The lofty homes of Seraphim —
The pure bright stars.

The viewless winds need not the light
To wage their fearful war;
And all their subsidies that night
Wreak vengeance fiercer far,
In darkness wrapt.

Where is the tome wherein ye 're named?
Spirits sent forth from every sea
To join the conflict proudly aimed,
For all the world's wide mastery —
Matter and mind!

From Equatorial seas, Atrope,
Phloisbos and Tormentoso grim
From Afric's cape, miscalled Good Hope;
Boron, Euroclydon, and Hym,
From either pole:

All, all — from every gulf and bay,
From maelstroom, reef, and key;
Driven forth by Boreas on their way,
Monsoon, Typhoon, Chamsee,
And hot Siroc!

Ah, fatal Congress! spare your gibes,
Your gibberish and your glaring eyes;
Enough — enough the fiendish tribes
That guilty Conscience bids to rise,
In hours like this.

Cling, cling, poor helpless shivering souls,
To the icy masts and ropes!
For now the Troop a huge wave rolls,
Must crush your lingering hopes,
And whelm you all!

A shriek of despair through the fear-rent air,
And a crash of the quivering prow,
Go up with the yell from the watery lair
Of the fiends that are triumphing now —
Then all is hushed!

The wreck drifts tenantless along,
Swept by the ingulfing flood;
Save one, who cheats the vengeance strong
Of all the hellish brood,
Lives, if 't is life.

On, on — all helmless, mastless, riven,
The sport of winds and tides,
From hope of rescue widely driven,
That iron-bound hull still rides
From sea to sea.

Locked in an iceberg's cold embrace,
  On which, as on some rock-bound shore,
Wash the wild waves and leave no trace,
  That ship, with fixed, unheeding prore,
    Is southward borne.

That lone man sitteth like a king
  Of realms of ice : the sun at morn,
The moon at night, around him bring
  Such splendors as put all to scorn
    The thrones of earth.

Do the Ocean-spirits bid him bear
  The sceptre of the deep ?
To be of the frosty isle the Czar —
  A diamond foot-stool keep,
    And crystal throne ?

Lone mariner, 't is mockery all !
  The waves th' illusion whelm ;
Deep unto deep doth loudly call,
  And plough through all thy realm
    An ocean-path !

The loosened ship drifts on again
  To peril worse than storm,
Or prison of ice ; th' unbounded main,
  The air, and every form,
    Are still as death.

A withering calm enfolds the bark
  In hot embrace of air
And sea, as if it were the mark
  On which all things should bear,
    That could oppress.

He prayed the air might just be stirred
  If but by a wren's small wing ;
He would have wept could he have heard
  The gentlest wavelet sing
    Around the keel.

Stillness and Silence ! ye are strong
  To bind in awe the soul ;
Ere morning stars had learned their song,
  Or orbs began to roll,
    Ye sovereign were.

In your dread presence trembled he ;
  Your mystic shadows stole
O'er his awed breast ; and vacancy
  Came cloud-like o'er his soul,
    Deep, like your own.

Spirits of ocean and the air,
  And allies infinite !
Your triumph now ye may declare ;
  Ye plunge the Mind in night,
    And mock its powers !

Ye conquer now, but not for aye ;
For Mind, though thrust from Eden's bowers,
Quailing beneath the tempter's eye,
Slave to the luscious fruits and flowers,
Your sport and prey ;

Has vanquished one by one the foes
From Evil's legion sent ;
Nor from its triumphs shall repose,
Till all have humbly bent
Beneath its sway :

Till it all elements, all things,
To its strong will shall mould ;
And sweet, high, searching questionings
Shall with least atoms hold,
And loftiest stars !

SKETCHES OF THE COUNTRY.

NUMBER FIVE.

THE good old custom of observing Saturday evening as the commencement of holy time is fast going into disuse. In the cities and larger towns of New-England it is already done away with, and the next twenty years of our innovating age will hardly leave a relic, in the most sequestered hamlet of the mountains, of what was half a century ago universal custom. I have called it a ' good old custom ; ' and I believe that no one who has ever beheld its practical effect upon the condition of a community, or upon the individuals composing that community, will be disposed to deny that it is so. Aside from the ties which all customs handed down to us from our fathers and which are associated with the memory of the Puritans, have over us, binding us to the holy principles which they loved and honored, there is something I believe in the very nature of the sacred observance of Saturday evening ; in its calm preparations and unusual stillness ; which fits us better for the duties of the Sabbath, and tends to render the day a more holy one ; ' sacred to the Lord, and honorable.'

There are places in New-England where the custom is still observed in all its pristine strictness. They are not the manufacturing villages which are studded thickly along her wild and rapid streams, and which forever crowd the bustle and noise of Labor's appointed hour into the night as well as the Sabbath ; nor are they the large towns whose business facilities have drawn streamlets into them from the great tide of emigration ; nor the capitals of the States, nor the market towns of the rich intervales and meadows, nor the new settlements on the borders of the forest ; but they are the quiet old homes of the peasantry of the mountains ; the ancient farming towns of the Commonwealth, whose soil, too rough to tempt the avarice of the indolent, has been handed down with the staunch virtues of its first cultivators from sire to son, from the earliest settlement of the country. The external appearance of some of these old agricultural towns makes a singular impression upon a stranger. The time-worn church is situated most likely on the highest and bleakest hill where its builders could find a public road, and behind it run off the long sheds, numbering as many stalls as there are chaises and waggons in the parish. Low gable-roofed farm-houses of every shade and color stand like decrepit patriarchs among the huge barns which have grown up around them. Red school-houses in the centre of each district; old cemeteries, with the slate head-stones half sunk in the earth or hid in the rank luxuriance of the grass; whole miles of moss-covered stone walls; the road, without regard to hills or points of the compass, winding from farm to farm; the powder-house, the pound, the poor-house, and the county-house, are all objects of notice to the traveller. The antique garb of the inhabitants may strike him strangely; but if he be in a pleasant humor, the rustic civility which accompanies it, and which he meets with everywhere, cannot fail to delight him. The urchins, trudging homeward from school, greet him with doffed hats and ready bows; the checked frocks and aprons in their rear render the graceful courtesy; while the complaisant smile of the parasol'd and gloved school-ma'am betrays her pride in the good breeding of her little flock. If it chance to be a pleasant afternoon of Summer, he will find bright faces looking after him from every door; the grandame plying her knitting-needles or turning the foot-wheel, less for gain than as a thrifty pastime; the careful mother making ' auld claes look amaist as weel 's the new ; ' the daughters carding the white rolls of wool or rapidly shifting the bobbins of the lace-pillows; and all listening meanwhile to the simple ballad or fast chattering of the neighbor's news from the market town. The boys suspend their ball game while he drives over the green; the veteran 'Squire, the patriarch of the place,

> ' With his old three-cornered hat,
> His breeches, and all that,'

respectfully uncovers his head, with the true dignity of the old John Hancock courtesy; the rustic maid, full blown as the Summer rose, glances a coquettish look from beneath her dark eye-lashes, and hastens home to tell of the handsome stranger whom she met; and not least, the fat landlord — mine host of the Sun for forty years — meets him at the door, and welcomes him with most gracious air to the well-sanded parlor.

You are in truth reminded at every step that Nature is not out of date here, and that the standard which art and fashion have introduced over the world, which, like the bed of Procrustes, reduces redundances and racks out deficiences, to suit its dimensions and measurement, has no dwelling-place among the people. Take your fishing-rod in your hand and travel through all the country; sit down by the huge sirloin of the farmer's table or take pot-luck at the more simple meal of his daily workman; plant your cold and dripping limbs against the peat embers of the cottager's hearth or before the roaring beacon of the landlord's hall; trace every stream from its mouth through all its

windings to its source, and chat with every one you meet; and the
same unaffected simplicity; the same honest and manly frankness; the
same independence of thought and manner, will arrest your attention
every where.

The week-day life of these dwellers upon the old farms of New-
England is to be sure one of wearisome and unceasing labor. But then
it is the labor of contentment and innocence, where pride has not dissatisfied the heart, nor luxury enervated the spirit. Nor is it unvaried
by bright hours of mirthfulness and enjoyment. Beside the satisfaction with which the owner surveys his thick hay-cocks and waving
grain, his fatted herds and heavy fruit-trees, he finds scenes of frequent
enjoyment in the regularly-observed customs which each season brings.
Harvest-time, from the earliest haying to late in the Autumn, is to the
young men and maidens a perpetual scene of merry-making. The
berrying parties in the dull days of July; the roast-corn frolics; the
apple-gatherings; and above all the long round of husking-bees, with
their rich fun and well-earned forfeits; the shows of white linen and fat
cattle at the annual fair, and the nobly won premiums of the young
housewife, furnish sources of enjoyment, long remembered, and anxiously counted on in the future. But from all the scenes of merriment,
the day of raising a new building bears off the palm. For weeks before the event arrives, the day is set, with the proviso of an adjourn-
ment to the first fair day, if bad weather should prevent, and invitations
are sent by the owner of the building to the whole neighborhood, for
miles around, so that oftentimes an hundred helpers will congregate to
the gathering. If the enviable aspirant for the new building should
chance to be a bachelor who is preparing his house for the reception
of a wife, the merry-making is multiplied fourfold. Custom makes it
imperative that the bride-elect should be upon the ground at the close
of the work, and to drive the last pin into the main-brace of the corner
beam. The frame is all complete; the last 'heave yo, my men!' of the
master carpenter has been given; each stud, and joist, and main-stay,
and king-post, is fitted and fastened to its place; the workmen have all
descended, and ranged themselves in long file in front of the work;
when the bride-to-be steps forward with uncovered head from her
concealment, and taking the pin from the master, drives it with mallet
in hand merrily home. As soon as the last blow rings from the beam,
she hastily retires, to send in the banquet which she is expected to
furnish; and loud huzzas are repeated, till the welkin rings again. The
hearty meal and liberal drink :

> ———— ' the brown October, drawn
> Mature and perfect, from his dark retreat
> Of thirty years ; '

wind up the day — the merriest day of the farmer's calendar.

On Saturday evening, whatever may be the season of the year, no
festivities ever take place   The work and the play of the farmer's boy
have then ceased, and young and old all prepare for the approach of holy
time. Early in the afternoon, an attentive observer might notice something differing from the ordinary avocations of the week, for the workmen are earlier by an hour in quitting the field; the heavily laden wains

are more rapidly drawn to the granaries; the cows come by broad sunlight from the pastures, and the oxen are turned out upon the meadows
long before the usual time of ceasing from labor.   In-doors the female
part of the household are equally forward with their work.   The house
has been thoroughly cleansed and 'put to rights,' from the disorder
which the week's movements have occasioned; the long rows of shining
pewter upon the dresser have been newly scoured; the proceeds of the
last churning have been thoroughly worked and neatly put away; the
new-made cheese is placed under the press; the beer has been brewed;
and the batch of Indian bread, with its Sunday-noon concomitants of
baked pork-and-beans, is safely deposited in the oven.

As evening comes on, the children are called into the house to
undergo the thorough weekly ablution, and then, one after the other,
are called to learn the Bible-questions for Sunday-school.   The men
drop in, as each one finishes his duties; the boy has collected and put
by all the farming utensils for the next week; the rich store of milk is
brought in from the barn-yard; and sunset finds the whole family partaking of the evening meal.   All loud talk or boisterous merriment is,
as if by common consent, suspended; and throughout the whole
neighborhood, so strict is the custom of the observance of the evening
upon all, no visits are made, nor unnecessary work engaged in.   At
dark the merchant has closed his store, and the mechanic has locked
up his shop; and a stranger might well suppose that some fearful calamity was impending over the town, so silent is the whole scene around
him.

Go into that low moss-roofed dwelling, whose Summer walls are covered with the richest honeysuckle, or into the large painted one in whose
shadow it stands, where the vast barns and thick out-houses indicate
the owner's wealth, and you may have in either a picture of every
family in town.   In each the affairs of the household are arranged for
the night.   The clock strikes audibly in the corner; the lights shed
their bright beams over a quiet and thoughtful circle; the very house-dog
himself learns to know the evening, and has lazily stretched himself to
sleep beneath the master's chair; while on the wooden chimney-piece
lies an open Bible, ready for family worship.   At eight o'clock the old
church-bell rings, the chapter and the prayer close the evening, and all
retire to rest for an early rising on the day of our blessed Lord.

It was my fortune to visit the old house of my grandfather during
the month of July, in 1840.   He had long since passed away with the
generation in which he lived, not a relic of which remained save the
old pastor, who had been settled over his flock for more than sixty years.
I knew he was to meet me at the corner of two roads, where the stage-
coach turned off toward the next post-town, and I had been reflecting
at times, all the day, upon scenes which twenty years had not effaced
from my memory, and speculating upon the changes which I should
find the lapse of time had made upon the vigorous frame of my old and
earliest friend.   He had been before my mind's eye as he was during
my childhood; a noble, venerable man, the Father of his people,
habited in the most plain and homely manner; not less loved and
respected at home than venerated and esteemed abroad; carrying along
with him into all the intercourse of life 'a mind void of offence;' a

sincerity and earnestness which extended over every religious duty, from the blessing at the frugal meal to the higher ministrations of the pulpit. I remember him in his Sabbath services giving to his flock the simple food of the Gospel; his grave demeanor as he walked from the house of God to the parsonage; the easy and unassumed familiarity with which he greeted the poorest even of his charge; and the total absence of all selfishness which his whole life showed. I thought of him in his visitations; his quiet and cheerful aspect at the sick-bed; his grave and solemn tones in the church-yard; his relief to the poor, his comfort to the afflicted, his reproof to the wandering; and I felt that to no man more than he, could the apostle's description be applied: 'Blameless, vigilant, sober, of good behavior, given to hospitality.'

I found him still the same; unchanged save in the increased whiteness of his thinning locks; and his hearty welcome made me forget the long years of absence which had passed. Leaving my trunk at a house near by, to be sent after from the parsonage, I took a seat by the old man, in the very same chaise, as it seemed to me, in which my boyhood used to rejoice, and turned with him down a deep shaded lane, which led to a remote part of the town. He was going to perform the last solemn rites at the funeral of a young member of his congregation; and as we rode along, he took occasion to narrate to me some of the incidents connected with her death.

Her father, who was a respectable and independent farmer, lived in a very charming but retired situation. I had known well in childhood that lonely farm-house, so far off among the beautiful wild green hills; and some of the brightest hours of my holydays from school had been spent in sailing over the lake that lay just below it, or in rambling through the woods that stretched far away to the eastward, over a long range of rough mountains. An elder sister of the one who now lay dead had been my school-mate and playmate, and I had not forgotten the bright faces of brothers and sisters to whom she used to bring me on Saturday afternoons; nor the pleasant greeting of the parents, that made me sure of a welcome whenever I could get permission to accompany her. The other sons and daughters had grown up, and left one after another the old homestead; until Agnes, the youngest, the petted child of old age, now fast creeping on the parents, was the only one who was left to cheer the once merry fireside.

She had just out-grown the mere unthinking gladness of childhood, but had not yet reached that time when selfishness mixes with the pure current of love. Unlike the others, nature had endowed her with the richest charms of beauty, as if to add a new link to the chain which bound her so strongly to her parents. With dark eyes and jet-black hair, set off by a luxuriance of health which gives such a light and bloom to the countenance; full of buoyant mirth and gayety, softened by a mildness and propriety that won every beholder; she had been the pride and loved one of the village at every rustic gathering. From among her numerous admirers she had selected one who was in every respect worthy of her, and who, engaged in a course of collegiate study, in which he was gathering the brightest laurels, had led her to look forward to a preparation for a higher sphere of action than she had yet filled. His college vacations were spent at her father's house; and the beautiful scenery of woods and mountains around them, where they sought out every fairy knoll and heath-covered fell, and among which they passed many a long Summer afternoon,

> 'While time seemed young, and life a thing divine,'

increased and strengthened the pure and devoted love which had grown up between them. Indeed no one could see her, in her neat and simple dress, with a profusion of dark glossy tresses escaping from her sun-bonnet, so unsuspecting and innocent; now hanging upon his arm, with her soft dark eyes fixed upon his manly face, and anon bounding away over the hills or along the narrow beach with the lightness of a roe, laughing at his vain attempts to overtake her; without confessing that here surely was real, unselfish attachment.

It was during one of these walks, in the Autumn before, that they sat down upon the side of a large rock, the extreme end of which shot out into the deepest part of the lake, forming a bluff and bold shore for nearly a quarter of a mile. Wearied with the excitement of a long walk and the warmth of the day, Agnes had laid her bonnet in a crevice of the rock just above them, and was parting back her ringlets from her brow, when a light gust of wind lifted it from the rock, and rolled it over the side, toward the water. Both sprang from their seats to grasp it, and the lover, in his haste to save it, unconsciously stepped upon a slippery part of the rock, and was precipitated at once into the lake. The poor girl sprang to the edge of the bank, but he had sunk, and probably becoming entangled in the weeds at the bottom, never again rose! With the most pitiable screams she alarmed some men who were at work near by, one of whom dived several times near the spot where he had disappeared, but without success; and the poor girl was taken home a raving maniac.

Months had passed after this heart-rending event, before Agnes had sufficiently recovered to be able to leave her room. And then how changed! The elastic step, and bright eye, and laughing face, were gone, without leaving a single relic of her beauty. The Winter came and went; and the beautiful Spring, too, with its fresh breezes, and bright flowers, and soft tones, without waking one glad feeling in her heart. Never again was her bright and noble spirit lifted up; for her heart lay buried in her young lover's grave. And the Summer month was to witness the last office which her friends could pay her. She had been calm and unmurmuring under the whole, but it had long been too evident to all her friends that the heart was gathering about the citadel of life every drop of the vital current, and must ultimately burst in the struggle to relieve itself.

Declining the invitation of my friend to enter the house, I seated myself on a rustic bench beneath some beeches, some rods below the house, and out of sight of the mourners. It had evidently been a favorite resort of her who was departed. Around the sides and back woodbine and ever-greens had been tastefully intertwined, and wild rose-bushes were thickly clustered all over the little hillocks behind. The view which it commanded of the scenery around was eminently beautiful. Below you, the hill swept off toward the lake with a gentle descent, covered with the brightest green-sward and interspersed with frequent copses of large forest trees. The waters were unruffled by a single wave, and one little wooded island, just off the shore, seemed hung in mid-air, and looked like a fairy resort of coolness and beauty. Beyond were the deep blue mountains, over which the shadows were flitting like winged messengers, while their broadly indented summits were bathed in a flood of purple light. It was one of those delicious evenings which occur only during the long droughts of midsummer, when the rapid evaporation from the bodies of water during the day gives fragrance and coolness to the atmosphere of the coming night, and softens the light which the sun throws over the landscape just before setting, into a mellowness and radiance which no words can describe. It was in sweet unison with my own feelings and with the burial scene. As the procession moved slowly round the side of the hill, preceded by twelve maidens of the age of the deceased, dressed in white, and carrying wreaths of white roses in their hands, as they passed on to the old burial-place, far up the ascent, with a slow and measured tread over the grass-grown pathway, while the summons of the distant bell struck faintly on the ear ; as they listened around the grave to the solemn words of the gray-haired pastor, and casting their fresh flowers upon the coffin, turned to retrace their steps ; the whole was in such harmony with the spot, the hour, and the Saturday-evening stillness, that it thrilled to the heart with inexpressible power. It was like a whisper from the spirit-land, summoning the weary from the cares of earth, and bidding the mourner rejoice that the lost one had carried with her the warmth of the young affections, the youth of the soul, the beauty and freshness of the spring of being.

A FAREWELL.

We may not meet again :
　Yet oft, when lost in sleep,
The olden hopes will rise,
　Like spirits from the deep :
While not a bird that wings
　Its flight o'er earth or sea,
But whispers, as it sings,
　Some thought, loved one ! of thee.

We may not meet again :
　For earth has many ways,
And lips in other lands
　Are voiceful in thy praise :
But thy sweet lute and songs,
　The places where we met,
The glen, the fount, the tree,
　All bid me not forget.

We may not meet again :
　But oh ! from round my heart
The ' light of other days '
　Alas ! will ne'er depart :
But like some lonely star,
　That lights the deep blue sea,
Thy beauty shines upon
　The wave of memory.

A FATHER'S PRAYER.

A SCENE IN THE CHAMBER OF AN INVALID POET.

BY MRS. E. C. STEDMAN.

I.

Oh! Thou, whose watchful eye
Doth slumber not, nor sleep, look down on me;
In sickness and in sorrow, hear the sigh
My soul breathes out to Thee!

II.

For *me* 't is better far
From all these earthly shadows to depart,
And dwell with *her* who was the guiding star
That led aright my heart.

III.

And yet a tender tie
Fastens to earth my chastened spirit still,
And doubly needful doth it seem that I
The parent charge fulfil.

IV.

Deign then, O God of love!
This ' harp of thousand strings' to tune again;
Let thy restoring breath upon it move,
And wake the healthful strain.

V.

But if thou dost refuse —
If wasting sickness shall its chords destroy,
O, hear me while its waning strength I use
As suppliant for my boy!

VI.

Thou temperest e'en ' the wind
To the shorn lamb ' — and wilt thou not defend
The innocent that I must leave behind,
And be the orphan's friend?

VII.

Upon thy page I see
Rich promises his lonely lot to bless;
That *more* than friend — a FATHER thou wilt be,
Unto the Fatherless!

VIII.

And in ' the trying hour,'
May I my boy resign with tearless eyes,
And by the strength of Faith's all-conquering power,
Die as the Christian dies!

Cedar-Brook, Dec. 1840.

THE SERENADERS.

A SKETCH OF TINNECUM.

' We confess ourselves utterly at a loss to account for them. The beautifullest noises piercing our chamber at midnight, perfectly delighting our ears with their harmonies, and coming apparently from nowhere. Far be it from us to lend any sanction in these columns to a belief in witchcraft or haunted houses. Once for all, we beg it to be distinctly understood that we entirely repudiate the idea. *Ne plus ultra* — that is our motto. Still we shall forbear to speak of this matter until it has been investigated by our scientific citizens.'
TINNECUM GAZETTE.

LIFE, in its daily routine, would be dull and tasteless without a little seasoning of romance. How languid would be its current, stirred scarcely by a ripple or a wave, and bearing us on to the regions of death. Among the utilitarians of the present age, addicted almost entirely to sober realities and the plainest matters of fact, we sometimes look back to the vanished heroic ages with a sigh; we hail any vestige of them with delight; and turning from the toils of life, or the pursuit of mere utility, with disgust, we hold it pleasant, as it is rare, on the highways, or on the thoroughfares, or in the fields, or in any of our wanderings, to meet with aught in the shape of a Quixotte, or armed knight, or minstrel, or troubadour, speeding on any errand of mercy, love, tenderness, music, or romance.

TINNECUM AND ROMANCE! When we began to compose these ANNALS, it never occurred to us that these words would be found in juxtaposition. Nor could they ever have been, without the instrumentality of Mr. BRUFF. He, by his chivalric conduct, instituted a new order of affairs. He first introduced nocturnal serenades into Tinnecum, and to the astonished rustics revealed, by the light of the pale moonbeams, the unknown, elegant guitar, swung over his shoulders with consummate grace, and trembling in all its strings beneath his masterly touch. He first taught how delicious music is, when it steals on the wakeful ear at midnight; sudden, unlooked-for, involuntary as a sigh out of the bosom of darkness; or when, too gentle to abolish sleep, it causes smiles to flit over the repose of beauty, and marshals sweet images in dreams. From that hour the progress of refinement was visible. A tender sensibility, a Della Cruscan sympathy, pervaded the hearts of all the women of Tinnecum, and the reign of sentimentalism commenced. The way had been already somewhat prepared for this; but those who will have the patience to peruse these annals, if indeed it be worth our while to carry them out, will be astonished at the rapid transition of society, and how prone men are to pass from one extreme to another, forsaking the paths which their fathers trod, and keeping up with the spirit of the age.

This Mr. Bruff, an inhabitant of the great town of Gotham, came to Tinnecum early in the spring-time, when Nature had clothed the fields with verdure, and the ' gentle zephyrs fanned the creek.'* For

---

* Tinnecum Gazette.

a long time the cause of his visit was a source of serious doubt and conjecture; nor were there wanting those who made it their main business to observe his motions and to deduce his motives. By some it was said that he came to spy out the country, and to write his observations in a book. There were many things worthy of note in Tinnecum; it was a wonder that no traveller had ever mentioned its name. Many imagined that he came to pay attentions to Miss Sharkey, who always blushed when the subject was alluded to; (interesting gëirl!) while others said that he only came 'to go a-crabbing, or may-be a-eeling in Swan Creek, or to shoot yellow-legged snipe,' or to hunt conies in their refuges, upon the high hills, and among the rocks. To us it is little matter of astonishment that the appearance of a gentleman wearing spectacles and a Panama hat, and white pantaloons fastened under the feet, and walking through Tinnecum on a fine Spring morning, should be an object of attention. It would be a matter of greater astonishment if he could manage to get through *without* exciting attention. And if during his continued stay he should still remain the object of curious solicitude and inquiry, it would only prove that there must be something about him worthy of regard. But without stopping to meddle with his conduct, suffice it to say that he was an exemplary young man; in proof of which we will barely state the fact that before he had been in the town a week, the youth of Tinnecum all wore straps under their pantaloons.

Mr. Bruff was a musical amateur of some eminence, and being of a romantic turn, was in the habit of putting an octave-flute in his pocket, and wandering out after night-fall in retired spots, where its exquisite fitful breathings, coming out of grove, and thicket, and sweet recess, were conveyed to the ears of those who listened admiringly in the distance. There was a charming mystery and magic about this, which at first baffled explanation. The superstitious circulated a tale. They said that some places were haunted; that sounds were heard in the middle of the night, which were neither the voice of man, whippoorwill, nor nightingale, but were like the moanings of a spirit, and they fancied that they proceeded from some dead musician of the Tinnecum band. While this affair was yet the subject of much conversation, and underwent the scrutiny of the curious, Mr. Bruff revealed the whole truth, and played 'Moll Brook' most charmingly in open day. Thus was a fruitful topic brought to an untimely end.

This accomplished gentleman was likewise wont to accompany his voice with a Spanish guitar, which he had brought into the country; and it was to this instrument, and to a little romantic expedition which had been projected, that the learned editor, in the great dearth of other news, thus alluded in his columns:

' ON DIT. — We have been favored by our distinguished friend, Mr. BRUFF, with the sight of a *fiddle* of peculiar construction. Let the ladies of this town keep their eyes open, and their ears too. We have been confidentially informed that a great musical treat is in store.'

This exposé was unfair, and very much out of place; and it raised expectations to so high a pitch, that there was great danger of disappointment. Mr. Bruff had written to his friend Thwackit, of the town of Gotham, to bear him company for two or three days at Tinnecum, during which he meditated a serenading party on a considerable scale, out of compliment to the belles of the place. Mr. Thwackit promptly complied with the request, and putting on his sporting-jacket, took his guitar-case in one hand and his double-barrelled fowling-piece in the other, and depositing both in his curricle, drove tandem into Tinnecum, followed by an immense crowd. That very night the serenade came off.

At eight o'clock the parties met in the apartments of Mr. Bruff, and were shortly reïnforced by the arrival of Mr. Dawkins of the Gazette, and Tunnecliffe, a Tinnecum beau of the first water. The doors were then locked, and the work of preparation began. Thwackit overhauled his carpet-bag and drew forth his Spanish song-book; he then opened a case and revealed a guitar of rosewood and ebony, sumptuously inlaid with pearl. It was a piece of furniture on which he doted with all his heart. He never ruralized without it, but made it the sweet companion of all his wanderings. Dawkins' eyes glared and glistened the moment that he got a sight of it. 'Ha!' said he, snatching it up, and giving one of the strings a pull; 'that's fust-rate! That beats Cram's tunin'-fork.'

'Have a care,' said Thwackit; 'do n't bruise it.'

'No, I wo' n't. What's it made of? Black wornut?'

'Strike a light,' said Bruff, ill-humoredly, fumbling for his flute by the moonbeams, and upsetting a flower-vase which stood on the table; 'do n't let us commence operations in the dark.'

A little blue star hung for a moment in air, upon this order, accompanied by the sulphureous smell of a Lucifer match, and presently turning to a yellow flame, was communicated to two mould candles. At the same instant fifty thousand musquitoes started from Swan Creek in the direction of the illuminated windows, to serenade the serenaders. There they were encountered by the nets, and forced to stay without.

When Dawkins saw the music-books spread out, the guitars and flutes, and all the preparations for rehearsal, he had a foretaste and presentiment of 'fairy-like music;' and striking his heels together he sprang from the floor with a cry of delight, and danced a Tinnecum hornpipe. When he had done cutting up these capers, and his exuberant joy had a little subsided, he flung himself at full length cn a cot in the room, propping up his greasy head with Mr. Bruff's pillows. The musician frowned. Mr. Dawkins smiled. 'Go ahead,' said he; 'give us a touch, will you?'

And now commenced a preludial tuning, and strumming, and humming, and thrumming, which lasted for several minutes, and an attempt to make Bruff's flute chord with Thwackit's guitar. Tunnecliffe lamented the flute of the dead TOOTLE. He would have been the greatest musician that Tinnecum ever produced, and beyond question fell a victim to his passionate devotion to the art. He was one of those who never wearied in his favorite pastime, but sat in an open window and from morn to night doled upon the same notes, 'rich as a cuckoo.' It is pleasant to live in the neighborhood of such. The very air which you breathe is impregnated with music. If you read, it hovers around you, sweeter than the poetry of your page.   If you think, it mingles itself with your waking visions, and if you sleep, with your dreams. But mark the expense at which your gratification is obtained.   Tootle fell into a consumption.   First, he blew away one lobe of his lungs, then another, with equal prodigality; after which, melancholy to relate, he 'breathed his last.'   Let the promising young men, who wish to prolong their swan-like notes, take warning.

The evening wore away pleasantly in rehearsal.   'We must be off,' said Thwackit, pulling out his watch, and expressing surprise at the lateness of the hour.   It was nearly midnight, and the Bear was turning at the hand of Boötes.   The members of the party sprang from their seats, and seized their hats, anxious to sally forth.   Thwackit screwed up his guitar to concert-pitch.   It was arranged that he and Bruff should play the accompaniment alternately, and both should sing. Tunnecliffe was to 'jine in' with them in 'Oft in the Stilly Night.' The other songs were unknown to Tinnecum.

Thus prepared, they extinguished the candles, and groped their way down stairs into the street.   They debated for a moment where to go first.   Probably every eye in Tinnecum was closed in slumber.   All was still, and nothing appeared to be abroad except a few dissolute cats, who kept late hours.   Dawkins led the way, followed by the rest of the party.   They crept stealthily along under the shadows of the trees and hedges, without saying a word, and presently came to Swan Creek.   They were going to serenade Miss Chubbs, who lived in a meadow on the opposite side.   A narrow plank was thrown across the stream, and Mr. Thwackit hugged his guitar close as he crossed over the perilous bridge.   All however reached the bank in safety, and proceeded over the fields in the direction of the house, which lay in a hollow or valley at the distance of a quarter of a mile.   There happened to be no pathway; the fields were rough, and presented many obstacles; but what were all these compared with the pleasure of serenading Miss Chubbs?   Bruff scratched his shins with the blackberry bushes and brambles; Thwackit stumbled, and barely recovered himself and his guitar.   These were incidents to be expected in an expedition of this kind, and formed the matériel of laughter and merriment to those who were novices.

'I hope you can climb fences, gentlemen?' said Tunnecliffe.

'Trust us for that,' replied the amateurs.   'And take to your heels, if it be necessary,' added he, in sober earnest.

'Why so?' exclaimed Bruff and Thwackit, in a breath.

'Only I forgot there was a dangerous fractious black bull in this neighborhood, that sometimes attacks strangers.'

'By all the powers!' shouted Dawkins, 'there he comes!'

The musical gentlemen barely turned their heads, when they discovered a black monster of a bull plunging onward, bellowing and heaving up his tail, as if he meant to demolish the whole party, who in fact ran for their very lives.   Never was there such a scampering.   All reached the fence in the nick of time.   Thwackit and his guitar went over with all possible speed; the Tinnecum youths next, and Bruff last, falling at full length, and bruising his heels against a rock.   It took the party some minutes to recover breath. Little damage was actually done, but they reasoned that the affair might have proved very serious. It was a wonder that Thwackit had not broken his guitar, and that its love-resounding strings had not all been snapped. 'Rocks and briars,' said Mr. Bruff, 'are nothing; but it is intolerable to be attacked by the Tinnecum bulls.' That gentleman trembled in every limb, having never met with such a fright in all his moonlight crusades.

At last they reached the house, which seemed to be rather forbidding in its external aspect, and in attempting to enter the gate found it locked. It happened that Chubbs, the master-spirit of the house, had remained up later than usual that night, and had just blown out his candle; but before getting into bed, he looked out of the window, as was his wont, when to his extreme fright and astonishment he discovered four men singularly armed, apparently making an attempt to enter his premises. On the impulse of the moment he threw up the window and hailed them; but as they made no reply, and rather seemed to persist in their effort, he could not stand still and see his house robbed; so he prepared to act promptly. Going down stairs into the kitchen, he took down a musket from the wall, coolly examined, loaded, primed it, and carried it up stairs. Finding that the men had now got into the yard, and were holding a consultation on the porch, no doubt as to how they should break into the house, he watched them yet a little while, that he might do nothing in haste, and that his conscience might be free from blame. When he became thoroughly satisfied what their intentions were, he held the gun out of the window, directed the muzzle of it toward the unfortunate young men, placed his hand upon the trigger, took aim, and ——

Just at this moment a soft strain of music arrested him in the very act of firing on the intruders. He listened attentively for a moment, at a loss to conjecture what it meant, but presuming it to be the work of some wild young blades, and in order to solve the riddle, he put his head out of the window, and again hailed the party. 'Holla there!' said he, in a savage voice; 'what do you want?'

'Only come to serenade Susannah,' replied some one underneath.

'Oh! is that you, Mr. Dawkins? You better go home, young man. Do you know it's a very late hour? You had better be in your beds, all on you, and not go round disturbing folks at this time o' night.'

'Very well; then you do n't want any music?' said the same spokesman.

'No, my friend, not now. Come in the day-time; very happy to see you in the day-time.'

Upon this the whole party turned upon their heels, greatly wondering at this repulse, which was without a parallel in all the annals of serenades. They however made the best of it, making merry with this incident, as they made good their retreat. Undaunted in spirit, they now went to serenade a belle, a beauty whose surpassing charms had been the theme of all, and at whose shrine the Tinnecum youth bowed down in admiration. No doubt she was sleeping sweetly, unmindful of the new homage which was to be paid her, and those beautiful eyes were closed, whose glances had wrought so much destruction. Ah!

how many had lived and would have died for her, led captive at her will! The hearts of the musicians beat quickly, as they drew the little wicket-gate, and entered those sweet precincts, where in the midst of many flowers Beauty had chosen for herself a fitting abode. They sat down under the windows of the small cottage, on a green mound which a willow tree overhung, through whose boughs the stars twinkled. It was a select and silent hour, whose loveliness made it suitable for deeds of romance. The rural landscape lay in the voluptuous light of the high-risen moon, shed down on stream and meadow, and on the dappled herds; and whether in the unbroken silence of the crowded city or the small hamlet, no one looked abroad to contemplate the glorious night; no one, unless the poor wanderer, with no sweet home for a refuge, and no couch on which to lay his weary head in forgetfulness, or the sick man tossing on his feverish pillow, or the dying man who looks out of his casement for the last time upon the light of stars; and there they all shone in their own places in the firmament, satellite, and star, and planet; Jupiter with his peculiar glory, Mars with his red light. Oh! ye orbs, sweetly glimmering, who can gaze at you without rapture?—without smiles, without tears, without prayers to God? without gushings of fond affections, deep thoughts, ardent hopes? Whence and what am I? Whither going? And Thou who wast the dearer part of my soul, whither hast thou fled as with the wings of a dove, and where dwellest thou in all yon regions of space? Almost do we forget the present, the finite, gazing heavenward, transported and lost among those bright stars which seem like islands of the blest. What a study!—what a page! Pure, sparkling, full of poetry seldom read by the many. And this is true of the effulgent noon-day not less than of the solemn night. Then the voices of Nature are drowned by the cries of humanity. The devotee is absorbed in the pursuit of gain, and the artisan struggles for his daily bread: and when the night comes, and the music of the spheres is heard, they shut their eyes for very weariness.

We indeed are not astronomers. We know not to trace the courses of the planets; we know not Orion or Pleiades, except to behold them, as would a poet, in the chambers of the sky. But there is a heaven which we love to gaze at, whose pure lights are reflected into the very soul; where the young, the beautiful, fill up the zodiac of its bright sphere; passionate orbs, differing from one another in glory; yet pure, spiritual, distant, shining with their own light, the centres of their harmonious systems, around whom thoughts, feelings, loves, passions, and affections circle; the lights of a true science, the controllers of many destinies, gazed at adoringly while they shine upon earth — tenderly wept when missed from heaven: these are the stars which we could ever worship, and this the astronomy we love.

Listen! What sounds are those which steal out softly on the midnight air, enchaining me to earth, and breaking in upon my rhapsody?

> ' Auditis? an me ludit amabilis
> Insania? '

Lo! in the depth of the still night, in the obscurity and shades of Tinnecum, the *Cachucha* is played with surpassing grace, awaking sensations in the minds of all who ever witnessed the Mistress of the Dance; and just where the moonbeams break through the chinks and chasms of the overhanging foliage, and strike with contrasted lustre on the green lawn, forth from the darkness of the side-thickets, a nymph comes bounding on the silvan theatre. What motions! what extatic comeliness! We see the glancing of her steel-clad feet, and listen to the sound of castanets. Is it imagination, or is it one of the many fantasies which the witchery of moonlight always conjures up to ardent souls? It is not difficult to decide; but we will say, so rapidly does Fame fly to the remotest places of the earth, that the great enchantress, to whose twinkling feet so many hearts have kept measure, had been heard of even here. Her fame is indeed coëxtensive with the world, having escaped the dreaded obscurity which hovers over the natal hour of many. But had she lived alway in this place, instead of being born on the banks of the Rhine, nurtured by the Academy, caressed by the nobles, applauded by the populace, crowned with roses, and dragged in triumphal chariots, she might have been doomed to *blush*, if that were possible, unseen, and waste her sweetness on the desert air. On the other hand, we doubt not there have been heels born at Tinnecum which have degenerated into graceless movements and the heavy tramp; confined in their sphere of action, compelled to move only in the rustic dance, or beat the earth at harvest-home; when with a sufficient education, with a just developement of the joints and muscles, and elastic attributes, they might have bounded at once on a proper stage; captivating lofty intellects, and subjecting the whole world:

> ' Toll her that's young,
> And loves to have her graces spied,
> That had she lived
> In deserts where no men abide,
> She must have uncommended died.' *

Ever since the *début* of the Chipps at Tinnecum, the inhabitants had been apprized of theatrical intelligence, and felt an interest in the drama. It formed a prominent topic in all circles, (Chubbs' excepted,) and such important bits of news as the following were read with eagerness in the Gazette:

' The season has closed brilliantly at Bangor.
' Tho authorities at New-Lebanon have turned the drama out of town.
' Bruin, the black bear, has gone to Sag-Harbor. The wonderful pig will follow shortly.
' The learned goat is dead. *De mortise!*
' Hervio Nano has taken passage for Tuscany.
' Jim Crow is rusticating on Long Island.
' The Crummles are expected in this country in the course of the next season. We regret to learn that Miss Snevellici has been seriously ill of the fever-aig.
' The Chipps have got back to the metropolis.
' That capital fellow, Jo Annis, has taken the theatre at Buffalo. Success to him.
' The Callithumpians are at Cow-neck.
' We cannot inform our readers of the whereabout of Dickey Suett.
' We now add to the above, the astounding intelligence, which has this moment reached our ears, that THE ELSSLER may be confidently expected to dance at Tinnecum! Chipp has been written to, to engage her at all hazards, and to bring her on with his own wife, all three to form a superb *corpse-de-ballet*. She is to have the most liberal terms. Half the proceeds of the whole house, after paying for the candles, to board around among the farmers during her stay, and to be dragged around in a two-horse wagon, to which Squire Sharkey and the Board of Selectmen have in the most obliging manner consented to be harnessed.'

---

* WALLER.

Such was the triumph anticipated for the Elssler. It was a happy thought in the musicians to open with the *Cachucha,* which would have sounded deliciously, but for the presence of a cow with a bell round her neck. This vexatious creature, who was lying quietly down on the grass when the party arrived, chewing her cud, pretty soon got upon her legs, and went stalking about, with a ding-dong at every step. The soft notes of the flute were no match for those of the cow-bell, and as every pretty turn in the air was thus destroyed, Thwackit's lip, which was rolled down over the débouchure of the flute, assumed a malignant expression, dimly perceptible by moonlight. 'Stupid brute!' exclaimed he, stamping on the turf in the height of vexation.

'Ding, dong!'

'We might as well return home—'

'Ding, dong!'

'And hang up our fiddles.'

'Ding, dong!'

'I think so too,' said Bruff.

'Ding, dong!'

'Hold on, gentlemen!' said Dawkins, volunteering, and moving off after the cow.

'Ding, dong! ding, dong! . . . ding, dong! ding, dong! . . . ding, dong—dong! . . . ding, dong! . . . dong!'

Fainter and fainter sounded the tinkling of the bell, and at last became pleasantly distant, when Mr. Dawkins returned breathless, making his way through the bushes. 'Hist!' said he, leaning against the trunk of the willow, and pointing upward; 'only look! I see her. She's a-sittin' at the window with her hair done up in papers. Shall I holler? I'm a good mind to holler.'

Bruff shook his flute in a threatening manner over Mr. Dawkins, who forthwith faltered in his inclination to 'holler;' and all things being now still, and the musicians hearing the sash raised higher overhead, and conscious that they possessed the ear of Beauty, raised their voices, and to Mr. Thwackit's accompaniment thus sang :

'Una paloma blanca
Como la nieve
Si, madre cita,
Como la nieve, si,
Me ha pecado en el pecho
Si, madre cita, si.'

The last echoes of the music died away, and all was again hushed. Not a murmur was heard, not a ripple stirred, not a leaf moved, and the stars shone down through the stilly night; but she who was the guiding-star to the faith of so many, looked down from her casement, having admired the song; but she mistook it for low Dutch, in her innocent heart, and did not know that it was about a white dove, as white as snow. 'Janet,' whispered she, turning to her fair-haired sister, 'it is the beautifullest music! I'm sure it is the very song that old Hans Carvel's widow used to sing when she sot at her spinning-wheel in the old porch. I wonder if they're going away yet.'

'No, no, no!' exclaimed Mr. Dawkins, audibly; 'not by a jug-full! How-de-do, Susan?'

At this astounding impudence, Thwackit sprang back a foot or two
upon tip-toe, and grappling his guitar, club-like, in both hands, was in the
act of splitting it on the cranium of Mr. Dawkins of the Gazette, when
catching a glimpse of the glittering pearl and elaborate workmanship
of the instrument, he remained statue-like in the threatening attitude,
and exacted a promise from that gentleman to repress for the remainder of the evening his propensity to ' holler.'   This being settled, Mr.
Bruff now seized the guitar and attuned it anew with as little ado as
possible.   During this process, a slight clanking of chains met the ears
of the amateurs, and the noise as of some beast arousing from his lair,
followed by a low monotonous growl.

' Ha!' said Bruff, ' do you hear that?'

' B-wow!'

' No matter,' answered Dawkins, ' he 's chained fast; he 'll stop as
soon as he hears the music.'

' Bow — wow — wow — wow!'

Lulled by a false hope, the musicians began, and the dog at the same
time; but the former persisted in spite of interruption, and sang in
plaintive accents, lifting their eyes up steadily to the casement, as follows :

> ' Thou, thou reign'st in this — bow — wow !
> There, there hast thou thy throne ;
> Bow — wow ! — know'st that I love thee —
> Am I not fondly thine own ?
> Yes, yes — bow ! wow !
> Am I not fondly thine own ?'

' Curse that dog !   Bruff, shall we go on?'

' Bow — wow — wow — wow !   Bow — wow — wow — wow !'

' Go after him, Dawkins, that 's a good fellow :'

> ' Speak ! speak ! speak, I implore thee,
> Bow — wow — wow !
> Say, say, thou wilt love me ;
> Thoughts, thoughts, tender and — bow — wow !
> Say thou wilt cherish for me :
> Yes, yes — bow ! wow !
> Say thou wilt cherish for me.'

' Too bad! too bad!' exclaimed all the members of the party, when
the song was finished.   ' We 'll sing ' Oft in the Stilly Night,' and
then go.'   But the dog became perfectly outrageous during the last
performance, and was assisted by another dog who ' jined in' with him,
producing an intolerable concert of sounds, in the midst of which the
sensitive ears of the musicians appeared to distinguish the suppressed
titter of the lady at the window.   They therefore opened the little gate,
and passed out; and were it not for the extremely pleasant events
which followed, we are certain that this would have been the first and
last serenade ever given at Tinnecum.

The party had the good fortune to find all things silent in the heart
of the village; and when they halted the next time, undisturbed by
cows and dogs, cats and owls, or any other sounds which make night
hideous, they took possession of a clear field, and sang with a clearness
and spirit which struck immediately on the ears of the sleeping inhabi-

tants. The Tinnecum belle, whose head had scarcely been restored to its pillow, started up again at the first revival of the notes, and leaning on her elbow, while she listened attentively: 'Janet,' said she, 'hark! they're playing again! I wonder if they play the same tunes everywhere?' Miss Chubbs could faintly distinguish the music from the other side of Swan Creek, and felt a degree of vexation and disappointment which marred her whole countenance, hanging over it like a heavy cloud when she came to breakfast next morning, and dissipated by no sunshine during the rest of the day.

When the amateurs had sung 'Una paloma' over again, they looked around and found their party reïnforced by a fifth person, of curious physiognomy, who had hitherto slept in a barrel, but rolled out fully dressed when he heard the music, and began to peer with such intense earnestness into the faces of the performers, that they faltered, and were fain to break through with the Cracovienne in the very midst. Jimmy Hayden, son of Erin, hod-carrier, was ordered to go about his business forthwith; but his face beamed with pleasant smiles, and he stuck to the party like a leech. He was hoarse, and could hardly speak except in a whisper. 'God save the Queen!' said he, seizing Bruff by the elbow, and looking up significantly under his Panama hat. 'St. Pathrick's in the Mornin'.' The musicians laughed, and did not gratify his wishes, but they sang 'Home, sweet Home;' whereat Jimmy Hayden sat down on a stone and cried profusely. The drops were visible in his eyes. By this time all the windows along the street were lifted up, and several night-caps fell down. On one of these was inscribed in a neat hand, 'Amelia Sharkey, No. 3.' While the amateurs curiously inspected this article, a door was thrown open, and the 'Squire made his appearance in the street, with a pleased countenance. 'Gentlemen,' said he, 'your music does honor to you. It was unexpected. Accept our thanks. Never, in my recollection, has Tinnecum experienced such a treat.'

'You're welcome, 'Squire,' replied Mr. Dawkins; 'we thought you'd like it.'

'You thought right, Sir. I'm happy to see you, gentlemen; it's oncommon to hear music played on, in the middle of the night: it's oncommon.'

'We've been attackted by dogs onc't,' said Mr. Dawkins.

'And met with other adventures,' said Mr. Bruff.

'And came near scratching our guitar,' added Mr. Thwackit.

'Jus' so, jus' so,' replied the 'Squire. 'You may play before *my* door as long as you'm a-mind to—you may: there's not the slightest objection, rest assured, gentlemen. There's no difficul'.'

''Squire,' said Mr. Dawkins, 'you haven't got a little cool water, right out of the well, have you? Dry work, this singin'.'

'*Water*, indeed! Walk in, gentlemen; I'll give you somethin' better than water. Walk in, walk in.'

So saying, the 'Squire led the way, and conducted the whole party into his best parlor. Absenting himself for a few moments, he returned with a pitcher of cider, some crackers, and some cheese. These he pressed upon the gentlemen in the most obliging manner, conferring upon them the highest compliments, and assuring them that his daughter had listened to every word, and would be pleased to hear some of the songs repeated. After a gratifying and congratulatory visit, the musicians returned again to the street, where they sang until they were hoarse, and Mr. Dawkins cut sundry shines, having become exhilarated with the cider. Time would fail me to record all the pleasant adventures which befel them; how many lively faces peered out upon the serenaders; how many dark visages looked down astonished from the attic stories; and how they all came flocking like clouds and doves to their windows. Had poor Tootle have lived, how delighted he would have been to have joined that exhibition, and like Mr. Swiveller, to have fluted it all night! A kind reception met the serenaders wherever they went; and when they reached home, and laid their heads upon their pillows, the first faint streak of light had appeared in the eastern sky, and the impatient birds were welcoming in the new day with their sweetest notes.

THE PARTING OF THE WATERS.

On the hill of the ridge that separates the basin of the Lakes from that of the tributaries to the Mississippi, two springs gush out within a short distance from each other, one to lose itself in the bosom of the Saint Lawrence, and the other to mingle its wave with the great Father of Waters.
          'LETTERS FROM THE WEST.'

I.

Twin founts! from the same rocky caverns ye burst,
On the same verdant bosom your wavelets are nurst;
And the sunbeams and shadows upon ye have played,
Where the same lofty forest hangs o'er you its shade.

II.

Ye list to the songs of the same wild wood-bird,
Your own merry music together is heard;
Nor can Echo, sweet sisters! amid the rocks tell
Your voices apart in her moss-covered cell.

III.

Together ye sport, and together ye start,
Yet, springs of the mountain! how quickly ye part!
How widely ye flow till ye melt in the main:
Sweet streams! will your waters there mingle again?

IV.

How like are our lives, gentle streamlets! to you,
How transient the joys that our infancy knew!
How far are we torn from the friends we deplore:
O, loved ones and lost! shall we meet you no more?

          P.

We stay not ; for we seek again
Each his own native mountain glen ;
And there, when some kind bird will share
Our fondest loves and parent care,
Near the same spot we 'll build a nest,
Where erst our infant dreams were blest :
And when the mower whets his sithe,
  He 'll listen to the Boblink's song :
Earth cannot boast a bird more blithe,
  When June's gay hours are bright and long.

SCENES IN HOLLAND.

BY AN AMERICAN.

EVERY country has some distinguishing mark, which separates it from all others, and renders it note-worthy. France has her delightful climate, and beautifully-undulating surface ; Italy her romantic scenery and fading ruins ; Switzerland her soul-swelling, snow-capped mountains ; and Egypt her pyramids, coeval with the soil ; but none of these surpass Holland in *originality* of appearance to the eye of an American traveller. She has not the hilly surface of France, but she has the surface of a floor ; she has not the romance of Italy, yet she often surpasses it in the ' still picturesque.' She has not the pyramids ; yet may the Hollander point to his sea-wrested plains as a monument more glorious and more lasting than a pyramid that should o'ertop the Andes. To the lover of the past, she has not the plains of Pharsalia nor Actium ; yet she has a greater than either — a Waterloo ; that is, she *had*, before the separation of Belgium. To the connoisseur, she does not present the names of Raphael or Michael Angelo ; yet there are the names of Rubens, and Van Dyke, and Rembrandt. She cannot point the traveller to a Paris, nor a Versailles ; yet the Hague and Brussels are very, *very* delightful towns. Where now men, women, and children live, move, and have their being, and where the smoke of their pipes ascends for ever and ever, formerly spouted the whale, darted the shark, flew the flying-fish, leaped the dolphin, cosily lay the oyster and the crab, in thoughtful quiet, little dreaming of the short, thick-set race of men, who with pick-axes and spades were to colonize among them, and banish them from their kingdom.

Such were the miscellaneous thoughts which crowded my brain as I stood in that ' valley of the shadow of death,' beneath the level of the sea, and thought of its redemption thence, and all its curious history. If the Hollanders did expel the sea, it was not that they loved water less, but land more ; for they still permit old Ocean to visit his ancient domain, through their ten hundred canals, yet not to overwhelm. Approaching the coast, you see no lofty highland, indeed nothing, until you are almost upon it ; and then all that meets the eye is the handiwork of man.

My first place of landing was at Niew-Diep, the entrepôt of Amsterdam for vessels not desirous of ascending to the city. The harbor is very fine, though somewhat difficult of access. At the time of my arrival, there were several government vessels in port, whose beautiful models completely nonplused me; associating, as I had always been taught to do, every thing Dutch with grossness or deformity. But if the government vessels agreeably disappointed my previous conceptions, the smaller craft, sailing or rather *tumbling* about the bay, tended little to remove them. They were emphatically what we should term *fat ;* approaching more nearly the form of the Dutch belles, who are chosen rather for what they can bear, than for their symmetry. I mean only the ' lower orders ' of the inhabitants ; for Heaven forfend that I should disparage the beauty of the higher class of Hollanders, for the women of few nations on the Continent can compare with them in symmetry of form, beauty of face, and grace of manner. These vessels are seldom painted ; but are varnished over, and apparently very loosely put together ; yet in an encounter with a rock in the ocean, it is somewhat doubtful which would go down ! The rudder is hooked upon the outside, as represented in antique Dutch paintings; so that they can easily be unshipped ; a provision often taken advantage of, when the government or individuals are desirous of detaining the craft. Taking possession of the rudder is equivalent to seizing the vessel.

The town of Niew-Diep, as I have said, was my first place of landing ; and here the first features which arrested my eye, were the erections of Napoleon ; the navy-yard, of great extent ; the town, which he caused to be paved, and its buildings erected. Here it was that he hoped to build a fleet to cope with England. Landing for the first time in a monarchical government, I prepared myself for many little vexations ; such as examination of passports, as though one were a spy ; of your luggage, as though you were a thief; of your person, as if one had the plague. That I was free of the last, a mere glance of the doctor soon convinced him; of my luggage, he either took no notice, because he did not esteem it note-worthy, or else he read honesty in my face ; and the passport I never presented until I reached Amsterdam, and even there, not until three or four days after my arrival. As for *gens-d'arme*, there were not more than three in either city, except at the government buildings. Indeed, Holland may be considered a pretty free country. The people openly discuss political and social matters, and express their likes and dislikes in very democratic style.

The country, however, is most enormously taxed ; nearly one-half or one-third going to the government, and mainly for the purpose of paying the interest of debts incurred in filling in the sea. The only reason for their not taking immediate possession of another small sea, is the want of money ; although some assert that they do not wish to disturb some fifty or sixty fishermen who yet float there ; and that they are waiting patiently until they shall die off, when ' the restoration ' will at once take place.

Once again on shore, weary enough of the sea, I shook myself and proceeded ' to observe.' The houses stand with their sides to the street, and are of one story, built of the little home-made bricks which were formerly brought to our goodly city, and are still to be seen in one or two old KNICKERBOCKER houses. Each dwelling has a little 'stoop' before, or more correctly speaking, beside it. All the streets are paved with brick, turned side-wise, which resist wheels very well. The side-walks are wide enough for a good-sized Dutch dame. Most of them, however, prefer to walk in the street itself, always as neat and clean as brooms and all the cleansing paraphernalia can keep it.

Whether it is that the Hollander* is more humane or civilized than the Americans, or whether it is because there is a lack of loose stones in the streets, I know not; but certain it is, the thoroughfares are filled with little birds, skipping gaily among the feet of the inhabitants, and living in the eves of the houses, which you can generally reach from the ground; but on my approach, I noticed that they scanned me with an evil eye; as though they knew that I came from a country where stones were plentiful, and where their race was little respected. Several storks'-nests, a principal feature in all Dutch paintings, also attracted my attention; but none of the young were supporting on their backs their venerable sires.

Coming from a consumptive city like New-York, I was naturally led to regard the state of the disease in this country; but owing to the practice of allowing the person to 'run to waist,' or in other words, not *corsetting*, as with us, I could discover no symptoms of this fatal, incurable malady. All appear as GOD made them. The women are round and plump. There are no waspish bodies and dwindling waists, which one is really afraid to clasp, lest they should part in the middle. Some of the women, as I have said, are truly beautiful, but none *pretty ;* that is something too *dollish* a term for their circumference; with faces as fresh as the morning, as full as the moon, and fair as the heavens. Yet, dear creatures! they *do* have to work; sometimes dragging a wagon-load sufficient for a horse, and at others bearing the burden of a pannier'd mule on their heads. The women wear a head-piece, made of gold or silver, worth often fifty or a hundred dollars; mostly too among the lower orders; servants, who have not apparently a change of stockings. But I am informed it is the only out-fit they have in life. As they generally wear only caps, these head-pieces are less distasteful than they would appear on the heads of our American 'helps.'

'Laborious as a Dutchman' has become a proverb, and the race richly deserve the appellation. 'As honest as a Dutchman,' is another proverb, equally true; for they are a miracle of honesty. The women and men work in the fields together. The former appear lively, the latter dull and heavy. The Dutchman's ideas move like his canal-boat; the Anglo-Saxon's like a locomotive. A mixture of Yankees in the race would be a God-send with them. Dutch industry and Yankee ingenuity! The very ocean would be filled out, and one could ere long walk to America!

Regularity is another distinguishing trait of the Hollander. Everything moves like clock-work. Were a coach-spring to break, the mail

---

* This is his proper name. These people are as grateful to you for calling them *Dutchmen*, as we should be to be designated by our own countrymen as *Yankees*.

would be stopped six months, unless an entire new spring were inserted, or a new coach obtained. There is no invention. All is experience. As their fathers were, so are they. They revolve ever in the same circle. A new idea only bursts upon them every half century, completely dumbfounding them. Promptitude is another trait. Should one of them contract for building a house within seven years, on that day seven years, at twelve o'clock, the house would be finished; and though he trebled the number of workmen, yet it would not be in the least expedited; while in the same time a Yankee would have finished his contract and the half of another.

After spending several days at this agreeable little town, visiting the region round about, I took leave of its inhabitants, with many of whom I had become quite intimately acquainted; and among the number, with several excellent and interesting Dutch girls. I left Niew-Diep at sunrise. It was quite a novelty to the inhabitants, judging from the numbers assembled, although the same scene takes place every day. Such farewells, such waving of handkerchiefs, such elongating of round faces, I never saw before. It reminded me of those felicitous times when men made their wills, and added codicils to them, before trusting their persons across the Tappaan-Zee to Albany. Hoisting sail, (for this they carry, the wind having free scope over the plane-country,) and stirring up our two horses, along went our *treckschuyt*, at the rate of four miles an hour, perhaps more. These boats are very commodious. They are divided into three parts; the foremost for steerage passengers, the central part for ladies and gentlemen in general, and the latter or hinder part, as was proper, for ' exclusives' *par excellence.* The forward-cabin passengers were continually singing national airs — tunes which I never before had the honor of hearing — and that during the whole voyage, while a Frenchman was blowing on the French horn. Oh, doleful day! The air was cold; the windows were closed, of course; and there sat some two dozen men, puffing, puffing, ever puffing away. I remained seated while I could discern the opposite side of the cabin; but when I could only fairly see the end of my nose, ' the force of nature could no farther go.' I rushed on deck, where I remained, promenading in the cold, for the remainder of the passage. The Dutch may have altered in some respects; but they maintain all their old renown as smokers.

But a word touching the country through which we are passing, On all sides appears a low, level meadow, well cultivated, and of excellent soil, yet beneath the level of the canal. Often fifty or sixty windmills are visible at once, mostly used for draining the land, which is continually filling with water. What an army for Don Quixotte! Villages lie scattered in every direction, of the most picturesque description, so diversified are the colors used in painting the dwellings. Out of every one, as we passed, would rush a half-dozen boys and girls, turning somersets, and singing their unmusical airs. The passengers, sticking a potato full of half-cents, throw them on shore; when a scrambling scene ensues, that would do credit to office-seekers; and thus village succeeds village. The only place of any interest which we passed was

Alkemar, once the scene of a great battle, but where there was now nothing remarkable, save a ceaseless chiming of bells.—But I am at Amsterdam.

THE MISSING SHIP.

BY EPES SARGENT.

' What sighs have been wafted after that ship !— what prayers offered up at the deserted fire-side of home ! How often has the mistress, the wife, the mother, pored over the daily news, to catch some casual intelligence of this victim of the deep ! How has expectation darkened into anxiety — anxiety into dread — and dread into despair ! Alas ! not one memento shall ever return for love to cherish ! All that shall ever be known is, that she sailed from her port, ' and was never heard of more ! '

WASHINGTON IRVING.

I.

God speed the noble PRESIDENT !
A gallant boat is she,
As ever entered harbor,
Or cross'd a stormy sea.
Like some majestic castle
She floats upon the stream ;
The good ships moor'd beside her
Like pigmy shallops seem !

II.

How will her mighty bulwarks
The leaping surges brave !
How will her iron sinews
Make way 'gainst wind and wave !
Farewell, thou stately vessel !
Ye voyagers, farewell !
Securely on that deck shall ye
The tempest's shock repel.

III.

The stately vessel left us
In all her bold array ;
A glorious sight, O landsmen !
As she glided down our bay :
Her flags were waving joyfully,
And from her ribs of oak
' Farewell ! ' to all the city
Her guns in thunder spoke.

IV.

Flee, on thy vapory pinions !
Back, back to England flee !
Where patient watchers by the strand
Have waited long for thee ;
Where kindred hearts are beating
To welcome home thy crew,
And tearful eyes gaze constantly
Across the waters blue !

v.

Alas, ye watchers by the strand!
 Weeks, months have roll'd away,
But where, where is the President?
 And why is this delay?
Return, pale mourners, to your homes!
 Ye gaze, and gaze in vain;
Oh! never shall that pennon'd mast
 Salute your eyes again!

vi.

And now our hopes, like morning stars,
 Have one by one gone out;
And stern despair subdues at length
 The agony of doubt:
But still Affection lifts the torch
 At night along the shore,
And lingers by the surf-beat rocks,
 To marvel, to deplore.

vii.

In dreams I see the fated ship
 Torn by the northern blast;
About her tempest-riven track
 The white fog gathers fast;
When, lo! above the swathing mist
 Their heads the icebergs lift,
In lucent grandeur to the clouds —
 Vast continents adrift!

viii.

One mingled shriek of awe goes up,
 At that stupendous sight;
Now, helmsman, for a hundred lives,
 Oh! guide the helm aright!
Vain prayer! She strikes! and thundering down,
 The avalanches fall;
Crush'd, whelm'd, the stately vessel sinks —
 The cold sea covers all!

ix.

Anon, unresting Fancy holds
 A direr scene to view;
The burning ship, the fragile raft,
 The pale and dying crew!
Ah me! was such their maddening fate
 Upon the billowy brine?
Give up, remorseless Ocean!
 A relic and a sign!

x.

No answer cometh from the deep,
 To tell the tale we dread;
Nor shall it, till the trump shall sound,
 And the sea give up its dead.
Oh, then may that lost company,
 From earthly haven driven,
Meet where the weary are at rest,
 And storms reach not — in heaven!

THE COUNTRY DOCTOR:

AN AUTOBIOGRAPHY: WRITTEN AT THE REQUEST OF GLAUBER SAULTZ, M. D.

CHAPTER SEVENTH.

ONE day a gentleman in sportsman's attire knocked at the gate, and asked for a glass of water. He received the boon from my man Flummery, and while he extolled its purity and delightful coolness, I seemed to recognize a familiar voice, and on looking up, discovered indeed my old friend and fellow-student, Dr. Hawkins. He was not less surprised than glad to see me; and being prevailed on to walk in, related whatever of adventure had befallen him, and was pleased in turn to listen very obsequiously to the mishaps and trials of a country doctor. A half an hour passed very agreeably in this way, when he was compelled to resume his pouch and gun, and proceed on his journey, being anxious to return home from a long excursion on the island. Previous to his departure, he related that he had discovered in his rambles in the woods an old Indian, lying alone in his hut, in the last stage of life, whom he besought me, according to the kindness of his nature, to go and see; and having described the locality, and exacted this promise, Dr. Hawkins bade me farewell.

A season of more than ordinary leisure, somewhat of curiosity, and somewhat I hope of a better principle, induced me to set out immediately on this errand, which indeed led me very far from my customary route. But the beauties of the country cheerfully beguiled the way. It was a pleasant way, such as I have heretofore described it, leading over sweet valleys, and little hill-tops, through shadowy lanes, and along the brows of eminences which overlooked the varied landscape. The year had indeed begun to decay, but the leaves took the deep tints and more gorgeous hues of autumn, too soon to perish, to be trodden under foot, and sported with by the winter winds. It seemed but yesterday since I saw them budding in the spring-time, ere they burst forth in all their luxury of shade. How rapidly do the seasons wax and wane! How soon the flowers vanish, and the blossoms are matured to fruit! The harvest is past, the summer is ended; and while we search diligently where the late roses linger, the cold winter locks up the earth. Nevertheless the spring comes round again, and restores the glory of the season; but, as the poet has expressed it, when *we* go whither our ancestors have gone, we are but dust and shade.

I entered the thick forest, striking soon upon a path which would conduct me to my destination, and then I began to reflect earnestly on that race of men who have indeed flourished and passed away like leaves. Where are they, in all the wide land which was once their birth-right and their heritage? What monuments remain of them on the mountains or in the valleys, or on great battle-grounds, where the chieftain and his exploits are alike unremembered, for the want of an historian or sacred bard? There, instead of a perpetual stillness, broken only by the terrific war-cry, is heard the hum of the populous city, and the architect and the sculptor work out the memorials of their own genius, and the heroes of a later age. What a phenomenon is presented in the fate of the Indian! Other races have been deprived of national existence, and trampled under the feet of the conquerer; have remained slaves for ages, and their ancient spirit has been forever quenched. But their descendants still live upon the earth, and although despised and degenerate, linger within the shadows of their old monuments, which still rise to heaven to tell of a former age, and to reproach them with their ignominy. But these wholly perish. Day by day the whole race diminishes and fades away from the earth, and the places which once knew them, know them no more for ever.

He who has a human heart, cannot but think it a melancholy spectacle to mark the continual procession of these poor children from the sea to the mountains, and from the mountains to the Great River, and from the Great River to the opposite sea; and to behold the process of annihilation steadily going on. What part has the white man borne in their many sorrows, and how far will a just Heaven hold him responsible for oppression? It is an unpleasant office to forbode evil; yet we sometimes remember that innumerable tribes still live in their own wilds beyond the Mississippi, where the tide of emigration has never rolled. To their bosoms is confided a knowledge of the wrongs which their race has sustained, and a sense of foul injustice; and the time may yet come when they shall strike one blow for vengeance, and settle the arrears of the great debt which is due. The Gauls once knocked at the gates of Rome, in her palmy days, and she repulsed them from her capital. Centuries passed away, and she had subdued the whole world, and the wealth of many kingdoms contributed to her luxuries; and then the Goths came and destroyed her temples, and works of art, and burned up the city. And so with us, if the same causes operate, the barbarians may again pour down upon us; startle the ears of the defenceless with the obsolete war-whoop,; ravage the country; pluck down the star-spangled flag which may have waved for ages over the Capitol, and trample the statue of WASHINGTON in the dust. And it may be at a time when there shall be none to deliver; when all of Roman virtue shall have departed; when the republic shall have glided into the empire, and when the empire shall have fallen upon the venal days of Julianus, when there shall be no Brutus to wield the sword of the avenger; no Mutius to devote himself to his country; no Cocles to defend the passage of the bridge; no Curtius to leap into the flaming gulf.

But although I believe the Indian to have been the victim of accumulated wrongs, I am not one of those who are disposed to extol beyond its deserts the character of the American savage, or to place him on the score of intellect and the higher attributes of mind, above other untutored men. The grand and solemn state with which he roams his native wilds, the oriental imagery of his language, and above all, a just sense of his misfortunes, may have led to a too lavish praise of his intellectual character. He is not without some virtues and noble traits; but unlike other savage tribes, he is not prevailed on to yield up his barbarous habits, but resolutely refuses to sit down within the pale of society, or to acknowledge the institutions of civilized men. It seems impossible to mitigate his nature, except at the expense of all which before ennobled him. Where civilization is, there he is not. He steadily melts away at its approach. He is corrupted by all its vices, he is benefited by none of its rich blessings. Place him in the midst of a country where christianity has modified and refined the habits of external life; where villages have arisen, and temples are erected to God, and the cultivated landscape smiles every where : though it be impossible to flee entirely from the sight of human habitations, the noise of the farm-yard and the hum of industry, he will still have the semblance of solitude, and is enamored of the scanty woods which the axe has spared. Place him in the heart of cities; subject him to the polish of education and refined life ; bind him there by strong ties, and suffer him to remain for years ; yet when occasion offers he revolts with gladness to his barbarous life ; recurs to his former nakedness, banishes letters, prefers the spear to the pruning-hook, and goes glooming in the deepest forests, until he dies within their melancholy shades. What wonder, that being so constituted, he should give way before the restless energies of the Saxon race ? — that the latter should possess themselves of the whole land, and that he should waste away and die?

Such thoughts, and others of a like nature, were suggested to me as I proceeded on my journey, very naturally by the nature of my errand, and the thick gloom of the woods. For here, on the very ground over which I now passed, the powerful Montauks once reigned. The island tribes knew the prowess of their brave warriors, and fled before them in the battle. Here they once roamed. The very trees then lived, whose old branches waved over me ; and the surrounding thickets afforded them a refuge and an ambuscade. Not many years have passed away, since a handful of the tribe occupied a small neck of land. They were miserable beings, almost in a state of nature, living on shell-fish and the fruits of the earth, and never cultivating the little land which they possessed. The fire-water had consumed them : day by day they perished. Presently their number was reduced to six ; then only one was left, the representative and last man of his tribe. He now lay dying. On turning an angle of the path I started, as what man is not startled on coming suddenly on a rude habitation in the thick woods?

The abode of the Solitary was before me. It was a wigwam, constructed in the usual way. The door was closed, and there were some indications on the outside that it might recently have been inhabited. A pitcher lay broken at a spring, which gushed at the foot of an aged oak. But I saw no one. None cared for the old Indian. No brother came to administer to him in his last hour ; no minister of God to point the way to heaven. I only discovered the retreating footsteps of my friend.

I dismounted, approached the threshold, softly drew the latch of the door, and entered the one apartment. It was blackened with smoke, and disorderly. A few articles of rude furniture were strown about. A rusty rifle hung upon the wall. On a low and miserable pallet, covered with scanty clothing, guarded by a wolfish half-starved dog, who was extended at his master's feet, lay the red man, worn out with old age and disease. For eighty years he had willingly lived in these woods, and here he was content to die. I drew near his hard couch, gave water to him, which his parched lips rejected, and spoke a few words, of which he took little notice. His candle of life just flickered in its socket. As I stood over him, and gazed upon his furrowed brow, and reflected that he was the very last of his once powerful tribe, and that in a few moments I should see him breathe his last, the thought almost overpowered me. Here was indeed a lesson and a moral, to which the most impressive orator could hardly add any weight. What eloquence was equal to the eloquence of that silence, and those dumb, closed lips? Nor could the ruins of the desert, and all the relics of a voluptuous people, the shaft, the obelisk, and the temple prostrate, so touch the heart, as this living, dying memorial of a past race.

He who has occupied a position similar to my own, must have seen death in its many forms of terror or alleviation; whether it violently tears the soul asunder, or steals over the eye-lids like a pleasant sleep. He must have seen the old and the young perish; the poor man relinquishing the abode of penury; the rich man tossing on soft pillows, loath to go down from his palace of luxury to the grave: yet methinks that in the midst of those lone woods, in the melancholy time of autumn, gazing on that death-bed, I beheld a rare spectacle. Elsewhere I may have looked upon the last pangs of individuals; well-beloved it may be, and whose absence renders desolate many hearts. But what was *this*, but the wish of Caligula accomplished, and to see a whole nation struggle and die? Yes; in that bosom which yet heaved instinct with life, methought I beheld the concentrated throes of the race; in that faded form the impersonation of all which made the savage noble; his fierce valor, his unconquered spirit, his lofty pride; in those lips which moved not, an expression of vindictive scorn; in those eyes, which were yet lustrous, an eloquence which spoke of injustice unatoned for; of treaties broken, of lands wrested, of graves rifled, and which heaped contumely from him, the last of his race, on myself, who stood there as the representative of my own.

It is accounted hard to have outlived one's own immediate kindred; yet I have seen such an one die pleasantly. Though he may have laid successively in the grave all who were most near to him; the dear companion whose tender beauty first captivated his young heart; the sweet images of children who bloomed like flowers through a short summer, and then died; the manly form of sons who should have been the prop of his last years; nay even children's children; yet when he dies, his own race are around him; soft hands smooth his pillow; true mourners follow him to the grave, sprinkle the fresh sod with many tears, and find a place for him in their memory. He dies, but his country liveth; and that makes the patriot's heart throb once more.

But here was one who perished unwept, unpitied; the *last man* in his own solitary world! A hundred years ago, and he could have called up a thousand warriors to do his slightest will. Now he had none to close his eye-lids, and happily no foe to contend with but the last Enemy. Ha! he was even now in the grasp of the Destroyer. See! he lifts up his skeleton arm; he waves it in the direction of the setting sun; his eyes stare wildly around; they are fixed! — his arm drops nerveless at his side!

I hastily opened the door of the hut, and looked out, if haply I might see any one. All was solitary in the grove. I almost fell into a reverie. I imagined that I saw among the trees dark and naked forms, flitting, who were come to offer lamentations over the dead, and to perform the rites of burial. I was startled, and listened attentively to catch the sound of their footsteps. I heard nothing but the fall of the sere leaves, the squirrel mending his dry nest, and the water dripping from the stones. It was growing dark; the evening air felt chill; I had still to go forth and communicate the tidings of the red man's fate. I turned to gaze at him once more. A change had come over him. He had stretched his limbs as he would wish them decently to repose. I felt his brow, and it was cold; I passed my hand over his lips, but he had ceased to breathe. He had gone up to the bar of the Great Spirit, THE LAST MONTAUK!

LESSONS OF NATURE.

'Go forth under the open sky,
And list to Nature's teachings.'   BRYANT.

HEARD ye the whisper of the breeze,
    As soft it murmured by,
Amid the shadowy forest trees?
    It tells, with meaning sigh,
Of the bowers of bliss on that viewless shore
Where the weary spirit shall sin no more.

While sweet and low in crystal streams
    That glitter in the shade,
The music of an angel's dreams
    On bubbling keys are play'd;
And their echoes breathe, with a mystic tone,
Of that home where the loved and the lost are gone.

And when at evening's silent hour,
    We stand on Ocean's shore,
And feel the soul-subduing power
    Of its mysterious roar,
There 's a deep voice comes from its pearly caves,
Of that land of peace which no ocean laves.

And while the shadowy veil of night
    Sleeps on the mountain side,
And brilliants of unfathomed light
    Begem the concave wide,
There 's a spell, a power, of harmonious love,
That is beckoning mute to the realms above.

And Earth in all her temples wild
  Of mountain, rock, and dell,
Speaks with maternal accents mild,
  Our doubting fears to quell,
Of another shore and a brighter sphere,
Where we haste on the wings of each flying year.

On nature's bright and pictured scroll
  A speaking language see ;
. A pantomime the seasons roll,
  Of glorious imagery,
That reveal a *life* in this fading clay,
That shall wake again to a brighter day.

c. s. m.

OUR 'PALLADIUM OF LIBERTY.'

JURY TRIALS OF CIVIL SUITS.

THE English have been led by their rulers to believe that they are the freest and happiest people on earth; that their jurisprudence infinitely surpasses that of any other nation; and that their jury trial, in particular, is above all praise, in fact the *ne plus ultra* of civilization. America naturally imbibes her principles and customs from them, and has consequently adopted their jurisprudence, in most cases to the letter, and looks upon jury trial as the 'palladium of liberty.'

The antiquity of trial by jury in England renders the period of its introduction uncertain; and this circumstance proves that it must have occurred when the people of England were in a state of barbarism; when they were under the entire control of their barons or manor lords, who were their sole judges, both in civil and criminal cases, and no doubt exercised great partiality and injustice. To grant therefore to a people thus situated, the liberty of being judged by those of their own caste, was certainly an immense favor, and which seems to have been duly appreciated, for its praises have rung from generation to generation, down to the present time.

It is not denied that there may be just cause for continuing jury trial even in civil cases in England, where society is arbitrarily divided into what are called nobility, gentry, and common people. The judges being necessarily of the aristocratical classes, and receiving their commissions from the Crown, might naturally, or from interest, be biased in favor of the caste to which they belong. But this reason for jury trial does not apply in America. Here we have but one class of citizens, and the judges are appointed by them through their representatives, and are therefore identified with the mass of the people, and can be no more liable to partiality than jurymen. Judge BLACKSTONE, in his Commentaries, has indeed given reasons for the propriety of jury trial in a monarchical government; but they do not of course apply to a republic: and however well adapted the practice may have been to a people like the rude and ignorant Anglo-Saxons, it is unworthy the imitation of a civilized age. In England, the jury it seems were not to be 'threatened,' except with *starvation*, which the judge had a right to inflict in case of non-concurrence. What a tremendous power! Our juries do not 'cast lots for whom they shall find,' but they do what is equivalent. In case of agreeing to find for the plaintiff, but differing as to the amount to be awarded, they club the different sums proposed, divide the amount by twelve, and the result is returned as a true verdict! A device better suited to defeat the ends of justice than that which requires the unanimity of twelve jurymen, could not well be invented. The absurdity of requiring the entire panel of a jury to agree, which could scarcely ever voluntarily happen, arose from the merest accident. The practice formerly was to empanel more than twelve, in order to increase the chance of obtaining the unanimity of that number; and in case of failure, to add others till twelve should be found to concur. But this rule was sometimes neglected, perhaps from the difficulty of conveniently finding talesmen; and when only twelve were sworn, says Justice Christian, '*their unanimity became indispensable.*'

But the enigma of insisting on twelve to make up a verdict, remains to be solved. Justice Christian finds this to have been the custom 'from immemorial antiquity,' and he endeavors to persuade himself of its propriety. He will however convince no one who permits himself to think on the subject, that in cases of petty larceny, or disputes about property, there can be the least shadow of reason for requiring twelve men to pronounce judgment. Causes in which large amounts of property are at stake are taken out of court and submitted to three referees to decide. In these cases we hear nothing of the mystical number twelve. Reference of causes to individuals out of court, it may be presumed, was not practised at the time jury trial was first introduced; otherwise twelve would doubtless be the number of referees required.

There must have been some hidden cause, some talismanic virtue, supposed to exist in the number twelve, which has brought it into such high estimation. It is well known that the Pagans worshipped all the heavenly bodies, 'the whole host of heaven,' as expressed in Scripture; and the twelve signs of the zodiac were supposed to be the residence of the twelve greater gods, the *Dii Majores* of antiquity. They were very powerful, subject however to king Osiris, the sun, who passed through their dominions in his annual course. Hence the mystic sacredness of the number twelve. The highest court in England, composed of twelve judges, was no doubt formed upon the same principle as the jurymen. It was believed, no doubt, that this *perfect* number would insure righteous judgment.

Neither Judaism nor Christianity could entirely do away the superstitious notions and customs of ancient paganism. Many instances might be cited of their prevalence to this day. The numerals iii, vii, x, xl, are sacred cabalistic numbers, which have commanded the highest respect. The number *four* was sacred with Pythagoras, which he called the *tetractys*, as containing the principles of geometry; namely, a point, a line, a superfice, and a solid.

The judges of our courts are selected from the professors of law, for their uprightness and legal attainments; and their characters are staked upon the correctness of their administration of justice. They take notes of the evidence produced, and from habit are more capable than others of detecting error in conflicting testimony. Why draw men from the mass of the community, ignorant, *quoad hoc*, ignorant of the law, as it were to preside over the court, to superintend its proceedings, to see that nothing is done contrary to law; in short, to determine as to the law and the facts of cases argued before them? If they, in the opinion of the court, decide contrary to law, which, as might be expected, is often the case, a new trial, it is true, may be granted. The next jury however may do the same, and so on *ad infinitum*.

The consequent expenses attending these new trials added to those of appeals to higher courts, which are doubtless much more numerous than they would be were causes submitted to the courts, are evils of no small consideration. Two thirds of the time now consumed in trials at law are taken up by lawyers in talking to the jury, commenting on the testimony, and on the law applicable to the cases in hand; the counsel on both sides of course arguing in direct opposition to each other, till many of the jury often become completely confounded, and unable to form any opinion on the case at issue. After the pleadings are finished, the presiding judge in his charge endeavors to remove the veil that has been drawn over the eyes of the jury; *hoc opus, hic labor est*. Those of the jury who have formed any opinion, have come to different conclusions, and no reasoning will avail to shake their first impressions. What is to be done? Either sit up all night at least, or as before observed, compromise; divide the difference existing between them, which is generally preferred; that is, when the jury are agreed to find for the plaintiff, but differ as to the amount to be awarded. This is certainly a very loose way of administering justice, or rather, it is a perversion of justice; for men of the clearest perceptions are often induced, rather than suffer the consequence of non-concurrence, to surrender their judgment to others less capable to form a correct opinion, and consent to a verdict incompatible with their oaths as well as unjust to one of the litigants. This is well known to be done daily, and must be expected from the arbitrary rule, or law, requiring twelve men to think exactly alike, which is akin to the Roman Catholic inquisition.

Nothing but the most stupid veneration for the cabalistic number twelve could have induced men, even in a savage state, to adopt so absurd a rule. We have not inherited the superstition; but the practice, from the mere force of habit, has descended to us. I am informed by a well-read lawyer, that in France, under the Napoleon code, the majority of a jury in civil cases prevail, without regard to a specific number. But if the decision of law-suits were submitted to professors of law, without the intervention of men ignorant of the science, an infinite benefit would accrue to the community. The delay, the harrassing vexation, which now prevail, would be avoided. Suits would soon be determined, and with more justice and far less cost than at present. Perhaps in cases of trespass, and some others, a jury would be desirable, which might be granted by the court, a majority of whom being empowered to decide; or the cause might be submitted to referees. No one, not very conversant with our courts of justice, could conceive of the immense saving of time that would arise from this arrangement.

The boast of 'the glorious uncertainty of the law' would in a great measure cease, as the issue of suits might with far greater accuracy be calculated upon when the decisions depended upon judges of law, which would also tend greatly to lessen the number of suits; as lawyers would hardly risk their reputation in bringing or defending causes before judges, evidently against law and justice, when they had not a jury to operate upon. But as a consolation for the diminution of suits, they would find the practice more pleasant, in being relieved from the labored declamations now required in 'addresses to juries.

The eulogies that have been passed upon the British jurisprudence by Judge Blackstone, and others interested in its administration, seem to have obtained the entire approbation of Americans, without examination of that of other countries, over which it is pretended a vast superiority prevails. The Napoleon code, which the improvements of the age and the learned men employed in its compilation ought to render superior, is scarcely spoken of, much less read. This tenacity for old customs and precedents can only be accounted for by the influence of habit.

When the system is impartially examined, what do we find but vexatious delays and enormous costs? Some one in praise of it observed, that 'in England the courts are freely open to all of every condition;' to which Horne Tooke replied, 'so is the London tavern, to all who can pay the expense.' In fact, it is a common saying, that the longest purse generally wins the cause. The chancery suits are often continued for twenty and thirty years. Soame Jenyns said, 'if any one denied that there was evil in the world, he referred him to a fit of the gout, or to a suit in chancery!'

As to the trials by jury in criminal cases, so much vaunted, has there been any difficulty in obtaining convictions under them? The jury are sworn to return a verdict according to law and evidence : if therefore sufficient proof appear against the accused, they are bound to say so; and the judge passes sentence according to the laws, in the enactment of which the mass of the people have very little share. Thousands of men and women have been executed in England for petty larceny, of which they were found guilty by juries composed of their equals; which, according to the eulogists of the system, sanctifies the deed. The attention of the English people has been artfully drawn from the cruel severity of the laws, to the plausible method of procuring convictions for a breach of them. Colquhoun in his 'Police of London' states the average of yearly executions in that metropolis alone to amount to about fifty. Enough, in all conscience, to satisfy the cravings of the most despotical government.

Judge Blackstone found the people were flattered by the little brief authority conferred upon them by being permitted to sit in judgment upon their fellow subjects, and he made use of it to the great advantage of the government; as thereby the governed were more easily induced to obey the laws, good or bad.   Blackstone was well rewarded for his services, being made king's counsel, and solicitor-general to the queen; and afterward a judge of the king's bench and of the common pleas. A writer of a sketch of his life, says : ' Like almost all English lawyers, he leans to the side of prerogative; nor is there much more enlargement in his principles of religious liberty.   For this reason he was exposed to attack from Priestley, Bentham, and Junius.'   His pretence, therefore, of advocating the liberties of the people, is hypocritical and vain.

The great advantage supposed to accrue from jury trial certainly does not appear to be realized in practice.   The sympathy of caste, supposed to exist among the mass of the people in monarchies has no reality.   They feel more for the sufferings of those they deem their superiors than for themselves.   They can witness with unconcern scores of their equals turned off from the gallows at once.   But if a tyrant king happens to lose his head in a revolutionary struggle, the people cheerfully risk their lives to revenge his death.   Rousseau says : ' If a nobleman, travelling in his carriage, happens to get into a slough, the laborers in the neighboring fields eagerly run to his assistance, for which his lordship does not even thank them, thinking they have done no more than their duty ; but if one of their own caste meets with the like misfortune, they set up a horse-laugh, and let him extricate himself in the best way he can.'

Liberty consists in the right to make laws, not in their execution. Jurors at the time trial by jury was instituted probably had the power to determine not only the guilt of the accused, but also the punishment to be inflicted.   But being deprived of that authority by modern legislators, trial by jury is now not inaptly compared to the wooden image of Pallas in ancient Troy, called the *palladium*, whose eyes seemed to move.   The Trojans fancied it fell from heaven into an uncovered temple ; and were told by the oracle that Troy could not be taken while that image remained there ; which Diomede and Ulysses hearing, they stole into the temple, slew the keepers, and carried it away ; after which the destruction of the city soon followed.   Trial by jury seems to have met with a similar fate, while English jurists extol it in the same manner as did the oracle the Trojan palladium.   The ceremony of opening our courts shows the influence of habit in continuing a practice the cause for which no longer exists.   All persons having business with the court are called upon with, ' *Hear ye !* ' three times repeated ; to ' *draw near*,' and they shall be heard ; while at the same time the representatives or counsel of those on whom the call is made are at the place assigned for them ; and there is no necessity, nor is it expected, that they should approach nearer to the court.   The sheriff, who has already made his return according to law, and the jurymen, who are duly informed in their citations of the consequence of absenting themselves on the opening of the court, are unnecessarily called upon in like manner.

I apprehend the following historical fact will account for the origin of this custom : ' Justice,' says the Abbe Pluche, ' was anciently administered in Europe in the finest of our months, namely May.   We still find in a multitude of places remains of this custom, in the practice observed by the farmers of the duties and receipts of lords, of setting up branches, or a green arbor before the chief or manor-house, where the assizes were formerly held. All this preparation is founded in the circumstance of the season in which justice was administered in remotest antiquity. The above-mentioned green arbor is still called 'the May.' The terms of magistrate and majesty seem to be borrowed from the name of the month in which these venerable assemblies were held. This month received its name from the Pleias or Pleiades, anciently called Maïa, which then disengaged itself from the rays of the sun, distant thirty degrees, and passed under Gemini.'

It is reasonable to suppose that the vassals of the manor were not permitted to enter the arbor till his lordship made his appearance to open the court, and that in the mean time they sheltered themselves in out-houses, and under neighboring trees, when the crier called on those who had business to prefer to come forward, and they should be heard. In this case, the propriety and even necessity of the custom is apparent : but at this day, in halls prepared for the court, where all are supposed to be present who have business with it, the practice is out of place, and in fact is not intended to produce any effect.

Monarchies are conservative, avoiding as much as possible to disturb the existing state of things connected with their grand machine, fearing thereby that the whole might tumble into ruins ; and as this trifling ceremony tends in some measure to mystify the practice of law, England will be apt to retain it, as well as the other more important absurdities above-mentioned. But as our republic has no cause to be influenced by such motives, it is to be hoped that it will ere long brush away useless customs derived from antiquity, and which tend to check the onward march of the human mind.

J. P.

THE MESSENGER OF PEACE.

BY MISS M. A. BROWNE.

THE dove went forth on her pinions fair,
  Across the waters wide ;
And now she cleft the sunless air,
  And now she swept the tide :
And all day long her form around,
  Like a star, was seen to shoot ;
Yet on the pathless waves she found
  No rest for her weary foot.

She turned her from the billows dark,
  And from the curling foam ;
She turned her to the saving ark,
  And it took the wanderer home.
' Go forth again, fair dove ! and see
  If thy gentle eye can scan
A place in all the world, to be
  A resting-place for man.'

Again she went — again she sought
  The far-spread ocean round ;
And she returned : what hath she bro't?
  What hath the white dove found ?
The olive-branch ! — the type of peace
  She hath borne from the stormy earth ;
And soon the raging flood shall cease,
  And man himself go forth !

Oh, be my soul like thee, fair dove !
  In passing on through life,
Still by its faith borne far above
  The world's tumultuous strife :
And when by weariness 't is driven
  To rest where tempests cease,
Bearing, on its return to heaven,
  The sign of hope and peace.

LITERARY NOTICES.

The Life and Times of Red-Jacket, or Sa-go-ye-wat-ha : being the Sequel to the History of the Six Nations. By William L. Stone. In one volume, 8vo. pp. 484. New-York and London : Wiley and Putnam.

We alluded in a brief notice in our last number to this very entertaining volume ; and now propose to enter upon a more detailed consideration of its merits. Aside from its main historical features, which are agreeably interwoven with interesting incidental narrative, to trench upon which would exceed the limits of this notice, the volume is remarkable for the number and variety of speeches of its renowned subject, in collecting which our author has evidently exercised the most unwearied industry and research. It is to these speeches, and to the circumstances out of which they arose, that we shall ask the attention of the reader. Those among us, and especially our readers abroad, who have been accustomed to derive their impressions of the oratorical efforts of our aboriginal chiefs in council from the wordy and inflated imitations of second-rate native *romanticists*, will here see the difference between eloquent nature and fustian art ; and while they set down our be-Indian'd novel scenes at their proper valuation, will do justice to the terse, energetic, and poetical ' utterances ' of the legitimate sons of the forest.

We remember to have heard our correspondent, Colonel M'Kenney, who was for more than twenty years an Indian agent or commissioner on the part of the United States, remark, that in the whole course of his experience, every war with the natives and every savage outrage had been *provoked* by original aggressions on the part of the whites. When posterity shall ask, as ask it will when all this has become history, whether these things were so, and how our treaties with the Indians were kept, the reply will be found in the unanswerable records of the speeches of our aboriginal chiefs. ' Your forefathers,' said Red-Jacket, speaking to the whites in council, and on behalf of the Six Nations, ' your forefathers crossed the great water, and landed on this island. Their numbers were small. They found friends and not enemies. They told us they had fled from their own country for fear of wicked men, and had come here to enjoy their religion. They asked for a small seat. We took pity on them, and granted their request. They sat down among us. We gave them corn and meat ; they gave us the fire-water in return. The white people had now found our country. Tidings were carried back, and more came among us. Yet we did not fear them. We took them to be friends. They called us brothers. We believed them, and gave them a larger seat. At length their numbers had greatly increased. They wanted more land — they wanted our country ! Our eyes were opened, and our minds became uneasy.

Wars took place. Indians were hired to fight against Indians, and many of our people were destroyed. They also brought strong liquor among us. It was strong and powerful, and has slain thousands. BROTHERS : our seats were once large and yours were small. You have now become a great people, and we have scarcely a place left to spread our blankets!' 'Look back,' said the same orator on another occasion, 'to the first settlement by the whites, and then look at our present condition. Formerly, we continued to grow in numbers and strength. What has become of the Indians who extended to the salt waters? They have been driven back and become few, while you have been growing numerous and powerful. This land is ours, from the God of Heaven. It was given to us. We cannot make land. Driven back and reduced as we are, you wish to cramp us more and more. You tell us of a preëmptive right. Such men, you say, own one reservation, and such another. But they are *all* ours — ours from the top to the bottom.'

The celebrated chief CORNPLANTER, in one of his speeches, complains that the concessions of the treaty of Fort Stanwix were yielded only to force. 'You told us,' said he, addressing the whites, 'that we were in your hand, and that by closing it you could crush us to nothing ; and you demanded from us a great country as the price of that peace you had offered us — as if our want of strength had destroyed our rights. There were but few chiefs present, and they were compelled to give up the lands; and it is not the Six Nations only that reproach us for having given up that country. The Chippewas, and all the nations which lived on those lands westward, call to us, and ask us: 'Brothers of our fathers! where is the place which you have reserved for us to lie down upon?' What they agreed to has bound our nation ; and though our strength has not increased, nor your power become less, we ask you to consider calmly, were the terms dictated by your commissioners reasonable and just?' And yet, unjust as was this treaty, we find RED-JACKET entreating on behalf of the Six Nations, that its terms may be maintained. 'We wish that in respect to these lands, the treaty of Fort Stanwix may not be broken. You white people have increased very fast on this island, which was given to us Indians by the Great Spirit. We are now become a small people. You are cutting off our lands, piece after piece. You are a kind-hearted people, seeking your own advantages.'

A commissioner on behalf of the whites, when speaking of the small worth of these lands while in a wild and unproductive state, observed, that the only value they could have in the eyes of the Indians, must arise from the consciousness that they *owned* them; to which RED-JACKET replied: 'That consciousness is every thing to us. It raises us in our own estimation. It creates in our bosom a proud feeling, that elevates us as a nation. Observe the difference between the estimation in which a Seneca and an Oneida are held. We are courted, while the Oneidas are considered a degraded people, fit only to make brooms and baskets. Why this difference? It is because the Senecas are known as the proprietors of a broad domain, while the Oneidas are cooped up in a narrow space.' 'Have you voted?' said a political 'drummer' to a vagabond, as he thrust a ticket into his hand. 'No I hav'n't, and I do n't *mean* to, that's more, till the *third day*, about sundown. No body shakes hands with me, or treats, *after* I've voted. You do n't catch me!' and he wandered off to test the 'purity of elections' in another quarter. RED-JACKET seems to have understoood the application of this man's argument, in the comparative cases which he cites.

RED-JACKET took an early and a lasting dislike to the missionaries, who were sent from different societies to the Six Nations, to ameliorate their spiritual condition. His aversion, as we learn from our author, was perfectly natural. According to his testimony and that of Rev. Dr. BRECKENRIDGE, the early efforts of the missionaries were badly conducted. Men of more ability ought to have been selected for so peculiar and difficult service. It is stated, in justice to the Indians, that many of these ministers were destitute of any practical knowledge of human nature; that they had little talent and less information; and moreover, that they were bigoted, over-zealous, and lacked temper and patience. Instead of preaching simple discourses, bringing down to the level of the ignorant, and in relation to religion, child-like minds of the Indians the elementary principles of christianity, in their simplest and most winning forms, they were regaled, says Mr. STONE, with long argumentative sermons upon divine decrees, and the dark mysteries of foreknowledge and predestination; more repulsive themes than which, he adds, 'even for many enlightened congregations, reared in the bosom of the church, could hardly have been selected,' but for Indian auditors, especially unhappy. We have collated a few passages from the speeches of RED-JACKET, in reply to the importunities of various missionaries to be permitted to come among the Indians, 'to instruct and strengthen them in religion :'

'BROTHER: We have listened with attention to what you have said. You request us to speak our minds freely. All have heard your voice, and all speak to you now as one man what we think. Our minds are agreed. You say you want an answer to your talk before you leave this place. It is right you should have one, as you are at a great distance from home, and we do not wish to detain you. BROTHER: You have got our country, but you are not satisfied: you want to force your religion upon us. You say that you are sent to instruct us how to worship the Great Spirit agreeably to his mind, and if we do not take hold of the religion which you white people teach, we shall be unhappy hereafter. You may say that you are right and we are lost. How do we know this to be true? We understand that your religion is written in a book. If it was intended for us as well as you, why has not the Great Spirit given to us, and not only to us, but why did he not give to our forefathers, the knowledge of that book, with the means of understanding it rightly? We only know what you tell us about it. How shall we know when to believe, being so often deceived by the white people? You say there is but one way to worship and serve the Great Spirit. If there is but one religion, why do you white people differ so much about it? Why not all agreed, as you can all read the book? We do not understand these things. We are told that your religion was given to your forefathers, and has been handed down from father to son. We also have a religion which was given to our forefathers, and has been handed down to us, their children. We worship in that way. It teaches us to be thankful for all the favors we receive; to love each other, and to be united. We never quarrel about religion. Brother: we do not wish to enjoy our religion, or take it from you. We only want to enjoy our own. You say you have not come to get our land or our money, but to enlighten our minds. I will now tell you that I have been at your meetings, and saw you collect money from the meeting. I cannot tell what this money was intended for, but suppose that it was for your minister; and if we should conform to your way of thinking, perhaps you might want some from us. BROTHER: we are told that you have been preaching to the white people in this place. These people are our neighbors. We are acquainted with them. We will wait a little while, and see what effect your preaching has upon them. If we find it does them good, makes them honest, and less disposed to cheat Indians, we will then consider again of what you have said. You have now heard our answer to your talk; and this is all we have to say at present."

On another occasion, at Buffalo, RED-JACKET thus replied to a delegate from the State Missionary Society, who was endeavoring to establish a mission among the Senecas :

"BROTHER: We listened to the talk you delivered to us from the council of black-coats in New-York. We have fully considered your talk and the offers you have made us. Great numbers of black-coats have been among the Indians, and with sweet voices and smiling faces have offered to teach them the religion of the white people. Our brethren in the east listened to the black-coats, turned from the religion of their fathers, and took up the religion of the white people. What good has it done them? Are they more happy and more friendly one to another than we are? No, brother, they are a divided people; we are united. They quarrel about religion — we live in love and friendship. They drink strong water, have learnt how to cheat, and to practice all the vices of the white men, which disgrace Indians, without imitating the virtues of the white men. Brother, if you are our well-wisher, keep away, and do not disturb us. You wish us to change our religion for yours. We like our religion, and do not want another. Our friends the Quakers give us ploughs, and show us how to use them. They tell us we are accountable beings, but they do not ask us to change our religion. We are satisfied with what they do. We cannot receive your offers : we have other things to do, and beg you to make your minds easy, and not trouble us, lest our heads should be too much loaded, and by and by burst."

'Humanity weeps,' says our author, 'that the conduct of civilized men should put such arguments as the following into the mouths of the Indians, against their own best good :

"BROTHER: we pity you: we wish you to bear to our good friends our best wishes. Inform them that in compassion toward them, we are willing to send them missionaries, to teach them our religion, habits and customs. We would be willing they should be as happy as we are, and assure them that if they should follow our example, they would be far more happy than they are now. We would gladly know that you have relinquished your religion, productive of so much disagreement and inquietude among yourselves, and instead thereof that you should follow ours. Accept of this advice, brother, and take it back to your friends as the best pledge of our wishes for your welfare. Perhaps you think we are ignorant and uninformed. Go then and teach the whites. Select, for example, the people of Buffalo. We will be spectators, and remain silent. Improve their morals and refine their habits. Make them less disposed to cheat Indians. Make the whites generally less inclined to make Indians drunk, and to take from them their lands. Let us know the tree by the blossoms, and the blossoms by the fruit. When this shall be made clear to our minds, we may be more willing to listen to you. Brother — farewell ! "

The Indians could not be made to understand the doctrine of the atonement, or the death of our SAVIOUR for the redemption of the world. 'If you white men,' said RED-JACKET to one of the missionaries, speaking in behalf of his people, 'murdered the son of the Great Spirit, we Indians had nothing to do with it, and it is none of our affair. If he had come among us, we would not have killed him; we would have treated him well, and the white people who killed him ought to be damned for doing it. You must make amends for that crime among yourselves.' One of the converted Indians, however, at the Oneida castle, in addressing his red auditory, in his first discourse, drew such a picture of the sufferings and death of the REDEEMER, that many of his female hearers, 'albeit unused to the melting mood,' actually shed tears. The inexperienced preacher, seeing this result, began to think he had gone too far; and he proceeded to qualify the vivid sketch he had been limning : ' It was a great way off,' said he, ' a long while ago — and may be 't was n't so ! '

In some conversation with Rev. Dr. BRECKENRIDGE, who was well acquainted with RED-JACKET, that chieftain contended that the red man was of a totally different race, and needed an entirely different religion. The reverend gentleman pressed the points of resemblance in every thing but color, and argued that in the case of the christian Indians there was a common mind on religion. RED-JACKET waived the debate by saying, 'that one thing was certain, whatever else was not; that white men had a great love for Indian women, and left their traces behind them wherever they could ! ' He was frequently heard to murmur, that whereas before the approach of the white men, the eyes of the Indian children were all black, yet now they were becoming blue. We believe it was our swarthy hero who, in reply to an inquiry by a pious clergyman, to what tribe a bright boy, whose face he was admiring at the Oneida settlement, belonged, said : ' Ugh ! — part *'Neida*, part *Missionary !* '

Strangers in Buffalo used often to visit RED-JACKET at his residence near by, or send for him to come into the town to see them :

"On one occasion, not many years before his death, a gentleman from Albany, on a visit to Buffalo, being desirous of seeing the chief, sent a message to that effect. The gentleman was affluent in money and in words, the latter flowing forth with great rapidity, and in an inverse ratio to his ideas. He had also a habit of approaching very near to any person with whom he was conversing, and chattering with almost unapproachable volubility. On receiving the message, RED-JACKET dressed himself with the utmost care, designing, as he ever did when sober, to make the most imposing impression, and came over to the village. Being introduced to the stranger, he soon measured his intellectual capacity, and made no effort to suppress his disappointment, which indeed was sufficiently disclosed in his features. After listening for a few moments to the chatter of the gentleman, RED-JACKET, with a look of mingled chagrin and contempt, approached close to him, and exclaimed, ' *Cha, cha, cha!* ' as rapidly as utterance would allow. Then drawing himself up to his full height, he turned proudly upon his heel, and walked away in the direction of his own domicil, ' as straight as an Indian,' nor deigned to look behind. The gentleman with more money than brains was for once lost in astonishment, and stood longer motionless and silent than he had ever stood before."

The following anecdote is strikingly characteristic of Indian shrewdness and satire. RED-JACKET, it should be premised, is indignant at the verdict of a court at Buffalo, in which a Seneca had been convicted of stealing, and sentenced to the State's-prison:

"After the proceedings were over, in passing from the court-house to the inn, in company with a group of lawyers, RED-JACKET discerned upon the sign of a printing office the arms of the State, with the emblematical representation of Liberty and Justice, emblazoned in large figures and characters. The chieftain stopped, and pointing to the figure of Liberty, asked in broken English: ' *What him call?* ' He was answered ' LIBERTY.' ' Ugh!' was the significant and truly aboriginal response. Then pointing to the other figure, he inquired: ' What *him* call?' He was told ' JUSTICE;' to which with a kindling eye, he instantly replied: ' *Where him live now?* '

Our hero must have possessed a full developement of the organ of self-esteem, if one may judge from the following, and numerous kindred passages of the volume under notice:

"Toward the close of his life, he was present by invitation at the launching of a vessel at Black Rock, bearing his name. He made a short address on the occasion, showing the estimation in which he held his own high merit. In the course of his speech, addressing himself directly to the vessel, he said: ' You have had a great name given to you. Strive to deserve it. Be brave and daring. Go boldly into the great lakes, and fear neither the swift winds nor the strong waves. Be not frightened nor overcome by them ; for it is by resisting storms and tempests, that I whose name you bear, obtained my renown. Let my great example inspire you to courage, and lead you to glory."

Whatever doubts RED-JACKET may have had of the advantages likely to accrue to his race from the promulgation among them of the christian religion, certain it is that he was no skeptic — no blind adherent to the doctrine of chance, or a faith in heathen deities. 'I believe,' said he, a short time before his death, 'in the Great Spirit, who created the heavens and the earth. He peopled the forests, and the air, and the waters. He then created man, and placed him as a superior animal of this creation, and designed him as governor over all other created beings on earth.' It is a melancholy spectacle to us, acquainted as we are with the Indian character, and often a spectator of their wrongs, to survey their past history, and to look upon their present decline:

> ' A noble race ! but they are gone,
> With their old forests wide and deep,
> And we have built our homes upon
> Fields where their generations sleep.
> Their fountains slake our thirst at noon,
> Upon their fields our harvest waves ;
> Our lovers woo beneath their moon —
> Ah, let us spare at least their graves ! '

Well may the scattered remnants of the Six Nations exclaim, in the language of their noble orator: ' We stand a small island in the bosom of the great waters. We are encircled — we are encompassed. The evil spirit rides upon the blast, and the waters are disturbed. They rise, they press upon us; and the waves once settled over us, we disappear for ever. Who then lives to mourn us ? None. What marks our extermination? Nothing. We are mingled with the common elements.' There never was a more eloquent epitome of the ' marks of their extermination,' than is furnished by our orator himself in a brief review of his own career. ' RED-JACKET,' said he, ' was once a great man, and in favor with the Great Spirit. He was a lofty pine among the smaller trees of the forest. But after years of glory, he degraded himself by drinking the fire-water of the white man. The Great Spirit has looked upon him in anger, and his lightning has stripped the pine of its branches ! '

LETTERS FROM ABROAD TO KINDRED AT HOME. By Miss C. M. SEDGWICK. In two volumes, 12mo. pp. 572. New-York : HARPER AND BROTHERS.

WITH all the draw-backs that naturally attend the traversing of beaten ground, our gifted countrywoman has here presented us with two volumes of fresh and charming reading. Miss SEDGWICK needed no instruction from her friend Miss MARTINEAU, to teach her 'how to observe.' With a heart open as the day to the finest impulses of humanity, she has in all her journeyings given us her first warm impressions of *the people*, of 'the mass ;' and it is delightful to note, how their *welfare* always comes uppermost in her benevolent heart. Some of the London journals, we observe, while they award abundant praise to the 'Letters,' and speak in flattering terms of the author, yet complain loudly that they are 'something too familiar' in those portions which throw open, as it were, the doors of English society. Thus the 'Athenœum' does not hesitate to say : 'There is the stamp of individuality upon these Letters. Yet we cannot say, that to read them is as pleasant as it was to hear their writer *talk* of the impressions to which they are devoted. If America or England sent forth more travellers like Miss SEDGWICK, it would be better for the mutual good understanding of both countries. Simple to homeliness in her appearance and dress; of that 'certain age,' the graceful wearing of which is not given to every woman ; denied even the possession of that most winning gift, a sweet speaking voice ; national in her accent, and quaint in her phraseology ; there was nevertheless about her an upright and unpretending truthfulness, which commanded respect ; a thing rare, and therefore precious, in the feverish atmosphere of London saloons ; beside a poetical freshness of mind, which, throwing itself abroad upon the myriads of new objects around her, could not fail to captivate. Beyond the respect which attaches itself to all who have the courage to be as clear of affectation as Miss SEDGWICK, it was impossible not to conceive an admiration for one whose enthusiasm was so healthy, and whose admiration bestowed itself so justly and so liberally.' Now after such exceedingly relevant and impersonal matter as this, in a merely literary critique, it is especially modest, and in pleasant keeping, to hear the same reviewer complain, that 'it runs in the blood of the Americans *to gossip*,' and that Miss SEDGWICK has seen fit to follow the example of scores of British tourists in this country, and to carry her researches into the dwellings of private individuals, estimating their incomes, numbering their servants, etc. 'There is an amount of offence of this sort in her book,' adds the Athenœum, 'passing all former offences of the same nature.' All these complaints, however, are only note-worthy, as confirming the justice of Miss SEDGWICK's remark, that an unfailing concomitant of an Englishman's immense love of approbation, is a certain uncomfortable consciousness of the presence and observation of others.

Our author certainly seems to have had every opportunity afforded her to study the English character ; for her reputation and letters secured her access to the highest society in England, and her own benevolent inclinations prompted her to examine the condition of the lower orders ; and she records her warmest gratitude and admiration in favor of many of the noble traits of our brethren 'on the other side.' Yet when we find her on the Continent, looking leisurely back upon her experiences, comparing her impressions, and conning the qualities of our 'mother people,' she comes with evident reluctance to the conclusion, that there is no flexibility about an Englishman; no adaptation to circumstances and exigences. 'His face and demeanor always betray him. His muscles are in a state of tension; his nerves seem to be on the outside of his coat; his eye-brows are in motion; he looks as if he felt that all the people about him were *rats;*' his voice is quick and harsh, and his words none of the sweetest. The contrast between the English and German character is sufficiently striking, if one may judge from the following passage, the truth of which has been confirmed by all our travelled countrymen whom we have heard speak upon the subject:

"The English race, root and branch, what with their natural shyness, their conventional reserves, and their radical uncourteousness, are cold and repelling. The politeness of the French is conventional. It seems in part the result of their sense of personal grace, and in part of a selfish calculation of making the most of what costs nothing; and partly no doubt, it is the spontaneous effect of a vivacious nature. There is a deep-seated humanity in the courtesy of the Germans. They always seem to be feeling a gentle pressure from the cord that interlaces them with their species. They do not wait, as Schiller says, till you 'freely invite' them to 'friendlily stretch you a hand,' but the hand is instinctively stretched out, and the kind deed ready to follow it. And this suavity is not limited to any rank or condition, but extends all the way down, from the prince to the poorest peasant."

Our author records abundant proofs of the fidelity of this national sketch, several of which we had marked, with the hope of extracting, and *one* of which, a little group for a painter, we cannot avoid copying:

"Beneath my window, in a small triangular garden, is a touching chapter in human life; the whole book indeed, from the beginning almost to the end. There is a table under the trees in the universal German fashion, and wine and Seltzer-water on it; and there in his arm-chair sits an old blind man, with his children and grand-children, and the blossoms of yet another generation around him. While I write it, the young people are touching their glasses to his, and a little thing has clambered up behind him, and is holding a rose to his nose."

We close our brief quotations with the annexed sketch of our author's 'first impressions' of the Alps:

"We had read descriptions of them in manuscript and print, in prose and poetry; we knew their measurement; we had seen sketches, and paintings, and models of them; and yet I think if we had looked into the planet Jupiter, we could scarcely have felt a stronger emotion of surprise. In truth, up, *up* where they hung and shone, they seemed to belong to heaven rather than earth; and yet, such is the mystery of the spirit's kindred with the effulgent beauty of God's works, that they

—— 'seemed a part
Of me and of my soul, as I of them.'

The whole range of the Bernese Alps was before us, unclouded, undimmed by a breath of vapor. There they were, like glittering wedges cleaving the blue atmosphere. I had no anticipation of the exquisite effect of the light on these aërial palaces, of a whiteness as glittering and dazzling as the garments of the angels, and the contrasts of the *black* shadows, and here and there golden and rose-colored hues. I have no notion of attempting to describe them; but you shall not reproach me, as we, so soon as we recovered our voices, reproached all our travelled friends with: 'Why did they not tell us?' 'How cruel, how stupid, to let any one live and die without coming to see the Alps!'

If Miss Sedgwick before leaving America could have heard, as we had the pleasure the other day to hear, an accomplished correspondent of this Magazine describe the varied beauties of the Bernese Alps, she could hardly have said, even while gazing upon them, that 'the half had not been told her.' Next, we are confident, to a view of the Alps, may be esteemed a picture drawn of them by a tasteful observer, a poet, and a christian. We have now, we think, at least a *forcible* appreciation of these mountains; 'their shadows, dark at the base; the sun-light resting like a cincture upon the topmost peak, which rears its imperial head above most of the chain; thè magical effect of the delicate and fading pink upon the precious whiteness of the Alpine snow, and the clear blue ether that borders on it.'

AMERICA: HISTORICAL, STATISTIC, AND DESCRIPTIVE. By J. S. BUCKINGHAM, Esq. In two volumes. pp. 1030. New-York: HARPER AND BROTHERS.

'AN huge man,' says a quaint English author, 'and a book of monstrous size, generally fall short of what they seem to promise. An ordinary mind can no more inform an over-large body, than an ordinary genius can enliven a big book.' This criterion will certainly hold good in relation to the two corpulent volumes before us; in which there is more smooth verbosity than we remember ever to have encountered in the same number of pages, in any score of kindred works. Judging probably from the success at home and abroad of the gossipping publications which have appeared from time to time from the pens of second-rate English tourists, our author was perhaps justified in inferring that twattle was our only wear, and that common-place would find the readiest market. Mr. BUCKINGHAM has merely 'skimmed the superfices' in all his journeyings, taking care only, as is his wont, never to let the public eye lose sight of the private 'I.' So far from his volumes being the result of a searching examination and comparison of our institutions, 'men, manners, and things,' they exhibit little exertion of thought, and less labor of investigation. The work is neither suggestive nor comprehensive. To be sure, it has no very gross or ludicrous errors, but there are *no* striking beauties. In fact, its main characteristic is a sort of decent debility, relieved only by an excessive egotism, which is 'lugged in by ear and horn,' on every possible occasion. The style is a model for a mere book-maker. No man ever covered a larger piece of bread with a smaller piece of butter than Mr. BUCKINGHAM. Dilution is his forte. We verily believe, that if he were to describe a southern negro singing 'Such a Gittin' up Stairs I never did See,' he would write the passage thus: 'I was struck, on the morning before my departure from the hotel, where I had been, as I have already remarked, tarrying for a considerable period or more of time, with a species of song or chant, proceeding from the thick lips of a dark-skinned negro, the burden of which, so far as I was enabled to gather it, from hearing it on one occasion only, seemed to me to be, that at no previous period of his existence had he ever witnessed so difficult an ascension of a stair-case. The origin of this local song, chant, or ditty, I was not so fortunate as to be able to trace with sufficient certainty to justify its insertion in my journal.'

After all, Mr. BUCKINGHAM is one of the best of that species of elaborate and 'soft recorders,' whose minute descriptions, patiently mastered, will convey to the reader who has neither seen nor heard of the objects which he depicts, a very good idea of them. *This* praise we render with pleasure; and since our author is kind enough to say that 'the KNICKERBOCKER is quite on a par with the best of the magazines in Great Britain,' and to add other complimentary words, which our modesty forbids us to quote, we can only regret, in our gratitude for his praise, that we cannot conscientiously increase his own commendation. We remember to have met Mr. BUCKINGHAM often in society, while in this country, and to have found him an entertaining and not over-ostentatious person. Hence it is, that we fear there is something in the pen, that 'mighty instrument' in hands like his, which leads him to the display of himself, and of that *cacoethes scribendi* for which his very name has become a synonym. In justice to the worthy publishers, we should state, that they have done their part for the volumes. They have illustrated them with upwards of seventy wood-engravings, together with a fine portrait of the author, on steel. One or two of the cuts can scarcely be said to reflect their originals, as for example the picture of Utica, which the inhabitants of that beautiful town will assuredly repudiate ; but in the main, the pictorial features of the work are of a creditable character.

The Ancient Régime: a Tale. By G. P. R. James, Esq. In two volumes, 12mo. pp. 416. New-York: Harper and Brothers.

Mr. James, in the volume before us, in the hope of producing a certain moral effect upon the minds of his fellow-men, while at the same time he afforded them amusement, has deviated in some degree from the usual plan of his romances. 'A subject,' says he, 'of no slight interest, was to be found in the education of a girl from infancy to womanhood, by a man unconnected with her by blood, together with the results to both; but at the same time to treat it properly was not an easy undertaking.' In attempting it, he has striven to depict the fine shades of character and emotion, rather than the broader contrasts, the scenic light and shade, and the somewhat melo-dramatic effects for which there is such a fondness at the present day. We think Mr. James has not over-estimated the good taste of the public, in believing that quiet paintings of the human heart, executed with fidelity and vigor, will find no lack of admirers, among those especially whose praise is worth the having. Leaving the other characters of the novel, (including that of the abbé, Count de Castelneau, a most spirited delineation,) we need only call the attention of our female readers to Mr. James' *chef-dœuvre*, the character of Annette de St. Morin, concerning which he remarks : 'I have had here the peculiar difficulties to contend with which every man must encounter when he endeavors to depict the many fine gradations of thought and feeling produced in a woman's bosom by the different events of her life ; and certainly the circumstances in which I have placed her have not made the task more easy. Nevertheless, I trust the picture is a true one, and I believe it to be so. The rule that I have gone by in painting this character is, to have all the observations that I have made through life upon the nature and conduct of woman present to my mind, like colors ready on a palette; and I have never asked myself what would be my own sensations in any particular circumstance alluded to, but what would be the feelings of a woman, of such a woman, and of one so educated. Whether I have divined right, or whether I have made a mistake, women alone can judge.' To an attempt like this, by such a writer as Mr. James, it would be superfluous to call the attention of our readers; if indeed the 'Tale' shall not have been perused long before these pages pass to the public. One thing is especially remarkable in almost all our author's productions; and that is the frequent moral lessons deduced, in brief passages, from his spirited paintings. Thus, speaking of the vices of the higher class of the Parisian people, he says:

"Oh would but man remember that he is but a steward of all that he possesses ; that his wealth, his honors, his talents, his genius, his influence, are all merely lent to him by the one great Possessor, not alone for his individual benefit, but for the benefit of the whole ; would he but remember this, such terrible accounts of the stewardship would not be taken, as are often demanded on this earth by agents that seem little likely to be intrusted with such a commission ; and the after-reckoning too might be looked for in peace, knowing that it is to be rendered to a mild and merciful Lord."

EDITOR'S TABLE.

MODERATION *vs.* TEETOTALISM. — We have received several communications *pro* and *con* upon these themes, suggested by an article entitled as above in a late number ; but they have been, some too long, some too violent, and others quite too disengenuous and question-begging. But the writer of the following, gathering from these pages most likely a knowledge of our time-strengthened affection for 'The Pilgrim's Progress,'

> ——'that curious book of BUNYAN's
> All strung together like a bunch of onions,'

has touched our weak point ; and we surrender a good seat at our table for him, because he is a 'warm friend of an intimate friend of ours : ' ' I read the paper entitled ' Moderation *vs.* Teetotalism,' ' he writes, ' and certainly found in it many things of which I could approve, but yet more that I am compelled to condemn. And without entering into an argument with your contributor, who may and doubtless does deserve the personal commendations which you have bestowed upon him, I would respectfully invite him to turn over the leaves of ' The Pilgrim's Progress ' of BUNYAN, till he reaches the 'Third Part,' which I desire him to read. He will there find the Lady INTEMPERANCE, the wife of CARNAL SECURITY, inveigling TENDER-CONSCIENCE into her sumptuous dwelling, where with her daughters Wantonness and Forgetfulness, he would finally have perished, but for the secret and wonderful virtues of his crutch, with which he hit himself a blow, while turning in his sleep, which awoke him. He escapes the wiles of Intemperance and Wantonness, and arrives at the house of the good INTERPRETER, who thus 'improves' upon the temptations to which he had been exposed : ' And as to INTEMPERANCE, that common vice which this age does so much and so shamefully abound in : men think they may safely venture into company without being obliged to drink ; and when they are in company, they think they may drink a little without doing themselves any harm ; not considering that that little does but embolden them to venture on more, *every glass they pour down depriving them of so much of their resolution and strength to resist* : and when they come to be doubtful whether they shall let this one glass more go down, they throw down the fence of their soul, their reason, and expose her to be polluted by the height of madness and folly ; letting into their unguarded breasts a flood of vain passions with their superfluity of drink. *Thus by little and little, the poor soul suffers shipwreck.* In such a case, the only remedy is, to *flee the first occasions and temptations ;* to stop the avenues of the soul ; to set a guard upon the senses, and to restrain the imagination within its proper limits. A man ought not so much as to fancy that company pleasant or delightful, by keeping of which he runs the hazard of his soul's health; much less ought he to follow them and court them: nay, rather let him refuse when courted by them: 'tis much better to be thought ill-natured and uncomplaisant to others, than to be really so to one's self, by ruining one's self to oblige an acquaintance. There are some souls that are naturally so affable and courteous, so soft and pliant, that they comply oftentimes with company, more through the flexibleness and sweetness of their own disposition, than out of any real inclination to debauchery: nay, while they loathe the drink, they cannot forbear obliging their unreasonable companions. This is a great weakness: and though it may be capable of admitting some excuse, on the account of that sweetness of temper from whence it flows, yet 'tis never the less dangerous, and therefore must not be palliated, lest in so doing, we turn advocates for vice.' . . . Here the conversation of the good Interpreter was interrupted by the bell ringing for dinner; and I wish your 'moderate-drinking' correspondent could have accompanied Tender-conscience into the 'refectory,' and sat down with his companions to that repast. 'Temperance carved out for the rest, and Decency waited at the table.' There was no boisterous mirth, no offensive or unseemly jests; but a modest cheerfulness crowned the entertainment. There was plenty without riot, and variety without extravagance. They ate to nourish nature, and rose from the table lightsome and well refreshed; and in company with a virgin named Health, retired to take the air of the garden, where, sitting down under the shade of a broad-spreading sycamore, they fell afresh into discourse upon the beauty of 'temperance in all things.'

THE POET'S ORIGINAL. — We have often thought that it would be a curious and instructive book, which should give us the originals of the great pictures drawn by the ancient and modern English poets; and it is pleasant, ever and anon, to encounter them in biographies or 'hand-books of genius.' The following is from a very beautiful volume upon 'Wyoming,' heretofore referred to, and published recently by Messrs. WILEY AND PUTNAM. It is an extract from a letter written by THOMAS CAMPBELL to a relative in America, and affords us the 'first impressions' of the 'Battle of Hohenlinden:' 'Never shall time efface from my memory the recollection of that hour of astonishment and suspended breath, when I stood with the good monks of St. Jacob, to overlook a charge of KLENAW's cavalry upon the French under GRENNIER, encamped below us. We saw the fire given and returned, and heard distinctly the sound of the French pas de charge, collecting the lines to attack in close column. After three hours' awaiting the issue of a severe action, a park of artillery was opened just beneath the walls of the monastery, and several wagoners who were stationed to convey the wounded in spring-wagons, were killed in our sight. My love of novelty now gave way to personal fears; and I took a carriage, in company with an Austrian surgeon, back to Landshut.' 'I remember,' he adds, on his return to England, 'how little I valued the art of painting, before I got into the heart of such impressive scenes; but in Germany I would have given any thing to have possessed an art capable of conveying ideas inaccessible to speech and writing. Some particular scenes were rather overcharged with that degree of the terrific which oversteps the sublime; and I own my flesh yet creeps at the recollection of spring-wagons and hospitals; but the sight of Ingolstadt in ruins, or Hohenlinden covered with fire, seven miles in circumference, were spectacles never to be forgotten.'

'POOR POWER!'—How many thousands of times in England and America have these expressive words been repeated, within the last two months! A fine scholar, a thorough gentleman, and a *perfect* artist, went out of the world with TYRONE POWER. We have had his many noble qualities freshly brought home to us recently, by a perusal of his correspondence with one who well knew and warmly esteemed him, and who has since followed him to the 'undiscovered country;' one who never awakened of a morning, as he said, without seeing the President, in his mind's eye, struggling with the waves, 'towering to o'erwhelm,' on the horizon of a stormy ocean. Now that the peerless actor has gone, and we feel that his place can never be supplied, we turn with a fond affection to those master-pieces of art in which he won our admiration. In his own play of '*St. Patrick's Eve*' we remember always to have asked ourselves, as he is about to die, 'Where and when *will he*, who is now anticipating death, receive the dread messenger?' In the opening of the third scene, where in his sweet voice he is singing the touching song of 'Tobacco is an Indian Weed,' he pauses suddenly, and exclaims: 'There's a deal of morality in that little song; though, often as I've sung it, it never struck me till now. To be sure, I don't remember ever before giving my mind to serious thoughts on my latter end. Not but I've often had a smart tap on the door from the same leaden messengers, but then they always came unlooked for, and in hot blood: there's the difference. I wish old Fritz had sentenced me to be killed in the next general action! I'd have engaged to manage it, I dare say, by hook or by crook! It would have been all the same to him, and *much* more agreeable to me.' Who that has heard POWER in this fine play, can soon forget it? How beautiful the touch of nature with the shamrock, which 'Mrs. Blitz' had forgotten to get for him on the morning that he was to die, her husband thinking it was but nonsense: 'Nonsense?—is it nonsense?—the ever-green trefoil of ould Erin, the most pious, most poetical of national emblems, *nonsense?* Why,' he exclaims, 'you heathenish ould dragoon!—there's more meaning in that simple——But where's the use of expounding what is beyond your limited comprehension? Present my love to Mrs. Blitz, and tell her to bring me in the morning the neatest bunch of shamrock she can find. Though I couldn't *live* by the green, I'll *die* by it. It will serve in my last hour to recal to my memory the land of my birth. In my life I have never ceased to remember it; I'll not forget it in my death!' Words cannot describe the touching union of pathos and humor in this and similar scenes.

But it was in the overflowing spirit and richness of his *comedy*, that Mr. POWER was especially preëminent. He was a *national benefactor;* for when our country sat in ashes as it were, almost in utter despondency, he made the disheartened roar with temporary mirth, from Maine to Louisiana. What convulsions of laughter he created in the '*Irish Lion!*' See him on his little stool, in Mr. Wadd's shop, with his shocking bad white hat, short pipe, red nose, and *inexpressibly* comic and *espeigle* leer! His dinner-hour is not up by the 'ould Dutch clock at the bar ov the Bull'—which is 'an illigant clock, barrin' it's always too slow;' a fault on the right side when he is coming back to work by it, but 'a mighty great inconvanience' when he 'laves off to go to males be the time ov it'—and the journeyman smokes his pipe, and holds a few minutes' conversation with his employer. 'You know, Misther Wadd,' says he, 'when I hired you as my master for a job of journey-work a fortnight ago, I told you I was a rowling stone; that I was on me travels through furrin parts, to observe the manners and customs of barbarous nations; and that when I had 'arned two weeks' wages, I should show you the full front of me back, and proceed on me voyage ov discivery.' He goes on to awaken his employer's interest in his history, who at length inquires why his parents happened to mistake his genius so wofully : 'What made 'em put you to a tailor ? ' asked Mr. Wadd. ' *Put* me to a tailor? Is it *put* me to a tailor? Misther Wadd, I *inherited* me position in society. It was me father's profession at Tipperary. When me respectable progenitor became a bankrupt, I succeeded him in his flourish-ing business; but a young gentleman from Ireland, o' the name o' M'Kinzie, who expected a fortune but did n't get it, got into me debt, and I got into other people's. He ran away ; I ran after *him*, and me creditors ran after *me ;* but divil a bit did they catch me ; and here I am, a pedestrinatin' travellin' tailor, writin' me obser-vations ; and Misther Wadd, when you see 'em in print, ivery chapter peppered with a bit o' poethry of me own composin', to give the prose a flavor, you may say 'Tom 's gone home, and wid his money out of the book has paid every body his own.' But me ten minutes are up ; now for a stitch.' Who that saw it, could *ever* cease to remember his jumping upon the board, dropping his slippers from his feet as he leaped ; his most natural stitches ; and his cheerful song of :

> ' Brian O'Linn had no breeches to wear,
> So he took him a sheep-skin and made him a pair ;
> With the skinny side out, and the woolly side in,
> They 'll be nice and warm, says Brian O'Linn ! '

And then his soliloquy touching his book and its records : 'There 's one obser-vation that I must pen down, that 's a disgrace to civilization. I persave that in general society this h'athen paple *peels* their petatis before they *biles* 'em ! This must go under the head of ' Barbarous customs of the English aristocracy ! ' Ob-serve him too at Mrs. Fiz-jig's *conversazione*. Could any thing be richer than the 'eccentric lion-poet's ' behaviour ? How *Irish* his exposition of 'drinks ' to the Mrs. Leo-Hunter of the evening : 'You wish to know what I 'll take? Well, see : Port is the dacent thing for a person in middling circumstances. Sherry is no great shakes, unless you bate it up with an egg, to give a tone to the voice or the stomach, which ever you plase. As for claret, it 's the darlin' when an indi-vidual wants an azy and a coolin' beverage ; while champagne is the rale gintle-man's drink, when he 's takin' his rump-steak wid a lady — and barrin' the head-ache that 's at the bottom of the tenth bottle, I 'd as lieve have that as any thing. But whist ! — it 's not that I 'd take at this present ; with your good will and pleasure, I prefer the fluid that contains the soul o' *all* them drinks ; which has the dacency of port with the tone of the sherry ; the coolin' quality of the claret combined with the inspiration of champagne, and divil a bit o' head-ache ; and that 's a jolly good jug o' WHISKEY PUNCH ! ' 'Splendid ! beautiful ! delicious ! dem'd foine ! ' exclaim the company. 'Be me sowl it *is*, Mr. Dem'd-Foine ! ' replies the enthusiastic tailor-bard.

In ' *The Omnibus* ' he was particularly felicitous. Every town reader will remem-ber the story. He is an obstinate Irish valet, who will have his own way, and is continually getting his master into trouble. He is the ' dirtiest owld man that ever lived,' and Pat Rooney has the 'cl'anin' of him,' having his clothes to brush. After one of their quarrels, they encounter each other in the parlor. The master thinks his servant is abundantly penitent for recent and glaring faults, while *he* imagines that his master is bursting with contrition for 'ballyraggin' him : and each has determined to forgive the other; when the former says: ' Well, Rooney, think no more of what has passed; only let us endeavor to understand each other in future.' ' That 's enough, Sir,' answers Rooney, ' that 's enough; it is n't dacent for the likes o' you to be axin' my pardon.' ' *I* ask your pardon!' exclaims the exasperated employer. ' I forgive you, Sir!' interrupts Rooney, ' out an' out! You are off o' me corns, and I 'm azy. Do n't say another word about it!' Who does not remember this, and the kindred touches of subdued art in ' *How to Pay the Rent,*' where he gives his references to the sordid landlord, who returns quite satisfied, having received a good character of his new lodger from a similar Shylock, who has absolutely hired his troublesome tenant to go away, promising, as an additional inducement, to be his reference. ' You found it all right with old Fustian, eh?' asks Morgan Rattler of his new landlord, on his return. ' Oh, yes — perfectly. He seems much attached to you.' ' Exactly; oh, yes — *he was*. Do you know, I think if I 'd staid with him a year, he would *have kept me for nothing?*' ' I think it quite likely,' replies the new landlord. ' I KNOW IT!' adds Rattler, with an expression of mouth and eye that was perfectly irresistible. But at length our new landlord finds himself duped. His lodger's furniture, upon which he had relied as security, proves not to be worth two-and-sixpence; and Rattler frankly tells him: ' I 've sworn revenge against your whole tribe. There is n't a landlord within the London bills of mortality that can put his hand on his heart and say I ever paid him a rap o' rent!' The new landlord is perfectly frantic with rage. ' Do you take me, Mr. Rattler, for a fool?' he exclaims. ' If you ask me as a friend,' replies Rattler, coolly, ' I *do*, and a knave!' We are at the end of our tether, for this month.

ACTING AND ACTORS. — We have given in preceding pages an article upon this ' dual' subject, for the reason that in our judgment it contains several truths, well and forcibly set forth. We refer to it here, however, for the purpose of expressing our dissent from some of the writer's opinions. We are especially glad of an opportunity to lift our voice against the injustice of a portion of the public, who judging of the career and character of an actor from the disreputable members of the theatrical profession, set down the drama itself as an evil, and its votaries indiscriminately as unworthy of esteem. Nothing could be more false in theory or more ungenerous in practice than this. While objectors scout the grimacing mountebanks from the low suburban theatres of London, who come to this country to sport a patched-up theatrical style, stolen from *real* English artists, whom our countrymen have never been privileged to see, we have nothing to say against the just retribution. But are *these* persons to be classed with such artists and gentlemen as Mr. FORREST, Mr. HENRY PLACIDE, Mr. POWER, Mr. ABBOTT, and others of their superior stamp? By no means. These men are *gentlemen;* not vulgar buffoons, of the worst moral character; compelled ever and anon to call upon the American public to disbelieve the disgraceful facts concerning their characters which come well authenticated at intervals from the country which they have left for that country's good. We have spoken of Mr. FORREST. Our correspondent has imbibed a common error in relation to this exemplary gentleman and distinguished dramatic artist. Is it not *because* Mr. FORREST has a noble *physique* and surpassingly handsome features, that his fine tragic conceptions, his tasteful and effective readings, the results of close and discriminating study, are underrated by certain critics? We verily believe this to be the fact; and that our correspondent's groundless position, that a very good-looking man cannot be a superior artist, is seriously maintained by many. A discriminating critic, a ripe dramatic scholar, yet still an unwearied student, we consider Mr FORREST a striking argument *against* the correctness of our contributor's conclusions. But this apart. It is certain that 'J. N. B.' is sustained in his estimate of the imitative and extrinsic show-men of the stage, whose moral career is on a par with their vulgar social bearing, and both of which need only to be known to be despised. We have more than once been tempted to sketch the life of one of this class, from ample materials which have been furnished to our hand, that the public might see how much injustice is done to the profession by counting the wheat with the tares.

A distinguished dramatic author, describing his 'First Play' in a late London magazine, has shown up the stage and the character of the sort of theatrical persons of whom we speak, to the very life. Here is his picture of the green-room of Drury Lane Theatre :

'How mistaken had I been! I had always imagined the green-room was a luxurious chamber, adapted by every luxury of furniture and taste to receive the gay and gaudily-bedecked beings who here resort. It is in this room alone that the clown shakes hands with the queen, and his satanic majesty is graciously pleased to flirt with 'angels robed in white.' The lord, in every-day costume, is snubbed by his coachman's daughter, bedizened in all the glory of a ballet girl, and the pale ghost of Hamlet's royal father starts back with affright at the chance entrance of some heavy creditor. In Drury Lane there are two green-rooms. The right to enter, the line of aristocracy being strictly drawn, is according to the salary of the performer. A husband and wife are sometimes thus divided, and compelled to move in different circles. The first of these chambers, into which I now entered, is a large, bare place, something like a billiard room without a table ; a row of benches running around, on which the actresses sit, stuck up in all the fears of gown-spoiling, either by sitting down on their splendid stage dresses, or injuring them by coming in contact with the green-washed walls, or dusty, denuded floors. At one end there is a large mirror, before which a *figurante* was practising, as I entered, by the light of two miserable lamps.'

The writer is awaiting the production of his first play; and there is just the difference in the situation of a man occupying a box under such circumstances, compared with the calm observers around him, that there is between 'sitting at a table as a guest, or as *a meat*' in a country of cannibals :

'The first piece was over, and now came mine! It is all very well for those who have never felt them, to talk of the heart-throbbings of a young author, especially a dramatic author, whose fate is decided in a small short hour before his face ; but I defy any one, who has not yet gone through this ordeal, to imagine the choking anxiety, the quick pulse, the worse than heart-burn and apoplexy put together which I felt, when I found that the moment was come when my first literary production was about to be submitted to the taste of the public. Nothing save the awful time sometimes employed by a jury to decide on the fate of a felon, can equal a moment of this sort. I am sure no person under trial for his life ever felt more anxious than I now did.'

He is suddenly summoned by the call-boy to the dressing-room of his principal performer :

'I followed the lad through a thousand labyrinths, till he opened a door, and showed me into the gentleman's dressing-room, which, like every apartment of the kind in the theatre, was redolent with the fumes of brandy-and-water, while a brother actor was dressing in an opposite corner, and their united garments hastily thrown off, lay scattered on the floor, with sundry wigs, hare's feet covered with rouge, burnt corks, and many other dramatic assistants to the toilette. Never did I dream such smart-looking personages could issue from such dreary rooms !
'Will this dress do?' said the actor.
I felt flattered, and instantly replied in the affirmative.
'I fear I have scarcely had time to study the part. Bunn only got me out of the Bench this morning.'
I started with horror.
'And even now, I'm afraid I shall scarcely do justice to it ; for there is an infernal tailor waiting at the door for ten pounds, who swears he'll serve me with a copy of a writ as I go out ; which makes me so nervous that I really do dread I shall not play with spirit.'
'Oh, if that's the case,' said I, smiling, 'it is scarcely worth while to think of it more. I value

your services far beyond a trifle of this kind;' and I instantly handed him a note to that amount which he gave to his dresser, or valet, and ordered him to run over the way, pay the rascal his nine pounds odd, and bring three double glasses of brandy-and-water, 'which,' added he, blandly, 'I hope you will stay and partake of.'

After the performances are over, the players of this class, vulgar alike on and off the stage, retire to an adjoining tavern, 'a principal haunt of all the actors,' says the writer; but he corrects himself: 'When I say *all* the actors,' he adds, 'I am far from including such men as MACREADY, LISTON, POWER, and CHARLES KEMBLE. This class of performers seldom associate with their inferior brethren, and rarely address them, save at rehearsal, but seek more refined enjoyments in the upper society of the metropolis, in which they are always welcome guests.' This is equally true of the relative positions of the professors of the dramatic art in this country.

MYTHOLOGY: THE MYSTIC NUMBER TWELVE. — Since penning the article in preceding pages upon *Our 'Palladium of Liberty,'* the writer, a distinguished member of the New-York bar, has sent us the following extract from, and comments upon, one of CARLYLE's lectures on 'Hero-Worship,' which touches upon a collateral theme of our correspondent's paper. 'I should judge Mr. CARLYLE to be,' he says, 'well acquainted with ancient mythology; but really, his style is often so confused as to be scarcely intelligible to a plain man. He has however shown the channel in which the sacred character of the number *twelve* has descended to the English nation. His remarks on this subject, you will perceive, confirm my own observations:

'Our English blood, in good part, is Danish-Norse; or rather, at bottom, Danish, Norse, and Saxon have no distinction, except a superficial one. But all over our island we are mingled largely with Danish proper, from incessant invasions; and this, of course, in a greater proportion along the east coast; and greatest of all, as I find, in the north country. From the Humber upward, all over Scotland, the speech of the common people is still in a singular degree Icelandic; its Germanism has a peculiar Norse tinge. They too are 'Normans,' Northmen.
'Of the chief God, Odin, we shall speak by and by. Mark at present so much; that the essence of Scandinavian, and indeed of all Paganism, is a recognition of the forces of Nature as godlike, stupendous, personal agencies — as Gods or Demons. It is the infant thought of man opening itself, with awe and wonder, on the ever-stupendous universe. To me there is in the Norse system something very genuine, very great and manlike. A broad simplicity, rusticity, so very different from the lightness and gracefulness of the old Greek Paganism, distinguishes this Scandinavian system. . . . 'I think Scandinavian Paganism, to us, is more interesting than any other. It is, for one thing, the latest; it continued in those regions of Europe till the eleventh century; eight hundred years ago, the Norwegians were still worshippers of Odin. It is interesting, also, as the creed of our fathers: the men whose blood still runs in our veins, whom we resemble in so many ways. . . . 'Who knows to what unnameable subtleties of spiritual law all the Pagan fables owe their shape! The number *Twelve*, the most divisible of all, which could be halved, quartered, etc., — the most remarkable number — this was enough to determine the signs of the Zodiac, the number of Odin's sons, and innumerable other Twelves. Any vague *rumor* of a number had a tendency to settle into Twelve.'

'That is, twelve is often used for a vague, indefinite number; as we say, for example, 'I have called upon him a dozen times,' when perhaps half that number would be nearer the truth. Mr. CARLYLE, I think, has not been very fortunate in accounting for the celebrity of the number twelve. He puts the derivative in the place of the cause. There is nothing inherent in the number that could entitle it to preëminence. It owes this entirely to the circumstance of this number of clusters of stars having been fixed upon as stages or marks of the sun's progress through the heavens, denominated 'Signs of the Zodiac,' in which the twelve greater gods were supposed to be located; hence Odin is fabled to have produced these gods, called his sons.' Our correspondent adds farther, touching his remarks upon the expenses of new trials, and the time consumed by advocates in talking to the jury : ' In the diffuse state in which our laws now are, nobody can comprehend them ; neither practising lawyers nor judges of our courts. Many cases, to come to any thing like a definite understanding of the law applicable to them, require three or four days' debating and reading the various English and American reports of decisions of causes bearing some analogy to those in question, after which the judges make up an opinion upon them, which may be reversed by higher courts. A complete law library is computed to cost about ten thousand dollars. When lawyers therefore have to make such an exorbitant outlay for the implements of their trade, it is necessary for them to charge their clients extravagant prices for their services. And of the reports of cases there seems to be no prospect of coming to a close. Every year produces new batches ; so that lawyers of thirty and forty years' standing are obliged to keep a bright look-out to prevent being circumvented and cast by some quirk or novel turn given in recent trials, contrary to former decisions. Reform in this matter is imperiously demanded.'

GOSSIP WITH READERS AND CORRESPONDENTS. — We acknowledge our obligations to the author of the article on the ' *Influence of Lyceums*,' although our file does not permit us to avail ourselves of his kind intentions. We have pleasure, nevertheless, in endorsing the annexed passage, and passing it to our readers : ' As the dew the earth, so do these institutions fertilize and enrich the moral soil ; without interruption, without noise or bustle, or expense. Can you calculate, reader, the oceans of water that fall in the bright, starry summer nights ? — for the dew is most abundant when there are no clouds, as moral influences are most effective when there are no political strifes ; then may you calculate the fruits of these literary institutions upon our country. That our liberties rest upon the intelligence of the people, is an old saying. Let us realize it. How ? Can there be equality where men are unequal ? Can it be that a small portion of the American people can be intelligent, moral, and industrious, and the great mass the contrary in all respects, and that still we can preach about our republican state ? — and compare ourselves triumphantly with the governments of the old world ? Oh no ! I care not about names. Who can care for *names* ? Give me the *thing!* Give me liberty ; give me enlightened equality. Let me stand side by side with the hard-working, well-educated, strong-principled fellow-citizen, and I can then feel that I am living in a republican government. But when I am forced to hear the huzzas of brute force and numerical majority ; when I hear the sacred name of liberty desecrated by men who are slaves to their passions and prejudices ; I sicken at the sound, and already hear the clanking of the chains as they are being forged and riveted, to shackle the limbs of future Americans. Every lyceum in our land is an arch that strengthens the edifice of our government ; and every academy is a pillar of the Corinthian order, for it is a great adornment.' . . . ' *The Modern Anacreon*,' although the two songs introduced in the text are gracefully enough written, we cannot publish. ' May the writer's heart never be less light ! ' is our sincere but vain desire. His ' *Dum Vivimus Vivamus* ' is well answered in these lines of DRYDEN :

> ' And is one day of ease too much to borrow ?
> Ah, sure ! for yesterday was once to-morrow :
> That yesterday is gone, and nothing gained,
> And all thy fruitless days will thus be drained ;
> For thou hast more to-morrows yet to ask,
> And wilt be ever to begin thy task !
> Who like the hindmost chariot-wheels are curst,
> Still to be near, but ne'er to reach the first ! '

' The Era of Societies ' has been turned over to the ' larger medium ' intimated in the proviso of the writer, and for the reason he anticipated. Previously, however, we took the liberty to segregate a passage, for the wholesome truth which it conveys : ' Men pledge themselves to a party in morals, as they would to a party in politics ; as if they could n't afford to be philanthropic but in one direction. Your temperance societies, your dietetic societies, your abolition societies, your ameliorating-the-condition-of-the-Indian societies, are generally formed of different and distinct classes of men ; zealous enough in the cause to which they are pledged, but evincing little or no interest in the objects of the others; nay, often looking upon these others with an evil eye, as hostile parties. Shivering their lances, with superfluous courage, against every wind-mill in their way, or making internecine war with the spectres conjured up by their own inflamed imaginations, they rashly spur on after some favorite dogma, and greatly marvel when their hobbies have thrown them in the mire.' . . . ' *One who has Suffered* ' has our cordial thanks for her kind sympathy. Her ' *Lines* ' await an early insertion. It is doubtless true, could the mourner but realize it, that there *is* consolation in the thought, that the Departed has been taken ' from the evil to come.' ' He died young,' says our friend, ' and his spirit had been ' made perfect through suffering.' Had he lived, he would but have realized the truth, that as each scene of life passes away, never to return, we are made to feel that youth and hope are vanishing with them; that although the fair world be as bright, and its pleasures as rich in abundance, yet our capacity of enjoyment is daily, hourly diminishing; and while all around us smiles in beauty and happiness, that we, alas! are not what we were! The picture drawn by SWIFT, and for which he himself sat, of Old Age, is not unworthy to be considered in reference to the ' early lost.' It loads our declining years with many sufferings; with diseases and decays of nature; with the death of many friends, and the ingratitude of more; sometimes with the loss or diminution of our fortunes, when our infirmities most need them; often with contempt from the world, and always with neglect from it; with the death of our most hopeful or useful children; with a want of relish for all worldly enjoyments, and a general dislike of persons and things. And then, it is good to reflect that the *repose* of the ' poor body ' is perfect. It is OLLAPOD himself who has said, that ' when the hurly-burly of life is over, it is sweet to believe that there is rest in the tomb. The heart shrinks indeed from its breathless, pulseless, and ' cold obstruction;' but there is comfort to the care-worn bosom in the thought of its repose. When the ' fitful fever ' of earth has frenzied heart and brain; when the sad breast is surcharged with groans and sighs; it is not melancholy to believe in the rest of the grave:'

> ' The languishing head is at rest,
> Its thinking and aching are o'er
> The quiet, immovable breast
> Is heaved by affliction no more.

> ' The heart is no longer the seat
> Of sorrow, or shaken with pain;
> It ceases to flutter and beat —
> It never will flutter again!

> ' The lids he so seldom could close,
> By sadness forbidden to sleep,
> Sealed up in eternal repose,
> Have strangely forgotten to weep!'

' Again, remember that he has at length satisfied the ' longing aspirations breathed in the still night beneath the silent stars; the dread emotions of curiosity; the deep meditations of joy; the hallowed imaginings of purity and bliss!' Ah! Sir,

> ' He is happier than we,
> Howsoever blest we be!'

' *The American's love of Change* ' is a good theme, well handled; but we perceive that the MS. has been so long mislaid that some portions of it are no longer applicable — a fact which is of itself a forcible comment upon the writer's arguments. The following, however, will show the drift of our correspondent: ' The question is often asked, why are ministers so itinerary in their lives? The Methodist clergy are so professedly. Their ministers are not allowed to stay longer than two years at most in one place as pastors; and they oftener than otherwise change every year. The days are gone in our country, we fear, when the same hand that bathed the infant forehead with the baptismal water, joined the hand of its early care with another in the bonds of marriage; when he who invoked the blessing of heaven on the marriage rite, said the consecrated words over the same person at the grave. We have no longer shepherds, for there are no flocks. Our clergy are hunters, seeking those they may save, and not venerated fathers, watching the early years, guiding the passions of manhood, and soothing the old age of their people. We are moving, changing, unstable. Our country craves excitement, not truth. Having for a few years heard a preacher, and become accustomed to, and of course tired of him, they seize those faults which every man has, be he preacher or not, and magnify them into unpopularity. He, feeling himself no longer a favorite, and in love perhaps with novelty himself, seeks some new field of labor, and is happy in the excitement of change. He lives an easy life, because he can preach over his old sermons; he sees the country, becomes acquainted with variety, and gets to love it. Thus the character of public teachers is itinerary. There is no principle in all this. It is a custom which has resulted from the impulses of men, not from their judgment. The farmer's wife had rather *trade* with the pedler than the village store-keeper, because she sees a new face, and can at her leisure turn over his (to her) new goods. She can haggle and beat down at her leisure, and indulge to its full extent her curiosity. The father had rather send to a *new* teacher, if one can be found, in hopes that in some way his son will acquire a more novel species of improvement.' . . . 'C.,' who sends us '*I age I*,' lashing the transparent self-laudatory notices to imaginary correspondents of an old and popular weekly journal, must pardon us for suspecting *personality* in his clever satire, which we wish always to eschew. He speaks so flatteringly however of some kindred 'hits' by a late lamented correspondent of the KNICKERBOCKER, that we are tempted to present a few more from the same pen, which we chance to have in our possession:

'*Phila Clamus*' may rely upon the fact, which proceeds from his interrogation —'Is there an instance in sublunary history, where an oyster has spoken!'—that there is. Sir Christopher North, in his 'Crustaceous Tour,' describes the fact of ordering at a shop in Dublin ten dozen oysters 'on the shell,' or rather *in* the shell, to be opened at his leisure. They were sent into his private room and laid in a pile. Before he began to open them, the largest one of the heap got slowly to the top like an awkward terrapin, and opening his shell, announced himself as the chairman, we think, of the *Peldoody Association*. The speech was of some length, and eloquent. It spoke of grievances and losses. At the end of it, the professor, liking the speaker, took him upon his plate; removed his testaceous hat; gave him a traitorous kiss, and swallowed him whole. 'Never,' he adds with enthusiasm, 'did I ingulph so succulent and illustrious a bivalve!' This however is an isolated case; and like the whale in the Scripture, (who said to Moses in the bulrushes, 'Almost thou persuadest me to be a christian,' and to whom Moses, stretching out his hand, observed, 'Thou art the man!') does not by any means establish the garrulity of the oyster. Two swallows do not make a summer. . . . '*An Agriculturalist*' is informed that the gourd of Jonah, which grew in a night, was probably about three times as long as one of the crooked-necked squashes of the present day. Taking the circumstance of its nocturnal growth as a datum, and estimating the longitude of that vegetable by the mathematical principle of a plain third and half a third, multiplied by two, and the important fact is required at once. Historians are silent with respect to the *size* on which this gourd grew; but Sir Hookham Snivey, A. S. S., in his 'Dissertation' on that subject, (Vol. III., page 329, *et passim*,) has applied the same mode of calculation triumphantly, both to vine and gourd. Its correctness we think is indisputable. . . . In reply to '*A Druggist*' we are enabled to state, after assiduous inquiry, that *arsenic* takes a prominent rank among the poisons. Even in Homoeopathic doses it is highly disagreeable: the stomach rejects it; and when taken *inwardly*, (the most dangerous mode indeed of taking it,) the article has frequently been known to produce death. . . . We can assure '*Curiosus*' that he is entirely in error in what he has written. The breeches in which Shakspeare eloped from Stratford are *not* shown to the traveller in the British Museum: the hypothesis, therefore, that they were *split* in the long strides of the poet, as they took him from the scenes of his youth, falls of course to the ground. . . . '*Grunt*,' we think intends to be facetious. If he does not, and propounds his query in good faith, 'What and when was the origin of roasted pig?' we reply, in China, year '3. According to Lamb, (Young Mutton, *versus* Juvenile Bacon,) *Ho-ti* burned several houses down to get at the mystery, and accomplished it to perfection. The minutiae our limits will not admit. The curls or kinks in pigs' tails date from Confucius.'

Perhaps '*P. C.*' of Vermont, who scores us soundly for certain slighting words spoken of COLERIDGE's interminable 'preachments,' will do us the favor to read this passage from a recent London work: 'POLIDORI, the author of the 'Vampyre,' was a prey to nightmare: he died with a laudanum bottle in his bed. And COLERIDGE might have thus left a sad and pointed moral; blazoning his wretched suicide to that world which unconsciously has pored with a thrill of admiration over those fruits of his delinquency, the romantic and unearthly stories of 'Christabel' and the 'Ancient Mariner.' There was a vast deal of laudanum, in more senses than one, in much of COLERIDGE's conversations, which those admired most who understood the least. SOUTHEY admits that he was 'always saying startling things to amuse himself and to astonish others.' No doubt. . . . '*Midnight Thoughts*' will appear, *minus* one of its stanzas, the third, which contains an anti-climax, that made us laugh a good hour by as correct a clock as that of Shrewsbury. It reminds us of Dr. JOHNSON's well-known lines:

'Hermit, hoar, in solemn cell,
 Wearing out life's evening gray,
Strike thy bosom, sage, and tell
 What is bliss, and which the way?'

'Thus I spoke, and speaking sighed,
 Scarce repressed the starting tear,
When the hoary sage replied,
 'Come, my lad, and drink some beer!''

We respectfully decline the '*Criticism of Boz*,' which reaches us from Hudson, as we have already declined similar papers from other sources. And we beg leave here to offer it as our humble opinion, that much of the elaborate pen-and-ink criticism of the day is excessively dull reading. A barren, plodding person, incapable of producing anything original, shall sit down, and serve you up a series of dry commentaries upon well-known authors, long and in long succession; advising his readers what *he* thinks of writings with which they are familiar, and which are treasured in their heart of hearts; as if *his* opinion were necessary to the reader or to a favorite author's fame. There is a sensible article in BLACKWOOD for August on this species of 'literature upon literature;' a formal architecture of rules, attempted to be raised up by the understanding out of written books; all done 'in the way of business,' and for the *purpose* of criticising, by those who are '*nothing if not* critical.' 'Young minds,' says the writer, whom we judge to be Mr. CARLYLE, 'beginning with criticism, generally ripen into conceit, and end in ignorance. With small ideas, a clever critic may succeed in playing off a fine game of words; but when he attempts to lay hold of large thoughts, he is like a dog snapping at the air. A *merely* critical man is a mere pedant.' . . . In reading '*The Strife of the Ocean-Spirits*,' from the pen of an esteemed correspondent, elsewhere in the present number, we have been led to regard it as a matter of astonishment and regret that philosophers of former times, who were so familiar with the science of Demonology, should have left us so poor a *nomenclature!* Even LORD BACON, who in his '*Sylva Sylvarum*' and other works discourses largely of spirits, their nature and influence, and exhibits the spectacle of a gigantic intellect struggling with old errors, like Laöcoon with the serpents, unable to loose their coils, furnishes his readers with very meagre accounts of the different names and orders of spirits, whose control over the elements of the material world he recognizes and approves. Although it may appear presumptuous to attempt to walk where such men feared to tread, yet in these modern days, when all sciences are expected to possess a certain degree of exactness, our correspondent may be pardoned, we think, for presenting the initiative of a demonological nomenclature. . . . The '*Albany Evening Journal*,' referring to the '*Vision of the Coffin-Maker's Apprentice*,' and its illustration in the last number of our monthly contemporary, '*Arcturus*,' observes: 'The number was sent to us with a request that it should be noticed. Opening it for this purpose, a strong feeling of disgust was excited by the engraved illustration which fronts the first page. If the grave, and such as have been gathered to it, are suitable subjects for carricature and buffoonery in a literary periodical, we confess our inability to appreciate or enjoy either the taste or the wit.' This is somewhat too severely said; and had we written the paragraph we should have changed the phraseology. The writer of the 'Vision' has doubtless only not suffered the loss of near and dear friends; and by him the grave could not be regarded with that sensitive sympathy which thrills the heart of the mourner. Mr. DICKENS, who probably suggested the 'Vision' in his sketch of the Undertaker's Apprentice, being himself a recent sufferer, would doubtless have worked out the excellent *moral* of the writer in a different manner. The artist, in our poor judgment, has not done justice to the grotesque text. His imagination has borrowed from the sarcophagi and the figure of JACK REEVE, in the play of '*The Mummy*,' much of its originality. . . . A city correspondent commends our '*True Gentleman*' of Saratoga to a consideration of the following passage from ADDISON: 'When a gentleman speaks coarsely, he has dressed himself clean to no purpose. The clothing of our minds certainly ought to be regarded before that of our bodies. To betray in a man's talk a corrupted imagination is a much greater offence against the conversation of gentlemen than any negligence of dress imaginable.' This is all very well, but could n't 'M.' infer that *satire* and not *fact* was intended? . . . Several communications, some of them from esteemed correspondents, will receive early attention. Our readers will hear soon again from our entertaining friends 'FLANEUR,' 'HARRY FRANCO,' their old favorite the author of '*Odds and Ends*;' and may we not hope also from the chaste author of '*Childhood*,' and our excellent contributor, the '*Georgia Lawyer?*' Surely his escape from the populous city has been productive of *something* for the 'OLD KNICK!' Where, too, is our '*American in Paris*' and London?

LITERARY RECORD.

THE GREAT OF ITALY. — Messrs. LEA AND BLANCHARD, Philadelphia, have recently published two volumes, containing the lives of eminent literary and scientific men of Italy; by Mrs. SHELLEY, Sir DAVID BREWSTER, JAMES MONTGOMERY, and others. The first volume contains the lives of Dante, Petrarch, Bocaccio, Lorenzo de Medici, etc., Bojardo, Berni, Ariosto, Machiavelli; and the second those of Galileo, Guicciardini, Vittoria Colonna, Guarini, Tasso, Chiabrera, Tassoni, Marini, Filicaja, Metastasio, Goldoni, Alfieri, Monti, and Ugo Foscolo. A glance at these rich biographical themes, with a knowledge of the writers who treat them, will insure attention to these volumes.

'THE YOUNG PEOPLE'S BOOK.' — We predict for this publication an unexampled popularity, and a career of unsurpassed usefulness. We know well the excellent and competent proprietor, MORTON M'MICHAEL, Esq., of Philadelphia; and of the editor, Mr. FROST, it is sufficient to say that he is every way worthy to be his coadjutor in a good cause. 'The Young People's Book' is intended to furnish to those from whom it takes its title that which will be suited more particularly for them, and it is meant to do it in such a form as will make it most attractive and pleasant. By means of this book the youth of both sexes will be supplied with reading matter which will not only yield immediate instruction and amusement, but which will be suggestive of instruction and amusement for the future. Nor will it be the youth alone who will derive advantage from such a publication. In a new country like ours a large proportion of the adult population are still in the condition of learners. They have not had those opportunities of acquiring knowledge which the present generation possesses; and to them, therefore, a work which in a plain way conveys practical information, and points out what is most useful to know, must prove invaluable.' We shall take another occasion to refer more particularly to this laudable enterprise.

FOURTH OF JULY ORATIONS. — We have before us two orations, delivered on the recent national anniversary; the one 'before the Fencibles, Guards, Light Guards, Hussars, Light Artillery, and citizens of Natchez, (Miss.,) by THOMAS FLETCHER;' the other at St. Louis, by the Rev. J. VAN DE VELDE, S. J., President of the St. Louis University. The spirit and tendency of the first are altogether excellent; but the execution impresses us as partaking too much of the extra-florid, to be in good taste. It was an occasion, certainly, for the true American patriot's 'bosom to swell, and heave, and gush with joy and admiration;' but it would have been in better keeping to have expressed this and kindred sentences in less plethoric phrase. In this regard, it is as impossible to read Mr. FLETCHER's oration without regret, as it is in all other respects without respect for his uncompromising Americanism and ardent enthusiasm. Mr. VAN DE VELDE's discourse is in a style of greater purity, and well enforces the necessity of cementing the bonds of social union, through the exalted agency of religion and morality, which are its best safe-guards against invasion from without or discord within.

'GEORGIA ILLUSTRATED.' — We have heretofore adverted in terms of warm commendation to this very beautiful work. The third and fourth 'Parts' are before us; and it is only necessary to say, that the high character of the illustrations is in all respects sustained. We have the 'Falls of Taccoa,' a picturesque and beautiful scene, the original of which is well described by our excellent correspondent, ('whom we miss,') Hon. R. M. CHARLTON; a view of the Pulaski Monument and Episcopal church at Savannah; the romantic Falls of the Towalga; and a second charming view of Rock Mountain, from another point of observation. The engravings are all on steel, and by the first artists in America.

'THE PEASANT AND THE PRINCE.' — This is another of the excellent series of 'Tales for the People and their Children,' written by Miss MARTINEAU, and published by Messrs. APPLETON AND COMPANY, to which we have before alluded. As a writer, Miss MARTINEAU has much in common with Miss SEDGWICK. Her style is less attractive, certainly; but the same benevolent feeling impels her pen, and even her imagination is made subservient to the amelioration of the condition of the poor and the lowly.

THE WIDOW'S BOOK. — Among the recent issues of the Messrs. APPLETONS, there is one by the well-known religious author, JOHN ANGELL JAMES, entitled 'The Widow directed to the Widow's God,' which deserves especial mention, as being the only book devoted especially to the consolation of the widow. The author has most happily performed his task, for which indeed he was preëminently qualified, by the possession of a warm and generous heart, a clear and discriminating intellect, fervent piety, and moreover, large experience in a similar grief. We commend the volume with confidence to the afflicted mourner ; to whom we may only offer the consolation of our author : 'Time is short!' Solemn expression ! The death of the worldling's joy, but the solace of the christian's sorrows. Widow, you cannot weep long, even though you go weeping to your grave. The days of your mourning are numbered, and must end soon. The vale of tears is not interminable. You are passing through it, and will soon pass out of it.'

CHURCH MUSIC. — If this paragraph should chance to meet the eyes of Mr. PETER CRAM, late 'Singing-master to the village of Tinnecum,' he will greatly oblige himself by calling with his 'tunin'-fork' at the publishing-office of this Magazine, where he may be favored with a sight of one of the finest collections of new church music that ever met his great green eyes. *Such* a variety ! — psalm and hymn tunes; anthems, chants, sentences, and other set pieces; original, and selected with great care from the most eminent composers in the world; the whole calculated and intended for Congregational and the Church service, and arranged for the organ and piano-forte, by the Organist of the King's Chapel, Boston, and President of that preëminent establishment, the Boston Musical Institute. These tunes are all 'nice ones to look at,' being clearly printed, and 'good ones *to go,*' since *nine thousand copies* of the work have been sold by the publishers, Messrs. OTIS, BROADERS AND COMPANY, Boston, in the short space of six months.

OLD ENGLISH LITERATURE. — The valedictory oration on this theme, before the Senior class at Yale College, by Mr. WILLIAM E. ROBINSON, is a very creditable and spirited performance, indicating both industrious research and good taste. We should like to have stood at the orator's elbow, when copying from the 'old masters,' to have added two or three passages to his citations. We like the writer's hearty defence of the venerable worthies whom he loves, and his equally sincere sympathy with the social ties of the 'Brothers in Unity,' in his own case so soon to be sundered.

USURY. — A little book has just appeared from the press of Messrs. WILEY AND PUTNAM, entitled 'Remarks upon Usury and its Effects : a National Bank a Remedy.' The author writes in a style of great terseness and perspicuity, and is evidently a person of sound practical views ; and if one half of what he states be true, Wall-street should be closed, and an investigating committee at once convened '*in bank,*' to examine his charges, 'with power to send for persons and papers.'

To Correspondents.

COMMUNICATIONS, addresses, orations, periodicals, etc., intended for insertion or notice in this Magazine, should be addressed, *post-paid,* to 'L. GAYLORD CLARK, Editor of the KNICKERBOCKER, 124 Broadway.' The publishers, it should be understood also, are not entitled to a *free* exchange with newspapers and periodicals, as are the editors of the daily and weekly journals.

THE KNICKERBOCKER.

| Vol. XVIII. | OCTOBER, 1841. | No. 4. |

DURANTI ALGHIERI, OR DANTE.

BY A NEW CONTRIBUTOR.

'DANTE! Homer of the christian age; the sacred poet of Faith's mysteries; hero of Thought! whose gloomy genius played in Styx, and pierced to Hell, and whose deep was like the abyss it fathomed!'

FLORENCE, during the thirteenth century, was disturbed by a series of cabals and divisions, which for a time threatened it with destruction, and rendered it an unmeet residence for the quiet and peaceful. The rival factions of the Guelphs and Ghibelines, the Bianchi and Neri, were almost as fatal to the beautiful city, the Italian Athens, as the desolating war of the 'Roses,' which not long after deluged fair England with the blood of its bravest and best. Daily skirmishes took place in the city, between the adherents of the different parties, and the councils of state were disturbed by the angry disputes of the factious leaders, too intent upon the struggle for favor, to care for the real interest of those who looked to them for guidance and support. Happy was it for those who living retired from the city could avoid the daily conflict; and many of the wealthy nobles who took no decided interest in either faction retired to their mansions in the country.

Among the most lovely of the retreats which studded the banks of the Arno, was the palace Portonari, alike remarkable for its tasteful elegance and beauty of location. Its owner had in early years engaged in public life; by turns the senator, the warrior, and the ambassador; but wearied at last with the constant exertion, and with the ingratitude and deception he had found among men, he retired in disgust, and sought happiness in the country, where he could enjoy, undisturbed by political excitement, the pleasures of domestic life. His son had taken his place in the public arena, and was one of the principal leaders of the Guelph party; but the Count himself found sufficient enjoyment in the society of his beloved wife and daughter. The leisure he had, gave him an opportunity for the cultivation of his tastes, which were of a high order. He delighted to pore over the works of Virgil and Homer, and would often amuse himself by painting upon canvass the scenes so vividly depicted by them; and though he guided not the pencil of a Romano nor a Guido, he was no mean proficient in an art which *he* practised for amusement — *they* for immortality and life. Beatrice, his daughter, was the companion of his studies; and she gathered from him more classic lore than was the common possession of ladies of that period. Hers was a richly cultivated mind; and its progress and developement were a never-failing source of enjoyment to her father.

When not engaged with her father, or embroidering with her mother, it was her chief delight to wander about among the beautiful grounds attached to her father's residence; and her eye never wearied, nor did her heart ever cease to drink in the loveliness with which she was surrounded. On one side the silvery Arno glided along in tranquil beauty, bordered by the rich vineyards and dark olive-trees which give such peculiar depth of light and shade to an Italian landscape; on the other, the undulating surface, dotted with lovely villages, formed a *coup-d'œil* seldom surpassed. But Beatrice's favorite resort was the ' Lady's Bower,' where her father in his fondness had clustered all things bright and beautiful. Bocaccio himself could not more luxuriously or tastefully have arranged the scene. Birds of the rarest plumage and sweetest notes were confined in nets so delicate and extended, that they could not feel themselves prisoners; shrubs from all the known world; the English primrose and hawthorn, the Frenchman's darling mignonette, the fragrant rose and the graceful clematis, were wreathed with the myrtle and acacia into a foliage so dense that they were a perfect shelter from the noon-day sun. Marble vases filled with fresh flowers were scattered around; and in the centre of this little paradise was a *jet-d'eau*, which threw its sparkling dew-drops high in air, to be caught as they fell by vases held by fairy maids, whose beautiful proportions even Collini need not blush to have chiseled. On a little knoll which rose to meet the sun's rays stood a dial, on which was the motto, ' *Floras non numero nisi serenas ;*' ' I count only the hours that are serene;' and but few others had it counted for Beatrice Portonari; and yet a cloud not bigger than a man's hand had passed over the edge of the dial, and she feared it might increase and cover its whole surface.

It was Beatrice's invariable custom to pass the time given by her parents to their siesta in this sweet spot, where with her lute and books she whiled the time away; yet not alone with them : her fancy was ever busy with those fairy castles, ' chateaux d'Espagne,' which give so much delight in the raising, but which are crushed by the first cloud which hovers over them; and often were her silent meditations interrupted by a visitant from the distant city, in the guise of a carrier-dove, who had been trained to bear the messages of love to the fair girl. The bird seemed to know his errand would give pleasure. When he came, he always hovered a few moments in the air, rustling his wings and chirping, to attract her attention; an object quickly gained, for her ear seemed ever intent to catch the first sound of his approach. With a low whistle, she brought him to her hand, when he would raise his wing and show to her eager gaze the precious billet which he had borne for many a weary mile, and which unerring instinct taught him to deliver alone to her. He was always repaid for the faithful discharge of his duty with fond caresses.

On a lovely day in October, Beatrice was reclining on the soft turf, watching the fleecy clouds that wreathed themselves into a thousand fantastic shapes, when her feathered visiter broke upon the reverie which her fancy had conjured up. She had not expected him that day, but he was none the less welcome. With a trembling hand she untied the silken string that confined his precious burden, and with eager haste perused it. There was that in its contents which moved the maiden with strong emotion. As she read, the rose-tint flushed her usually pale cheek, and then retreated, leaving her fairer than before. It told of perils and escapes ; of the fear of faction ; of the sudden insurrection in the unquiet city ; but above all, it breathed a spirit of tenderness which hallowed even this painful picture of unhappy Florence. The messenger-bird had nestled in her bosom to find there a rest for its weary wings ; but as if anxious to speed on its homeward course with some message of love, it flew to the water, dipped in its pretty head and soft wings, then smoothing its ruffled plumage, and completing its rustic toilet with as much coquetry and far more grace than the fair belles of the cities of earth, it rested again upon Beatrice's shoulder, and chirped forth a few farewell notes. ' Stop, pretty pet,' she said ; ' I cannot let thee go without some token of remembrance ; else will thy master deem that thou hast been rifled by another.' So drawing a turquoise ring from her finger, she tied it with the silken riband that confined the bouquet in her girdle to the wing of the dove, who circled round a few times in the air, and then his rapid wing was cleaving the way in the direction of Florence.

Again and again did Beatrice read the scroll where ' thoughts that breathe' were expressed in the glowing language of the poet. She might be pardoned if a feeling akin to pride swelled her heart, as she felt that she alone was the inspiration of the youthful poet. ' No one knows him as *I* do,' she murmured ; ' to the world he is Duranti the Guelph ; to *me* DANTE, the lover-poet, the impersonation of my day-dreams. Would that I could but separate him from the cabals in which he is engaged ! I tremble at the thought of the danger to which he has but now been exposed. I will make one more effort to obtain my father's consent to our marriage, and *then* I can induce him to relinquish these ineffectual struggles to establish the liberty of Florence !'

With the letter in her hand, Beatrice sought her father. When very young she had attracted Duranti Alghieri by her extreme beauty, which was altogether different from that of her country-women. Her fair hair fell in rich profusion over a face which it was for the poet not the painter to depict. Its ever-flitting expression could not be caught upon the cold canvass. The heavenly purity which beamed from her eyes gave her so spiritual a look, that no one who gazed upon her could think of the beauty of the woman. She was well fitted to inspire the poet in this world, or to be his guide in his visits to another and more mysterious existence. To his early love for her, which aroused his spirit, and afforded images and figures for his poetical mind, are we indebted for the most beautiful of Dante's creations. This attachment had at first been repulsed by Beatrice's father, owing to some early prejudice ; but finding that his daughter's happiness depended upon his consent, he had reluctantly yielded it, though he deferred their union from time to time, upon the plea that Duranti was too much engrossed by the politics of his native city to make a good husband.

A few months previous to the period of which we are writing, a memorable battle had been fought between the Ghibelines and Guelphs at Campaldino, in which Duranti distinguished himself by his bravery; but he received a severe wound which his friends hoped would extinguish his fiery zeal. It only served however the more to excite it; and on his recovery he plunged with even more ardor into the excitements of the times. Count Portonari was seriously displeased, and represented to Duranti so vividly the consequences of his rashness, that he promised to withdraw himself as soon as possible from the coils in which he had become entangled. It was at this period that Beatrice received the letter we have mentioned, informing her of a new outbreak in the city, where he had himself been attacked by a party of the Ghibelines, and would have been sacrificed but for the opportune arrival of some of his friends. She could not endure to think of him as exposed to so many dangers which she could not share; and when she sought her father, it was with a determination to prevail upon him to give his consent to their union.

The tender parent could not resist the entreaties of his fair child; and he promised that when they repaired to Florence to celebrate the carnival, he would make the necessary arrangements for their nuptials.

It was the time of carnival. The whole world of Florence, save the few who were sick, who bitterly lamented that Azrael should be then looking upon them with an evil eye, and the two lovers, 'the world forgetting,' were enjoying that passionate intercourse which had been so long denied them. Dante read many of his compositions to Beatrice, and listened with delight to her playful criticisms. They were indeed but the germ of the plant which was to bear such glorious fruit; yet the promise of its strength and beauty could be read in these its first leaves. He had already conceived the idea of writing an epic poem that should elevate the Italian language, which had not been thought to possess sufficient power for any great literary composition; but Dante felt that the '*lingua vulgare*' was capable of much; and it was his aim to raise it to the rank of a classic tongue. How well he succeeded in his great endeavor, each succeeding age bears witness, in the immortality which it has given to him and the gentle being whom he has made his guide in the world of spirits.

How full of happiness were these few days, but oh, how brief! A world of tender emotions and deep heart-feeling was compressed into them; and all his life long did Duranti Alghieri turn a backward look upon these, the only truly happy days which his stormy life permitted him to enjoy. The last day of the carnival came. On the next Beatrice was to return home; for her father kept sacred the days of fasting and penance which followed, and preferred passing them in the privacy of his own palace. The arrangements had been made for Beatrice's marriage at an early day in the bright and sunny month of May. There was comparative peace in Florence, and Alghieri had promised to withdraw himself from its divisions. He was not to accompany them home, having many arrangements to make previous to resigning the offices of trust which he held under the Guelph party. With a light heart though a tearful eye Beatrice bade him adieu. She thought they were soon to meet, never again to be separated. No shadow cast its gloom upon the dial of her young heart ; but Duranti was sad. A cloud was upon him which he could not remove ; and a chillness as of death crept over him, while he watched the graceful guiding of her spirited jennet, as she rode away ; and he could scarce return the smile which she gave him with the parting glance before she was lost to his view.

The travellers did not leave Florence until late in the afternoon, for the day had been hot, and they preferred to await a less fervid sun. Gaily passed the first hour or two, for Beatrice's heart, relieved from the anxiety which she had long felt for her lover, was blithe and buoyant, and the elation of her favorite exercise made her almost unnaturally gay. As soon as they were out of the city, in the beautiful open campania, she removed the velvet mask which had partly shaded her exquisite face, and which it was the custom for ladies of her rank ever to wear when desirous to escape observation, and yielded herself to the ' abandon ' of the hour. Her father listened with delight to her playful sallies, and her bright picturings of the happiness she should enjoy when united to Duranti. With love's prophetic hand she sketched a future of undying fame. He was to immortalize not only himself but his age ; he was to be the founder of a new school of Italian literature, and she was to place upon his brow the laurel chaplet which would be decreed him by the general voice.

But now the air became oppressive ; the horizon gathered clouds, first beautiful and bright, and varying in color like the dying dolphin, then growing deeper and darker, until the whole heavens were covered with a sable pall. The party on horseback became alarmed. They were still at some distance from their home, and the servants were sent forward to find a carriage, or to ask some shelter for the Lady Beatrice, who though terrified kept her jennet to its speed, and clung almost breathless to the saddle. But the storm burst upon them ; the heavens were rent with the forked lightning ; and the thunder, reverberating from the distant hills, was terrific ; while the horses dashed on, maddened by the war of the elements. Beatrice was almost exhausted when they were met by their own carriage, which her mother, knowing they were to return, had despatched to meet them. The half-fainting girl was lifted into it, and they soon arrived at home, well-nigh dead with fatigue and agitation, and shivering with cold.

Beatrice's angelic spirit had been enclosed, as is often the case, in too frail a casket ; and those who looked upon her often prophesied that she was a flower destined in its bud for heaven ; meet offering for that holy shrine ! It was soon evident to all about her that Disease had laid his withering hand upon her. The unnatural excitement of her spirits ended in delirium. A messenger was despatched to Florence for an eminent physician, and to Duranti, informing him of her illness.

The physician arrived the same night, and his sad looks, as he surveyed the fair girl, indicated his fears; but there was hope that the youth of the patient would enable her to triumph over the malady. The servant brought back the letter for Duranti: he was not in Florence, having been suddenly summoned to Pisa by the illness of an uncle to whom he was much attached Portonari hesitated whether to send for him thither; but at length decided that it might be unnecessary thus to alarm him.

For several days Beatrice continued delirious, and in her wanderings she fancied Dante by her bed-side. She talked to him ever of love and of poetry; exhorted him to immortalize himself by some great work. Again she would reproach him for not being near her, and in such agonizing tones, that her father despatched a messenger to bring him to his villa without delay. But the days of his daughter were numbered. Her delirium ceased, but every hour wasted her little strength. Very beautiful it was, and yet most sad, to see that fair girl sinking so gently to her last sleep! She asked once for her lover, and being told that a messenger had been sent for him, she did not again speak of him, although her countenance brightened, and her glance was eager and anxious at the least sound without. She felt that the sands of life were wasting swiftly, and her only aim seemed to be to administer comfort to her parents; to reconcile them to her irreparable loss.

Toward evening of the eighth day of her illness, she begged to be placed upon a couch near the window, and to have the curtain undrawn, that she might once more see the beautiful sun, which was never more to gild those loved scenes for her eyes. She gazed upon it long and earnestly; and as she lay with the last rays of the sinking god upon her features, she looked like the angel she was so soon to become. All earthly taint seemed gone; when suddenly a painful shade crossed her face, and she murmured: 'Mother in Heaven! holy and pure! for thy blessed Son's sake, bless him, bless him!' Then turning to her weeping parents she said: 'Will you be father and mother to him — to my beloved? Would I could once more have seen him — only to bless him! But it may not be! Tell him to live for Beatrice. She will watch over him: though her mortal body has left him for ever, her soul will still be in communion with his. She will be his guardian, his friend. And now your blessing, my beloved parents! Forgive me if I have ever been undutiful. The cold grasp of death is upon me! . . . I must leave you! . . . I must be gone!'

She closed her glazing eyes; her lips moved as if in prayer; one slight shudder passed over her frame; and that angelic spirit had left its beautiful tenement for its native home.

The passionate grief of the mother and the agony of the father it were impossible to depict. Life had lost for them its charm; and they longed to lay themselves beside the cold insensate marble, which was all that was left them of their heart's best treasure. But even in this most trying hour they thought of Duranti Alghieri; his long attachment, and the heart-rending surprise which awaited him. They dreaded his arrival, which they knew could not long be delayed. That night he came. His impatient summons at the door was soon answered; and breathless with agitation he demanded of the trembling servant : ' How is the Lady Beatrice?' Before he could answer, Count Portonari met him in the hall.

With a strong effort the father composed himself and said : ' Come with me, my son, and you shall see her; but be calm, and pray for strength.'

The fearful truth flashed upon Dante's heart ; but there was that in the father's deportment which awed and silenced the stern conflict of his soul. They passed on through the various apartments until they came to Beatrice's door. Portonari paused for a moment ; then opening it, he turned to Dante : ' Enter my son,' said he, ' and behold all that is left us of our earthly treasure!' A veil must be drawn over the agony of that hour. Dante could scarcely believe that his soul's idol, the ' pulse of his heart,' had indeed gone. But the sad paraphernalia of death surrounded her. The wax tapers were burning at her head and feet, and the black cross lay upon her bosom. A changed being was Duranti Alghieri, when he went forth from that silent chamber of death.

Love has been often said to form the whole of woman's being, while it is but an episode in the busy, bustling life of man. But if Duranti Alghieri's love for Beatrice Portonari was an episode, it was one that colored his whole after-existence, and deepened the violet hues of his poetical temperament to darkest purple ; casting gloom and shadow over all his stormy and unquiet life. Had Beatrice lived in his own happy home, the spirit of unrest in Dante's bosom would have been exorcised, and his interests centred there. He would not have plunged headlong into the political divisions and excitements of Florence ; but this very circumstance probably brings him down to us a greater man than if he had been nursed in the lap of repose. The noblest works of genius have been produced in times of tumult and confusion, and the most powerful minds have been developed by those trying occasions which crush the weak ; when every man must be his own master, and the boldest heart can alone take precedence. Dante and Milton afford striking examples of the effect of political excitements upon a high order of epic mind. They were similarly situated, both struggling for liberty ; both suffering neglect and persecution for their principles ; and both finding a resource against enemies and the world's struggles in the creations of their fancy.

MACAULEY, with his diamond-nibbed pen, has drawn a beautiful parallel between these gifted men. ' Their poetry,' he observes, ' has in a great measure taken its character from their moral qualities. They are not egotists. They rarely obtrude their idiosyncracies on their readers. They have nothing in common with those beggars after fame who extort a pittance from the compassion of the inexperienced by exposing the nakedness and sores of their own minds ; yet it would be difficult to name two writers whose works have been more completely though undesignedly colored by their personal feelings. The character of Milton was distinguished by loftiness of thought ; that of Dante by intensity of feeling. In every line of the Divine Comedy we discern the asperity which is produced by pride struggling with misery. There is perhaps no work in the world so deeply and uniformly sorrowful. The melancholy of Dante was no fantastic caprice. It was not, as far as at this distance of time we can judge, the effect of external circumstances. It was from within. Neither love nor glory, neither the conflicts of the earth nor the hope of heaven, could dispel it. It twined every consolation and every pleasure into its own nature. It resembled that noxious Sardinian soil, of which the intense bitterness is said to have been perceptible even in its honey. His mind was, in the noble language of the Hebrew poet, ' a land of darkness, as darkness itself, and where the light was as darkness ! ' The gloom of his character discolors all the passions of men and all the face of nature, and tinges with its own livid hue the flowers of Paradise and the glories of the Eternal Throne. All the portraits of him are singularly characteristic. No person can look on the features, noble to ruggedness, the dark furrows of the cheek, the haggard and woful stare of the eye, the sullen and contemptuous curve of the lip, and doubt that they belonged to a man too sensitive to be happy.

' Milton was, like Dante, a statesman and a lover, and like Dante had been unfortunate in ambition and love. He had survived his health and his sight, the comforts of his home and the prosperity of his party. Of the great men by whom he had been distinguished at his entrance into life, some had been taken away from the evil to come, some had carried into foreign climes their unconquerable hatred of oppression ; some were pining in dungeons, and some had poured forth their blood on the scaffold. That hateful proscription facetiously termed the ' Act of Indemnity and Oblivion' had set a mark on the poor blind, deserted poet, and held him up by name to the hatred of a profligate court and an inconstant people. Venal and licentious scribblers, with just sufficient talent to clothe the thoughts of a pander in the style of a bell-man, were the favorite writers of the sovereign and the public. It was a loathsome horde, which could be compared to nothing so fitly as to the rabble of Comus ; grotesque monsters, half bestial, half human, dropping with wine and bloated with gluttony. Amidst these his Muse was placed like the chaste Lady of the Masque, lofty, spotless, and serene ; to be chattered at, pointed at, and grinned at, by the whole rabble of satyrs and goblins. If ever despondency and asperity could be excused in any man, it might have been in Milton. But the strength of his mind overcame every calamity. Neither blindness, nor gout, nor age, nor domestic afflictions, nor political disappointments, nor abuse, nor proscription, nor neglect, had power to disturb his sedate and majestic patience. His spirits do not seem to have been high, but they were singularly equable. His temper was serious and stern, but it was a temper which no sufferings could render fretful or sullen. Hence it was that though he wrote the Paradise Lost at a time of life when images of beauty and tenderness are in general beginning to fade, even from those minds in which they have not been effaced by anxiety and disappointment, he adorned it with all that is most lovely and delightful in the physical and moral world. His poetry reminds us of the pinnacles of Alpine scenery. Nooks and dells, beautiful as fairy-land, are embosomed in its most rugged and gigantic elevations. The roses and myrtles bloom unchilled on the verge of the avalanche.'

Such is the distinction between these two great poets. Had they changed birth-places, their peculiar dispositions would have seemed adapted to or influenced by the varying climates. Milton's radiant and beautiful spirit seemed to have been born under the sunny skies of Italy, where no cloud dims the brightness of the heavens; while Dante's fitful, gloomy temperament seemed more fitted to be the child of the fogs and storms of England.

Dante's early life was a happy one. His family was one of the most ancient in Florence. Some records say that Eliseus, the father of the race, existed in the time of Julius Cæsar; but this idea has been rejected; yet it is allowed that he acquired great distinction in the reign of Charlemagne, when he removed from Rome to Florence. One of the descendants of this Eliseus married into the noble family of the Aldighieri or Alghieri of Ferrara, and his son assumed his mother's name, and became the immediate ancestor of Dante, who was born at Florence in the month of May, 1265, and christened by the name of Duranti, afterward abbreviated to the one he has rendered so immortal.

Visions, prophecies, dreams, and many remarkable events, pointed him out for a wonderful child; and according to Bocaccio this light of Italy, by the special grace of God, was welcomed at his birth by as many lofty hopes as tender caresses. His father died too early to see any of the predictions verified; but his mother cherished them in her heart, and strengthened by them, performed with unwearied faithfulness her maternal duties. Dante was placed very early under the tuition of Brunetto Latinti, one of the first scholars of the age, and he fostered and developed with great care the powers which early showed themselves in the young Duranti. He had not only a great taste for poetry, but a decided talent for music and painting, which he cultivated with great success. One of his early and strong friendships was formed with Giotto and Aderigo, then the universal themes of admiration for their paintings, the taste for which art was just beginning to revive in Italy. Giotto begged as a favor that he might be permitted to take his portrait; so that we have the portrait of the first poet of his age drawn by the first painter of his time.

Like the head of our modern satanic school of poetry, Byron, Dante was very young when he first felt that love which has indelibly associated the name of Beatrice Portonari with his works and himself. In his ninth year he was invited to keep May-day with several young companions at her father's, when the quiet, gentle beauty of the young 'Brice,' as she was called, attracted him; and the sentiment in a few years became the absorbing passion of his being. To this he attributes the early exercise of his muse, and the following sonnet is the first of his printed ones. It is an address to the initiated in love, who could alone be supposed to understand him:

> 'To every captive soul and gentle heart,
> For whom I sing, what sorrows strange I prove!
> I wish all grace; and may their master Love
> Present delight and happy hopes impart:
> Two thirds of night were spent, but brightly clear

The stars were shining, when surprised I saw
Love, whom to worship is my will and law !
Glad was his aspect, and he seemed to bear
My own heart in his hand, while on his arms,
Garmented in her many-folded vest,
Madonna lay, with gentle sleep oppressed ;
But he awoke her, filled with soft alarms,
And with that burning heart in humble guise
Did feed her, till in gloom the vision fled my eyes.'

We cannot but believe that the acount which Dante has himself given of his early passion was too much exaggerated by the warmth of his imagination ; but it shows what an absorbing power it had upon him ; and we can imagine how deeply the severing of a tie which had been cherished for so many years must have affected him, although he says he was prepared for it by visions and prophecies. But he struggled with his grief, entered again into the service of the republic, and instead of brooding upon his loss, kept his mind active with politics or his literary pursuits. But he was not happy; and his friends, deeming that marriage would be the most effectual cure for disappointed affection, persuaded him to receive a wife at their hands; an undertaking compared by Bocaccio to that of ' a physician who should endeavor to cure an acute fever by fire, or an ague by immersion in snow or ice; or to refresh any one sick and feeble by carrying him from the sweet air of Italy into the burning heats of sandy Lybia or the eternal gloom of Mount Rhodope; ' for certainly,' says he, ' no one else would ever have conceived the notion of curing amorous tribulations with a wife ! '

On this homœopathic principle Dante married Gemma di Monetto di Donati, a woman of high birth and fortune, and one who would improve and strengthen his political connexions; but her jealous and imperious temper kept him constantly unhappy. His heart was devoted to the memory of Beatrice, and he could not give that love which Gemma herself yielded, and which her heart craved. This early sowed the seeds of discord between them, and they reaped a whirlwind of unhappiness, which blighted their lives, destroyed all harmony and domestic comfort, and made Dante an alien from his home as well as his country, and so embittered his existence that even the sweet bonds of parent and child lost their power over him, and he became a neglectful and unloving father. But he suffered less from this cause, from the active occupation of his mind in the affairs of the republic. It is reported that he was sent on fourteen embassies, and in all he is said to have had distinguished success.

But unfortunately for Dante's political prospects, an under-current of discord and faction was at work, which soon welled up, destroying the delusive peace which had rested for a short time upon Florence. New difficulties broke out between the Neri and the Bianchi ; the hatchet was unburied, and daily aggressions were committed by each party. Dante, whose superiority of intellect placed him at the head of the Bianchi, was deputed to Pope Boniface to implore his aid in their cause; but the pontiff secretly favored the Neri, and though he received Dante kindly and promised him his influence, it was only to lull his suspicions and to transfer the power to his own hands. This it was that gave Dante his hatred of the priests, and excited him to the burning satire against them all, the pope and cardinals especially, which is found in his ' Commedia.'

The sentence of banishment was soon pronounced upon six hundred of the Bianchi, and to that of Dante was added a fine of eight thousand livres; and in default of payment his estates and goods were confiscated, on the trivial excuse of mismanagement of public money; but the high name which he bore for integrity refutes the charge.   This severe sentence was pronounced on the 27th January, 1302; and on the tenth of March in the same year it was repeated, with the addition that if he was found within the territories of Florence he should be burnt alive.   What a disgrace to the republic was this act, which from political motives alone proscribed the noblest ornament of the age, and banished the poet and the patriot from his country!   Not all the statues, paintings, and inscriptions which were afterward offered to his memory could atone for this injury, which was not so much a disgrace to Dante as to the country which, blinded by prejudice, could not appreciate him.

From this time Dante, an exile from his beloved Florence, was a wanderer over Italy, and none of his chroniclers have been able to trace the exact course of his various pilgrimages.   His first sojourn however was at Arezzo, where a party of the Bianchi had fortified themselves.   Here they formed the plans which resulted in the sudden attack upon Florence, which took place the very night that Petrarch was born.   Their hopes of success were very sanguine, but they were totally discomfited; and with this failure Dante lost all the little hope he had nourished of being restored to his home.   While at Arezzo he formed an intimacy with Basone da Gubbio, a nobleman of great merit, whose friendship cheered and solaced him under his misfortunes. After wandering about for two or three years, now at Padua, then at Lunigiani, where he was kindly received by the Marquis Morello Malaspina, he went to Gubbio; and there tradition reports that in the convent of St. Croce, near the place, he composed a large portion of his poems.   His chamber is even now shown; and a marble bust with a suitable inscription has been placed in it, to commemorate the spot.

Some portion of his ' Commedia' was composed in Florence; and it is said that his wife rescued seven cantos with difficulty from the populace, when they pillaged his house, and sent them to him while he was with the Marquis Malaspina.   After leaving Gubbio he went to Verona, to which place he was attracted by the kindness of Francesco and Alborno Scaligori, who jointly exercised the sovereign authority. They were patrons of all literary merit, and felt a peculiar sympathy for Dante's distressed state; but although honored by them, his restless spirit could not be content.   He was unfitted by his irritable feelings for a residence at court; and annoyed by some fancied coldness on the part of his noble patrons, he withdrew to the French capital, which was during the thirteenth century more celebrated than any other city in the world for its learning and philosophy.   While here, Dante's mind was not unemployed; for by constant training he had prepared it for the discussion of the most abstruse questions; and his reputation having preceded him, he was called upon by the literary institutions for theses on many subjects connected with theology and logic.

The constant excitement, however, and the restless feeling of being without a home, had now almost worn him out, and he ardently wished for some place where he might repose in quiet, and pursue undisturbed the studies to which he now devoted himself. He had resigned all hope of rescuing Florence from its state of degradation, and his mind turned with loathing from all farther political excitement. He was therefore well prepared to accept the invitation which he at this time received, to find a home with Guido Novello da Polenta, lord of Ravenna, a nobleman of distinguished worth, who had truly sympathized with the sufferings of Dante, and who feared that his unsettled life would extinguish the torch which had lighted up so brilliantly the Egyptian darkness of Italian literature. Here at last, in the beautiful city of Ravenna, soothed by the assiduous kindness of his friend and patron, did Dante find that peace which he had so long sought; and his freed mind poured itself forth in psalms and penitential hymns, which still remain as monuments of his piety, and beautiful specimens of his poetical taste.

But Dante could not long enjoy this happy state of repose. Guido became involved in a war with the Venetians, which he found so injurious to his state, that he determined to negotiate if possible with the haughty republic; and knowing the experience of his guest in all these matters, he solicited him to undertake the embassy. Reluctantly did Dante once more come forth on the arena of public life; but he could not refuse Guido's request, and accordingly with a suitable retinue he proceeded to Venice; but so determined was the opposition of the Venetians to Ravenna that they would not even admit the ambassador to an audience; and he was obliged to return without having succeeded in the object of his mission. No blame attached to him, but the mortification sank deep into his susceptible heart; and from this time an unconquerable sadness oppressed him, which so wore upon his frame, debilitated as it was by previous suffering, that in September, 1320, he died.

His death was bitterly lamented by Guido and all Ravenna, and they showed their love and respect for him by the honors which were rendered him. The coarse Franciscan robe which he had worn for some time was replaced by rich garments, suitable to his birth and genius, and the trappings of the funeral were as gorgeous as if he himself had been the lord of the land rather than a travelling exile. Guido pronounced an eulogy upon him, and he was laid in his long rest in the Franciscan church at Ravenna. Cardinal Bembo a few years after erected a splendid monument to his memory, a tribute scarcely needed; for the writings of Duranti Alghieri will remain a fitting monument to his genius, long after the costly pile reared by his friend shall have been destroyed by the elements.

It was nearly a century before Italy was aroused to a sense of the greatness of Dante's genius, and the vast debt which she owed to him for exhuming the Muse, who, covered by the lava of ages, was forgotten and unsought, even in the asylum to which she had fled when exiled from her native Greece. But though tardily accomplished, the *amende honorable* was at length made to Dante's memory; and the fifteenth century saw Florence humbly begging for his hallowed remains, that they might rest in his loved birth-soil, and that she might atone to the honored dead for the neglect of the exiled and discarded living. But vain was the petition! Ravenna valued too highly the relics of the poet, and Duranti's body was permitted that repose which his living spirit so vainly sought. The disappointed Florentines were obliged to content themselves with causing his portrait, painted by Giotto, to be hung with a suitable inscription in a public place; and they instituted a professorship to explain the divine mysteries of the Commedia, the chair of which was filled first by Bocaccio, then successively by the most learned men in Florence. Bologna, Pisa, Venice, and other towns soon followed the example of Florence; and all Italy resounded with the name of DANTE, the creator of their poetical language and the father of their poetry.

THE PILOT OF THE ERIE.

'One deed of heroism on board this boat should not be left unrecorded. A letter from Buffalo informs us that the pilot stood by his post at the wheel, keeping the head of the steam-boat to the shore, until he burned to death! His name we believe was LUTHER FULLER.'

ALBANY DAILY ADVERTISER.

1.

THE lake's broad bosom gently met
  And fondly clasped its bride,
As fair a bark as ever yet
  Was wedded to its tide.
How few of all that vessel bore
Deemed as they skimmed the waters o'er
  And saw the bright sun set,
And gazed upon the fading shore,
That they should see that land no more!

11.

A smother'd sound the pilot heard —
  Full suddenly it came,
And quicker than his anxious word
  Forth flash'd the living flame!
A painted sky above him glow'd,
Purple the waves around him flow'd;
  He heard them call his name,
As hovering between fire and flood
The hapless, trembling victims stood!

111.

'Turn, pilot! turn us to the land!'
  Nor needs the pilot more;
The faithful bark obeys his hand,
  And seeks the distant shore:
Not for himself his skill he tried;
For his *own* sake he might have plied,
  Like his compeers, the oar;
But for the forms that clung beside
The wreck, with none but him to guide!

IV.

The boats have left the vessel's side —
  Will *he* forsake it too?
The helmsman turn'd away in pride,
  The bravest of the crew:
He only heeds the bitter prayer,
Love's last embrace, in sad despair —
  These wrung a heart full true:
What agony to perish here,
With home and help so *very* near!

v.

Ye who can feel for others' wo,
  Who mourn the many lost,
For *him* shall no sad tear-drop flow,
  Who perish'd at his post?
O DEATH, these are thy triumphs; these
Attest thy kingly sovereignties:
  Thou rul'st the human host
Upon the land, and on the seas,
Where'er the white sail woos the breeze!

vi.

But yet there is, which scorns thy art,
  Unconquer'd, unconfin'd,
The purpose of a noble heart —
  A brave heroic mind!
Though storms may gather, fears beset,
And hope depart, there lingers yet
  A strength thou canst not bind;
Which wakes yet soothes our sad regret,
And which we never can forget.

THE GRAVE.

AN EARLY POEM OF THE LATE WILLIS GAYLORD CLARK.

How many hopes are laid to rest within DEATH's chill abode!
How many down that shadowy vale in life's dull eve have trode;
And many, torn from hours of bliss when all was bright and blest —
A mighty power which none may quell hath hushed them into rest!
While life was in its spring-time glow, while Joy unfurled his wing,
And all the themes of young delight were fresh and blossoming;
When the promise of existence shone a rainbow to the view,
And over green and sunny spots Time's fleeting pinion flew!

Look to the past! — what multitudes have to the dust gone down!
Age with its pale and silvery brow, Youth with its flowery crown;
Love with its deep and burning sighs, its broken chain of bliss —
How doth the cold and gloomy tomb shut out its happiness!
Ambition with his eye of pride, the Victor with his wreath,
Mark how his crimson chariot-wheels sink in the surge of Death!
Lo! the dark clouds around him close, dim waves above him roll;
The casket perishes in death — but where's the gem, the SOUL?

But till the heavens shall be no more, the unconscious dust shall lie;
What though its mould was beautiful as summer's tinted sky?
What though the rose-lip curled in smiles — though light was on the brow?
Ye that have loved the faded dead, what is their beauty now?
The eyes whose kind and kindling glance like sunshine fell around,
In hours of youth's untroubled year, when earth was Eden-ground;
How hath the seal of Death eclipsed their light for evermore,
Which shone so brightly eloquent on childhood's pictured shore!

With embryo buds the spring may come, and in the o'er-arching sky
Through fragrant airs on golden wing its birds may wander by;
They may waft their blithesome cadences to man's delighted ear,
As they dance along like living flowers through the blue atmosphere;
But will their chant within the halls of the 'last conqueror' be,
And will the tuneless ear of Death e'er drink their melody?
Will the gale bear fragrance on its wing, and dust receive it not? —
Dust, which is all insensible, with every dream forgot?

What though the calm luxuriant bowers in summer beauty wave,
And fresh contented fields lie green around the noiseless grave?
What though the gorgeous clouds are piled along the sunset sky?
Oh! can they rouse that dreamless sleep — unseal the slumberer's eye!
Though the autumn leaves are eddying by, borne on the mournful wind,
Have they the power that awful spell of silence to unbind?
Will the sleeper answer unto sighs to the night-breezes given,
When Sorrow lifts her musing eye, to pierce the depths of heaven?

Then when the time is long and sad wherein the dust must lie,
Shut from the changing scenes of earth and the more varying sky;
When by the dull unseemly worm pale Beauty's form is pressed,
While the fluttering thrills of joy and hope stir not the moveless breast;
When the lessons of earth's vanity is on the marble writ,
Why should the careless sons of men cease to remember it?
Why should the spirit's eye be closed, when Faith can point the way
To a 'better land' where care is not, in Heaven's unshadowed day!

THE QUOD CORRESPONDENCE.

The Attorney.

CHAPTER VII.

As WILKINS went through the streets, there was that busy within him which made him shun the face of man. For in his mind and heart and soul there was a depth of misery mingled with hate, fear, and fury, that beggared all that he had ever felt before. Yet his course was onward. He would not pause ; he would not think. He was like the stricken beast that dashes madly on, tracking its path with its own blood, but bearing the arrow in its side. When he left the attorney's office, although it was late at night, and but few were stirring, he shrank from the frequented streets. He sometimes walked rapidly on and sometimes ran. At one time a solitary man was coming along, and Wilkins darted through a dark alley like a hunted malefactor, to avoid meeting him. Another time he stopped and looked listlessly at the black sky ; and then went on muttering and talking to himself, and uttering curses low and deep, which sent a chill to the heart of the few stragglers who happened to brush past, and made them quicken their steps until they were far away from so ill-omened a neighbor.

Yet with all his wretchedness there was no swerving from his course ; no shrinking from his task. With a feeling of desolation that was eating into his very heart ; with a consciousness of crime that was truly fearful ; with the awful conviction that GOD himself had raised his hand against him, and had written his malediction upon him in characters that every man could read ; with a love for his wife which poverty and suffering for a time had stifled, but which was now kindling into fresh existence ; together with remorse acting upon a disposition fierce, wayward, and yet irresolute, had driven him half mad ; he still breasted his way on, cursing and cursed ; wretched in his own heart, and a source of wretchedness to others. He went on his way blindly, without caring what direction he sought, but instinctively he took the course to his own house.

All was dark. He paused and looked up at the window, where he was in the habit of seeing his wife watching for his arrival. But no one was there. Muttering something between his teeth, he strode through the narrow passage and tried the door. It was locked, and resisted his efforts. Thrusting his hand in his great-coat pocket, he drew from it a key, unlocked the door, and with the air of one who expected and was resolved to meet something disagreeable, flung it open until it struck the wall and rattled on the hinges. The room was dark, with the exception of the light which struggled in from the dim lamps in the street. Slamming the door behind him, he groped his way to a cup-board, and taking a flint and steel, succeeded in striking a light. Holding it high above his head, he looked wistfully about him, examining every part of the room, and pausing at every sound. All however bore the mark of desertion. The fire-place was filled with ashes, and one or two half-burnt brands of wood were lying on the hearth. The table remained as it was on the night that he had driven his wife from him. The bread, the cold meat, the very chair in which she had sat, and the peg from which she had taken her hat and cloak, were all there.

So she was gone, and there was no chance of her return! He had buoyed himself up with a faint and half-acknowledged hope that she would come back, and would humbly beg to be forgiven. He had expected a severe struggle; that when they parted, it would be amid tears, supplications, and protestations on her part; and that he would stand before her in the light of a husband whom deep wrong had rendered stern and inflexible. For this he was prepared. He had expected to choose his own time for the consummation of his purpose. She had borne so much, so long and so patiently, that he thought there was no limit to her endurance. But he had overtasked her at last. She had deserted one who had broken his vow to love and protect her, and had thrown herself upon the charity of a world — the poor and wretched only know how 'cold and heartless.' He searched, in hopes of finding something to tell where she was; but there was nothing of the kind. Every thing was undisturbed as he had left it; and all so quiet and so sad! And there was something so solemn yet reproachful in the dead silence, that he experienced a strange sensation of fear, and scarcely dared to remain alone in that melancholy room. He opened the closet, looked under the bed, behind the chairs; and yet he could not tell why, he was strangely restless. His foot struck against something on the floor, and he picked it up. It was a small needle-case which he had given to his wife a long time previously. There was nothing either curious or uncommon about it; and he had often seen it; but he held it to the light, and examined it again and again, and then laid it gently on the table, as if he feared the slightest touch might break it. He felt an unusual thickness gathering in his throat. Walking across the room, he flung himself on a chair, and folding his arms, attempted to whistle; but the same feeling of suffocation rose in his throat and stopped him. Muttering a curse upon himself, he sprang up, and pulling his hat over his eyes, paced rapidly up and down the room. Once or twice he paused, as he heard a female voice. But it was only that of some person in the street, and shaking his head, he continued his walk. At length he again went to the cupboard and opened it. A few shillings and some copper coins were lying on the lower shelf.

'She has not even taken that!' muttered he; 'gone without a cent to keep her from starving! God! — what will she do! She must die, or ——.' As the thought of *her*, driven by hunger and distress to something worse, flashed across his mind, his eyes glared; he gasped for breath, and his limbs shook so that he could scarcely support himself. 'It must not be. It *shall* not! No, no! — Lucy driven to *that!* No, no! — by G—d! it would make me mad! I'll look for her. Ha! what's this? — a tear! Poh! this is mere weakness. Let her go;

yes, *let* her ! It 's what I *want*, and will save me trouble in what I 've got to do.'

Mastering the better impulses which were unnerving him, he seated himself, and leaning his head on the table began to reflect in what manner he might best effect his purpose. It was long before he could sufficiently command his feelings even to think. His mind was filled with strong misgivings ; for although his wife had hitherto been almost his slave, yet the resolution displayed by her on the preceding night convinced him that she would not sit silently under an attack against her fame. Jack Phillips too, whose name he intended to link in guilt with hers, he feared. He had once been his friend, and professed to be so still, and he knew him to be bold and resolute. He felt sure that he would resist a charge which was to be made against him to the last, and would hurl back upon him accusations which he dreaded to meet. No alternative however presented itself ; for there was no other upon whom he could fix it with a sufficient coloring of truth to justify even suspicion. But how to commence !

The more he reflected on it, the more difficult it seemed. He had just settled in his mind that the next time he met Phillips he would accuse him to his face, and then trust to the tried sagacity of Bolton to pilot him through, when a sharp knock at the door interrupted him. ' It might be Lucy ! ' His face brightened, and he said : ' Come in ! '

The door opened, and in walked a young man of about four-and-twenty. If ever a face bore the stamp of frank and open honesty, his did ; and as he entered the room and saluted Wilkins, his voice was full of that honest gladness which the heart instinctively springs forward to meet, even in a stranger.

' No fire, and all dark ! ' said he after his first salutation. ' Where is your wife ? '

Wilkins attempted to look him in the face, but his eye quailed, and he made no answer.

' Are you deaf, George ? ' asked the other ; ' where is your wife ? '

' No, I ain't,' said Wilkins sullenly. ' She 's out. I suppose you can *see* that, can 't you ? '

' I 'm not blind,' said the young man calmly, looking steadily at Wilkins, but without the slightest appearance of anger at his harsh language. There was a pause.

At last Wilkins said in a low tone : ' You said you were not blind, Jack Phillips.' He fixed his eyes on the face of the young man with the cowed yet dogged stare of one who has resolved that he *would* look his opponent down. Phillips quietly answered :

' I did say so.'

' Nor am *I*.'

' What do you mean ? Speak out ! ' said Phillips, with more impatience than he had hitherto shown.

Wilkins turned deadly pale, and rose to his feet. He tottered as he did so, and his fingers clutched convulsively. He walked straight to the door, locked it, put the key in his pocket, went back to the table, up to Phillips, and stood in front of him, face to face. The young man watched him without a word ; and when he had locked the door, and stood thus menacingly before him, neither muscle nor feature evinced the slightest emotion.

Wilkins opened his vest, and with his fore-finger touched the handle of his dirk, and then buttoned his vest to the throat.

'Did you see *that?*' said he, watching the effect of the action upon his visiter.

'I did,' replied Phillips, quietly.

'Well; what answer have you to make to it?'

'*This!*' said Phillips, for the first time warming into anger: 'I deal not with such cut-throat weapons as that; nor do I know what the devil you would be at to-night; but here's my answer.' He held before him a fist which equalled in size the head of a small child; 'and by heaven! if I see your fingers approaching that dirk again I'll strangle you on the spot! I can do it — you know it; and by G—d I will! *That's* my answer!'

As he spoke he drew nearer to Wilkins, to be ready to execute his purpose; but after eyeing him for a moment, he said:

'I didn't come here to quarrel. It's a late hour, I know; but I knew you'd be up, and I wanted to see you about a matter of some consequence: I've been here later than this, before now.'

'I *know* you have,' said Wilkins; 'I know that. I'm glad to see some honesty left; you admit *that*. He *admits* that! Ha! ha!' He laughed so savagely that Phillips looked at him, and began to debate within himself the propriety of strangling him at once; but seeing no immediate danger, he deferred it for the present, and answered:

'Of course I do. Why not?'

'Oh! no reason in the world — none at all; especially if it's true. Go on — go on; *do* go on!'

'What ails you?' exclaimed Phillips, surveying him from head to foot. 'You seem out of your senses. Are you drunk, or mad, or what?'

'What ails me?' exclaimed Wilkins fiercely, and gradually working himself up to a pitch of anger, to enable him boldly to make his intended charge; 'perhaps you don't know, and perhaps you would like me to tell you.'

'Yes, I would.'

'Well then,' said he, 'Lucy, my wife; I thought her all she should be. I was a cursed blind fool — had no misgivings. I let her have her own way; was away most of the day, and never suspected any thing amiss until a friend gave me a hint.'

'Who was that friend?' demanded Phillips, in a clear, calm voice.

Wilkins hesitated, and at length refused to give the name.

'Well — go on,' said Phillips in the same cold tone.

Wilkins went on. 'I wouldn't believe it at first, but it was made too clear, and I found *him* out too.'

'Who's the man?' demanded Phillips, sternly.

Wilkins was silent; but he set his teeth, and his eyes glowed as he fixed them on the face of his questioner.

'Who's the man?' repeated Phillips.

'You — *you* — you!' screamed Wilkins, springing forward and striking him a violent blow at each word. 'You are the man!'

Phillips grasped him by the wrists, and pinioning them with a strength which he could not resist, held him off.

'I would half murder you for that, but that I think you are mad or drunk. There 's not one word of truth in what you have said. It 's a lie from beginning to end; and you know it!' He flung him from him as if he had been a child.

Wilkins sprang up and clenched his fists. His dark, sallow complexion grew almost black, and his eye wandered over the person of his opponent with a malignity of purpose that would have made one less courageous tremble.

'Do n't strike me again!' exclaimed Phillips, in a quick stern tone; 'do n't do it; or I 'll crush every bone in your body!'

For a moment the two stood on the eve of collision; but Wilkins knew too well the strength of the man he had to deal with; and with an attempt at moderation he said:

'Now I 've told you who the man is, I suppose you 'd like me to tell you where she went to when she cleared out, and why she went?'

'You need n't tell me that,' said Phillips. 'If that is n't a lie too, I know the reason. I wonder she did n't do it before; for if ever man gave woman cause to hate and curse him, you gave it to that poor girl. If she left you last night it was because you had filled the cup of her bitterness to the brim, and treated her as man never treated woman. What you did, God only knows. You must have goaded her almost to madness. Perhaps, perhaps,' said he, drawing in his breath and clenching his fist, while with the other hand he grasped Wilkins by the arm, and speaking in a whisper, 'perhaps you *struck* her!'

'No, I did not,' said Wilkins, shrinking from the angry eye that encountered his, and feeling as powerless as a child in the iron grasp of his questioner.

'I 'm glad of *that*. Now give me the key of that door. I 'll not be in the same room with such a d — d scoundrel as you are.'

Without the slightest opposition, or a single word in reply, Wilkins drew the key from his pocket and gave it to him. Phillips paused as he took it, as if about to say something; but apparently altering his mind, unlocked the door and went out.

As soon as he was gone, the wretched man who remained went to the door and turned the key. He then closed the window-shutters, flung himself listlessly on a chair, and intertwined his fingers together. All trace of the passion which but a moment before had flashed in every feature was gone, and he groaned aloud in the very bitterness of his soul.

'That d — d attorney!' said he, shaking his hand menacingly, as if he saw the object of his hatred before him; '*he* led me on; *he* made me what I am; and I 'll pay him off some day!' For some time he sat brooding over a scheme of revenge; then his mind wandered until he thought of the main object of all his plans. He fancied himself successful, and surrounded by wealth. ·He thought of his wife, seated at his side, with her soft eyes looking fondly in his own, and of her joyful voice! He started up and wrung his hands. 'If he succeeded, his wife must be another than *her*!' Oh! the bitter and constant agony of crime!

CHAPTER VIII.

LATE on the night that Lucy had separated from her husband, an old gentleman, who was a physician, came out of a large house in the upper part of the city, where he had been lingering at the bedside of a sick person. The night was pitchy dark ; not a star in the sky, no moon and no light, except a solitary lamp, the result of the private enterprise of an apothecary, which gleamed like a green planet at the far end of the street. The old gentleman felt his way cautiously down the steps, one by one, until he came to the last, when he very deliberately fell over some one apparently asleep there, and both rolled on the side-walk together. The person thus disturbed remained perfectly motion-less, uttering no sound or cry. The old gentleman however did not take matters so quietly, and in the first burst of his surprise let off a volley of testy exclamations : but being naturally good-tempered, and withal hale and hearty, and brisk for his years, he picked himself up and trotted merrily on, wondering what could have induced any one to sleep on a stone step ; it was very inconvenient, and on a dark night like this not a little dangerous. 'Suppose I had broken my neck?' thought he ; 'or suppose I had broken his?' He stopped, for it just then occurred to him that something of the kind had happened ; the sleeper had not stirred after the accident, nor even spoken. As this idea presented itself, he paused in front of the green lamp before men-tioned, to make up his mind. This was soon done, and he trotted back to the person, who lay just as he had left him. Taking hold of an arm he shook it smartly. 'Wake up, my good fellow!' said he. There was no motion nor reply. He raised the arm and it fell back lead-like and heavy, like that of a corpse.

'Drunk!' said he, 'and a *woman* too! Good God! what will they come to!' As he spoke, he slowly passed his fingers over her features, which were as cold as ice ; held the back of his hand to her mouth, then took her by the wrist and felt her pulse.

'Dead! God of heaven grant that I have not killed her!' exclaimed he earnestly, with his fingers still on her wrist, scarcely breathing lest he should not detect any sign of animation.

A pulsation so faint and fluttering that it would have escaped one less intently anxious, was felt beneath his fingers. Springing up the steps, two at a time, he pulled the bell until the house echoed ; then running down, he lifted the object of his solicitude in his arms, and reached the door just as the servant from the inside exclaimed :

'Who 's there? and what do you want? Speak quick! You 'd better, or I 'll fire!' And something which looked more like a poker than any kind of fire-arms was protruded from behind the side-light.

'If you do n't open the door I 'll give you something to fire for,' exclaimed the Doctor, on the outside.

The voice of the speaker was apparently recognized, for the next moment the door opened, and a red-eared servant, with a considerable abatement in the ferocity of his tone, said : 'Oh! Doctor Thurston. It 's you, is it, Sir?'

'To be sure it is. Hold the light here — quick!'

The servant however had heard strange stories about how doctors amused themselves in the night-time ; how they stole into grave-yards and carried off dead people, all in their shrouds ; how coffins which ought to have been tenanted were found empty ; how a black man who had set fire to a house and roasted an old blind lady, and was hanged for it, was buried in Potters-Field, and nothing was found when they went to look for him afterward except a foot with a wart on it. With these and many other facts of the same kind floating through his mind, the servant became strongly impressed with the belief that the elderly gentleman before him had stolen a corpse, and had brought it there in his arms for dissection ; and having no great predilection for the company of dead people, he had sprung across the entry with an agility quite singular in one usually remarkable for the great perseverance with which he was slow in every thing.

'Bring back the candle, you fool, will you?' said the Doctor, staggering under his burden, and finally depositing it in a chair ; 'I'm afraid she's dead.'

'Of course she is. I know'd it from the fust, Sir,' said the servant, extending the light as near to, and his body as far from, the object of his fears as a man exactly one inch over five feet conveniently could. 'I hope it was n't a small-pox she died of, Sir ; I never had it myself, and I've seven young 'uns at home as has never been 'noculated.'

The Doctor stared at him for a moment, and not being aware of the train of ideas which had been passing through his head, told him to hold his tongue, and bring the light so that he could see what was the matter with the woman. 'There, that'll do. Let it shine in her face. How beautiful she is!— but how thin! Bring some wine ; then wake up the cook, and let her make something warm, and let a fire be kindled in one of the bed-rooms. Be quick! How lucky that I stopped! She'd have been dead in an hour.'

A ray of light gradually found its way into the mind of the slow servant, like a sunbeam through a thick fog or a stray ray into a cave of bats, and he began to mutter something about the streets being 'good enough for the likes o' her ; he guessed she was used to it ; and if she had a died, he supposed she was n't the fust that did so ; and he did n't see why the kitchen was n't warm enough. When *he* was sick, he'd never had a bed-room ; nor little Tommy 'nother, although he'd had the measles awful.'

Catching the Doctor's eye in the midst of these undertoned mutterings, he put the light on a chair, and paced off with as much exactitude as if a duel was to be fought in the entry, and he was appointed to measure the distance.

Notwithstanding the slowness of the servant and the lateness of the night, but a short time had elapsed before the Doctor's instructions had been obeyed. When Lucy opened her eyes, (for it was she,) it was broad day-light ; and she found herself in a large bed-room handsomely furnished, with an old gentleman sitting at the foot of the bed, reading a newspaper, and a young girl, scarcely older than herself, standing at the side of it, bathing her forehead.

'How do you feel, my good girl?' said the old man, putting down his paper and taking her hand; 'are you better?'

Lucy was bewildered at all she saw: the two strangers; the rich and costly furniture; everything so different from what she had been accustomed to. She closed her eyes, and endeavored to think. Like one who has been stunned, the past was confused and indistinct to her. Strange figures and fancies, wild, distorted, and fanciful, flitted through her mind like the fantastic forms in a dream. But one by one the occurrences of the preceding night grew upon her; stronger and stronger, until they became fearfully distinct. She attempted to answer the inquiries of the physician, but she could not, and her head sank back on the pillow.

'God bless me! poor thing!' exclaimed the old gentleman; 'completely exhausted!' Hurrying across the room, he brought a wine-glass containing something, which he placed to her lips: 'There, drink that; do n't be afraid of it; it'll do you good. Miss Crawford,' said he, turning to the young lady who sat near the bed, 'you doubtless think it strange, very strange, that I should thus unceremoniously bring this girl into your house; no doubt you do; but you see it was necessary, absolutely: she would have died before morning. She'll do very well now; so I'll just step down stairs and see what you've got for breakfast.'

For a long time after the old gentleman had eaten his breakfast, and read the paper through, he sat at the table, balancing his spoon on the edge of his cup, and looking very intently at the fire.

'It's very strange,' said he, taking his handkerchief out of his pocket, and blowing his nose very hard; 'it *is* strange;' and then he got up and walked to the window, and looked abstractedly out in the wet streets. 'I can't bring myself to think what this poor girl must be: appearances are much against her — *very* much against her;' and he blew his nose very hard again. 'Well, Mary, how's your patient?' said he, addressing a girl who came in at that moment.

'She's better, Sir; but she takes on sadly. She does nothing but cry. She's been sadly used, Sir; I'm sure of it.'

'Poor thing!' said the old man; 'they *are* horribly used — all of them.'

Without saying any thing more, he went up stairs, and going to Lucy's bedside, mechanically felt her pulse; then sat down without speaking.

'You are very kind!' said Lucy, faintly, 'to trouble yourself about one like me.'

'It's as I feared!' thought the Doctor; but still he looked kindly at her.

'You must have thought very badly of me, from where you found me — you and the lady,' said she, looking toward the young girl, with a sadness that made her very heart ache. 'I'm very poor, and have suffered much; but that's all; and you wrong me if you think any thing worse than that.'

'I knew it!' said the Doctor, emphatically; 'I said so from the first. Did n't I, Miss Crawford?'

The young lady did not recollect any communication of the sort, so she only smiled and said nothing, and Lucy went on. Her tale was a long one, and sad enough. She told it all. She told how she had left the home of her childhood and her kind mother. She told how they loved her ; how they grieved at their parting, and what kind things they said and did when she bade them farewell, and went off with one who had promised to love her, and to make her new home a happy one ; how buoyant and confident she felt, and how gay and light-hearted she was, when she left them all ; and how her mother laid her hand upon her head and blessed her, and blessed *him*, and hoped God would prosper them in life, and make them love each other.

She laughed then, and *he* (she would not mention his name) laughed too, and they went away to her new home. Then her sorrows began. The news came that her little brother was ill. Then came a letter ; he was worse ; and then another ; he was dead. But her husband was kind to her then, and soothed her, and did all that he could to make her forget her grief, and she was happy again. But one by one her brothers grew ill and died, and last of all her mother died too. She thought she should never have got over that, but she did ; and she lived on, although she was now alone, with no one in the wide world but *him*. She told how they had lived together long after the death of her mother ; but her husband soon began to change toward her ; somehow he grew more and more cold. He went away from his home oftener, and staid from it longer. He grew stern and savage ; talked frequently of his poverty, and spoke to her as if she were the cause of it. One by one they sold every thing, and as they became poorer he grew more stern and fierce ; until the night before, when his treatment had been such that she had left her home ; and now she knew not where to turn or whither to go. She refused to tell her husband's name ; and when she had finished, she turned her head upon the pillow and sobbed as if her heart would break.

' You have a home, lady, and those about you who love you, and would go to the end of the world barefoot to serve you ; but I, GOD knows, I wish I was in my grave ! There 's not a soul will care for me — not even *he !* '

Her hearers had listened in silence, until she got through. They did not doubt the truth of her story — not for an instant. Her frail figure, her anxious eye, her faded cheek ; her wasted hand, so white and thin that they could almost see through it — all confirmed it.

For some time after she stopped, Miss Crawford and the Doctor sat watching her agitated face, as if they expected to hear something more ; but she had finished. At last the Doctor got hastily up, walked to the window, looked out, cleared his throat with great emphasis, took a pinch of snuff, and then came back and seated himself.

' My God ! my poor girl ! this is dreadful treatment ! ' exclaimed he.

Lucy said something, which they could not hear.

' And that husband of yours,' exclaimed he, growing excited ; ' what an infernal scamp he is ! Why, I' ll ——— '

Lucy laid her hand on his arm : ' Ah ! Sir, you do n't know what want and suffering will do. Poverty with the rich is not like poverty with the poor. The first want a few luxuries or some little matter of convenience or pleasure. The poor have not food. It is *that* that eats into a man's soul. Sometimes the more he loves the worse he is. That's the way with *him*. Don't speak as you were going to. He was driven to what he did, and is sorry for it now. I know he is.'

' God bless me!' exclaimed Dr. Thurston, in the greatest surprise, and perfectly nonplussed. ' God bless me! did you ever hear the like? I 'll be d—d (I beg pardon,' said he, bowing to Miss Crawford,) ' but I 'll be d—d if she is n't standing up for that rascal who kicked her out of doors! She 's mad — must be. It can't *be*, that any one in her senses would justify such an infernal good-for-nothing ——'

' Doctor,' said Miss Crawford, interrupting him and leading him across the room, and speaking in a low tone, ' this poor girl is completely exhausted. Would it not be better to keep quiet ourselves, and keep her so? I think she needs sleep.'

' Always considerate, Miss Crawford; always like yourself;' said the warm-hearted old man, pressing the hand that rested on his arm; ' I hope you 'll get a husband who *deserves* you — that 's all.'

It is probable that the young lady had some ideas and hopes of her own on the subject, for she colored up.

Both used their utmost endeavors to soothe the patient, and they soon had the satisfaction of leaving her in a deep and quiet sleep. ' She 'll be better when she awakes,' said he; ' and now Miss Crawford, do you go to your room, for your watching here and at your father's bedside has been too much for you. You too want rest. It will never do for those eyes of yours to lose their brightness.'

The young lady suffered herself to be led from the room; but just as the Doctor was preparing to leave her she laid her hand on his arm, and said with a trembling voice:

' Doctor, I must now ask a question, which I conjure you to answer me truly, on your honor. My father ' — she paused to recover her calmness — ' what do you think of his situation? Will he recover? '

The old man took both her hands in his, pressed them together, and in a solemn tone, that went to her very heart, said: ' God's will be done! ' and hurried away.

The girl reeled as if she had received a sudden blow; but recovered herself, went to her own room, locked the door, and throwing herself on the bed, lay as one stunned.

AN EPITAPH.

He saw whatever thou hast seen,
  Encountered all that troubles thee;
He *was*, whatever thou hast been,
  He *is*, what thou shalt be:
Then let thy heart, whoe'er thou art,
  To Wisdom's voice incline;
Use well this hour, while in thy power,
  The next may not be thine!

L I N E S

TO A LINNET FRIGHTENED FROM HER NEST.

BY AN OLD CORRESPONDENT.

WEE lintie, stay, an' dinna fear me,
It is nae i' my heart to steer ye,
Ye needna flee, tho' I am near ye,
    Frae lounie nest,
But i' your broomy shelter hear me
    Wi' unscathed breast.

I hae na come by ill inclined,
Keekin' ilk leafy bield behind,
As, I wad fain wee tremblers find
    In hedge or brier ;
If I had kent ye here reclined,
    I 'd nae come near.

But tired o' Glasgow's wark an' wile,
I 've wandered mony a weary mile
To see the knowes sae blithely smile
    Wi' wealth o' flowers ;
The burns and braes my thought beguile
    O' dreary hours.

I 've come to sit by Grieto's linn,
To hear its pleasing prattling din,
To spy the trout wi' rapid fin
    Dart 'neath a stane,
As frae its green banks I peep in,
    Amused, alane.

The lark sings to the rising day,
The black-bird to its latest ray ;
Frae morn till night on ilka spray
    Sweet wild notes ring :
My heart exults at every lay
    The warblers sing.

An' weel I loe your cheerfu' sang
The bloomin' whin or broom amang,
I 've listened aft the morning lang,
    Wi' 'raptured ear :
Puir thing ! I wad na do ye wrang
    For warlds o' gear.

Then wherefore, lintie, leave your bield ?
Mair mither-like to stay an' shield
Wi' a' the art that ye may wield,
    Your yaupin' things,
Than flee atour yon stibble-field
    Wi' flurried wings.

If man possess a selfish heart,
Our mithers wadna act thy part,
To drive awa' at ilka start
　　Sae heedlessly ;
They 'd save their bairns, or share their smart,
　　Or wi' them dee.

Come, lintie, to your sheltered nest,
An' cuddle 'neath your downy breast
Your unfledged young ; their needfu' rest
　　I 've broke ower lang ;
I 'm gaun awa', but this request —
　　Sing me a sang.

　　　　　　　　　　　　　　　　　　J. L.

L I F E   I N   H A Y T I.

BY AN AMERICAN.

HAVING passed nine years of my life in the Republic of Hayti, the only country on earth short of Africa where the blacks have rule, I have thought that an account of the present state of that island would offer some themes of interest ; more especially since the American residents, by a system recently adopted, have been driven from its shores, and it is not probable that there will be any addition to the half dozen individuals who still linger there. A fresh interest would seem to attach to this island from the late emancipation in the British islands, and from the fact that France, while the bloody struggle which tore her brightest jewel from her crown is still fresh in the memories of many of her sons, is deliberating whether or not to follow the example of Great Britain. An affirmative decision would leave the large islands of Martinique and Gaudaloupe on a footing with Jamaica, Trinidad, Barbadoes, Antigua, etc. The difference in their situation as freedmen, compared with the freedmen of Hayti, I shall attempt to show.

Soon after leaving school, I was invited by a gentleman who was established in business in a small port in Hayti, to accompany him on his return. Strong inducements were held out to me, and I accepted the offer. I entered with alacrity upon the new life I had marked out for myself. A considerable trade from my native town had made me familiar with the name of the place, but of any knowledge of the present state of the country I was entirely guiltless ; being more familiar with the exploits of Jugurtha than with those of Christophe and Toussaint L'Ouverture. I had afterward much reason to regret that I had not more thoroughly perused its terrible history, for such information would have enabled me to understand many things which were at first incomprehensible in the manners of the people.

My preparations were soon made ; and in the heyday of youth I embarked at Philadelphia, to seek my fortune beneath the burning sun of

the tropics.   Our passage had something of novelty, even to those who
have read the thousand journals of tours and voyages which have issued
from the press of late years.   It is not on board a splendid packet-ship
that he embarks who is bound for those shores.   He has no stately
cabins and elegant state-rooms to luxuriate in, like those which accommodate the voyagers between Europe and our country.   West-India traders are small craft, and those to Hayti particularly, as they have not the
bulky article of molasses to bring home, which employs such a multitude of vessels in the Cuba trade.   The little craft which received us
into her snug quarters showed by register only seventy tons burden,
and six individuals composed her whole crew, including captain, mate,
and steward.   Beside two passengers in the cabin, we had two upon
deck, a pair of large horses; so that with a full cargo, and the boisterous month of December, our little vessel had as much as she could
do to keep herself 'right side up.'   This she managed to accomplish,
however, in spite of wind and weather; and the noble animals lived to
arrive safely, to be launched over the side, and to swim on shore;
and there they lived for many years, the tallest and handsomest specimens of their race within a hundred miles.

There was not a dry spot upon our decks until we had reached the
latitude of Turks'-Island; our fowls were fairly drowned in their coops
by the sea washing or dashing over them, with the exception of some
three or four, which the cook managed to preserve, and which he converted into such delicate fricos, that when we had seen the last we
mourned over their departed comrades, and refused to be comforted.
It is now many years since I performed this my first voyage, 'across
the Atlantic' I suppose I may say to landsmen, although 'an old salt'
once took me to task for the expression : 'Poh!' said he, 'it 's only a
trip; you make it before you can smoke a pipe out!'   Men look at
things always comparatively.   To the old sailor a voyage of fifteen
hundred miles is a trip; to the landsman it is an important and dangerous enterprise.   How 'freshly remembered' are the incidents of
our first voyage!   The starting from the wharf and stopping for a night
at Newcastle; then farther down the bay at Port Penn, inside of Reedy
Island, where we went ashore on a dark and cold night, and replenished our larder with a large basket of oysters; the pleasure anticipated
from feasting on them, and after-disappointment, by reason of a horrible
sea-sickness which came on as soon as we encountered the waves of the
ocean; and before I had recovered, the shells of the oysters had been
returned to their natural resting-place.

When I crawled on deck on the third day, the big waves were rolling
and tumbling about us like monsters at play; now raising us on their
crests and anon dropping us into an abyss; and though we were not
swallowed up in their green maws, yet there was a constant struggle
between them, which should make a mouthful of our devoted bark.   At
length on a fine morning, when we had exchanged the cold storms of
the north for the softest airs which poet ever sang, the glad sound of
'land ho!' was heard from one of the crew.   It was a long time before
my inexperienced optics fixed upon the faint clouds in the distant horizon, which I was at length convinced was neither more nor less than a

mass of mountains. When well in with the coast of Hayti, of which these mountains were a part, so as to be able ' to define our position,' we ascertained that we had the night previous run the gauntlet of one of the most dangerous places in the Atlantic Ocean ; and perhaps the turn of a single spoke by the helmsman would have wrecked us on one of ' the Silver Keys.' These dangerous rocks and sands lie just beneath the surface of the sea, one hundred miles distant from the north shore of Hayti, and about the same to the windward of Turks'-Islands. I have known many vessels to be lost on them, whose crews have usually escaped in their boats and landed at Port-au-Plat in Hayti. An instance has occurred indeed within a few weeks, in the French brig ' Jeune Theodore,' from New-York ; but in rough weather the boats would inevitably swamp, which has doubtless often happened. But here we were in a clear sea, with our ' native element ' once more in view. Let him who is dragging out a semi-torpid existence, without a moment of excitement to make the blood circulate with a more lively current through his veins, go a voyage to sea. If the sound and the sight of ' land ho ! ' does not electrify him, his nature is too sluggish to know enjoyment.

We were now abreast of the Tortugas, an island renowned in the early history of the new world, and immortalized by IRVING as the grand rendezvous and head-quarters of those bold rovers who were the scourge of Spain, and whose ill-defined occupation, half pirate, half man-of-wars men, procured for them a hangman's rope from the enemy or knighthood from their own sovereign. Such were Cavendish, and Morgan, and Dampier. These were the Bucaniers of America, whose dreadful flag carried terror to the cultivator of the Spanish soil or to the crew of the Spanish ship ; now planted on the captured walls of Panama and Porto Bello, and now floating over the vanquished galleon loaded with treasure. Tortugas lies along the shore of Hayti, from which it is separated by a good ship-channel a league wide. Its length is not far from six leagues, and each extremity forms what is called in the West-Indies a porpoise's-snout, from which the land rises uneven and hilly to the centre, the highest part, and apparently a thousand feet above the level of the sea. How many watch-fires have gleamed out from that summit, warning the rover of the approach of his enemy !

A law of Hayti forbids settlements on the islands, which it owns, and the bones of the bold and cruel Bucaniers sleep peacefully beneath its shady and deserted sod.* From their mode of life one can easily believe that many a broad gold-piece also lies buried beneath that soil. After capturing their prize in the neighboring seas, they returned to their favorite haunt, and there the sailor buried his surplus treasure in the silent forest, and acquainted no confidant of his hiding-place save the queen of night. Again he departs on a marauding expedition, attacks some Spanish settlement on the main or some well-filled galleon ; his life falls a sacrifice ; and his gold still rests beneath the deserted soil of Tortugas.

---

* FOR an account of tho Bucaniers, soo the ' Voyages of the Early Navigators,' in No. XXX. of HARPER's ' Family Library.'

Our ideas of the West-India islands are of broad and cultivated plains of the sugar-cane.   We associate with them rich crops and a burning sun rather than sublime natural scenery.   Our surprise is therefore great to find the larger islands composed of huge masses of mountains, thrown together in separate groups and ridges, their steep woody sides descending to the very edge of the ocean.   Soon after leaving Tortugas we were sailing along one of the few level spots to be seen on the shores of Hayti ; a little plain six or eight miles square, just west of cape Nicola Mole.   Its even surface looks quite unnatural, where every acre of land around has its slope of greater or less abruptness.   The seaward edge of this little prairie is lined with dwarf trees resembling the box, which must be very strong to stand against the heavy winds that sweep over them continually in the winter northers.   A solid wall of rock prevents the encroachments of the ever-beating sea, and the site is altogether admirably adapted for a large town, whose harbor would be that of the little town ' La Mole,' which is at the bottom of a bay three miles deep, at the western extremity of the prairie.   As we opened upon this harbor, we saw on the sides of the hills over the town what to the naked eye seemed chalk-cliffs, but by the aid of a glass we made out the vast proportions of the fortifications which the French had built to protect their shipping in this their great naval rendezvous in the new world.   Nothing in fact ever impressed me with the former presence of a powerful nation on these shores so vividly as the view obtained of this harbor.   The forts and castles were spread over acres of ground, and their castellated battlements, lofty arches, and thick walls, now crumbling to ruins, were only a page in the world's history. What is that history but that of empires rising into lofty grandeur and then crumbling away ?   ' 'T is distance lends enchantment to the view.' So true is this, that we saw no signs of ruin as we looked, but every battlement appeared perfect in all its parts ; and had it been an unknown country, we should have expected to see the national banner flying from ' the outer wall,' and to hear a gun pealing over the waters from those marble forts.   They are of dazzling whiteness, and are probably built of the white soft stone which is here so abundant.   It was not easy to conceive that these splendid works are now the mockery of the barefooted negro, and that a nearer approach would show us broken parapets and ruined ramparts choked up with the weeds and rubbish of decay.

The little town which lies under the guns of these ruins, and which a half century ago saw floating in its harbor the war and merchant ships of France, with the white flag of the Bourbons flaunting gaily in the breeze from their mast-heads, is now an inconsiderable place, rarely visited save by the little coasters plying between Port-au-Prince and Cape Hayti.   Close around this cape of Nicola Mole pass all vessels bound to Europe or the States from Jamaica, several ports in Hayti and Cuba, the Spanish Main, etc. ; so that there are always more or less in sight, and sometimes a large fleet.

We were now within eighty miles of our destined port, and fancied we had surmounted all dangers, for we had a bright sky above and a clear sea before us.   But we had still another ' peril of the sea ' to encounter. We were becalmed all night, and in the morning found we had a day's work with a good breeze before us. Soon after breakfast, while ragged and squally clouds were flying, a water-spout was observed to shape its mysterious column not far off, and to bear down upon us. At first we were rather interested in watching the process of formation than apprehensive of danger; but when it had drawn so near that we beheld the water foaming and breaking at its base, and could see it twist and twirl like a huge serpent, we began to be alarmed : next we silently cast off shoes and coats, and began to ask in a voice suppressed with awe, if the vessel would probably sink beneath the shock! We remained in a state of horrible suspense for a few minutes, which seemed hours, when we were relieved by a change in its course. It passed off on our quarter, and faded away as we gazed, like ' the baseless fabric of a vision.'

I have met with these phenomena often on the ocean since, and always with awe and breathless anxiety. They usually formed in wild and unsettled weather, and their formation, as well as could be seen, was in this wise : a pipe, perfectly round, and tapering at its lower end to a point, crept down from a ragged cloud, while directly beneath it the surface of the water appeared agitated, boiling and foaming like a caldron. The trunk soon began to rise from the midst of this hurly-burly, stealing up to meet its other half. During this time a swaying movement in each part is perceptible ; and they each seem to be filling with water. This however could not be the case with the upper portion, as the cloud was usually quite small, and could hold but a small quantity suspended. Before the two parts united, the appearance was that of water forcing its way up in a spiral direction, and the columns began to twist and bend with a terrific gracefulness. At length, by an union of the two parts, a column is formed as round and perfect and clearly defined as a ship's mast, resting on the sea, and supporting on its summit a cloud. I have here attempted to describe a water-spout by combining different parts of the process from different times and points of observation. It is believed that few persons have beheld the beginning and the end of the same column's formation, as not one in a hundred arrives at perfection : they fade away in different stages. The progress of the vessel and that of the column itself also prevent such an opportunity.

Soon after our encounter with this magnificent pillar in Neptune's temple, we took the sea-breeze, which wafted us to our port, in front of which we were boarded by a black pilot and his crew, in a small-boat, who conducted us to the anchorage, a quarter of a mile from the shore. As the sun sank behind the hills, we left our narrow quarters and set foot upon terra firma, with a feeling of expansion and elasticity which those only can understand who have landed under similar circumstances. In three minutes we were in the balcony of our new abode, looking down upon the busy street below, illumined by a bright moon, which commences her faithful guardianship the moment the sun has disappeared, there being little or no twilight in those climes.

What a change! A few minutes before we were upon the broad ocean, gazing upon the lofty hills which formed the back-ground of the little town of Jeremie, whose houses lined the shore, overtopped here and there by the cocoa-nut, waving its long leaves far above the roofs. Every thing was still around save the low murmur of the sea. And now, as if by magic, we were in the midst of the bustle and stir of *life*. Troops of black boys and girls, with bundles of grass upon their heads, and some of them driving an ass before them, bearing an immense load, were wending their noisy way to the market-place. Before each door sat groups of people, discussing with their usual volubility the news of the day, of which the arrival of ' a vessel from America ' was probably an important item. Others were looking out for their daily stock of grass, the venders shouting ' *z'herbes !* ' ' *z'herbes !* ' at the top of their voices, and the purchaser stopping them by as loud a cry of ' *Portez venez !* ' The little donkeys stepping stoutly along, buried under their green load so that nothing was visible but their ears, were as strange beasts doubtless to my wondering eyes as were the guanacas of Brazil to Pinzon and his crew.

But thoughts soon arose which rendered even the novel scenes before me comparatively uninteresting. I was in the far-famed isle where COLUMBUS lived many years, and in which he died, after laying the foundation of the vast Spanish empire in the New World. This very port he had probably touched at, and his caravels had anchored in these waters. This was the island to which Europeans flocked as an El Dorado, whose mountains concealed beds of gold, and whose rivers flowed over golden sands! On these hills the Spaniard and his blood-hounds hunted to death the harmless Indian; and these blacks were the children of Africans who were torn from their homes as valuable substitutes for the exterminated aborigines. What seas of blood had deluged the soil! First the native Indians fell like ' leaves in Vallambrosa ' before the ruthless Spaniard; the Bucaniers and the French revenged the Indians' massacre; the negroes poured out the life-stream of their French masters like water; and to finish the checkered tragedy, the blacks and the yellows gorged themselves with each others' blood; and the soil had scarcely yet drank the red streams which had last flowed!

Bright and early the next morning I awoke, and much to my satis-faction, in a spacious chamber; not cramped up between the side of a vessel and a berth-board, rolling and pitching to suit the humor of the sea, but with every thing solid and *stationary* around me; no extra hands or feet required to brace up with, while the operations of the toilette were performed; no shadeless deck to mount upon; no mis-chievous waves to dodge; and no sea-coffee to anticipate for breakfast. Who *ever* drank good coffee at sea? Perhaps in the packets, where Brindle goes passenger, something passable may be prepared; but I doubt, and with reason. The house-wives put a bit of fish-skin or egg-shells into the boiling liquid to settle it; but what is the *use* of a settle where it cannot from the nature of things *stay* settled? Tea does not require a settler, neither does chocolate; and both, but particularly the former, are very palatable. But as for coffee ——

Our house was a large square two-story building, having a broad covered gallery or balcony running along the front and rear, and on one side of the second story, forming a wide promenade above stairs and a covering to the pavement below. The lower story comprised the store-rooms and the upper the dwelling-house. The frame of the building was made in my native place, and Yankee carpenters went out to put it up. Great was the wonder of the natives when they saw for the first time a New-England 'raising,' and beheld the whole broad-side of a house going up at once!

Stepping out upon the balcony, I had the first day-light view of my new home. I was much struck at the well-worn surface of the streets. Not a spire of grass grew any where, and every part was like a frequented thoroughfare in a large city. This slight circumstance surprised me, and evinced a deal of passing to and fro: the actual movement was not however large, until Saturday and Sunday, when the crowds of blacks flocking in to market accounted for the matter. The houses were generally of one story, having the roofs projecting over the side-walks, forming a continuous and most grateful shade to pedestrians, and serving also as a parlor to the inmates, for they *live* under them. It may be imagined that families sitting the livelong day before their front-doors, separated from their neighbors only by the distance from door to door, which is from fifteen to twenty feet, cannot have a great many secrets from each other. The shore formed a semi-circle, and a street ran parallel with it from a river at the south to a rocky point at the north of the harbor. The houses on the sea side of the street had but scanty room for yards, and old Ocean sometimes broke into the back-doors, when very angry; while on the other side, for some distance, the yards were cut off by a precipitous hill, which overhung the backs of the houses on that side. The crackling sound of the cocoa-nut tree, as it waved its long limbs to the land-breeze, was heard in the stillness of morning. On one the fruit hung within reach of the hand; on another it was at the top of a tall spar, fifty feet from the ground. It is wonderful how so slight a column bears such a weight of fruit and such a spread of foliage even at its very summit; especially as it never 'takes a reef in its topsails,' even in a hurricane.

Our little schooner lay in full view in front, reposing quietly on the smooth water like a sea-bird resting itself after a weary flight. By her side was a big down-east brig, which had touched for a market, and found a sale for her cargo of lumber. Though the first rays of the sun were but just darting upward from behind the Cayemitto Island, her crew had already commenced making a raft, thus wisely taking advantage of the cool of the day. At this moment the stripes and stars were run up to the mast-head of the little F——, and I gazed upon them with feelings entirely new. We may look upon our flag at home, performing its daily duty from the top of a ship-house or an arsenal, or floating in the hot dust of a fête-day, without any great stirring of the soul. But when we are treading a strange soil, and are surrounded by an unsympathizing and it may be a hostile people, *then* we look to it as to a talisman which wards off evil; as a friend and protector, whose every star and stripe says significantly, 'Beware!'

L I N E S

ON REVISITING A FAVORITE LAKE, AFTER AN ABSENCE OF MANY YEARS.

BY WILLIAM PITT PALMER.

FROM these thronged haunts, where Nature's trampled germs
Ne'er feel the touch of Spring, nor wake to wear
Her green and perfumed garniture again,
Escap'd at last, like vassal from his thrall,
I stand upon thy sylvan marge once more,
O fairest mirror ! where the charmèd Morn
Surveys her blushing loveliness, or Eve
The wondrous glory of her starry train !
Yet bears the image gazing at me now
Far other aspect than was wont to smile
On boyhood's bending vision ; though the boy
And he that sighs to mark the mournful change
Are still the same.   Sad change, indeed ! — yet thanks,
Thanks, dear magician ! in whose faithful glass
I read that Time may pale the flush of youth,
May blanch the raven locks, and earthward bend
The wan and wrinkled tablet of the brow,
Yet leave the heart's first records uneffaced,
And all its Geyser-fountains bubbling still.
Therefore to thee and these associate scenes,
Whate'er this outward seeming, I have brought
The fresh, warm feelings, and the memories dear
Ye nursed within my breast in vernal years.
Despite the past, I *am* a boy again !
And soon from yon dim grotto as of yore
A fairy bark shall leap into thy waves,
And fling its white folds bravely to the breeze,
In gay defiance ; nor shall he whose hand
Directs its billowy fleetness heave a sigh
For broader ocean or diviner isles
Than these my own dear native hills embrace.
And when the stormy spirit of the North
Has hushed thy liquid murmurs, and consigned
Thy dimpled beauty to a rigid waste,
The boy of two-score winters oft shall join
The hamlet's merry troop, careering wild
On steel-shod sandals o'er thy smooth expanse,
While ring the echoing dells with louder mirth
When sheer beneath their swiftly-gliding feet
Thunders the sudden cleft from shore to shore !

And she who bends in childhood's strange delight
Above the pale sweet face soft mirrored there,
As if thy loveliest naiad's sister eyes
Were smiling up in hers, shall haunt with me
Thy winding bays, green isles, and headlands bold,
And deem that Eden in its vernal prime
Could boast no charm that were exotic here.
To her erewhile in urban durance pent,
Earth's verdant lap, perfumed with floral hues,
And laced with silver streams, was all unknown :

Nay, yonder sun, bedimmed by sulphurous clouds,
And shorn of half his realms by Art's proud piles
Upheaved in gloomy grandeur to the sky,
Has never taught the wondering soul till now
With what a god-like glory he comes forth
From morning's rosy portals, and at eve
Smiles from his golden chambers of the west.
The time has been when one poor sickly flower,
One dwarf'd shrub pining in the dim damp court,
And one pet bird, unconscious as herself
Of bloomy lawns and many-minstrelled groves,
Were all she knew of nature ; but henceforth
Her path shall wind through fields so pranked with flowers
That oft her fairy foot shall seek in vain
For space whereon to light, nor harm the bee ;
Or steal through warbling wilds so arched with boughs,
And roofed with myriad leaves, the noon-day sun
Ne'er sees the moss on which their shadows sleep.
And ah ! should that young cheek's too lingering flush,
Like autumn's hectic hues, presage decay,
Still hope is ours, that Thou who sendest forth
Thy cooling mists upon the evening winds
To bless with gentle showers or gentler dews
The lowliest herb that withers in the waste,
Hast yet a healing balm for this dear flower,
Snatched from the rough Zahara of the world,
To bloom in thy glad presence, fairy lake,
And crown the glory of thy perfect charms.

New-York, August, 1841.

THE HOLY WARS OF STOKEVILLE.

A VERITABLE HISTORY.

STOKEVILLE at one period boasted of two churches only — the Presbyterian and Episcopalian. These were erected at the first settlement of the village, and had grown with its growth. In the days of their adversity they maintained a proper degree of harmony within their borders; but when they became prosperous they were often convulsed by internal and external commotion, both as respected their own affairs and their relations to each other. In short, as they waxed fat they kicked.

The first distinctive recollection I have of these churches was during the ministerial labors of Parson BRUSH, at the Episcopal, and ' old Mr. BETTS,' as he was called, at the Presbyterian. When Mr. Brush was first installed, and preached his initiatory sermon, he captivated the whole congregation. It was averred by all the villagers, far and near, that he was ' the most remarkable young man that the age had produced.' Every body said it was providential that they had been so fortunate in the selection of a clergyman: that they might have searched the world over and not have found another such a man as Mr. Brush; and the vestry-men in particular deemed him just *the* man of all others to fill the pulpit. All passed off in the happiest manner for two or three months. Every sermon was 'better and better.' The whole congregation were sure that they should keep him for ever. All the ladies in the parish were continually making presents to him, and all the gentlemen were applauding them for their liberality. At length the people thought the church was not good enough for him to preach in, and the vestry-men were called together to concert measures to repair it. It was finally resolved to overhaul the edifice completely. A subscription paper was set on foot, and every body subscribed; and very soon the old church which had withstood so many winters was 'rent in twain from top to bottom.' New slips were put in; a glaring pulpit, blazing with red velvet and elaborate tassels, was erected; a new organ was purchased, and a new bell swung high in the steeple, to call the people to their prayers.

Every thing in short was put in complete order, and the churchmen of Stokeville prided themselves upon having the finest church and the most eloquent preacher for fifty miles around.

Now it chanced about this time that Mrs. Miranda Meeks and several other church-going 'ceruleans of the second sex' had a tea-party. There was Mrs. Miranda Meeks herself, Mrs. Lucinda Dow, Mrs. Mary Brown, Polly Sly, an old maid, together with some others. While sitting around the table, they freely canvassed all the affairs of the village from one end to the other. When they had disposed of the temporal, they very naturally took up spiritual things, and Parson Brush's name came frequently in question. Miss Polly Sly said 'Mr. Brush was a fine man;' that she always *had* liked him, and she did n't know but she still liked him as well as she ever did; she *had* heard stories about him, 't was true, but she did n't believe them; and therefore she should n't repeat them.

This set the whole tea-table on fire. 'Heard stories about Mr. Brush!' exclaimed Mrs. Meeks; 'why Miss Sly!—how can you say so? *What* stories, pray?'

'Oh, it 's of no consequence,' replied Miss Sly, with an air of great indifference; 'I do n't believe a word of it; though I must confess it looks strange—*very* strange.'

'Do tell us!' said all the tea-drinkers, with suspended cups, and in one breath; 'you know *we* shall never circulate it. Let us know who *could* have the heart to slander Mr. Brush!'

'Oh, but then,' said Miss Sly, 'if it should get out, it would be reported as coming from *me;* and you know I never want to make no mischief.'

But it was of no avail. The gossips *en masse* besought Miss Sly to repeat the reports which she had heard.

'Well,' said Miss Sly, 'upon your word and honor that you do n't say a word to a living soul about it, I do n't know but I 'll ——'

'Oh no! no! no!' burst from a dozen voices at once. '*We* would n't do any thing Miss Sly, *you* know, to get you into trouble.'

'Well then,' said the maiden-innocent, reducing her voice to a whisper, and looking carefully around the room, 'they say Mr. Brush *drinks;* and that he is under the influence of liquor every Sabbath; and John Noakes told me t'other day he saw him purchase a quart of gin at Mr. Tape's store; and beside that, he has been seen in the tavern bar-room several times lately.'

'Why Miss Sly! You do n't say so!' 'Law me!' 'Why how *can* you!' were the exclamations which followed this precious bit of scandal.

'Oh yes!' continued Miss Sly, 'I 've known it for a great while, but I did n't want to say any thing about it, because I was afraid it would make difficulty.'

'Well, now *there!*' broke out Mrs. Meeks; 'that just puts me in mind of something. I *thought* Mr. Brush's face looked very red in church last Sunday; and he *acted* queerly too, 'pears to me. Did n't *you* observe it, Mrs. Dow?' asked Mrs. Meeks, turning round; 'I 'm sure you must.'

'Well, come to think,' answered Mrs. Dow, '*I did!*'

'Oh, ho! that 's it then!' exclaimed Mrs. Meeks.

'Yes, that 's it,' replied Miss Sly.

And now the whole company 'set in with a steady stream of talk' about the awful disclosure. All was hubbub and uproar; each one trying to drown her neighbor; and before they closed the discussion Mr. Brush's character was annihilated.

The tea-party at Mrs. Meeks' broke up at a late hour; and each one went home with visible 'marks of wonder and surprise' ('as O the folly of sinners!') depicted on her countenance.

When Mrs. Meeks' parlor was entirely cleared, and all was quiet, she sat down before the fire with her respectable husband, Mr. John Meeks. She was unusually taciturn for her, and Mr. Meeks seeing it, inquired the cause.

'Oh nothing — nothing,' said Mrs. Meeks, starting up suddenly; 'that is, nothing of importance. I was only thinking.'

'So I perceived,' said Mr. Meeks; 'you seemed to be quite *lost* in thought.'

'It 's very strange, aint it?' said Mrs. Meeks, glancing round to her husband.

'Very *strange?*' inquired Mr. Meeks, looking up in amazement; '*what 's* very strange?'

'Why Mr. Brush.'

'What of Mr. Brush?'

'Why, HE DRINKS!' exclaimed Mrs. Meeks.

'Mr. Brush drinks!' exclaimed Mr. Meeks, with astonishment; 'Mr. Brush *drinks!* Who has been circulating *that* slander?'

'I mus' n't tell,' said Mrs. Meeks; 'but I believe it, and a great many others believe it; and some have observed his intoxication while in the pulpit; and Tom Noakes see him get liquor at Mr. Tape's store; and he has been seen in the tavern and other places! Any thing but a drunken clergyman!'

'A base slander!' said Mr. Meeks, rising up and walking the floor; 'a base tea-table slander. Fine business for a pack of women to be engaged in! Could n't your company find any better employment?'

'Well, well!' replied Mrs. Meeks, with an ironical smile; 'do n't believe it; keep a drunken clergyman! I 've cleared *my* conscience, and that 's enough. I shan't say any thing more about it. You ain't compelled to believe me. Go on your own way.'

When Mrs. Meeks closed the last sentence, she rose up and threw herself out of the room as if the ten Furies impelled her; and thus put an end to the conversation.

Mrs. Mary Brown, Mrs. Lucinda Dow, and the other ladies who were present when Miss Polly Sly made her developement, hurried home and told *their* husbands; and when the sun rose next morning, Stokeville was ringing from one end to the other with the awful tale that Parson Brush was a drunkard! And not only that, but that he had *been* a drunkard from the time he first came to Stokeville! And some said they had heard of his intemperance even *before;* that he always had been intoxicated in the pulpit; and that his best discourses were delivered when under the influence of liquor, there was now no doubt. There were more than an hundred persons to be found who recollected to have seen him in a state of unnatural excitement; 'though,' as they said, 'they did not suspect any thing *at the time.*' Every little fit of sickness with which the parson had been visited during his sojourn in the village was attributed to drink; and there was a determination with man, woman, and child, to dismiss him forthwith, even without the formality of a trial.

Parson Brush, as may be anticipated, could not get a hearing in this small maëlstrom of excitement. He was condemned by all Stokeville; and what could he do single-handed with the multitude against him? He demanded a trial before an ecclesiastical tribunal, that he might exculpate himself; but his church refused him the privilege; its members declaring that 'his usefulness was destroyed, guilty or innocent;' and that 'clergymen ought to be above suspicion even.' He protested against such arbitrary proceedings, but his remonstrances were of no avail. He was *dismissed;* and thus ended the labors of Parson Brush in Stokeville, after a residence of eight months and fourteen days; and he departed with as many curses upon his head as there had been blessings showered upon him at his arrival.

When the public mind had settled down, the people began to reflect upon what they had done. They inquired into the charges which had been alleged against Mr. Brush, and found them totally without foundation in truth. The gin which Tom Noakes declared he saw Mr. Brush purchase at Mr. Tape's store was found to have been used for horse-medicine, and all the other sights and conjectures were in like manner accounted for. Not a solitary charge was substantiated, and not an individual in Stokeville could be found who was not convinced that Parson Brush had been dismissed for crimes of which he was never guilty, and which had their existence only in the brain of a pack of mischievous and gossipping women.

AFTER the dismissal of Mr. Brush, the church in Stokeville remained for a great length of time unopened. The excitement had been so furious, and the feelings of the religious portion of the community so exasperated, that there seemed to be an indifference whether the church was *ever* resuscitated. But when they found that Mr. Brush was innocent, and that *they* only were in the wrong, there was a movement immediately manifested to procure another clergyman.

No one was more forward in this work than Mrs. Meeks, Mrs. Dow, Mrs. Brown, and Miss Polly Sly; the evil spirits who had by their venomous tongues first poisoned the congregation. It was resolved that an *old* man should be procured; one whom slander could not touch; one who had been tried in the fiery furnace; one in fine whose age should render him invulnerable to all the shafts which malice could forge or slander direct.

After some weeks, ' old PARSON GERRY ' was hit upon as the very man of all others to fill the pulpit in Stokeville. He was about sixty years of age, and as venerable in appearance as the pictures of the apostles. His fine head, quick piercing eye, wrinkled brow, and thin gray hair, gave to him a reverend and holy aspect. He was installed, and with a family of ten children, comfortably located in the parish house. He was one of those whose fortune it had been, as is too often the case with members of the clerical profession, never to be settled; to be tempest-tossed through the world, without ever finding port. He had preached in every State in the Union, and almost in every town. He had never been in one spot long enough to take root; and when he came to Stokeville, with his children swarming around him, he seemed jaded out of all spirits; as one indeed who looked to the grave as his only resting-place.

Old Parson Gerry was the town's talk for some months. Every body called upon his family, and every mouth was open in their praise. The old man was extolled as ' a saint, if ever there was one;' his wife was a female Samaritan, and his daughters were all beautiful. ' What a good old man Parson Gerry is!' said Mrs. Meeks. ' What an amiable wife he has!' rejoined Mrs. Dow. ' What lovely daughters!' said Mrs. Brown. The whole public sentiment had changed. There was at length a delightful calm after the late terrible storm. Several large parties were given on Parson Gerry's account, and his daughters were hailed as the spirit and soul of them all. Presents were made to the family; and it really seemed for some months that it was impossible to do too much for, or exalt too highly, old Parson Gerry and his incomparable family.

Mr. Meeks, husband of Mrs. Meeks, was the first man to break in upon the quiet of the church the second time. It so happened that the old parson, on one or two occasions, omitted a portion of the service. Mr. Meeks detected this at once, and of course was struck dumb with horror. He said he ' had been brought up a churchman, in the severest sense of the word; and it wounded his feelings, and roused his astonishment, to find Parson Gerry guilty of such sacrilege! There must be something wrong about him; he was either *no* christian, or else his faith in the discipline of the church was sadly perverted.' Of course a flame was soon blown up, which spread wider and wider; but before it had entirely consumed the old gentlemen, some friendly band extinguished it, harmonized the congregation, and tranquillity was restored.

It was soon observed, that in spite of the harmony restored, there was a growing dislike to Parson Gerry and his preaching. The people were about ' getting tired ' of him, as the phrase is. His congregation began to drop off one after another, until scarcely an apology for an audience was left. Every member had his own excuse for not attending church. Some did not like his discourses because they were so long; others disliked them because they were prosy and dull; and many said he did not preach the true orthodox doctrine. There were a thousand objections to him; and each one who had an objection found in it an excuse for deserting the church, until, as we have said, he had scarcely an apology for an audience left.

It was necessary to find some grave charge to justify the removal of Parson Gerry; and the ingenuity of Stokeville soon framed one. After torturing every act that had ever been committed by the minister or his family, they discovered that 'Parson Gerry's wife and daughters were extravagant in their dress;' and it wounded the feelings of the congregation to behold christian simplicity so outraged.

This was enough. All the church snapped at the bait. The family of Parson Gerry was so extravagant that they were running themselves 'head over ears in debt.' It would never do; the church would be ruined.

'Oh!' said Miss Polly Sly, running breathless into Mrs. Dow's, just for an afternoon's call; 'oh, Mrs. Dow! *have* you heard the news?'

'Why, what!' exclaimed Mrs. Dow, looking up in astonishment.

'Why, Parson Gerry! — about Parson Gerry! He owes every body!' exclaimed Polly, holding up both hands, with a holy horror.

'Why how you talk!' said Mrs. Dow.

'Yes, every body! — every body! He owes Mr. Tape ten dollars for that beautiful satin his daughter Mary wears; and Mr. Shalley for the gingham; and Mr. Broadcloth for three new suits; and Mr. Worsted for the Lord knows how many goods! And every body says, Mrs. Dow, that he 'll never pay; and they say he owes all the merchants where he comes from. Did you ever hear the like?' said Polly. 'Did you ever in all your born days? And they say ——'

'But perhaps he has the means to pay,' interrupted Mrs. Dow.

'Pay?' said Polly; 'not he! He never *means* to pay. Why that 's the way every body says he gets through the world. Folks, you know, trust to his honesty because he is a clergyman; and then he runs away and cheats them. Such men as we have to fill our pulpit is really too bad.'

'Yes, but do n't let us condemn him until we are assured of his guilt,' replied Mrs. Dow, trying to pump up a christian spirit of forbearance.

'But do n't you believe me?' exclaimed Polly; 'every body says 'he is condemned already.' Your husband, Mr. Dow, and Mr. Meeks, and Brown, and Mr. Jones, and two-thirds of the church members, and every body else, thinks so. He do n't never *mean* to pay. And there 's his girls; I saw them flirting through the streets this very day with their silks and satins, all of which he owes for. And he 's got a new sofa, and I dare say he owes the cabinet-maker for *that ;* and his wife keeps a hired girl, and pays her a dollar a week. There never *was* such a man;' and Polly Sly, running out of breath, sank back for a moment, completely exhausted.

Just as Polly closed, in came Mrs. Meeks. 'Did n't call to stay,' said Mrs. Meeks. Polly heard Mrs. Meeks' voice, and up she jumped, caught her by the hand, and was *so* glad to see her; it was so comfortable to see one's friends; there was *so* much trouble in the church, it 'was rejoicing to find a person who could revive her spirits.'

Mrs. Meeks was out on precisely the same business, to cry down Parson Gerry's extravagance. Mrs. Meeks had been 'making calls' for two hours, talking all the time as fast as her tongue could rattle. She was as happy to meet Polly Sly as Polly Sly was to meet her.

'What *are* we to do with our minister?' exclaimed Polly to Mrs. Meeks, as soon as she got through welcoming her. 'Mrs. Dow and I have been talking about it. I've been telling her all about him; how he owes every body and can't pay; how the church is disgraced, and how every body talks about it — and ——'

'And how,' said Mrs. Meeks, suddenly cutting Polly short, 'heavy demands have been sent on for collection from abroad to Lawyer Brief, who holds them in his hands, but do n't want to make trouble!'

'Mercy sakes!' roared Polly; 'is he going to be sued! Well, I expected it. I told them he owed where he come from. Do n't say any more, Mrs. Meeks; I shall go distracted.'

'What a man!' exclaimed Mrs. Dow, who just began to enter into the spirit of the occasion.

'Well,' said Polly, 'I must be going.' And Mrs. Meeks said '*she* must be going too;' and both, bidding Mrs. Dow 'good afternoon,' talked scandal to the door, and then to the gate, and finally broke off the subject, by bidding Mrs. Dow 'good *morning*,' and departing.

The next day the storm of scandal raged still higher. Several persons were to be seen talking at the corners of the streets, berating Parson Gerry and his family. Some said that the old man ran away from the last parish where he preached, to avoid the service of civil process for debt; others said that the Bishop had dismissed him for the same cause, and that he was preaching without license. Wherever he had been, the same extravagance, it was said, had been indulged in. The story was revived which originated with Mrs. Meeks, 'that heavy demands were sent on for collection from abroad to Lawyer Brief;' and two or three of the church vestry-men visited the Lawyer, to inquire into the matter. Lawyer Brief pronounced the charge false, but no one believed him, for they thought he acted from interested motives; that he was fearful of endangering the collection of his debt, by adding fuel to the fire of persecution which was already consuming their victim.

The excitement in Stokeville lasted for some weeks. It was finally resolved that the good old man must be dismissed at once. He had of course heard of the charges which were in circulation against him; he pronounced them untrue, and was willing to submit them to an investigation. He admitted that he was somewhat in debt, but it was necessity alone that had driven him into it. He nevertheless declared himself able to pay all. He denied that he owed a cent to any one abroad, or that prosecutions had been commenced against him. But it was of no use. The fiat had gone forth. It was determined that old Parson Gerry should leave the parish forthwith.

A covered wagon was shortly after seen moving out of Stokeville, containing the scanty furniture of Parson Gerry. His family were seated in a couple of carriages, which followed behind. They had been absolutely driven out of the place; and driven out too by those who were so sensitive in matters of religious duty that they considered themselves doing GOD service, in the course they had taken. They supposed they had purged the church, and cleansed it for the reception of another pastor.

———

WE have said that old Mr. BETTS was the minister in what was called the Presbyterian church. He was indeed ' old,' and had officiated in Stokeville for several years. Like all other men, he had his friends and enemies. This church, like its neighbor, was subject to periodical revulsions, which at times threatened its ruin. Parson Betts was too orthodox to suit some of his members, and they declared it ' perfect agony' for them to listen to him; and many had absolutely abandoned him, with a view of forming another congregation. Yet the old gentleman preached on. He heeded not the wreck which he at times made; but solaced himself with the conviction that he was in the discharge of a christian duty, and that was enough.

It so happened that Mr. Betts on a certain Sabbath spiced his sermon rather higher than usual with ' the doctrine of election;' and a majority of the congregation were determined to submit to it no longer. Accordingly, he was waited upon the following Monday by several members of his church, who told him that they were sorry to say it, but they should forever hereafter be under the necessity of absenting themselves from his preaching, provided he did not qualify or retract what he had said, in a sermon to be preached on the following Sabbath.

Now it so happened that there was a minority party who subscribed exactly to the doctrine contained in the sermon which had raised such confusion, and were just as hotly opposed to the recantation. They said it was the first sermon they had heard which came *entirely* up to the standard of their faith; and they would see the church blown into atoms, before a qualification or retraction should be made. They too appointed *their* committee, and waited upon Mr. Betts, and commanded him not to retract one ' jot nor tittle,' under fear of their displeasure and consequent desertion of the church.

The old gentleman was in a quandary. He was between Scylla and Charybdis; if he avoided the one he must inevitably be swallowed by the other. He ' must qualify or retract,' and he ' must neither qualify nor retract.' Finally, as his best plan in the premises, he determined to pray for an extension of the time allotted him to determine his course in the matter; and after some correspondence between his Janus-faced opponents, his day of grace was extended to four weeks. On the fourth Sunday he was to ' choose whom he would serve.'

The war now opened in Stokeville in good earnest. Every family that attended old Mr. Betts' church arrayed itself either on the one side or the other. No one was permitted to take neutral ground in the contest. The women were out every afternoon, running up and down the streets, impressing their friends with their various opinions, and drawing in all the converts they could convince by their zeal and eloquence; while the men were warring together on the corners, in the tavern, and in the stores.

The first week had passed away, and the excitement was tremendous. On the second, it had engendered so much bitterness between members of the same church, that all communication was stopped. The Retraction party did not speak to nor trade with the Anti-retraction party. Entertainments were given for the sole purpose of manifesting the spirit of exclusiveness; and there was a degree of life and mock-merriment exhibited in Stokeville that had never been paralleled.

When the third week came round, the two parties fell pell-mell to scandalizing each other. First, the Retraction party assailed one of the deacons who belonged to the Anti-retraction party. They said he was 'a dishonest man, and if justice had been done him, he would have been churched years ago; that he had been charged with keeping false weights, and thus swindling the public — the widow and the orphan; that he had been known to swear, and that proof could be furnished of the fact; that a great many years ago he cheated a relative out of the very property he was now holding; that he had always made difficulty in the church, wherever he had been connected with it;' and a hundred other allegations were brought against him, and circulated from mouth to mouth, increasing in magnitude as they acquired age and notoriety.

The Anti-retraction party were not to be out-done, and they retaliated with double severity. They assailed in turn one of the deacons of the other division, and after charging upon him all the crimes mentioned in the moral and divine law, fell upon other members of the party, and dissected them in like manner. This bitterness was met on the opposite side again, until at last every person's character who was in any manner connected with the excitement, however unsullied, was completely blackened, and to all appearances forever ruined.

Finally the Sabbath came round when old Mr. Betts was to recant or adhere to the doctrine which had spread such desolation over the church. There was a fearful intensity of feeling on the subject. The house was crowded to overflowing, and eager eyes were directed to the old man, as he ascended the pulpit. After the preliminary exercises were gone through with, Mr. BETTS arose. He said that it had been his misfortune to differ with a portion of his congregation upon some points of doctrine, and that he had been called upon to make a recantation, and that this day had been assigned to him for that purpose. He said he was glad that an excitement had been produced in the church by the course he had taken, as it was the first one within his recollection for the last ten years. He had preached against *practical* sin and wickedness, and it had all passed off harmless; but so soon as he touched the *faith* of his people, they were all on fire. He said it appeared to him that his hearers were determined to save themselves by 'faith *alone*,' as he had never been able to discover any very great abundance of good works; and in that particular he differed materially with the course pursued by all his congregation. If he understood the position he was placed in, he said, he must qualify or recant, or half of his congregation would desert him, and if he *did* qualify or recant, the other half would do the same; the two parties differing with each other in point of christian duty, and both differing with him.   He said '*both*,' and it was in preferring 'faith' to 'good works;' and unless they reformed, and walked more uprightly in the path which they had marked out for themselves, he should at once desert *them*, and leave them to the error of their ways.   He should give them four weeks to make up their minds; the same space of time which had been allotted him for a similar purpose.   He had no more to say.

These words shivered their way among the congregation like a thunderbolt.   All was silence and solemnity.   The heart of every one was struck with conscious guilt.   The old man proceeded with his discourse as usual, closed, and dismissed his people.   And this was the last that was ever heard of the Retraction and Anti-retraction parties, and the last of the HOLY WARS OF STOKEVILLE.

STANZAS.

VAIN lord of golden-mirror'd halls,
    And pictured galleries,
Whose sculptured grandeur often palls,
    Whose gems not always please;
Unlearn thy self-conceit, nor deem
    So partially of Fate;
There 's many a wanderer's wild day-dream
    Worth all thy pomp and state.

'Tis true, no marble vestibule
    My homeward glance allures;
For me there waits no servile fool
    To ope the noiseless doors;
But sweet, beyond what words may tell,
    The lips that warmly greet,
Of one who loves the echoes well
    Of my returning feet!

How dark soe'er and cold and sad
    The lot of man appears,
Some light benign still shines to glad
    The winter of his years;
The veriest wretch whose withered form
    Totters before our sight,
Hath garnered from the powerless storm
    Some hoard of calm delight.

The clime of arctic frost and gloom
    Hath yet its summer dream,
And brightly do the roses bloom
    By Zenglio's winding stream;
Strange beauty wraps Niemi's mountains
    And legendary lake,
And by the visionary fountains
    Her favorite haunt doth make.

Richmond, (Va.,) 1841.   BON-ROSNI.

LINES

DESCRIPTIVE OF A VOYAGE OVER LAKE SUPERIOR BY STAR-LIGHT.

FROM A MANUSCRIPT POEM.

THE twilight deepens : but the skies
Still show some soft celestial dies
  Where the departing day hath set ;
As, when have fallen the shades of death,
And calmly passed the christian's breath,
Unto the eye of sorrowing Faith
The confines of two worlds are given,
Bright with the glorious hues of heaven,
  Where Time Eternity hath met :
And just above the darkening west
Pale Dian lifts her faded crest,
That all the day a heavenly path serene
Hath silent trod, content to be unseen ;
And now, like some fair victim of decay,
Hovers above her grave with sad, sweet ray.

Along the winding coast awhile
Their course they swept with easy toil,
And down Keweena's shadowy shore,
That hears the western waters roar ;
Then sped them fearless, far and free,
Forth on that wide and silent sea !
Soon land was lost, nor aught around
Save dimness could the distance bound ;
  Vanished the glory of the day,
And heaven grew pale ; the distant wave
Received the meek moon to her grave :
  But soon, with more prevailing ray,
The stars came forth : a deeper blue
Now all their silent courts imbue.

The stars came forth !   Upon his throne
Each watched his realm prescribed, alone,
With calm and radiant countenance ;
And from their gaze, o'er all the expanse
Of waters, like a mighty spell,
A strange and awful stillness fell !
All was the deep repose of thought ;
No sound the ear of listener caught :
The waves were hushed ; the pure, clear air
Awoke no creeping ripple there ;
Just stirred, all infinite and lone,   .
Like breathings of the world unknown.
So still above, around, beneath,
It might have seemed the reign of Death,
But that with an unfailing light
The stars' immortal brows were bright,
And with their glorious presence made
That solemn and mysterious shade
O'er sky, earth, air, and waters given,
A spiritual life.   All heaven
Came down upon the deep, and glassed
In its unruffled mirror vast,

Swelled far below, as boundless, clear,
Into another hemisphere,
And with as bright a firmament
Around its dim horizon bent,
Whence upward gazed its host of stars
Upon those moving mariners.

As when the parted soul doth stray
From earth beyond the solar way,
Till in the deepening distance far
The spheréd sun becomes a star ;
The circling vastness, awed and stilled,
All, all with countless orbs is filled ;
And wheresoe'er that spirit turns,
One wide, immortal radiance burns :
So moved they, hung two heavens between,
Whose crowded worlds on worlds were seen,
Where'er they gazed, in awe profound,
The bright circumference around !
Amazed they moved ; all sounds forbore,
Save the light dipping of the oar ;
And scarce their hearts dare beat to tell
Their spirits yet within them dwell :
For as they glide, the Indian deems
He passeth to the Land of Dreams.

G. H. C.

The Crayon Papers.

AMERICAN RESEARCHES IN ITALY.

LIFE OF TASSO: RECOVERY OF A LOST PORTRAIT OF DANTE.

TO THE EDITOR OF THE KNICKERBOCKER.

Sir : Permit me through the pages of your Magazine to call the
attention of the public to the learned and elegant researches in Europe
of one of our countrymen, Mr. R. H. WILDE, of Georgia, formerly a
member of the House of Representatives. After leaving Congress,
Mr. Wilde a few years since spent about eighteen months in travelling through different parts of Europe, until he became stationary for a
time in Tuscany. Here he occupied himself with researches concerning the private life of Tasso, whose mysterious and romantic love for
the Princess Leonora, his madness and imprisonment, had recently
become the theme of a literary controversy, not yet ended ; curious in
itself, and rendered still more curious by some alledged manuscripts of
the poets, brought forward by Count Alberti. Mr. Wilde entered into
the investigation with the enthusiasm of a poet, and the patience and
accuracy of a case-hunter ; and has produced a work, now in the press,
in which the 'vexed questions' concerning Tasso are most ably
discussed, and lights thrown upon them by his letters, and by various
of his sonnets, which last are rendered into English with rare felicity.
While Mr. Wilde was occupied upon this work, he became acquainted

with Signor Carlo Liverati, an artist of considerable merit, and especially well versed in the antiquities of Florence. This gentleman mentioned incidentally one day, in the course of conversation, that there once and probably still existed in the *Bargello*, anciently both the prison and palace of the republic, an authentic portrait of DANTE. It was believed to be in fresco, on a wall which afterward, by some strange neglect or inadvertency, had been covered with white-wash. Signor Liverati mentioned the circumstance merely to deplore the loss of so precious a portrait, and to regret the almost utter hopelessness of its recovery.

As Mr. Wilde had not as yet imbibed that enthusiastic admiration for Dante which possesses all Italians, by whom the poet is almost worshipped, this conversation made but a slight impression on him at the time. Subsequently, however, his researches concerning Tasso being ended, he began to amuse his leisure hours with attempts to translate some specimens of Italian lyric poetry, and to compose very short biographical sketches of the authors. In these specimens, which as yet exist only in manuscript, he has shown the same critical knowledge of the Italian language, and admirable command of the English, that characterize his translations of Tasso. He had not advanced far in these exercises, when the obscure and contradictory accounts of many incidents in the life of Dante caused him much embarrassment, and sorely piqued his curiosity. About the same time he received, through the courtesy of Don Neri dei Principi Corsini, what he had long most fervently desired, a permission from the Grand Duke to pursue his investigations in the secret archives of Florence, with power to obtain copies therefrom. This was a rich and almost unwrought mine of literary research ; for to Italians themselves, as well as to foreigners, their archives for the most part have been long inaccessible. For two years Mr. Wilde devoted himself with indefatigable ardor, to explore the records of the republic during the time of Dante. These being written in barbarous Latin and semi-Gothic characters, on parchment more or less discolored and mutilated, with ink sometimes faded, were rendered still more illegible by the arbitrary abbreviations of the notaries. They require in fact an especial study ; few even of the officers employed in the ' *Archivio delle Riformagione* ' can read them currently and correctly.

Mr. Wilde however persevered in his laborious task with a patience severely tried, but invincible. Being without an index, each file, each book, required to be examined page by page, to ascertain whether any particular of the immortal poet's political life had escaped the untiring industry of his countrymen. This toil was not wholly fruitless, and several interesting facts obscurely known, and others utterly unknown by the Italians themselves, are drawn forth by Mr. Wilde from the oblivion of these archives.

While thus engaged, the circumstance of the lost portrait of Dante was again brought to Mr. Wilde's mind, but now excited intense interest. In perusing the notes of the late learned Canonico Moreri on Filelfo's life of Dante, he found it stated that a portrait of the poet by Giotto was formerly to be seen in the Bargello. He learned also that Signor Scotti, who has charge of the original drawings of the old masters in the imperial and royal gallery, had made several years previously an ineffectual attempt to set on foot a project for the recovery of the lost treasure. Here was a new vein of inquiry, which Mr. Wilde followed up with his usual energy and sagacity. He soon satisfied himself, by reference to Vasari, and to the still more ancient and decisive authority of Filippo Villari, who lived shortly after the poet, that Giotto, the friend and contemporary of Dante, did undoubtedly paint his likeness in the place indicated. Giotto died in 1336, but as Dante was banished, and was even sentenced to be burned, in 1302, it was obvious the work must have been executed before that time; since the portrait of one outlawed and capitally convicted as an enemy to the commonwealth would never have been ordered or tolerated in the chapel of the royal palace. It was clear then, that the portrait must have been painted between 1290 and 1302.

Mr. Wilde now revolved in his own mind the possibility that this precious relic might remain undestroyed under its coat of white-wash, and might yet be restored to the world. For a moment he felt an impulse to undertake the enterprise; but feared that, in a foreigner from a new world, any part of which is unrepresented at the Tuscan court, it might appear like an intrusion. He soon however found a zealous coadjutor. This was one Giovanni Aubrey Bezzi, a Piedmontese exile, who had long been a resident in England, and was familiar with its language and literature. He was now on a visit to Florence, which liberal and hospitable city is always open to men of merit who for political reasons have been excluded from other parts of Italy. Signor Bezzi partook deeply of the enthusiasm of his countrymen for the memory of Dante, and sympathized with Mr. Wilde in his eagerness to retrieve if possible the lost portrait. They had several consultations as to the means to be adopted to effect their purpose, without incurring the charge of undue officiousness. To lessen any objections that might occur, they resolved to ask for nothing but permission to search for the fresco painting at their own expense; and should any remains of it be found, then to propose to the nobility and gentry of Florence an association for the purpose of completing the undertaking, and effectually recovering the lost portrait.

For the same reason the formal memorial addressed to the Grand Duke was drawn up in the name of Florentines; among whom were the celebrated Bartolini, now President of the School of Sculpture in the Imperial and Royal Academy, Signor Paolo Ferroni, of the noble family of that name, who has exhibited considerable talent for painting, and Signor Gasparini, also an artist. This petition was urged and supported with indefatigable zeal by Signor Bezzi; and being warmly countenanced by Count Nerli and other functionaries, met with more prompt success than had been anticipated. Signor Marini, a skilful artist, who had succeeded in similar operations, was now employed to remove the white-wash by a process of his own, by which any fresco painting that might exist beneath would be protected from injury. He set to work patiently and cautiously. In a short time he met with evidence of the existence of the fresco. From under the coat of white-wash the head of an angel gradually made its appearance, and was pronounced to be by the pencil of Giotto.

The enterprise was now prosecuted with increased ardor. Several months were expended on the task, and three sides of the chapel-wall were uncovered; they were all painted in fresco by Giotto, with the history of the Magdalen, exhibiting her conversion, her penance, and her beatification. The figures, however, were all those of saints and angels : no historical portraits had yet been discovered, and doubts began to be entertained whether there were any. Still the recovery of an indisputable work of Giotto's was considered an ample reward for any toil; and the Ministers of the Grand Duke, acting under his directions, assumed on his behalf the past charges and future management of the enterprise.

At length, on the uncovering of the fourth wall, the undertaking was crowned with complete success. A number of historical figures were brought to light, and among them the undoubted likeness of Dante. He was represented in full length, in the garb of the time, with a book under his arm, designed most probably to represent the ' Vita Nuova,' for the ' Comedia ' was not yet composed, and to all appearance from thirty to thirty-five years of age. The face was in profile, and in excellent preservation, excepting that at some former period a nail had unfortunately been driven into the eye. The outline of the eyelid was perfect, so that the injury could easily be remedied. The countenance was extremely handsome, yet bore a strong resemblance to the portraits of the poet taken later in life.

It is not easy to appreciate the delight of Mr. Wilde and his coadjutors at this triumphant result of their researches; nor the sensation produced, not merely in Florence but throughout Italy, by this discovery of a veritable portrait of Dante, in the prime of his days. It was some such sensation as would be produced in England by the sudden discovery of a perfectly well authenticated likeness of Shakspeare; with a difference in intensity proportioned to the superior sensitiveness of the Italians.

The recovery of this portrait of the ' divine poet' has occasioned fresh inquiry into the origin of the masks said to have been made from a cast of his face taken after death. One of these masks, in the possession of the Marquess of Torrigiani, has been pronounced as certainly the *original*. Several artists of high talent have concurred in this opinion ; among these may be named Jesi, the first engraver in Florence ; Seymour Kirkup, Esq., a painter and antiquary ; and our own countryman Powers, whose genius, by the way, is very highly appreciated by the Italians.

We may expect from the accomplished pen of Carlo Torrigiani, son of the Marquess, and who is advantageously known in this country, from having travelled here, an account of this curious and valuable relic, which has been upward of a century in the possession of his family.

Should Mr. Wilde finish his biographical work concerning Dante, which promises to be a proud achievement in American literature, he intends, I understand, to apply for permission to have both likenesses copied, and should circumstances warrant the expense, to have them engraved by eminent artists. We shall then have the features of Dante while in the prime of life as well as at the moment of his death. ᴏ. ᴄ.

TO MY WIFE THAT IS TO BE.

O FAIR Unknown! we have not met —
  We ne'er have seen each other;
Nor in this heart hath love been yet,
  Save that of son and brother :
But close though these affections twine,
  There 's one that twineth nearest;
One that will knit my heart to thine,
  Of all dear things the dearest!

I know I cannot love too well
  These kind ones now around me;
To these true friends I cannot tell
  How many ties have bound me :
Yet oft when vacant seems this breast,
  A consciousness will thrill it,
That there is room still unpossess'd,
  And your sweet self should fill it!

I miss thy smile of quiet mirth,
  When other friends are merry;
But more I miss thee from my hearth,
  When sad and solitary.
It blunts the ills that life annoy,
  From Sympathy to borrow
That charm which heightens every joy,
  And lightens every sorrow.

Should sadness rule my heart's deep chords,
  Or wrongs that wildly stir it,
How strong shall be thy gentle words
  To soothe the wounded spirit!
And yet to hush thine own alarms
  Will be employment dearer :
The more they trouble thee, my arms
  Shall fold thee, love! the nearer.

How wilt thou, dearest! win my view?
  With form for love's entwining?
And brightly dark, or deeply blue,
  Thine eyes, of tender shining?
Wilt thou be fair? Will midnight be,
  Or sunshine, on thy tresses?
Thy voice of witching melody,
  And lips that woo caresses?

But oh! I care not for the hue
  Wherewith thine eyes shall greet me,
If but the soul that trembles through,
  Sincerely, warmly meet me!
A noble mind within the brow,
  Who heeds what locks enwreath it?
The bosom may forget its snow,
  When pure the heart beneath it.

But vain are these imaginings !
  My phantom spouse soon perishes ;
And fades before the ' truth of things '
  Each picture Fancy cherishes :
How dull our life-substantial seems,
  Compared with life-ideal !
'T is with a sadness from its dreams
  We waken to the real.

Farewell then, love ! already dear :
  It will perchance be pleasant
To read in some far distant year
  The vows I write at present :
Fair be the world before thy feet,
  Serene the sky above thee ;
And when we (if we ever) meet,
  How dearly will I love thee !

'OUR FATHERS, WHERE ARE THEY?'

IT was a stirring time in the Island of Grenada during the period
that Sir George Young had command of the Colony.   His Excellency,
(for he was governour,) had served with distinction upon the Continent,
been in several engagements under the immediate notice of the great
Frederick ; had been promoted by him ; and at last, upon retirement
to his own country at the return of peace had had the honor of Knighthood conferred upon him at the hands of that veteran monarch.

Thenceforth, Prussian manners, customs, tactics and absolutism
took possession alike of the heart and the imagination of Sir George
Young ; and when unhappily as it afterward proved, his friends procured for him the government of our beautiful Island, he became in
the performance of his duties almost as peremptory as old Frederick
himself.   There was no ebullition about him, however.   The tropical
climate, before which every thing else vailed, or faltered, or effervesced,
in him found one imperturbable impassive subject.   The same cocked
hat, the same long thick military queue, and heavy boots, coat, vest,
yellow breeches and gloves, the dress of his landing, was, whatever
might be the state of the weather, the dress of his administration.

So also with the exact erectness and discipline of his carriage ; the
length of his marching-step every morning at the same hour upon the
esplanade in the shade of the Government House ; the halt ; the backward movement four inches of the right foot ; the military turn upon
the heels which brought him into the third position, and the renewed
march left foot foremost back to the place of beginning and then again
to the right-about ; it was all without change or variation, or display,
apparently without thought ; and the reason that a smile never passed
across that dark fixed visage I suppose to be, that a smile was never
laid down in any Prussian manual of exercise nor included in any written strategy of war.

This was not a comfortable person for a Governour, particularly among

the free-hearted planters of our little gem of the world, who regarded
life as too short for the observance of much form or ceremony among
a brotherhood of Gentlemen.   And so at the end of some six or eight
months there grew up at the Council-board at which His Excellency pre-
sided and where the Colonial affairs of the Island were chiefly regulated and despatched, a respectful but decided opposition to some of his
favorite measures.   .

Among the members of the Council was a bland and estimable Gentleman, a planter, who had formerly been attached to the medical profession, and still bore the title of Doctor Bl —— n.   Mild, gentle, refined,
of an inquiring and philosophic temperament, he was more fond of
discussion than of action, and of examining the expediency of the
Governour's plans than of voting at once in favour of them.   He was a
person of good address, spoke freely and at his ease, and in this had
greatly the advantage of His Excellency, whose expressions were almost
limited to words of command ; or, when he dwelt upon any subject,
seemed to be first translated from the German into his own proper
vernacular and then uttered with difficulty and hesitation.

By degrees Doctor Bl —— n came to be regarded in the eyes of the
Governour as leader of the opposition in the Council-Chamber, and as
exercising an influence that in his military mode of judging things was
to be summarily put down.   And one morning during an animated
debate, His Excellency made use of some remarks of a nature too
closely personal to be entirely passed over ; and Doctor Bl——n said,
perhaps rather indiscreetly :

'I can have no reply to make ; • Your Excellency represents the
King.'

'I do Sir, while in this chair,' retorted Sir George ; 'but the moment I leave it I am Sir George Young, very much at your service.'

Now this happened at a time before deliberative bodies had hit upon
the invention of explaining away words in the felicitous manner that
obtains at present on both sides the Atlantic, to such a degree as that
any two members on opposite sides of the house may indulge in the
bitterest invective against each other, and then upon the intervention
of friends, or a call from the Speaker, made before they separate,
mumble a few words about having differed upon 'a seventh cause,' or
something else that nobody can understand, and then go home to supper without any unpleasant result.   No, this was not the way with our
Fathers ; and the consequence was, that mine was hardly seated, before
his friend Doctor Bl——n was announced.   As soon as they were in
private, the Doctor said :

'Well my friend, you heard what passed between the Governour and
myself.'

'I did, and regretted it very sincerely.'

'The affair can, I suppose, be settled only in one way.'

'I am sorry to say that I do not perceive any other.'

'Can you aid me in it?'

'Not as your second.'

'Why not?'

'I am the oldest member of the Council-board ; we are at present without a Lieutenant Governour; and if Sir George should fall, very important duties will devolve on me until his successor should arrive, and I might expose my character to the severest animadversion if I were to take any active part in a rencontre that should result in his death. I hope that this reason may appear sufficient to you. I have thought the whole matter over, for it seemed to me probable that you might apply to me.'

'What then do you advise me to do?'

'I would have you consult our neighbor Colonel Williams without a moment's delay.'

Colonel Williams, as the name portends, was a Welchman. He commanded the regiment at that time stationed in the Island; and he was not exempt from a certain native vivacity of temperament which has been ascribed as a characteristic to his countrymen. 'Our army' says my Uncle Toby 'swore terribly in Flanders;' and the provocation for the use of intensives is greater in the tropics than in the Low Countries.

However, the Colonel received Doctor Bl——n with singular quietness and even a certain mysteriousness of manner; conducted him on tiptoe into an apartment that was at once library, dressing-room, workshop, and head-quarters; seated him; and then bringing another chair placed himself opposite so closely as that their knees almost touched. 'We must speak very low,' said he. 'The walls of these d——d barracks are not thicker than cartridge-paper, and my wife, who fancies she has to answer for all my sins as well as her own, is crying her life out over a cursed book called 'Hervey's Meditations among the Tombs:' she goes to it every now and then, and I always think if there's any thing in the wind she hears clearer then than at any other time. But now to business. So! you and Frederick the Great have got at it, eh? It is very odd what luck some men are born to! I could have sworn that he and I were to have it together!—but indeed there has been very little communication between us of late. Tell me what has taken place since the Council broke up. I have heard of his overture to you.'

Doctor Bl——n then informed the Colonel of his unsuccessful application to my father, and to another of his friends; and that he was quite at a loss to know in what manner to proceed.

'I have no doubt,' replied Colonel Williams, 'that His Excellency will have his own difficulties in the choice of a second, unless he determine upon some subaltern. It is something like getting into a scrape to have any thing to do with shooting a Governour in command who has been bred up in the Prussian service and ——' I shall omit the Colonel's expletives.

'There is not the remotest chance of that being the issue of our meeting,' said Doctor Bl——n. 'I am entirely unacquainted with the use of a pistol, and do not even possess a pair. I shall stand no chance whatever with him; but life is of no value with a brand upon it.'

'Are you quite out of practice with the pistol?' asked the Colonel.

'I never fired a pistol in my life?'

'Then I would not give a guinea for his!' replied Colonel Williams; 'a man's first shot is the best in the first hundred. Here is a pair that

have never missed since they were manufactured.   You will take them
home with you.   Stand before the largest mirror you have in the house.
Look well at your shadow.   Raise the pistol from your knee, here in
this way, with a stiff elbow, ranging along the shadow in the glass, and
when you get the muzzle to the height of the hip, draw the trigger.
When you come upon the ground—take care to be there in good season—plant yourself at one end of the saw-pit.   You will fight in Glenn's
saw-pit, that 's the common place, and there there is no choice of light
or shade : be early on the ground.   Glance your eye along the sides of
the pit, and get yourself used to it ; and when he comes opposite to you,
think of the man in the glass ; raise your muzzle as you did before,
always with a stiff elbow, and pull as soon as it ranges with his hip.
Now will you recollect all this?   If you drop your pistol and level
at him from above you will overshoot him.   If you coolly bring up the
piece with a stiff elbow from the knee, you cannot miss him, by ——— !

  'When he comes upon the ground, ten to one he will talk to you about
marching, and facing to the right-about, and give you a lecture on the
Prussian mode of doing things.   Tell him you are fixed to your spot,
but that he may march, and countermarch, and be ——— '

  'Now, will you remember all this?   Let me see you handle your
pistol.   Very well, quite well.   Accustom yourself to the grasp.   Fix
on five in the afternoon ; it will be better for you both, as there are
no strong lights there then.   The field is not far from you.   My orderly
will be with you at four and load your pistols, so that you will have
nothing in the world to do after you get upon the ground but take one
careful glance at the priming, and see that the powder lies well upon
the touch-hole.   I believe you understand it now.   Let me see you
raise it once more.   Very well ; that was quite well.   When you get
upon the ground, remember you have only one thing to do after examining the priming, and that is, to raise the muzzle as high as His
Excellency's hip, and then pull as quietly as you did before the glass,
and always with a stiff elbow.   You have two things to think of, recollect,
and only two, after you get upon the ground.   First the priming, and
then the man in the glass.   Now go out this way, that my wife may not
see you.   I should like you to have had a second, but in your card you
can state to Sir George the impossibility of procuring one ; and that
you are content to rely upon any arrangement that he may make in this
respect.   You may safely do this.   After all, he is a Gentleman, and if
he had been bred up in our own service he would have been a soldier,
instead of being as he now is, a —— martinet.'

  The hour of five in the afternoon of the following day had nearly
arrived, when Doctor Bl———n was stationed at one extremity of Glenn's
saw-pit.   The saw-pit had not for some time been in use, and the slight
structure that had formerly sheltered the workmen had been removed,
except a remaining stick or two of timber that lay longitudinally over
the pit.   Vegetation, with the luxuriance of the tropics, had sprung up
around the borders, and when the Doctor looked upward from his
sheltered position into the rich azure sky above him, the Heavens had
never seemed to him so beautiful as then, and a thought passed across
his mind that his spirit might in a few moments be wending its way

through the depths of that celestial blue.　The hard necessities of life, the stern conditions of the laws of honour, and the want of charity between man and man, began to occupy his mind, when he suddenly recollected Colonel Williams's charge to him that he had only two things to think of after he had got upon the ground.　The first was the priming; he opened the locks and found the caution an useful one. He looked at his watch; it was ten minutes beyond the time.　Where could Sir George be?　How long should he wait for him?

Just then he heard the Governour's voice: 'There, that will do; give it me; now drive quietly home, and see that you do n't blow the horses.'　And in a moment after, he entered the pit, bringing with him a case of pistols.　He walked close up to his antagonist before he spoke. 'Doctor Bl——n, I have a thousand apologies to make to you.　The truth is that I had some official matters to perform very unexpectedly just before I left the Government House, and I preferred throwing myself upon your courtesy to postponing what was really important, or doing it in a slovenly way.　I fear I must have made you wait some time.'

The Doctor received his explanation gracefully, and then observed: 'Your Excellency has brought no second?'

'No,' he replied; 'on the Continent I have known difficulties arise from such circumstances, and the honour of Gentlemen called in question when two have gone out against one.　No, you have confided in me; surely I will confide in you.'

During this time, Sir George had opened his pistol-case, and prepared one piece to his entire satisfaction, examining and sharpening the flint before he loaded the pistol.　The Doctor also took his pistol in hand.

'Doctor — Bl——n,' said Sir George, 'I suppose this business is no novelty to you?'

'On the contrary,' replied the Doctor, 'it is, thank God, the first occasion of the sort that I was ever yet engaged in.'

'Different people have different ways of settling it,' replied the Governour; 'but *in the Prussian service* the practice is to stand in the centre of the field, back to back, march off three paces, or four paces, then to the right-about, then level and fire; and it has been in reference to that practice that I have had the ground of this pit cleared of all obstructions, and put in the condition for marching in which you see it.'

'As I have never had the honour to be in the Prussian service,' replied Doctor Bl——n, 'and am utterly unacquainted with military movements, Your Excellency will I hope excuse me from any such evolution. I am placed; either here, or if you please, at the other extremity of this pit; but,' added he, perceiving a shade of dissatisfaction on the Governour's face, 'my course need not I think prevent Your Excellency from the practice to which you are accustomed.'

'Doctor Bl——n,' said Sir George Young, his countenance brightening at the suggestion, 'you are in all respects a Gentleman — permit me to say it.　Well then, as I have your leave, I shall march up to you; go to the right-about, march off eight paces, and then again face you; at which time, we fire.　And as in this method I must necessarily turn my back upon you, I desire explicitly to say, that I do it strictly as a military manœuvre and without the remotest idea of conveying toward you the least personal slight or indignity.'

'There is only one thing more,' said Doctor Bl——n ; 'and that is, the exact moment at which I should fire. Your Excellency will excuse my inexperience in these matters, but it is not to my perception so nicely defined as I could wish it might be.'

'Now how very well thought of that is !' said Sir George Young. 'I shall make it perfectly obvious to you. I shall march and countermarch with my handkerchief—you perceive it is a white one—in my left hand, and when I drop it, you will fire.'

His Excellency performed his part accordingly, marching with a very gracious air toward Doctor Bl——n, then turning to the right-about he counted aloud in German, as he marched them, the eight paces; faced again to the right-about; dropped the handkerchief, and two discharges were almost simultaneously heard. The ball of his pistol had lodged in one of the timbers directly over the head of Doctor Bl——n, while that of his opponent, guided by a surer aim, had pierced his heart. He sprang convulsively upward, and fell lifeless without a groan.   JOHN WATERS.

THE BROKEN HEART.

BY MRS. E. C. STEDMAN.

DEAL gently with the broken heart ! It is the 'stricken deer,'
That turneth from the herd aside, to bleed where none is near ;
Or like some tender flower, that shrinks before the coming blast,
And drooping 'neath big rain-drops, hangs, when the storm is overpast.

O, lightly touch the broken heart ! It is a harp unstrung,
And rudeness, from its shattered chords, but dismal notes hath wrung :
Yet let the gentle hand of LOVE those heart-strings tune again,
And at the touch of tenderness 't will pour a grateful strain.

The broken heart ! Say not that THOU hast never oped anew
Its hidden wounds, by aught that words or looks unkind could do ;
For if indifference or neglect forgot the stricken one,
Hast thou not left undone the deed which kindness should have done ?

The broken heart by Heaven is seen ! and HE who will not break
'The bruised reed,' shall bid that heart His healing love partake ;
And when it bleeds in solitude, will pour the Gilead-balm,
Which can assuage its keenest pang — its midnight throbbings calm.

Go thou, who hast not felt before, and learn of HIM to feel !
Catch the pure spark of sympathy — its heaven-born tear reveal ;
Weep with the sufferer ; or at least, the kindly *word* impart,
Which meets a sure reward from Heaven, and ' heals the broken heart.'

THE POLYGON PAPERS.

NUMBER THREE.

WHAT a scene would be presented to our eyes could we congregate beneath some vast and shadowy dome the spirits of the illustrious dead! How would all the might and majesty of living men shrink into nothing before so glorious an assemblage! The spectacle would be imposing beyond all that earth can display, all that imagination can embody. Even were we to select the mental and moral princes from among the nations of contemporary men, and bring them together while yet in their imperfect corporeal existence, it would be such a meeting as the world has never beheld. But what if we could command the spell of Endor's sorceress to evoke from their silent dwellings and gather in ghostly convention all the noble souls which have quickened these frames of clay for nine score generations! What a general assembly of earth's first-born children would be there! A spiritual congress of what unparalleled magnificence and power! How would the man who has imbued his soul with the spirit of the Past, and paid his intellectual worship at the universal shrine, stand fixed and rooted in over-mastering awe before this grand œcumenical council; this senate of nations; this parliament of ages! From all climes they come; all tribes, all dynasties — unsexed, unbodied; divested of their temporal distinctions, and preserving only the original worth and energy of their natures. They come! — the imperishable essences of those who lived and walked and suffered among their fellows; who labored for the welfare of humanity, and toiled to build themselves a name 'the world would not willingly let die.' They come! — the light of intelligence beaming in their eyes, and the atmosphere of immortality shining around them. They come! — scions from all branches of the tree of Adam; those who opposed the tyrant and upheld the right; those who fed the fires of Truth amidst gloom and darkness; and those who, self-tutored, touched the chords of human sympathy, and breathed immortal strains of poetry and feeling; recalling for a while the hardened hearts of men from war and bloodshed, tumult and distress.

But among all the spirits of this regal congregation who are those with eyes of deeper meaning and faces of more radiant lustre? They are the Lords of Song. And who form that trio of celestial shapes, of whom the foremost has shaded the effulgence of his features with a pitying veil; the second, of princely port, strikes with golden key a ten-stringed harp, accompanying its notes with psalms and hymns and spiritual songs; and the third from burning lips pours strains of music, which rise like a pealing anthem above the flight of eagles? The first is Moses, the out-cast of the Nile, who 'talked face to face with GOD,' and rehearsed in simple majesty the tale,

'In the beginning how the Heavens and Earth
Rose out of Chaos.'

The next is David, the poet-king, who sang on the harp of Judah the aspirations of a pious soul, and mourned over the sins and sorrows of rebellious Israel. The last is Isaiah, the minstrel-seer, whose lips were touched with a live coal from the altar of JEHOVAH, and whose spirit on the wings of prophecy flew sublimely forward into uncreated. Time, chanting the downfall of triumphant tyrants and the advent of millennial peace. Wonder not that they are of loftier stature and more kingly bearing than the minstrels who surround them ; for these latter are Pagan bards, and have drunk their inspiration from the streams of earth. And how could the shell of Hermes or the lyre of Apollo vie with that heavenly harp, swept by the fingers of prophets and animated by the breath of GOD ? How could they whose loftiest intercourse was with poor frail beings of their own conception rival them who talked, as man to man, with the angels of an unfabled heaven ? Or how could they who received their warnings from lying spectres through the ' ivory gate,' equal them who heard the oracles of truth in dreams and visions of the night ?

Yet though inferior to the Hebrew poets, from the nature of their subjects and the source of their inspiration, these heathen harpers and the christian minstrels who have succeeded them are great and beautiful beings. Their forms have ' not yet lost all their original brightness,' and in their faces we may trace the ' excess of glory obscured ' by earthly passions, weaknesses, and woes. And who among this throng of almost super-human spirits are worthiest the love and reverence of those who would indoctrinate their minds in earth's loftiest wisdom, and refresh their fainting hearts at times with a draught from the purest and most invigorating fountains of song ? This is the point on which I wish to speak, and this the cause why I have arrayed this company of ' Nature's noblemen ' before you.

To the mere English scholar I will speak on another occasion. I now address myself to the sensitive and eager youth who possesses the leisure and the will to acquire other languages than his vernacular, and has the desire to discover and the taste to appreciate the beautiful wherever it exists. I shall not throw my remarks into the dry and repulsive form of a syllogism ; a mode of reasoning as ill adapted to so light and intangible a subject as it would be distasteful to the character and habits of my reader. I shall rather transcribe my thoughts on paper as they paint themselves upon my mind in that Mosaic mixture of argument, belief, and feeling, which constitutes the only attainable evidence on so delicate a theme, and is most congenial to the nature of poetry — that inexplicable compound of reason, sentiment, and impulse.

Now I shall not display the unpardonable presumption of deciding on the separate claims of Virgil and Homer ; a question which has engaged the pens of the most eminent critics for centuries, and which Dryden, Pope, and Rapin, all competent judges, have left in trembling equipoise. Nor will I attempt to settle the point long mooted in the literary courts, whether Milton be superior to them both ; or whether he and all others save Shakspeare must cast their crowns before one of the Italian trio. I have no critical spirit-level to ascertain the altitude of genius, or poetic square and compass to measure the magnitude of the marvellous palaces which 'rose like an exhalation' beneath the waving of its wand.

'Non nostrum inter vos tantas componere litos.'

Leaving the stature and proportions of these giants to be taken by mightier giants than themselves, I dash at once into the heart of my subject, and affirm that these with four or five similar Philistine shapes are immeasurably superior to their bulky and overgrown competitors. Yes! supporting my weak judgment by the authority of nations, and bowing in implicit deference to the mature and impartial verdict of mankind, I will indicate who are and *must be* the chief gods, the ' Dii Consentes,' among the deities of song. But before taking this irrecoverable plunge, I have an exordium to make by way of enlisting the benevolence of my readers, and obviating some prejudices and misapprehensions which might obstruct the avenue to their minds.

Let me premise that I am not exposed to the captious question, ' Who made thee a ruler and a judge over us?' For I pretend not to the dogmatic positiveness of criticism; since, alas! I am no Frederic Schlegel, William Hazlitt, or Kit North. Would I were! Then, instead of talking about the wealth of others, I would dive into the chambers of my own bright spirit and draw glittering from its golden depths such treasures as never sparkled in the palace of Aladdin, or were guarded by the jealousy of ' gloomy gnome.' I merely aim in the first place to suggest a few thoughts to the young and the ardent; thoughts with some of which they may not coincide, for tastes will differ, but of which others must meet their assent; for I am sure they are just. Secondly, as Steele wrote ' the Christian Soldier ' (or ' Hero,' I do n't know which, and pray be liberal to my references, as I generally quote from memory,) to amend his own irregularities of action, so do I, who have bowed the knee to Baal as often and as fervently perhaps as any of my readers, wish to correct, at least on paper, my own heterodox sentiments, that I may be able hereafter

'To quote my proverbs to refute my life.'

I next remark, that as I detest all sailing under a false flag, and should be ashamed to pretend to knowledge which I had not, I must frankly confess that with two or three of the authors whom I shall mention I am acquainted only as Sancho Panza had seen the peerless Dulcinea, ' by hearsay!' For all the purposes of my argument, however, it is immaterial whether I have read them or not. Lastly, I have at present nothing to do with the humorous in poetry, if indeed poetry in its true sense embrace the humorous; consequently all the versifying Heracliti, Aristophanes, Plautus, Molière, and Hudibras, fall without my scope.

Warm-hearted enthusiast, worshipper of Genius, young neophyte of the Muses, you know not the perils that surround you! You cannot guess, experience, ruinous or saving, can alone inform you, how pregnant of momentous consequences is this your transition state. Your infant wings are just bursting from their chrysalis envelope, and when you first begin to flutter among the flowers of Fancy, and sun yourself in the warmth of passion, and revel in the airs of poesy, you know not what you would be at. In the extacies of your new birth the simple sensation of existence is a delightful poem, an exquisite Midsummer Night's Dream. To your inexperienced senses, entranced by bewildering beauty and drunk with new-born joy, each common herb is a glorious blossom, and each common breath a heavenly ' afflatus.' And thus it often happens that you sip poisonous nectar to intoxicate and weaken, and inhale a pestilent miasma to wither and destroy. The feast of intellect is spread in inexhaustible profusion before you. You are dazzled, blinded. Unable to distinguish the healthful from the deadly, you grasp with indiscriminate avidity at both. You seem to yourselves admitted at the table of the gods. Each imp that presents a savory viand you think a golden-haired Ganymede, and you devour his offering in thankful haste. Each sorceress who pours out her sparkling goblet appears to you a blooming Hebe, and you quaff the libation and thirst for more. You may awake as from a surfeit, with prostrate spirits, a loathing stomach, and an aching head. You may discover to your infinite surprise that you have been at a demon's banquet, and instead of supping on phœnix' tongues and sipping the grape-blood of Elysium, have been masticating *devilled* Harpies of the Stymphalion brood, and guzzling aqua-fortis distilled from the lake of Avernus. You may never recover from the diseased cravings consequent on that intemperate meal, and may continue to relish high-seasoned meats and inebriating liquors more than moderate nourishment and simple beverage, till at last,

> ' Like to the Pontic monarch of old days,
> You feed on poisons and they cause no harm,
> But are a kind of nutriment.'

I feel to you as a brother, for I have been similarly situated; and believing as I do that poetry of an immoral or sneering or hopeless or super-passionate character is, in the words of a holy father, ' the wine of devils,' and knowing as I do know, that a free potation from that infernal cup will envenom all your blood and taint your whole moral constitution with incurable disease, I would lay my hand on your shoulder and affectionately whisper in your ear : ' Child of Time and heir of Immortality ! listen to the words of a suffering invalid, convalescent it is true from the Byronic fever of misguided sentiment, but still hypochondriac, spiritless, and enervate from the mastery of morbid feeling and the dearth of healthful thought. If you have the time to become familiar with Poetry in her most original and worshipful essence, and the wish to feast on veritable nectar and genuine ambrosia, let Homer, Æschylus, and Sophocles; Virgil and Horace; Dante, Tasso, and Ariosto; Shakspeare, Spencer, and Milton; Racine, Schiller, and Goëthe, be ever present at your table, constituting your daily food and your hourly beverage. This is no pedantic or fastidious or arbitrary selection of my own. It rests on no shallow pride of knowledge or pretended infallibility of criticism. For were I perfectly familiar, from the title to the coronis, with all the poems of all languages, obsolete or living, it would be utterly impossible for my dazzled eyes and unaided discrimination to decide on their respective claims to priority. But this is a judgment which sinks its foundations deep in the general and irreversible consent of men; and a judgment thus founded on the rock of irrefutable reason, and supported by all the pillars of human sympathy and feeling, can never be shaken, but like a well-compacted arch will only be strengthened and consolidated by the gathering weight of superincumbent years.

I am aware that many other poets at various times, and especially during the freshness and effervescence of their fame, have been thought to have equalled or surpassed those whom I have mentioned. Many of the departed minstrels, and many living singers, American, English, and Continental, have uttered strains so beautiful that their sounds linger in our grateful ears like harmony from the cherubic choir. But I maintain the superiority of some dozen great poets, scattered throughout the world's history from B. C. 800 to A. D. 1800, over all their competitors, however admirable the latter may have been. For there are none on whom the suffrages of nations are so unanimously united as on these. These have received their unquestioned apotheösis, and never will they be undeified while taste and feeling shall remain on earth. To each and all of them may be applied the charming line addressed by the pious Æneas to the unhappy Dido:

'Semper honos, nomenque tuum, laudesque manebunt.'

'So then, the stars in that galaxy of genius which has blazed over our heads for the last half-century are to be 'shorn of their beams?'' By no means. Although some of them have been baleful comets, shooting malignant rays, and afflicting their deluded worshippers with 'pining atrophy or moon-struck madness,' yet far be it from me to detract from their beauty or their brightness. Let them still retain their respective glories and pursue their sparkling track in the orrery of mind; but let them hide their diminished heads before superior lustre; for there are lights in the vivid firmament, of purer essence and lovelier radiance than they.

For myself, I think there have been some among the earlier and later poets of genius no less sublime and a taste perhaps more exquisite than those whom I have named; but a neglected education, desultory habits, unhappy circumstances, an adventitious bias, or an ill-judging age, misdirected and frittered away their noblest energies. Burns derived from nature a spirit enkindled with fire as etherial as ever flamed on mortal altar; but his knowledge was too limited and his heart oppressed by too crushing a sorrow, to allow the completion of any thing truly great and extensive. His sweet spontaneous warblings may call tears of tender sympathy and sorrowful delight to the eyes of all who read or utter his 'land's language;' and his name be linked in history with those of Dante and Tasso, as a kindred instance of the everlasting struggle between genius and affliction; yet though equally exalted by nature and equally distinguished by misfortune, he shares not the world-wide celebrity of those immortal sufferers. Lucretius possessed native faculties not at all inferior to those of Virgil, who was partially his copyist; but his language was roughened by the rudeness of his age, and the fire of his spirit quenched by the cold skepticism of his creed. Scarce do we behold his wings gilded by the lovely light of natural affection and unsophisticated feeling, before he plunges into the clouds and darkness of false philosophy. The harp of Melpomene was never swept by a more masterly hand than that of Pindar; but the opulence of his wealth was wasted on the narrow Hippodrome, and the magnificence of his powers lost in hymning the praises of skilful charioteers and stalwart athletæ. With subjects so confined and so uninteresting to posterity, his genius might indeed rescue his name from becoming his own 'shadow of a dream,' and place his statue in the temple of eternal fame, but could never enshrine his image in the glowing h_art of man.

All these then, and many others, according to your time and taste, are worthy of perusal, *after* you shall have studied their masters. I unchurch them not; for they too are priests. They are still in the temple; but go not to them, young catechumen of Apollo, for your first purification or rudimental teachings; because they are not of the pontifical family, and must discharge an humbler office. Moreover, many of them have defiled their hands among unclean things, and soiled their robes by contact with pollution, and burned sensual incense in the desecrated censer. How then can they sprinkle the lustral waters and kindle the sacred fumigation, to prepare your spirits for initiation in the mysteries of the 'Bona Dea'—'Nature, our gracious and awful Mother!'

I shall not throw myself among the combatants in that eager war which has so long been waged between the advocates of the ancients and the partisans of the moderns. Poetry has never fallen, like the scriptural manna, exclusively upon one favored age or people, leaving all others to glut their gross appetites on the flesh-pots of Egypt; but rather at all times and on all regions, it descends from the Father of Bounties; like the genial sunshine or the fertilizing rain, refreshing the thirsty earth and purifying the noxious air. Common sense then decides that the ancients and moderns have their respective and probably equal merits; that if the former be distinguished for depth, the latter cover an amazing extent of surface; and that, while the fathers are more simple, original, and striking, the sons have a wider range of thought and illustration.

Shall I gild thy refined gold, oh! 'blind Mæonides?' Shall I carry brass to Corinth, and toss my silver change into the mines of Potosi? Shall I take my lonely taper, first lighted at thy blaze, and by its glimmer reveal to a world of laughers thy matchless radiance, bright morning-star of song? There are, who say thou never didst exist; that the site of Troy is the local habitation of an airy nothing; and that all the warriors who gleamed in armor around her heaven-built walls were but the spectres of a poet's dream. Yet hast thou a life whose tenacity is interwoven with the fibres of all our being, and identified with the destiny of Poetry herself. Yet have thy Hector and Achilles, thine Ajax and Agamemnon, a vitality imperishable as the essence of feeling, and pervading as the subtlety of thought. And yet have Ilion's wild figtree, and her winding rivers, and her Scæan Gate, a most real and permanent place assigned them in the geography of the heart, and her ten-years' siege is an ineffaceable epoch in the chronicles of the soul. There are skeptical critics who conjecture that thy poems are not thy legitimate offspring, but are the compositions of rhapsodists, who charmed the ears of Greece by their itinerant improvisations. As well deny the symmetry of the planetary system to be the production of one grand Intelligence. But whether thy music flow from one or from an hundred harps, its 'wingéd words' have swept with the careering winds over all the earth, and like the melody of the stars, 'there is no nation nor language where their voice is not heard.'

Yet I cannot coincide with the extravagant lines of Buckingham :

> 'Read Homer once, and you can read no more ;
> For all books else will be so mean, so poor,
> Verse will seem prose ; but still keep on to read,
> And Homer will be all the books you need.'

The frequent perusal of Homer will indeed increase your admiration of him, but can never so stultify your mind as to incapacitate it for the appreciation of the Beautiful, wherever else it may be found. He must be acknowledged as the fountain of almost one half the poetry in the world; yet, infinite as was his spirit, and copious as were the streams wherewith it watered the fields of human thought, there is in the nature and history of man many a sunny valley and many a wild ravine where they never flowed. He has left the most exquisite pictures of implacable Hatred, waiting patiently for its revenge ; unwavering Constancy, periling life for friendship ; anxious Tenderness, smiling through her tears ; and majestic Grief, drooping cold and comfortless above the bed of death. But you may find in Shakspeare paintings of deliberate courage, unscrupulous ambition, crafty malice, touching sorrow, and passionate affection, as perfect as any image portrayed by the photogenic pencil of genius on the mind of old 'Simplex munditiis.'

'But how can you judge whether this great master be justly or unjustly exalted to so high a rank unless you study him diligently and long?' You must read him often, and read him too as easily as you read Milton, before you can grasp all the greatness of his perfection. This intimate knowledge is not to be gained by pondering on enclitics, dialects, or digammas ; nor yet by devouring fifty volumes of German prolegomena. Homer and Shakspeare have been more encumbered with hindrances in the shape of helps, and more exsiccated of their vigor and essence by the cataplasms and sudorifics of doctors, than any other writings save the Bible ; and it is my belief that all three need no other aid than a glossary, a historical index, a concordance, and above all, a sincere and earnest spirit. I can certify that the best method of mastering Homer is to study the first book deeply, with all the appliances of grammar, lexicon, and commentary. Read this book a dozen times with microscopic attention ; and then peruse the rest of the Iliad and Odyssey, with few or no notes, and without stopping to remove every minor impediment. Read the whole work again with increased care, and then a third time, with a minutely laborious search after the delicate proprieties and hidden sense of your author. You may afterward peruse this sublime bard with unfettered facility, and skim over his vivid pages, and embrace the scope of his poem, as you glance through a newspaper paragraph, or seize the gist of a bon-mot. And I am convinced from experience, and from the nature of the case, that this is the very surest and fastest mode of mastering a great production in any foreign tongue. Accurate and repeated study of the first few pages will give you an insight into the style and spirit of the author, and the only remaining difficulties will be an occasional obscurity of phrase or remoteness of allusion.

In regard to the extraordinary merits of Homer and the other great classics, I know not whether it be greater madness to deny them or folly to attempt to *prove* them. To reason upon the beauties of the ancients with those who know little or nothing of them would be like arguing with men upon an unknown subject in an unknown language. To uphold them to stubborn utilitarians, who discard all relics of the past as so much useless lumber, were an idle and a thankless task. And to demonstrate them to those who are familiar with them would be to convince them of what they already feel in their inmost hearts. But to the sincere young student, not yet inoculated with the vanity of imaginary wisdom, but whose natural repulsion to laborious studies is fortified by the reckless denunciations of antiquity, so prevalent of late, a brief argument may be addressed ; an argument which, appealing to his deference for age and experience, may fix his wavering purpose and cheer his faltering steps. The claims of those ever-venerated worthies have long been perfectly and irrevocably settled by the best species of evidence the matter will admit; the coincident testimony of all who have read them enough to judge of them. If you reject this criterion of merit, you are out at open sea, with neither chart nor compass. You have never seen them decried in an author of tried solidity and established fame. They are never denounced by old and prudent dignitaries, whether in Church or State. The few who raise their voices against them are either shallow sciolists, depreciating what they understand not, or bold innovators, theorizing for the sake of theory, and uttering absurdities as their only chance of being original. Grimké is the only able writer of this country who has opposed the cultivation of classic knowledge ; and he presented the singular spectacle of an eminent man striving to dry up the fountain whence he derived his eminence. Could he have ' seen himself as others saw him,' he would have perceived that his arguments were specious only from their classical splendor of embellishment, and his eloquence captivating only because he had studied with a diligence seldom equalled the bright pages whose brightness he denied. It is utterly impossible to suppose that all the great minds which have been so sweetly enthralled by these productions; minds too of the most various endowments, and far remote from all suspicion of prejudiced partiality ; can have been mistaken in their enthusiasm. They were not the men to shout ' Great is Diana of the Ephesians ' to an imaginary goddess. The most eminent characters of modern times, while mingling in the affairs of court and camp, and when thoroughly conversant and often largely participant in the literature of their day, have stolen many a delicious hour from care and toil, and jealousy and strife, and renewed their vows in the serious devotion of age at the shrine of their youthful idolatry. After making all due allowance for the influence of association and the force of early habit, there still must remain something marvellously great and fine in these remnants of antique art, to have held these powerful and polished intellects in such charming bondage.

Young classical student! have you just laved your feet in the waters of the Jordan, and do you murmur for the streams of Abana and Pharphar? Their current may be more voluminously rapid, and their color more dazzling to your eye; but have they the virtue to cleanse your mind from the leprosy of perverted feeling and wash away the filth collected by daily contact with selfishness and meanness? Know you how presumptuous it is in you, when standing at the very threshold of the temple, to declare that you have seen it all and there is no splendor there? If you have passed through college, learning nothing but upon compulsion, and turning off an exercise in Greek mechanically, as a smith turns off a horse-shoe, of course at the conclusion of your *studies* you exclaim with the delight of an Eton 'whip' or an Oxford 'blood,'

'Then farewell, Horace, whom I hated so!'

But how can you assume the unutterable impudence of deciding on him or other ancients, of whose merits you are as well fitted to judge as an ass is of any music save his own braying? You have been charmed it may be with Anacreon, because the gayety of his sentiments chimed in with the laxity of your morals; but you could not penetrate that truly Greek simplicity which constitutes his beauty and sanctifies his faults. You have dived as far as the 'Evoe, Bacche' and 'O Venus, regina' of heathen song; and you have exemplified your appreciation of its spirit by getting drunk on adulterated wine which would have sickened the jolly old Silenus, or by ogling a bar-maid Cyprian whom Cytherea would disown, were it only for her anti-Grecian pug-nose. Instead of adorning your mind, you have been decorating your body; instead of wooing the Muses, you have smiled in beardless tenderness on boarding-school goddesses; instead of dwelling with eager eye on the classic pages, you have looked in lack-lustre earnestness on the fifty-two sheets of Hoyle; instead of listening to the swelling voices and catching the kindling inspiration of the glorious Past, your ears have been stunned by the roar of tipsy revelry, and your senses fuddled by the steam of 'long-nines,' hot punches, and juleps. At the conclusion of each lagging term, you have joined in the 'uproarious' saturnalia of rejoicing to commemorate your brief emancipation from the round of the daily tread-mill and the clanking of the college chain.

And after all this murderous waste of time and faculties, how dare you come forth and soil in the eyes of the young and earnest the lustre of those works which have been the pride of ages? How dare you scoff at the enthusiasm of those who have gazed through the mist of distance at the awful Grecian goddess, till her veiled face has grown distinct and lovely to their vision, and her shrouded form, at first cold and death-like as the yet unbreathing statue of Pygmalion, has heaved

before them in the might of passion, and swelled with the energy of
life? Walk in a sphere more subject to your knowledge, and more
congenial to your taste. Stuff your mind to apoplectic fulness with the
precious namby-pamby which will render your words so palatable when
you bow before the daughters of Fashion or mingle with the sons of
Pride. Warm your faculties with the poetry of small-beer genius, that
you may fill with feeble sentiment the ear of simpering Beauty; or heat
your spirit with those monstrous mixtures which quicken the droning
blood, and relieve the yawning listlessness of the halls where congregate
the vain, the vapid, and the vile. This will not be 'above your bent.'
But disturb not the repose of ancient Art. The austere beauty of its
sleep might shock your nerves, and fright you from your propriety.

Yet no! Go bury yourself for toilsome years in your solitary chamber; surround yourself with books, 'those mute yet eloquent companions;' transport yourself to the days of old, and sit a sympathizing
mourner among the graves of nations; familiarize yourself with their
thoughts, their habits, their history, their poetry; compare their specious
miracles, point by point, with the wonders of modern times; and then
come forth and proclaim your judgment to the world. If you think the
moderns their equals, I complain not; for in the aggregate I believe
they are. If you deem the ancients men of narrow genius, unworthy
of our attention, and likely soon to perish with other relics of a barbarous age, I still complain not; for you have earned the right to form
and promulgate your opinion. Yet when you thus oppose your judgment to the adjudication of a world, I would also request you to inflate
your lungs and blow against a tropical hurricane, or brace your limbs
to stem the torrent of the ocean tide. Be not amazed if your breath
turn backward to swell the tempest of applause which sweeps before
the wings of rushing years, or if the gulf-stream of Time bear you to
the oozy cavern where old Homeromastix sleeps on mouldering bed of
graduses and grammars; his brain embalmed in juice of the cuttle-fish,
and his head encircled with the pseudo-critic's crown of dripping owl-
quills and the dank Sardinian weed.

'Let us return to our sheep.' 'Can it be possible,' you ask, 'that
Homer, Æschylus, and Sophocles in Greek, Virgil and Horace in Latin,
and the poets you have mentioned in the modern languages, are the
only ones worthy of perusal?' Certainly not. But as beyond all
question the opinion of men has stamped these as the first, and as this
opinion is your only guide, while yet a mere freshman in literature it is
the dictate of reason to study these till you can thoroughly appreciate
them. This will hardly leave you the time to dwell equally long on the
other authors. Euripides has left several tragedies, particularly the
Medea, which can hardly be overrated; and Theocritus and the An-
thology contain much that is most worthy of attention. In like manner
you would choose to be acquainted with the graceful Catullus, the
fanciful Ovid, the elegiac Tibullus, and the wrathful Juvenal, not less
for their intrinsic merits than because they are so widely known and so
universally referred to among the literati. Among the moderns there
are countless poets, French, Spanish, German, and Italian, which are

more or less replete with beauties, and you may read them all if you can. I shall not try the toilsome task, or bear the cumbrous load. Those which I have read have pleased me; but I have no lease of life, and therefore, except to amuse an idle hour, I am content to dwell among those poets whose merits depend not upon the *dixit* of one great man or a dozen, but which have on them an inspection-mark indubitably good — the stamp of Father Time! The poems of Dante and Tasso have received the *imprimatur* of King Antiquity, and Prince Posterity will never repudiate their claims. Why would you forsake these acknowledged fountains of nature, sublimity, and passion, for the ideal tenderness of Petrarch to an imaginary Laura, or the elaborately-polished fancies of Guarini in the 'Pastor Fido?' These elegant writers have always enjoyed high reputation among polite scholars and learned lovers; but their fine conceits and manufactured passion have not built them an enduring home in the sympathies of our nature. When the names of Schiller and Goëthe have already far overstepped the limits of their native land and taken rank among the denizens of earth, why would you subtract your time from them, to expend it on their successors, of narrow fame and doubtful inspiration?

The deep interest I take in my subject has made me prolix; and therefore I leave unsaid much that presents itself to my mind on the *moral* preëminence of these great artists. I wished to tell you that you can hardly find one vicious or sickly sentiment in all their writings, and hardly even an indecorous *word*, except in Horace and Shakspeare. For despite the cant of the fastidious, these two writers are sound moralists almost throughout. But I hasten on to remove a stumbling-block over which I fell, and which may trip you up; and to point you to an infallible guide, which I hope we both shall have the grace to follow. The impediment I speak of is that all-grasping spirit which is at once a glorious proof and an ever-agitating consequence of the divinity of our origin and the immortality of our existence. This spirit, so visible in our insatiable thirst for riches, power, and glory, is no less apparent in our ceaseless craving for *all* that is touching, beautiful, or great, in the dominions of the mind. The Ciceronian maxim that we should always aim at the 'immensum infinitumque' must be received and acted upon with an important restriction. We are to aim at that which is immense and infinite in its character and kind, not in its diversity and extent. Otherwise we transform this career of life into a chase after the unattainable, and are mere children, idly spreading our tiny hands to span the immeasurable vault. The limited cannot grasp the limitless, nor infinitesimal fractions swell to the compass of an integer whose vastness defies the arithmetic of angels.

The world contains more grand and beautiful thoughts, more poetry in verse and prose, than would suffice to feed and intoxicate the most insatiate heart through ten antediluvian lives. Do you covet it *all*, because it is all desirable? Well. Apply the same principle to other matters. There is not a country, not a spot on the globe, where you may not meet something of surpassing interest, either in the character of its people, the beauty of its scenery, or its monuments of antiquity.

Will nothing satisfy you, therefore, short of circumnavigating the earth and visiting all that can enlist the feelings or elevate the soul? If you have prayed with Coleridge in the valley of Chamouni, and rhapsodized with Byron at the foot of Parnassus, must you plant yourself on every rugged mountain-top and 'heaven-kissing hill,' Rhodope and Ætna, Hybla and Ben Nevis? If you have sailed down the Rhine's 'exulting and abounding river,' must you also float on the waters of every other stream which has beautiful green banks and broad majestic waves? Why, there is not a blade of green or withered grass, not a budding or fading flower, not an earthly or aërial bird, from 'the hidden to the apparent pole,' which has not its charm to the poetic or scientific view. Will you therefore botanize over fifty million square miles? Shall every herb reveal to your gaze its curious texture? — every mountain-flower and prairie-blossom display its coloring and exhale its perfume for your senses? — each winged existence of the forest and the cloud pour its melody in your ear and unfold its plumage to your eye? Dear friend, be content with that which is perfect in its kind and equal to your time and capacity, though it should not comprise in itself *all* that is excellent. A sufficiency is enough, and simple fulness is as good as the redundancy of a deluge. You who have stood dumb in the dizziness of wonder and thrilled with the ecstacy of awe at the Falls of Niagara, have no need to visit any other cataract ; for you have already witnessed the sum and mightiness of physical grandeur, and the others are but cascades of a second-rate magnificence.

Reason, then, and the common principles of life, and more than all, inexorable necessity, bid you make a selection. By what standard will you select? The opinions of *individual* great men are but a doubtful guide; for they are as various as the poetry from which you would select ; and while they almost all unite in their estimate of some poets, they have each their private household gods, whom they would force on your worship as prime divinities. Dr. Johnson considered Milton's Lycidas a poor unnatural affair ; a strange decision to be sure; but it is delivered *excathedrâ* by Sir Oracle himself, and 'let no dog bark.' Schlegel thought Ariosto unworthy the name of genius. Landor thinks Voltaire and Boileau have written no true poetry. Jeffrey considered Wordsworth a very inferior poet, while Coleridge and Southey esteemed him the greatest of the last century. Sergeant Talfourd and Professor Wilson view Coleridge as his equal if not superior, and Byron places Campbell at the head of them all. Now will you puzzle your yet unfurnished brain in striving to reconcile these jarring judgments? The discussions and cavils in the chancery court of criticism far outdo the glorious uncertainty of the law's delay ; and nothing remains for you but to withdraw these cases from that disputatious moot-court, and refer them for decision to a supreme, impartial, incorruptible tribunal. I refer to the tribunal of ages, constituted by the men of all time, and where your own good mind must sit as a coördinate judge. Here all artists receive a full and patient hearing, and their contending claims are settled by its final and unimpeachable award.

This tribunal bases its conclusions not upon the Grecian Code or

Roman Pandects; it adopts exclusively neither the ecclesiastical nor the civil, nor yet the common law of any particular age or nation. It regards no partial decrees, no temporary enactments. It guides itself not by the legislation of Aristotle, the Commentaries of Quinctilian, the dogmas of the Sorbonne, or the statute-book of the Della Cruscans. It laughs to scorn the musty doctrine that every epic must be modelled after the Iliad and Æneid, with just twenty-four or exactly twelve books, and episodes to match; or that a tragedy must observe all the unities of time and place, precisely as they may be found in a pattern-drama of Sophocles. It fetters not the flight of Genius; it clips not his wing to the size and shape of Homer's pinion. It decrees not that rhyme is a necessary adjunct or a paralysing weight to poetry. It does not even assert that metrical numbers are essential to her existence. It considers these peculiarities in her external developement as the mere accidents of time and place; neither constituting her life nor occasioning her death. These mutations in the fashion of her dress, with all their incidental appendages of ornament and taste, may indeed lessen or enhance her beauty, but can neither create nor annihilate the inspired spirit and the etherial form. It believes that through all these transfigurations her vitality and identity consist in the rapture of exalted feeling and the utterance of immortal truth; and that the bane which consumes her energies and blights her beauty is frigid exaggeration and specious falsehood.

This tribunal listens not to the special pleading of Englishmen alone; for they believe scores of their tragedians to have eclipsed Racine; nor does it confide in the arguments of Frenchmen merely; for they would exalt Voltaire and De Lille above Milton and Pope. It rejects the estimates of national pride and professional vanity. It melts up and amalgamates the sentiments of all nations and of all times; its valuation results from the fusion and combination of the *dicta* of the learned and the feelings of the populace. It admits no arbiter but itself. It summons Dionysius and Longinus, and Scaliger and Heinsius, and all the learned, as intelligent witnesses; it listens to their testimony with respectful attention; but they are only witnesses and can pass no definitive sentence. Nor does it reject the evidence or disregard the carpings of Zoilus and Aristarchus, ignorant and malicious though they be; for ignorance may stumble upon truths, and malice reveal failings to the world; while on the other hand Fancy, wild will-o'-the-wisp, and Theory, delusive meteor, may lead Genius and Learning into the pitfalls of extravagance and error.

In short, this tribunal is a grand court of equity, whose sessions are never intermitted, and in whose unexclusive halls all poets are tried and sentenced; tried by the unpurchased evidence of human hearts, and sentenced upon the invariable principles of international and universal literary law. On matters of religion, philosophy, and government, this court has often erred and may often err again; for these matters have been subjected to the head rather than the heart; and our minds, though composed of the same elements, are yet infinitely diverse in their proportionate mixtures. But on the beautiful and the sublime in poetry and her sister arts the decisions of this court are infallibly correct; for these things follow not the track of our wandering reason, so darkened by the mists of prejudice and swayed by the tide of interest and shattered by the fury of conflicting passions. Their appreciation depends on the sympathies of the soul, which, though inexplicably strange and unfathomably deep, have yet been at all times unchangeably the same. The sentences of this tribunal are usually lingering in their promulgation. They are rarely passed, ratified, and recorded before at least a century after the death of the litigant; for it requires that time to extend the merits of his cause to foreign nations and collect the suffrages of men. But when this unanimous verdict has once been rendered in, History receives it in her faithful keeping, and Memory engraves it, not in permanent and changeless characters on brass or marble, but in ever-deepening letters impressed by the old and wise on living tablets in the hearts of young and happy generations.

POLYGON.

THE MISER.

I.

THE mouse crept out of the old stone wall
　　To search for the precious store,
And he wandered silently through the hall,
　　And gnawed at the bolted door;
And the gray-haired miser turned his head —
　　He turned his head and swore!

II.

And there he sat with his sunken eyes,
　　That old man thin and pale,
While the wind in broken symphonies
　　Through the creaking blinds made wail,
And the raven croaked on the battlement
　　In the rising autumn-gale.

III.

Over his shoulder a direful look
　　At the bolted door gave he,
And his knees in his thread-bare breeches shook
　　Like the limbs of a withered tree,
When the shrill wind shrieks on the mountain-top
　　In its midnight agony!

IV.

Ah! sad and fearful to look upon
　　Were those glassy eyes of his,
For a soul shone out of them, had done
　　Much in its day amiss,
And thought was a dark and bitter thing
　　Unto that man, I wis!

V.

A dark and a bitter thing it was,
　For his heart was dry and cold,
And he had been deaf to the widow's cause,
　For the sake of his precious gold,
Counting it o'er, year out year in,
　In that room so dim and old.

VI.

The old man gazed at the bolted door
　And muttered to himself,
For he thought of his heaps of shining ore,
　And all his ill-got pelf
In the good strong chests that, side by side,
　Stood locked on his cellar-shelf.

VII.

Then paler and paler waxed his cheek,
　For the storm-wind fiercer grew,
And the raven with a dismal shriek
　Against the window flew,
And the lightning through the pitch-black night
　The glare of a demon threw !

VIII.

And the gloomy thunder moaned on high,
　As the huge clouds, dark with rain,
Like an army of ragged fiends swept by
　From the wind-tossed ocean-main ;
Slowly and solemn, and black as death,
　Mid the roar of the hurricane.

　.　　.　　.　　.

IX.

Long years passed over that lonely house,
　But the foot of man no more
Was heard by the small gray garret-mouse,
　That gnawed in the shattered floor,
Till a wild grim-visaged outlaw came
　And unbolted that oaken door.

X.

But he rushed from that room with cheeks as white
　As the cheeks of dead men are :
Ah me ! — such a sad and woful sight
　That strong-nerved man saw there !
'T would have curdled the blood in his flinty heart
　Had it been like the heart of a bear.

XI.

For his arms had clasped a skeleton cold,
　That sat in the solemn gloom
Beside a coffer of precious gold,
　In that dark and lonely room ;
And this was all that was ever known
　Of the gray-haired miser's doom !

Utica, (N Y.,) September, 1841.　　　　　H. W. ROCKWELL.

A WEEK IN NEWPORT.

BY A SOJOURNER.

This fine old place loses none of its attractions after repeated visits. It seems as though one could never grow weary of admiring the beautiful scenery, and enjoying the delicious softness of the climate. Here are no east winds, nor suffocating heats, like those which by turns render the rest of New-England uncomfortable and unhealthy. Although in summer the early part of the day is often close and warm, producing in those who are not acclimated an almost irresistible feeling of drowsiness, yet it does not last long. The breezes which spring up in the forenoon and continue to blow until evening, impart vigor and buoyancy to the languid frame. Nothing can surpass the transparency of the atmosphere in the latter part of the day. An afternoon's ride over the island is of itself worth coming here to enjoy. Beside the serenity and freshness of the air ; the rich green meadows sloping to the shore ; the smooth roads, waving crops, and farm-houses so embowered among trees that the eye catches but occasional glimpses of them, leaving the imagination to fill up the picture ; beside these, there are beautiful views of the harbor and bay ; of the main land stretching far away in the distance, and

—— ' Poured round all,
Old Ocean's gray and melancholy waste.'

This last never loses its sublimity, yet there are some who complain of its wearisome sameness. Those who make this complaint however are mostly fair-weather visiters, who pay it a morning call, or come upon it in their rambles at particular hours, when the sky is clear. But let them stand upon the beach when the rays of the rising sun paint the water and the sky till they seem to be involved in one red conflagration, and when the moon, lingering above the horizon, spans as it were with a pathway of gold the fathomless expanse. Let them listen to the swelling and falling billows, as they play with the smooth pebles in some retired nook among the rocks, and hear the deep bass thundered upon the shore, when storm and tempest have roused old Neptune from his slumber, and they will find that the ocean has variety enough. The scarcity of trees, of which the island was despoiled by the English during the war, is often felt to be a blemish in the landscape. In truth these alone are wanting to render it complete. Efforts are making, by transplanting, to supply this deficiency ; and many of the roads are already lined with rows of the beautiful sycamore, which is found to flourish better than any other tree.

The town has little of wealth or enterprise to boast, the citizens apparently being satisfied that they were *once* industrious and prosperous. Newport was a flourishing city when New-York was in its infancy. She had her merchants who trafficked in the products of both the Indies, of China, and Europe, and had at one time a line of packets to Liverpool. Previous to the war she ranked second only to Boston, among the New-England towns, in enterprise and population. But her glory as a city has departed. The town presents a rusty and decayed appearance. 'They build all old houses;' and the piers at which heavy merchantmen were once moored are now occupied by a few fishing smacks and coasting sloops; and the warehouses once filled with merchandise are deserted and in ruins.

But the contrast which it presents to other places, where American enterprise is more operative, is not unpleasant to those who are tired of the din of trade which fills all our large cities, and who are seeking repose and quiet. Though devoid of interest to the mere man of business, few places in our country possess more materials of interest to the historian and antiquarian. From the earliest settlement of Rhode-Island this place has furnished an asylum to the persecuted from other countries, and even from some parts of our own country; while the salubrity of the climate has attracted not a few from different parts of the world to fix their residence here. It has always been a place of resort for the votaries of wealth and fashion. In its better days, they took up their residence here, and in its decline they come to enjoy its beauties for a season, and then flit away to a more extended and brilliant scene. These visiters brought with them each his peculiar habits and notions, and many of them had interesting histories of their own which have been interspersed in the history of the place, and have added much to its value.

Bishop Berkley, after the failure of his benevolent project for establishing an institution to educate the Indians, resided here two or three years. The house built and occupied by him is still standing about three miles from the town. It is a small dwelling of wood, stands very low, and has a gloomy appearance. The parlor and study of the philosopher are still shown, but not a fragment of his furniture; nor does any memento of him exist, except an organ presented by him to one of the churches of Newport. The Bishop led a very secluded life, passing much of his time among the rocks, a short distance from the house, which command a fine view of the ocean. It was here that he composed the greater part of that ingenious work, 'The Minute Philosopher,' which the late Dr. Payson admired so much that he could repeat whole chapters. It is an admirable place for contemplation and study; for analyzing and describing the intricate operations of the mind. The favorite nook of the Bishop is pointed out to visiters, a kind of shelf high up among the rocks, open only toward the ocean; where no sound disturbs the quiet save the solemn monotone of the waves breaking upon the shore.

In that gloomiest hour of our struggle for liberty, when the long-prayed-for succour from France arrived, Newport again presented a smiling appearance. The French troops on landing were received with every possible demonstration of joy. But a short time before, the island had been in possession of the enemy, who were quartered among the citizens; and their customary haughtiness added to their bitter contempt of the rebels, had rendered them any thing but agreeable guests. Now, they welcomed their enthusiastic allies, who had quitted their homes to bleed in their defence; and their gayety and courtesy banished for a time all their gloomy apprehensions. The contrast between the rude and insolent Hessians and the flower of French chivalry, with Count Rochambeau at their head, produced a deep impression on the minds of the citizens. That joyous occasion has not yet been forgotten. Elderly matrons and maidens can still remember the polished manners and unrestrained merriment of the polite strangers, as they turned them in the dance, or escorted them along the crowded streets.

The story of the destruction of the 'Gaspee' and the capture of Prescott would have been sufficient vouchers for the courage of the people of Rhode-Island, had no Perry nor Greene made them illustrious in the eyes of the world. There are many instances of daring exploits performed by her citizens, which have not yet been made public. One of these it is our good fortune to be able to record, and it is well worthy of a page in the history of this patriotic little State, should she ever have a historian to do her the justice she deserves.

During the reign of Queen Anne, a piratical ship of three hundred tons appeared off the harbor of Newport, and cruising between Block-Island and Point Judith, levied contributions upon every vessel that attempted to pass. The commerce of the colony suffered severely from these depredations, until at length two resolute young men, John and William Wanton, formed a plan to capture or destroy the vessel. Courage on such occasions is contagious. No sooner was their purpose made known, than thirty other young men of their acquaintance offered to accompany them. A sloop of sixty tons was engaged for the enterprise. With no other armament than their muskets, this spirited company sailed out of the harbor to all appearance on a coasting voyage, every person being below except a sufficient number to navigate the vessel. As they approached the pirate, and appeared to be anxious to avoid her, a shot was fired at them. They were hailed, and ordered to come alongside. They immediately dropped the peak of their mainsail, in token of their compliance, and luffed up for the ship. Instead of bringing the sloop alongside, they came directly under and in contact with her stern. The men below sprang upon deck, and instantly grappled the sloop to the ship. With wedges prepared for the purpose, they made the rudder immovable, thus rendering the ship totally unmanageable. Having succeeded thus far to their entire satisfaction, they were prepared to contend with the superior number of the enemy. The large guns of the pirates were of no use to them, as they could not be brought to bear upon the sloop, while the latter, having chosen her position, was able to keep up a galling fire, raking the decks of the ship from stern to bowsprit. The young men were all good marksmen, and every pirate who exposed himself was instantly shot. After a great variety of unavailing efforts to disengage themselves from their awkward situation, and after losing a great number of men, they surrendered, and were brought back in triumph to Newport. The fame of this brave achievement reached the Queen, who in testimony of her appreciation of their generous self-devotion, presented the brothers Wanton with a large silver bowl and salver, having a suitable inscription.   D. T. M.

THE THREE MESSENGERS.

BY S. D. DAKIN.

'Religion and Science shall lead Freedom through the world, and neither shall lack worshippers.'—LORD BACON.

THERE 's a glow in the west o'er the mountain's crest,
  On the folds of the rosy clouds ;
And afar mid the sheen of the sky's apple-green,
  Like the stars its soft lustre enshrouds,
Two figures of light are growing more bright
  To the gazers in ecstacy here ;
On a mission of love from the high court above,
  They come to this dark rolling sphere ;
With stars for their torches, the sky for a dome,
Oh ! welcome them here to a temple and home !

Ye Messengers sweet, your mission complete
  In the fields of the heart and the mind ;
Prepare ye the way for the coming bright day,
  That follows in glory behind ;
When the dew from your wings a redolence flings
  On the white flag around you unfurled,
And Freedom ye guide, with a generous pride,
  Through the uttermost realms of the world ;
While worshippers flock to your shrines with delight,
And Love fans Devotion with pinions of light !

As ye pass there is mirth o'er the wide-smiling earth,
  And the mountains are ringing with glee ;
New life in the air as it plays with the hair
  On the brow, wide, expanded and free ;
And valley and stream, glowing bright in your beam,
  Rejoice in each other's embrace ;
For, from sunniest nooks by the murmuring brooks,
  Where they loved their foul dwellings to place,
The minions of Might and Oppression ye 've hurled,
And swept with a besom of light from the world !

Ye bowed ones arouse, and take the bold vows
  That bind all the brave through the earth ;
Baptize the stern front in Freedom's blest font,
  And claim the new heavenly birth ;
While your serried souls one ardor controls,
  As heat-lightning the serried clouds ;
And its flashes shall daunt in each blood-crimsoned haunt
  Proud kings mid their cowering crowds ;
And world over, the flag of your victory stream,
As o'er storm-clouds dispersing the bright morning beam !

Mid Niagara's roar shall Columbia pour
  The first shout of the free to the sky ;
Th' Alleghanies shall bear the high sound through the air,
  And the Ural and Alps shall reply !
And the Messengers bright shall behold with delight
  The gladness that springs in their path,
And folding their wings o'er the beautiful things
  That grow where were terror and wrath,
Like the dove from the ark, to return shall refuse,
And the earth for their dwelling shall cheerfully choose !

LITERARY NOTICES.

THE DEERSLAYER: OR THE FIRST WAR-PATH: A TALE. By the Author of 'The Last of the Mohicans,' 'The Pioneers,' etc. In two volumes 12mo. pp. 549. Philadelphia: LEA AND BLANCHARD.

WE take it for granted, that so long as Mr. COOPER shall continue to lay before the public works like 'The Deerslayer,' just so long will he find no lack of readers to reward his endeavors to entertain them For our own part, we have perused these volumes with deep interest. The pictures which our author has here drawn of nature, we contend are second to none of those vivid limnings by which he has won his reputation. The wide, solemn forest, varied by the season's changes; the lake embosomed in its recesses; and the groupings of objects in this great framework, are admirable examples of Mr. COOPER's close observation and fine powers of description. And without going into a detailed review of the characters and events of the tale — for which indeed, even supposing them to be what they cannot be, at this late period, *new* to our readers, we yet have not the room — we desire especially to record our high admiration of one of our author's finest creations, DEERSLAYER. This noble conception Mr. COOPER tell us is the 'study' from which the successive portraits of LEATHERSTOCKING, in his former works, were drawn; and the series in which this personage appears, now forms something like a drama in five acts, complete as to material and design. We pass at once to our extracts, fearing at the best to be able to indicate a few only of the passages which have afforded us the highest gratification. The following is one of those strikingly beautiful delineations of nature to which we have alluded:

" ' Land ahead, Deerslayer,' said March, ' and open the bushes; the rest I can do for myself.'

" The other obeyed, and the men left the spot, Deerslayer clearing the way for his companion, and inclining to the right, or to the left, as the latter directed. In about ten minutes they both broke suddenly into the brilliant light of the sun, on a low gravelly point, that was washed by water on quite half its outline.

" An exclamation of surprise broke from the lips of Deerslayer, an exclamation that was low and guardedly made, however, for his habits were much more thoughtful and regulated than those of the reckless Hurry, when, on reaching the margin of the lake, he beheld the view that unexpectedly met his gaze. It was, in truth, sufficiently striking to merit a brief description. On a level with the point lay a broad sheet of water, so placid and limpid, that it resembled a bed of the pure mountain atmosphere, compressed into a setting of hills and woods. Its length was about three leagues, while its breadth was irregular, expanding to half a league, or even more, opposite to the point, and contracting to less than half that distance, more to the southward. Of course, its margin was irregular, being indented by bays, and broken by many projecting, low points. At its northern, or nearest end, it was bounded by an isolated mountain, lower land falling off, east and west, gracefully relieving the sweep of the outline. Still the character of the country was mountainous; high hills, or low mountains, rising abruptly from the water, on quite nine-tenths of its circuit. The exceptions, indeed, only served a little to vary the scene; and even beyond the parts of the shore that were comparatively low, the back-ground was high, though more distant.

" But the most striking peculiarities of this scene were its solemn solitude and sweet repose. On all sides, wherever the eye turned, nothing met it but the mirror-like surface of the lake, the placid view of heaven, and the dense setting of woods. So rich and fleecy were the outlines of the forest, that scarce an opening could be seen, the whole visible earth, from the rounded mountain-top to the water's edge, presenting one unvaried hue of unbroken verdure. As if vegetation were not satisfied with a triumph so complete, the trees overhung the lake itself, shooting out towards the light ; and there were miles along its eastern shore, where a boat might have pulled beneath the branches of dark Rembrandt-looking hemlocks, ' quivering aspens,' and melancholy pines. In a word, the hand of man had never yet defaced or deformed any part of this native scene, which lay bathed in the sun-light, a glorious picture of affluent forest-grandeur, softened by the balminess of June, and relieved by the beautiful variety afforded by the presence of so broad an expanse of water.

" ' This is grand — 't is solemn ! — 't is an edication of itself, to look upon ! ' exclaimed Deerslayer, as he stood leaning on his rifle, and gazing to the right and left, north and south, above and beneath, in whichever direction his eye could wander ; ' not a tree disturbed even by red-skin hand, as I can discover, but every thing left in the ordering of the Lord, to live and die according to his own designs and laws ! ' "

Such transcripts from nature as this require not our poor praise to insure the admiration of the reader. We have observed that one or two critics have spoken of the dialogue portions of ' The Deerslayer' as dull and tedious. Nothing, as it seems to us, could be more erroneous than this judgment. Saving that in one or two instances they may be deemed a little too protracted, we are compelled to regard them as the most felicitous and attractive parts of the romance. We proceed to fortify our opinion by a passage or two. The first which we shall present succeeds a description of an unsuccessful shot at a deer, by a conspicuous companion-voyager of Deerslayer on the lake :

" When about half-way across, a slight noise drew the eyes of the men towards the nearest land, and they saw that the buck was just emerging from the lake, and wading towards the beach. In a minute the noble animal shook the water from his flanks, gazed upward at the covering of trees, and bounding against the bank, plunged into the forest.

" ' That creatur' goes off with gratitude in his heart,' said Deerslayer, ' for natur' tells him he has escaped a great danger. You ought to have some of the same feelins', Hurry, to think your eye was n't truer — that your hand was unsteady, when no good could come of a shot that was intended onmeaningly, rather than in reason.'

" ' I deny the eye and the hand,' cried March, with some heat. ' You 've got a little character, down among the Delawares, there, for quickness and sartainty, at a deer ; but I should like to see you behind one of them pines, and a full-painted Mingo behind another, each with a cock'd rifle, and a-striving for the chance ! Them 's the situations, Nathaniel, to try the sight and the hand, for they begin with trying the narves. I never look upon killing a creatur' as an explite ; but killing a savage is. The time will come to try your hand, now we 've got to blows ag'in, and we shall soon know what a ven'son repitation can do in the field. I deny that either hand or eye was onsteady ; it was all a miscalculation of the buck, which stood still when he ought to have kept in motion, and so I shot ahead of him.'

" ' Have it your own way, Hurry ; all I contend for is, that it 's lucky. I dare say I shall not pull upon a human mortal as steadily, or with as light a heart, as I pull upon a deer.'

" ' Who 's talking of mortals, or of human beings at all, Deerslayer? I put the matter to you on the supposition of an Indian. I dare say any man would have his feelin's when it got to be life, or death, ag'in another human mortal ; but there would be no such scruples in regard to an Indian ; nothing but the chance of his hitting you, or the chance of your hitting him.'

" ' I look upon the red-men to be quite as human as we are ourselves, Hurry. They have their gifts, and their religion, it 's true ; but that makes no difference in the end, when each will be judged according to his deeds, and not according to his skin.'

" ' That 's downright missionary, and will find little favor up in this part of the country, where the Moravians do n't congregate. Now, skin makes the man. This is reason ; else how are people to judge of each other The skin is put on, over all, in order that when a creatur', or a mortal, is fairly seen, you may know at once what to make of him. You know a bear from a hog, by his skin, and a gray squirrel from a black.'

" ' True, Hurry,' said the other, looking back and smiling, ' nevertheless, they are both squirrels.'

" ' Who denies it? But you 'll not say that a red-man and a white man are both Indians ? '

" ' No ; but I do say they are both men. Men of different races and colors, and having different gifts and traditions, but, in the main, with the same natur'. Both have souls ; and both will be held accountable for their deeds in this life.'

" ' You 're a boy, Deerslayer, misled and misconsaited by Delaware arts, and missionary ignorance,' he exclaimed, with his usual indifference to the forms of speech, when excited. ' You may account yourself as a red-skin's brother, but I hold 'em all to be animals ; with nothing human about 'em, but cunning. That they have, I 'll allow ; but so has a fox, or even a bear. I 'm older than you, and have lived longer in the woods — or, for that matter, have lived always there, and am not to be told what an Indian is, or what he is not.' "

Here ensues a dialogue between the same artistically-contrasted characters, upon the propriety of the whites ' doing as they were done by' in the matter of scalping their red enemies :

" ' The savages scalp your fri'nds, the Delawares or Mohicans, whichever they may be, among the rest ; and why should 'nt we scalp ? I 'll own it would be ag'in right for you and me, now, to go into the settlements and bring out scalps, but it 's a very different matter as consarns Indians. A man should 'nt take scalps, if he is 'nt ready to be scalped himself, on fitting occasions. One good turn desarves another, all the world over. That 's reason, and I believe it to be good religion.'

" ' You must fight a man with his own we'pons, Deerslayer,' cried Hurry, in his uncouth dialect, and in his dogmatical manner of disposing of all moral propositions ; ' if he 's f'erce, you must be f'ercer ; if he 's stout of heart, you must be stouter. This is the way to get the better of christian or savage : by keeping up to this trail, you 'll get soonest to the ind of your journey.'

" ' That 's not Moravian doctrine, which teaches that all are to be judged according to their talents, or l'arning ; the Indian, like an Indian ; and the white man, like a white man. Some of their teachers say, that if you 're struck on the cheek, it 's a duty to turn the other side of the face, and take another blow, instead of seeking revenge, whereby I understand —— '

" ' That 's enough ! ' shouted Hurry ; ' that 's all I want, to prove a man's doctrine ! How long would it take to kick a man through the Colony — in at one ind, and out at the other, on that principle ? '

" ' Don 't mistake me, March,' returned the young hunter, with dignity ; ' I don 't understand by this, any more, than that it 's *best* to do this, if *possible*. Revenge is an Indian gift, and forgiveness a white man's. That 's all. Overlook all you *can*, is what 's meant ; and not *revenge* all you can. As for kicking, Master Hurry,' and Deerslayer's sun-burnt cheek flushed, as he continued, ' into the Colony or out of the Colony, that 's neither here nor there, seeing no one proposes it, and no one would be likely to put up with it. What I wish to say is, that a red-skin's scalping don 't justify a pale-face's scalping.

" ' Do as you 're done by, Deerslayer ; that 's ever the christian parson's doctrine.'

" ' No, Hurry, I 've asked the Moravians consarning that ; and it 's altogether different. ' Do as you *would* be done by,' they tell me, is the *true* saying, while men *practyse* the *false*. They think all the Colonies wrong, that offer bounties for scalps, and believe no blessing will follow the measures. Above all things, they forbid revenge.'

" ' *That* for your Moravians ! ' cried March, snapping his fingers ; ' they 're the next thing to Quakers ; and if you 'd believe all they tell you, not even a 'rat would be skinned, out of marcy. Who ever heard of marcy on a muskrat ! ' "

We shall make only one more extract, but to that we invite the especial attention of the reader. It is a dialogue between Sarpent, the familiar *nom de guerre* of a Delaware chief, and Deerslayer, and involves one of the most characteristic and beautiful illustrations of *faith* that we remember ever to have encountered :

" ' There 's one thing, however, chief, that *does* seem to me to be onreasonable, and ag'in natur', though the missionaries say it 's true ; and bein' of my religion and color, I feel bound to believe them. They say an Indian may torment and tortur' the body to the heart's content, and scalp and cut, and tear, and burn, and consume all his inventions and deviltries, until nothin' is left but ashes, and they shall be scattered to the four winds of heaven, yet, when the trumpet of God shall sound, all will come together ag'in and the man will stand forth in his flesh, the same creatur' as to looks, if not as to feelin's, that he was afore he was harmed ! '

" ' The missionaries are good men ; they mean well,' returned the Delaware, courteously ; ' they are not great medicines. They think all they say, Deerslayer ; that is no reason why warriors and orators should be all ears. When Chingachgook shall see the father of Tamenund standing in his scalp, and paint, and war-lock, then will he believe the missionaries.'

" ' Seein' is believin', of a sartainty — ah 's me ! and some of us may see these things sooner than we thought. I comprehend your meanin' about Tamenund's father, Sarpent, and the idee's a close idee. Tamenund is now an elderly man, say eighty, every day of it ; and his father was scalped, and tormented, and burnt, when the present prophet was a youngster. Yes, if one could see *that* come to pass, there would 'nt be much difficulty in yieldin' faith to all that the missionaries say. However, I am not ag'in the opinion now ; for you must know, Sarpent, that the great principle of christianity is to believe *without* seeing ; and a man should always act up to his religion and principles, let them be what they may.'

" ' That is strange, for a wise nation,' said the Delaware, with emphasis. ' The red man looks hard, that he may *see* and understand.'

" ' Yes, that 's plausorble, and is agreeable to mortal pride ; but it 's not as deep as it seems. If we could understand *all* we see, Sarpent, there might be not only sense, but safety, in refusin' to give faith to any *one* thing that we might find oncomprehensible ; but when there 's so many things, about which, it may be said, we know nothin' at all, why, there 's little use, and no reason, in bein' difficult touchin' any one in partic'lar. For my part, Delaware, all my thoughts hav 'nt been on the game, when outlyin' in the hunts and scoutin's of our youth. Many 's the hour I 've passed pleasantly enough, too, in what is tarmed conterplation by my people. On such occasions, the mind is actyve, though the body seems lazy and listless. An open spot on a mountain side, where a wide look can be had at the heavens and the 'arth, is a most judicious place for a man to get a just idee of the power of the Manitou, and of his own littleness. At such times, there is 'nt any great disposition to find fault with little difficulties, in the way of comprehension, as there are so many big ones to hide them. Believin' comes easy enough to me, at such times ; and, if the Lord made man first, out of 'arth, as they tell me it is written in the Bible, then turns him into dust, at death, I see no great difficulty in the way to bringin' him back into the body, though ashes be the only substance left. These things lie beyond our understandin', though they may, and do, lie so close to our feelin's. But of all the doctrines, Sarpent, that which disturbs me, and disconsarts my mind the most, is the one which teaches us to think that a pale-face goes to one heaven, and a red-skin to another ; it may separate in death, them which lived much together, and loved each other well, in life ! '

" ' Do the missionaries teach their white brethren to think it is so ? ' demanded the Indian, with serious earnestness. ' The Delawares believe that good men and brave warriors will hunt together in the same pleasant woods, let them belong to whatever tribe they may ; that all the unjust Indians, and cowards, will have to sneak in with the dogs and the wolves, to get venison for their lodges.'

"' 'T is wonderful how many consaits mankind have consarnin' happiness and misery, hereafter!' exclaimed the hunter, borne away by the power of his own thoughts. 'Some believe in burnin's and flames, and some think punishment is to eat with the wolves and dogs. Then, ag'in, some fancy heaven to be only the carryin' out of their own 'arthly longin's; while others fancy it all gold and shinin' lights! Well, I 've an idee of my own, in that matter, which is just this, Sarpent. Whenever I 've done wrong, I 've ginirally found 't was owin' to some blindness of the mind, which hid the right from view, and when sight has returned, then has come sorrow and repentance. Now, I consait that, after death, when the body is laid aside, or, if used at all, is purified and without its longin's, the spirit sees all things in their ra'al light, and never becomes blind to truth and justice. Such bein' the case, all that has been done in life is beheld as plainly as the sun is seen at noon; the good brings joy, while the evil brings sorrow. There 's nothin' onreasonable in that, but it 's agreeable to every man's exper'ence.'

"' I thought the pale-faces believed *all* men were wicked; who then could ever find the white man's heaven?'

"' That 's ingen'ous, but it falls short of the missionary teachin's. You 'll be christianized one day, I make no doubt, and then 't will all come plain enough. You must know, Sarpent, that there 's been a great deed of salvation done, that, by God's help, enables all men to find a pardon for their wickednesses, and *that* is the essence of the white man's religion. I can 't stop to talk this matter over with you any longer, for Hetty 's in the canoe, and the furlough takes me away; but the time will come I hope, when you 'll *feel* these things; for, after all, they must be *felt*, rather than reasoned about. Ah 's! me; well, Delaware, there 's my hand; you know it 's that of a fri'nd, and will shake it as such, though it never has done you one-half the good its owner wishes it had.'"

We have purposely refrained from allusion to the main incidents of 'The Deer-slayer,' by which it is constituted a romance proper, or to the minuter machinery by which its dramatic scenes and plot are evolved. These we commend our readers to seek in the work itself; asking them only to judge how far, if the passages we have quoted be from the 'dull' and 'tedious' portions, they may be likely to find entertainment in those parts which were invincible against the ready censure of lynx-eyed and hostile critics.

Confessions of an English Opium-Eater. From the last London Edition. In one volume. pp. 190. Boston: William D. Ticknor.

Brief reference has heretofore been had in the Knickerbocker to this remarkable and exciting work, which had its origin some twenty years ago in the pages of the 'London Magazine.' It purports to be 'an extract from the life of a scholar.' The authorship of these 'Confessions' has been frequently attributed, and so far as we know without denial, to De Quincy, and their authenticity is believed to be unquestionable. Indeed, no reader can rise from a perusal of the book, with any doubt in his mind on *this* subject. We have only refreshed our memory of records which it would be impossible, having once read, ever entirely to forget; but as many of our readers may not have encountered them, we shall venture upon one or two extracts. The first is from 'the pleasures of opium,' which a friend informs us, who was once for a few hours under the influence of the drug, can scarcely be depicted, so ravishing are the sensations, and so exquisite the joys which belong to the incipiency of the habit:

"Arrived at my lodgings, it may be supposed that I lost not a moment in taking the quantity prescribed. I was necessarily ignorant of the whole art and mystery of opium-taking; and, what I took, I took under every disadvantage. But I took it; and in an hour, oh! Heavens! what a revulsion! what an upheaving, from its lowest depths, of the inner spirit! what an apocalypse of the world within me! That my pains had vanished, was now a trifle in my eyes: this negative effect was swallowed up in the immensity of those positive effects which had opened before me — in the abyss of divine enjoyment thus suddenly revealed. Here was a panacea — a φαρμακον νηπενθες for all human woes; here was the secret of happiness, about which philosophers had disputed for so many ages, at once discovered; happiness might now be bought for a penny, and carried in the waistcoat pocket; portable ecstacies might be had corked up in a pint bottle; and peace of mind could be sent down in gallons by the mail-coach." · · · "The town of L—— represented the earth, with its sorrows and its graves left behind, yet not out of sight, nor wholly forgotten. The ocean, in everlasting but gentle agitation, and brooded over by dove-like calm, might not unfitly typify the mind and the mood which then swayed it. For it seemed to me as if then first I stood at a distance and aloof from the uproar of life ; as if the tumult, the fever, and the strife, were suspended ; a respite granted from the secret burdens of the heart ; a sabbath of repose ; a resting from human labors. Here were the hopes which blossom in the paths of life, reconciled with the peace which is in the grave ; motions of the intellect as unwearied as the heavens, yet for all anxieties a halcyon calm ; a tranquillity that seemed no product of inertia, but as if resulting from mighty and equal antagonisms ; infinite activities, infinite repose."

The pleasures of opium-eating are painted less elaborately than the 'pains' of the practice, which are dashed in with a rich brush. Take for example the following :

"The first notice I had of any important change going on in this part of my physical economy, was from the reäwaking of a state of eye generally incident to childhood, or exalted states of irritability. I know not whether my reader is aware that many children, perhaps most, have a power of painting, as it were, upon the darkness, all sorts of phantoms ; in some that power is simply a mechanic affection of the eye ; others have a voluntary, or semi-voluntary power to dismiss or to summon them ; or, as a child once said to me when I questioned him on this matter, ' I can tell them to go, and they go ; but sometimes they come when I do n't tell them to come.' Whereupon I told him that he had almost as unlimited a command over apparitions, as a Roman centurion over his soldiers. In the middle of 1817, I think it was, that this faculty became positively distressing to me : at night, when I lay awake in bed, vast processions passed along in mournful pomp ; friezes of never-ending stories, that to my feelings were as sad and solemn as if they were stories drawn from times before Œdipus or Priam, before Tyre, before Memphis. And, at the same time, a corresponding change took place in my dreams ; a theatre seemed suddenly opened and lighted up within my brain, which presented nightly spectacles of more than earthly splendor." · · · "The changes in my dreams were accompanied by deep-seated anxiety and gloomy melancholy, such as are wholly incommunicable by words. I seemed every night to descend, not metaphorically, but literally to descend, into chasms and sunless abysses, depths below depths, from which it seemed hopeless that I could ever reäscend. Nor did I, by waking, feel that I had reäscended." · · · "The sense of space, and in the end, the sense of time, were both powerfully affected. Buildings, landscapes, etc., were exhibited in proportions so vast as the bodily eye is not fitted to receive. Space swelled, and was amplified to an extent of unutterable infinity. This, however, did not disturb me so much as the vast expansion of time : I sometimes seemed to have lived for seventy or one hundred years in one night."

After remarking that Southern Asia in general, the cradle of the human race, was the seat of awful images and associations, and the dreams of oriental imagery and mythology those of unimaginable horror, the opium-eater says :

"Under the connecting feeling of tropical heat and vertical sun-lights, I brought together all creatures, birds, beasts, reptiles, all trees and plants, usages and appearances, that are found in all tropical regions, and assembled them together in China or Indostan. From kindred feelings, I soon brought Egypt and all her gods under the same law. I was stared at, hooted at, grinned at, chattered at, by monkeys, by paroquots, by cockatoos. I ran into pagodas, and was fixed, for centuries, at the summit, or in secret rooms ; I was the idol ; I was the priest ; I was worshipped ; I was sacrificed. I fled from the wrath of Brama through all the forests of Asia : Vishnu hated me : Seeva laid wait for me. I came suddenly upon Isis and Osiris : I had done a deed, they said, which the ibis and the crocodile trembled at. I was buried, for a thousand years, in stone coffins, with mummies and sphynxes, in narrow chambers at the heart of eternal pyramids. I was kissed, with cancerous kisses, by crocodiles ; and laid, confounded with all unutterable slimy things, amongst reeds and Nilotic mud. Sooner or later, came a reflux of feeling that swallowed up the astonishment, and left me, not so much in terror, as in hatred and abomination of what I saw. Over every form, and threat, and punishment, and dim sightless incarceration, brooded a sense of eternity and infinity that drove me into an oppression as of madness. Into these dreams only, it was, with one or two slight exceptions, that any circumstances of physical horror entered. All before had been moral and spiritual terrors. But here the main agents were ugly birds, or snakes, or crocodiles ; especially the last. The cursed crocodile became to me the object of more horror than almost all the rest. I was compelled to live with him ; and (as was always the case almost in my dreams) for centuries. I escaped sometimes, and found myself in Chinese houses with cane tables, etc. All the feet of the tables, sofas, etc., soon became instinct with life : the abominable head of the crocodile, and his leering eyes, looked out at me, multiplied into a thousand repetitions : and I stood loathing and fascinated. And so often did this hideous reptile haunt my dreams, that many times the very same dream was broken up in the very same way ; I heard gentle voices speaking to me, (I hear every thing when I am sleeping,) and instantly I awoke : it was broad noon ; and my children were standing, hand in hand, at my bed-side ; come to show me their colored shoes, or new frocks, or to let me see them dressed for going out. I protest that so awful was the transition from the damned crocodile, and the other unutterable monsters and abortions of my dreams, to the sight of innocent human natures and of infancy, that, in the mighty and sudden revulsion of mind, I wept, and could not forbear it, as I kissed their faces."

Other passages in connexion with these we had pencilled for insertion ; but the printer, more mindful of our available space, 'brings us up with a round turn,' forcibly reminding us how much larger is our desire than our ability to entertain our readers longer with the experiences of an opium-eater.

THE HISTORY OF CONNECTICUT, FROM ITS FIRST SETTLEMENT TO THE PRESENT TIME. By THEODORE DWIGHT, Jr. New-York: HARPERS' Family Library.

MR. DWIGHT has given us an entertaining volume, which perhaps we may take another occasion to review in detail. We refer to it at present only to defend our worthy and world-renowned progenitor against the serious charge of falsifying history, *implied* in the records of our author. Either Mr. DWIGHT or DIEDRICH KNICKERBOCKER is mistaken. To doubt *which* of the two is wrong, would be sacrilege. The modern historian has followed the example of his predecessor, BENJAMIN TRUMBULL, and evidently considers the Dutch to have been 'mere intruders' in the land of steady habits. The leading Dutchmen at Manhadoes, says Mr. DWIGHT, came to America for trade, and not for religious purposes; and he dwells upon the notice given by KIEFT, that the people of Hartford were no longer to be permitted to trade with the Dutch at Fort Good-Hope, and upon the protest against the settlement of New-Haven, as evincing little sympathy with the colonists. Now KNICKERBOCKER's veracious history contains not only proofs that the Dutch had clear title and possession in the fair valleys of the Connecticut, and that they were wrongfully dispossessed thereof, but likewise that they have been scandalously maltreated ever since by the misrepresentations of the crafty historians of New England. Even in the reign of VAN TWILLER, the pacific cabinet of that renowned monarch bore the impertinences of the losel Yankees 'with a magnanimity that redounded to their immortal credit; becoming by passive endurance inured to the increasing mass of wrongs; like that mighty man of old, who by dint of carrying about a calf from the time it was born, continued to carry it without difficulty when it had grown to be an ox.' And in the matter of Fort Good Hoop, did not the Weathersfield squatters extend their onion-plantations under the very noses of the garrison, insomuch that the honest Dutchmen could not look toward that quarter without tears in their eyes? Talk of 'sympathy!' What sympathy had *they* with the redoubtable VAN CURLET? They paid no attention to his protests, and even less to the two proclamations of his new sovereign, WILHELMUS KIEFT, although the second missive of that sturdy executive was of heavy metal, written in thundering long sentences, not one of which was under five syllables. 'It forbade and prohibited all commerce and connexion between any and every of the Yankee intruders, and the fortified post of Fort Good Hoop; and ordered, commanded, and advised all his trusty, loyal, and well-beloved subjects to furnish them with no supplies of gin, gingerbread, or sour-crout; to buy none of their pacing horses, measly pork, apple-brandy, Yankee rum, cider-water, apple-sweatmeats, Weathersfield onions, tin ware or wooden bowls.' What was the consequence? The first that was heard of the result of this proclamation was the sudden arrival of the gallant Van Curlet, who came staggering into New-Amsterdam at the head of his crew of tatterdemalions, bringing the tidings of his own defeat, and the capture of the redoubtable post of Fort Good Hoop by the ferocious enemy, which happened in this wise: 'It appears that the crafty Yankees, having heard of the regular habits of the garrison, watched a favorable opportunity, and silently introduced themselves into the fort, about the middle of a sultry day; when its vigilant defenders, having gorged themselves with a hearty dinner, and smoked out their pipes, were one and all snoring most obstreperously at their posts, little dreaming of so disastrous an occurrence. The enemy most inhumanly seized Jacobus Van Curlet and his sturdy myrmidons by the nape of the neck, gallanted them to the gate of the fort, and dismissed them severally with a kick on the crupper, as Charles the Twelfth dismissed the heavy-bottomed Russians, after the battle of Narva, only taking care to give two kicks to Van Curlet, as a signal mark of distinction. A strong garrison was immediately established in the fort, consisting of twenty long-sided, hard-fisted Yankees, with Weathersfield onions stuck in their hats by way of cockades and feathers; long rusty fowling-pieces for muskets; hasty-pudding, dumb-fish, pork and molasses for stores; and a huge pumpkin was hoisted on the end of a pole as a standard, liberty-caps not having as yet come into fashion.' It will behoove modern historians of Connecticut to consult *authentic* records, before they sit down to write away the reputation of the Dutch fathers of our city. Having put our readers upon their guard, we take leave of Mr. DWIGHT's volume for the present.

WILSON'S AMERICAN ORNITHOLOGY: WITH NOTES BY JARDINE. To which is added a Synopsis of American Birds, including those described by BONAPARTE, AUDUBON, NUTALL, and RICHARDSON. By T. M. BREWER. In one volume. pp. 744. Boston: OTIS, BROADERS AND COMPANY.

WE are indebted for the delightful 'spirit of life' which pervades the ornithological descriptions of WILSON, to the ardent love he bore his favorite study. We have stood by his grave, near the old Swedes' Church at Philadelphia, and have heard there the fulfilment of his last wish, that he might be buried where the birds could come and sing above his ashes their anthems of praise to the great CREATOR; and we never peruse his pages without a thorough conviction that this last prayer was dictated by no love of eccentricity, nor by affectation, but by a ruling passion so strong that even death had not the power to lessen it. But it is too late in the day to speak of WILSON. His work has attained and maintained an unequalled popularity; and constitutes, with the additions included in the handsome and comprehensive volume under notice, by far the cheapest and best publication of its kind extant. The volume is illustrated with fine copper-plate engravings of the birds described, embellished with an exquisite vignette title-page, than which we scarcely remember any thing more soft and beautiful, and printed upon a clear neat type and fine white paper. It is in short just such an edition as has long been wanted; and while it supplies a present desideratum, will secure for it a future patronage commensurate with its merits and the liberal outlays of the publishers.

MISCELLANIES OF LITERATURE. By the Author of 'Curiosities of Literature.' A new edition, revised and corrected. In three volumes. pp. 1170. New-York: G. AND H. G. LANGLEY.

THESE are rare and entertaining volumes, and as such we commend them warmly to the acceptance of our readers, without having either space or leisure to assign the reason of the faith which is in us that they will surely confirm our judgment on a perusal of the work. The mass of facts, the numerous anecdotes, and the authentic gossip, in the collecting of which the author is so remarkable, render it one of those take-downable series from one's library shelf, which are certain to reward even a desultory and hurried examination. The first volume is devoted to literary miscellanies, the 'calamities of authors;' the second to the literary character and character of James the First; and the third to the quarrels of authors; a more various and prolific theme than the reader may imagine. The volumes are well and carefully printed.

EDITOR'S TABLE.

'OLD PUT. DISCHARGED' is the title of a very long communication which we have received from an eastern correspondent, a relative of the renowned General PUTNAM, in reply to the article entitled 'Old Put. at the Bar,' in our issue for August. In a note to the Editor, the writer says: 'Many of Gen. PUTNAM's descendants are among the most honored and respected of our land; and a score of them would start up instantly, if the attack in the KNICKERBOCKER should meet their eyes. Perhaps you have already received replies. If you have any better than the enclosed, please insert them without regard to mine.' We have not as yet received any reply to the article complained of; but as a friend and defender of Gen. PUTNAM has desired us to keep our pages open for the publication hereafter of a few sufficient yet brief rebutting facts, which he is about collecting and rendering press-worthy, we shall substitute them for the communication before us, which is very long, written with great feeling, and contains much that is foreign to the subject in question, with misplaced and it seems to us injudicious reflections upon the writer of the paper whose statements it aims to refute. We may state here, that it was with 'unwilling willingness we gave a faint consent' to the publication of the original article. It was the first reflection we had ever heard of or ever seen upon the character and services of Gen. PUTNAM; and nothing but the most positive assurance that every material statement which it contained was or could be established by the most irrefragible testimony, induced us at length to yield its reluctant admission into our pages. Our correspondent now informs us that the story is an old one of Gen. DEARBORN's, re-vamped for the occasion; and we learn from him that this officer, whom we have always supposed to have taken Little York and Fort George, and to have been a rather successful general, was of no great consequence in any man's opinion save his own. But it is not with Gen. DEARBORN that we have to do. We wish to confine the reply to the FACTS of the case. Our correspondent says that the wolf-story is *true*; that a man, when the Pomfret cave is full of dry leaves, *can* be drawn out with safety, as he himself has tested; that Gen. PUTNAM's horse, being 'well-trained and sagacious, *did* slide down the rocky steep of Horse-Neck on his haunches;' and what is of more importance, that Gen. PUTNAM *was* an active belligerent in the battle of Bunker-Hill, and was in fact the hero of the action. But he takes no notice of Gen. HEATH's statement that the gallant PRESCOTT was the commanding officer; nor of the evidence of the three clergymen and the judge of probate, who affirm that PRESCOTT never ceased to condemn Gen. PUTNAM for having kept his men back when their presence in the action might have changed the fate of the day. We wish only to advise the friends of Gen. PUTNAM what reputed facts it will be necessary for them *specifically* to refute, so that the controversy may be terminated in a single responsive communication. Col. TRUMBULL in his celebrated picture makes PUTNAM commander in the redoubt; but has he not since stated that he is now satisfied that the General had little or nothing to do with the battle? Distinguished generals, clergymen, judges, and officers of the church, we find sustaining this testimony, as heard by them personally from the lips of PRESCOTT himself; and this evidence we hope to see met, and if possible refuted, but not slurred over with mere denial. Col. HUMPHREYS himself makes no mention of the action of his hero in the battle, but speaks of his brave conduct in the retreat, halting at Winter-Hill, and driving the enemy back under cover of their ships. But even this the *editor* of HUMPHREYS' work afterward states was without foundation; that there was no pursuit beyond Bunker-Hill. It is admitted that PUTNAM was at the redoubt before the action commenced, and ordered the intrenching tools removed, but soon disappeared. We would have the reply which is to be prepared to what is here termed a 'puerile pop-squirt attack' made broad enough to cover the whole ground, and to take nothing for granted as true, which has such testimony against it as we have indicated. Our correspondent, for example, asks: 'Did not PUTNAM satisfy the expectation of WASHINGTON in *all* his military services?' To which we must certainly answer, '*No;*' and yet a month since we could not have gainsaid the implied fact. WASHINGTON's remarks against PUTNAM's taking command of our Highland posts we quoted in our 'Gossip' for the August number; and we have since discovered, in looking over the pages of the admirable life of ALEXANDER HAMILTON, by a son worthy of such a father, a passage from one of WASHINGTON's letters to Congress, concerning the evacuation of Red-Bank, after the fall of Fort Mifflin, which affords a still stronger reply to our correspondent's query. Gen. WASHINGTON mentions the movement of the enemy to Chestnut-Hill, and their sudden retreat, and expresses a regret that they had not come to an engagement. An obedience of HAMILTON's orders by PUTNAM must not only have saved the defences of the river, so long and gallantly maintained, but by enabling the Americans to take a strong position in the vicinity of Red-Bank, would have cut off the communication between the British army and fleet, and fulfilled WASHINGTON's well-known prophecy. Howe would have been reduced to the situation of Burgoyne, and the war would probably have been terminated in the second year of our independence. 'The conduct of PUTNAM on this occasion,' says HAMILTON, 'entered deeply into the breast of WASHINGTON; and in a letter from Valley Forge, some months after, he thus expresses himself in relation to the command at Rhode-Island: 'They also know, with more certainty than I do, what will be the determination of Congress respecting General PUTNAM; and of course whether the appointment of him to such a command as that at Rhode-Island would fall within their views; it being only incumbent on me to observe, that with such materials as I am furnished, *the work must go on;* whether well or ill, is another matter. If therefore he and others are not laid aside, *they must be placed where they can least injure the service.*' Thus it will be seen that in the proposed reply, assertion should be *fortified*, that a prolonged controversy, to which we cannot give place, may be avoided. It is needless for us to say — whose immediate ancestors were of the men whose souls and bodies were tried in the fires of our revolution — that we seek only THE TRUTH; and that we would shrink from disturbing the laurels of a brave American patriot, save justly to divide the honors with one equally brave, whose fame has been less cherished.

EDITOR'S DRAWER.—We retire in a good degree from our 'table,' with a satisfaction that will doubtless be shared by the reader, to make room for several guests whose seats have previously been occupied. Other friends, whom we are loath to place 'below the salt,' await their turn at our board.

WE give the following without being sure that we are quite aware of the writer's drift, which we have feared might have a personal bearing. We are advised, however, that it is 'intended to lash a small class of pretenders to mechanical science, who bring its exalted purposes into contempt, and confound its honored votaries with ignorant charlatans.' 'For the *true* mechanic,' says the writer, in his note to the Editor, 'I have a respect that amounts almost to reverence. With the Rouen carpenter, I ask: 'What have GOD's noblemen, MECHANICS, not done? Have they not opened the secret chambers of the deep, and extracted its treasures, and made the raging billows their highway, on which they ride as on a tame steed? Are not the elements of fire and water chained to the crank, and at the mechanic's bidding compelled to turn it? Have not mechanics opened the bowels of the earth, and made its products contribute to their wants? The forked lightning is their plaything, and they ride triumphant on the wings of the wind! To the wise they are the flood-gates of knowledge; kings and princes are decorated with their handiwork. HE who made the universe was a great Mechanic!' *Such* laborers are dishonored by association in the minds of any with that class whose prototype I enclose for your pages.'

HUMBUGEOUS 'MECHANICS.'

'THE science of Mechanics, Mr. EDITOR, is a noble one; and that it is so considered in most American communities, is evident from the fact, that those who have nothing else to do, emulous of its honors, are ever and anon spreading before the public, from their teeming brains, the crudest possible contrivances, which can never be reduced to any purpose of practical utility, and which derive their only claim to attention from the mystery which at first envelopes them, and their utter absurdity when understood. How many such schemes, from ignorant pretenders, have we seen broached in the newspapers within the present summer! I could point you, Mr. EDITOR, were the game worth the candle, to an inflated theoretical pseudo-mechanist, who 'from his seat in the country' has frequently of late favored the public with a view of his 'plans' and 'systems,' with no other result than to be temporarily wondered at by the ignorant, and ridiculed by men of intelligence. His vague and wordy communications are so *perfectly* represented by Professor MYSTIFIER, whose picture I find sketched to my hand by an English writer, that I cannot forbear sending it to you for insertion. The learned humbug, it will be understood, is giving an explanation of a few of his theorems connected with mechanical science; and he elucidates them in the following clear and felicitous manner: 'Mechanics,' he said, 'were founded upon that well-understood law of gravity which connected the Copernican system of botany with the invariable impetus given to the piston by means of domestic economy. If a lever were fixed in the Thames during the season for partridge-shooting, the result would be, that the mechanical action of the water would impede the centrifugal force of the capillary glands to be found in all well-seasoned wood. So that a steam-engine of forty-horse power could hardly counteract the combined force of a single-acting spinning-jenny. When a cylinder was so fixed as to present an entirely flat surface, the interstices of the safety-valve would expand with the refrigerating rays of the sun, and the caloric properties of the matter so introduced would of course harden the cogs of the wheels. Thus it would be easily perceived that the plane of the cylinder would be diametrically at right angles with the air-pump; which, not having power to evaporate, must necessarily create a vacuum. If this vacuum were examined with a microscope, it would be found to be filled with a stratum of globules, which caused the mist. This was the reason why pneumonic pumps would not act in the winter time. He however had discovered a simple remedy for restoring the action of the gasometer. The gasometer must not be pushed too forward during the motion of a stationary locomotive; for if so, the hinges of the self-acting apparatus, whether worked by steam or horse-power, would assuredly impinge themselves on the points of the rails, and there would be a danger of too strong a rotatory power in the boiler. He had discovered that this was the reason why steam-boilers burst. If anti-corrosive paint were used in forming the uprights of the beams of patent axletrees, the horses would be greatly relieved; for it was a well-known principle of mechanics, that no complete action could be given to turning-lathes, unless the height of each section of the hydraulic pumps exactly corresponded with the level of the sea. A diagram was here exhibited, by which it appeared that centrifugal force could only be imparted to fire-engines with the Archimedean screw, made upon the principle which Bolton and Watt applied to the diving-bell.' I am sure, Mr. EDITOR, that this lucid sketch will recall to the minds of your metropolitan readers several descriptions of a similar character, of matters equally clear and practical.'   J. T.

WE suppress the name and suburban *locals* of the author of the following lines, that we may quote the explanatory private note which accompanied them: 'The respected Editor of the KNICKERBOCKER may be assured that the enclosed ' *Stanzas to Memory*' are not to be considered the mere effort of a diseased imagination, a sickly fancy, or a capricious mind; but a true and unvarnished transcript of individual suffering, perhaps unequalled in the American world, and even now brought to a climax of distress, which obtains utterance in the enclosed lines.' Who alas! can estimate the bitterness of heart which finds vent (in a hand-writing that seems itself to stagger with distress) in aspirations like these:

STANZAS TO MEMORY.

THOU fixed tormentor of my lonely hours,
Hard MEMORY! with thought-contracted brow,
Hence all thy cormorant brood and giant powers!
Leave these sequestered, peace-devoted bowers,
And let the waters of oblivion flow!

Why must thy stony fingers still portray
Some banished comfort, never to return?
Why the racked soul at rude unkindness burn,
Dreaming that Pleasure smiled but one short day,
While crushed Affliction had whole years to mourn?

Or why recal the summer-seeking crow
Who with the sinking sun in clouds withdrew,
Pouring cold counsel on the suffering heart;
O'er the torn breast imbittered poisons threw,
Or flung with iron hand the secret dart.

Too faithful painter of each colored scene,
Hide thy full tablets from my aching sight!
Let Sleep's dark veil thy tortured victim screen
From the sharp radiance of their growing light,
And plunge each phantom in the deep of night!

Yet thy dread arm no fatal scourge uprears
From heartless deeds, or sacred laws profaned,
By no deep wound is the calm conscience pained,
Nor do thy wrongs extort these trembling tears,
This weight of sufferance, and this world of fears.

In vain mild Patience breathes her matin prayer,
Soothes the worn soul, and gives the heart to bear;
She cannot give one sacred tear to break
O'er the hard lines of Pride's averted cheek,
Nor light the dark cold bosom of Despair!

Let yon starved idiot yield his laugh to me,
And take this adamantine memory!
Or thou, lost victim of the moon's full beam,
Come! I resign weak reason's transient gleam
For the blest transport of the maniac's dream!

But fly, thou traitor, with thine arrowy hand!
No longer pierce this desolated breast,
Since by thy side thy great Destroyer stands,
(Of grief the refuge and of toil the rest,)
Spreads his long arms, and bares his hollow chest!

Hope of the wretched ! solace of the good !
To peace and bliss, and fame the only road,
Healer of wrongs ! kind source of rectitude !
Lorn ' Misery's love ! '   I woo thee to my arms,
Inhale thy earthy breath, and claim, with muse of fire,
    Thy frozen charms !

LOOKING once more over a ' Fox Story,' for which we were some months since indebted to a new correspondent, and which we had laid aside on a first perusal, fancying it to be a tale of mystery, written after the model of MATTHEWS' celebrated Scotch anecdote, we have been struck with the annexed characteristic illustration of the sly nature of Reynard.   The writer it should be premised is ' sitting on a rail ' fence that encloses a country church-yard, rapt in meditation :

' IN this mood I was gazing upon the grave-yard, when one of the ghostly shapes I had conjured up seemed gradually to lose its ethereal nature, and to assume a sort of furtive locomotion ; and the form of one of the ' brutes that perish,' the figure of a fox, moved among the tomb-stones.   The apparition startled me from my communion with phantoms.   It *was* a fox, and my romance was over.   I had long cherished an ambition to kill a fox ; and I betook myself forthwith to the house for a rifle, determined to ' do death ' upon the sacrilegious trespasser.   He was still wandering among the tombs when I returned, slowly and desultorily, and appeared at a distance as if he might be reading the inscriptions, and musing upon the uncertainty of life.   He moved away, however, at my approach, but with great deliberation, trying to look as if he did not see me, but was retiring of his own accord.   I passed around the hill to cut off his retreat, and succeeded ; but he kept warily out of gun-shot, upon the opposite side.   In this way he lured me on to chase him for half an hour, around the hill, over to the next one, and back again ; but never going far from the grave-yard.   Vexed and excited as I was, I could not help wondering at his singular fancy to be near the church-yard.   His managing to keep out of my reach was not so surprising.   It was ' the nature of the beast.'   But his cool indifferent *manner* had its usual effect upon a man in a passion.   He did not move fast, but seemed only desirous to avoid having any thing to do with me ; like a gentleman upon whom a bully is trying to force a quarrel.   At last, however, seeing me bent upon proceeding to extremities, he retired among the graves, and seemed to be expecting me with the calm and settled resignation of one who feels conscious of having done all that his duty demanded to avoid a rencontre.   I approached cautiously to within reasonable distance, levelled my piece upon an intervening fence, and fired.   He was sitting quietly upon a grave-side at the time, but he moved not.   He was dead.   Gratified beyond measure at my success, I ran hastily up to the spot.   The body retained its sitting position, with the head reclining upon the tomb-stone, with that placid expression of features which distinguishes those who die of gun-shot wounds.   I looked to see where I had struck him.   No blood appeared to have been shed.   He had bled inwardly, perhaps.   I examined him more closely.   It was very strange !   I could find no mark of violence.   It was *very* singular !   But there must be a ball somewhere.   At last I discovered fresh marks of violence upon the nose of a sculptured cherub that adorned a grave-stone some six feet from where the animal lay.   Searching, I found the ball ; flattened, with evident traces of the stone, but without the slightest ' mark of the beast ' upon it !   ' Now what,' said I, ' could have killed the fox ?   Did he die of fright ? '   I leaned upon my rifle, in great perplexity ; looking alternately upon the fox, the flattened ball, and the disfigured countenance of the cherub upon the tomb-stone.   It was barely possible that the animal was dead before I killed him : he fell, a victim perhaps of some honest disease, or of old age.   And thus I speculated.   But reader, *what killed that fox ?* '

THIS seems an appropriate occasion to gratify the wishes of a correspondent who regrets that our hurried and imperfect ' notice of poor POWER ' did not include a reminiscence of his admirable manner in the capital play of ' *Rory O'More*, and especially in the third act.'   We cannot better fill the hiatus complained of, than by endeavoring to present in this connexion the fox-story which Rory relates to the credulous ' Devilskin,' as he terms De Welskin, the French smuggler, whose attention he is beguiling while he matures an Irish plan of escape from the subterranean retreat into which he has been inveigled :

' AN Irish fox, Mounseer Devilskin,' says he, ' would sthrip a French fox of his skin, and sell it before his face, and th' other not know it !   You do n't know, Mounseer, what divils thim Irish foxes is. D' ever you hear of the fox of Ballybotherum? Oh, *that* was the fox in airnest! Divil such a fox ever was, before nor sence, as that same fox; and the thing I 'm going to tell you happened to a relation of mine, one Mickee Rooney, that was a ranger in the service of the Lord-knows-who, a great lord in them parts. Mickee lived in a small taste of a cabin, beside the wood, all alone by himself, barrin' the dogs that was his companions.' 'De daugs!' exclaims the smuggler. 'Yes, *de daugs;*' himself and the dogs was the only christians in the place; and one night, when he kem home, wet and wairy wid the day's sport, he sot down beside the fire, just as we 're sittin' here, and begun smoking his pipe to warm himself; and when he tuk an air o' the fire, he thought he 'd go to bed; not to sleep, you persaive, but to rest himself, like; so he took off his clothes and hung them to dhry forninst the fire, and then he went to bed, and an illigant bed it was; the finest shafe o' sthraw you ever seen, lyin' over in the corner as it might be there;' (and here Rory points to the place where several kegs of gunpowder are stowed;) 'and as he was lyin' in bed, thinkin' o' nothin' at all, and divartin' himself with lookin' at the smoke curlin' up out o' the fire, what should he see but the door open, and a fox march into the place, just as bowld as if the house was his own; an' he went over and sot down on his hunkers forninst the fire, and begun to warm his hands like a christian; it's thruth I 'm tellin' you.' 'Bah!' interrupts De Welskin; 'staup! Sair, staup! Vere vas de daugs all dis time, eh!' 'The dogs?' says Rory; 'oh, the dogs it is? Oh, I did 'nt tell you that! Oh, sure the dogs was runnin' about the wood at the time, ketchin rabbits; for the fox was listenin', you see, outside the door, and heer'd the ranger tell the dogs to go and ketch him a brace o' rabbits for his supper; for I go bail if the fox did n't know the dogs was out o' the place, the divil a toe he 'd put inside the ranger's house; and that shows you the cunnin' o' the baste. Well, as he was sittin' at the fire, what do you think, but he tuk the ranger's pipe off the hob, an' lights it in the fire, and begins to smoke, as nath'ral as any other man you ever seen.' 'Smoke! — de faux smoke!' — sneers the smuggler. 'Oh, yes!' replies Rory; 'all the Irish foxes smoke when they can get bakky; and they are mighty fond o' short-cut when the dogs is afther them! Well, Mounseer, the ranger could hardly keep his timper at all when he seen the baste smokin' his pipe; and with that, says he, 'It 's fire and smoke of another kind I 'll give you, my buck,' says he, takin' up his gun, to shoot him; but the fox had put the gun into a pail o' wather, and of coorse the divil a fire the gun would fire for the ranger. And the fox put his finger on his nose, just that-a-way, and laughed at him. 'Wow! wow!' says the fox, puttin' out his hand and takin' up the newspaper to read.' 'Ha! ha! — sacre! De newspaper!' exclaims 'Divilskin: ' 'de faux read de newspaper!! No, no! my boy!' 'Why man alive!' interrupts the ready hoaxer, 'how would the fox know where the hounds was to meet next mornin' if he did n't read the paper? Sure that shows you the cunnin' o' the baste! Well with that, the ranger puts his fingers to his mouth, and gives a blast of a fwistle you 'd hear a mile off, for to call the dogs. 'Oh! is it for fwistlin' you are?' says the fox; 'then it is time for me to lave the place,' says he, 'for 't would not be good for my health to be here when the dogs come back.' So he lays down the pipe in the hob; but, before he did, I must tell you he wiped it with the end of his tail; for he was a dacent baste, and used his tail as nath'ral as a christian would use the sleeve of his coat for a cowld in his nose; and then he was goin' to start; but the ranger seein' him goin' to escape, jumps out o' the bed and gets betune him and the door, and 'Divil a start you 'll start,' says he, 'till the dogs come back, you red rascal, and I 'll have your head in my fist before long,' says he, 'and that 's worth a pound to me.' 'I 'll hould you a quart o' porther,' says the fox, 'I 'll make you leave that.' 'Divil a lave,' says the ranger. 'Wow, wow!' says the fox, 'I 'm a match for you yet;' and what do you think, but he whips the ranger's breeches off the back of the chair, and throws them into the fire; and he knew the divil another pair the ranger had to his back! 'That 'll make you start,' says the fox. 'Divil a start,' says the ranger; 'my breeches is worth half a crown, and your head 's worth a pound, so I 'll make seventeen and sixpence by the exchange.' 'Well, you 're the stupidest vagabond I ever met,' says the fox, 'and I 'll make you sensible at last that you must let me go, for I 'll burn you out o' house and home,' says he; and wid that he takes up a piece o' lighted stick like this,' (and here Rory takes a burning brand from the smuggler's fire at which they are sitting,) 'and runs over to the ranger's bed in the corner.'

Upon this, as all who have ever seen the play will remember, Rory upsets De Welskin, and runs to the gun-powder. The smugglers and their chief exclaim, 'Gun-powder! gun-powder!' and retreat to the opposite corner of the cavern; but Rory stamps his heels through one of the kegs, upsets it, and the powder falls out; while he stands in an attitude of triumph upon it, and roars out: ''Wow wow!' says the fox!' — this is the match for you; a lighted stick and a barrel o' gunpowther! See, Divilskin! get into that room there,' pointing to a grated door, 'all of ye; lock yourselves up, and bring me the key, or I 'll blow you all to the Ould

Nick, your relation!' The smugglers comply with Rory's direction, save in the last Irish clause; the locking in and bringing the key being necessarily confided to other hands. The mere *reader*, who may not be counted among the tens of thousands who once heard the lamented POWER in this character, will find it difficult perhaps to appreciate the rich burlesque which characterizes this ludicrous story in the hands of Rory O'More; but all who have seen the play represented on the stage will thank us for recalling to their minds a scene which in its inception, progress, and dénouement, was not less effective than the best in which POWER won the universal suffrages of American theatre-goers.

THERE is a class of synonyms in English, which deserve more attention than has usually been paid to them. We refer to words which were once identically the same, and which of course present the same etymology, but which by usage have now acquired a difference of signification. The nature and causes of such difference are well explained by a correspondent in the examples which follow :

ENGLISH SYNONYMS.

1. BALM: Heb. *basâm*; Arab. *balsâm*; Gr. βάλσαμον; Lat. *balsamum*; Ital., Span., and Portug. *balsamo*; Fr. *baulme* and *baume*: in several popular acceptations : 1. the name of a fragrant tree or shrub; 11. its juice or sap; 111. any fragrant ointment; and 1v. whatever mitigates pain.
BALSAM: immediately from the Greek and Latin, in more definite scientific acceptations: 1. the name of a plant producing an unctuous resin; and 11. the unctuous resin.
2. BASE: Gr. βάσις; Lat. *basis*; Ital. and Span. *base* and *basa*; Portug. and Fr. *base*: the bottom or foundation in various physical and technical senses.
BASIS: immediately from the Greek and Latin. 1. in the same acceptations as *base*; and 11. in a more refined metaphorical sense, as the *basis* of all excellence is truth. NOTE. In other cases, these redundant forms are used without any difference of signification: as, *ellipsis* and *ellipse*; *periphrasis* and *periphrase*; *phasis* and *phase*.
3. CAPTIVE: Lat. *captivus*; Provenç. *caitiu*; Ital. *cattivo*; Span. *cautivo*; Portug. *cativo*; Fr. *captif*; fem. *captive*: made prisoner, enslaved.
CAITIFF: Fr. *chaitif* and *chetif*: vile, roguish; immediately from the Ital. *cattivo*, a rascal, villain.
4. CORD: Gr. χορδ,'; Lat. *chorda*; Ital. *corda*; Span. *cuerda*; Portug. *corda*; Fr. *corde*; a string or small rope; also a quantity of wood originally measured with a cord.
CHORD: immediately from the Greek and Latin; the string of a musical instrument; also a technical term in music and in geometry.
5. COMPLEMENT: Lat. *complementum*; Ital., Span., and Portug., *complemento*; Fr. *complement*; fullness, or that which fills up.
COMPLIMENT: Ital. *complimento*; Span. *cumplimiento*; Portug. *comprimento*; Fr. *compliment*; also from the Lat. *complementum*, an expression of civility.
6. CUSTOM: Lat. *consuetudo*, gen. *-inis*; Provenç. *cosdumna* and *costuma*; Ital. *consuetudine* and *costume*; Span. *consuetud* and *costumbre*; Portug. *costume*; Fr. *coustume* and *coutume*: habit, usage.
COSTUME: Fr. *costume*; from the Ital. *costume*, a technical term in painting, for mode of dress, etc.
7. FLOWER: Lat. *flos*, gen. *floris*; Ital. *fiore*; Span. and Portug. *flor*; Fr. *fleur*: a blossom.
FLOUR: from the same Latin and French words; the edible part of corn, or the finest part of grain pulverized.
8. FLOURISH: Lat. *floresco*; Ital. *fiorire*, pres. *fiorisco*; Span. and Portug. *florecer*; Fr. *florir* and *fleuvir*, gen. *florissant* and *fleurissant*: to thrive.
FLORESCE: in *florescence*, *effloresce*, *inflorescence*: immediately from the Latin; used in a peculiar botanical, chemical, or medical sense.
9. GATE: Germ. *gat*; Anglo-Sax. *geat* or *gat*; from *ga*, to go: a way, passage.
GAIT: merely a different orthography for *gate*, a manner of walking.
10. GENTLE: Lat. *gentilis*; Ital. *gentile*; Span., Portug., and Fr. *gentil*: well born, mild.
GENTEEL: with French accent; well bred, polite, graceful.
GENTILE: immediately from the Latin; in an ecclesiastical sense, a heathen, pagan.
11. GRACE: in *graceful*; Lat. *gratia*; Ital. *grazia*; Span. *gracia*; Portug. *graça*; Fr. *grace*: elegance, dignity.

GRATE: in *grateful*; more resembling the Latin, gratitude.

12. HUMAN: Lat. *humanus*; Ital. *umano*; Span. and Portug. *humano*; Fr. *humain*: relating to man.

HUMANE: with French accent; kind, tender.

13. HYPERBOLE: Gr. ὑπερβολή; Lat. *hyperbola*; Ital. *iperpola*; Span. *hiperbole*; Portug. *hyperbole*; Fr. *hyperbole*: the name of a rhetorical figure.

HYPERBOLA: Span. *hiperbola*, with Latin termination; the name of a conic section.

14. LOYAL: Lat. *legalis*; Ital. *leale*; Span. and Portug. *leal*; Fr. *loyal*: faithful to a prince or superior.

LEGAL: Span. Portug. and Fr. *legal*: immediately from the Latin; relating to or according to law.

15. NOT: compounded of *ne*, not, and *aught*, any thing; comp. old Germ. *niowiht*, compounded of *ni* and *iowiht*; Anglo-Sax. *nawiht*, compounded of *ne* and *awiht*: a word expressing negation, denial, or refusal.

NAUGHT or NOUGHT: retaining more of its etymological signification; I. nothing; II. of no worth, worthless.

16. NATIVITY: Lat. *nativitas*; Ital. *nativita*; Span. *natividad*; Portug. *natividade*: Fr. *nativité*: birth.

NAIVETE: Fr. *naiveté*; also from the Latin *nativitas*: natural simplicity, naturalness.

17. OF: Sansc. *apa*; Gr. ἀπό; Lat. *ab*; Goth. *af*; Anglo-Sax. *of*: a preposition denoting from, or out of.

OFF: the same word used as an adverb.

18. ONE: Gr. εἷς, γία, ἕν; Lat. *unus*; Goth. *ains*; Germ. *ein*; Anglo-Sax. *an*: single in number.

AN or A: the same word feebly enounced or accented, to enable the stress or force to fall on the following word, thus becoming what is usually called the indefinite article.

19. ORAISON or ORISON; Lat. *oratio*; Ital. *orazione*; Span. *orazion*; Span. *oracion*; Portug. *oraçaõ*; Fr. *oraison*: a prayer.

ORATION: immediately from the Latin; a public discourse.

20. PARABLE: Gr. παραβολή: Lat., Ital., Span., and Portug., *parabola*; Fr. *parabole*: a continued metaphor in the form of a narrative.

PARABOLE: the same word less perfectly Anglicized; a similitude, comparison.

PARABOLA: with Latin termination; the name of a conic section.

21. PENITENCE: Lat. *pœnitentia*; Ital. *penitenza*; Span. and Portug. *penitencia*; Fr. *penitence*: repentance.

PENANCE: from the same Latin and French words; pain voluntarily undergone for sin.

22. PIETY: Lat. *pietas*; Ital. *pieta* and *pietade*; Span. *piedad*; Portug. *piedade*; Fr. *pieté*: affection, devotion.

PITY: Fr. *pitié*: also from the Latin *pietas*: compassion, sympathy.

23. PLAINTIVE: Fr. *plaintif*, fem. *plaintive*; from Lat. *plango*: lamenting.

PLAINTIF: from the same Latin and French words; one who commences a suit in law.

24. ROYAL: Lat. *regalis*; Ital. *regale* and *reale*: Span. and Portug. *real*; Fr. *royal*: relating to a king; also magnificent.

REGAL: Fr. *regale*; immediately from the Latin; relating to a king.

REGALE: with French accent; the prerogative of monarchy.

REAL or RIAL: Fr. *reale*; from the Span. *real*: the name of a Spanish coin.

25. SEIGNIOR: Lat. *senior*; Ital. *signore*; Span. *señor*; Portug. *senhor*; Fr. *seigneur*: a lord.

SENIOR: immediately from the Latin; older.

26. STRAIT: Lat. *strictus*; Ital. *stretto*; Span. *estreecho*; Portug. *estreito*; Fr. *étroit*: narrow, close.

STRAIGHT: merely a different orthography for *strait*, direct.

STRICT: immediately from the Latin; rigid, severe.

27. SURFACE: Lat. *superficies*; Ital., Span., and Portug., *superficie*; Fr. *surface*: the exterior part of any thing.

SUPERFICE or SUPERFICIES: Fr. *superficies*: immediately from the Latin, used in a more exact and scientific sense.

28. THAT: Sansc. and Zend *tat*; Gr. τό for τύτ; Lat. *tud* in *istud*; Goth. *thata*; Germ. *das*; Anglo-Sax. *that*: a demonstrative pronoun.

THE: the same word feebly enounced or accented, to enable the stress or force to fall on the following word, thus becoming what is usually called the definite article.

29. TO: Lat. *ad*; Goth. *du*; Germ. *zu*; Anglo-Sax. *to*: having various uses; I. as a preposition with its case; II. as the sign of the infinitive mode; III. as an adverb with meanings corresponding to the preposition; and IV. in the phrase *to and fro*.

TOO: old Eng. *to*: the same word employed, I. as an adverb, denoting excess; and II. as a conjunction; also, likewise.

RECORDS like the following we are always well pleased to preserve in these pages; and the writer has our thanks for his considerate attention. His non-resistant progenitor reminds us of a kindred non-combatant, of the city of Brotherly Love, who during the excitement which several years since divided the Society of Friends into two hostile parties, mounted the archway that admitted entrance to a grave-yard which was in litigation between the Legitimates and Seceders, and when the 'adverse faction' attempted to pass to bury their dead, liberated a brick or two from under his feet upon the heads of those below, accompanied with a word of advice to the most persevering, something to this effect: 'Friend THOMAS, I think thee had better stand from under the gate-way, or peradventure some of these bricks may fall upon thy head! Look out Thomas!' — and down toppled the non-resistant missiles :

UNWRITTEN HISTORY.

'THERE are incidents in unwritten history which by frequent repetition as anecdotes lose their historical character. This rarely fails to be the case, if the incident has been made use of by some novelist, to weave into the light web of romance. Such an incident I wish to redeem from the province of fiction, and place it where it properly belongs, with history.

'It is perhaps not generally known, even by the reading public, that the celebrated ADMIRAL WAGER of the British navy, when a boy, was bound apprentice to a Quaker by the name of JOHN HULL, who sailed a vessel between Newport (Rhode Island) and London; and in whose service he probably learned the rudiments of that nautical skill, as well as that upright honor and integrity, for which he is so much lauded by his biographer. The circumstance of running his master's vessel over a privateer first recommended him to an advantageous place in the British navy. The facts of this encounter, as near as I can gather them, are these : The pirate was a small schooner, full of men, and was about boarding the ship of Captain HULL, whose religious scruples prevented him from taking any measures of a hostile nature. After much persuasion from young WAGER, the peaceable captain retired to his cabin, and gave the command of his ship to his apprentice. His anxiety however induced him to look out from the companion-way, and occasionally give directions to the boy, who he perceived designed to run over the pirate; saying to him : '*Charles, if thee intends to run over that schooner, thee must put the helm a little more to the starboard!*' The ship passed directly over the schooner, which instantly sunk, with every soul on board.

'The Admiral appears in after life to have borne a grateful remembrance of his former master, to whom he sent occasionally a pipe of wine. Letters advising of the shipment of the wine are still preserved in the family. On one occasion when the Admiral was in Newport, Captain HULL called at the coffee-house to see his former apprentice; and observing a lieutenant there, asked him 'where is CHARLES?'' At which the lieutenant took umbrage, and threatened to chastise the old Quaker for his insolence, in not speaking more respectfully of his Admiral. When WAGER heard of it, he took occasion to reprove the lieutenant, before Captain HULL, saying, 'Mr. HULL, Sir, is my honored master.'

'JOHN HULL died at Conanicut, on the first day of December, 1732, aged seventy-eight years.' H.

A FRIEND writing from Rome, in just such a gossiping epistle as we delight to receive, has recorded two or three passages which we have thought would not be without interest to our readers. 'The second week after our arrival,' says he, 'a grand ceremony took place at St. Peters. To an American eye, it was imposing enough. It was the ceremony of blessing the holy candles; and the whole power and wealth of the Pope were in requisition for the occasion. His Holiness, borne upon the shoulders of four persons, passed within a few feet of me, and I had a good opportunity to see him. He seems about sixty years of age, and is rather hale and good-looking. I wish you could have stood with me, as the procession of cardinals, bishops, and priests, dressed in richest state, swept gorgeously by; attended by plumed troops, and followed by foreign noblemen, strangers, noble and beautiful ladies, etc., etc., all robed in costly apparel, brightening and flashing in the sun of

Rome! An American friend at my elbow said he had 'seen a handsomer procession in Louisville.' He has caught the *nil admirari* of the English, and vows that Kentucky is worth all Italy, 'including Rome and Vesuvius!' It must have been him, I fancy, who admitted, while standing upon St. Pauls in London, and looking around upon a forty-mile circumference of brick and mortar, that 'it *was* a pretty fair village — rather thickly-settled here about the meeting-house!' · · · 'Did E —— write you about passing himself off for *Lord Yankeedoodle* to the time-serving, sychophantic beggars, near one of the Italian towns through which he passed? They actually took the horses out, and dragged the carriage which contained him and his friends into the city; but the 'lord' had to pay after the English fashion for his thoughtless imitation of 'Signor G — D D — N,' as the surly London tourists are called in Italy. It was a good joke, and well kept up.' · · · 'I heard LISZT perform twice at Hamburgh. No praise can be too extravagant, when applied to him. I remember thinking, while reading the admirable description given of him by your correspondent, Mr. WATERS, that it was 'too good to be true;' but not so. I believe he would depict the Falls of Niagara, and set its solemn under-tones to music, in his matchless mastery of an instrument which I really never *heard* before. A plaintive passage from BELLINI made me moan all night, from sheer sympathy. · · · By the way, 'speaking of Bellini:' I saw at Dresden the house where the original 'Somnambulist,' contrary to the operatic version of the story, met her melancholy fate. It seems that very early one morning a female was seen walking on the roof of one of the loftiest houses in the city, apparently occupied in some ornamental needle-work. The house stood as it were alone, being much higher than those adjoining it, and to draw her from her perilous situation was impossible. Thousands of spectators had assembled in the streets. It was discovered to be a beautiful girl, nineteen years of age, the daughter of a master-baker, possessing a small independence, bequeathed to her by her mother. She continued her terrific promenade for hours, at times sitting on the parapet, and dressing her hair. The police came to the spot, and various means of preservation were resorted to. In a few minutes the streets were thickly strown with straw, and beds were called for from the house; but the heartless father, influenced by the girl's step-mother, refused them. Nets were suspended from the balcony of the first floor, and the neighbors fastened sheets to their windows. All this time the poor girl was walking in perfect unconsciousness, sometimes gazing toward the moon, and at others singing or talking to herself. Some persons succeeded in getting on the roof, but dared not approach her for fear of the consequences if they awoke her. Toward eleven o'clock, she approached the very verge of the parapet, leaned forward, and gazed upon the multitude beneath. Every one felt that the moment of the catastrophe had arrived. She rose up, however, and returned calmly to the window by which she had got out. When she saw there were votive lights in the room, she uttered a piercing shriek, which was reëchoed by thousands below, and fell dead into the street.' · · · 'There are a good many American artists in Rome, and they are revelling in the treasures of art with which it abounds. Here have been or are CRAWFORD, DURAND, CASILEAR, TERRY, WAUGH, and others, mingling socially and pleasantly together, once a-week at least, in a Saturday evening reunion at the American consul's. *Apropos* of consul GREENE. He is preparing, he informs me, a series of '*Letters from Rome*' for the KNICKERBOCKER, in which I venture to say you will find vivid descriptions of *aspects* and *results*, instead of reasoning and conjectures. No American has ever painted Rome as Mr. GREENE will be able to paint it; and this your readers will discover.'

'THE POET'S ORIGINAL.'—We spake in our last of the interest which in general attaches to the original 'study' of a writer who has transcribed his limnings directly from nature. Standing lately upon the Heights at Brooklyn, with the gay gardens that sprinkle her midst, and verdant fields and woodlands in the back-ground, and before us the glorious panorama of our noble metropolis, with its peerless bay and harbor, and undulating coast, we remembered anew that here it was once stood *one*, (and reader, it seemed to us that he stood there *then*,) and while we talked together, with the city's voice rising in a subdued murmur from below, sketched the following scene :

'Who that hath stood, where summer brightly lay
On some broad city, by a spreading bay,
And from a rural height the scene survey'd,
While on the distant strand the billows play'd,
But felt the vital spirit of the scene,
What time the south wind stray'd thro' foliage green,
And freshened from the dancing waves, went on,
By the gay groves, and fields, and gardens won ?
Oh, who that listens to the inspiring sound,
Which the wide Ocean wakes against his bound,
While, like some fading hope, the distant sail,
Flits o'er the dim blue waters, in the gale ;
When the tired sea-bird dips his wings in foam,
And hies him to his beetling eyry home ;
When sun-gilt ships are parting from the strand,
And glittering streamers by the breeze are fanned ;
When the wide city's domes and piles aspire,
And rivers broad seemed touch'd with golden fire ;
Save where some gliding boat their lustre breaks,
And volumed smoke its murky tower forsakes,
And surging in dark masses, soars to lie,
And stain the glory of the uplifted sky ;
Oh, who at such a scene unmoved hath stood,
And gazed on town, and plain, and field, and flood—
Nor felt that life's keen spirit lingered there,
Through earth, and ocean, and the genial air ?'

Looking over the original sketch of '*The Spirit of Life*,' by the late WILLIS GAYLORD CLARK, from which the above passage is taken, we find that portion of the MS. which touches upon Autumn much more elaborate than in the printed version. But who loved this sad and solemn season like the Departed ? Whose eye surveyed the many-colored woods, the pomp of autumnal clouds, pavilioning the setting sun, with a more overflowing fulness of calm delight ? Whose ear drank in the plaintive voice of fall-blasts with more 'joyful sadness ?' But that eye is dim, which looked abroad upon decaying nature, and that accurate sense of sound is now but the 'dull, cold ear of death !' Yet are the gorgeous hues of Autumn around us, and the wail of expiring Summer resounds through the fading woods. Solemn monition ! But let us, like him whom we mourn, in another passage of the poem from which we have quoted, regard aright the season and its lessons :

'Change is the life of Nature ;' and the hour
When storm and blight reveal lone autumn's pow'r ;
When damask leaves to swollen streams are cast,
Borne on the funeral anthems of the blast ;
When smit with pestilence the woodlands seem,
Yet gorgeous as a Persian poet's dream ;
That hour that the seeds of life within it bears,
Tho' fraught with perished blooms and sobbing airs ;
Though solemn companies of clouds may rest
Along the uncheer'd and melancholy west ;
Though there no more the enthusiast may behold
Effulgent troops, arrayed in purple and gold ;
Or mark the quivering lines of light aspire,
Where crimson shapes are bathed in living fire ;
Though Nature's withered breast no more be fair,
Nor happy voices fluctuate in the air ;
Yet is there life in Autumn's sad domains—
Life, strong and quenchless, thro' his kingdom reigns.
To kindred dust the leaves and flowers return,
Yet briefly sleep in winter's icy urn ;
Tho' o'er their graves in blended wreaths repose
Dim wastes of dreary and untrodden snows—
Though the aspiring hills rise cold and pale
To breast the murmurs of the northern gale ;

Yet, when the jocund spring again comes on,
Their trance is broken, and their slumber done ;
Awakening Nature re-asserts her reign,
And her kind bosom throbs with life again !

. . . . . .

'T is thus with man. He cometh, like the flow'r,
To feel the changes of each earthly hour ;
To enjoy the sunshine, or endure the shade,
By hopes deluded, or by reason sway'd ;
Yet haply, if to Virtue's path he turn,
And feel her hallowed fires within him burn,
He passeth calmly from that sunny morn,
Where all the buds of youth are 'newly born,'
Through varying intervals of onward years,
Until the eve of his decline appears :
And while the shadows round his path descend,
As down the vale of age his footsteps tend,
Peace o'er his bosom sheds her soft control,
And throngs of gentlest memories charm the soul ;
Then, weaned from earth, he turns his steadfast eye
Beyond the grave, whose verge he falters nigh ;
Surveys the brightening regions of the blest,
And, like a wearied pilgrim, sinks to rest.'

Let those, reader, who mourn the loved and lost, remind you that the solemn influences of this 'sweet Sabbath of the Year' may be made fruitful of good;

awakening anew remembrances of our frail mortality; bringing home to careless bosoms the thought, that 'Death is continually walking his tireless rounds, and sooner or later stops at every man's door.' Truly says the eloquent GREENWOOD, 'you cannot raise your eyes, but you look upon the dying; you cannot move, but you step upon the dead. Leaves and flowers are returning to the dust; can you forbear thinking, that in this universal destiny they are like yourself? Dust *thou* art, and unto dust thou shalt return. Can you forbear thinking that the successive generations of men, like the successive generations of leaves and flowers, have been cut off by the death-frost, and mingled with common earth? And are not individual names whispered to your memory by the dying fragrance, and the rustling sounds; names of those who flourished, faded, and fell in your sight? Perhaps you think of the fair infant, who, like the last tender leaf put forth by a plant, was not spared for its tenderness, but compelled to drop like the rest. Perhaps your thoughts dwell on the young man, who, full of vigor and hope, verdant in fresh affections, generous purposes, and high promise, and bearing to you some name which means more to the heart than to the ear, friend, brother, son, husband — was chilled in a night, and fell from the tree of life. Or perhaps there rises up before you the form of the maiden, delicate as the flower, and as fragile also, who was breathed upon by that mysterious wind, lost the hues of health, and though nursed and watched with unremitting care, could not be preserved, but faded away. You are not alone in the brown woods, though no living being is near you. Thin and dim shades come round you — stand with you among the withered grass — walk with you in the leaf-strewn path. Forms of the loved, shades of the lost, mind-created images of those who have taken their place with the leaves and flowers of the past summer — they speak not, they make no sound; but how surely do they bear witness to the words of the apostle and the prophet, till you hear their burden in every breeze — the spontaneous dirge of nature. 'The grass withereth, the flower fadeth,' is the annually repeated strain from the fields and woods; and man's heart replies, 'All flesh is grass, and the goodliness thereof is as the flower of the field.' The listening Psalmist heard the same theme and the same response, and he too has repeated and recorded them. 'As for man, his days are as grass; as a flower of the field, so he flourisheth; for the wind passeth over it and it is gone, and the place thereof shall know it no more.' · · · Oh bond unbroken between Nature's fairest children and ourselves! who is not conscious of its reality and its force! Oh primitive brotherhood between herbs and blossoms and the sons of men; between the green things which spring up and then wither, and the bright things which unfold and then fade; between these and the countenances which bloom and then change, eyes which sparkle and then are quenched, breathing and blessed forms which appear in loveliness and then are gone! who does not acknowledge its claims of kindred? 'Surely, we *are* but the grass of the field, which to-day is, and to-morrow is cast into the oven!'

MUSICAL INSTRUCTION. — Miss BLUNDELL, who has been mentioned heretofore in terms of praise in the KNICKERBOCKER, we are glad to learn meets with the amplest patronage from our most eminent citizens. We allude to her fine acquirements here only to say, that in addition to the piano-forte she now gives instruction on the guitar, and to express our admiration of her musical compositions, two or three specimens of which are in course of publication by Mr. ATWILL in Broadway.

GOSSIP WITH READERS AND CORRESPONDENTS. — Our warm acknowledgments are due to ' R. M. C.' for his touching and beautiful lines. We *feel* and are deeply grateful for his kind sympathy. · · · ' F.'s ' ' *Translation from the German* ' is not well chosen, although it may be as ' faithful ' as he believes it. It is one of those passages of the German mind in which, whether owing to the beer or the tobacco, there is something so vague, cloudy, and floating, that it would be ' caviare ' to American readers. It would suit the ' English Opium-Eater,' who tells us that after a thousand drops of the precious narcotic, he could even read KANT, and understand him ; or *fancy* he could, which was perhaps as well. · · · We do not remember to have received the ' *Loves of the Birds.*' If we did, it has gone to the vast region of *somewhere*, and is quite beyond the reach of our hand. · · · ' *My First Gong* ' has good points, but it is ' *written to death.*' Why *will* correspondents be so prolix ? Interest is thus frittered away, and curiosity killed outright. The three foolscap pages of our contributor do not after all express so much as three lines of an English Magazine writer, who, speaking of the noise of the gong, says : ' It sent up a sound as if it sold thunder by retail, and was now putting up a sixpence worth ! ' · · · The lines on ' *Crossing Lake Superior by Moonlight*,' in preceding pages, will attract attention. They are from a MS. poem, portions of which we have been permitted to read ; and if, when it shall appear entire, it does not find favor with the public, we shall have small confidence thereafter in our literary judgment. But, to employ a very novel phrase, *Nous Verrons.* · · · Our position that the Chinese edicts were *inimitable*, is not weakened, but rather strengthened by the labored effort of '*Philo-Lin.*' Let the writer run his eye over the last imperial mandates received from China. They are in *terms* unlike their predecessors, but how *infinitely* Chinese ! ' It is reported that on the sixth day the Tiger's Gate was laid in ruins : now this intelligence has *riven my very heart and liver !* The English barbarians, also, taking occasion to enter far into the river with large forces, have advanced upon and attacked Woochung, near to Whampoa, wounding our great generals, and slaying our troops. Such wickedness and guilt as this it would be most difficult indeed for the waves of the ocean to wash out ! I, the Emperor, have therefore specially summoned my imperial younger brother Meenfang, together with the high minister Hoo, to lead forth a grand army fifty thousand strong, and by journeying day and night, to repair to Canton with all haste ; and let the vengeance of Heaven be exhibited by not allowing a single English sail to return, but sweeping them clean from the face of the seas (shade of VAN TROMP !) in order to fill my imperial mind with gratification. I will most peremptorily make an entire end of the *whole* of them, not allowing one barbarian to escape back to his country. KESHEN, having received bribes, and hired troops not to fight, I order that he forthwith be *cut in sunder at the waist!* Decidedly these are the dreadful orders ! ' Does Philo-Lin fancy this style can be imitated without the feeling that dictated it ? Decidedly not. A confirmed opinion. Respect it. · · · Our correspondent ' *Democritus* ' says that he agrees with FRANKLIN, that a ' laugh is better than a groan, in any state of the market ; ' and begs, if we are of opinion with himself that ' an inch of mirth is worth an ell of moan,' that his passage may be committed to the public. ' Man,' says he, ' is the only animal that can laugh. To laugh is one of the prerogatives of his nature. After a hearty laugh, he feels better ; he *is* better ; more sociable, more friendly, more humane, more courteous, more benevolent ; has a better appetite, requires less physic, sleeps more sweetly, and has better dreams. ' Laugh and be fat,' says the old adage. I never knew a fat man that was a melancholy one, nor a dyspeptic that was not. Melancholy is not only a consequence, it is often a cause of disease. A laugh gives exercise to a part of our system that requires it as much as any other, and yet that can get it in no other way. When we wish to take an airing, we resort to a carriage ; but if we wish to give our spirits an airing, a hearty laugh is the only vehicle. A man that has a hearty laugh for your trifles, is more agreeable than one who has a great many good things of his own. Gay people love him from sympathy, and grave people for the relief and relaxation which he brings to grave spirits. The thoughts of solitude are always grave. We run into company very benevolently to shoulder upon others the burden of ourselves. A laugh is to conversation what music is to rhyme ; it makes that pleasing which would otherwise often be silly. Unless a man sometimes utter nonsense, well seasoned with laughter to make it palatable, he forces upon you the severe duty of always being sensible in turn. He forces you to station a sentry on your thoughts, and put them under guard, lest a silly one escape. You are compelled to think twice before you speak once, which reduces very much the occasions and the probability of your ever speaking at all. Conversation thus becomes a task levied by society upon a man's intellect, and instead of being an agreeable relaxation, becomes a severe study. Then, *Vive la bagatelle !* The good humor that gives birth to a hearty laugh infects a company with mirth ; and Old Father Time, laying by for the moment his sithe, uses only his wings.' · · · We regret that the first of a series of ' *Letters from Rome*,' from our esteemed correspondent, GEORGE WASHINGTON GREENE, Esq., American Consul at the Eternal City, and ' *The Day Dream of a Grocer*,' by HARRY FRANCO, reached us too late for insertion in the present number. Both will appear in our next. The following

are among other articles filed for insertion, or awaiting consideration : ' *The Pioneers*,' an essay
descriptive of some of the events and hardships in the life of a western settler ; ' *My Father's House*,'
a New-England Sketch ; ' *Ave Maria* ; ' *Lines on the Loss of the Erie* ; ' *The Mariner's Song on a Wintry
Night*,' etc. ; ' *Hidron, or the Call to Rest* ; ' *Lines to Trenton Falls* ; ' *Twenty Years* ; ' ' *Faces*,' an
Essay. · · · ' *The Drama*,' and notices of several new works, including the beautiful *Boston Token*
for 1842, the recent publications for the young, by the Messrs. APPLETON AND COMPANY, and the ' French
and English Reading Book,' published by COLMAN, are unavoidably deferred until our next. · · · Several communications, from unknown correspondents, with heavy postages marked, remain in the post-
office. One from Petersburgh, (Va.,) another from Saint Louis, and a third from Pittsburgh, we may
especially mention.

LITERARY RECORD.

' THE AMERICAN ECLECTIC ' for September is well calculated ' we do n't think '
for general perusal by our countrymen. We have among other things the Epis-
tolæ Samaritanæ, addressed to their brethren in England in 1672 ; ' Monumenti
dell' Egitto e della Nubia disegnati della Spedizione Scientifico-Literaria Toscana in
Egitto ; ' a review of the ' Seaow Low,' from the Chinese, a work every way equal
we are told to the *Hung-Low-mum*, in the Pihking dialect, so familiar to our countrymen ; a very profound article on the ' Svea Rikets Häfder,' by that well-known
author, Erik Gustaf Gejer, Berättellser ur Svenska Historien ; Talvis' recent book,
' Versuch einer Geschichtlichen characteristick der Volkslieder,' is exceedingly
rich ; so too is the ' Entziklopeditchesko Leksikon : ' reference is also made to the
' Slovar ' of Snigerev, or rather that of the original projector, Balkhovirev, who
should not be robbed of his laurels. We are favored with a notice also of ' Der
Kampf des Reformirten und des Jesuistischen Katholicism,' and several other very
readable and entertaining works — to such as peruse and affect them.

HARPERS' FAMILY LIBRARY. — No. 132 of Harpers' ' Family Library ' is a work
upon the ' Manners and Customs of the Japanese in the Nineteenth Century ; '
taken from the accounts of recent Dutch residents in Japan, and from the German
work of Dr. VON SIEBOLD. The publishers do not claim too much for the themes
of this work, when they assume that ' there is no people with any claims to civilization of who n so little is known as of the Japanese. Their policy in regard to
foreigners is even more jealous and exclusive than that of the Chinese ; the Dutch
being the only Europeans allowed to trade with them, and their intercourse being
extremely limited, and subject to severe restrictions.' Within the last two or three
years several publications have appeared in Holland, by members of the Dutch
factory, descriptive of the institutions, character, etc., of that most singular people.
These however have not been translated, and this we are informed is the first
attempt to present to the English or American reader a compendium of the curious
and interesting facts which they contain.

COLONEL TRUMBULL'S LIFE AND TIMES. — The ' Autobiography, Reminiscences,
and Letters of JOHN TRUMBULL, from 1756 to 1841,' which we have heretofore
mentioned as in the press, has been published by Messrs. WILEY AND PUTNAM,
New-York, and Mr. B. L. HAMLEN, New-Haven. We shall aim to do justice to
the volume in an ensuing number. It is superbly executed, illustrated by numerous
elegant engravings, and in its records replete with interest. We can do no more
at the late hour at which the work reaches us than to recommend it to the public
as a volume worthy of success, and well calculated to command it.

RELIGION AND THE STATE. — We tender acknowledgments to our friend the author for a copy of a handsome pamphlet, containing an Oration entitled ' Religion and the State, or Christianity the Safeguard of Civil Liberty,' delivered before the members of St. Paul's College and St. Ann's Hall, College Point, on the 5th of July, by JOHN FREDERICK SCHRÖEDER, D. D., Rector of St. Ann's Hall, Flushing, (L. I.) It is a comprehensive and well-written essay, evincing study and forcible rhetoric, and establishes and illustrates the following important principles: that GOD is the supreme ruler of men; that His will is the fountain of all Law; that the State is essentially dependent on Religion; that Christianity is the religion of our land; and that Christian Education is the best guaranty for the preservation and permanent continuance of our civil and religious liberty. To principles such as these, enforced and illustrated by the mind and pen of Dr. SCHRÖEDER, we scarcely need ask the attention of the moral and religious or even the general reader. The pamphlet, as we have had occasion to remark of other publications from the same press, is very neatly executed by Mr. LINCOLN, printer to the New-York colleges at Flushing.

A RARE WORK. — We regret that the early period of the month at which the s' eets of this department of our Magazine pass to the press, has prevented a notice of a rare work from the pen of our correspondent, the popular author of ' The Palmyra Letters.' It is in two volumes, and is entitled ' Julian, or Scenes in Judea.' It will be enough to secure the attention of our readers to these admirable volumes to state, that the same glowing pencil which so vividly painted ancient Palmyra, has here depicted the scenes and events in Judea in the time of our SAVIOUR; bringing the past before us as in a solemn slow-moving panorama, with its time-hallowed incidents, the greatest and altogether the most important that the world ever saw. We shall take an early occasion to do these volumes more elaborate justice; and in the mean time commend them warmly to our readers.

' BA-A-A-H !' — Messrs. WILEY AND PUTNAM have republished from the English edition, a ' Treatise on Sheep,' with the best means for their improvement, general management, and the treatment of their diseases; with a chapter on wool and the wool trade, and another on the management of sheep in Australia. The author, AMBROSE BLACKLOCK, a surgeon of Dumfries, Scotland, has evidently a feeling sense of the interest of his subject, if we may judge from his motto, for which he is indebted to a Swedish proverb: ' Sheep have golden feet, and wherever the print of them appears, the soil is turned into gold.' Several good engravings, some of them colored, illustrate the ' internal economy,' modes of washing, shearing, etc., of that gentle animal which JOHN RANDOLPH said he would go ten miles out of his way to kick.

THE CHEAP EDITION OF SCOTT. — Mr. C. S. FRANCIS, Broadway, who is giving to the public, in continuation of PARKER's well-known edition of the Waverley Novels, all the poetry of SIR WALTER SCOTT, as well as LOCKHART's Life of the ' Northern Wizard,' has just issued in a handsome form and on good paper the third volume of the ' Life,' and two volumes comprising the ' Lady of the Lake.' All who have secured copies of PARKER's edition, will serve their best interest by purchasing at the same small price the issues of Mr. FRANCIS, which will thus form a *complete* library of the works of SCOTT, with the best history of his life extant, or doubtless that could possibly be written.

THE KNICKERBOCKER.

VOL. XVIII.   NOVEMBER, 1841.   No. 5.

LETTERS FROM ROME.

BY GEORGE WASHINGTON GREENE.

LETTER FIRST.

THE first view of Rome should be taken from the tower of the Capitol. There are other points which command prospects equally extensive. From the top of St. Peters the eye embraces at one glance the city and the mountains, and may distinguish upon the verge of the horizon the blue waters of the Mediterranean. From the Janiculum you look upon it as upon a map at your feet, and may count its streets and edifices one by one. But in both of these views the ancient city and the modern, the past and the present, are too closely blended; and while you are seeking for some record of distant ages, your attention is distracted by the fabrics of yesterday. But upon the tower of the Capitol you stand midway between ancient and modern Rome; the republic and the empire; a waste of ruins before, and behind you the gorgeous residence of the pontiffs. The tide of population has swept around the base of the Capitoline hill, leaving it as a land-mark in this wilderness of thought, from which you may almost count the footsteps of Time, and gather up one by one those scattered links which bind us to the great and the good of every age.

The first glance that you cast around you embraces nearly the whole extent of primitive Latium. A plain, in whose unbroken surface you can scarcely distinguish an undulation, fills the landscape on your right, and upon its extreme verge the horizon reposes with so soft and so pure an outline, that you almost fancy it the blending of sea and sky. Following this line toward the east, you meet, at a distance which varies from nine to fourteen miles, the Alban mount. It rises from the midst of the plain with a gradual elevation, broken here and there by gentle eminences, that you hardly know how to designate, until, with a sudden change in the character of its outline, it swells up into the wooded cone of Monte Cavo, three thousand feet above the level of the sea. This elevation continues with but trifling variations along the west of the mount to the summits of Pila and Algidium, which, although bearing different names, are parts of the same group. From thence it slopes downward to the plain, with a descent somewhat more rapid than that of the south-western declivity, but with the same peculiarities, and an equal softness of outline. An opening is here left in the landscape of about five miles in breadth, which serves to give a striking relief to the peculiarly insulated and complete contour of the Alban mount.

Beyond this and directly opposite to the Alban, the Sabine mounts, themselves a branch of the Apennine, commence their rugged and undulating chain. They form on the north-east the natural boundary of the Campagna, with every variety and gradation of height, from elevations that seem made for a castle or a villa, to peaks that retain their mantle of snow under the sun of midsummer. For more than thirty miles the plain follows the course of this continuous chain, in an undulating line, as a lake the windings of its shores. Here and there the chain bends inward with a slight or a broader curve, and a few gentle eminences that cluster around its base serve to soften the asperity of its rough and precipitous sides. It is on one of these that stands Tivoli, and the headlong Avis still borrows a part of its rapidity from the descent. A broader valley is formed where the mountains approach the Tiber, and one of their crests is crowned with the ruins of Cures, the birth-place of Tatius and of Numa.

In turning to trace the northern boundary of the plain, you are struck by the change in its surface. Instead of the flat, unbroken level which it has hitherto presented, it rises on every side into hillocks and ridges, which, although they never attain to the height of even the lowest of the adjacent mountains, give it the aspect of a troubled sea. Soracte, like the Alban mount, stands alone :

> ——'a long-swept wave from out the surge,
> That on the curl hangs pausing.'

Like waves too, the mountains of Etruria rise one above the other, with a successive flow, and shut in the landscape on the north. It is only toward the west, and there but in part, that the view is limited. The boundary here is the Janiculum, whose verdant summit, decked with villas and vineyards, overhangs Rome herself, and like the ivy that once encircled the arches of the Coliseum, forms a screen and a garland for the desolation that lies below.

It is only upon the map that you can trace the course of the Avis and of the Tiber, much less distinguish the smaller streams which flow from every direction into these two principal currents of the Campagna. The sea is not visible on either side ; the view of that portion of the coast which is nearest to the city being cut off by the intervening heights of the Janiculum.

If now you confine your observation more directly to the precincts of the ancient city, your attention will first be arrested by the irregularity of its surface, and the intermingling of hills and valleys. One of these, and evidently of the largest, lies directly at the foot of the tower on which we are standing. The triumphal arches, the fragments of porticoes and temples and massive walls, tell you at once that it is the Roman Forum. The hill beyond still preserves the peculiarity of conformation which obtained for the primitive city of Romulus the epithet of ' The

Square.' You can almost trace its boundaries with the naked eye, and follow in imagination the course of the shepherd-king, as he traced out with his plough-share the original limits of the future sovereign of the universe.* You may take as a starting-point the arch of Janus, not far from the river, and follow the line of the valley to the three columns which were so long supposed to have belonged to the Temple of Jupiter Stator, upon that side of the Forum which fronts the Capitol. A line drawn at right angles with this will pass under the Arch of Titus, and between the foundations of the temple of Venus and Rome on the one hand and the imperial structures of the Palatine on the other. The opposite line runs along the valley that separates the Palatine from the Aventine, and may be distinguished by a row of trees, of a fresh green, which grow in what once was the ancient *Maximus.* The remaining boundary is invisible to the naked eye, but may be easily traced in a line which begins amid the gigantic remains of the palace of Nero, and skirting the base of the Cœlian, leads you beneath the Arch of Constantine to the collossal amphitheatre of the Flavians.

That portion of the Aventine which overhangs the left bank of the Tiber is the only one of the seven hills which like the Palatine stands sufficiently in relief to be distinguished from the neighboring eminences. You can trace a part of its course by the ruins which lie scattered among its verdant festoons of vineyards and shrubbery. The gray walls of a convent mark the point nearest to the river, and farther on the eye rests on the naked halls of the Baths of Caracalla, at whose feet the earth teems with verdure, while scarce an ivy-vine or a shrub has found a footing in its walls, from which to weave its flexile veil and cover their fearful desolation.

The Cœlian is separated from the Palatine by a narrow valley, and stretches southward in a long ridge of shapeless fragments, from the Arch of Constantine to the church and palace of the Lateran.

The Esquiline, Viminal, and Quirinal, seem, as you look down upon them from this height, to form one broad flat of table-land rather than a succession of hills. The Baths of Titus, within bow-shot of the Coliseum, designate the first rise of the Esquiline, and serve to mark the termination of the valley that divides it from the Cœlian. You may distinguish too the highest point of elevation, by the Basilica of Santa Maria Maggiore.

Turning now to the north-east, the last of the original valleys of Rome lies before you. The eye still falls upon broken arches and crumbling walls; but you here begin to distinguish the approaches of the modern city, and the structures of another religion and another age. They spread through the valley in its full extent, clustering closely around the Forum of Trajan, and ascending in a succession of churches and palaces and convents to the summer residence of the pontiffs upon the summit of the Quirinal. All the rest is modern Rome. Even the northern declivity of the Quirinal is without the

---

* TACITUS in the twenty-fourth chapter of the twelfth book of his Annals has given us a minute account of the course taken by Romulus. My readers may trace this, by reversing the order of my description, and beginning with the valley between the Palatine and Aventine. The order I have adopted is the clearest for the point of view from which my sketch was taken.

limits of the walls of Servius, although it still retains dim traces of the Circus of Flora.　Beyond it rises with a gentle ascension the 'Hill of Gardens,' a favorite resort of Lucullus and of Sallust, where Belisarius held his head-quarters during the Gothic siege, and whose shady coverts, in times though less remote, yet still old and classic to us children of a newer world, afforded a shelter to the wearied limbs and care-worn mind of Gallileo.

The Pincian, or 'Hill of Gardens,' forms, together with the Quirinal, the eastern enclosure of a spacious valley, which converges upon the Capitoline as its base, and following the curve of the Janiculum for its south-western boundary, expands at midway into an ample plain, until the waving line of the mountain again bends inward with a gradual contraction, leaving it girded on every side but one, like the arena of an amphitheatre.　The Tiber enters this valley at its northern extremity, winding its way through the heart of the city in curves that can be likened only to the folds of a serpent.　On its western bank, at the point of broadest expansion, stands the Vatican, and the mountain-like dome of St. Peters swells up above the crest of the Janiculum itself. The greater portion of the remainder of this valley, between the left bank of the river and the hills which we have designated as its boundaries, was once the tumultuous scene of the Comitia, and is now the chief seat of modern Rome.　Squares and streets intersect it in every direction, and the eye falls bewildered upon thick-woven masses of temples and palaces, of spires and domes.

LETTER SECOND.

FROM this general survey of the exterior of the Eternal City I must now ask you to follow me beneath its surface, and with Geology for our guide, contemplate the works of those mighty agents whose powers were so long a secret even to the eye of Science.　Few spots have been the scene of greater natural revolutions than the soil of Rome.　The sea once flowed in lonely grandeur amidst the windings of her valleys; the summits of her highest hills were washed by the waters of the Tiber; and earthquakes and volcanoes united their resistless energies to the silent action of those milder elements.　Remote as the earliest epoch of her authentic history may seem; bewildering as the glance we have just cast upon these scenes, hallowed by the most ennobling recollections of our race, may appear; time itself shrinks to a point in the contemplation of these mysteries of nature, and you lose sight of man, as if more immediately in the presence of his Maker!

Geology teaches us that the plain of Latium, like all the low-lands of the Italian peninsula, was originally covered with the sea.　It was while in this state of submersion that the action of its volcanoes commenced, and by a series of eruptions, of which science no longer pretends to fix the date or the duration, gradually raised the first layers of the future valley above the level of the waters.　The streams which descended in every direction from the adjacent mountains united their currents as they approached the plain, and the first general inundation was succeeded by a partial deluge of fresh-water rivers.　The gradual accession of matter thus washed down from the mountains, and the successive induration of the original marine and volcanic deposits, formed by degrees a more solid soil, which opposing a greater resistance to the impulse of the rivers, gradually reduced their dominions to a narrower compass, and at length, after many a violent outbreak and transient inundation, confined their currents to determined channels. The casual inequalities of the primitive formation, and the greater or less resistance thus offered by different parts of the passage of the fresh-water streams, gave rise to irregularities in the surface of the soil, which became more defined with each new accession of matter, and finally imprinted upon it that rough and broken exterior which characterizes the immediate precincts of Rome.

These inductions of science, which might seem to savor somewhat too strongly of theory, are warranted by facts that cannot be called in question. Actual examination has every where verified in the lower parts of Rome the existence of a substratum, which can only be accounted for by the preceding supposition. Every appearance leads to the belief that the basis of the hills is of the same nature and consequently derived from the same cause.

The materials which compose the soil of Rome are of two classes, distinguished alike in their nature and in their origin. Those of the first class are derived from the agency of water; those of the second from fire, or more strictly speaking, from volcanoes. Of the first there are three kinds, which, in various proportions, enter into the composition of the soil of the lower city. The first of these is clay combined with a certain portion of calcareous carbonate, the presence of which is detected by its instantly effervescing upon the application of acids. Properly speaking this is a marl; and from the predominance of the clayey portion, should be called clay marl. It is to the peculiar adhesiveness of this substance that the lower city is indebted for its numerous wells. The water which flows in upon its layers from the surrounding hills, and finds an easy passage through the beds of less tenacious earth, meets an impenetrable barrier in this, and is thus retained in pools, or obeying the inclination of the strata, flows onward toward the Tiber, with whose current it unites in rivulets or drops that filter through the banks. Hence upon the rise of the river, its natural outlets being closed, it collects in larger masses and inundates the cellars and lower parts of the city.

In addition to this marl, and sometimes in immediate mixture with it, is found a calcareous gravel of a yellowish color, which also in some places contains calcareous pebbles of considerable magnitude.

The third element of the soil of the plain is a sand composed of pebbly grains, and more or less intermixed with clay. It is of a color inclining to yellow, spotted with small scales of a silverish mica and grains of pirossena, and apparently, though of dimensions too subtile to be clearly distinguished even with the aid of the microscope, containing crystals of feldspar. The origin of these strata is made evident by the frequent discovery of fossil shells and calcareous tufa, both of a kind found only in layers of fluvial formation.

Among the volcanic elements of the soil of Rome is a kind of tufa to which the most distinguished of the native geologists has given the name of *tufa litoide*, or the stony. This material was in great request in the early ages of the city for the construction of arches and walls, and was even occasionally used as a paving stone for the streets. In ancient writers it is called *saxum quadratum, saxum rubrum*, and by similar terms, indicative of some peculiarity in its form or its color.

The *tufa granulare* is a distinct species, which forms the basis of five of the hills of Rome. It is in this that the catacombs, so renowned in the early history of the church, and of which so many openings still remain, were excavated, and the original Latin denomination of *arenarii* is still preserved in the *arnare* of Seguid Frosinone. A third species of tufa, or to speak with more precision, a variety of the species last mentioned, is the *tufa torroso*, or earthy. It is little else than the tufa granulare in a state of absolute decomposition. Beside these varieties of volcanic formation, pumice is also found in several of the hills, and that of the Janiculum is not inferior to the pumice of Lipari.

While the formation of the hills upon the left bank of the river is chiefly attributable to the agency of volcanoes and of fresh-water streams, the action of the sea itself is equally apparent in those of the opposite shore. Marine substances have been found in each of the three hills which compose the chain of the Janiculum, and oysters of the largest size may be seen intermingled with the soil of Monte Mario, four hundred and forty feet above the level of the sea. The presence of fluvial deposites in the midst of these creations of the deep is a confirmation of the theory so briefly sketched in the beginning of this letter. In such clear and indelible characters has Nature recorded the labors and the revolutions of her infancy.

I shall not attempt a detailed description of the fossil remains which have from time to time been discovered both in and out of the city. The zoological cabinet of the Sapienga contains a valuable collection, some of them belonging to species long since extinct. Among these is a portion of the tusk of an elephant, thirteen palms in length, which was found at the depth of thirty feet below the soil of the sacred mountain. Seven distinct species of the Delex have been identified among the shells, of which there are two that are not mentioned in the catalogue of Linnæus.

The copious water-courses which flow in every direction below the surface form undoubtedly one of the most interesting features in the subterranean history of this remarkable spot. Many of these, once known to the ancients, now wander with an uncertain current, and every trace of their rise and outlets is lost. Others still serve to supply the fountains of several edifices, both public and private, and have been proved by a rigorous analysis to be among the most salubrious of potable streams. Wells are found in the valleys at a depth varying from ten to twenty feet, and afford an abundant supply of the purest water. Upon the hills their sources lie much deeper. The greatest depth before reaching the water is that of the well in the Villa Spada on the Palatine, which is one hundred and twenty-two feet, Parisian measure. The greatest depth of water is thirty-six feet eight inches, and in this instance the well itself is eighty-two feet deep.

Beside the streams which irrigate the subterranean regions of Rome, we know by the concurrent testimony of all antiquity, that many parts of the exterior surface which are now united by dry land were originally covered with large bodies of water. The valley between the Palatine and Aventine was filled by a spacious pool, known among the early Romans as the Velabrum, and which was crossed as the Tiber now is, by a ferry. Propertius even goes so far as to represent the boatmen as employing a sail in the passage : in this, however, he may justly be suspected of a poetic exaggeration. A portion of this pool, which extended around the base of the Palatine to the Capitol, was distinguished from the main body by the epithet of the ' lesser Velabro,' a name which it in part retains to the present day, although every trace of its primitive state has long since disappeared. It was chiefly for the draining of these bodies of water that the Cloacca Maxima was constructed, and more than one of their original subterranean tributaries still flow through this same passage to the river.

In the Forum there was a pool celebrated in the early annals of the city as the ' Lago Curzio,' and which, though but a branch of the lesser Velabro, has given rise to various conjectures and much learned disquisition. Nor has the position and history of the ' Lago Caprea,' the scene of the death or disappearance of Romulus, been agitated with less ardor. And difficult as it is to ascertain with precision the location of objects of which every vestige has been effaced, the mass of citation and reasoning is sufficient to show that it must have covered that part of the plain which lies between St. Andrea della Valle and the river.

To complete this picture of primitive Rome, you must fancy every hill as covered with thick grown woods, and here and there along their rocky declivities some cavern looking gloomily forth from a shroud of dark shrubbery and trailing vines. The fable of Cacus is familiar to every reader of Virgil, and tradition still points you out his cave at the base of the Aventine. A spacious grove of oaks crowned the Capitoline and Cœlian ; laurels and myrtles were interwoven in dark masses upon the summit of the Aventine ; the beech, that favorite of Latin pastoral, spread its broad shade over the Esquiline ; and even the least credulous etymologists will acknowledge the correctness of the interpretation which traces to its willow groves the origin of the name of the Viminal. Religious associations, which have never yet been satisfactorily explained, imparted to these groves a character of sanctity which in part secured their preservation long after every other portion of the city had lost all traces of its original aspect under the busy hand of man. They were the favored haunts of the Dryads and Guino, and Diana herself loved the freshness of their cool retreats. Beautiful must they have seemed amid the temples and palaces of the imperial city, relieving the sombre majesty of their massive walls, and extending a grateful shade over their squares and fountains. Some traces of them still remain in the vicinity of the city, if not enough to shelter you, as in the days of their prime, yet showing how gracefully they followed the windings of the valleys, and with what a garland-like verdure they encircled the brows of the hills. But the same causes which had been their protection during the reign of paganism, proved fatal upon the public adoption of christianity, and it is generally believed that but few remained to share in the desolation of the middle ages.　　　　G. W. G.

Rome, 49 Via del Quirinale,
　　June 20, 1841.　　————

THE best work upon the Geology of Rome is Brocchi's treatise '*Dello Stato Fisico del Molo di Roma.*' It is accompanied by an admirable geognostic map. It may perhaps be fair to state that BREIS-LAK supposes Rome itself to have been the seat of a volcano. I have adopted the more propable opinion of BROCCHI.

————

TWENTY YEARS.

FOR twenty years we 've passed, dear Kate!
　Down Time's full tide together,
And proved all changing chance and scene,
　And met all kinds of weather;
Since when — 't was on your birth-day, Kate —
　We vowed eternal truth;
Two laughing girls, with all the mirth
　Of gay and careless youth.

And we have kept our promise, Kate,
　In spite of youth's decaying,
While Time with other's fortunes hath
　All sorts of freaks been playing;
Nor has it left *us* changeless, Kate!
　Mine eye has lost its brightness,
And your once graceful form hath not
　Its former fairy lightness.

For twenty years will make, dear Kate!
　In maiden beauty, changes;
And many a head it layeth low,
　And many a heart estranges:
Full forty years are on your brow,
　And some few more on mine,
Where shining threads of silver gray
　Begin with brown to twine.

And we are spinsters both, dear Kate!
　Yet happy ones, I trow;
There 's many a wedded wife I know
　Who wears a sadder brow:
And blessings on your birth-day, Kate!
　And blessings on your lot;
You 're blest indeed with loving friends,
　For oh! who loves you not!

And far off be the day, dear Kate!
　When one of us lies low;
And one is left behind to mourn,
　And strive alone with wo.
We 've lived in love, while twenty years
　Have flown full swiftly past;
And when the parting summons comes
　May I not be the last!

Albany, September, 1841.　　　　　　　　ANNE RIVERS.

THE DAY-DREAM OF A GROCER.

BY HARRY FRANCO.

' A-BUBBLE, a-bubble, a-bubble, rubble, rubble, rubble, ubble, ubble, ubble, ble, ble, and a half, and a half, and a half, alf, alf, alf, f — f - f - f, and a half; *did* you say a half? — *will* you say a half?　I mean to give you the wines, gentlemen; I *mean* to do it; I *will* give you the wines; a half it is; thank you, Isaac; I *must* have my commissions, gentlemen; I *must* have 'em: thank you, Isaac — jolly old soul! Isaac bids twelve; a-rubble, a-rubble, a-rubble, and a half; go it strong, Isaac! go it *strong*, I say; and a half, and a half, and a half, alf, af, af, af, f — f - f - f; wo n't *you* give any more? — wo n't *you?* nor *you?* Then I must give it to Isaac at twelve and a half; put it down to Isaac at twelve and a half.'

These were the identical words that came rattling from the throat of the rich and portly Walter Windmill, Esquire, the auctioneer.　Every body is a squire in these days, but above every body else rich auctioneers. Mr. Windmill was a Falstaff in his profession; he had enormous jowls, the most comical crispy hair conceivable, and a pair of the funniest hazle eyes that ever an auctioneer was blessed with; but they were entirely useless to him without the aid of a pair of gold-mounted spectacles, and even with this aid the owner of them could not distinguish a hawk from a hand-saw at any respectable distance.　The occasion on which the emphatic words above recorded were uttered was a sale of wines, by catalogue and sample; and the gentleman whose name was repeated with such unction by Mr. Windmill was ISAAC DEMIJOHN, Esquire, a rich old grocer of Coenties Slip, who had breathed the atmosphere of that favored spot ever since he came into this breathing world.　Isaac was very rich, rich enough, every body thought but himself, and he enjoyed all the honors that belong to that happy condition.　Nobody, at least no poor body, ever had the audacity to call in question the correctness of his opinion.　All his sayings had an orphic tendency; and his jokes were always sure to command an explosion of mirth.　This is one of the choicest blessings that wealth can bestow; to know that your wit will be appreciated by discerning listeners, and that should you chance, through forgetfulness, to tell a funny story a second or third time, your auditor will kindly receive it as though he had never heard it before.　Isaac's sons were the greatest rakes about town, and gave unquestionable evidence of ending their lives in an alms-house: his daughters too, having been stinted in their education, because their father was determined upon dying a rich man, were idle, extravagant, and silly, and much sought after too.　If one had a desire to be completely wretched, he could not attain his object more surely than by taking one of the Misses Demijohn to wife; and yet many young gentlemen whose sole pursuit was happiness, paid them the most assiduous attentions, with the hope of winning their favor. Such are some of the blessings attached to riches.

Isaac was a first-rate judge of liquors. You would have thought he held the destiny of all the states and territories in his hand, if you could have seen with what profound deliberation he drew his proof-glass from the bung-hole of a brandy-pipe and applied it to his plethoric lips; and then with what a solemn shake of his head he intimated a forthcoming veto on the quality of the liquor. You would have sworn that nothing short of a constitutional scruple or a Virginia abstraction could induce such a mighty caution. But Isaac never troubled his head with such unprofitable articles as abstract ideas: the main question with him was which of two brands would bear the most mixing; whether ' Pellevoisin' or ' A. Seignette' would take the greatest quantity of pure spirits without losing its flavor. This was an important point to decide; and the deliberation with which Isaac considered the subject was undoubted proof of his sincerity. He had scruples, beyond a question, conscientious scruples too; for Isaac was a communicant in a fashionable Dutch church, and he had frequently been called upon to hand round the plate for missionary purposes. As the flavor of good wine will remain in the cask long after its contents have been emptied, so will an odor of sanctity hang about a man engaged in such pious pursuits, even when employed about mere worldly matters. And no one who saw Isaac deliberating over a pipe of brandy or a hogshead of molasses, and knew what a lively interest he took in the welfare of the heathen, could doubt that he had the good of souls at heart.

The day on which we introduced him to the notice of the reader he had been engaged in tasting, smelling, and comparing an unusually long catalogue of choice wines; and he no sooner seated himself on one of the wooden benches in Mr. Windmill's auction-room, than a heavy drowsiness came over him, which he tried in vain to shake off. Let him change his position as he might, or open his eyes ever so wide, he could not resist the disposition to slumber which overpowered him. Sleep seemed to rain its influence upon him; and in spite of his anxiety to bid, he was forced to yield to its resistless but gentle power, and be borne off to the Land of Nod like a manacled slave. There he sat with his catalogue and pencil in hand, his back against the wall, and his head kept upright by his fat double chin, unable to move or speak a word. His spirit had passed away from the spot in which his body was located, and while all around were conscious of his corporeal presence, he was not himself conscious of any thing that was passing near him. In all save appearance he was like a skeleton at an Egyptian feast. He had purposely placed himself in a corner where no one but the auctioneer could see his motions; for he knew that when younger grocers saw him bid upon a particular lot, they would try to out-bid him, to show their superior judgment to the rest of the world. And there he sat, every now and then nodding at the auctioneer, whose imperfect vision did not allow him to discover that Isaac was stuck fast in an apoplectic slumber; so he took all his nods for bids, and knocked down to him some terrible hard bargains, that would have ruined the credit of a younger grocer.

Who would have guessed that the soul which inhabited that happy-looking corporation was then undergoing a probationary residence with the troubled spirits in Tophet? So little of an index to the mind are the outward developements of the person. Although Isaac was asleep in the auction-room, he was wide awake in another place. Though he was deaf to the winning voice of Mr. Windmill, he could not shut the ears of his soul to a terrible voice that none heard but himself.

Lord! what an uncomfortable position a man is in when left alone *tête-à-tête* with his conscience! But if it is terrible in a day-dream, with the blessed light of day shining full upon you, and many voices chattering around you, what must it be when one is lying with the cold earth upon his breast, and dismal night-winds howling around his solitary biding-place! It is too fearful for thought; and so it appeared to Isaac Demijohn, Esq., while like a guilty coward he tried to shun his accuser, but dared not offer a word in his own defence. Rich as he was, Mr. Demijohn would have given all he was worth if some kind hand had but touched him and delivered him from his troublesome condition. But no one discovered that he was asleep, or a dozen hands would instantly have been raised for his rescue; and the auctioneer rattled away with his lubble, a-lubble, a-lubble, a-lubble, and a half, and a half, and a half, af, af, af, as other men in other places will rattle away at their various employments, wholly regardless and careless of the sufferings and griefs of those around them.

But what could possibly disturb so respectable a person as Isaac Demijohn, Esq.? He occupied a very elevated position in society; he was a bank director, and a subscriber to all the charitable enterprises of the day; he was looked up to by his neighbors, and when men spoke of him in the street he was said to be ' as good as old wheat.' Yet in spite of all these things Isaac would have sold himself for a sixpence. A monstrous weight was lying upon his breast, compared with which one of the granite pillars of the new Exchange were a feather; and yet, oppressive though it was, it was only a *false* weight; and the spirits that so troubled him were pure spirits; yes *pure spirits*, that he had mixed with brandy. Where was the harm in that? He could always aver with exact truth to his customers that he sold nothing but a *pure* article. Then there were tares springing up all around him, choking his path whithersoever he turned, and entangling his feet; but these were *false* tares. How horribly he was beset by these things, which, though they took no fixed shape, were so palpable and unquestionable that he knew them at a glance; and furthermore, he knew them to be his own. It never once occurred to him to shift them off upon somebody else.

After a while these passed away, and then a poor wretch came along with suffering in his looks, and Isaac trembled at his cruel glances. It was an unfortunate neighbor, from whom he had taken usury many years before, and who had been in his grave a long time. What a malicious creature he must be to bear malice so long! Close upon his heels came a maddened multitude of wo-stricken beings, every one of whom gave him a reproachful look, which seemed to say, ' But for you we had been happy and blessed; it was you who sold us rum; it was

you who wasted our bodies and drugged our souls with sin and misery!'
Isaac, it should be known, had begun trade as a retailer.   Lord! how
they grinned and chattered!—how they gnashed their teeth upon him!
What a dismal howling they set up, and how they glared upon him with
their red and swollen eyes!   The sweat started in big drops upon his
forehead and rolled down his unconscious cheeks, which looked as red
and as jolly as though their proprietor were reclining upon a Sybarite's
bed of roses.   As this miserable multitude gradually melted away into
the dim space whence they emerged, there came others, mute but
mournful beings, whose down-cast eyes and sad features were a thousand
times more harrowing to him than the noise of the excited and chattering
creatures who had just left him.   These were unfortunates who had
appealed to him for help in their adversity, and whom he had refused
with hard words and abuse; widows, orphans, and cripples; the most
feeble of all feeble folk, whose very helplessness gave them now the
power of giants over him.   'O, if they were only to come to me again!'
thought Isaac; 'I would give them my last penny.   Would n't I shell
out to them?   I would give my coach-horses for the use of these lame
people, and my idle and profligate sons should labor for those wretched
women.   But they glided silently away, seeming to say, 'It is too late;
we are very happy now.'

And then Isaac was left all alone to his thoughts.   How dreadfully
dark it was!   How vast the empty space in which he hung!   How
dreadful to be deserted, even by his tormenting persecutors, and left all
alone to the reproaches of his conscience!   He tried to call for help,
but in vain.   His voice was choked.   Why did not the heathen for
whom he had given so much money come to his assistance?   Why did
not the reverend doctor under whose preaching he had slept so many
Sundays come and speak a consolatory word in his ear?   This was
more terrible than all, to be left alone in that black abyss of nothingness.
He could not endure it; and yet he did.   'O!' he said, 'is this the
end of all my speculating?   Is it for this that I have toiled night and
day through a long life, and denied myself all the bright and pleasant
things that I saw around me?—the cheap luxury of doing good, and
all?   Did I wrong those poor people only that my sons should squander
my earnings upon wantons and profligates, and that I might myself be
wretched at last?   How exact I would be in my weights and measures,
if it were to do over again!   How contentedly I would live upon a
mere crust and a cup of water rather than wrong a human being out
of a penny!   And how devout I would be in my religious duties!
Instead of going to church in a coach, I would walk, that my coachman
might enjoy the blessed privileges of the Sabbath as well as myself; and
I would take the lowest seat, and give to the poor all that the velvet
cushions and gaudy furniture of my pew have cost!'

But now a cool breeze swept across his face, and he began to breathe
easier.   The terrible load upon his chest grew lighter; and although
he heard strange noises ringing in his ear, they did not appeal with
such terrifying distinctness to his fears.   'After all,' thought Isaac, 'I
have only followed the example that was set me.   I have been quite as
good as my neighbor.   I *must* provide for my family.   I pay my debts,

and others must do the same, or take the consequences. I do not see why I should be bound to provide for all the poor devils in the world. Let them take care of themselves, as I do. And as for walking to church, when I can afford to ride, that's a doctrine that I wo'n't subscribe to.' Thus he began to comfort himself, as his breathing grew freer; and instead of his short struggling respiration he fairly snored aloud; and as he drew a good long breath from the depths of his capacious chest, all the vile phantoms that had been harrowing his soul took flight. It was a short respite, however; for the next moment he felt a shock that sent the blood in a tumultuous current from his head into the extremities of his body. Now he thought his time was indeed come, and that the Enemy of Mankind had him fast in his clutches.

'Hallo! Isaac!' said Mr. Windmill, as he struck the grocer upon his back; 'what! asleep?'

'Save me! save me!' exclaimed Mr. Demijohn, starting upon his feet.

'Ha! ha! ha! — ho! ho! ho!' roared a multitude of voices.

'Where am I! — what have I been doing!' exclaimed the amazed grocer. 'Has the sale commenced? Has lot forty-one been sold?'

'Lot forty-one been sold?' repeated the auctioneer; 'bless my precious picture! — what a question that is for *you* to ask! Why you bought it yourself, and two thirds of the catalogue beside.'

'I? — I bid two thirds of the catalogue? Sir, I have not bid at all!' said Isaac.

And here, as the novel writers have it, an *eclaircissement* took place, but not a settlement; for Isaac refused to take the wines that had been knocked down to him, and Mr. Windmill forthwith commenced a suit against him, which having been instituted only four years has not yet been brought to a close; consequently we cannot at this time lay the result before the reader. But as far as Mr. Demijohn himself is concerned it is a matter of small moment how the affair may terminate, as that respectable gentleman took his departure very suddenly from this wicked world a few months after the events recorded in this essay occurred; and the anxious reader may find his many virtues recorded on a very tall marble pillar erected in the Honey-Suckle Cemetery, on the banks of the Hudson, a few miles from the City Hall.

HUMAN HAPPINESS.

O THOU whom all admire, adore,
    Pursue, but ne'er possess,
Away! — delude some easier fool,
    Thou phantom, Happiness!

Thou art Life's long disastrous game,
    That can the craftiest beat;
While Death looks on, but to reveal,
    When 't is too late, the cheat.

Safe is the whirlwind's boding calm,
    And true the treacherous sea,
And real all the mirage paints,
    Compared, thou Dream! with thee.

PASSAIC:

A GROUP OF POEMS TOUCHING THAT RIVER.

—

BY FLACCUS.

> ' Oh could I flow like thee, and make thy stream
> My great example as it is my theme ;
> Though deep, yet clear, though gentle yet not dull,
> Strong without rage, without o'erflowing, full.'
>
> DENHAM'S COOPER'S HILL.

—

INTRODUCTORY MUSINGS ON RIVERS.

I.

BEAUTIFUL Rivers! that adown the vale
With graceful winding journey to the deep,
Let me along your grassy marge recline
At ease, and musing, meditate the strange
Bright history of your life.   Yes! from your birth
Has beauty's shadow chased your every step :
The blue sea was your mother, and the sun
Your glorious sire : clouds your voluptuous cradle,
Roofed with o'erarching rainbows ; and your fall
To earth was cheered with shout of happy birds —
With brightened faces of reviving flowers,
And meadows ; while the sympathizing West
Took holiday, and donned her richest robes.
From deep mysterious wanderings your springs
Break bubbling into beauty ; where they lie
In infant helplessness awhile, but soon
Gathering in tiny brooks they gambol down
The steep sides of the mountain, laughing, shouting,
Teasing the wild-flowers, and at every turn
Meeting new play-mates still to swell their ranks ;
Which with the rich increase resistless grown,
Shed foam and thunder, that the echoing wood
Rings with the boisterous glee ; while o'er their heads,
Catching their spirit blithe, young rainbows sport,
The frolic children of the wanton sun.

Nor is your swelling prime or green old age
Though calm, unlovely : still where'er ye move
Your train is beauty ; trees stand grouping by
To mark your graceful progress ; giddy flowers,
And vain, as beauties wont, stoop o'er the verge
To greet their faces in your flattering glass.
The thirsty herd are following at your side,
And water-birds in clustering fleets convoy
Your sea-bound tides ; and jaded man, released
From worldly thraldom, here his dwelling plants ;
Here pauses in your pleasant neighborhood,
Sure of repose along your tranquil shores.
And when your end approaches, and ye blend
With th' eternal Ocean, ye shall fade
As placidly as when an infant dies,
And the death-angel shall your powers withdraw
Gently as twilight takes the parting day,
And with a soft and gradual decline,
That cheats the senses, lets it down to night.

II.

BOUNTIFUL Rivers! not upon the earth
Is record traced of GOD's exuberant grace
So deeply graven as the channels worn
By ever-flowing streams: arteries of earth,
That widely branching, circulate its blood:
Whose ever-throbbing pulses are the tides.
Amazing effort for the good of man!
The whole vast energy of Nature, all
The roused and laboring elements combine
In their production; for the mighty end
Is growth, is life to every living thing.
The Sun himself is chartered for the work:
His arm uplifts the main, and at his smile
The fluttering vapors take their flight for heaven,
Shaking the briny sea-dregs from their wings:
Here wrought by unseen fingers soon is wove
The cloudy tissue, till a mighty fleet
Freighted with treasures bound for distant shores
Floats waiting for the breeze: loosed on the sky
Rush the strong tempests, that with sweeping breath
Impel the vast flotilla to its port;
Where overhanging wide the arid plain,
Drops the rich mercy down.   And oft when Summer
Withers the harvest, and the lazy clouds
Drag idly at the bidding of the breeze,
New riders spur them, and enraged they rush,
Bestrode by thunders, that with hideous shouts
And crackling thongs of fire urge them along.

As falls the blessing, how the satiate Earth
And all her race shed grateful smiles!   Not here
The bounty ceases: when the drenching streams
Have inly sinking quenched the greedy thirst
Of plants, of woods, some strong invisible arm
In bright perennial springs pumps up again
For needy man and beast: and as your brooks
Grow strong, apprenticed to the use of man,
The ponderous wheel they turn, the web to weave,
The stubborn metal forge; and when advanced
To sober age at last ye seek the sea,
Bearing the wealth of commerce on your backs,
Ye seem the unpaid carriers of the sky,
Vouchsafed to earth for burden; and your host
Of shining branches spread from land to land
Seem purposed, like the silver bands of love,
To hold the world in unity and peace.

III.

PRIMEVAL Rivers! ancient as the hills!
From immemorial ages have ye run
From mountain unto sea: your busy brooks
Still singing endless songs; your solemn falls
Pealing aloft their ever-during hymn,
Unwearied: mightiest thine, Niagara!
The loudest voice which Earth sends up to Heaven.

Back to the primal chaos fancy sweeps,
To trace your dim beginning; when dull earth

Lay sunken low, one level plashy marsh,
Girdled with mists; while saurian reptiles, strange
Measureless monsters, through the cloggy plain
Paddled and floundered; when th' Almighty voice
Like silver trumpet from their hidden dens
Summoned the central and resistless fires,
That with a groan from pole to pole upheave
The mountain masses, and with dreadful rent
Fracture the rocky crust: then Andes rose,
And Alps their granite pyramids shot up,
Barren of soil; but gathering vapors round
Their stony scalps condensed to drops, from drops
To brooks, from brooks to rivers, which set out
Over that rugged and untravelled land,
The first exploring pilgrims to the sea.
Tedious their route, precipitous, and vague,
Seeking with humbleness the lowliest paths:
Oft, shut in valleys deep, forlorn they turn
And find no vent, till gathered into lakes
Topping the basin's brimming lip, they plunge
Headlong, and hurry to the level main
Rejoicing. Misty ages did they run,
And with unceasing friction all the while
Frittered to granular atoms the dense rock,
And ground it into soil: then dropped — oh! sure
From heaven! — the precious seed: first mosses, lichens
Seized on the sterile stone; and from their dust
Sprang herbs and flowers; whose death deepening the mould,
Uprose to heaven at last the princely tree,
And earth was fitted for her coming lord.

Thus in those ancient channels still ye run,
Enduring Rivers! — thus will run, till earth's
High places be laid low: ye haughty hills!
Had not th' Almighty word the solemn truth
Elsewhere revealed, I know your days are numbered:
Yes! streams, the gentlest of God's messengers,
Though late, yet sure, will bow your stubborn heads,
And bring your honors level with the plain!

Whenever upon mountain peaks I stand,
And mark the broken and disordered scene,
The wreck, the crumbling crags that stone by stone
Have tumbling piled the rubbish-heaps that choke
The deep ravines, while up their hoary sides
Rash vines and bushes clamber where they can,
Clinging with hungry, desperate roots — it seems
To Fancy's eye that earth is one wide ruin,
And vegetation but the ivy-wreath
That crowns and beautifies its mouldering walls:
Unworthy dwelling for aspiring souls
That crave perfection; yet there be who deem
The charms of earth enhanced by ruggedness —
That without contrasts Beauty's self were tame:
If true of Nature, yet that better land
Exists where order without change can charm,
And universal beauty needs no foil
To yield perpetual rapture to the soul.
Not unattainable this perfect clime,
Even by the weakness of ignoble man,
If rightly sought, as rivers seek the sea:
With humbleness that loves the lowliest ways,

With patience under crosses, and withal
Enduring courage, faithful to the close —
The crowning close! — when on the wondering sight
Opens th' eternal sea, lit by the Sun
Of Righteousness, whose vivifying ray
Cheers the awed spirit, quickens, purifies,
And lifts it like a virgin cloud to heaven!

THE PIONEERS.

" THOSE matted woods where birds forget to sing,
But silent bats in drowsy clusters cling ;
Where at each step the stranger fears to wake
The rattling terrors of the vengeful snake ;
Where crouching tigers wait their hapless prey,
And savage men, more murderous still than they :
Far different these from every former scene,
The cooling brook, the grassy vested green,
The breezy covert of the warbling grove,
That only sheltered thefts of harmless love "

GOLDSMITH.

How few among you, O ye sons and daughters of civilization! know any thing of hardships and sorrows! In quiet enjoyment of neighborhood and home, in the peaceful pursuit of business, or in the varied rounds of pleasure, your lives are passed; and little troubles you save the insignificant nothings recurring daily, amidst which your lives are frittered away. Sickness, and occasional loss of property and loss of friends indeed you may have — as who have not? But who among you can endure even the thought of long years passed in insecurity, alone, far in the wilderness; dead to the great living, moving world and all its concerns; your view circumscribed by a gigantic wall of trees, from which come nightly the howl of the wolf, the screech of the panther, and the growling of the bear; with no sympathizing friends around; in sickness, woman relying only upon the assiduous but rough carefulness of man; in health, for both to labor from morn till night, with patient weariness, for the benefit of those to come after you; trusting only to the future years for earthly recompense, and to the infinite future for final reward?

O ye who 'dwell in palaces,' with the luxuries of every clime at your command; who amidst the graceful drapery of the theatre weep nightly at imaginary grief, exhibited with all the pomp of scenic show; who pursue the phantom Fashion, and are ready to expire if you have not obtained the latest style in dress or ornament; come with me to the far-off West, in solitudes almost unbroken, and I will show you *real* life; I will exhibit to you a *real* scene of patient endurance of hardships, of cheerful toil, which knows not nor ever dreams of praise. I will show you not only how noble hearts have baffled and braved the sternest realities, but also, ye 'Mothers in Israel,' how freemen are brought forth and nurtured, and given to the world for its safety and regeneration.

In the remote West, many miles from any settlement, rose a small log-cabin, surrounded by a few acres covered with piles of logs and massive trees, recently felled. Many a blow had been given with the axe before the sturdy arm of the woodsman had accomplished so much. The logs and trees, with piles of brush and leaves gathered around them, were on fire, crackling and sparkling; the brilliant flames ascended in wreaths to the mild autumnal sky, its glare driving the wood-birds from their evening rest in the adjacent forest, while columns of smoke arising in various shades, and in many a fanciful form, created a picture to which the pencil of WEIR could alone do justice. A patch of corn grew thriftily near the rude dwelling, and showed that no idle hands were there. Unyoked oxen browsed in the bushes hard by, and the faint tinkling of a cow-bell was heard at intervals, its patient wearer meanwhile watching the spreading flames, as if lost in wonder at the sight of so much fire and smoke. Within and around the house were strewed a few necessary articles of furniture; a shining rifle with powder-flask and bullet-pouch were suspended from wooden hooks; a long hunting-knife, more formidable still, a ponderous axe, worn bright with use, were visible; and two modest beds, covered with whitened linen, invited the weary to repose. A huge mastiff, the guardian of the night, with protuberant lip and threatening eye, lay at full length by the door-sill, snapping at the large blue-winged flies which disturbed his slumber. Three little children, their hands blackened with coal and smoke, were building mimic houses of brake and brush, and seemed the very impersonation of health and enjoyment. The father was a stout, stalwart man, in the prime of life; and was evidently well fitted to ' dare the wolf, and grapple with the bear.' He looked out from the open door, enjoying the scene, and gazing complacently upon the result of his day's labor, while his wife, a fair-haired delicate woman in cleanly dress, busied herself with careful skill in preparing the evening meal.

This was their first year in the woods. Over a long and weary way they had travelled the preceding winter, and here they had pitched their tent, to build a goodly heritage for their children. His axe had since made the old forest ring with the sound of falling trees : and her gentle song, learned in her father's home, made glad the heart of one whom she had sworn to love and obey through life. It was not without many tears that she left friends and companions for a home in the *new world* of the West. She parted with them as if for ever; and her woman's heart was almost broken as the word farewell lingered on her tongue. That she should no more see her father's face nor hear her mother's voice was a sad thought; but this was not the sum of her grief. There was the trysting-place of her youthful love; the hills and vales which first greeted her infant eye; the venerable church in which were gathered weekly the good and beautiful for prayer and praise; and there also were the buried dead; friends whose graves her tears had watered. These were forsaken; and with fortitude though not without sorrow she had left them all. But when, after weeks of journeying through scattered settlements, she passed what seemed the *bounds* of the civilized world, and entered still farther into the wilderness, she remembered the frightful tales of savage life which had been poured into her childish ear, and her heart shrunk within her; and she peered into the gloom around their way, as if expecting frightful forms to arise from every side. Still she fainted not, nor faltered, nor complained. Her course was taken, and she felt that her destiny was fixed. She trusted much to the strong arm of her companion, but more to the stronger arm of Him who protects alike the dweller of the forest and of the crowded city.

As evening came on, their frugal repast finished, the husband sat gazing from the door-way, half dreaming, half watching the crackling fires : the wife came and seated herself by his side, and laid her hand with a woman's gentleness in his outstretched palm, and looked into his face with such a look as only deep feeling and affection can bestow. At the twilight hour a sense of loneliness is most burdensome ; and she felt then how far, how *very* far off they were from that busy world of which they had once formed a part. She spoke of home, and friends, and by-gone days, and old-remembered scenes, which they should see no more, until even his rugged nature was moved, and he felt it not unmanly to weep. Blinded with falling tears, not of grief nor of penitence, nor of awakened guilt, but of sweet and melancholy remembrances, she reclined her head upon his shoulder, and her thoughts flitted alternately between the past, the present, and the future, until the present and the future were lost in the visions of her home and her youth.

When the stars were up, and the night had closed in upon them, from that humble abode arose a manly, deep-toned voice of praise and supplication, for the pioneer was a prayerful man. A descendant of the Pilgrims, he had in him that ' faith which was once delivered to the saints.' It is needless to speak of the eloquence of that forest devotion : it was a prayer for pardon of transgressions, a thanksgiving for life, and health, and many blessings ; a supplication for peace and protection, and for strength and firmness to endure whatsoever of suffering or of evil remained in store for them. And most assuredly far-off friends were not then forgotten. Over the whole wide earth, and in all its temples ' made with hands,' no devotion more heart-felt, simple, or affecting, was ever offered :

> ——— ' For his simple heart
> Might not resist the sacred influences
> Which from the stilly twilight of the place,
> And from the gray old trunks that high in heaven
> Mingled their mossy boughs, and from the sound
> Of the invisible breath that swayed at once
> All their green tops, stole over him, and bowed
> His spirit with the thought of boundless power,
> And inaccessible majesty.'

Quietly they slept that night ; and if no sweet dreams visited them in their slumbers, it was because the weary labor of the day had overpowered them, and banished from the brain all the ' thick coming fancies ' of an ideal world.

And thus the time wore on. The winter day saw the pioneer amid the snow, felling the great trees around him, or pursuing herds of deer, or some grisly bear prowling among the thickets. Meanwhile, her household labors over, the mother was treasuring up in the infant minds of her children such lessons of instruction as her store of knowledge

allowed.   At evening how anxiously did mother and children watch
the first approach of husband and father!   They were to each other
friends, companions, the world ; and when the huge logs blazed up from
the hearth through the open-mouthed chimney, lighting up every corner
of the snug cottage, the winds howling and roaring among the trees,
and the drifting snow, were all unheeded.   There around that fire-side
old legends were rehearsed, old friends were talked of, and all the events
of their former days were brought up anew.   Evening after evening
too their few books were brought out, and read over and again, as if
their contents were never heard before.   A file of old newspapers,
which had somehow been packed up with their little stock of goods,
was re-perused with as much avidity as if the sheets were damp from
the press : the marriages and deaths recorded years before were to
them as events of yesterday ; old advertisements were faithfully pored
over from time to time ; and it must be confessed some of them
rekindled in the good wife a half-forgotten idea of caps, ribands, and
laces ; of shops, and their long shelves filled and surrounded with many
an article of female finery.

Spring came again, and with it also the scourge of a new country,
racking agues and burning fevers.   The strong man was bowed low ;
his frame drooped, his eye rolled delirious, and his tongue spake strange
things : the tender child too was confined to its couch of pain.   Then
came the trials of life upon that lone wife and mother.   No physician
was near, with healing medicine ; no friend to keep with her the long
watches of the night ; but the ' Lord of the whole earth ' was there,
and He inspired her breast with fortitude.   The simple remedies which
she had learned from some old prudent house-wife she prepared with
an earnest care ; she culled the wild herb, and made cooling drinks ;
and after long months of patient watching and nursing she saw her
husband slowly recover.   But meanwhile the summer solstice had come
and gone ; and that they might not be left destitute of provisions, her
own hands had planted the earth with corn ; had pulled up the rank
weeds which clogged its growth ; and when the harvest was ripe, she
had gathered it in.   Thrice had she travelled, alone, a long day's
journey through the woods to the nearest settlement, for medicine and
advice ; and thrice a longer distance to a rudely-constructed mill, and
from it carried back sustenance to her sick household.   It was a weary
way for a woman who in her girlhood would have been scared by the
sound of her own light footstep.   Saddest of all, came Death into that
lonely abode — and the youngest and fairest child was no more !   A
rough box was all the coffin its feeble father could make : a few shovels
of loose mould was thrown up, and the pale child, borne to its resting
place by the hands of its mother, its father faintly following, was covered
with moist earth and matted leaves.   Not a word was spoken, but tears
fell like rain.   The scene was more solemn than if loud-sounding
requiems had been sung, or long. procession drawn out to bid the little
sleeper farewell.

The cool breeze of autumn brought healing on its wings ; and the
pioneer, strong once more, made the old woods resound again with his
thick-falling blows.   He carefully put seed into the ground for the

ensuing year, and dreamed of prosperity. But another enemy was at hand. The war-whoop of the Indian sounded fearfully in their ears one dark night, and they fled, lighted by the flames of their own cottage, with their little *one* — for one of the remaining two whom sickness had spared was butchered almost in its mothers arms, and left unburied on the ground. After a toilsome and dangerous march they gained a shelter in the settlements; and when from scattered neighborhoods hardy men gathered together to protect and defend their homes, the husband bade his wife adieu, and went forth against the foe. Peace came, and the settler and his wife revisited their deserted home. Anon a new dwelling arose; their household gods were gathered once more; and amidst various vicissitudes of fortune, the forest gradually fell around them, and other sons and daughters grew up to bless them.

Years rolled swiftly by, and the adjacent woods, which once bounded the view of our humble friends, were partially cleared away. A settlement had been formed; adventurers like themselves had come in: need it be said how grateful to them was the sight of man, and the pleasant sound of voices near or remote? Roads were opened; a modest school-house of hewn logs was erected, used on week-days to teach and train the budding intellect, and on Sundays for mutual communion of the few who with mingled fear and faith trusted and waited upon their God. Now it has become like an old country: fine fair fields extend on either side, waving in summer with yellow grain; with pastures from which one may hear the neighing of horses and the lowing of sleek-skinned kine. The deer and the panther have been driven farther west along with the savage, the aboriginal lord of the land.

The traveller who now passes the spot may think, as he looks upon all this, and sees the husbandman gather his harvest in peace, and witnesses the evening's merry-meeting of brave youths and fair-haired maidens, that peace, security, and ease had always smiled upon the pioneer; and while he sips his coffee in graceful indolence, should he perchance hear from that gray-headed pair (for such have our friends become) a brief history of the perils and trials of a new settlement, he may possibly turn away half-displeased, as if a nursery fable had been breathed in his ear.

———

DWELLERS in cities! who rejoice in the 'security of streets,' think occasionally of him who toils many and weary months, and makes one spot of this great earth the greener by his exertions. While you enjoy your luxuries, think of the brave band of men who are making our common country great and glorious, and by whose labor you thrive and fatten in at least *comparative* ease. If you are in debt, and curse your stars for your fortune, or the government for the too-much it promises or the too-little which it performs, or if, being rich, you fear that in the future your possessions may 'take to themselves wings and fly away;' contrast your situation with that of the hardy pioneer; weigh your troubles in the balance with the dangers which *he* braves, with the labor and suffering which *he* endures, and for the honor of man repine no more!

c.

EPITAPH ON A BARREL OF FLOUR.

Thou art departed! — gone the way of all
  The things of earth. Peace to thy quiet manes!
We deeply grieve; and many a tear shall fall
  In thy remembrance: we sorrow for the pains
With which thou didst so oft the stomach wrong;
We weep — to think that thou shouldst last so long!

Thou wert a fruitful source of many ills,
  Of which our tortured bodies sore complained;
And all those frequent heavy doctor's bills,
  That always kept our slender purses drained:
To thee we owed, beyond the slightest question,
Our head-aches, night-mares — blues, and indigestion.

Thou wert most stubborn! — never wouldst thou shape
  Thyself to crust or cake, or any thing
That 's eatable; and many a luckless scrape
  Upon my housewife-sister's guests wouldst bring;
For spite of all the care she could bestow,
Whene'er she cut her cake, she found it dough.

No fire so hot, could bake thee into bread;
  The 'seven-times' heated 'furnace' lurid blast
Thou didst defy — the oven's glowing bed:
  The cooks, confounded, all declared at last,
' Should they thy loaf in Ætna's crater throw,
Even then, thou wouldst come out but heavy dough!'

I 'm not o'er-dainty in my daily diet,
  As many landlord's know, or ought to know;
For I have paid outrageous bills in quiet,
  Through all the States, from Maine to Mexico.
For hunger often makes the trav'ller prize
What all the chemists ne'er could analyze.

I 've lived in steam-boats, if you 'll call it living,
  Where travellers are oft obliged to cope
With strangest compounds; stewards often giving
  To passengers what they should save for soap.
I never question; 't is a dangerous habit:
A cat tastes best when you suppose it rabbit.

I 've lived in Southern inns; and there I ate
  A dubious manufacture, miscalled bread;
'T was ' bread by courtesy;' whose clammy weight
  Upon the o'ercharged stomach lay like lead;
And e'en like the coiled incubus oppressed it,
Defying every effort to digest it!

In tough ship-biscuit, GRAHAM's saw-dust bread,
  I 've had some sad experience in my day,
And rough 's the food on which I 've often fed;
  But as for thee, in justice let me say,
Of all the fare I 've known, from last to first,
Thou wert the roughest, toughest, soggiest — worst!

Brimfield, August, 1841.   F.

THE BURNING OF THE SHIPS.

A STORY OF THE REVOLUTION.*

IN TWO PARTS.—PART I: CHAPTER FIRST.

On a bright morning in May, 1778, a young man, dressed in the uniform of the Continental service, was seen walking slowly along the high-road leading from the interior of New-Jersey toward the village of Bordentown, and about two miles from that place. His gait I have said betokened no great haste; on the contrary he stopped repeatedly to gather wild flowers, which he tore in pieces without remorse or ruth. His walk was to and fro before the opening of a shaded by-path, leading through a wood that skirted the high-road; and ever and anon, as he passed that retired path, he cast an anxious and eager gaze along its narrow vista. I would have waged any sum that he expected some one from that direction; but whom? Gentle reader, if you guess not already, you will be at no loss when I describe the outward appearance of that youth. He was tall, erect, well proportioned in figure, with an open and expressive countenance and healthy complexion, browned by exposure to the sun; in fact, the very man to be in love with some romantic country girl, against the unreasonable wishes of her friends, and in defiance of the stern commands of a proud and ambitious or mean and money-seeking father. Were I writing a fictitious tale, such a man should have been my hero, and I consider myself fortunate in finding him ready furnished to my hand. For though common enough in novels and other fictitious and unprofitable stories, this sort of character is hard to find in real life.

Our youth thus continued to pace backward and forward, to the great damage of the aforesaid wild flowers and his fingers' ends, (which he gnawed as if the arrival of his sweet-heart depended upon the annihilation of the same,) for the space of half an hour, though in his estimation it was a half day at least, or some period of duration between that and eternity. But he did not wait in vain. Suddenly he quickened his pace, turned rapidly down the shaded by-path into the wood, trampling unheeded whole beds of violets and arbatus in his course. It would have puzzled an indifferent observer to guess the cause of that sudden impulse. But lovers, as all who have acted in that capacity know, are

---

* Nearly seventeen volumes of the Knickerbocker have appeared since this admirable tale was written for its pages; and there are few of our readers, numbering thousands now where they counted hundreds then, who will not here peruse it for the first time. Its publication has been often urged upon us within the last two years, even by time-honored subscribers, who had themselves failed to obtain it entire; and we confess that at length we turn even from present liberal stores to comply with these repeated requests, with a gratification which we are sure will be shared by *all* our readers. We may add here, that we have so often borne cordial testimony to the excellences of the Society of Friends, that it is deemed quite unnecessary to state that no offence is intended toward the religious sect whose early strait-lacedness only is here pleasantly satirized.   Ed. Knickerbocker.

blessed with a special keenness of vision, or a peculiar instinct, teaching them with the certainty of demonstration the approach of that object 'dearer to them than life.' The waving of a shawl, the glancing of a riband t rough trees, which no human vision under other circumstances could penetrate, is enough, and was for our hero. They met; there was a taking hold of hands and a kiss, followed like all stolen kisses by a conscious and half-guilty look around, to be sure no envious eye gazed upon the scene. This ceremony performed, the gentleman drew the lady's arm within his, and the happy pair, leaving the path, walked to a clump of pines, under which they found, upon an old log, a rural and lover-like seat.

But why this mysterious meeting in the loneliness of the silent wood? Can that erect and noble bearing belong to some proscribed outlaw, endeared by his misery and his guilt to the gentle lady? Can that open and engaging countenance cover the false heart and base purposes of a villain? Or, less guilty if not less miserable, is poverty his only but unpardonable crime in the eyes of a hard-hearted father? Surely, some unexplained, some horrible obstacle disturbs as usual the never smooth 'course of true love;' else why this secret meeting beneath the deep shadow of yonder ever-greens, with no better seat than a gum log, instead of comfortably courting on the parlor sofa, or behind the more congenial concealment afforded by the honeysuckles that twine so gracefully over the nice summer-house at the foot of the garden?

Were mine a tale of the imagination, I would reserve the developement of this mystery for the last chapter. But I write history, and must tell truth as I go along. The gentleman I have said was a soldier. The lady, I must now inform the reader, was a Quaker, 'by the world so called.' It was against the 'testimony of early Friends' to paint likenesses, and the rule was not so often infringed in the time of Emma Richie's youth as it is at this day. I cannot therefore give a minute description of her appearance, without drawing upon fancy for the materials, which I am determined not to do in this true story. I only know, as all will take for granted, that she was beautiful, and that her complexion was of the transparent kind usually attendant upon light hair and eyes. But *her* hair was brown, and her eyes of a color so dark that they were generally supposed to be black. The hair, as it curled naturally over her white and rounding forehead, was surpassingly beautiful, but like all other beauty proved a source of serious trouble to its possessor. It had long been a cause of uneasiness of mind to all the straight-haired members of the women's meetings, and was finally declared to be against the discipline by that body. A delegation of two old Friends was sent 'to treat' with her parents about the matter, and authorized to set it straight. The father declared that he had nothing to do in the business; the mother professed 'great concern on her mind;' but the hair contumaciously continued to curl, and it was shrewdly guessed by many that no very effectual measures were ever taken to reform the beautiful error.

There was an air of real or affected demureness about Emma's mouth, which but for the contradiction of her eyes, would have given too prim an expression to her face. As it was, her friends were often puzzled to determine when she was in fun or earnest, sober or mischievous. But her smile left no longer room for doubt. It shed over her face a joyous but sweet and composed expression that was perfectly irresistible. It broke upon her features like a June sunbeam upon the fields of green grass and yellow grain and waving forests, or like that beautiful and gladdening effect of early day, before his rays have reached the valleys and the plain, which the prophet so poetically terms 'the morning spread upon the mountains.' These particulars are to a great extent matters of record. The curling hair appears to have been the subject of grave discussion at more than one 'meeting of business;' and the case of two young men is also recorded, who were 'dealt with for too frequent gazing' at the same, and the appurtenances thereunto belonging, during silent meeting, instead of directing their attention to some more profitable subject. The young men pleaded guilty, and 'submitted to treatment;' urging as some palliation the strength of the temptation and the weakness of poor humanity. Upon acknowledging that they were 'sorry they had disobliged Friends,' the culprits were readmitted into favor.

Emma's dress comported with the rules of her Society, and was as fine in its texture, as neatly fitted to the figure, and had received as much care in its arrangement, as ever was bestowed on the dress of a fashionable belle, or the strictest member of the Society of Friends. In this there was no non-conformity to rules, which although they proscribe all gay colors, cannot alas! divert the woman's attention from her attire. The fault is not in the rules, which are excellent, but the passion exists in the female bosom and must have indulgence. Refuse her the colors of the rainbow, forbid her to deck her person in its dyes, and she will devote equal attention in devising herself dresses out of white muslin, drab merino, and fawn-colored silk.

Emma's consisted of a white silk bonnet, very small, and close to her face, tied with white riband; white muslin gown, and a white crape shawl around her shoulders, and gathered up so as to show the graceful rounding of her figure. The only colored article upon her person was a pink riband, which she wore around her neck; an indulgence for some reason allowed to the young members, while all other colors are most especially eschewed. Even this is not *recommended*, but only *permitted*, and that much against the weight upon the minds of the strictest of the sect. If they *can*, the young friends are advised to do without the indulgence; but if that is impossible, a pink riband, provided it be not too long, is allowed in consideration of the weakness of the younger sisterhood. Some of the other rules concerning dress are apparently less reasonable. Why the women are allowed to dress in black, while that color is denied the men, is incomprehensible. But that man who would presume to clothe his shoulders in a black coat, might as well deny the inspiration of George Fox. A set of heterodox Quakers exists in the neighborhood of Boston. The principal point in which they differ from the Society, and the only one by which they can be *outwardly* distinguished, is that of being addicted to black coats.

But my reader must be anxious to hear what is going on all this while between the lovers. I give notice that I mean to detail no private conversation, except what concerns the story, and which he has therefore a right to know. The rest I shall consider sacred.

'But what in the world kept you so long?' inquired the lover.

'Indeed I could not help it, William. We are to have the English Friends at dinner, and mother wanted my aid. I should not have got off at all, if she had not sent me to neighbor Comstock's for a basket of *Fifth-month dukes.*'

'What in the name of nonsense are *they?*'

'That is the way with you world's people. You are so given to the heathenish appellation of days and months, that you cannot understand a christian language.'

'If your eyes would keep your counsel, Emma, you might make a capital quiz; but *they* always tell the truth. But what do you mean by Fifth-month dukes?'

'Cherries that ripen in the fifth-month, by the world's people called ' May dukes.''

'Nonsense!'

'I see thee thinks us fools; but in truth we are not so *very* particular. But friend Comstock is a little more so than the rest of us. He does not feel easy to call one of Heaven's gifts after a heathen idol.'

'Friend Comstock is right then, and consistent. You would not call the month after the heathen god, and why should you the fruit? Is it not quite as absurd to say '*Fifth-month*,' as '*Fifth-month dukes?*' The only difference is, that you are used to the first and not to the second.'

'I would not have said a word to thee, William, about the foolish cherries, had I supposed they would have put thee in such a pet. But if thee will promise to be pleased again, I'll adopt friend Comstock's expression, since thee prefers it. I am always glad to oblige thee.'

'Well, no matter, Emma. I'm a fool, and you shall say what you please. Here is a little present for you. You must wear it for me. I bought it of a French pedler. It was the prettiest he had.'

''I'll *keep* it for thy sake, William; but only think of my going to meeting with a blue riband round my neck! What could I say to old Friends? If it were pink, now!'

'Why so? Is it less gay?'

'Oh! pink is the color of the rose, thee knows.'

'And blue that of the sky. But why are you so fond of drab? That is not the color of the rose!'

'Oh! drab is the natural color of the wool.'

'Did you ever see a drab sheep, Emma?'

'Well, I do n't know what is the reason; and farther, I do n't care. Early Friends wore it, and we choose to.'

'Exactly; and you have given the only good reason I ever heard yet; *you choose to.* In a free country it is unanswerable; but it is only so as far as you *do* choose, and should not operate upon those who do *not.* This only convinces me of what I have often told you, that you are the veriest slaves in Christendom. That invisible pope, the weight of the meeting, holds you in more than inquisitorial awe. You must needs practice what you see no reason for, and abstain from enjoyments you deem innocent; and if you venture to ask a reason for the one or the other, your mouths are stopped by the information that such was the practice of early Friends, or by some other argument equally convincing to a reasonable and reasoning mind. You remind me ———'

'Now, William, hold thy tongue; for if thee sets fairly under way on that subject, thee will never stop until it has made me angry. Beside, thee cannot convince me.'

'Convince! No indeed; I'm not fool enough to hope *that*. There is one reason why no one of your Society ever *can* be convinced. It is part of the discipline, I believe, never to listen to any reason that makes against its errors. *I* convince! Moses and the Prophets, the four Evangelists, with St. Paul to boot, have failed, and *I* can scarcely expect to succeed!"

'Do they say any thing against Friends?'

'They do not mention the Society by name, I believe, but are pretty hard upon some of its errors.'

'Come, William, we have had enough of this. Thee is too fond of the subject, and want discretion in urging it so far. Why should thee be so anxious to change my views upon this subject? There are no essential differences between us. Why cannot thou adhere to thy forms, thy bishops with their white sleeves, and thy steeple-houses, as George Fox called them? If I do not feel able to adopt them, I shall not scold thee for doing so. Thou art unjust in thy abuse of Friends' principles. I am attached to them; then why should I change them? Our difference need neither divide our hearts here nor separate our destinies hereafter. We both adore one God and Father, both trust in the merits and intercession of one Saviour, and pray for the sanctifying influence of the same Holy Spirit, to guide us into all truth. Our peculiarities are harmless, if not meritorious. My parents, *all* whom I love, except thee, are Friends. It would be a sore cause of grief to them, especially to my mother, were I to leave their faith. Then why urge me? My principles shall never clash with thine. I am satisfied to see those who can, consistently with their own feelings, practice its forms, while in conformity to that portion of inward light given to me, I prefer the principles and bear the testimony of Friends. But I'll promise thee one thing, William; I will never turn preacher, that is if I can help it.'

'That would be a pity; for you have a copious gift. I never heard so full an outpouring from the gallery. I hope you feel easier. But is it possible you have not felt the curiosity to ask what urgent reason induced me to send for you this morning?'

'Why, there is nothing to be curious about. Thee's always crazy to see me. Thee never wrote me a note in thy life without having an urgent cause to see me.'

'Yes, but I have a *seriously* urgent one this time. If you will promise not to faint, I'll tell you. You need not turn so pale, you goose. It is not much after all. Only we expect an attack upon the ships at Bordentown.'

' When ? — not to-day ? '

' No, but to-night. A considerable force, in small vessels, has reached Burlington, and we have no doubt they are designed to destroy the property here.'

' At Burlington ! — they may be here in an hour.'

' We have taken measures to be advised by signals of the moment they leave Burlington. The wind is adverse, and they cannot beat up here in less than two or three hours.'

' But you do not mean to contend with them ? '

' It is true we cannot hope to protect the ships ; but M'Cauley will not give up without firing a gun or two, by way of compliment. We have made preparations to annoy them, without giving them much chance to hurt us.'

' Dear me ! I shall have no peace until it is over. Why did thee tell me, William, since I can do no good ? '

' Yes, but you can. Emma, you know how obnoxious your father is to the enemy. His Quaker feelings have kept his hands from blood, but not from aiding us rebels in many important particulars. He has set a bad example to his Society, who have generally been as submissive as the king's people could desire. It is believed that the opportunity will be taken to strike terror unto all evil-doers through him. I fear this is part of the duty assigned to the force at Burlington. We must avoid a repetition of the Caldwell tragedy. Your father must remove his family into the interior. I was on my way to see him, but heard he had gone to Crosswick's meeting. As I could not wait, I resolved to intrust the secret with you. Wait till he comes home, and then communicate the news in private.'

' But why keep it secret ? Should not our neighbors —— '

' No, they are in no danger.'

' Oh, dear ! when will the war be over ! Thou art surely Quaker enough to desire peace.'

' Oh, yes ! honorable peace. And then, that farm we talked about.'

' Yes, but first, thy profession of Friends' principles ; the exchange of these gaudy regimentals for a drab coat reaching to thy heels, and broad enough to cover both of us of a rainy day. How respectable thee will look ; may-be seated in the gallery ! '

' Very pleasant indeed, to Fancy, but like most of her pictures, not likely to be realized.'

' Not realized ! How are we to be married then, and go upon that farm ? Does thee expect me to disoblige Friends, and offend my parents, just to pleasure thee ? I thought there was nothing hard or impossible to lovers ! '

' Emma, you are incorrigible. Is there no article in the discipline against malicious mischief ? Your father would not care if we were married to-morrow, provided he knew nothing of it till it were done, and was not compromised with the meeting. Your mother would not be pleased, I know ; but after awhile she would remember that I am *not* a Presbyterian, and might have been worse than I am. Then as to Friends, they would read you out, and after a month or so, read you *in* again, and there would be an end.'

'That is true; I should only have to express my sorrow, which before a month I may truly do, and the fold would be open to the wandering and repentant lamb.'

'Emma, I must bid you good-by, for my time has expired. Remember what I have told you. I shall not feel easy till you are gone. Do n't fear for me. I 'll dodge the balls for your sake. Good-by!'

'Farewell, William; I did not think thee would go so soon. I will do all thee said. Farewell!'

The young soldier brought a horse from the wood, and rode away at full gallop. The lady wiped divers tears from her eyes, and quietly pursued her way to neighbor Comstock's house, where she procured a supply of 'Fifth-month dukes,' and returned home.

CHAPTER II.

WHEN Emma reached home she found her mother and all the family busy in preparing a grand dinner for the expected strangers. The English Friends, Joseph Dido and Martha Nazleby, were that morning holding meetings at Crosswicks, where it may gratify my readers to learn they were favored, (see their Journal, page 37,) with a 'comfortable sitting and a plentiful opening.' Joseph and Martha were, as their names prove, *not* man and wife; and though to the world it may seem strange that a rosy English gentleman of forty should leave his wife and children to visit Friends in America, with a companion young and handsome, of the softer sex, whose husband also remained in England, let not the Philistine scoff nor the daughter of the uncircumcised sneer thereat. Such things are not uncommon among Friends; and be it spoken to the credit of this moral people, I never heard of any harm coming of the practice. A visit from a travelling Friend, more especially when he is also an *English* Friend, is esteemed a great honor, and calls forth the most solid testimonials of hospitality.

At twelve, then the usual dinner-hour in the country, all the preparations were completed, and Jonathan Richie's equipage was seen approaching up the avenue of young poplars. This valuable exotic had been lately introduced into the country, and Jonathan was as eager as any of his neighbors to ornament his grounds with their stiff and lofty forms. There they stood straight and tall, like some maiden ladies I have seen, neither useful nor ornamental. I need not describe the equipage : every body has seen a Jersey wagon, and knows what it was of old and is now. It approached, drawn by two of those fat, lazy and lounging horses which rich farmers always drive, and at the slow gait to which they are accustomed. Joseph Dido and Martha Nazleby were accompanied by Nathaniel Comstock and Samuel Robertson, two public Friends, connected with Crosswick's meeting, and Jonathan Richie.

Friend Dido was a handsome comfortable-looking Englishman, with the appearance and manners of a gentleman ; Martha, his companion, a tall fine looking woman, of dignified appearance, and rather comely face. Nathaniel Comstock looked, as he was, the quintessence of

Quaker formality. He scorned all form, though without being aware that in his studied opposition to 'the world's ways' he had slipped to the other extreme, and was as much a slave to a formal avoidance as the 'world's people' can be to an observance of them. It was with him a point of conscience to keep his hat on in the house, during the most oppressive weather and under the most inconvenient circumstances. When he accosted a Friend in the street, he would double brace his sinews and stiffen his body, and pronounce his 'How's thee do?' through his inmost nose, as if the whole ceremony were a part of his religion. Nathaniel was a selfish, money-loving, worldly-minded man, incased in the outward covering of a Quaker. I desire to do no injustice to this respectable community, but such persons exist among them as well as among other societies of Christians. It is no argument against a good thing, that it is liable to abuse. Nathaniel knew that a strict conformity to its discipline would insure him the countenance and support of his Society, provided he could keep his inward rascality to himself. In this he succeeded, though his character was not above suspicion with the wiser portion of the meeting. Still he was rich; and wealth is power, with all men, or societies of men, civil or religious, and with the self-denying and world-contemning Quakers as well as others. So long as Nathaniel was contented to remain in a lay capacity, he found no opposition, but he was suddenly bitten with that restless flea, ambition, and aspired to the ministry. Friends did not approve the proposition, and the candidate was advised to wait and test the call more fully. But the 'weight on his mind increased' so fast, and 'his uneasiness' became so pressing, that he was at last permitted to 'relieve his mind.'

Accordingly, on the first ensuing First-day, being the seventh of Eighth-month, 1770, he took his seat among the ministers, and before long arose. Great expectation was excited, as usual, at the 'opening' of a new public Friend; and while Nathaniel stood in silence for a minute before he began to speak, you might have *heard* the profoundest stillness that reigned around. A pin which dropped from Sybella Hoskins' starched neckerchief was distinctly heard as it struck the floor, to the extreme end of the men's meeting. At length the words began to drop one by one from Nathaniel's *nose*, (I had like to have said mouth,) with an interval of about thirty seconds between each. 'It has — been — on — my — mind . . . for a — long time, to address Friends. The thought weighs heavy on my mind . . . and I can't feel easy to suppress it. It appears to me . . . that it would be more consistent and becoming for all Friends to mind . . . their own business.'

The pronunciation of the first six words occupied three minutes. The next clause was delivered with more rapidity, one or two words at a time, like water from a full porter-bottle: as the speaker proceeded, the matter continued to flow more readily, like the aforesaid bottle when having lost some of its contents it bolts out the remainder as fast as the internal vacuum can be supplied. The rest was given forth freely: the voice was raised, and the words were pronounced at its highest and most discordant pitch, the bottle having nearly emptied itself.

This was not esteemed a very *reaching* sermon; but as Nathaniel was just opening, it was hoped he would become 'much enlarged.' He made several subsequent attempts, but not much 'to approval:' as he had received, he gave but little. The best attempt was his last, and it is still quoted and deemed worthy of preservation in the country. He rose one day, and without preamble or addition, he expressed the following elegant and appropriate sentiment: 'Young folks *thinks* old folks fools, but old folks *knows* young folks to *be* fools.' This was his last public testimony. His wife met him at the door of the meeting-house, and before the congregated elders, the very weight of the meeting, thus accosted him: 'Oh! Nathaniel, why *will* thee make such a fool of thyself!' Whether this gentle remonstrance had the effect, or he received a hint from the old Friends that he was not approved of, is not known; but he never felt moved again. He continued however strictest of the strict in his deportment and conversation. He it was who always addressed an old tinker, by name 'Munday,' as 'neighbor Second-day;' and of whose 'Fifth-month dukes' the reader has already heard enough.

So much for Nathaniel's history and character. I cannot forbear some description of his outer man, for it was original and unimitated. He was very tall and very spare. His small head was thinly covered with gray hair, and attached to a nose of immense proportions and singular conformation. It was an isoceles' triangle, resting on its shortest side as its base, and of course stuck out almost directly from his face, with the air, as he walked head and chin erect, of a grey-hound when he hears the horn of a morning. An old Indian of the Brotherton tribe styled it the 'father of all noses.' Beneath this phenomenon opened as singular a mouth. In its quiescent state it did not look very large, being puckered up like the mouth of Nathaniel's purse. Like it, too, its openings were little profitable to his neighbors, though both possessed a capacity for reception wonderful to behold. Imagine this mouth and nose fixed by a long and thin neck on as long and thin a body, and this supported by a pair of the merest spindle-shanks, attached to two of the heaviest and most ill-shaped feet in New-Jersey, and you have Nathaniel Comstock; of whom enough for the present.

Samuel Robertson was the very reverse of his thin neighbor in disposition and in person; and clearly demonstrated in his life and conversation that all the usages of his Society might be strictly and religiously observed, without offending those from whom he differed in sentiment, or infringing one rule of true and genuine politeness. Samuel was a gentleman by nature and education, in heart and in manner. In his day he appears to have been considered rather a phenomenon among his people. In point of education, there were probably few among them equal to him; but doubtless many possessed his other good qualities. If it were not so, the Society of Friends have made a rapid improvement. For where we could show one wolf in sheep's clothing, like Nathaniel, we could produce ten who have imitated Samuel Robertson in his gentlemanlike deportment, his liberal feelings, and his generous philanthropy.

Jonathan Richie was never meant by nature for a Quaker; and

though he wore the dress and observed the outward practices of the sect, was totally deficient in that spirit of forbearance under insult, or to speak more correctly, that suppression of the irritable feelings, which forms an important part of the practice of its professors. Still, though quick he was easily appeased, true-hearted, and intelligent. He had taken great interest in the Colonial cause, and itched to have his hand in the work. But the influence of his wife and Friends had sufficed to keep his fingers from fight and himself from expulsion.

Rachel Richie was a fat and prejudiced, but at the same time kind and hospitable old woman, perfectly satisfied with herself and 'Friends,' and firmly convinced that all the rest of the world were in the bonds of iniquity and the depths of ignorance. This good opinion of herself and her judgment showed itself on all occasions, and sometimes provoked our young acquaintance, William Vallette, (Emma's lover,) beyond forbearance, though he had every reason to desire her good feelings. She would take frequent occasion to observe upon his religious opinions, the form of prayer, written discourses, and observance of Christmas, Easter, etc., all which she termed 'heathen superstitions,' evidently without entertaining any idea of the meaning of the charge. This invariably brought on an argument, in the course of which, while she always displayed a sorrowful ignorance of every thing in the shape of books, except the contents of two or three 'Journals of Travelling Friends,' Rachel would express a provoking and condescending pity for her young friend's blindness, which invariably threw him out of his argument into a passion. If he stood this unmoved, she was sure to conquer him. After he had exhausted all his ingenuity upon some (in his opinion) absurdity of her creed, and nailed it with Scripture, she would dress her face in a half-contemptuous half-pitying smile, and complacently answer, that she 'did not feel easy to adopt that opinion;' that 'the light within her was sufficient for her;' or, to his equal satisfaction, that 'Friends thought otherwise.' This in answer to a plain injunction of Scripture would inevitably throw poor Vallette into a fever, which was only increased by the placid and still contemptuous and pitying smile with which his petulance was received.

Upon one occasion he was tempted to retaliate upon her the disrespect she had expressed toward a venerable clergyman of the episcopal church, by denying the inspiration of John Stokes, a highly-gifted minister whom Friend Rachel almost adored and quite worshipped. He persuaded her to admit that though John's inspiration might be fully equal to that which dictated the Bible, yet that since the Bible was *certainly* an inspired production, all other inspiration must unite with it; and all which should differ from or be in any particular unlike the inspiration of the Bible could not be inspiration at all. 'Well then,' said he, 'show me that holy men were ever inspired to speak nonsense, and I will believe the nonsense of John Stokes to be inspiration; but not *till* then.' There was an end of all calmness and placidity upon the countenance of Friend Rachel in a moment. Contempt gave way to rage, and Vallette was glad to escape the presence. As he valued his chance for Emma's hand, he took care to avoid theological disputes with her mother from that time forward.

Here, as I write for the instruction of my fellow-men, I must be permitted to waste a little upon them. Dr. Franklin used to say that if all things lost on earth went to the moon, how full she must be of good advice! Nevertheless, I am resolved to do my duty, and to wash my hands of the blood of all men.

First then, ye aspirants after and pretenders to the light of inspiration, never admit the Bible to be the true standard by which your claims shall be weighed. It will prove a dangerous test, and ten to one you will suffer by the comparison. You have heard of that celebrated philosopher who in pity for the blindness of this dark world hung his rush-light upon a tall post. It gave no great amount of radiance, it is true; yet as it shone at midnight amid pitch darkness, and was hung above the heads of his neighbors, it passed among them for a new star or a comet. But the philosopher became ambitious with partial success, and resolved to lend his powerful aid to the sun, and having so effectually lighted the night, proposed to illuminate the noon-day. As might have been predicted, he made but a poor business of it. His lamp burned, but gave forth darkness rather than light, since the only visible evidence that it continued to blaze was the smoke it evolved. Its fire evidently was not of the same essence with the heaven-born radiance of the glorious sun; and even his neighbors perceived how little claim his paltry taper had to a communion with the stars of the firmament, when they saw it perched scarce out of their reach, on the top of a twenty-feet pole.

Then take wisdom from the philosopher's failure, ye who would hold up the light of your vaunted inspiration to aid the beams of the Sun of Righteousness. Keep your candle from his rays: hide it by day; bring it forth only by night.

Secondly: You who are given to religious arguments with bigoted and ignorant partisans, beware how you insinuate aught against the purity of their creed or the perfection of their prophets, but content yourself with defending your own. You will find it sufficient occupation. You may naturally conclude, that since they take all sorts of liberties with your creed and your teachers, you may with propriety express your sentiments in return. You will find yourself mistaken, and give unpardonable offence. If you have no reason to regard the good or ill opinion of your adversary, it may be very well and very satisfactory to speak your mind; but if you are courting his daughter, or wish to borrow his money, by all means keep it to yourself.

The visiters were ushered into the parlor, opened specially for this occasion, and received by Emma and her mother.

'Joseph Dido, my wife, my daughter; Martha Nazleby, my wife, my daughter Emma.'

'Pleased to see thee, Joseph; pleased to see you *all*, friends. Emma, take friend Nazleby's bonnet. Samuel, how's thee do? Well, Nathaniel, how's *thee*? And Rebecca? I heerd she was poorly.'

'Complains of being some better this morning, thank thee, Rachel.'

'Come, Rachel,' said Jonathan, 'has thee got nothing for these Friends? They have ridden far this morning.'

'We can give them something, but poor to what such travellers have been used to.'

'We are not used to any thing better than thou art, Rachel, I assure thee,' said Friend Dido, as they walked into the room where dinner was prepared.

It may be as well to remark here upon one peculiarity by which an English Friend may be distinguished. He speaks good English. It must be from disinclination to take the necessary trouble rather than from ignorance, that American Quakers so universally commit high treason against the Queen in her capacity of Defender of the Grammar. 'How's thee do,' 'thee would,' etc., certainly come much easier to the tongue than 'how dost thou do,' and 'thou wouldst.'

Being seated at the table, our Friends assumed that solemn manner and perfect silence which always precedes their meals; an appropriate and affecting ceremony, when the form is accompanied and sanctified by the inward and spiritual grace. The dinner advanced without much conversation, except an occasional passing remark between Joseph and Samuel, and the brief and oft-repeated exhortations to eat, addressed to the guests on the part of their host and hostess.

'Why, Friend Dido, I declare thee does not eat at all. *Do* take some more of the roast pig! Well then, try the boiled beef; thee'll find it very good. No? Well, this is a very tender young chicken. Martha, I am afraid thee finds nothing thee likes. Why, thee eats nothing at all.'

Nathaniel did not open his mouth to speak, except to say 'Yes, thank thee,' when Jonathan offered to replenish his plate; but sat with his tall figure bent to the table, his nose almost touching it, and poured the food into his capacious mouth with a rapidity and energy truly miraculous. When the meal was finished, the conversation began.

'Thou wert at Burlington Quarterly Meeting, Joseph, I believe,' said Samuel Robertson, who though an American, was conscientiously scrupulous of speaking ungrammatically, and was almost a solitary exception to the general rule.

'Yes,' said Joseph.

'Was Robert Dot at meeting?'

'Yes, and Susan Sacherville. We had a profitable meeting, and experienced a great state of inwardness.'

'I thought so,' said Nathaniel, wiping his mouth. 'Robert Dot was highly favored on that day. The power accompanying his words was very reaching. Did thee not feel it so, Joseph?'

'Yes, at first; but Robert himself told me he over-stayed the motion, and persisted to speak, though he felt an inward inclining to sit down; and so it came to pass that great flatness and uneasiness ensued. The latter part reminded me of George Fox's prison, 'the savor whereof was very grievous to be endured.''

'Was there not some difference among Friends at that meeting?' inquired Friend Rachel.

'Yes,' said Martha. 'John Pearce, as soon as the meeting was gathered into an inward waiting state of mind, felt constrained to address Friends. He felt some concern on his mind on account of backsliding of certain former members, calling themselves Free Quakers, and violating the testimony concerning war, holding what they termed defensive war to be allowable. John had it on his mind to confer privately with Joseph Haywood on the matter.'

' Was Joseph at meeting ? '

' Yes, and John had opportunity with him afterward, and let him know his uneasiness; but it was not removed.'

' Did Joseph speak ? '

' He expressed himself under weight. But it was signified by Friends that as he was under dealing, it would not be to approval.'

' I hear Tobias Haley opened as a public Friend.'

' Yes, and a new woman Friend appeared in supplication, but not to edification of Friends.'

At this period of the conversation, Jonathan, who would much rather have talked with the Englishman about the wonderful things in the old country, of the events and prospects of the struggling Colonists, and had attempted in vain to turn the current, left the room on pretence of business. Emma, who had been watching for an opportunity to speak privately with him, soon followed and delivered her message.

' That was kind in William, and I will not forget it. He is a fine fellow; don 't thee think so, Emma? I thought so. I must go to Bordentown, and see about the matter. Tell Quommino to put the horses to the wagon.'

Jonathan, having informed his friends that urgent business called him to Bordentown, prepared to depart alone; but Nathaniel, having some purchases to make of Amos Smith, the principal store-keeper and moneyed man of the vicinity, offered, to his great annoyance, to accompany him. PART TWO IN OUR NEXT.

THE NAMELESS GRAVE.

BY MISS M. A. BROWNE.

'T is but a fragment of a tomb,
  Spared when the rest was clear'd away;
Its sculpture gone; the name of whom
  It covered perished in decay:
But though it bears nor name nor date,
  I have wild fancies of my own,
And well I love to contemplate
  That old and shattered stone !

I wander near it when the dew
  Of morn is dripping from the eaves,
And the church window glistens thro'
  Its curtain green of ivy leaves.
The marble shines, when o'er its white
  Smooth surface is the sunlight thrown;
But oh! I love, though not so bright,
  That old and shattered stone !

I love to think, ' Perchance some head
  Of peerless beauty there may rest;
That monument perhaps was laid
  Upon a fair and lovely breast !
And even while I gaze, perchance
  Some spotless spirit looketh down,
And casts its pure celestial glance
  Upon the old gray stone !'

If such things be, what vanity
  This earth and all therein must seem
To those who dwell in bliss on high,
  Whose name on earth is but a dream !
And while we strive with care and pains
  To leave a name when we are gone,
May we remember what remains
  Of that sepulchral stone.

THE PASSAGE OF THE SEA.

WRITTEN IN THE GULF OF MEXICO.

WE have journeyed far o'er many a land,
    O'er many a sunny plain;
And now our steps have left the strand —
    Our path lies o'er the main!

It lies across the waters drear,
    Far o'er the lone blue sea :
In perfect love there dwells no fear —
    Then pass the waves with me.

Our vessel like a broad-winged bird
    Lies on the watery track ;
The springing breeze her sails hath stirr'd,
    And streams her pennon back.

We hope for many happy hours
    Upon that silent deep ;
Our hearts, like long unfaded flowers,
    Shall still Earth's freshness keep.

We 'll watch the white and leaping spray
    Curl'd from our cleaving prow,
And the wild breeze shall kiss away
    The dark locks from each brow.

And when the stars of midnight o'er
    The waves shine gleamingly,
We 'll speak of those who dar'd of yore
    The passage of the sea :

The inmates of the early ark,
    Floating a world above,
Till o'er the space of waters dark,
    Returned the peace-fraught dove :

And Pharoah's bands that came in wrath,
    With clashing cymbals tost ;
Fiercely on fleeing Israel's path,
    A dark and angry host :

Till on those red and rolling waves,
    Those ancient waters lone,
Chariot and horsemen found their graves,
    And Egypt's might was gone.

The passage of the classic deep,
    When Grecian spears were met,
And Fate for destined Troy might weep,
    And eyes in Heav'n were wet.

And the fleeing of that bark by night,
  That bore Æneas' fate,
When Illium's flames were red and bright,
  And the Trojan — desolate.

We 'll speak of days when mighty Rome
  Her eagle wings unfurled,
When the passage of the sea brought home
  The conquerors of a world :

The Cæsars and the Antonies,
  And the Nile's captive green :
Freighted with god-like destinies
  The ancient seas have been !

A bark went forth, a bark from Spain,
  In the knightly days of yore ;
A frail bark o'er that mighty main
  No sail had swept before.

The mariner that held the helm
  Was bound in fervent dreams ;
In visions of the unknown realm,
  Its gold, its gushing streams.

Oh ! strong was faith, a faith sincere,
  To guide that lonely ship,
When through each storm and doubt and fear
  COLUMBUS passed the deep !

They too, whose memory yet can thrill,
  The Pilgrim Fathers' band,
Whose faith in quenchless embers still
  Burns on, from land to land :

Each gray head bore its anguish deep
  From the rest of its native sod,
And the passage of the sea to them
  Was a passage unto GOD !

And there are darker memories,
  That I could call to mind,
Till fraught with startling histories
  Seems every ocean wind.

The legends of the Spanish Main,
  Of cruisers stern and bold,
Of deeds that madden on the brain,
  And tales of blood and gold.

We traverse the wild ocean o'er,
  A cold and careless race,
Remembering not the hosts of yore
  That swept the water's space.

But oh ! let *one* great memory
  Be graven on the deep,
Let not thy tides, tumultuous Sea !
  That record darkly sweep.

'T is written on each billow's crest,
  Each white surge rolling free,
That HE who fram'd, who sav'd the world,
  Once passed the darkened sea.

He passed not with the cymbals' clash,
  Mid ships of sound and flame ;
No herald was the battle's flash —
  In simple guise HE came.

Clad in the fisher's garb, alone,
  He came, at close of even,
Who spread the waves from zone to zone,
  And set the stars in Heaven !

Thus let the path of those who rove
  Over the dark waves be :
Fearing not, in HIS might of love,
  The passage of the sea !

Big Prairie, (Miss.) ＼ ELLEN PERCY.

MY FATHER'S HOUSE: A REMINISCENCE.

'DOMOS ANTIQUITAQUE, RUSTICA.'

I HAVE a great affection for every thing which brings to mind my boyish days. I believe that if by any possibility I could obtain the identical rod with which my father whipped me for the first time, I should cherish it as the apple of my eye. It would afford occupation for many a quiet hour, to gaze upon that dry, knotty, barkless stick. A few weeks ago I passed by chance through the village in which I was born. It is situated in the south-western part of good old Connecticut, and is just such a place, both in the character of its inhabitants and in its general appearance, as one would expect to find in that 'land of steady habits.' The main feature of the country around it is hills; some with barren, naked summits, standing in bold relief against the distant sky; others crowned with the hardy birch and dark solemn pines; and not a few covered with bright yellow fields of ripe and waving grain.

My father's house stood (or stands, but it is his no longer,) at some distance from the centre of the village. I remember that in my boyhood he used to rejoice at this circumstance, for it kept me from all intercourse with the wild, mischief-loving youngsters of the place. When I passed through the little settlement, I was astonished to find the building which had been my home for the first fifteen years of my life, still standing, as it had stood eighteen years before, save that the trees around it were somewhat larger, and its old dilapidated chimney was a shade or two blacker. It was an old-fashioned building; originally of a red color ; but time had sprinkled moss upon its sides, and here and there where a board had fallen off a new unpainted one had been hastily nailed on, contrasting strongly with its weather-stained fellows. The roof was of the kind peculiar to all old country houses ; narrow in front, but reaching almost to the ground in the rear.

The trees before the house had almost grown out of my recollection. They were no longer the trees at which I used to wonder in my infancy ; which I climbed in my boyhood ; upon whose branches I loved to sit and be shaken by the wind ; under which I built my play-house, and fed my young birds, and conned my morning lessons. They were familiar to me as connected with the dwelling, and for that I loved them ; but my *childish* regard for them had disappeared. I used to think that there were no trees like them ; but now — I had been abroad, and the dreams of infancy were dispelled.

My father had moved from the place shortly after I left home, and the house had fallen into the hands of strangers. A ragged urchin, who was playing in the street before it, informed me that it had been untenanted ever since he could remember. I entered the little yard by its side, and passing through it, gazed upon the narrow plat of green-sward in the rear. There was the well with its long pole and ' moss-covered bucket ; ' the very bucket from which I had slaked my thirst when a merry, heedless boy. The garden-fence was just as I had left it. Its chestnut pickets, embrowned by long exposure, and here and there whitened by the hoary moss, had withstood the storms and tempests of eighteen years ; but it was the same as when I looked upon it last. The garden was sadly changed. In my father's time it had been devoted to culinary vegetables ; now it was covered with rank, unchecked weeds. The white-flowered stramonium struggled for a place with the nettle and thistle ; and the bright yellow-flowered ear-drop and blue-crested virvane sprang up in the corners in wild luxuriance. That garden which my father had kept so neat and clean ; where not a vestige of a weed was to be found ; which in my infancy I was forbidden to enter, and in my boyhood commanded to cultivate ; that garden thus to be overspread with the offscouring of the fields and road-sides — it was sacrilege ! In the roaring cataract or the majestic ocean, the murmuring rivulet or the foaming cascade ; in the wide-spread landscape, or the grotto whose arched and fretted roof reflects a thousand sparkling colors ; Nature may be more impressive than Art ; but if you bring down the rule to the cultivation or neglect of a garden, the ancient dame must yield to her younger rival.

I tried the door of the house. It was not locked, and I entered. Passing through a sort of hall, I found myself in the kitchen. There was the wide fire-place, in whose ample corner I used to sit during the long winter evenings, and read by the yellow fire-light strange tales of ' ghosts and goblins and chimeras dire ! ' How often had I piled the oaken sticks upon the huge andirons which here used to ' sprawl on iron feet ! ' The fire-place was now empty, and the chimney was rough and blackened by the smoke which I had watched as it curled upward in dark wreaths into the wide aperture above. A few ashes lay upon the hearth. I touched them; they were cold and damp. I knew not but that I myself had kindled the fire whose remains were before me. In one corner of the room was the old cup-board. The door had fallen from the hinges; and the empty shelves, upon which I had so often seen rows of shining crockery and huge pewter-platters neatly arranged by my mother's hands — those shelves, now empty and covered with the collected dust of years, sent a thrill of desolation to my heart. As I turned away, a gust of wind rushing through the open door behind me with a crash, blew open with a hollow sound the door of the old-fashioned parlor. I could not choose but enter. Before me was the window at which my mother used to sit in the summer evenings, and relate strange, wild stories to her wondering boy. I left the apartment with a vague choking sensation in my throat. For ten years had that kind mother slept in her silent grave! God bless her for ever!

Passing once more through the hall, I mounted the wide winding stair-case, and gained the top. On my right hand stood what had been the Haunted Room. The good people of the village told strange stories concerning that apartment. It was before my father bought the house, before I was born, they said, that Satan had played his wild pranks there-in. Those who lived in the house deserted the apartment; for it seemed that although his Infernal Majesty could easily creep through blinds and glass, yet if a curtain were drawn, it greatly impeded his progress. Hence it was that the house-keeper was unable to keep a curtain on the windows. She nailed up strong cloth, but it was of no avail. So surely as the witching hour of night came, so surely would the windows rattle and shake; and at last, crash! down would come the curtains, with no visible agent, and in the sight of many an honest neighbor. The plain inference was, that His Highness thus announced his coming; and one or two were heard to declare that precisely at the moment the curtains fell a strong sulphureous odor pervaded the room. Certain it is, that as soon as the curtains were fairly down, the chairs commenced a general waltz, whether there were sitters in them or no; and the result generally was, that every body was frightened out of the apartment, and Satan was left to flourish as he pleased. This state of affairs continued until the room was entirely deserted; and even after that, when every article of furniture was removed and the door double-locked, strange unearthly noises were heard to proceed from it at dead of night; and it was at length branded as the Haunted Room.

One day, however, a kind of half-crazy, half-cunning man in the village was taken ill. He assured his friends that he never should get well until he was carried to the Haunted Room; he must lie there till his disease should pass away. His relatives, knowing the force of imagination, yielded at last to his entreaties, and the apartment was once more opened. A bed was carried into it; the cobwebs were brushed from the walls; curtains were again put upon the windows; and the sick man was brought and deposited there. The first night of his stay several of the bolder spirits of the neighborhood remained with him until morning. Midnight came; and just as the clock struck twelve, with a tremendous crash down fell or rather flew the curtains, into the middle of the room! The affrighted neighbors would have fled; but the sick man, leaping from the bed, stationed himself between them and the door, and commanded them to remain. He desired them, he said, to stay and see him conquer the foul fiend. They tarried reluctantly; when he seized the curtains in his hands, advanced toward the grate, where a bright fire was burning, thrust them into it, and exclaimed with a loud voice: 'SATAN, AVAUNT!'

Instantly a loud roar of laughter was heard, and the curtains, unharmed by the fierce flame, flew up the chimney. The neighbors rushed out of doors, and gazed earnestly into the air. They saw or thought they saw the curtains flying over the distant trees; and one bolder than the rest affirmed that he plainly perceived a little horned imp sitting snugly ensconced in the folds. They returned to the room; but the sick man was gone. The next day he was found pursuing his usual occupations in the village. The room was haunted no more. The owners of the house mended the broken sashes, and put new curtains over the windows, which ever after remained unmolested. It was subsequently hinted by many around the village that the pretended sick man had once exhibited himself as a juggler; that the sulphureous smell existed only in the imaginations of those who had experienced it; that in a windy winter night the draught might easily draw a pair of curtains up the chimney; and that as for seeing them flying over the distant trees with a devil in each corner, why — there *could n't be* much truth in it. But the ghost-believing inhabitants scouted such unreasonable suppositions; and they still cherish with awe a reverential belief in the Haunted Room.

As I entered this apartment, a vague indefinable feeling came over me; the same sensation with which I used to enter it when a boy. I looked at the walls and the windows. The former were damp and covered with cobwebs; the latter dusty and dim. A soiled and tattered curtain still hung to one of them. I glanced at it, and left the room with a shudder. The superstitions which are instilled into our minds in infancy cling to us till the very latest breath of life. We may strive to shake them off, but they will *sometimes* creep over us. I felt them creeping over me while I surveyed that tattered curtain. In my boyhood I had been accustomed to gaze at those windows, and wonder whether 'old Clootie,' as Burns calls him, ever *had* come through them; and half wish that he might and half fear lest he should appear before me in veritable *propria persona.*

My visit to the old mansion has often since afforded me a theme for pleasant contemplation, especially when the twilight is just disappearing, and one by one the stars go up upon their watch in the deep blue vault of heaven. Fond thoughts of the past, of youthful dreams and of bygone pleasures, are awakened within me; cherished recollections come back upon me, of my early friends; some wandering in other lands and some fallen asleep upon the bosom of the earth; all serving to throw a hallowed influence around my spirit, when I think of MY FATHER'S HOUSE.

IMITATION OF HORACE.

BY A NEW CONTRIBUTOR.

REST of the gods does he implore,
Who, on the Ægean, far from shore,
  Is tossed, when tempests veil the moon :
When stars, that pilot o'er his way
The mariner, afford no ray
  To cheer the darkness in its noon.

For rest the warlike Thracian pleads,
For rest the quiver-bearing Medes,
  My Grosphus, rest, which none can buy,
Not with the diamond's sparkling light,
Nor sands of Tagus shining bright,
  Nor robes that drink the purple dye.

The glittering dust which men demand
And haughty consul's fascial band
  Secure no quietude of mind ;
Cares hover round the palace gate,
The vaulted ceilings of the great,
  And in a bitter bondage bind.

What cheerful days does he prepare,
Who takes his father's humble fare ;
  How sweet his slumbers in the shade !
No sordid, avaricious schemes
Disturb him in his lightsome dreams,
  Or pierce his soul with Envy's blade.

Ah ! why do we, whose hours are few,
Ten thousand futile plans pursue ?
  Why seek for peace in foreign lands ?
What voluntary exile may,
As he forsakes his country, say
  That he from self dissolves the bands ?

The brass-beaked ships corroding Care
Ascends ; her pallid form is there ;
  Where'er the horseman spurs his steed,
Swifter than stag she flies along,
Swifter than Eurus with his throng,
  The gloomy tempest-gathered seed.

Pleased with the present, let the soul
Refuse to wander o'er the scroll
  Where Fate the future may portray ;
In sorrow seek a just relief ;
With gentle laughter temper grief,
  Nor look thou for a cloudless day.

The noble son of Peleus died
While coursed his blood in youthful pride;
   Tithonus mourned Aurora's plea:
And thou perchance mayst vainly lift
Thy prayer to Fortune for the gift
   The fickle goddess grants to me.

Thy hundred herds their lowing raise,
And in thy meads the race-horse neighs —
   Thy robes with Tyrian purple shine;
A narrow farm and lyric flow
Did Destiny on me bestow,
   A spurner of the crowd malign.

M. T. D.

PASSAGES FROM JEAN PAUL.

BY JOHN BRINCKMAN.

I.

FEELINGS are stars which guide only when the sky is cloudless; but Reason is a magnetic needle attracting the vessel surely, even though the stars are hidden and no longer shining.

II.

MAN never delineates more truly his own mind than by the manner in which he draws that of another.

III.

LIKE the water of the ocean, life becomes really sweet only by rising heavenward.

IV.

Do not throw thy anchor into the depths of the mud of earth, but into the height of the clear blue heavens; then thou wilt be well moored, though there blows a gale.

V.

EVERY man of genius is a philosopher, but not every philosopher a genius.

VI.

THE arrows of misfortune pierce the deepest into gentle hearts. The tears of man are the larger and flow the faster, the less Earth is able to give him, and the higher he himself stands above her; even as a cloud rising higher than the rest from the globe, sends forth the largest drops.

VII.

To be happy we require little less than every thing, and to be unhappy, a trifle more than nothing.

VIII.

TWO noble souls first discover their relation by the corresponding love that joins them to a third.

IX.

MISFORTUNES are like thunder clouds. Far away, they look black; over head, they are only gray. As gloomy dreams are harbingers of a joyful future, so the dream of life will prove on our awaking from it.

X.

THERE is no work of art which can do greater honor to the talents and taste of a married woman, and which she ought more readily to improve and to polish, than — her daughter.

XI.

Do you believe that there exists no smaller rock of liberty or republic than St. Marino in Italy? There is a republic that finds room in a bosom : or do you lack a heart?

XII.

WOMEN love energy without imitating it; men, tenderness without returning it.

XIII.

FATE deals with nations as Heliogabalus did with his cooks. If one of them served a dish, the ingredients of which were bad, he forced him to live on it until he had invented a better.

XIV.

CHILDREN stand very near God, as the smallest sphere is nearest to the sun.

XV.

IN the cave of the mountain the drop falls gently, but betrays a lasting existence by growing hard, sharp, and rough. The tear of man is more beautiful. It cuts the eye that is sore while giving birth to it; but the diamond once wept away at length becomes soft : the eye looks for it — and lo! the diamond is the dew of a flower.

XVI.

HUSBAND and wife ought to pass through life like the sun and newmoon which rise and set together. For although the sun sparkles and burns, while the moon shows only the dark side to the world, burning the bright one to her own sun, yet she attracts in a stronger degree than he, influencing weather, growth, and fertility.

XVII.

IN this miserable life of disappointment, where our wishes and aims are but steps leading to no real summits, we are soothed only by love, as by some second world; and in the midst of the charnel-house of perishableness, a heart loving and beloved feels the true immortality.

XVIII.

THE most innocent caress is liable to become a guilty one by repetition. Women ought to confide in their heart, but not in their weak nerves. Alas! in spite of the most beautiful and noble feelings, it happens to many unfortunate sisters, on account of a want of energy of will and body, as it did to the Mexicans who were vanquished by the Spaniards, because they possessed only weak *gold*, and no *iron*.

xix.

IT is true, ' art is not the bread of life,' but its wine.

xx.

YOUNG men fall upon the knee before their adored, but only like foot-soldiers before the cavalry, in order to vanquish and to kill.

xxi.

WE detest our faults soonest and most strongly, when we have got rid of them ; even as the secretions of the body are not loathsome to us till they are no longer parts of the body.

xxii.

' WEEP on ! weep on ! ' once said a scholar to his betrothed, who wept her life away, withering like her dying lover. ' Tears are the best comforters ; for they are taken from the river of Lemnos, which alone causes forgetfulness of the beloved object.' ' Can tears effect this ? ' she asked, in dismay ; and with determination she dried her eyes, and raised them joyfully toward Heaven, until the drops were exhausted and dried up for ever.

xxiii.

HERDER and SCHILLER intended in their youth to become surgeons. But fate said : ' No ! there are deeper wounds than those of the body.' And both wrote.

xxiv.

EVIL desires clip the wings instead of the beak of their Promethean vulture, and thus the latter ever eats the heart.

xxv.

MANY flowers open themselves before the sun, but there is only one which always follows him. My heart ! be thou like the sun-flower ! Not only open thyself to God, but obey Him also.

xxvi.

GIFT of Genius ! thou art like the dew descending from the heavens while the evening-star is there. Invisibly and silently it strengthens the flower, and keeps her honey cool for a whole starry night. But if morning come, and the dew begins to sparkle more brightly than the flower, the holy sun takes it away from out it. Gift of Genius ! thou art like the dew. Veiled by the bosom, thou keepest it pure and cool a long time ; but if thou throwest colors and brightness upon the world thou art soon dispersed, and leavest a sick heart behind thee.

xxvii.

PAST and future veil themselves to us. But the former bears the veil of the widow, the latter that of the bride.

xxviii.

A NOBLE-MINDED prince, silvered with age, at whose feet his lands flourish, is like a high snow-covered mountain, beneath which the meadows and valleys, watered from its summit, are spread full of flowers and harvests.

xxix.

Do not say, 'I will suffer,' for it is necessity. But say, 'I will act,' for nobody can force you to do so.

xxx.

WE wonder why love of God should occupy and warm oftener the weak woman than the strong man. Did not the giants among all nations fight the gods?

xxxi.

SOME people live like the eleven apostles and die like the twelfth.

xxxii.

THOSE have the least time to walk the way of heaven, who repair it; and he who carries the lantern stumbles much more easily than he who follows it.

xxxiii.

WE generally find that the dagger of Fanaticism has done no greater injury to reason than the dagger of Criticism to genius.

xxxiv.

HE who travels toward the west, loses one day; the traveller toward the east gains one. Therefore start for the orient of the heart and the rising sun, and you will gain instead of the day the year, and instead of the year an eternity in time.

xxxv.

LIKE the vulture of Prometheus the panting for love seizes upon the heart and wounds it, only in order to increase it.

xxxvi.

ONLY very weak people become instantly friends of every one they meet with; like arsenic which unites with every metal, and like portraits which appear to gaze with attention upon every one who looks at them.

xxxvii.

'THAT was my happiest time,' we often say in looking back on some portion of the past. But the single days and even the single hours we then lived, and in which that happy time of course must be divided, cannot be accounted as truly happy ones. Thus an age or a great portion of life is like an annual with gilt margin. The whole of it sparkles like gold, but if you open it, how little brightness is on the single leaf!

xxxviii.

No country grows rich and powerful (rather the contrary) by that which it gains from abroad, but only by all it brings from out itself. Only the healthy and leafy tree bears every year its blossoms full of honey, but that tree in which the bees accumulate their honey is hollow and decayed, and soon stands without any honey-comb.

XXXIX.

THE oracle predicted the blind Orion should have his sight again, if unceasingly he would go to meet the sun. Ye searchers after truth! seek evermore the sun, and an eye will be given to you.

XL.

To describe great deeds properly is well nigh as sublime as to enact them; and there is little difference between an author and a hero.

XLI.

AUTHORS dressing and hiding their thoughts in unintelligible language imitate cunningly those hosts who serve thick ale in untransparent cups.

XLII.

EVERY love believes in a double immortality, that of itself and the other. If it fears ever to cease, it has ceased already. To our heart it is the same whether the beloved disappears, or only love.

XLIII.

EARTH, in which all of us are going to lay down our sunken heads for repose, is but the broad block of execution for pale and worn-out men coming from out the prison.

XLIV.

IF women converse about women, they will particularly notice mind where there is beauty, and beauty where there is mind; in the peacock, the voice; in the nightingale, the plumage.

XLV.

OLD age is not gloomy because our *joys* but because our *hopes* then will cease.

XLVI.

WHERE the end appears divine to us, the road to it must have been the same, because the end was the road, and because the road becomes the end. We perhaps are nearer to thee, Eternal Being! than we think, for thou only canst know it; and we live not only on Thee but in Thee, as our earth moves in the midst of the atmosphere of the sun, while it appears to turn far off around his brightness.

XLVII.

GIRLS should talk with their friends as though a man overheard them; and with men as though girls were present.

XLVIII.

THE greater love of God and men, the less self-love. The quicker a planet moves about the sun the slower it turns round itself.

XLIX.

CAN any thing be more lovely than beauty and innocence united? What charms still can a beautiful and innocent virgin borrow, that are not less than those she already possesses? Yet she borrows even the smallest; for she resembles the Roman who, according to Pliny, had the white lily and the white lamb painted in motley colors.

L.

THE true man opens himself still with faith and hope to heaven, though he no longer beholds or possesses it; even as the flowers that open to the sun continue so still, although he be clouded.

LI.

TOO violent sorrow is suicide of the heart; and as in Silesia suicides are buried with the face turned toward the earth, thus he who grieves too much has his face turned in the same way toward the earth, although he be not in her, and though he ought to raise it to look about him, to gaze upon something higher, and something that is more cheerful than earth, worms, and the black mould. Not to enjoy but to be merry is our duty, and it ought to be our aim. In a soul full of gloominess and vexation, the sultry and heavy air chokes all mental flowers and all moral growth. To a soft melancholy and to compassion the heart should open, but not to cold ill-humor and dejection; as the flower remains open to the dew, but closes before the rain. To feel unwell is so little and to feel well so strongly congenial with our nature, that by the same degree of delusion we only are sorry for that which gave sorrow but not for that which gave joy.

LII.

OUR sufferings exist only in moments; for they form time. One most painful moment we readily would bear. Then why not the second and third, and every next that is just as short? Therefore all who perplex themselves give to every pungent moment two fresh thorns, those of the past and future; and thus bleed thrice at the same time. Shall we then like children ever fear the thunder, and even its lengthened roar, though the moment of the lightning shall have passed away?

LIII.

WHO is the greater? the sage, who rising above the stormy time gazes at it without action, or he who throws himself boldly from the summits of repose into the battle-crowd of time? It is sublime if the eagle flies through the thunder-cloud up to the serene heavens; but far more sublime if, soaring in the blue above the dark vaults of the gale, he rushes through it upon his mountain-seat, where his featherless family gather and tremble.

THOUGHTS OF THE BLEST.

O! sweet is the thought of the loved who have flown
　On the spirit's bright wing to a covert on high;
Where the sorrows of earth shall be ever unknown,
　Where clouds shall ne'er gather, nor moaning winds sigh;
No! rapture's full song stirs those Eden-like bowers,
　And the gush of Life's fountain comes soft to th' ear,
While the incense of praise is like breath from the flowers,
　And Infinite Love is the light of the sphere!
But sweet is the thought that they do not forget,
　Though affection's bright chain at this moment is riv'n,
That unbroken its links will encircle us yet,
　When we meet, a blest band, in the mansion of heaven.

w.

THE MARINER'S SONG.

A WINTER NIGHT AT SEA.

I.

'T is a bitter cold night on the wintry sea,
  And cheerless the winds are blowing,
But I know that at home there 's a heart for me
  With the warmest true love glowing.
Then here 's to the lassie of sweet sixteen,
With her rosy lips and her bright blue een,
      God bless her!
Oh! how I long, on this wintry night,
To throw my arms round that form so light,
      And to my bosom press her!

II.

'T was a summer eve, when the day was done,
  And the sun had sunk in the billow,
That I met my love by the brook alone,
  Down by our trysting-willow:
The big tear stood in her lustrous eye,
And her white bosom heaved with a heavy sigh,
      God bless her!
She laid her head on my breast and wept,
And the warm tear down my bosom crept,
      As to my heart I press'd her.

III.

'I know, I know,' thus the dear one spake,
  'That you will love me ever;
But oh! my bursting heart will break,
  If now for aye we sever!'
I bade her dry her gushing tears,
And give to the winds her foolish fears,
      God bless her!
'The fleeting year will soon pass by,
And then to my love I 'll return,' said I,
      As to my heart I press'd her.

IV.

Then what though the wind is blowing cold,
  As we fly o'er the freezing billow?
I know as we sweep past each land-mark old,
  I am nearing my home and the willow:
And soon, oh! *soon* on my native shore
I shall meet my love — we shall part no more —
      God bless her!
And then what words can paint the bliss
Of the warm embrace and the rapturous kiss,
      When again to my heart I press her!

Providence, (R. I.,) Sept., 1841.   C. O. F.

THE QUOD CORRESPONDENCE.

NUMBER SIX.

DEAR SIR: I have just returned from the green fields, the blue skies, and the rich, glowing sun-shine of the country. I spent my time in lingering through the dark shadowy woods, or in sauntering along the borders of a brook that wound through copse, meadow, and woodland; sometimes gliding in unruffled smoothness between fringed banks, and at others indulging a very choleric sputtering where stones or rocks stood in its way.

All was so fresh and gay and glowing, that I could scarcely persuade myself it was nature and not myself that was young. The flowers, the fields, trees, birds, all seemed the self-same that I had seen when a boy. A small, busy, bustling wren had her nest at the window of my room, and the first note that I heard at day-break was the loud, joyous, gushing voice of that little bird. Oh! how my memory floated back on that tide of song to the days of childhood! A wren sang at my window then; and when I awake now, and hear the loud, glad note of this merry little chorister, I fancy myself still a child; that this long, long, weary life is a dream, and that I am not a decrepid, broken-down old man.

Yet when I once turned my face to the city, how I longed to reach my old home! With what an affectionate eye I looked at the old house! Its ruined walls, its small narrow windows, its creaking stairs and gloomy chambers, each had a corner in my heart; and it was with a glow of secret pride that I once more seated myself in my own chair, and felt that I was at home at last.

I found a number of letters awaiting my return; and among them the following from my former correspondent, Mr. Snagg:

'*Sept.* 9th, 1841.

'MR. JOHN QUOD, ESQ.

'MY DEAR OLD BOY: Some folks like what 's pathetic — some do n't; and I am one of them. Do n't take it hard; but it 's high time you should know you are going it too strong in that line. As for your heroine, she has done nothing but snivel and weep, from first to last. We found her at it, and left her at it. It 's too much pork for a shilling. Now do give us something jolly — there 's a good fellow! Sprinkle in a few chaps like that Higgs; or give us a little more of him. He knows a thing or two. The way he come it over the man in the eating-house was not so bad : but I could have given him a few hints in that line, which would be very useful to one of his standing in society. Perhaps you do n't know it; but that dog Wommut is your great card. Bring him forward often; he 's a general favorite : ' My bowels fairly yearn toward him,' as some one says, somewhere — he 's so like Slaughter! How he would pin a bull!

'As for Lucy — could n't you kill her quietly? If you could, it would be judicious; if you can 't, dish her up in small quantities, or by G — d! you 'll turn some one's stomach. I 've a sister who hates the name. She took to her bed when she first saw it: but now we scratch it out with a lead pencil and write Mary over it; and then with the assistance of a smelling-bottle she contrives to survive the reading of your correspondence. 'What 's in a name,' etc., is all gammon.

'But all this is neither here nor there. I commenced this letter to say that several very respectable gentlemen of my acquaintance would be highly delighted to open a correspondence with you, on things in general: and that we have determined to make you a member of our club of 'Infant Roarers.' It would have been done at the last meeting; but one of our most distinguished dogs baited a bull in the upper part of the city; and two imported cocks were pitted against each other the same evening. So that no one was present except myself, (who came on purpose to nominate you,) and one other very respectable gentleman, who was unable to attend either exhibition, owing to an infirmity in one leg, which he lately broke in a fight with a watchman.

'Of course, as you are an old man, you wo n't be expected to do much in the fighting way. Just drop in at the meetings, when it 's convenient. The dog-fights, bull-baits, etc., of course your own taste will lead you to attend; and between you and I, if you should happen to be out on a lark with us, you might occasionally knock down a small watchman or a sickly one, just for the name of the thing. I 'll attend to the big ones. Yours to the back-bone, ISAAC SNAGG.

'P. S. I copy an extract from the minutes of the last meeting of the Club of 'Infant Roarers:'

'RESOLVED: That we have read with the highest satisfaction the letter of ISAAC SNAGG, Esq., to Mr. JOHN QUOD, contained in the fourth number of that last gentleman's correspondence with the NEW-YORK KNICKERBOCKER, and that with all due respect to that worthy gentleman, we consider the letter the most interesting portion of the correspondence, and that it does honor to the head and heart of the gentleman who penned it.

'RESOLVED: That to show our high regard for the talents of Mr. SNAGG, and for the merits of the valuable animal whose virtues he commemorates, the said letter be recorded among the minutes of this Society. I. S.'

About a week after the preceding letter, the following notice was left at my abode, as I was informed, by a small boy with one eye not a little damaged from having recently come in contact with some hard obstacle — possibly a fist:

'*Sept.* 25, 1841.'

'SIR: I have the honor to inform you that at a regular meeting of the Society of Infant Roarers, held at their 'Den,' on the 21st day of September instant, you were unanimously elected a member of that Society.

'By order of the Trustees. JOHN SQUAIL, Sec'y.'

'To JOHN QUOD, ESQ.

'A special meeting of the members of the Society will be held at the 'Den,' on the first day of October proximo, to take into consideration matters of much importance. A punctual attendance is requested, as it is desirable that the meeting should be as full as possible. JOHN SQUAIL, Sec'y.'

A day or two afterward I received the following letter from Mr. Snagg:

'*September* 27, 1841.'

'MR. JOHN QUOD, ESQ.

'MY DEAR BOY: Before this you will have received notice from the Secretary of the Society of I. R's, informing you that you are one of us. You went in by an unanimous vote; for you 've no idea of the sensation your last number created among us — particularly my letter. There 's to be a special meeting of the Society, on the first of next month. Do n't fail to be there. All the best bull-dogs in the country are to be produced, and a game-cock of a famous strain, the closest hitter and best mouther in the State; and it 's said a match is to be made up between Big Ben and Raw Pete. Excuse my breaking off abruptly; but it wants a quarter to six, and I have appointed the hour of six precisely for a dun to call here, so that I might know exactly when to be out. Yours, t. t. m., ISAAC SNAGG.'

In reply to the critique in the first letter of Mr. Snagg, I can only say that the web of the story is woven in truth, and it must take its course; but for the kindness which he has evinced toward me, I return my warmest thanks: as also for the honor conferred upon me, through his influence, by the Society of Infant Roarers; an honor which to say the least was most unexpected. My time however is so much taken up, that I fear I shall scarcely be able to attend their meetings with the punctuality which the rules of the Society and the importance of its objects requires: but at all times, I shall be happy to receive any communication from the members of that respectable society, or from any other person who numbers Mr. Snagg among his friends. JOHN QUOD.

The Attorney.

CHAPTER IX.

It was one of those bitter nights that almost cut one to the heart. Oh! how coldly the sharp wind went hissing through the streets, mocking the shivering limbs, and breaking the hearts of the wretched and homeless! There seemed no shelter from its fury. Up and down the streets, through alleys and along broad avenues, it swept with the same intense rigor. But the night before, the streets had been drenched with rain: puddles were standing in every hollow, the whole city was teeming with moisture, when this fierce wind came sweeping along. Every thing disappeared before it: pool after pool of water went as if by magic, no one knew where. The pavements were dry, parched as in the very heat of summer. The streets, which at that hour of the night were generally peopled with a living multitude, were empty. A desolation like that of a pestilence had come over them; and the cold winter wind went rushing madly on its course, moaning and sighing and howling through old buildings and dark entries and over chimney-tops, its own wild voice drowning the groans which it wrung from thousands.

What a night it was for those who owned no home but the world, no shelter but the sky! Into what wretched holes they shrank! — in stables, in kennels, in sheds with beasts. Shivering boys gathered at the doors of blacksmiths' shops, and looked wistfully in at the red fire; and wretched old men stole up to the windows of rich dwellings, and peered in, hoping to cheer their icy hearts by the comfort which they saw within. Oh! could we but distinguish the sighs and groans which mingle in the wild melody of the north wind, as it comes careering along, how mournfully sad would be the sound!

The forbidding appearance of the weather was not without its influence upon a small elderly lady who dwelt in a snug house near the Bowery, and who was sitting in a state of great expectation in a high chair with a straight narrow back, in a small back parlor communicating with a front one by folding doors. This was Mrs. Dow, the widow-elect of Wilkins. She was a small thin woman, tough, wirey, not unlike a bundle of rattans; and many years ago it is not unlikely had been better looking. At all events she was to be pitied if she had not. But Time generally has his own way with the old and the young. He digs the graves of the first, and blights the bright promise of the second; and the widow had not escaped the general doom. She had resisted to the last; but the old gentleman of the sythe and hour-glass, finding that she was likely to prove a hard customer, and having plenty of leisure on his hands, instead of a storm commenced a siege; and at the end of fifty years Mrs. Dow had withered down into the small elderly lady just described. When she fell in with Wilkins she had retired from the combat, and though a little excitable, had betaken herself to meekness and prayer-meetings. Meek widows, however, are very apt to fancy reckless dare-devil men, especially if the widows are a little pious. It gives a flavor to their existence.

The whole room had an air of comfort, doubly so from the howling of the blast without. Heavy curtains reached the floor and shut out the cold air. A bright fire burnt cheerily in the grate, before which stood an arm-chair, at present unoccupied. The mantel-piece was decorated with two plated candlesticks of a spiral form. From the top of each a rose of green paper peeped coyly out, and between them two unknown shells, brought from a distant sea, were recumbent on a bed of green paper carefully scolloped out at the edges. Over these, in a very small gilt frame, hung the profile of the late Mr. Dow, cut from a card, with a piece of black silk introduced in the rear, and showing off to all advantage a pug nose and an ample shirt-ruffle. The chairs in the room were all of mahogany, and were Mrs. Dow's own. In truth the widow was well to do in the world, and it was this which excited the cupidity of Wilkins.

As she sat in her high-backed chair she glanced restlessly at the clock, then looked around the room. There was a speck of dust on one of the chairs, so she got up and wiped it off with her handkerchief. 'Ah me!' said she, pausing before a looking-glass and tenderly adjusting a very small curl which peeped from under her cap. 'Our present state of existence is a very precarious one — very.' And having uttered this moral apothegm, Mrs. Dow with equal tenderness bestowed a few small attentions on a fierce little riband, done up as a bow, which was perched on the highest elevation of her cap. 'Very precarious indeed,' continued she, turning first one side of her head to the glass, then the other, and making a desperate effort to catch a transient glance of the back of her neck. 'The world's a fleeting show; life's a dream; gracious me! how the wind whistles!'

Having finished her interesting occupation, Mrs. Dow drew a large chair near the fire, sank gently into it, and fixed her eyes pathetically on the profile of the late Mr. D. 'Ah! he was a dear good man — he was!' and she shook her head mournfully at the profile. Then she thought how that respectable gentleman one pleasant evening had thrown himself in that very arm-chair, and placing a small stool under each foot, and quietly observing that he intended to take a long nap, had subsided into a calm apoplexy, and was now finishing his nap in a neighboring church-yard — a neat marble slab, surmounted by two cherubs beautifully carved, with curly hair and wings growing out of the back of their necks, being carefully placed over him to keep him comfortable.

'He *was* a nice man, Mr. Dow; so kind — and he died so easy! It was *so* like him — so considerate! Never gave trouble. Poor dear! he always wanted to die on a suddent; and always hoped he would n't suffer when he died. Providence was kind to him, very; he was gratified in both wishes. I 'm sure he had every reason to be thankful.'

A very faint cough and a slight snuffle in the room startled the speaker.

'Who 's there?' demanded she, a little tremulously, and not altogether without apprehension that the late Mr. Dow, encouraged by her reflections, and finding his quarters in the church-yard a little cool, might have dropped in to warm himself at her fire.

'Me,' replied a solemn voice, emanating from a man-servant clad in a broad-skirted snuff-colored coat and rusty unmentionables.

'Oh! it 's *you*, Aaron, is it?' said the lady sharply, as the man-servant advanced, and paused, with a puzzled look, in the middle of the room. 'What brings you here? What do you want?'

The man-servant uttered the single word, 'sugar,' at the same time extending toward the relict of the late Mr. Dow a receptacle for that article, of the smallest credible dimensions.

'Sugar!'

The man nodded.

'Well, I never, in all my born-days! It was filled not (let me see, Monday, Friday, Tuesday, Monday, Friday,) not ten days ago, and more sugar! It 's sinful!' and Mrs. Dow raised her eyes to heaven in pious wrath. 'Many poor wretches,' continued she, fumbling in her pocket for the keys, 'never have sugar in their tea. That idea should make this little cup last a fortnight at least. You have n't a proper spirit, Aaron. If you had, the thought of the poor starving beggar in the street would sweeten your tea almost without sugar. I 'm sure of it.'

The man-servant seemed to entertain a different opinion on the subject; but as Mrs. Dow took the cup from his hand and proceeded to fill it, he kept his thoughts to himself.

'There,' said the lady, a little red in the face from bending over the sugar-barrel, and locking the door of the closet, 'take that, and I hope you 'll remember what I have said.'

'I will,' said the man, moving toward the door.

'Stop, Aaron. What did you give the lame boy, with a sick mother and three small sisters, when he called to-day?'

'Two cold 'taters and an inion,' said Aaron solemnly.

'That 's right. Always assist the poor;' and Mrs. Dow looked blandly at the solemn domestic. 'When he comes you may inquire how his poor mother is. You need n't give him any thing to-day. It might encourage gluttony; and gluttony, you know, is one of the great cardinal sins spoken against in Scripture.'

'Yes,' said the man-servant, shifting his weight from one leg to the other

'How it delights one to have done a charitable act!' said Mrs. Dow. 'Do n't you feel it, Aaron?'

'Is it a queer feeling about here?' asked the man-servant, pressing his fingers with an air of profound investigation in various parts of his abdomen. 'A sort of emptiness?'

'It's delightful!' ejaculated the widow, her face glowing with benevolence toward the whole human race, and toward lame boys with sick mothers and young sisters in particular.

'Then I do n't feel it,' said Aaron; and he shook his head disconsolately: 'I thought I did, but it could n't a-been. It must ha' been wind in the stomach.'

Mrs. Dow paid no attention to this matter-of-fact remark, but requested him to 'think of that sick mother and them hungry children when they sat down to the meal which their bounty had provided.'

'I do think on 'em,' replied Aaron, looking hard at the small sugar-cup, and edging off toward the kitchen.

'How the grateful tears will fill their eyes ——'

'Wo'n't they!' ejaculated Aaron; 'especially if they ventur' to eat that 'ere inion. It was a raw von.'

Mrs. Dow drew herself up with dignity, and told the man-servant that he might withdraw.

Aaron was already at the door, when suddenly he paused, and smoothing his hair straight over his forehead with his left hand, made a step or two toward the centre of the room, and looked earnestly in the fire. As these preparations generally indicated something, Mrs. Dow asked, a little sharply: 'Well, what now?'

'*In*, this evening?' said Aaron, with some vivacity, but making no other motion than a slight questioning nod of his head.

'In!' replied the widow with a slight increase of shrillness; 'of *course* I'm in.'

'To every body?' demanded Aaron, in the same tone.

'Yes, every body.'

'That Wilkins too?'

'Of course to Mr. Wilkins. Why not?' and now Mrs. Dow's voice became a little louder and a little sharper.

'Oh! no reason in the world — none at all,' replied the man-servant; 'but might I ventur'?'

Mrs. Dow paused to reflect; and then having made up her mind that an elderly man-servant in drabs was not likely to venture too far, she considerately assented.

'Well then,' exclaimed Aaron, advancing and extending his right hand in the energy of his speech, 'that chap Wilkins; you should guard ag'in' him; he's an owdacious cha-racter!'

'Aaron!' exclaimed the lady, sitting bolt upright; 'you alarm me! Speak! What have you learned? What do you know?'

'Nothing,' said Aaron. 'I wish I could;' and he shook his head mournfully; 'but I *suspects*;' and now the shake of his head was ominous.

'What do you suspect? I can't bear suspense. It excites me to a degree!' And to prove this last assertion she seized the man-servant by the coat-collar and shook him violently.

The man waited until she had finished, and then adjusted his collar. 'I suspect a great deal — a *very* great deal!' said he, looking impressively into the eyes of his mistress, and sinking his voice. 'I know it by a sign that never fails.'

'What is it?' demanded Mrs. Dow, nervously : 'quick — tell me. Oh my! oh my!'

'The sign,' replied Aaron confidently, 'I know it by, is the cut of his eye.'

'The what!'

'The cut of his eye,' reiterated Aaron, positively; compressing his lips and looking at his mistress with a stern impressive air. 'Try a man on all tacks, and they may fail ; but let me get the cut of his eye and I knows him at once.'

'Aaron,' replied the widow, recovering instantly, 'the cut of Mr. Wilkins' eye is no ground for suspicion against his respectability. I have never seen any thing at all unpleasant in their expression, or denoting a bad character ; and if he does sometimes sit with his feet on the new brass fender, and occasionally spit on the clean grate, these are trifles — flaws in a gem — spots in the sun. You must from this time cease your remarks respecting both his eyes and character, as he 's a friend of mine — a very *particular* friend.'

Mrs. Dow coughed slightly as she emphasized these last words, and the man-servant, who had nothing but mere suspicion, and that grounded only on a general dislike to Wilkins, drew back abashed.

'You may go.'

Aaron cast a disconsolate look at the widow, and shook his head mournfully.

'She 's a gone horse!' said he, as he shut the door, ' or my name 's not Aaron!'

A new course however was given to the current of Aaron's ideas by a knock at the door.

'There he is I s'pose,' muttered he, showing his displeasure in the only manner that he dared, by obeying the summons as slowly as possible. 'If I did n't know she was a-listenin', he would n't get in now, 'nother.'

With this muttered expression of dissatisfaction, he opened the door.

'Is your mistress at home?' demanded a voice which he knew to be that of Wilkins, although the darkness prevented his seeing his person.

'What 's your name?' demanded Aaron. 'I never lets nobody in without their name.'

The man made no reply until he had thrust the door violently open, jamming Aaron between it and the wall, to the great annoyance of that person, who being somewhat prominent in the region of the stomach, found the compass of six inches into which he was pressed rather more inconvenient than otherwise.

'D — n you! would you let a man stand there and freeze?' said the other, as he stepped in front of him. 'Do n't you hear the wind howling as if hell was riding on it? Is this a night to ask a man's name,

when you know it already? Get to your mistress and tell her I'm
here. Shut the door, and be quick!'

'You need n't wait for that,' said Aaron sulkily, passing his hand
tenderly over the aggrieved parts of his body. 'She's been a-waiting
for you these three nights. There's the door; you can go in.'

'So you've found out who I am, have you? It's well you did; or
it might have been put in your head in a way you would n't have liked
so well.'

As he said this, Wilkins turned from him and going to the room
door, opened it, went in, and shut it after him. As soon as the door
closed, Aaron paused, shook his fist violently at the third panel three
successive times; indulged in several strange and uncouth distortions
of the face, indicative of bitter hostility; then quietly went to the
kitchen to communicate his troubles and suspicions to an elderly
female with projecting teeth and red hair, who officiated as cook.

———

CHAPTER X.

WHEN Wilkins entered the room, he spoke a few words to Mrs.
Dow, strode directly up to the fire, and held his hands almost in the
flame. Cold, stiff, with his uncombed hair hanging loosely about his
face, and his beard of two days' growth, he seemed the very picture
of exhaustion. It had been a weary day for him. The whole of the
night before he had passed without closing an eye. He had paced his
room over and over again; he had counted every hour : he had
watched the dark gloom of night as it gradually mellowed into day,
and then the golden halo as it shot up in the east, growing richer and
richer, until the bright sun came flashing over the house-tops. Stragglers began to pass his window, in the early gray of the morning; then
they became more numerous, and then the steady tramp of feet told
him the day was begun, and that the thousands of souls who were to
strive and struggle for bread had donned their harness for the labor :
Yet like one in a dream the wretched man remained in his room.
Strange and unconnected fancies and forms and figures flitted to and
fro in his mind. Higgs, his wife, the attorney, presented themselves,
sometimes in turn, sometimes together, sometimes whirling and dancing
and flitting to and fro, and then vanishing as in a mist. But amid all
was a vague, indefinable consciousness that there was something on
hand; a strong oppressive feeling that there was something to be done
which demanded immediate attention, and that he must be up and
busy. Still he remained without stirring until late in the morning;
but finally he rose, left the room, and went out into the street. The
cold biting air, as it rushed over his hot forehead, partly brought him
to himself; but no sooner had he locked the door of his house, than he
fled from it with a feeling of terror. An undefinable guilt, a secret
dread of he knew not what, seemed connected with it. Want of rest
and mental anxiety had completely unstrung him, and he obeyed every
wild phantasy of his brain like a very slave. A weary day it had
been. He had wandered from street to street, in a kind of stupid

bewilderment. Wherever he saw a crowd stopping to gaze, he stopped and gazed with the rest. If they laughed, he laughed too, and then sauntered on. He went from shop-window to shop-window, gazing idly in. From one end of the city to the other he wandered that day.

He stopped once near a bright curly-headed child, who was playing in the street, and endeavored to coax him to him. The child looked up, drew back from the wild face that glared on his own, and shrinking farther and farther off, until he reached a corner, fairly took to his heels. Wilkins muttered something to himself, and went listlessly on. In the middle of the day he was hungry, and stopping at a baker's shop bought a roll, and ate it at the counter with a ravenous appetite. He threw a few cents to the baker, who eyed him with fear and suspicion, and felt relieved when he was gone. Several times he stopped in front of Bolton's office, looked up at the gloomy building, and counted the windows in its front, and thought how old and ruinous it was; wondered who built it; and then wandered off without going in. Several times he went to the corner of the street where he lived, and stood there, and watched his own house; and once he went to the window and peeped in; but all was empty; and whistling carelessly, he went away. But as the day waned he became wearied, and this unnatural state of feeling wore off. His mind gradually recovered its tone, and he became keenly alive to his own exhaustion. The cold wind, which had whistled around him the whole day unheeded, now became piercing: it stiffened every joint, and seemed eating into his very flesh. His own home was tenantless; and with little thought or reflection, he directed his steps to the widow's, where he entered as before mentioned.

He was too much at home, and Mrs. Dow too much accustomed to him, to note his peculiarities. But that night there was something in the appearance of the gaunt savage man that startled her. He drew long shivering breaths, and a cold shuddering passed spasmodically over him, as he began to feel the warmth. From head to foot, flesh and bone and blood were all cold. It seemed as if the current of his blood was congealed and flowed through his veins in a stream of ice.

'There's no heat in that fire, widow; it only makes one colder,' said he, still standing over it. 'More coal — more coal! The night's horrible.'

The lady, without remark at the rough manner of her visiter, heaped the fire with coal.

'There, that's something like,' said he gazing with childish satisfaction at the huge flame that hissed and roared up the chimney. 'One *feels* that.'

'Are you very cold, George?' asked Mrs. Dow sympathetically.

'Ay, widow, to the heart; all is cold, all except *here*,' said he, slapping his forehead with his open hand; '*that's* on fire! But never mind; here I am at last merry as ever, and gay as a lark. I *am* gay, widow, ai'n't I!' said he, looking her full in the face.

'Oh! Mr. Wilkins,' replied the lady, 'what a question! You know you are gay — *so gay*!'

'Of course I am,' said Wilkins: 'so gay,' continued he, setting his teeth, 'that I sometimes catch myself laughing until the room rings and rings. God! how merry I am then!' And a dark scowl swept over his face, as if a demon had passed and his shadow fallen upon it. 'But come widow,' said he, flinging himself in an easy chair and stretching his feet to the fire, 'let's drop this. I suppose you wondered where I was. Perhaps you thought I was dead, drowned, or had killed somebody, or something of that kind?'

Mrs. Dow looked slightly confused, and then admitted that she had wondered a great deal, a very great deal; but she really did not think he had killed any body, although folks did such things now-a-days: but she did n't think that of *him*. Oh no! But she had been worried about him; very much worried; and hoped he had not been ill, for he looked as if he had.

'Yes I have been,' said Wilkins, rising and taking a light from the mantel-piece and holding it to his own face. 'Do n't I look so? It was a fever, and that soon brings a man down. It eats up the flesh, drinks the blood, and leaves nothing but the bone. I would have been down to that, if it had n't gone off as it did. I'm weak enough; a child might master me now.' As he spoke, he placed the light on the table, and sank feebly back into the chair.

'Poor dear!' ejaculated Mrs. Dow; 'and I did n't know it! How agitated I should have been at the bare thought!'

'Would you, widow?'

'Would I!' exclaimed Mrs. Dow, in a tone which was intended to indicate to all intents and purposes that she most certainly would. 'Would I? Oh, George! Mr. Wilkins, I mean;' and Mrs. Dow colored slightly at the lapse into which the ardor of her feeling had led her.

'Well, I believe you,' replied Wilkins feebly. 'One likes to know there is some one to care for him. This feeling of loneliness is d — d uncomfortable. It sometimes almost chokes one. I've had it often.'

'Oh!' said Mrs. Dow, raising her eyes pathetically to the profile of the late Mr. Dow, 'it's bad enough. I can feel for you, that I can.' And Mrs. Dow shook her head mournfully, until the small riband on the top of her cap quivered like an aspen. 'When one is bereaved, Mr. Wilkins, then one knows what one suffers; then one finds out what bereavement is.' And again Mrs. Dow shook her head mournfully, and threw a tender glance at the profile of her late husband, and again the small riband quivered.

'That's true, very true,' said Wilkins, scarcely heeding what he said; for a feeling of deep drowsiness was stealing over him. There was a rich enjoyment in sitting in that deep easy-chair, with the warmth of the fire gradually spreading through his frozen frame! A deep luxurious languor seemed creeping over him, stealing from limb to limb, wrapping itself around him, and warming his very heart. His past troubles and suffering passed before him with a dreamy, shadowy indistinctness. The thin piping voice of the widow echoed in his ears with a lulling sound. He heard her moral reflections upon the virtues and resignation of the late Mr. Dow, as they dripped from her in a small, incessant and pattering stream; but his mind was far, far away.

He saw gorgeous avenues in the crumbling fire; houses, arcades, palaces, cathedrals; then an arch gave way, then a column; now a grove of trees sank down, down. He made a faint effort to do something. He muttered incoherently in reply to the widow; his head fell back in the chair, and he sank into the deep, death-like and dreamless sleep of complete exhaustion.

When Mrs. Dow saw that he was sound asleep, she forbore to talk; and sat watching his gaunt, haggard countenance with a look of deep concern. She occasionally stirred the fire cautiously, so as to keep it bright, without disturbing him; and she moved the light so that it might not flash in his eyes and awaken him.

The sleep of the exhausted man was almost like the profound and never-ending rest of the dead. Not a limb moved, not a muscle. There lay his hollow and sunken cheek, as if cut from marble; the light of the bright flame playing and flickering over his face, and giving a strange uncertain expression to its very wildness. The strong man had wrestled boldly with his fierce passions. There had been a bitter struggle between body and soul; but flesh and blood had given out at last, and sank to the ground, dragging all his energies with them.

Long, long did he sleep; and patiently did Mrs. Dow watch at his side. When he awoke he was an altered man; refreshed in body, and with his energies restored to their former vigor. Once more he was resolved, hardened, and unrelenting: with one fell purpose in view, and with a stern determination to carry it out at all hazards.

The widow had not been unmindful of his other wants during his sleep; and when he awoke he found a table spread, with a large joint of cold meat and a tea-kettle steaming away at its side.

Nothing could have been more acceptable to Wilkins than this sight, for he was famished to the very verge of starvation. Saying little, he drew a chair to the table and ate voraciously. For three days his body had been the slave of his passions; but his physical nature was resuming its sway; and now he devoured what was placed before him, like a famished beast. Whatever may have been the habits of economy with which Mrs. Dow habitually amused herself, there was no stint there; for with all her foibles and weakness, that savage man had really found a tender spot in her time-warped heart.

At last he threw himself back in the chair. 'Ah! widow,' said he, 'you know what's good for a sick man. When the illness is off, then comes hunger. It makes one ravenous. I could almost eat you, widow.'

'Lor! how you talk!' exclaimed the lady, moving a little restlessly in her chair, and assuming that orange tint which in widows of bilious complexions passes for a blush. 'You don't mean it. I know you don't.' And the lady had every reason to believe what she asserted; for she would certainly have made an exceedingly tough mouthful.

'But I *do*,' replied Wilkins, for the first time in the course of the evening casting at the relict of the late Mr. Dow one of those insinuating glances which had heretofore been so successful in worming their way into her heart.

Mrs. Dow turned away her head, and looked into a small tea-cup with an air of the most desperate unconcern; though it might have been remarked that the small riband on the top of her cap was unusually tremulous.

'And you are so snug here!' continued he, looking about the room; 'very snug. Ah, widow! Mr. Dow was a happy man! He *must* have been.'

'Ah! George — I mean Mr. Wilkins!' And the widow paused.

'Call me George; do call me George!' said Wilkins; 'I shall take it *so* kind in you.'

'Well then, if you *really* wish it;' and again Mrs. Dow paused to reflect, before committing herself upon so serious a point. She being a widow and Wilkins a single man, it was a matter of some moment.

'To be sure I do,' said Wilkins earnestly. 'If *we* can't be familiar, who can? If we ai'n't married, we soon shall be; as soon as this cursed business of mine is done for.'

'Ah! you men have so many troubles,' said Mrs. Dow, drawing a sigh so long that it seemed to come from her very toes, 'and so much to do, and so many secrets! It is n't right, Mr. Wilkins — George I mean; it is n't right. Now who would have thought it! — even *I* have never been able to find out what this business is, nor when it is to be ended.'

'It's in law,' said Wilkins, 'and you know what law is. If you do n't, you're lucky. One can never tell how a law-suit will end. If I succeed, why then, widow, in two days you are Mrs. Wilkins.'

Mrs. Dow shook her head despondingly, as she said: 'But suppose you fail?'

'I won't suppose it!' said Wilkins earnestly; 'I won't suppose it: but if I dò,' continued he, drawing in his breath, and forgetting to whom he was speaking, his black eye flashing, 'let her look to herself! She'll rue it, by G — d!'

'*She!*' exclaimed the widow, nervously; '*she!* Mr. Wilkins, is it a *she!* Who is *she?* Oh! I am *so* agitated!' This was doubtless true, for otherwise the lady would not have poured the boiling water from the tea-kettle on the smallest finger of her left hand, which she did. This slight incident aided her in regaining her composure, and also recalled Wilkins to himself. He replied rather doggedly:

'Well, this business is a law-suit. A woman is opposed to me in it. If she succeeds, I'm a ruined man. If she do n't, why then Mrs. Dow,' said he, sinking his voice and casting a tender glance at the lady, 'may become Mrs. Wilkins. That's the whole of it.'

'Is that all! Ah!' said Mrs. Dow, working her way through a crowd of small palpitations, previous to becoming composed, 'ah! I'm so excitable! I'm better now — much better. But it was a tender subject; and I really believe, George, that I *am* a very little jealous; the smallest morsel in the world, but yet jealous. I never had any thing to awaken the feeling during the life-time of the late Mr. Dow. I never was jealous of *him*; not for the tenth part of a single second.'

'I suppose not,' said Wilkins, fixing his eyes on the portentous shirt-ruffle of that gentleman's profile. 'You had no reason to be.'

'No, never,' said the widow mournfully; 'he was such a man; *such* a husband! Oh! George, I hope you'll resemble him! But I'm afraid you wo'n't.' Which last fear was a very reasonable one; for Mr. D. having been a short fat man with blue eyes and red hair, and Mr. Wilkins being a tall, gaunt one, with both hair and eyes coal-black, there was every likelihood of her fears being realized.

'Well, I'm glad he's dead!' said Wilkins, rising.

'Mis-ter Wilkins!' exclaimed the lady, starting from her chair in absolute horror.

'So I am,' repeated Wilkins. 'If he was n't, you could n't be Mrs. Wilkins. But I must be off. It's late, and I have much to do to-night. But before I go — one chaste salute.' As he spoke, he threw an arm around the widow's neck and gave her a hearty smack. Widows generally resist improprieties of any kind; and it is probable Mrs. Dow would have been governed in this matter by old-established precedent. But the consummation followed the annunciation so rapidly that she had not time to rally her energies before she found herself a kissed woman. Some rooms have very singular echoes. The echo to that chaste salute was a deep groan, which seemed to proceed from the key-hole of the door opening in the entry. Be that as it may, it escaped the attention of both parties concerned; and as the salute was not repeated before Wilkins left the house, of course there was no likelihood that the echo would be.

THE PEN.

AN EXTRACT FROM A COMMENCEMENT POEM.

WHEN in the childhood of the world a towering spirit sought
To bow Earth's struggling tribes before his own imperious thought,
He bade his banners ride the breeze, waved the red sword on high,
And soon the startling clarion sang his world-wide victory:
But to these later days is given a less pretending wand,
We wave an humbler symbol now of contest and command;
For 'the gray goose-quill' lords it o'er the destinies of men —
The triumphs of the SWORD forgot in triumphs of the PEN.
A feather wins more victories than e'er did stalwart steel,
Our authors are our bravest now — knights-errant of the quill!

 . . . . .

Mute chronicler of joy and grief, of peace and passionate strife;
Of virtue, vice; the gayeties and gravities of life:
Ally in Wisdom's palmiest hour; the veriest imp of Folly;
What gladdens, maddens into mirth, what drives to melancholy;
What bids the cheek or blanch or burn in childhood, manhood, age,
All that man's mighty soul conceives, it pours upon the page;
Shapes into speech the laboring thought, and moulds the glowing line,
By turns historian, orator, romancer, bard, divine.
  The scholar's book-girt home, the maiden's bower,
  The splendid dome where fatten wealth and power,
  The haunts of trade, the halls of lettered ease,
  Still rules the pen the master-spell in these.

'T is the true Proteus typified of old,
Sacred alike to genius or to gold;
To truth or scandal; meanness, mightiness;
To fact or fancy; glory or distress;
To cash or classics; debts or eloquence;
The world of poetry, the world of pence.

Lo! as the daily coach comes lumbering in
From lazy Ease, from Toil's, from Traffic's din,
How the roused rabble postward wend their way,
To greet the mail-borne message of the day!
Mark, at each broken seal what feelings speak
In the warm eye, and paint the changing cheek.
Thrift's careful look along the missive runs
That tells of bills and bargains, drafts and duns;
The partisan cons, or anxious or elate,
The sheet that warns him of the storms of state,
Of what may make or mar his own, his party's fate:
Of this so dreaded, and of that so sought
By statesmen sage — a veto or a vote;
The bankrupt reads and rails at fortune's fickleness
And simpering Beauty clasps the messenger of bliss;
Lo! has the message sad or stirring been,
Blessing or curse is poured upon the pen!
Perchance some breaking heart has turned away,
Sick at the long dispiriting delay,
Seeking but vainly, as how oft before!
The longed-for missive that will come no more;
Perchance some joyous one, with trembling breath,
Breaks the black-boding seal that tells of death.

.   .   .   .   .   .

The Pen! — sole scribe of mortal thought in that primeval age
When yellow faces bent above the crisp and yellow page;
When the rare lore of eld they traced, those gray and cloistered men,
On the piled parchment that proclaimed the triumphs of the pen;
Now to the groaning press it turns, the press whose bantlings fly
Thick as the snowy flakes that cloud our wild and wintry sky:
The press, in our rude fathers' day its weekly issue borne
By the slow post-boy o'er the land, with echoing hoof and horn,
Now daily speeds with swifter pace than fairy's in a dream,
For steaming carriers yield the road to carriers of steam.
It speeds on wings might shame Apollyon's 'sail-broad vans' of yore,
Their vastness, and the recking load of infamy they bore!
Mammoths of fiction, folly, fun, of wit and wickedness,
Of scurrile slanders on the great, of mockery at distress;
Heralds of skilful sin, the veriest calendars of crime,
To teach all tricks of hoary vice to childhood's guileless prime,
Garbage and jewels mixed they bring to Virtue's awful eye,
Trials and tracts, the last new sermon and the last new lie:
My country! 't is the words of him, thy boldest, brightest son,
The counsels of whose pen protect what his brave sword hath won,
When recreant both, the pen, the press shall 'gild the brow of crime,'
Thy gallant ship of state shall breast no more the sea of time;
But 'neath the wave that feeble keel go down when storms awake,
And o'er the swift and sullen plunge no tell-tale bubble break.
My country! may the pen, the press, thy blessing and thy bane,
Again fair Virtue's stoutest friend, Guilt's sternest scourge again,
No more each curious avenue to sin and sadness show,
Bid o'er thy hills and blossomy vales untainted pages go;
Be still the mightiest to break the towering demon's rod,
And win man's spirit back to peace, to purity and God!

The Mermaid Isle.

'THE Nereid Sisters and their Queen!
In grace earth's fairest daughters they excel;
Pure undecaying beauty is their lot;
Their voices into liquid music swell,
Thrilling each pearly cleft and sparry grot,
The undisturbed abodes where sea-nymphs dwell!'

WORDSWORTH.

PART I.

LORD EUSTACE lay on his dying bed,
   And death was nigh at hand;
And he had sent for his brother dear,
   From his home in a distant land.

'Brother,' said he, 'though circumstance
   For many years has set
Distance unnatural betwixt
Our homes, thy strong affections fixed
Our early love in boyhood's days
   Can never all forget.

'Motherless has my Mary been;
Nor longer in this earthly scene
   May I her father be:
O be thou a father unto her,
   And God will prosper thee!'

Sir Gerald took the solemn trust,
   Low kneeling by his side:
In joy serene the father smiled,
He blessed his brother, kissed the child,
   And then contented died.

Like Winter old, with wind and cold,
   The sire had passed away;
But after his long and dreary reign
He left, to cheer the earth again,
A maiden, blushing in excess
Of half-unconscious loveliness;
A blooming bud, or a budding flower,
Yet bright with the tears of a passing shower,
   In the year's youth, sweet young May!

The heiress sole was she of all
   Her father's wide domain:
From the castle that by the sea did stand,
Far inward stretched her fertile land;
   And all the wide champain;
Still scattering verdure as they ran,
   Did wide streams intervene,
That freighted flowed through meadow green,
   Or fields of yellow grain;
Through woods where spotted deer are seen,
And rustic hamlets peep between
   High hills, or dot the plain.

Sir Gerald was a tall, gaunt man,
  With dark and sunken eye ;
His sallow cheek for years had burned
  Beneath a southern sky :
And oft, when wandering alone,
Fair Mary's fields he gazed upon,
  And welcomed silently
The thought, that these were all his own,
(For the next of kin the prize would win,)
  Should Mary chance to die.

The unforbidden thought returned,
  The young desire grew strong,
Until within his heart said he,
' Why should not chance be certainty ? '
  God shield the maid from wrong !

There 's sickness within those castle walls —
  Soft is the menials' tread ;
Hushed is the lute in Mary's bower,
Untimely fades the fair May-flower !
And paid by the good Sir Gerald's gold,
A skilful crone, lean, withered and old,
  Is watching by her bed.

And kind Sir Gerald anxiously,
  And many times a day,
Exclaims, ' God grant she may not die ! '
Then upward turns his glistening eye,
His pale lips moving silently,
  And sighing, seems to pray.

But youth proves stronger than disease ;
And to give good Sir Gerald ease,
The crisis past, she will at last
  Perchance continue living.
His anxious prayers are answered now,
But gloom broods over Sir Gerald's brow :
Why do his grateful knees not bow
  In a devout thanksgiving ?

'T was a gloomy night, no moon no stars,
  But a vast rayless cloud
With breathless calm o'erhung the heavens,
  As with a sable shroud.

'T was in the ' small hours ' of the night,
  The early night of morn,
Three men stole through the castle hall
Up the winding stair ; and one is tall —
Hush ! hear how whisperingly he spoke !
And he wears meseems the cap and cloak
  That are by Sir Gerald worn.

The old crone was there at the top of the stair ;
  She opened the door and beckoned them in
  With her long finger, crooked and thin :
Lady Mary fair in her beauty there
  Lay sunk in dreamless sleep ;
The careful nurse had mingled up ,
An opiate in her sleeping-cup,
  That her slumber might be deep !

Few words and low they spake, and what
  They did I may not say;
But three there were that entered there,
  And four that went away:
And none but the crone sat there alone,
  In the bower, at dawn of day.

An holy anchoret, some tell,
Who built his solitary cell
On the neighboring crag's o'erhanging height,
Did hear strange sounds on that calm night,
  As he said his vigil prayer.
Footsteps, and many a hurried word,
And a dull plashing sound was heard
Reëchoed from the wave below;
But little did that good man know
  What doings foul were there!
There's mourning within those castle walls,
  And funeral preparation;
And meek and gentle as a lamb,
Sir Gerald's face reveals a calm
  And chastened resignation.

As the evening shades come glooming on,
  While vesper bells are ringing,
In solemn tones from the altar rolls
The requiem for departed souls,
  That holy priests are singing.

In the church-yard a sable pall
  Upon a coffin lies,
And many a tear upon the bier
  Falls from Sir Gerald's eyes.

Earth rattles on the coffin-lid;
  And then, to close the scene,
Fresh flowers, untimely plucked, are thrown
To die, like her, untimely on
  The little mound of green.

———

PART II.

THE sun sank down behind the sea,
  The evening-star shone soon,
And o'er the eastern hill-top trees
  Up rose the round red moon.

There sat a youthful fisherman,
  Upon a rock sat he,
The salt tears trickled down his face,
  And fell into the sea.

Ere morning dawn he took his seat
  To throw the baited hook,
But listless o'er the rock he leant
Forgetful of his first intent;
And there he sat till eventide,
His rod still idle by his side,
  Nor any fish he took.

But ever and anon the tears
 Were streaming from his eyes,
And sobs were bursting from his breast,
 And deep-drawn heavy sighs.

Oft-time he moaned, and moved his lips
 In motion still the same,
And oft he murmured o'er, in tears,
 Some well-beloved name.

All yesternight his weary feet
 The church-yard grass had trod;
A new-made grave lies under the yews—
 Who sleeps beneath the sod?

. . . .

From the west waves where the sun went down,
 Over the blushing deep
A rosy mist comes rolling on,
 With slow majestic sweep.

And from the mist afar, soft sounds
 Of music sweet are heard,
Half like a vocal summer-wind,
 Half like a warbling bird.

Slow winding through the mist, along
 The shore the cadence rung;
The Fisherman listed, and this was the song
 The gentle mermaids sung:

MERMAIDS' SONG.

I.

'O COME with me, young fisherman!
 My pearl-boat waits for thee;
Thy Mary sleeps with me afar,
 Beyond the deep green sea;
In the Mermaid Isle, the charméd isle,
 Far, far beyond the moon-lit sea!

II.

'She 's sleeping in her beauty-bower,
 And waiting there for thee;
O come with me, young fisherman,
 Beyond the deep green sea;
To the Mermaid Isle, the charméd isle,
 Far, far beyond the moon-lit sea!'

In long-drawn plaintive notes the song
 Over the waters stole;
The floating melody it sank
 Like hope into his soul.

The rosy mist rolled slowly on,
 Wide spreading more and more;
Till it circled round the Fisherman
 As he lay on the shore.

The pearl-boat touched the rock. He saw
 Three faces round the prow,
And, peering through the rosy mist,
 Dim shone each moony brow.

He heard the nearing music well
Its witching invitation tell,
And heaving with its hidden spell
He saw each snowy bosom swell,
    Saw curved each warbling throat :
And while he listened to the song,
    He slid into the boat.

Then over his head up rose the mist,
    Hiding the silver moon :
But another light, more softly bright,
    Relieved the darkness soon.

Moon-rainbows shone about the boat,
    Changeful as sparkling foam ;
Circle on circle round they rose,
    And formed an arching dome.

They flitted and twined among each other,
    Like the flashes of northern light ;
And the dome, mast-high, sailed over the boat,
Above and around, though it touched it not :
    It was a wondrous sight !

Under the dome, on the circled tide,
With tints reflected, multiplied,
    The dancing colors played ;
It seemed the waving waters were
    Of molten rainbows made.

Cleaving the many-tinted wave
    The choral mermaids swam,
Still chanting slow in sweeter strain
Their charmèd song — the while did reign
    O'er the sea a brooding calm.

Without a sail, or an oar, or a helm,
    How fast the boat did fly !
Yet the waves were silent before its prow,
And the air it breathed not on his brow
    As he passed it swiftly by !

A pilot there was below the wave,
    A pilot below the keel ;
He spun through the sea like a bird through the air,
And the light pearl-boat on his back he bare ;
Nor breath nor motion, in air or ocean,
    The Fisherman could feel.

———

PART III.

THE boat speeds on ! The boat speeds on !
    No boat e'er sped so well :
Hark ! o'er the still sea, soft and slow,
    The Triton winds his shell. .

Then swifter sped the pearly barque ;
    And soon the Fisherman wist
That the nearing shore was dimly seen
    Through the folds of the rainbow mist.

Sounded again the Triton's shell :
The dome then rising, wide did swell,
  The rainbows dimmer grew,
Till fading and expanding thin,
  They melted from the view.

And naught was left but the rosy mist,
  Transparent as the air ;
Yet it hid the Mermaid Isle, as if
  No island had been there.

Naught but the glimmering moon-lit sea
  Now met his wondering eye ;
Though a sound in the air did seem to tell
  The ear that land was nigh.

The Triton wound his shell again,
  'T was louder than before ;
And doubling echoes caught the sound,
  Answering as from a shore.

The three mer-maidens ceased their song
  At the Triton's third long peal ;
Then rose the spirit before the prow,
  That had swam below the keel.

A thin white wand was in his hand,
  And, when he rose to the air,
Naught was around but the boundless sea
  As vacant as eternity !
Silence was there, in the empty air,
The moon-lit waves looked chill and bare,
  Nor sight nor sound was there.

He touched with his wand the Fisherman's eyes.
  Oh, he had been blind before !
The air was filled with living things,
With spirits on their whirring wings,
And the sea was bright with glancing fins,
And faces were there of Undines fair,
With amber decking their sea-green hair ;
And their azure eyes were all turned with surprise
  To the stranger the pearl-boat bore.

Still deeper down were other forms,
  For the sea seemed as clear as the air ;
Half in the dark lurked the dusky shark,
The ' slid slimy eels ' glided over the strand,
And the star-fish spangled the ' ribbed sea-sand ; '
Rocked on the sea-swells, the porpoise rolled,
And a thousand bright fishes of silver and gold
  Peopled the waters there.

Before him was the Mermaid-Queen
  Enthroned in royal state ;
She sat on the back of a monster-whale,
Who spouted two jets of water, high
O'er her head, like two twin rainbows pale
On the sun-shower clouds of the evening sky :
  'Neath such canopy she sate.

Four ' Dolphins bared their backs of gold,'
All under her throne of pearl,
And the sea-weed green in festoons was seen
O'er its sides and back to curl.

Behind and above the rainbow sheen,
The serpent of the sea was seen
To rear his gleaming crest;
And the Kraken, with his thousand arms
Stretched up to heaven for thunder-storms —
For many a rood outspread was he,
Like a forest in the barren sea,
Like an army of giants at rest.

Suspended o'er the Kraken's form,
Was seen the shadowy spirit of storm
Inwrapped in growing gloom;
Half-veiled behind a lowering cloud,
Whence dull infrequent flashes rise
As if sleepily winking his lightning-eyes,
And muttering, from his sable shroud,
A sound as if he were sunk in sleep,
While the moon-light lay on the placid deep;
Yet, even in dreams, on mischief bent,
Stretched his black giant jaws, intent
To swallow up the calm still moon
Within his yawning womb!

Every spirit that roamed the deep
Or lived in ocean air,
Every fish and every bird,
That eye hath seen or ear hath heard,
And a thousand, thousand more beside
That man's dull sense hath ne'er descried,
Around their queen were there.

And the Mermaid-Queen, O who was she?
O she was wondrous fair!
A daintily-painted transparency,
Compounded of water and air:
Her eyes, that shone with a moistened light,
That was softly dim and yet was bright,
Were an azure green or an azure blue,
Or a something just between the two.
Her webbéd wings, woven of pale moonbeams
While twinkling on the mountain streams;
Their ribs, incrusted with gems that shone
With flashes that gleamed and then were gone;
A veil of the dripping sea-weed hid
Her bosom's wavy swell;
More cannot I sing — she was a thing
' To dream of, not to tell!'

The pearl-boat floated on alone,
Till the Fisherman stood before her throne.
She charmed him with her eyes' bright sheen;
Her azure eyes' soft glances, keen
They glided cold through his veins and skin,
A thrilling feeling — half, I ween,
Like Winter, and half like dread:
The pearl-boat changed to a mussel-shell,
And sank to the bottom like lead!

PART IV.

ALL above and around was water now
  That had been air before ;
It moved to and fro like a living thing,
And made a moan-like murmuring,
    Like the rough waves' distant roar
    Upon a rocky shore.

The sea-weed hung, swinging and waving,
    Swinging and waving green ;
And through the tall and bending flags
    The coral groves were seen.

Where were the shapes that flocked around
    Thronging the peopled sea ?
Save where some lagging half-seen sprite
    Through the distant flags might flee,
No living thing was anywhere,
But the mermaids fair, that brought him there,
    The mermaid sisters three.

Now, when under the wave, he saw
    How below their virgin breast
Their forms wound down like a fish's tail,
With purple and gold on every scale,
Now flashing bright, now glimmering pale ;
And their bright blue fins through the waves were seen
Plying, with golden ribs between,
    In glancing colors drest.

But the charméd glance of the Mermaid-Queen
    Had changed himself still more ;
He felt that his legs had run together,
    And fins were behind and before.

And scales were between his skin and the sea ;
The water slipped by them unfeelingly,
    Like streams o'er a pebble-stone :
His fins they plied of their own accord,
    By an instinct of their own ;
They seemed like part of another self,
As if they knew what he would do,
    And did it themselves alone.

One mermaid led the way before,
    One was on either side ;
'Swift as the thoughts of Love,' they cleft
    Their course through the yielding tide.

First they sped through the bending flags,
    And then through a coral grove
Whose boughs were intertwined together,
The white and the red met overhead,
    And formed an archway above.

Far down below, in his oozy bed,
The sea-snake's sinuous coils were spread;
The rank weeds covered his sleeping head,
    And he was couched before
An opening dark, in which were seen
The kelp's broad leaves of waving green,
And the crimson dulse flapped through the water,
Red as ' a banner bathed in slaughter : '
    It was a cavern door.

They entered in through a rift in the rock,
    And upward still they swam,
Till to a grotto wonderful
    And beautiful they came.

Here of a softly-perfumed air
    The atmosphere did seem :
With moon-stone were the walls inlaid,
Half in the light, half in dark shade;
The cavern was lofty, long, and wide,
And, opening in each indented side,
Were deep recesses, leading on —
A devious course through solid stone —
To other chambers, not less rare,
Nor favored less by sea-girls' care,
Which decked these arches crystalline
With wreaths of shells, in varied line
Of drooping sweep, or light festoon,
Or swelling curve of crescent moon.
The roof above its span revealed
With mazy intricacy ceiled ;
Resembling in its fretted style
Some ancient quaint cathedral pile :
Downward the sparry pendants hung,
And far the blazing radiance flung
Of carbuncles, set in their tips,
Giving the moon a half-eclipse.
The triple-moulded ribs they shone
With amethyst and beryl-stone ;
All waving seemed the rest of the roof
As of tissue made — the twinkling woof
Inwoven with stars. (A servant-sprite
Wrought the magic web in a single night.)
Wondrously gorgeous was the sight,
    As a ' youthful poet's dream ! '
And between the central pendants, through
A rich round window of deep sky-blue,
    Shone in the pale moon-beam.

Here in this twilight chamber fair
Shone all that ever ocean bare
Of beautiful, or rich, or rare,
    With self-born brilliance ; all
The natural wealth the waters boast,
With gems by shipwrecked mariners lost,
    Incrusted the spangled wall.

Below the water, the wrinkled sands
    Were studded with jewels bright ;
And up through the wave came glistering rays
    Of faintly-tinted light.

In it the self-illumined gems
Gazed on their twinkling diadems,
  Shadow with shadow dancing;
And the tide, with its thousand crystal eyes,
  Did twinkle back their glancing.

But the gayest of all was a deep alcove
Beneath the boughs of a coral grove,
  Where floated a couch, it seemed;
Its curtains were wrought of the Nautilus' sails
That sported once in ocean gales;
Festoons of pearls were hung around,
Pearls that of every hue were found;
They shone with a mild and misty light,
And from their mingled tints a bright
  And diverse radiance beamed.

A lovely form on the couch was laid,
  Each eye, in deep repose,
Was veiled behind a blue-veined lid,
Whose silken fringes but half hid
  What they would fain disclose.

One pale soft cheek on her snowy arm
  All motionless was laid:
Her tresses brown they hung adown,
Dipping their circlets in the tide;
Whence little ripplings, side by side,
  In the quivering moon-light played.
Her vest, of silver-vapor made,
(The warp was light, the weft was shade,
Woven cunningly by magic hand
In the tiny looms of faerie-land,)
With many a swell half visible,
Whose outline soft no tongue could tell,
  Inwrapped the slumbering maid.

  Like the beamy glory shed
  Round an infant Jesus' head,
The moonbeams shone on that lovely one,
  A silvery bright air-shower;
'T was Mary fair lay slumbering there,
  And this was her beauty-bower!

PART V.

HIST! Music with a witching tone
  The while is breathing round:
And yet in sooth I could not say
That *voice* e'er sang so sweet a lay;
O say not that it was a voice,
  But call it voiceless sound.

I could not tell the song it sung,
The words were of another tongue —
  They sounded soft and slow;
As when in sultry summer weather
The air and the sea are whispering together,
Waves rolling their regular lengths along,
The measured rhythm of ocean-song,
  Murmuring in ebb and flow.

The music had a deeper swell
Than Arion's dolphin-charming shell.
The various, omnipresent sound
Uttered itself from all around,
Clear, echoing, whisp'ring, circling, ringing,
As if the very walls were singing,
  All seemed so musical.
With open ears the rangèd shells
  Drank in the ' dying fall ; '
The curtained pearls they seemed to be,
Amid this melting melody,
By their own will so breathless still,
  As they were listening all.

Not palpable this melody,
Like human music, seemed to be :
For every note from a mortal throat
Doth come from some particular spot,
And fills as it were but one half of the air ;
This through the whole round atmosphere
  With sweet vibrations wound,
As if spirits that are themselves but air
Had gently wooed their brother-air
  To change itself to sound.

The mazy tones, forever new,
Crept lingering, loitering, winding through
The labyrinths of the wondering ear,
As if ever just beginning to hear
  A never-ending strain :
And when you thought that all was still,
  You heard the sound again.

The Fisherman in wonderment
  A moment listening stood ;
Then gazed on the couch with deep devotion,
As, rocked with undulating motion,
  It floated on the flood.

When lo ! the couch began to glide
Over the rippling, sparkling tide,
And the sea-girls swam on either side,
The sleeping fair in their arms to bear,
  And through the wave to guide.
Then the inarticulate music, swelling,
Following forsook its moon-stone dwelling ;
And, as they left the deep alcove,
And sped again through the coral grove,
And through the bending flags did flee,
They heard its warbling minstrelsy :
Thrilling the soul, through the waves it stole,
  And echoes faint replied.

And the sea-sisters three sang merrily,
  And waved their locks of green,
As gaily they bore their charge before
  The throne of the Mermaid-Queen.

'T was the early matin hour ; the time
Of the first watch after the midnight chime.
The Kraken's arms, below the sea,
Were folded all ; asleep was he.

The sea-snake, cased in glossy green,
Lay in slumbering coils of spotted sheen,
And the mer-women gay had glided away,
    In their coral caves to rest :
The Spirit of Storm, with his lightning eyes,
Lay, lulled to sleep by murmuring sighs,
    On a zephyr's balmy breast.

The young Queen reclined in a purple shell,
So gently rocked by the ocean swell,
    That scarce it seemed to move.
Her webbed wings, of the moonbeams moulded,
Arching over her head were folded,
And round her form half immaterial,
Fairies had wrapped a robe aërial.
Transparent as the pure blue skies,
The stars shone through her azure eyes,
    In which their tender twinkling light
Shone softer, sweeter, yet not less bright,
    Than from their orbs above.

And while he watched her beauty rare,
Soft sounds of silence filled the air ;
Such as in Nature's beauties fair
    Do a mute life betoken.
The sounds he can hear with his outward ear,
Though he feels and knows they cannot be
From the distant earth, or the air, or the sea,
But from within come echoingly,
From the caves of long-gone Memory,
    By wondrous charm awoken.
'T is as when, in the noon of a summer's day,
By the cicada's roundelay,
By the cool clear brook in its bubbling play,
Or by the murmuring wings of bees,
By whispering trees, or sighing seas,
    Silence is bred, not broken.

The lovely Queen of the Mermaid Isle
She gazed on the Fisherman the while,
With charméd glance and witching smile,
    When again his own form he wore.
Then a deep thrill came o'er his quivering frame ;
And loves, and longing, and fond thoughts thronging,
And burning hopes, sprang in his breast,
Such as had seemed to be at best
    But hopeless dreams before.

And Mary feels the charm that lies
Within those star-lit, cerulean eyes.
The marble-white from her cheek has fled
'Fore the blush of life, with its delicate red ;
And her heaving breast and flitting smile
Told tales of conscious love-dreams, while
(Still all by magic sleep oppressed,)
She sank on her lover's throbbing breast.
Then under the twain, from the depths of the main
    The pearl-boat rose again ;
And, gath'ring its folds from its island-home,
Over them rose the rainbow-dome.
With reflex hues the water played
Beneath its ever-varying shade :

Then, like a distant village bell,
The Triton wound his echoing shell,
And the sea-girls raised their choral strain,
    And away o'er the glassy main!

PART VI.

'Twas at the time of morning prime:
'Fore the dawn's gray light the shades of night
O'er the western hills began to flee,
And the eastern dim stars drowsily
    Were winking at the morn,
When the boat glided over the quiet bay
To the smooth rock, where the live-long day
In sobs and tears the Fisherman lay
    Despairing and forlorn.

The mer-maidens left them on that rock
    Where the setting moonbeams lay:
Then the rosy mist rolled over the boat,
And on the air sweet sounds did float;
A sad yet pleasing strain they sung—
Round the lone shore the cadence rung,
    And echoing died away.

The Lady Mary was now once more
    With her own green fields around her;
But she could not wake from her slumber yet,
    For the magic sleep still bound her.

The Fisherman watched her ruby lips,
    And the fringe round her closéd eyes;
And he thought of the time when, a child, he dreamed
    That he was in Paradise.

There lived near by a noble Knight,
    Who, at the peep of dawn,
Mounted his gallant hunting barb,
    And to the chase is gone.

But the hounds ahead, in the heat of the chase,
    Turned aside near the sea-shore, where
Round a sleeping form they silent stood,
    And all in wonder stare;
And the huntsmen crossed themselves, as if
    An angel had been there.

Amazed, the Knight in haste rode up,
    When lo! in sweet surprise,
Her blue-veined lids unclose before
    The brilliance of her eyes,
As at morn before the unveiling sun
    The white cloud-curtains rise.

The Knight was young and beautiful,
    With an eye of beaming blue;
The tender down upon his cheek
    Scarce dimmed its blooming hue:

His graceful form was gaily decked,
　His hand was small and fair,
And round his open smiling brow
　Fell his clustering light-brown hair.

The Fisherman's eye was deep and dark,
　And with weeping and watching dim :
His shagged locks were all unshorn,
His cheek sun-burnt and weather-worn,
　Could *she* deign to look on *him ?*

Lady Mary gazed on the noble Knight ;
And she knew by his broad plume, nodding white
　O'er his cap of crimson gay,
That under her window he thrice had sung
　Of love a tender lay.
And what could a maiden think of a knight
Who, by the young moon's mellow light,
With passioned love-songs waked the night ?
　Refuse to love him ?　Nay !

In his arm the young Knight deftly raised her,
Upon his barb he gently placed her,
　Then took the bridle-rein ;
And holding converse sweet, together
　They paced across the plain.

The Fisherman watched her form, until
They disappeared behind the hill
　That bounds the spreading lea ;
Then a tear-drop fell — and once he sighed :
'Forever lost !' he wildly cried,
　And plunged into the sea.

———

PART VII.

But during all this wondrous night
　How did Sir Gerald sleep ?
Did dreams of new wealth bring delight ?
　Was his slumber calm and deep ?

The night before the funeral
　Little I ween he slept ;
The first night after, his poignant grief
In sleepless mourning sought relief —
　Sir Gerald 'waked and wept.'

Now wearied nature claimed repose ;
　But he feared to sleep alone,
And he dared not sleep with another, lest
Unconscious mutterings in his rest
　Should tell what he had done.

Before he closed his aching eyes,
　He heard the midnight bell :
The solemn tones to him did sound
　The tolling of a knell !

He slept. In a dream he saw broad lands
  And gems of wondrous size ;
Vast heaps of coinéd gold did feast
  His avaricious eyes :
With greedy joy he stretched his hands
  To clutch the glittering prize,
When long worms with their slimy forms
Crawled cold and clammy round his arms,
  And clinched them like a vice ;
The chilly horror in his veins,
  It froze his blood to ice !

And ghast snakes' forkéd tongues and fangs
  Did hiss and grind in his face ;
While arms of crooked flame did stretch,
Burning to clasp the sordid wretch
  In their intense embrace !

In fear he started ! Along the wall
  Sadly the night-wind sighed ;
And slowly o'er the marble floor
  The cold moon-beam did glide.

He slept again. He was in a vault
Dim-lit by lantern dark : in thought
  From every eye close-hid,
Filling a coffin with stone and sod,
  And screwing down the lid.
When he looked up, and from on high,
Lo ! a serene and bright blue eye
  Was watching what he did !

Trembling he woke. Along the wall
  Softly the night-wind sighed ;
And nearer o'er the marble floor
  Did the quiet moon-beam glide.

He slept again. Before his eyes
The crag o'erhanging the sea did rise ;
And falling swift down to the wave below,
Was a woman's form in a robe of snow :
How he strained his eye and his listening ear
  To see the dim form disappear,
And the sound of the deep dull plash to hear !
But the sinking form, to his fearful stare,
Falls slower, and stops in middle-air !
From her fair neck the stone, unbound,
Drops alone in the wave with a deadened sound ;
While, struggling free from the twisted band,
For help was stretched a quivering hand,
  And a shrill shriek rends the skies :
More shrill, the sky echoes back the cry ;
  And, 'fore his starting eyes,
  The form begins to rise !

In terror he woke : his flesh did quake —
What sees he now ? Does he dream awake ?
  Standing before his bed
There 's a woman's form in a dank white shroud !
Round her snowy neck, by death-pains bowed,

Is a corded mark in a circle dark ;
Her rigid face is pale and stark ;
Her eyeballs glare — a glassy stare !
In wild locks hangs her dripping hair,
  And the sea-foam is on her head.

' 'T is she !' he cried ; and, quick as light,
From the casement he leaped — a fearful height !
  Ten fathom down he fell.
Yet started, flying, to his feet,
For fiends bore him up unhurt, to meet
  A death more horrible.

Like Panic, over the rocks he fled
  With wondrous speed and wild :
'T was startling strange to see a man
So furious, haggard, wild and wan,
  In the silent moonshine mild.

Aye backward staring, he descried
That awful form behind him glide,
  With a scowl on her pallid face ;
And her cold and skinny hands outstretchéd,
Urged fast and faster the maniac wretched
  On his terrific race.

Sir Gerald, hold ! the crags are here !
  But *she* follows close behind !
Sir Gerald ! Sir Gerald ! the sea is near,
  But nearer is SHE behind !

Ha ! ha !—o'er the cliff he 's plunged, hell-driven
  By the phantom-fiend, Remorse !
High from the green brine hungry sharks
  Leaped up at the caitiff-corse !

———

CONCLUSION.

THE old moon in the young moon's arm
  In shadowy slumber lay ;
And one short month, how enviously !
  Had swiftly passed away.

When, on the eve of a sunny day,
  To the village-church there hied,
With merry bells ringing, and young girls singing,
  A bridegroom and a bride.

And well I ween a sight was seen
  Both beautiful and rare,
When Sir Frederick, the noble Knight, gave troth
  To Lady Mary fair

There was jolly cheer in the castle-hall
  When the wedding-feast began ;
With dainties stored then groaned the board,
  And free the rich red wine ran :
And the Bridegroom gay and his lovely Bride
  —— Forgot the Fisherman !

But the mermaid-sisters had carried him
  Before their Island Queen;
With witching smile and magic eye
She charmed his bitter misery;
And by oblivion took away
The grief that in his bosom lay,
  With its gnawing anguish keen.
She changed his form; and now he roves
With the mer-women free through coral groves,
And the moon-stone cave, with its pearl-alcoves,
  Deep down in the ocean green.

And often at night, near that charméd shore,
  On the salt-breeze borne along,
The mariner hears, o'er the moon-lit wave,
  The sea-boy's distant song.

J. RESYN PINSOMB.

THE THUNDER-CLOUD.

'Intonnere poli, et crebris micat ignibus æther.' — VIRGIL.

A SONG for the Thunder-cloud, gloomy and dark!
Whose shafts never fail, never swerve from their mark:
Whose voice is far louder than Ocean's wild roar,
When his foam-crested waves lash the rock-bound shore;
A song for the Thunder-cloud, frowning and black!
Right onward it cometh, it ne'er turneth back.

O! heard ye that sound? 'T was a low rumbling jar,
Like the noise of the battle, when heard from afar;
And see yon dark mass, rudely piled in the west,
And mark the red lightning which glares on its breast!
Now swiftly it rises, its dark wings outspread —
It filleth the heart of the gazer with dread.

It rolls and it whirls, but it still presses on;
It o'erspreadeth the sky, it hath darkened the sun!
Its black wreaths unfold, and swift leaps out the flash,
With a rattle, a roar, and a deafening crash;
'T is the Thunder-cloud fierce! right onward it comes,
While men, terror-stricken, retreat to their homes.

The oak on yon hill-top, for many a year
Hath spread out his arms, without blenching or fear;
The trees of the forest which stood by his side,
Have bow'd to the axe of the woodman, and died:
The children beneath those huge branches that play'd,
Have grown up to manhood — are laid with the dead!

But mark yon red blaze, darting swift from the skies;
Down, down through the crest of the strong Oak it flies!
It wraps his broad branches in bright lurid flames —
A loud-roaring crash the proud triumph proclaims.
'Though long he had breasted the storm and the blast,
The Thunder-cloud conquers the brave Oak at last!'

F. G. F

LITERARY NOTICES.

THE TOKEN AND ATLANTIC SOUVENIR. AN OFFERING FOR CHRISTMAS AND THE
NEW YEAR. pp. 320. Boston: DAVID H. WILLIAMS.

IT seems a long time, in our memory, since the first number of the 'Atlantic
Souvenir,' the pioneer of the American tribe of annuals, made its appearance in
this country. It was a pompous, corpulent little volume; but it took the public
approbation captive at once, even as the 'Lady' held the 'Merlin' prisoner in the
frontispiece, by a delightful species of bondage. From the Bay of Fundy to the
Gulf of Mexico the 'press-gang' vied with each other which should say the most
flattering things of the first American annual. Since that period, how these
'painted bladders' have swarmed upon the public! Year after year saw them
increase, until at length they began sadly to deteriorate in literary merit, and
attraction, and the public to grow tired of their mere *prettinesses*, internal as well as
external. Their circulation began to decrease; and in the mean-time kindred
English manufactures, prepared mainly for the 'daughter country,' began to multiply in our markets, and the native article experienced a still farther decline. At
the present moment, two or three works of this description, of a sterling literary
character, alone hold sway among us, and command a deserved popularity. Foremost among these, we regard the 'TOKEN,' which presents this season literary
attractions of a high order and value. Of the illustrations, it will be sufficient to
say, that their execution in the first style of the art of celature was secured by the
employment of those eminent engravers, Messrs. RAWDON, WRIGHT, HATCH and
SMILLIE. The subjects are various and well chosen. We check them, as it were
by catalogue. The first, 'The Bracelet,' is a fine engraving, but the lady seems to
have just stepped from under the hands of a French hair-dresser. The frontispiece
has an atmosphere of softness suited to the character of the design; 'Rockland
Lake' is a faithful transcript of a most picturesque and beautiful scene; the
'Oaken Bucket,' with the enticing farm-house and the vista of quiet loveliness
opening beyond, is admirable; and 'The Outward Bound' is perhaps as good as an
engraving *can* be of BIRCH's matchless sea-sketches, which require his natural
coloring and ocean atmosphere, if adequate justice would be rendered them.
'Winter' is excellent; 'Metamora' by FORREST is portrayed with great faithfulness and spirit; and 'The First Ship' has many of CHAPMAN's beauties and not a
few of his defects. Who, for example, ever saw such a tree as the one he has here
depicted?

In its literary contents, the 'Token' is unwontedly rich, and quite superior to any of its rivals. 'The Seen and the Unseen,' by Rev. Mr. PEABODY of New-Bedford, is one of those thoughtful moral essays which come home to the hearts of men with all the force of a powerful and eloquent sermon. So admirable is the style and so just the sentiments of this article, that we should be tempted to copy it entire, but for the publisher's remonstrance against wholesale appropriation. 'The Two Locks of Hair,' a translation by Mr. LONGFELLOW, it is scarcely necessary to say, is a beautiful poem. 'The Teachings of Autumn,' too, by Mr. GREENWOOD, are worthy that gentleman's reputation. There is a winning tenderness, an easy grace, in the style, which it would not be difficult to trace to its true source, even though the name of the writer were not given. We have seen nothing better from the eminent pen of PERCIVAL, for many years, than the 'Classic Melodies' in this volume, which evince alike his fine ear for the melody of verse, and the variety and facility of his execution. Miss HARRIET BEECHER STOWE, whom we should class with Miss MITFORD as a graphic delineator of rustic life and manners, has furnished a pleasant story, in 'The Yankee Girl;' Mr. J. R. LOWELL, in the 'Ballad of the Stranger,' teaches consolation to the afflicted in a quaint yet touching poem; and Mr. PIERPONT has illustrated 'The Bucket' with some natural lines, which sparkle like the drops of the cool draught they celebrate. Many other writers, whom we lack space to indicate, add to the attractions of 'The Token,' which we take pleasure in warmly commending to the acceptance of our readers.

JULIAN: OR SCENES IN JUDEA. By the Author of Letters from Palmyra and Rome. In two volumes. pp. 691. New-York: C. S. FRANCIS. Boston: J. H. FRANCIS.

OUR readers, who are especially familiar with the writings of Mr. WARE, will need no additional incentive to the possession of the volumes before us. We shall not anticipate their enjoyment by following the author through his pages in our own; but simply indicate, by a few extracts, how well the spirit which pervaded the Palmyra Letters, and which secured their wide-spread popularity, is preserved in those under notice. The 'Scenes,' as we gather from the preface, are purely fictitious, with no foundation whatever in historical fact, except where an obvious agreement will be found with the Scriptures. Wherever the story deviates from the straight course of the New-Testament record, it is to be taken as imaginary — illustrative merely of the period chosen. We are again profoundly impressed with the life-like characteristics of our author's narrative and descriptive style. Indeed his 'Letters' are little less than a series of elaborate paintings, filled up with such care in all the minor accessories, as almost to do away the impression that the whole is after all but an illusion. We shall illustrate these remarks by one or two striking passages. In the following, the writer must be supposed to have crossed the Jordan, and to have approached by the barren wastes and rocky defiles beyond its western bank, near to the holy city:

"You will readily believe it was with no common emotion that I found myself drawing near for the first time to so celebrated a place. The sentiments which possessed me when I first beheld from the ocean the outlines of Lebanon and first set my foot upon the soil of Cæsarea, were again present. As I ascended the eastern side of the Mount of Olives, passing through Bethany, and knew that upon reaching its summit or coming to its descent the long-expected prospect would break upon me, I could with difficulty restrain my pace to that of Judith's mule, whose step seemed slower than ever before. But the hill was in due time surmounted, and soon as we had crossed a part of its summit, and passed from out the groves which clothe its western brow, the city, as it were in a moment of time, stood before us in its whole extent, no object whatsoever intervening to cut off the least portion of the prospect. Mount Moriah crowned with its Temple rising from the vast supporting walls that form a part of the hill on which it stands, Mount Sion with its shining palaces, Acra and Bezetha, the heavy walls of the city girding it about, with their gate-ways and frequent towers — all lay before me a vision of greatness and beauty not surpassed by any other I had ever beheld. The vast assemblage of temple, palace, and dwelling, with the swarming populace and all the thousand signs of overflowing and active life, struck the mind the more impressively too from standing, as it all did, in the midst of surrounding hills, whose bare and rugged tops and sides gave no token of aught but sterility and death. The eye beheld nothing upon them but flocks of sheep among the gray rocks, hardly to be distinguished from the rocks themselves, and so only adding one more to the other features of desolation. Another scene was, however, presented by fertile valleys at their feet thickly inhabited, their olive orchards, and their vineyards creeping a little way up the barren hill-sides. At the roots of the hill we were upon, and all along upon the banks of the Kedron, the white, pointed tents of strangers and travellers were visible, who had, like ourselves, come thus early to witness the events that should ensue, while the roads leading to the gates of the city, and crossing the plain in all directions, were filled with crowds of those who on horse and on foot or in vehicles of every various kind were arriving or departing. Clouds of dust, converted by the rays of the setting sun to a gaudy purple hue, rose and hovered over the whole scene, through which glittered the shining points of polished harness, or the steel trappings of troops of Roman horse as they shot swiftly along. We stopped and gazed ere we descended the hill, that we might enjoy awhile the beauty and magnificence that were spread out below. · · · I was filled with admiration as I drew nearer to the walls, and saw their immense height and thickness, and the strength of the gates with the defences of their vast towers, and considered that, owing to these things and to its natural position, it was a place absolutely impregnable. On this side, indeed, the city derives great advantage from the height of the ground on which it stands, in addition to that of the walls. But were there the walls alone, it seemed to me an impossible thing that they should either be surmounted by an enemy, or demolished by engines. Onias with a proud step, as he beheld my wonder, led me on to the gates, and through them into the city, pointing out as he went the buildings that were most remarkable, and the persons also whom we met, who were distinguished for their office or their power over the people. At length hastening along the streets, now thronged with those who were pouring also in the same direction, we reached the great object of my desire, that which from my infancy I had ever wished to behold, the Temple. Truly did Herod show his magnificence in this vast and beautiful structure. If in other cities, as I have seen, he did great things and well worthy of admiration, here he did greater still; so that, as I judge, all that together he had built in Cæsarea would not compare with what, for grandeur, perfect workmanship, proportion, and variety of beauty, he accomplished in Jerusalem in this single building. The marble of which it is built is beautiful and polished to the smoothness of crystal, yet are the separate pieces so large that it is surprising they should have been laid in their places safely and without injury at such heights. The innumerable columns surrounding the courts of the Gentiles and the Women, and supporting the porticoes which encompass the building, create unfeigned astonishment in the beholder.

"All parts of it on the morning of this Sabbath I found swarming with the numbers of those who had come up, some to worship, some, like myself, strangers from remote parts to wonder and gaze, and some to converse and learn the news of those who had recently arrived. The name of Jesus was heard from every one, as he passed talking with another, or as he addressed yourself. All were asking some question concerning him of those who, they supposed, might know better than themselves, or else answering those who had made inquiries, or else loudly and fiercely disputing concerning his character, authority, and works, and the designs of the Council. In the outer courts, where the meaner sort of people assemble, no measures were kept among those who disputed, but words often came to blows, and peace was restored only by the interference of officers of the Temple.

"The question put by all to all was, 'will he come up to the feast? who can tell!' As I stood upon the upper steps of those leading to the Treasury, I was accosted by one, who said 'Sir, can you tell me if Jesus will be at the feast?' I answered that I could not, but I trusted much to the general persuasion that he would come. Though none can say that he will from any certain knowledge, yet all feel assured that he will, and there are none to say nay. Such general convictions commonly turn out well founded.

"'What you say,' he replied, 'is true. Seeing you, however, but now in company with Onias of Beth-Harem, I looked for more certain intelligence at your hands, as Jesus has of late been in those regions.'

"'He has moved so fast,' I replied, 'from place to place, as if hasting to complete some work that he had to do in season, that it is likely none can tell where he has been, or where he now is, save those disciples, who, as I hear, never leave him.'

"'Some others know a little,' cried a voice at my side, 'as well as those of whom you speak. Two days ago he was in the Peræa, beyond Jordan — to be in the outskirts of Jericho on the Sabbath, where I doubt not he now is. And what is more, he will be in Jerusalem at the feast.' So saying he turned away, and passing from place to place, repeated his news to as many as would hear. 'This is news indeed,' said he who had first spoken. 'It will crowd the city more and more.'"

The approach of the SAVIOUR to Jerusalem is thus vividly described; and the reader will agree with us, that it well deserves to be classed among the productions of a great artist's pencil:

"Another day has come and gone — Jesus has entered the city — I have seen him.

"Early in the morning it became apparent, that that would take place which had been looked for. For so soon as the gates were open, the people began to pour forth, and throng the road leading by the house of Heber and over the Mount of Olives to Bethany. As the day advanced, the crowds increased of persons of all sorts and conditions, the old as well as the young, the rich and poor, women and little children. It seemed as if the whole city had come abroad to honor by its presence and welcome, at least witness, the entrance of one who was either to reign over it as King, or else, it might be, fall a sacrifice to the rage of the present rulers. If one might judge by the countenance, but especially by the language which continually fell upon the ear, they who had thus come abroad had come in the spirit of friendship, and with the intention to show that if Jesus would meet them in their wishes, they on the other hand would acknowledge and receive him. As these crowds passed by our tent, loud and ardent in their talk, their lively gesticulations, as well as their voices, showing what hopes and passions were ruling within, it was in vain that I longer tried to resist the contagion, but leaving Judith and Ruth at the tent door, threw myself into the midst of the living mass, and was borne along with it up the Mount, and on toward Bethphage and Bethany. When we had reached the brow of the hill and were about passing it, the sound of voices as of a great number caught our ears, and looking forward we beheld where, as the road suddenly turned, Jesus, surrounded by another multitude, came on toward us. The air was now filled with the exulting cries of the approaching throng, which, caught up by us and those who were behind, rolled on an increasing shout even to the gates of the city, announcing to those who covered the walls and the towers, that Jesus was drawing nigh. Never were a people, I believe, so carried away by what cannot be termed other than a sacred zeal. No language was too lofty and confident for them to utter, no acts of homage too expressive to render of their loyalty and devotion. The way was all along strewn with the leaves and branches of trees, which the eager populace tore from the groves that bordered the road ; branches of the Palm were waved over their heads, and ever, as Jesus slowly moved on, often wholly obstructed by the struggling crowds, they who were immediately about him cast their garments in the way as before a king. Many, especially such as had at any time received benefits of healing at his hands, or whose friends had been restored by his power, cast themselves down prostrate on the ground, as the only sufficient sign they could offer of their reverence and gratitude. · · · He seemed buried in thought for the most part as he rode along, save that now and then he briefly responded to the cries or the questions of those who pressed about him. But he spake not many words, or so that more than a very few could hear, until we were come to the descent of the Mount of Olives, and the city suddenly came into view in all its glory — its walls, and towers, and house-tops covered with her thronging inhabitants. He then paused ; and beholding with both astonishment and pity, as it seemed, the scene before him, tears fell from his eyes ; and though I could not hear with distinctness all that he said, he appeared to express apprehensions of great evil and disaster as about to overtake Jerusalem and Judea, of enemies who should assail and oppress them, and lay them waste. All who heard were struck with amazement, and one to another uttered in secret tones their astonishment. Thus while the innumerable multitude of those who encompassed him, and hailed him King and Deliverer, and could find no words of joy in which to give vent to the hopes that were within, he rejoiced not, but was evidently sad. The sight of the city with its populace all awaiting him, and the sounds of their tumultuous cries as they were borne to us from afar, and the waving of their hands in token of welcome, seemed to awaken no feeling of triumph in his heart, but, instead, drew forth tears. I confess that I was also astonished ; and could only say, the whole of this man is mysterious and impenetrable — we know him not — we do not comprehend what he is, nor what he has come to do.

" Thus we moved on — but hardly moving by reason of the constantly increasing throngs of people — to the sublime music of their acclamations, which without ceasing filled the air. As we came against the house of Heber, our humble tents I beheld swept away and trampled into the earth by the descending torrent, which, swelling beyond the limits of the road, spread far into the grounds on either side. No other end seemed to be regarded by those who composed these crowds, than, if possible, to keep within sight of the object of their worship or the hearing of his voice ; and but that a Divine Providence seemed to protect the people, great numbers would have perished, trodden into the earth by those who rushed madly on, forgetful, in their struggles for precedence, of the feeble and the young who filled their way.'

ADTOBIOGRAPHY, REMINISCENCES, AND LETTERS OF JOHN TRUMBULL, from 1756 to 1841. In one volume, large 8vo. pp. 439. New-York and London : WILEY AND PUTNAM.

WE have already announced this work, and spoken of the superior character of its numerous engravings, from original drawings by its distinguished subject, and its excellent typographical execution. It remains only briefly to characterize its literary attractions. All who know Col. TRUMBULL, or are familiar with his public career, are aware that in the wars of the American revolution he was not only a spectator but a participant ; that his pictures of the memorable battles between the Americans and their early foes have been cherished by his countrymen as graphic records of events 'all of which he saw and part of which he was ;' but it may not be as generally known to *all* our readers, that our author travelled much abroad, after the establishment of our independence, mingling in the best European ranks, sketching as he moved scenes and characters with his pencil, which are re-produced in the volume before us ; and that in London he was arrested and confined as an American prisoner, and finally liberated at the instance of an eminent British statesman. These matters and nameless numbers more we must counsel the reader to examine at large in our author's very beautiful book.

EDITOR'S TABLE.

THE BATTLE OF BUNKER HILL. — We have never seen a more clear, intelligible, and in all respects a better-written description of the Battle of Bunker-Hill than is contained in an Oration delivered at Charlestown, (Mass.,) in June last, in commemoration of that remarkable event, by Rev. GEORGE E. ELLIS. So graphic are the details, so complete the panorama which the orator causes to pass before the eyes of the reader, that we are almost tempted again to rehearse in these pages this oft-told tale. And as it is, we must be pardoned for presenting one or two spirited extracts. The annexed passage succeeds a description of the intrenchments thrown up in the night by the Provincials, a scene so finely depicted in COOPER's ' Lionel Lincoln : '

" The instant that the first beams of light marked distinctly the outlines of the Americans, and of their intrenchments upon the hill, the cannon of the Lively, which floated nearest, opened a hot fire upon them, at the same time arousing the sleepers in Boston, to come forth as spectators or actors in the cruel tragedy. The other armed vessels, some floating batteries, and the battery on Copp's Hill, combined to pour forth their vollies, uttering a startling and dismal note of preparation for the day's conflict. But the works, though not completed, were in a state of such forwardness that the missiles of destruction fell harmless, and the intrenchers continued to strengthen their position. The enemy in Boston could scarcely credit their eyesight. Prescott, the hero of the day, with whom its proudest fame should rest, was undaunted, ardent, and full of heroic energy. He planned and directed, he encouraged the men, he mounted the works, and with his bald head uncovered, and his commanding frame, he was a noble personification of a patriot cause. Some of the men incautiously ventured in front of the works, when one of them was instantly killed by a cannot-shot. This first victim was buried in the ditch, and his companions were fearfully warned of the fatality which the day would bring yet nearer to them.

" When the orders had been issued at Cambridge, the night before, to those who had thus complied with them, refreshments and reinforcements had been promised in the morning. Thus some of the men might have thought they had fulfilled their part of the work, and were entitled to relief, or were at liberty to depart. Some few, when the first victim fell, left the hill, and did not return. Those who remained were exhausted with their toil, and without food and water, and the morning was already intensely hot. The officers, sympathizing with their situation and sufferings, requested Prescott to send to Cambridge for relief. He summoned a council of war, but was resolute against the petition, saying that the enemy would not venture an attack, and if they did venture, would be defeated ; that the men who had raised the works were best able to defend them, and deserved the honor of the victory : that they had already learned to despise the fire of the enemy. The vehemence of Prescott infused new spirit into the men, and they resolved to stand the dread issue. Prescott ordered a guard to the ferry to prevent a landing there. He was seen by Gage, who was reconnoitring from Copp's Hill, and who inquired of Counsellor Willard by his side, ' Who is that officer commanding ? ' Willard recognized his brother-in-law, and named Colonel Prescott. ' Will he fight ? ' asked Gage. The answer was, ' Yes, sir, depend upon it, to the last drop of blood in him ; but I cannot answer for his men.' Yet Prescott could answer for his men, and that amounted to the same thing."

We give the first of three successive ' impressions ' which the King's troops received of the valor of the hitherto despised and contemned Provincials :

" It was of vital necessity that every charge of powder and ball spent by the Americans should take effect. There was none for waste. The officers commanded their men to withhold their fire till the enemy were within eight rods, and when they could see the whites of their eyes, to aim at their waist-bands; also to 'aim at the handsome coats, and pick off the commanders.' As the British left wing came within gun-shot, the men in the redoubt could scarcely restrain their fire, and a few discharged their pieces. Prescott, indignant at this disobedience, vowed instant death to any one who should repeat it, and promised by the confidence which they reposed in him to give the command at the proper moment. His Lieutenant-Colonel, Robinson, ran round the top of the works and knocked up the muskets. When the space between the assailants and the redoubt was narrowed to the appointed span, the word was spoken at the moment; the deadly flashes burst forth, and the green grass was crimsoned with the life-blood of hundreds. The front rank was nearly obliterated, as were its successive substi-tutes, as the Americans were well protected, and were deliberate in their aim. The enemy fell like the tall grass which grew around before the practised sweep of the mower. General Pigot was obliged to give the word for a retreat. Some of the wounded were seen crawling with the last energies of life from the gory heap of the dying and the dead, among whom the officers, by their proportion, far out-numbered the private soldiers. As the wind rolled away the suffocating smoke, and the blasts of the artillery and the musketry for a moment ceased, the spectacle was truly awful. The agonizing yells and shrieks of the sufferers were distracting and piercing. Prayers and groans, foul impious oaths, and fond invocations of the loved and the dear, were mingled into sounds which scarcely seemed of human utterance, by the rapturous shout of victory which rang from the redoubt.''

Mr. Ellis certainly confirms the statement of a correspondent who arraigned 'Old Put. at the Bar,' in our September number. There is no certainty, he says, that Gen. Putnam was at the intrenchments, even the night before the battle. 'He *may* have ridden over with or after the detachment, and *if* so, his presence must have been cheering and animating to those who knew his person and his-tory: he would have been a welcome counsellor. But if in the redoubt at all, it is certain that he left it in the night, or very early the next morning.' The hero of the day was the gallant Prescott; and to him should *due* honor at least be awarded:

"It was only when the redoubt was crowded with the enemy and the defenders in one promiscuous throng, and assailants on all sides were pouring into it, that Prescott, no less, but even more a hero, when he uttered the reluctant word, ordered a retreat. A longer trial would have been folly, not courage. Some of the men had splintered their musket-stocks in fierce blows, nearly all were defence-less, yet was there that left within them, in a dauntless soul, which might still help their country at its need. Prescott gave the crowning proof of his devoted and magnanimous spirit, when he cooled the heat of his own brain, and bore the bitter pang in his own heart, by commanding an orderly and still resisting retreat. He was the hero of that blood-dyed summit — the midnight leader and guard, the morning sentinel, the orator of the opening strife, the cool and deliberate overseer of the whole struggle, the well-skilled marksman of the exact distance at which a shot was certain death: he was the venerable chief in whose bright eye and steady nerve all read their duty; and when conduct, skill and courage could do no more, he was the merciful deliverer of the remnant. Prescott was the hero of the day, and wherever its tale is told, let him be its chieftain.''

But Mr. Ellis has no desire, as we trust no other true American has, to detract from the *deserved* reputation of the 'the old bear,' as the British are said to have termed Putnam. The following passage bears the impress of conscious candor:

"While such was the issue at the redoubt, the left wing, under Putnam, aided by some reinforce-ments which had arrived too late, was making a vigorous stand at the rail fence. But the retreat at the redoubt compelled the resolute defenders to yield with slow and reluctant steps, as their flank was opened to the enemy. Putnam pleaded and cursed; he commanded and implored the scattering bands to rally, and he swore that he would win them the victory. For his foul profanity he made a sincere confession before the church and congregation of which he was a member, after the war. On the day of the battle, his great and consuming purpose was to fortify Bunker Hill. To effect this, he passed and repassed between Cambridge and Charlestown, sending for tools to the redoubt, where he does not appear to have been present during the action, and endeavoring to rally the flying even when there was no longer a hope. His furious ardor may or may not have needed the control of deliberate judgment, and of that essential characteristic of the soldier, which is termed 'conduct.' His courage was unquestionable. I have fairly presented him and his services as a careful examination of all the authorities within my reach has enabled me to decide upon a point where writers better informed than myself have differed. I cannot regard Putnam either as the commander or the hero of the day; and while I would speak with great diffidence upon so delicate a point, I would still hope that my conclu-sions in reference to it partake as much of truth as I am sure they do of impartiality.''

'Prescott,' says Mr. Ellis, 'repaired to head-quarters to make return of his trust. He was indignant at the loss of the battle, and implored Gen. Ward to commit to him three fresh regiments, promising with them to win back the day. But he had already honorably accomplished all that his country might demand. He complained bitterly that the reinforcements which might have given to his triumph the completeness that was needed to make it a victory, had failed him. It is almost clear to our minds, that but for the unfortunate announcement in a loud tone by a Provincial soldier, that the ammunition of the Americans was nearly exhausted, and the discovery of the weak point in the works, alone nerved the British to a third attack, and gained them the victory, if such it could be called, which in its effects secured in time their total defeat. As apropos to this general theme, we may remark, that up to the time at which the sheets of this department are committed to the press, we have not received the promised rejoinder to the paper entitled 'Old Put. at the Bar.' If received in season, it shall have an early place in our number for December.

THE AMERICAN REVIEWS.—We have before us 'THE NEW-YORK REVIEW' and 'THE NORTH-AMERICAN REVIEW' for the October quarter. Both are various and entertaining, which could not be said of some of their predecessors. The first paper in our own Quarterly leads us to regret that the Life of JOHN JAY, which is its subject, should not have attained a wider circulation among our countrymen, by whom his exalted reputation should be cherished as a proud legacy to the national annals. The 'Relation of Platonism to Christianity,' which opens much to our taste, is yet in store for us, since we have not as yet found leisure for its perusal. 'The Earliest Ages of English Poetry' is a desultory essay, with extracts, upon the poetry of the earliest Anglo-Saxon writers, BEÖWOLF, CÆDMON, and their successors of the lyre. It evinces a fair share of research, and a general familiarity with the theme in hand, which could scarcely fail to result in an instructive and entertaining review. We passed Young's 'Chronicles of the Pilgrim Fathers' to arrive at the article upon 'Tasso, and his Writings,' which will naturally be traced to the classic pen of our accomplished contributor, Hon. R. H. WILDE, of Georgia. We ask the especial attention of our readers to this paper, to which indeed it will be attracted the more readily that it contains some additional particulars touching the Alberti Manuscripts, an extended notice of which, from a distinguished correspondent then in Florence, (and from which the reviewer says he has 'borrowed freely,') appeared some time since in this Magazine. We are well pleased to find so capable a pen as that of Mr. WILDE remonstrating with our countrymen against their servile adoption of British opinions in regard to the authors of foreign countries; our neglect of foreign languages; our impolitic duty on books printed in them; our want of an international copy-right law, and the consequent inundation of our country by all the trashy productions of the British press. The reviewer reminds his readers that taste and genius are not confined to one nation; that polite literature is successfully prosecuted by many; and he shows that it is a great folly to limit our vision to a single district of the Republic of Letters, however rich and highly cultivated it may be. And here we cannot resist the desire to say a word or two touching the short-sighted and narrow view which is sometimes taken in this country of the objects of a *national literature*. Many construe the term to mean, that an American writer should continue to reproduce pictures of his own country and countrymen, even as an artist who should never go out of his own family for subjects for his pencil. And nothing is more common than to hear or read querulous remarks like these: 'Why does not our countryman confine himself to *American* ground, in which he has been so successful? Have we not our romantic aborigines, our vast forests, our revolutionary struggles, our border strifes, our magnificent scenery every where? Why should an American leave his own country, to find themes for his pen?' We must get rid of this narrow, exclusive spirit. 'The whole boundless continent is ours;' and it should be for our writers, above all others, to carry their researches, as Mr. IRVING and Mr. WILDE have done, with so much honor to themselves and their country, into the rich stores, the unwrought mines, of other nations. Aloof as we are from the excitements, political or other, which agitate the countries of the old world; with our interest in their great authors fresh and unbiassed; and ourselves regarded with no suspicious eye by the people from whom we are so widely separated; our writers, we repeat, while they neglect not our own resources, are the very men to enrich our literature from the ample store-houses of other countries.

With the exception of a long and very able paper upon the 'National Defence,' evidently from the pen of one practically acquainted with the details of his subject, the remaining articles of the *Review* are of works which have been elaborately noticed in these pages; Mr. STONE's 'Life and Times of Red-Jacket,' Miss SEDGWICK's 'Letters from Abroad,' etc. Of this last paper, in passing, we must express our admiration. Unquestionably, the reviewer is correct in the kind and gentleman-like dissent which he renders against certain inferences drawn by our amiable and accomplished country-woman. The truth is, human nature must be taken as we find it. The distinctions of society — and we appeal to every gentleman whose observation and experience entitle him to be a competent judge — are *necessary,* and while the world stands *will* be, for the social order of a refined and well-balanced community. And in this, as we shall aim hereafter to show, consists a *true* republicanism. The tenth and concluding article is a cluster of 'Critical Notices,' in which brief but well-digested judgments are passed upon eleven current publications, including COOPER's 'Deerslayer,' TRUMBULL's Autobiography, Life and Remains of Miss LANDON, etc.

The NORTH AMERICAN has nine articles, the last including some dozen short 'Critical Notices.' The papers upon BEETHOVEN, the 'Early History of Ohio,' and the American Navy, are voluminous, comprehensive, and exceedingly well-written. There are matters in each of these papers which we have pencilled for reference, and to which we shall hereafter advert. The article upon 'Rural Cemeteries' we may hope to find widely influential in multiplying those 'gardens of bereaved Affection.' We must be permitted, however, to take exception to one judgment of the reviewer, uttered with an *ex-cathedra* air, and influenced no doubt by some interest incident to Mount Auburn. The writer inveighs against *vaults,* and contends warmly for the preference of graves over these repositories of the dead. But let us ask any mourner, who has seen a dear friend deposited in a 'narrow house of clay,' and heard the striking of spades into sand and gravel, and the rumbling of clods upon the coffin, of all sounds, says Mr. IRVING in his Rural Funerals, the most withering, whether he would not far rather see the last remains of the loved being left in a spacious marble apartment, white and clean, and below the influences of the upper air and the moist earth? For our own part, we consider vaults a vast improvement upon grave-burials. It is *not* a principal recommendation of this mode of sepulture, that the dust of our friend 'should be *accessible,'* a position which our reviewer first assumes, and then gratuitously combats; although if it were, the result would often be far from repugnant; since in many well-built vaults bodies often remain for many years apparently unchanged. As to the objection that vaults are insecure, it will not stand against arches, good materials, and sound workmanship. If the reviewer is convinced that vaults would disfigure

Mount Auburn, let him keep that point in view; but he is travelling out of the record when he denounces all vaults, in all places, in order to enforce a specious argument in favor of a local question. Our 'Relations with England,' the next paper, will attract much attention at this moment. It embraces among other matters a timely, comprehensive, and succinct history, obtained from all the authentic documents upon the subject, of the 'Affair of the Caroline,' and the preceding and subsequent events connected with that transaction. Following this, we have 'The Memorials of Oglethorpe,' that eminent Georgian, of whom, even at the age of ninety, Burke said: 'He perfectly realizes all my ideas of Nestor; his literature is great; his knowledge of the world extensive; and his faculties as bright as ever.' This article we must read again. A merely cursory perusal prevents our rendering it at present the justice it deserves. A review of Stephens' Travels in Central America, and Wright's Translations from Lafontaine, brings us to the 'Critical Notices,' which are imbued with a condensed spirit appropriate to their brevity. We observe that the Editor, in his notice of Combe's 'Phrenological Visit,' speaks of the stilted altitude in which the most unquestionable verities are often announced. He adduces a few examples, and adds: 'Dr. Channing, of whom Mr. Combe is a devoted admirer, sometimes writes in this way. But it requires all the graces of his eminent genius to make it tolerable. Smaller wits should beware of such experiments.' Excellent advice; and while the passage confirms a judgment of this Magazine which once gave some offence in certain quarters, it will also serve as a hint to sundry small critics and interminable literary *spin*-sters of the first sex, who are sententious only in *words*, and who think that short sentences, which make mince-meat of long and not very intelligible ideas, are veritable *terseness*. We have two or three specimens of these pretenders in our mind's eye, and one capital imitation of their style, from the pen of a correspondent, which we may present in a subsequent number.

The Gift for 1842. — Had we received this fine annual at an earlier hour, we could have rendered it that elaborate attention which is now impossible; since 'late accounts from the' printing-office bring us the unexpected intelligence, that we have already exceeded our wonted bound, and that several articles in type for this department must await another issue. We cannot omit to say, however, that in its embellishments and typographical execution, 'The Gift' is richer than any of its predecessors. 'The Country Girl,' the face in the vignette, and 'The Gipsy,' by Sully, are in that eminent artist's best manner. Leslie's 'Dulcinea' is of the same high order of merit. Mount's 'Tough Story' and 'The Raffle' are admirably engraved, and with those who have not revelled in their originals, will divide the admiration which 'the pictures' will elicit. 'Sliding down Hill' should not be passed unnoticed, for it is a very fine engraving of a good picture. In its literary contents, 'The Gift' is second only to the Token. It has a fine array of contributors, who have written up to their several reputations. Miss Mary Clavers, in 'The Bee-Tree,' presents us with one of her life-drawn sketches of western life; Miss Leslie has a story of 'The People that did not take Boarders,' which is well told, and inculcates a salutary lesson; Mr. Simms narrates a characteristic tale of Murder that 'would out;' and Mr. Seba Smith another 'Tough Story;' Mrs. Embury, Mrs. Osgood, the late gifted Miss Hooper, and several other female pens, still farther enrich a volume which reflects credit upon the taste and liberality of the publishers, Messrs. Carey and Hart.

THE SPIRIT-WORLD. — It is related by an elegant writer, once greatly admired, but we fear only occasionally talked of and seldom read in these days of the 'thrilling' and 'exciting' in literature, that there is a tradition among a certain tribe of our Indians, that one of their number once descended in a vision to the great repository of souls, or as we call it, the other world; and that upon his return he gave his friends a distinct account of every thing he saw among those regions of the dead. He stated that after having travelled for a long space under a hollow mountain, he arrived at length on the confines of the world of spirits, but could not enter it by reason of a thick forest made up of bushes, brambles, and pointed thorns, so perplexed and interwoven with one another, that it was impossible to find a passage through it. While he was looking about for some track or pathway, that might be worn in any part of it, he saw a huge lion couched under the side of it, who kept his eye upon him in the same posture as when he watches for his prey. The Indian immediately started back, while the lion rose with a spring, and leaped toward him. Being wholly destitute of all other weapons, he stooped down to take up a huge stone in his hand; but to his infinite surprise grasped nothing, and found the supposed stone to be only the apparition of one. If he was disappointed on this side, he was as much pleased on the other, when he found the lion, which had seized on his left shoulder, had no power to hurt him, and was only the ghost of that ravenous creature which it appeared to be. He no sooner got rid of his impotent enemy, but he marched up to the wood, and, after having surveyed it for some time, endeavored to press into one part of it that was a little thinner than the rest; when again to his great surprise he found the bushes made no resistance, but that he walked through briers and brambles with the same ease as through the open air; and in short, that the whole wood was nothing else but a wood of shades.

He immediately concluded that this huge thicket of thorns and brakes was designed as a kind of fence or quick-set hedge to the ghosts it enclosed; and that probably their soft substances might be torn by these subtile points and prickles, which were too weak to make any impression in flesh and blood. With this thought he resolved to travel through this intricate wood; when by degrees he felt a gale of perfumes breathing upon him, that grew stronger and sweeter in proportion as he advanced. He had not proceeded much farther, when he observed the thorns and briers to end, and give place to a thousand beautiful green trees covered with blossoms of the finest scents and colors, that formed a wilderness of sweets, and were a kind of lining to those ragged scenes which he had before passed through. · · · He had no sooner got out of the wood, but he was entertained with such a landscape of flowery plains, green meadows, running streams, sunny hills, and shady vales, as were not to be represented by his own expressions, nor, as he said, by the conceptions of others. This happy region was peopled with innumerable swarms of spirits, who applied themselves to exercises and diversions, according as their fancies led them. Some of them were pitching the figure of a quoit; others were tossing the shadow of a ball; others were breaking the apparition of a horse; and multitudes employing themselves upon ingenious handicrafts with the souls of departed utensils. As he travelled through this delightful scene, he was very often tempted to pluck the flowers that rose every where about him in the greatest variety and profusion, having never seen several of them in his own country: but he quickly found, that, though they were objects of his sight, they were not liable to his touch. He at length came to the side of a great river, and being a good fisherman himself, stood upon the banks of it some time to look upon

an angler that had taken a great many shapes of fishes, which lay flouncing up and
down by him.

The tradition goes on to say, that the Indian had not stood long by the fisherman,
when he saw on the opposite bank of the river the shadow of his beloved wife,
who had gone before him into the other world, after having borne him several
lovely children. Her arms were stretched out toward him; floods of tears ran
down her eyes; her looks, her hands, her voice, called him over to her; and at the
same time seemed to tell him that the river was impassable. Who can describe the
passion made up of joy, sorrow, love, desire, astonishment, that rose in the Indian
upon the sight of his dear departed? He could express it by nothing but his tears,
which ran like a river down his cheeks as he looked upon her. He had not stood
in this posture long, before he plunged into the stream that lay before him; and
finding it to be nothing but the phantom of a river, stalked on the bottom of it till
he arose on the other side. At his approach, the loved spirit flew into his arms,
while he himself longed to be disencumbered of that body which kept her from his
embraces. After many questions and endearments, she conducted him to a bower,
which day by day she had embellished with her own hands from those blooming
regions, expressly for his reception. As he stood astonished at the unspeakable
beauty of the habitation, she brought two of her children to him who had died some
years before, and who resided with her in the same delightful dwelling; imploring
him to train up those others which were still with him, in such a manner that
they might hereafter all of them meet together in that happy place. Bereaved
mourner! treasure this record in thy heart of hearts. To the untutored mind
even of this poor Indian was vouchsafed, in a vision of the night, a glimpse of that
spirit-land to which we all are tending. There we shall meet the loved and lost:

> ‘ The dear departed, gone before
> To that unknown and silent shore,
> Sure we shall meet as heretofore,
> Some summer morning.’

SOUTHERN AND WESTERN PERIODICAL LITERATURE. — We received not long
since the prospectus of a new literary periodical, to be published at brief and regular
intervals at St. Louis. We were struck with the manliness of its tone, and the
independence of position which it maintained. It scouted, and justly, the idea of
sectional literature, of which it said so much was prated at the South and West; a
distinction which had been drawn by the very presses that now complained of it.
American talent is not local nor provincial; and the existence of such works as the
‘ Southern Messenger,’ ‘ Augusta Mirror,’ Macon ‘ Companion,’ Savannah ‘ Mag-
nolia,’ Cincinnati ‘ Repository,’ and the like, abundantly proves the correctness
of the remark. But our remote contemporaries must avoid one thing. They
must not ask favor for, and claim a ready acceptance of, articles which may be
ill-written or otherwise objectionable, merely *because* they are of local manufacture; and this we are glad to see condemned in the appropriate quarter. The
public are the best judges of what pleases them, and all attempts to reason them into
a belief that they *should* be entertained, and that they are mistaken in their antipa-
thies, will in nine cases out of ten be found to result in a confirmation of precon-
ceived opinion. For our own parts, we would know no *sectional* literature. Our
contemporaries at the South and West have our warmest wishes for their success;
and that success we make no doubt they will command by deserving it. We see

on this side the Potomac none of the 'airs' which are sometimes charged as being put on by northern writers in northern literary journals; on the contrary, the cordiality with which such choice spirits and ripe, fertile scholars as WILDE of Georgia and LEGARE of South Carolina — gentlemen who are *really* eminent, without any personal display or offensive egotism, and who stand out prominently from the literary level, simply by reason of their unpretending genius and fine scholarship — the cordiality, we say, with which such writers and gentlemen are welcomed among us, in society not less than in our highest literary reviews and magazines, must convince *them* at least that the advocacy of a sectional literature cannot with truth be charged upon us. We have in our humble medium greeted with hearty good will writers from the south and west, and correspondents from every quarter. Often the pages of a single number of the KNICKERBOCKER have contained communications from every section of our noble and beloved country. We are a social, a political republic; and palsied be the hand that would make us less a 'Republic of Letters.'

GOSSIP WITH READERS AND CORRESPONDENTS. — We had sketched a report of '*A Trip to the Pleasant Land of Goshen,*' on the occasion of opening the New-York and Erie Rail-road, one of the noblest and most important enterprises of the day; but correspondents in preceding pages have anticipated our space, for which the reader will perhaps thank his stars. Still we *must* say that the occasion was one of deep interest and hilarious but chastened enjoyment. It was pleasant to meet such an assemblage of distinguished talent; religious, political, financial, literary. It was pleasant to mark the gay crowds gathered upon the rounded hills of rich and verdant Orange, watching the fire-horse, 'at first a speck, a cloud in the distance, then rapidly developing, with all its polished furniture, and brazen pipes, and long train;' now approaching, now sweeping by; a sublime sight, 'throwing up great volumes of smoke, and rumbling over the earth with the swiftness of a thunder-bolt;' and rushing onward to encounter the same constantly-recurring scenes. The effect of the engine on the beasts of the field might have been rehearsed from the vivid picture drawn by BOB KUSHOW. Grazing year after year in habitual quietude, 'they knew not what to make of the terrible course of this living, moving, fire-breathing machine. The meek-eyed horses, worn out with old age and the plough, who stood hanging their long straight necks over the rails, with a forlorn expression of countenance, or breathing in long-drawn sighs over the grass, threw off at least a dozen years of their age, and became colts again. Their eyes blazed like fire; they curved in their necks, pricked up their ears, looked on for a few seconds attentively, then snorting and rearing up, dashed into the fields, as if they had heard a trump of war. But the cows lost their senses altogether. In vain the bell rang, and the whistle whistled. They crouched down on their hind legs, awkwardly tumbling around in a circle, in a vain attempt to rise, or throwing out their long tails, with a vast muscular energy, stupidly galloped over the track, cracking their shins as they went, and turning neither to the right hand nor to the left. The joy was universal. Flags flouted the air from every hill-top, where a bevy could gather to look down upon the track; lonely dwellings were vocal with 'huzzas;' and at one point, from the high banks of a cornfield a sable Apollo, with a scooped pumpkin upon his head, from which flaunted a leafy vine, a green and waving plume, welcomed the rumbling train with his three-stringed violin. And thus we reached 'the pleasant town of Goshen,' the perfection of a quiet inland country village, amid the waving of flags, the roar of ordnance, the ringing of the bells, and the rejoicings of the populace. Greatly were we edified by the wondering remarks of the young lads from the neighboring country, who gathered about the '*locofocomotive,*' as they termed the engine. One sleepy-looking boy who had been 'touching off the cannon,' and had only glanced at the train whose advent he was honoring, was anxious to know 'where they hitched the horses to the p'ison critter;' and the explanation tendered by a fellow-urchin but little relieved his mind. 'The hoss in the b'iler!' he replied; 'Oh, git oŭut! How'd he *git* there?' There were more serious thoughts awakened — and they were shared we are sure by the renowned historian of Sleepy Hollow, who had seldom travelled through that wizard region at the pace we had journeyed hither — by the reflection, that rail-roads were 'removing the old land-marks' and making us another people. We thought too, as our worthy Chief Magistrate alighted in the land of his fathers, amid a crowd of plain townsmen and old play-mates, with a second generation around them, of the privileges of our glorious republic, which opens every where to talent and perseverance a path to distinction. But this is 'gossip' merely, and we forbear;

regretting only, that for all that followed — the good cheer, the brief but felicitous speeches ; the cordiality and warm hospitality of the good citizens of Goshen ; the pleasant journey to the Hudson, and the crowning entertainments (various in kind but all of the best) on board our fine ' sea-girt citadel ' — we have only space for the single word *delightful*, as embracing in a convivial, intellectual, joyous sense all that we had elaborated, in confess with some care, in testimony of our own unalloyed enjoyment. . . . 'T. R.' shall appear in December. His ' *Western School-Keeping*,' however, is not entirely new. The following is nevertheless too good to pass unnoticed. An ignorant *ci-devant* actor, dentist, and phrenological and animal magnetism lecturer, who has tried the entire range of humbug, finally presents himself before a convocation of school-examiners in an obscure town of the far West. The questioners, who are in intelligence about on a par with the questioned, proceed first to test his knowledge of general history : ' In what era, Mr. FLIFKINS, did NAPOLEON BONAPARTE flourish ? ' ' How 's that ? ' asks Mr. F., in reply. ' Wo'n't you jest *repeat* that question ? ' ' Certainly, Sir : in what ag·· did Bonaparte the warrior reign ? ' ' Umph ! ' rejoins the proposed school-master, with an insinuating smile, ' *You 've got me there, gentlemen !* ' ' Never mind, Doctor,' said one of the committee to his fellow-member, ' about *particulars*. Let *me* ask him the same question in a leetle dif'rent form. You hear'n the *fust* question, Mister FLIFKINS : now, was it before or after CHRIST ? ' ' Can I have the question ag'in ? ' asked Mr. F. ' I am 'fraid I did n't take it 'zactly as 't was put.' The querist repeated the question. The ex-dentist and lecturer scratched his head, looked imploringly first at one examiner and then the other, and made answer : ' *Well, re-ally, gentlemen, you 've got me ag'in ! I could n't say, re-ally !!* ' . . . The ' *Lines on the American Fall* ' are too sombre. We must have the contrasts of November and December, to enable us to appreciate the brighter days of more sunny months. We confess ourselves, with DE QUINCY, surprised to see people think it a matter of congratulation that winter is going ; or if coming, that it is not likely to be a severe one. ' On the contrary,' says he, ' I put up a petition annually for as much snow, hail, frost, or storm, as the skies can possibly afford me.' Surely every body is aware of the divine pleasures which attend a winter fire-side ; early candles, warm hearth-rugs, shutters closed, curtains flowing in ample draperies on the floor, while the wind and rain are raging audibly without :

> ' And at the doors and windows seem to call
> As heaven and earth they would together mell ;
> Yet the least entrance find they none at all :
> Whence sweeter grows our rest, secure in ample hall.'

We too are ' not particular ' whether it be snow or black frost, or wind so strong that you may loan your back against it like a post. We can put up even with rain, provided it rains cats and dogs ; but something of the sort we must have ; and if we have not, we think ourselves in a manner ill-used ; for why are we called upon to pay so heavily for winter, in coals, in candles, and various privations that will occur even to gentlemen, if we are not to have the article good of its kind ? No ! — a Canadian winter for *our* money, or a Russian one, where every man is but a co-proprietor with the north wind, in the fee-simple of his own ears.' . . . ' *Reflections upon the Career of Colt the Murderer* ' is an untimely and ill-judged sketch, and we are glad of an opportunity thus publicly to decline it. Without desiring to express an opinion touching the late melancholy event in which this unhappy man is charged to have been a participant, we have yet a word to say in behalf of his relatives, who have been dragged before the public in connexion with this painful transaction ; his parents' early care impugned ; the ' temper ' and character of his brothers canvassed, and reflections cast upon *them*, as if the sorrow into which they have been plunged were not enough for their almost breaking hearts. A craven-spirited tradesman even appears under his signature in the daily journals, assuring the public that a ' brother of the murderer ' — a man we are informed who is known and respected not less for his private worth than for his practical contributions to warlike science — has ' nothing to do with, and no interest in, his establishment ! ' If the public were of *our* mind, there would be hundreds *more* who would ' have nothing to do with ' the establishment in question. Another brother of the prisoner is known to us as a high-minded, generous, ingenuous young gentleman ; yet even he has been included as one of the ' passionate,' ' head-strong,' and ' ungovernable family,' by writers regardless alike of the truth, and of the sufferings of a collateral family and friends. Could any course be more cruel, we might say *inhuman*, than this ? . . . ' *The Manners of* JOHN BULL ' comes from one, we are quite sure, who never saw the English at home ; and hence his numerous errors, which we shall endeavor to indicate in our next. The *nil admirari* feature we admit. It is true ; and was finely illustrated by the short, plethoric John Bull, who, peering into the Great Fall at Niagara, conceded thus much . ' Well, 'pon me life, they *are* clever ! — they are, *really*. But they 're very disagreeable. Here 's my 'at, thoroughly wetted ; I 've *spoilt* me coat ; and Gad ! I prefer looking at a *picture* of 'em that 's in the 'ouse ! ' . . . ' *Faith and Hope, an Allegory*,' is too mystical for our plain comprehension. An allegory should be a picture. What it shadows forth of SWEDENBOURG's theory, darkens that which is not itself over-clear, yet delightful in theory. *Apropos* of this: That believer in his doctrine, who in voyaging across the Atlantic lost his only son when three days out, had *his* 'faith' thoroughly tested. He had his boy's vacant chair placed at his side at every meal, and his plate filled; declaring that though absent in the body, he was ever present with him. He discovered the extent of his mistake only when the captain insisted upon the payment of the lad's fare and passage money. · · · A correspondent enlarges in glowing terms upon 'a correct picture of QUEEN VICTORIA which he has seen, with the Lord's Prayer written around it, and the whole in the circumference of a sixpence;' a wonderful exhibition, he imagines, of 'native talent.' With due deference, we think the 'promising young artist' who prepared it might have been better employed; and we decline the proffered eulogium upon his performance. This silly manufacture is neither new nor indigenous. DRYDEN hints at it; and STEELE speaks of a miniature of Charles I., which had the whole book of Psalms written in the lines of the face and the hair of the head. He mentions having 'perused one of the whiskers' while at Oxford, and being vexatiously interrupted while reading the other, by a meddling personage, who told him of a portrait near by that had in its full-bottomed periwig all the Old Testament, and in the supernumerary locks half the Apocrypha; and of another picture of King William, that had the two books of Kings in the foretop! · · · We thought to have published the '*Essay on Contentment*' in the present number, but were overruled. Its spirit and teachings are praiseworthy, and we resign it, as requested, to a contemporary, with reluctance. And here let us commend to our friend, (who *should* have been our contributor,) the reflections of a London Essayist, who has followed out an idea of GOLDSMITH's in a late number of Blackwood. He is speaking, it should be premised, of life in the British metropolis: 'Whatever,' says he, 'may be the differences in our social or domestic positions; whether we repose under the roofs of palaces, or enjoy a slumber broken by the tom-cats caterwauling outside our garret tiles; whether our pocket-book suffers under a plethora of bank notes, or it is our worse luck to wander along the street jingling three-halfpence in the lining of our breeches; whether we are engaged to dine with Prince Albert at the palace, or Duke Humphrey in the park; whether we walk about in search of a dinner or an appetite — fore gad! as long as we are not out at toes or elbows: so long as we can keep the nap on our hat, the grease off our collar, and the gloves on our fingers, we are equally citizens of the great republic of London streets, and eligible with the first man in town to the highest honors of the *pavé*. Well, Sir, and pray what more would you have? Can the Duke of Northumberland eat more than half a pound of beef-steaks at a meal, or imbibe at a draught more than a pot of mild porter? Can Esterhazy wear more than a shirt at a time, though he may have dozens in his wardrobe? Could D'Orsay himself venture to sport three hats, one on the top of the other, like our friend Peter in the 'Tale of a Tub?' Can Cecil Forester put on more than a pair of primrose kids in the forenoon, and another in the evening? Contemplate, then, with the spectacles of good-humored contentment, how artificial and extrinsic to happiness are the superfluities of this life: thanks to a discerning public, we can command, while Heaven spares us the use of this right arm, as much food as satisfies the cravings of nature, which is all that the great or affluent can consume: while we have one shirt on our back, and *the* other at our washer-woman's, we have no occasion to make an inventory of our wearables. We contrive to procure, by hook or by crook, a good suit of clothes every year; and, unless a man chooses to roll himself in the kennel, he cannot wear out a suit of clothes in less time. We surmount our caput with *our* hat, (while D'Orsay does the same with *one* of his hats,) and, to all outward appearance, our heads are equally furnished.' There is a world of enjoyment, and good sense withal, in philosophers of this class. · · · 'B. L. S.'s' lines are grotesque, but not humorous. He has CANNING's measure, but not his spirit:

> 'Needy knife-grinder! whither are you going?
> Keen blows the cold wind; your hat 's got a hole in 't,
> So have your breeches!'

For ample reasons, elsewhere stated, we are compelled, very reluctantly, to omit an admirable article by CHARLES DE BERNARD, the BULWER of France, and a fine poem on Trenton-Falls, by a new and valued correspondent. The following articles are among those filed for insertion or under consideration: 'Journal of a Residence in London Seventy Years Ago;' 'Reconciliations;' 'The Country Doctor;' 'The Call to Rest;' 'To the Departed;' 'Translation from Béranger;' 'The Hunt;' 'The Christian Knight;' 'The Contrast,' Written on the wreck of the Steamer Erie; 'The Buffalo Hunter's Bride;' 'The White Rabbit, a Tale;' 'Life;' 'Fourth Eclogue of Virgil;' 'The Flower of Poesy;' 'The Poet's Evening Walk;' 'To an Old Horse;' 'On a Steam-boat Ascending Hudson River;' 'Night;' 'The Sun;' 'Flowers;' 'An Epigram;' 'Autumn;' 'The Complainer Reconciled,' etc. etc. · · · One or two errors, by accident not subject to the revision of the Editor, escaped the vigilance of the proof-reader in our last number. It was not so provoking as the substitution of freshly-blown *noses* for 'freshly-blown *roses*;' so that our excellent printer 'stands in some rank of praise.'

LITERARY RECORD.

THE 'AMERICAN BIBLICAL REPOSITORY' for October we have perused with more than ordinary interest. It embraces nine articles proper, various and interesting, including a collection of seventeen briefer critical notices of current publications, and the recent literary intelligence. We are glad to find here an adequate notice of the writings of Rev. DANIEL A. CLARK, particularly of a volume of sermons, which we early received from the writer's own hand, and the manner of which we have often admired. We are enabled to bear personal testimony with the reviewer to the kind heart and blameless life of this plain-spoken and eloquent divine. The following criticism is most just, and applicable alike to writers and speakers. There are two or three of the former among our second-rate litterateurs, whose redundant style rises to our mind, as we record this passage against it:

"There is uncommon compactness and condensation in our author's style. There are but few words which can be safely blotted out; nor, by recasting, can we diminish the space a thought occupies. There is a very sparing use of epithets and qualifying terms. The principal words are selected with so much precision generally, that he succeeds in conveying his idea without the aid of thronging expletives and adjuncts. When reading him, we are constrained sometimes to pause and admire the amount and pungent force of meaning, conveyed by some single word, or brief combination of words. This is one of the very highest excellences of style. It takes some a long time to get weaned from their love of the jingle of adjectives and adjuncts, though assured, from every quarter, that no other single thing does more to encumber and enfeeble the style. One of the great rhetorical sins in preaching, as well as writing, is overdoing, saying too much on the topics introduced, and especially taking up altogether too much time in saying what we do say. Mr. Clark has not only strength, he has frequently a simple elegance and harmony. The following is a fair specimen of the often easy and musical flow of the sentences: 'Individuals may prosper most when they are nearest destruction. The old world and the devoted cities were never more prosperous, than when their last sun was rising. Men may be ripe for the scythe of death, their cup of iniquity full, while yet their fields wave with the abundant harvest, and the atmosphere is fragrant with the odors of the ripened fruit and flowers, and echoes with the song of the cheerful laborers.' Another attribute for which our author's style is remarkable is vivacity. There is nothing about it dry, abstract, dead. Every thing is living, moving. He is almost constantly giving us vivid pictures. He shows great skill in gathering and grouping the interesting circumstances of a scene or case. It is this skilful touching of some characteristic circumstance, which brings before the mind the picture of a whole scene: 'How many, once as rich as you, are now poor; or as healthy as you, are now in the grave; had a home as you have, but it burned down: had children, as it may be you have, but the cold blast came over them and they died,'" etc.

The notice of the 'Travels' of Mr. BUCKINGHAM, a gentleman who is our *beau-ideal* of a Humbug, confirms our own estimate of their character:

'In reading a book of travels we are always pleased to find the narrative so conducted as to make us, as far as may be, the travelling companions of the author, seeing things in the order in which he saw them, and sympathizing with him in his vicissitudes. But when he becomes himself the hero of his own story, and magnifies every incident, and honors every person and institution just in proportion as they serve to give prominence to his own exploits, we are disgusted. Such we confess has been the effect, on our own mind, of this marked characteristic of the work before us.'

The 'Repository' is marked by evident editorial industry, and numbers among its collaborateurs many of our best writers. We trust it meets with deserved encouragement.

COLLEGIATE POEM. — The progress of Science is pleasingly illustrated in a poem by P. HAMILTON MYERS, ESQ., author of 'Ensenore,' delivered before the Euglossian Society of Geneva College, in August last, a copy of which is before us. In a rapid review, which is rather remarkable for melody of versification and general correctness of style than for striking originality or deep thought, Mr. MYERS traces the prominent scientific events and their effects, of the past and present ages. The defects; or more properly the *wants* of the poem are doubtless owing to the 'hasty composition' and 'lack of elaborate revisal,' against which the author warns the collegiate committee, in the letter granting permission to publish.

'ESSAYS FOR SUMMER HOURS' is the title of a small volume by Mr. CHARLES
LANMAN, of Norwich, (Conn.,) a large portion of which we have encountered in
some of the periodicals of the day within the last twelve months. We respect our
young author's enthusiastic love of nature and his admiration of literature; but we
cannot conscientiously affirm that we place a very high estimate upon his powers
as a writer. A few of his descriptions are natural and pleasing; but he sometimes
indulges in very common-place thoughts; he is frequently stiltish and apostrophi-
cal; and in his general style he is what LAMB terms '*scrappy;*' by which we
mean, that he jots down apparently every thing that passes through his mind while
his pen is in his hand; here oftentimes a hackneyed sentiment, there a verse of
poetry; and the next moment away he flies at a tangent after something suddenly
suggested and as suddenly forgotten. It must be admitted, however, that Mr.
LANMAN's miscellaneous reflections, quotations, and descriptions, all tend to inculcate a love of the beautiful in nature, and the correct in morals; and in this regard
they demand our praise. The execution of the volume, we should remark, is not
creditable to the Norwich press. Aside from its distasteful typography, it is disfigured by blunders, for which the author is compelled to apologize to the reader.
Since the above was placed in type, we learn that the present edition has been can-
celled, and that a new and better one, illustrated by original drawings from the pencil
of the author, will hereafter appear.

LIFE OF ALEXANDER HAMILTON. — We have omitted heretofore to mention the
publication, by the Messrs. APPLETON AND COMPANY, of the second volume of the
Life of ALEXANDER HAMILTON, by his son, JOHN C. HAMILTON, Esq. This work,
now complete, forms a portion of the national records and history, and should be
found in every American's library. 'HAMILTON,' says the profound GUIZOT, 'must
be classed among the men who have best known the vital principles and fundamental conditions of a government — a government worthy of its mission and of its
name. There is not in the constitution of the United States an element of order,
of force, of duration, which he has not powerfully contributed to introduce into it,
and to cause to predominate.' Mr. HAMILTON in the second volume seems to have
written with renewed vigor, and with such ease and freedom as to induce the belief
that he here felt the literary harness well upon his back.

'LONDON ASSURANCE.' — We have but a few words' space for the PARK THEATRE,
but that must be devoted, we are glad to be enabled to say, to unqualified praise of
one of the most effective and altogether magnificent plays with which we have
been favored for many a year. '*London Assurance,*' in the superiority of its action,
the splendor of its scenery, dresses, and appointments, and the spirit and variety of
the performance itself, deserves the warmest commendation. We shall advert to it
more at large hereafter; but for the present, we commend every town reader of
this hasty paragraph to lose no time in personally testing the justice of our enco-
mium. The thanks of the theatre-going public are eminently due, for the liberality
displayed by Mr. SIMPSON; and crowded houses nightly evince that *thanks* alone
are not to constitute the reward of his enterprise.

.*. NOTICES of the following works are in type: 'Incidents of a Whaling Voyage;' 'BROWN's Lecture on Education;'
'De Clifford;' 'Democracy in America;' 'The Retrospect;' 'CROSBY's Greek Grammar;' BUNYAN's 'Holy War;'
'Evenings with the Chroniclers;' 'BULWER's Miscellanies;' The 'Book Without a Name;' 'LANGLEY's' Literary
Advertiser;' 'Amenities of Literature;' Messrs. APPLETON's Publications; 'French and English Reading Book.'

THE KNICKERBOCKER.

Vol. XVIII.   DECEMBER, 1841.   No. 6.

RECONCILIATIONS.

' Be ye reconciled one to another.' — St. Paul.

MEN differ widely in opinion upon the various subjects that agitate society, the important questions of the age. They differ honestly and heartily in matters of religion, in politics, often in scientific views, in what is expedient, and sometimes in what is right. This proposition, in which we can hardly be mistaken, states a happy circumstance for the safety and health of our social condition. We do not stagnate and become blind in prejudice and bigotry, as might happen were there no agitation, no discussion of the important questions of our time by the public mind. All nature is full of health from the action of antagonistic powers. The centripetal and centrifugal forces which regulate the motions of the earth; attraction and heat, the one combining, the other separating the particles of matter; are common illustrations of the principle we state.

Take a mercantile view, and see how the spirit of accumulation of wealth in a republic is opposed by a tendency to equality. How is this? In our own country, I appeal to the observation of those who live in cities, a man amasses a princely fortune. In a monarchy this would perhaps be the cause of a title, and he might become a noble. In a republic it can give him no privilege, no public privilege, which he had not before. The most it can do for his family is, to exempt them for a time, it may be a life, from the toils of labor and from habits of industry. In many cases such a fortune, in common phrase, spoils the rich man's children. The money is squandered, or lost or misapplied — scattered to the four winds. Money like water tends to an equilibrium. It is collected in drops, in small sums, by the father, as the largest rivers are made up of the silent dews and the pattering rain, and is often spent in masses as the waters, seeking an equilibrium, find their level by torrents and cataracts. There is health in this. Were it not so, our republic would vanish. In order that a republic may exist, there must be more than the name of equality. To say that all men are created free and equal will not be enough. There must be something more than merely an acknowledged equality of rights. That would certainly be the happiest state where there should be no overgrown wealth and no abject poverty. Such a state would show a general state of knowledge and industry, philosophical and religious views of the objects of money and property. As we approach this condition we shall consequently be a happy nation. The tendency to this condition keeps us an active and thriving people. Sometimes this wealth seeks its level by a munificent gift to the people of a state, like that of STEPHEN GIRARD. Sometimes it is diffused abroad by a great public work, erected to increase this wealth; capacious stores and dwellings, bridges, turnpikes, rail-roads, new streets. The speculation fails for the individual, but the work stands to be used by the people. I hazard nothing in saying that in our social and moral condition, as well as in our physical, all things, by a great law of nature, are tending to an equilibrium. From the rise and fall of the tides of the ocean to the gentlest motion of the aërial tides, invisible, often hardly perceptible to us in their action, this is true. And is it not apparent that as social and intellectual beings we tend to this equality? Let an improvement be made in any of the arts of life; let some comfort or convenience be found out by the individual; even if he be a selfish and insensible man, the regard for his own advantage will induce him to throw it into the common stock, at a premium and by patent, so that all may have it. But how higher and nobler is this principle evinced in intellectual wealth! The scholar and thinker, the poet, the sage, must give utterance to the thought within them, or it burns and consumes away their very souls. As the heart of man is made to answer to the heart of man, so the desire of sympathy and its enjoyment is an essential part of the existence of the mind. The scholar must speak; the poet must sing. The thought, until it is uttered, is no more than the seed before it is planted. Its value, even to the originator of it, is chiefly in its capacity to free, to enlighten, to charm, perhaps to soothe. It is true then that the intellect diffuses itself, and seeks to produce in all what height or enthusiasm it may have gained for itself.

Since I am upon this topic, I cannot forbear to remark, that I believe the existence of our own happy republic is nothing more than the result of the action of this great law of equality. The wars and reformations, the revolutions and cabals of the other hemisphere were but the fermentation natural to any social and political condition where this law is contravened. There never can be peace and happiness where there is not justice. That some men should be nobles and others drones, sucking the life-blood from their fellow-men; that some thousands should live in luxury and ease, and many millions be plunged in poverty and want; some clothed in purple and fine linen, while others have not even rags to cover them from the cold, is no more in accordance with the laws of God than that water should run up hill. How idle to expect national prosperity where even an approach to such a state of things exists! To enjoy this natural equality, our fathers left their native land; the emigrant is seeking liberty and his natural state when he thinks he is only seeking bread for himself and his family. The action of the principle we refer to is producing the changes and revolutions about us, and it is at work here in our very midst. In this country is the fullest developement of political equality in the world. Let us take care that we do not mar our own fortunes.

The fate of our country naturally presents itself, in thinking of differences of opinion. If we have any thing to fear as a republic, we ought most to dread division caused by bigotry of political and religious opinion. I think I am not mistaken in stating, that no other cause is so prolific of strife and bitterness in our otherwise peaceful villages. There is harmony upon almost all other subjects; great unanimity and concert; until about the time of election, or some great religious movement. The noisiest actors in politics are not always remarkable for their patriotism, and the most strenuous advocates for some particular dogmas are by no means necessarily the most pious members of the community. But, at any rate, they have influence enough to set the people by the ears. In this way, where one common-sized church is more than large enough for the whole people, we see, in a population of one or two thousand souls, as many as three or four meeting-houses; ill-formed edifices, badly located, sparsely attended; the pulpit occupied by a poorly-paid minister, who is expected to do battle with his neighbors instead of Satan, and whose instructions make him more earnest to fill up his pews than to benefit the souls of his hearers. People who in fact often do love one another, meet coldly in the street; fail to exchange neighborly acts of kindness; and after a while goad themselves into positive belief that they hate each other. Little annoyances follow, and there begins to be some cause for aversion, until time widens the breach, and they are severed for ever who ought to love and cherish one another. Politics, being confined to the male part of the community, does not so much damage to the social order of things. Men are necessarily thrown much together in business, and they often agree to laugh off their little disputes about the great matters of state. Indeed the men of our country towns have generally too much good practical sense to suffer intricate questions of finance, about which they, on both sides, are aware they know next to nothing, to create any very lasting breach in their society, though bound by party feeling, and I am sorry to say, principle, to stand up strongly for the side their leading organ may mark out.

Therefore, from these considerations it seems to me that something ought to be said upon the real differences that divide men in sentiment, and moreover, upon those seeming differences, only so in name, which sever society, and cut up by the roots all concert of action; quite as effectually (perhaps more so) as those true lines of difference which mark various orders of mind. In the first place the natural differences of men do not create animosity and rancor. If the moon appear to one as large as a cart-wheel, from the great convexity of the crystalline lens in the eye, and to another no larger than a peck-measure, from an equally natural cause, these men will not quarrel about it, each being convinced that the other entertains an honest opinion, which he cannot help entertaining. But let these same persons get into an argument, more properly perhaps called a squabble, about the unity or trinity of the Godhead, neither being deeply read in divinity, but happening to belong to churches with opposite creeds, and they will show a fretfulness and over-earnestness incompatible with sound reason engaged in any discussion. Perhaps this chance argument may begin an enmity ending only with life.

We all know that people differ in taste, in dress, in food and furniture; in pictures, in styles of music, in colors; and these differences are allowed, with no interruption to the harmony of society. But these are the real differences that divide men. We wish to show that it is imaginary differences that create turmoil and trouble in society. It need hardly be said here, that when a man feels he has a bad cause, he almost invariably gets angry; partly through vexation at his ill luck, and partly with intention to brow-beat his adversary.

It will not be difficult to show that the true differences that exist among mankind are a cause of peace, harmony, mutual love, and convenience. What would be the consequence of a uniformity of taste in all the minutiæ of life, it is easy to see. Had we not different ideas of what is beautiful and engaging; did we not vary in taste, society would be a constant strife, and the friction of the social machine would be so great as to stop it altogether. We are constituted each one to be agreeable to some other. The notion of Dr. Watts that marriages are made in heaven is far more than a poetical theory. It is undoubtedly true, that for each male and female there exists a mate some where, with whom they could be supremely happy. A person plain to the eyes of one, may be beautiful in the eyes of another. No one may bear away the palm of beauty from the world. And this is true too of disposition and manner, which results in all being pleased and satisfied, and none having real cause for animosity. Some incline to one pursuit and some to another. Each one is apt to think, upon a superficial view, that his own choice is the right one, not only for himself but for others. The successful farmer, the plodding lawyer, with pursuits the most opposite, think they have hit each the true path to prosperity and happiness; while the artist shudders at the low aims of trade, and the merchant places below par the unsaleable products of the scholar. But how unnecessary to prove by farther instances the fact, that for the variety of human life, there is variety of taste; capacities adapted to all occupations of men, different and distinct; and that this difference of view and capacity is the cause of harmony and order.

More difficult is it to show, what is equally true, that the discords and contentions of society grow out of slight differences of opinion, rather than great ones; and that the blinded zeal and bigotry of men is oftener fostered by a point than a wide principle; as, some one has remarked, the smaller the point the sharper it is. Two persons or more might travel together for weeks, and indulge in general conversation upon politics, religion and literature; and such a chance intercourse might be delightful, and improving to all parties. If all were intelligent and educated people, the slight differences that might occur would only serve to give zest and spirit to the occasion. And this would be the case, because they would probably have the good sense to see that they were not thus thrown together to quarrel and disturb each other, but feeling a mutual desire for comfort and peace, each one might relinquish a little of his own peculiarity, until all would be astonished to find how much they felt alike, and what a deep sympathy exists in the human heart for every other human heart, if we will but give our nature fair play. These supposed travellers might the one call himself a monarchist, another a republican, a third might be a chartist, and a fourth Mr. Owen himself.

The Catholic believes in the being of a God, in a future state, in rewards and punishments. The Calvinist also believes in these points, and so does the Unitarian. Why, we ask, do these christians feel such dislike for each other? Why do they grow excited and get angry whenever the subject of religion, in its smaller divisions, is mentioned? Is it not plain that they do not differ widely in their religion? How then? They differ about the worldly part of the matter; about the success of their church; its glory and numbers; its monied interests; about the talent and eloquence of their several preachers. Let them meet in a storm at sea, and they pray to the same God; when the pestilence walks abroad, they look to the same power to stay its ravages. Let us suppose a case to occur that shall call out pity, and summon us to assist a suffering fellow-being. We bend around the couch of pain; we proffer alms; we feed and clothe these objects God sends to us to keep alive in our hearts benevolence and charity, without asking to what church these persons belong; and we feel a common joy in these good acts of kindness, and do in fact worship together at this best common altar — the altar of good works; conscious for the time of a bond of union stronger than all creeds. If we chance to meet these same persons the next day or the next hour, in a condition where no particular act is to be done, for the sake it may be of getting up excitement, we fall to hard words about minor points of difference in form of worship, even so small a matter as rising or sitting during prayer, and part with them in high dudgeon, and a most devilish state of feeling.

It is so in politics. Agreeing in principle, we fight about men; agreeing in men, we fight about principles. All loving one common country, ready to die for her, if need be; feeling the same pride in her greatness, offering the same prayer for her safety, we fall to abusing each other for no good reason certainly. We say for no good reason, because it has always been true that these party differences vanish when any thing vital is to be done, as all bitterness and sectarianism vanish when a real christian act is to be performed. We agree well enough when agreement is really necessary, and we are only at swords' point about nothing.

Mr. Editor, it is valuable sometimes to the public to hear homely truths stated. We do not claim great originality in our statements. We contend that it is well to recal such thoughts to the mind, and to put others in mind of them. It is well to try to feel united when our newspapers, for selfish purposes, are endeavoring to convince us that we ought to feel great indignation toward Mr. A. or Mr. B.; for this party and that junto; and the religious papers and the religious pulpits are quite as bad as the political papers and the political pulpits. It is there, in those holy places, in those (should be) sacred columns, that this rancor is fostered. There, in that church dedicated to the worship of God, are men taught to look with distrust and hatred upon their fellow-men. It is not pretended that such advice is given literally, but such is the natural consequence of the tone of remark in which our ministers often indulge; serving Satan when they delude themselves into the belief that they are doing God service.

Let us be reconciled to our brother man : let us believe that we have common bonds of sympathy with him. And as we wear a common form, feel common desires, and are all tending to a common home, these are arguments that should convince us of the virtue of union. Whenever excited to malignity, we may well distrust the soundness of our principles; and we would ask the denouncer of the pulpit or the press if he should not study well the ground-work upon which he stands, when he feels prompted by it to contradict ' love to one another.'

Is it a matter of wonder that our religion is so cold, and our love of country so dead, when instead of being fed with nourishing food, our minds are kept in an unhealthy state of excitement by little party questions? The youth starts enthusiastically in the service of God or his country, and soon finds all his nobler, higher feelings out of place in the wrangling schools of politics or divinity. He thinks : ' I will go forth to my fellow-men and persuade them to love and serve God; to do right; to avoid evil, to copy CHRIST; to be gentle and forgiving, self-sacrificing and self-forgetting in the great work we have each of us to do; and having labored and prayed and wept for his flock for a season, he goes to them and finds that all his preaching has created a strong party for some particular minor view he casually uttered, and also a strong party against this same view! The whole object of all his prayers and sermons is lost, swallowed up in this little sea of windy controversy; and he begins to learn a bitter lesson of human nature, and his enthusiasm begins to cool; in short, he doubts now what a little while ago he did not doubt, that he was beginning a course of preaching that was to evangelize the world.

But perhaps our young man enters upon life with a mind stored with examples of Roman patriotism and Spartan self-denial. He burns to signalize himself as a patriot : he is ready to die. No thought of self-aggrandizement enters his mind; he has never thought of the emoluments of office. He reads of the affairs of Congress, and knows the names of these great, (to him,) venerable men. They have in his imagination something, little if any, short of Roman senatorial dignity. They are virtuous, noble, and eloquent to him; for (thinks our unsophisticated young man who has not been at Washington) how can it be possible that they who have the interests of millions at stake can be any thing else? Poor youth! Sorry are we to undeceive thee. Patriotism now-a-days is a mere classical allusion; such names as Regulus, Brutus, William Tell, and Alfred are introduced by our speech-makers to tickle up retired parsons and secluded book-worms, or for euphonious effect upon the galleries; but the present school of politics teaches how to touch the hearts of men through the nerves that lie in their pockets. You will not find venerable, dignified men any more at Washington than elsewhere. There are noble exceptions to this remark, for there you may see JOHN QUINCY ADAMS; but Congress has become a field for party bull-fights, and a kind of canvassing-ground about who next shall fill the places of renown and money. All your fine enthusiasm is out of place; and if you would rise to political distinction, you must take sides; take the papers; cry aloud at every corner in answer to your leader; and instead of being a free man, in a free government, you must become a slave, and learn to smother your convictions. But you must not by any means neglect to enrol your name as a church member (and this is easily managed) in that sect in your county which is the most numerous; for no so great aid is found as *sect* to boost a man along in political glory. Take care not to commit yourself as a philanthropist. You, as a great man, can have no sympathy with the poor, the enslaved, the insane, and the blind. The less you say about any thing but the glory of your party, and the immaculate character of all those who constitute it, the better. You have nothing to do with your fellow-creatures now, but as members of your party. If pushed hard by some ignorant man among your constituents as to what you think upon the slavery question, you must say: 'How's that? — please to state that again;' and, while he is putting his question anew, jump upon the first fence you can find out of his reach and hearing. These are the modern precepts of rising in the world to political greatness. Poor youth! we say again: 'How hard it is to climb!'"

Be it known, then, to all religious wranglers, to all political sparrers, that there is but one God, whom we should all worship, and one country which we should all serve; that we all have the same rule of right written on our hearts; that there is but one standard of virtue and patriotism and goodness; that we may as well, and better than not, be reconciled one to another.   J. N. B.

DECEMBER.

I.

How fast the leaves, all brown and sere,
Desert the old and hoary year,
And withered fall, to deck no more
The bough their verdure covered o'er;
At last the snow, in dazzling white,
Hides them forever from our sight.

II.

Thus from our Tree of Life, each year
A withered leaf will disappear,
And unreturning, like the last,
Haste from the Present to the Past:
At length the shroud, in snowy white,
Hides us forever from the sight!

III.

But far beyond this vale of strife
There grows another Tree of Life;
Its verdure in the realms of Day,
Shall never fall or fade away:
And GOD shall clothe in robes of snow
The blessed souls that thither go.

FLOWERS.

At morn the flowers from under Night's dull pall
Peep laughing ; their reflecting dew-drops bear
Bright tiny suns, far twinkling through the air.
But some I 've seen, on whom, o'ershadowed all
By an old tower, no ray of light did fall ;
I pitied them — so cheerless sad they were.
I saw those smiling flowers in noon's hot glare,
Sun-struck, and faint ; while under the stern wall,
Fresh as at morn the shaded roses grew,
The dew yet in their bosoms. Thus when come
Deep sorrows o'er us, why should we upbraid ?
His hand o'ershadows us. The friendly shade
Shuts out the world's bright glare, and the soft dew
Of pure religion finds the soul its home.

T. R. H.

THE BURNING OF THE SHIPS.

A STORY OF THE REVOLUTION.

PART SECOND: CHAPTER I.

OUR travellers had not proceeded half a mile, when they perceived the road thronged with a motley and unusual cavalcade. There were wagons and carts, horses and men on foot, loaded with all sorts of household furniture ; beds, bureaus, pork-tubs, looking-glasses, and cider-barrels ; accompanied with women, children, and cattle, hurrying along in eager and ludicrous confusion, as if Bordentown had been warned, like Sodom of old, and her people were flying to some Zoar for refuge and safety. The foremost party informed Jonathan that Sir William Howe had sent his whole fleet and army to take possession of Bordentown, and spoil its inhabitants ; to which information, an old man solemnly added : ' I told Squire Smallhead so last fall, when our hogs turned out so heavy, that the enemy would hear of it, and never rest till they had every pound in their clutches. I knew it would be so ! '

' But how did you become apprized of the intended attack ? '

' Oh ! the Squire found it out and told us. So we thought we had no time to lose. We 'll cheat them, the greedy thieves, yet ! '

Jonathan heard pretty much the same tale from each party. Just as he was entering the village, he met a man running at full speed, and frightened out of his senses. It was with some difficulty he was brought to a parley.

' Why, Simon, what ails thee ? '

' Turn round for your life — run ! '

' But why ? what is the matter ? '

'The English have come, and killed all the people, and hung Squire Smallhead up before his own door, for impertinence and sass!'

'That's impossible, Simon. Some one has made fun of thee. Squire Smallhead has no impudence for those who are able to punish it. Who told thee?'

'Betty Meek.'

'Betty has been running her rigs on thee.'

Jonathan was quietly resuming his journey, without observing the horror and fear depicted on Nathaniel's countenance. 'Stop, Jonathan! Let me alight — *let* me!' And as he gasped and extended his mouth to its maximum size, his nostrils opened and swelled, and he looked more like a frightened horse than a human being.

'Nonsense! why, Nathaniel, there's nothing to alarm thee. Did thee not hear that Squire Smallhead had remained? Depend upon it, there is no danger. Beside, we have heard no firing. Smallhead has sent these people off that he may remain behind, and brag and bluster. Be sure, had there been danger, he would have led the retreat.'

These arguments, with the hope of getting his goods cheap in the present disturbed state of things, induced Nathaniel to proceed.

It was June, 1778. Sir William Howe had passed the winter in Philadelphia, and Washington with his army at Valley Forge. The latter, penetrating his enemy's design to evacuate Philadelphia, as he did only eighteen days later, had despatched General Maxwell into New-Jersey, his native state, in order to raise the militia, and be prepared to harass the enemy's march, should he retreat that way.

Captain M'Cauley, with his company, of which Vallette was lieutenant, and which numbered about sixty men, had been detached by Maxwell to take possession of Bordentown; ostensibly to protect a fleet of about twenty vessels, which had been sent thither when the British entered Philadelphia, but really to stir up and embody the militia, and keep an eye on the movements below. The fleet consisted of two frigates, belonging to Congress, not quite finished, and unarmed, and eighteen or twenty merchant vessels. M'Cauley's whole force, including one hundred militia-men, amounted to one hundred and sixty men. As these were very insufficient to man the ships, he had moored them close under the bank of the river, and erected on it, here unusually high for the Delaware, a breast-work, which afforded a pretty sure protection for his men.

On their arrival before Amos Smith's store, our friends alighted; and while Jonathan made haste in search of Vallette, Nathaniel entered the store to make his purchases. He found Amos in confusion, his shelves emptied, and their contents piled for removal on the counter.

'Well, how's thee do, Amos?'

'Why, well, Nathaniel; how's *thee*, and thy wife?'

'Why, well too, thank thee; how's thine?'

'She's well.'

'Thee's in confusion here?'

'Yes; Squire Smallhead says I must move my goods.'

'The Squire seems to be the greatest man in Bordentown. Between thee and me, Amos, I should not like it mentioned so that the Squire should come to hear of it; so thee 'll say nothing about it. He and me has dealin's. But to my notion, he is the greatest fool, as well as greatest man, so to speak, in the whole town; and Jonathan Richie says, though about that I do n't know, that he is also the biggest coward. Though may-be his opinion is not worth much in the matter.'

'I know something of the Squire too. But every body says that Sir William Howe, so called, has been meditating an attack on Bordentown all winter, and he has taken great pains to learn every thing that goes on here.'

'Well, but why need thee care? Thee never took any part. I never have been able to guess which way thy wishes take.'

'No, nor I either!—for I *do n't* care. But then I sold Captain M'Cauley, so called, seven and a quarter yards of buff-and-blue cloth, and if thee will believe me, he had it made into a regimental suit.'

Nathaniel was horrified. 'Why, Amos, how could thee do so?'

'Why, he did not tell me what he wanted with them.'

'But thee might have been sure what he *would* do with them. This must be laid before the meeting.'

'I shall take it very unkind in thee, if thee does so, Nathaniel. It would not be friendly.'

'Well, if thee 'll be more cautious in future, and remember the friendship in our dealin's, thee sees, Amos, why may-be I will not expose thee, though thee deserves it. I want some cloth, thee sees, and I must expect thee to let me have it cheap.'

'Cheap! these times; well, thee shall have it as low as I can afford. There now, there 's the very thing for thee. Joshua Collins bought a coat off that, last week. Thee shall have that,' (stroking the cloth down with his open hand,) 'thee shall have that at — it cost me one-pound-eight, sterling money — thee shall have it at cost. Just feel it. It 's a beautiful piece of goods; come, we 'll say one-pound-eight for that.'

'One-pound-eight! why it is the dearest cloth I ever bought at that price.' Here Nathaniel thrust his hand into his immense waistcoat pocket, and drew it out full of silver and gold coin, which, after picking from among it a small memorandum, he returned into their reservoir. Amos' eyes opened and glistened with delight at the unusual sight. Coin was rarely seen at that day, and the Continental paper was sadly depreciated. Nothing induced Amos to receive these 'rags,' as they were called, in payment for his wares, but the law which made them a legal tender, and imposed certain fearful penalties on those who by refusing to receive injured the credit of the national currency. He generally contrived to indemnify himself by laying double prices upon his goods when he expected to be paid in paper. The sight of the silver soon reduced the price. 'Well, Nathaniel, thee shall have it at one-pound-six. I shall lose by it; but thee 's an old customer.'

'That is quite too much, yet,' said Nathaniel, *accidentally* striking his hand upon the pocket till the money jingled again.

'Will thee say one-pound-four?'

'I see we shall not bargain,' said Nathaniel, returning his memorandum to his pocket, and turning to leave the store.

'Well, one-pound-three, then.'

'Say one pound,' said Nathaniel, pausing at the door and looking over his shoulder. Amos hesitated. Nathaniel ran his hand through the silver as he exclaimed, 'Come, Amos, thee wo n't stand on trifles with an old friend.' The gold conquered; and before half an hour had elapsed Nathaniel had by the same means made a large purchase, at a price which Amos really could not afford, except for hard money. The whole being completed, and the goods deposited in the wagon, Nathaniel very deliberately returned the silver into his pocket, and taking an immense roll of Continental paper from his pocket, (in those days it was carried in sheets,) cut from it with a pair of Amos' scissors the sum due to him, and calmly bade him 'farewell.' At first Amos was too much surprised and horror-stricken to remonstrate. Just however as the purchaser was leaving his store he found words: 'But stop! O surely, Nathaniel, I sold for silver!'

'What put that in thy head? I never *said* I would pay silver.'

'No, but thee as much as said so by thy acts. Return me my goods, then, and take back thy rags.'

'Amos, thee had better take care; thee knows the law.'

'The meeting shall hear of this, Nathaniel Comstock.'

'Amos, thee surely forgets the blue cloth thee sold to M'Cauley to go to war in.'

Amos was silenced: his custom came from his Society, and depended upon his conformity to its rules. So without more ado the *Friends* parted.

Jonathan, on his way toward the river, found the houses closed, and the town apparently deserted. The only *men* visible were Squire Smallhead and Betsey Meek, the latter a sort of privileged virago, whose name seemed to have been given because she possessed none of the quality it denoted.

'Why, Squire, as thee is not in the military, I wonder to see thee here.'

'True, I *am* not in the military — I am *not*. But as chief magistrate in this vicinity, and principal peace-officer, I thought it my duty to remain. But I wonder you venture here at this time.'

'I assure thee, Thomas, I fear no danger where thee is.'

The Squire not understanding the drift of this remark, mistook it for a compliment, looked complacent, and drew himself up as he condescendingly, after the manner of great men, replied:

'My presence would scarcely scare away a cannon-ball, Jonathan.'

'Thee mistakes me, Thomas. I mean I am not apprehensive that the enemy will send a ball in any neighborhood where thee is: or, to speak with more plainness, that thou wilt scarcely remain voluntarily where a ball is like to come.'

'That 's true, Jonathan Richie,' exclaimed Betsey, who stood by, with her arms a-kimbo, composedly listening to the conversation; 'that 's true, and the very reason I staid; for, says I, it will be time enough to run when the Squire does.'

The Squire eyed first one and then the other with an air of offended dignity, and a heart filled with real rage. But he was too great a coward to express his feelings to Jonathan, and dared not give them full

vent even to Betsey.   Assuming therefore an awful air of offended
dignity, mingled with as much contempt as his rage would permit him
to muster, he indignantly strode away.   Jonathan, having despatched
Betsey upon some pretext to another part of the town, proceeded to the
river bank, where he found M'Cauley, Vallette, and their men busily
completing their little breast-work.   There were but about forty militia-
men present, and no officers belonging to that department.   The rest,
on hearing they were likely to be wanted, had gone off in great haste,
in despite of the prayers of their fat captain, who besought them not to
go so fast, since he could not keep up with them if they did.   Jonathan
learned that there was not much prospect of a visit from the enemy
before morning.   The wind and tide were both adverse, and the latter
would not change before midnight.   With the little wind blowing, a
vessel could not beat up before five in the morning.   The party was
said to be five hundred strong, and therefore irresistible by any force
in the vicinity.   Most of the inhabitants of any standing around were
' Friends,' and non-combatants.   The most spirited young men had
joined Maxwell, and gone eastward to interrupt the enemy at an advantageous point in their expected line of march.   The rest were of the
sort commanded by the valiant Captain Ducklegs, whose prowess in
running away has just been detailed, and were not wanted, even if they
could be had.   A few however had already arrived on hearing the news,
and about sixty more were expected before sun-down.   With this force
M'Cauley was resolved to make what fight he could from the top of the
bank, taking care not to have his retreat cut off, and to be prepared to
annoy the enemy, should they send any marauding parties into the
interior.

Before taking leave, Jonathan called Vallette on one side.   ' William,'
said he, ' I think I will defer my departure till day-break to-morrow.
It is getting late, and I do n't like travelling at night, in these disturbed
times :   does thee think it best ? '   The young man assented.   ' Well
then, it shall be so.   Ahem ;   how are thy friends provided with powder ? '

' To tell the truth, very badly.'

' I guessed as much.   Could thee send two men as far as the big oak,
by the gate ?   They will find a keg in the corner of the fence.   No
matter how I came by it, only be quiet about it.   I have some left for
an occasion.   Do n't let the men come before dark ;   I must have time
to remove it there.'

' Never fear me, Sir ;   I 'll be secret.'

They separated, and Jonathan having deposited Nathaniel with his
ill-gotten merchandise at his home, proceeded to his own house.   The
keg of powder was found, and safely transported to the little camp.

On his arrival, Jonathan's first duty was to give his daughter, to
whom he confided all things, directions to be ready for a move to her
uncle William's, at day-break.   This being arranged, he desired
Quommino, his old black servant, to be called.   Quommino entered,
and stood respectfully waiting his master's commands.   For though
Friends do not approve of the title of master, where it is applied as a
compliment, they have no objection to its use where the relation of
master and servant actually exists.

'Quommino.'

'Masser.'

'Mind to have the horses to both wagons by day-break, and ready for a start to my brother William's.'

'Yes, Masser; trus' me for dat.'

'Well, go and see to it.'

'Yes, Masser.'

CHAPTER IV.

WE must now return to the river bank at Bordentown. It was near eleven o'clock. The men were generally asleep in an old house; the sentinels paraded on the edge of the bank, and three or four countrymen, who had lately arrived, with M'Cauley and Vallette, were sitting round a small fire, which, though it was June, the coolness of the night made pleasant.

'Have you observed, Vallette,' said his Captain, 'that the wind is changed? It is blowing up the river, and a pretty stiff breeze too.'

'Is it possible?—let us see to that.'

The officers walked aside for a moment. 'I say, Martin,' said a tall Jerseyman, who had just arrived, 'this Captain is a pretty cute fellow, considering he is from Pennsylvany. I rather wonder where he got his gumption.'

'He from Pennsylvany! No such thing; he's from Maryland. They's cute fellers down there; they live in the sand, and is most as smart as Jerseymen.'

'Well, it *is* odd,' said a third, musingly: 'what a difference it makes in people's sense, whether they's born in one place or another. I never could see why them Pennsylvany fellers is so dull and heavy like. I would not believe, if my own eyes did not see it, that that strip of water could make such a mighty difference between us and them.'

The return of the officers interrupted this interesting discussion. 'We must keep a good look out, boys, or we may be surprised by a visit from those Englishmen sooner than we expected. This wind will soon bring them up.'

Vallette was proceeding in search of some one by whom to send a message to his friend Jonathan, when the creaking of a vessel's boom against the mast, amid the stillness of the night, broke distinctly on his ear. 'What's that? Did you hear nothing, Captain? There is a vessel not a quarter of a mile below.'

'They might be within arms' reach, and we could not *see* them; these thick clouds have shut out all hope of that,' returned the Captain. The same sound was distinctly heard again; the rushing of a vessel through the waters, and the splashing of the ripples against her bow became audible. 'Vallette, let the men be mustered in silence; do n't let that fellow so much as touch his drum.'

The command was obeyed: the sounds before heard became still more distinct, though nothing could be seen. 'Scipio, is your piece loaded?' said the Captain.

'Yes, Cappin,' answered a very black negro, though that fact was not then visible.

'Well, keep ready to fire : that fellow will show himself directly ; and mind, we cannot afford to miss.'

'Nebber fear, Cappin.'

Scipio had been educated on board a man-of-war, and had acquired great skill in gunnery ; a science but little understood among the colonists, and accordingly much valued in those who possessed it. Scipio was a great man, and having the sole piece which the neighborhood owned, (and that had been left there by a party of British on their retreat after the battle of Trenton,) under his command, was looked upon as only one grade below the Captain himself. Being attached to his person as a body servant, he filled the double capacity of valet-de-chambre to the commanding officer and master of the ordnance.

For about five minutes the vessel continued to approach in perfect darkness. Suddenly however a light appeared moving slowly on the river, and then an anchor was heard to splash into the water. In less than a minute the light ascended as if drawn up the mast. During all this time Scipio was busy taking a most careful and deliberate aim.

'Take care, Sir ; let him have it ; put out his light for him.'

'Yes, Cappin.'

The gun went off : the lantern disappeared, and a crash was heard as if the whole mast had gone by the board.

'Gosh! put he candle out —— yaw, haw !' and Scipio's long, loud and characteristic laugh resounded over the water, almost as startling, considering the occasion, the pitch darkness, and deep silence which followed as it had preceded the report, as the roar of the cannon itself.

'Stop your laughing, you black rascal, and give him another.'

'Yes, Cappin, yes, Sir ; yaw, haw! guess put he candle out !'

It was useless to remonstrate ; so Scipio was allowed to take out his laugh, and with his usual composure, re-load his piece. By this time the vessel showed another light. Scipio, after a long and most particular aim, took up his match with a quiet chuckle and fired. The report was again followed by the noise of a falling spar, and then almost instantaneously by a shot from the vessel. Her fire enabled our friends to perceive the position of the leading sloop, and showed three other vessels now within a short distance of the first. The enemy were too near the shore to bring the top of the bank within range of their guns, and the ball dug its grave in the clay below. A volley of small arms followed, but the men being behind their breast-wall, the volley, sent at random, took no effect. Presently, one after another an anchor was let down from each vessel, and the light, having answered its purpose and guided her consorts to their proper stations, was lowered from the leading sloop, and extinguished. Scipio had just finished his preparations for a third fire, when this unforeseen and very provoking event put an end, for the time, to his fun. He held such conduct to be contemptible and unfair.

'Dam cowards! — 'fraid of one poor nigger ! — dam cowards!' and he sat down upon his gun in sullen and contemptuous silence.

'No matter, Scipio, you will have light enough directly. I hear them getting out their boats to board the ships : we 'll have fire enough to light hell before long.'

The splashing of oars and the striking of boats against the sides of the American ships were next heard; lights were appearing and disappearing on their decks. Whenever seen they were fired at, but with little effect, till the boats were again heard to move off, and a smoky flame crept from the hatchway of each vessel. Presently a blaze burst forth from a small sloop, loaded with some inflammable substance, and illuminated the scene with the splendor of noon. The ships and their smallest spars, the men on their deck, the river, shores, stood out to view, contrasted with the darkness in the background, with even more than the vividness and distinctness of day. On the edge of the bank, his piece depressed almost at an angle of forty-five degrees, stood Scipio, arranging his aim. He fired with his usual success, dropped his match, threw off his hat, sprang upon his gun, clapped his sides with both hands, and gave his accustomed laugh : ' Got him gin ! haw, haw ! Did he feel good ? Yaw, haw ! goo by ! pleasan journey ! Yaw, haw, haw ! '

Just then, the farthest vessel, which had weighed anchor and was drifting down the stream, was able to bring her gun to bear upon the top of the bank. She fired, and Scipio, in the midst of his last yaw-haw ! was seen to fly into two parts. His lower members stood for a moment on the gun, before they fell to the ground. But his face retained its grin, and he was actually heard to give two distinct explosions of laughter, as his head and shoulders went sailing through the air. A momentary horror seized his companions. Vallette flew to the gun and began to reload her, but all the balls were expended.

' What shall we do, Sir ? We have no more balls.'

' There is a pile of stones Scipio collected for the purpose ; he had but three balls : load with the stones.'

But before this order could be obeyed, it became evident that a retreat was necessary ; particularly as nothing was to be gained by remaining. The enemy's boats were again manning, in a cove, which formed the mouth of a small creek, just below the town. In a few minutes retreat would have been impracticable ; it therefore commenced forthwith. On reaching the outskirts of the town, M'Cauley divided his force, giving Vallette the command of one detachment, with directions to watch the upper road leading into the country, and be prepared to annoy the enemy's parties, if they should send any that way, while he kept his eye on the other.

It was past midnight when Jonathan Richie awoke and found his room in a blaze of light. His first thought was that he had overslept himself, and the sun was up ; his next, that his house was on fire. He sprang to the window, and finally concluded that all Bordentown was in a blaze.

' Rachel ! Rachel, I say ! awake ! Call Emma, and be ready to start. *Can't* thee wake ? '

' Why, Jonathan, thee 's very impatient ; what ail's thee ? Thee need not be in a hurry.'

' I tell thee the British have burned Bordentown, and are on their way hither.'

There was no need of farther remonstrance. Rachel was awake, on the floor, half dressed, in Emma's room, and back again in her own, with hands full of silver spoons, etc., in the space of ten minutes. All hands were alarmed and collected in the stairway, and Quommino despatched for the horses.

'Surely, Jonathan,' said Joseph Dido, 'thou hast worked thyself into an unnecessary turmoil : there can be no reason for *thee* to fear for thy property ; thee, a peaceable man.'

'I tell thee I do n't fear for my *property*, and I am not a peaceable man, as thee 'll see, if the bloody red-coats come to interfere with me.'

'Jonathan, thee forgets thyself ; hush thee,' said his wife.

'Masser, masser! here, masser,' said Quommino, who now made his appearance at the door, the whites of his eyes frightfully distended, and evidently in great alarm. Jonathan went to him : 'Masser it is too late ; they are come : I seed 'em, by light of the fire, though it be most out, stannin at the ledge of the wood.'

'Who? the English? How many?'

'Bout thirty, I guess.'

'Did you fasten the door?'

'Yes.'

'Where are John and Sam?'

'In kitchen ; just come down stairs.'

'Call them.'

When the men arrived, Jonathan took them into an adjoining chamber, and unlocking a large pine chest, took out five guns, with a supply of ammunition. The men stared with surprise. 'Boys you know how ; are you afraid to use these?'

'What, on them red-coats? No, I guess not!' said John.

'Well, fix yourselves at the front windows up stairs, but do n't shoot till I give the word.'

'But, masser, here be one to spare : shall I take him to Friend Didore?'

'Go about your business, you old fool, and see you do n't miss your aim.'

Jonathan's next business was with his woman-kind and the visiters, whose surprise at seeing him enter with a gun in each hand was infinite.

'Rachel, Friends, you must all go up stairs into the garret, and keep away from the windows.'

'Dost thou indeed mean to resist with force?' said Friend Dido, in a horror of wonder : 'remember, he that useth the sword shall perish by the sword.'

'I use no such weapon. But I will have no argument ; every thing I hold dear is assailed — more than my life,' and he looked at his daughter ; 'but I 'll not talk : do as I bid, or stay here and be shot.'

This last argument was sufficient, and all retired except Emma, who persisted in staying with her father. 'I shall be in no danger, father ; I 'll keep away from the windows.'

'Well, then, come with me ; thee can load one of my guns while I shoot the other.'

When Jonathan had arrived at the window, up stairs, at which he had stationed his men, he found all dark again. The fire had burnt out, or at least was nearly extinguished, so that coming as it did from behind the river bank, and intercepted by the house, it gave forth no light, to enable him to distinguish objects in front. He therefore neither saw nor heard any thing of his enemy, until a voice nearly under the window called his attention that way.

' Holla, the house! Open your door to the king's soldiers.' A loud rap at the window, which in the darkness had been mistaken for the door, accompanied this gentle salute.

' Shall I shoot?' said Quommino.

' No, do n't move; let him try again : we must gain all the time we can.'

' Holla there! I say, you old quaker wolf, let us in, or we 'll break up your silent meeting with a vengeance.'

' May I not shoot the skunk? I can see his red back where he stands beside the white fence; I have got capital good aim.'

' No, John, not yet.'

' Do n't you mean to open? Hubert, you and Johnson bring up that log I stumbled over just now, and break in the door.'

It was now time to take some notice of the strangers. Jonathan slowly raised the window. ' What means this? Who is thee that disturbs a peaceful family this time of night?'

'Open your door, Sir, and you will see.'

' But suppose I do n't?'

' Why then we will enable you to see us directly by the light of your own house.'

' But how do I know thee is not a common robber, assuming the king's dress for thy own purposes of robbery and murder?'

' This will not do, Sir. I put a plain question : will *you* open your door, or shall *we*?"

' Boys," said Jonathan, ' can you see the two fellows who carry the log?'

' Yes, the white fence shows them plain.'

' Shoot them. I 'll try the master; and Quommino, thee hit the other.'

The guns flashed. An officer, attended by two men carrying the log, and another; were distinctly seen for a moment. Then a still deeper darkness followed : there was no attempt to force the door, and one or two groans near it told the reason. Jonathan, however, had missed his aim; for the voice of the same officer was heard at a little distance, giving orders to his men.

' De Lancey, take ten men and break in the other side of the house. The d——d old Quaker has taken to fighting at last. Had I expected that, I would have come at him differently. Hubert — I forget; the sergeant is shot — Jones, go flash your musket in yonder hay-mow; it will give us a little light to work by. I do n't like this night-work.'

' But had we not better postpone that till we have secured our prisoner, and are ready to march? It will bring a hornet's nest round our ears,' said the lieutenant.

' Well, I believe you are right.'

The lieutenant moved off, and took his station as directed. This manœuvre, simple as it was, puzzled Jonathan considerably. He had not calculated on a double attack, front and rear at once, and he saw how deplorably it diminished his chance of successful resistance. He had given orders to divide *his* forces also, when a sudden report of fire-arms burst forth on the other side of the house.

'By jingo! them English must be great shots! I have heard of missing a barn door, but not to be able to hit a whole house is more than I can understand.'

The firing was repeated, though apparently with less force.

'That's queer,' added Sam; 'I'll just go to the end window and 'conitre.'

They all ran to the window, but could see nothing, as the firing had for the moment ceased. There was evidently something going on more than they could account for : a good deal of confusion prevailed, and voices of men running to and fro, mingled with groans, were heard. Presently a volley from the front of the house exhibited the state of affairs.

The royal forces had reunited, (the lieutenant's party having left several of their fellows on the grass,) and were firing at a number of men in a measure concealed by a clump of trees, and dressed, some of them in the continental uniform, others in none at all. The latter were rapidly loading and firing. Three red-coats lay between the hostile parties, two of whom seemed dead, while the other leaned on his arm, and frequently attempted to rise, but before he could get upon his feet, invariably reeled and fell. After this random firing had continued about five minutes, the fate of the conflict ceased to be doubtful. Almost every shot wounded some one of the royal forces, while the colonists, protected by the trees among which they were stationed, or favored by the unskilful aim of their enemies, escaped without any serious loss. The commander of the former was evidently getting tired of the amusement. His men ceased firing at his command, and having loaded their guns, formed in a line and charged rapidly upon the Americans, expecting to drive them, undisciplined as they were, at the point of the bayonet. The latter also withheld their fire, and silence and darkness again prevailed. The regular and rapid tread of the one party could alone be heard, till having reached within twice a musket's length of the trees behind which their foes were stationed, a blaze burst from among the leaves; the advancing party stopped, hesitated, and then in despite of the remonstrances of their officers, retreated at a much more rapid and less regular pace than they had advanced. The effect of the fire was not visible, nor were the movements of the hostile parties, as the one pursued the other. Now and then a shot was heard, each less distinct than its predecessor, till they ceased entirely. After an interval of half an hour, the steps of the victorious party again approached. They had followed their foes as far as prudence permitted, considering the powerful force in the neighborhood.

'William, we are glad to see thee; never were more so to see any one. A friend in need, thee knows; but come in; thy friends must want some refreshment.'

'Are you all safe ? Where is Emma?'

'Oh! she is well, and so are all; but come in.'

'In one moment, Sir. Jenkins, have these wounded men attended to: bring all of them into the house; leave the dead till morning.'

Three wounded men were found, and an old French surgeon, who was attached to the continental service in that capacity, prepared to attend to them. He was a man of great skill, and of still greater eccentricity.

'Doctor,' said the first man, whom they had laid on a bed, 'I shall die, if you don't hurry. I have already bled for half an hour.'

'Do you wish to die, Sir?' examining the wound.

'No, Sir, I would prefer to live.'

'I shall take off your right leg.'

'My right leg! for Heaven's sake, Sir, don't do that!'

'By gar,' said the doctor, throwing himself back in an attitude; 'I thought you said you prefere to live; no?'

'To be sure, I do, but ——'

'Take your preference; live with one leg, or go to hell with two.'

'Oh! take it off, if it must be so: I must bear it.'

'I shall have that happiness directly: your comrade seems more like to die than you.'

This man, who had been for some time groaning, as much in bitterness of spirit as from bodily pain, ceased his complaints as the doctor approached, and watched his countenance with an intense interest, while he proceeded to inquire into the wounds. Monsieur Vattel went through all the necessary examination with perfect coolness and professional composure, his face giving no indications by which the wounded man could estimate his chance for life. Having finished, he turned round, as if to leave him to his fate.

'Is there *no* chance for me?'

'No.'

'Indeed, indeed, Sir, I am not very weak: *must* I indeed die?'

'To be sure you die.'

'I tell you, Sir,' raising on his arms, 'I *must* not, *dare* not, *will* not die! Not *yet* — not *now!*'

'Ver well, if you can help it; if you can live with that hole through your guts, ver well.'

'Oh, Sir, if you knew all, you would *try* to keep me alive — a few hours at least. Oh, I shall go to hell!'

'Why for you go to hell?'

'Oh! there is no help for me! I have the business of a life to do, and five minutes to do it in! *Can* you not give me a day? But it is useless. I must go to hell.'

'But *why for* you go there? Oh, no! come, be compose; you will *not* go to hell: why for you go there?'

'I'll tell you, Sir, and you will believe me when I say, I am *lost* for ever. My uncle died. My elder brother was his heir; as there was no will, myself and two others offered to watch the corpse. We wrote a will in my favor, put a pen in the dead man's hand, and I guided the fingers and made him sign his name. My companions witnessed the will, and swore they saw my uncle sign it. We divided

the money.   Now, Sir, have I not forfeited all mercy, human or divine?
What do you think now?'

'By G——d! then you *do* go to hell!' said the doctor, dropping the
hand he had continued to hold.   The dying man fell back upon the
bed, gave one heavy heart-rending groan, and died.

The rest is soon told.   Vallette retained his men in the house, in
fear of another attack, until day dawned and rendered that precaution
unnecessary.   The enemy had left ten of their men, including the
wounded, around the house.   The two who carried the log were found
lifeless upon it.   The English Friends, Rachel, and the maids were
brought safe from the garret, from which they seemed very loath to
venture, until they were assured that the guns carried by Vallette's
friends, though loaded, '*would not go off.*'   On reaching the hall,
where the dead were all collected for interment, they were no little
horrified.

'How uncertain is life!   Vain and fleeting as the morning mist!
Verily, 'in the midst of life we are in death!' solemnly observed
Joseph Dido.

'Verily in the midst of life we are in *debt*,' solemnly answered the
doctor.

'He says true—too true.   But it is Congress' fault.   Why don't
they pay our dues?'

The next competent meeting dealt with Jonathan, and he *was read
out*, in due form.   He was never willing to confess the impropriety of
his conduct, and of course was not readmitted.   But this was not all:
it was clearly in evidence that Emma had not only carried, but actually
assisted her father to load, one of the guns, thus aiding and abetting
his contumacy.   She was, therefore, upon the principle that the acces-
sary is as bad as the principal, also ejected from the Society.   This
incident was very convenient to her lover.   There remained no longer
any impediment to their marriage.   The gordian knot was severed by
the very authority which had formed it.   Friend Dido and Martha
Nazleby experienced a sudden relief from that weight on their mind,
which had forced them to visit Friends in America, and felt easy to
return home.   The two worthies, Betsey Meek and Esquire Smallbead
lived long, and died lamented.   Betsey was for years a notorious dealer
in grog 'by the small,' without legal license, contrary to the act of the
state of New-Jersey, in that case made and provided, for which, after
having escaped innumerable indictments, she was at last convicted and
sentenced to imprisonment.   She died in prison, expressing with her
latest breath, her surprise that an ungrateful country so forgot the
important services she had rendered during the '*revolution war*,' as
she termed it, and declaring that had Gineral Washington or Gineral
Maxwell lived, they would never have seen her so hardly used.   The
Esquire met with a very different return for his valuable services, and
died '*a hero of the revolution.*'

The reader may be anxious to know what distinguished share he
took in the night's affair; thus far is known.   While Vallette was
hurrying through a wood on his return to Bordentown, to rejoin his
Captain, a man was seen to start at full speed from a bunch of bushes,

with his body almost bent double and his head sunk beneath his shoulders, shouting all the while, 'Do n't shoot! do n't shoot! do n't shoot!'" One of the men, in sport, discharged his gun in the air, and the man dropped as if dead. He proved to be the Esquire; and being raised from the ground, was with difficulty persuaded that he was unhurt, or even alive. He lived, however, to be a great man, and a valiant, according to his own representations, though the people knew how far to credit them, and laughed at his empty boastings. After a while, however, the actors in the scene, of which the Esquire always represented himself the hero, died off or removed from the vicinity, and the new-comers began to look upon him as really a soldier of the revolution, and entitled to the gratitude of his country. Accordingly he was sent to the legislature, and aspired to a seat in Congress.

After many years, his native town was elevated to the dignity of a borough, and it became necessary to choose a chief burgess. Who so well qualified for that elevated station as the patriotic and gallant Esquire? He was accordingly elected by the unanimous suffrages of his fellow-citizens, and became forthwith a great reformer of abuses. Wo to the man who left his wheel-barrow over night on the side path, especially if the chief burgess or his lady chanced to stumble over it! Wo to the boy who ventured, in defiance of the 'Proclamation' and the law, to fire a squib at elections or on the Fourth of July! Soon after he came into office he strove anxiously to obtain authority from the legislature to hold a quarterly borough court, for the trial of all offences committed within its limits. A friend modestly suggested that there did not appear to be an amount of business sufficient to warrant the establishment of the court. 'Oh,' said the learned burgess, 'oh, let me but establish my court, and I'll *create* a business! I'll soon create a business, Sir.' On hearing that such was the calculation of their chief magistrate, the people declined to further it, and it failed.

I remember to have been present on one occasion, at a concert given by a party of musical ladies and gentlemen, at which Mr. Smallhead and the clergyman of the church in which it was held were standing near me. 'Old hundred' was performed, and the reverend gentleman observed to me: 'Noble tune that, Sir, it was composed by Martin Luther.' Another gentleman who was near us did not hear the remark: 'By whom, Sir?' said he: 'By *Marshal Blucher*, Sir,' said the chief burgess, emphatically, 'by Marshal Blucher, Sir!'

But he is with his fathers; so rest to his ashes! peace to his memory! The country newspaper, in announcing his death, proclaimed that 'another revolutionary hero was no more.' The body was interred with great state in the grave-yard, and a volley fired over the senseless clay, that would have frightened the life out of its frail tenement had it not fled already. A column was erected very appropriately upon the scene of his imaginary glory, just over the spot on which Scipio had planted his cannon; engraved upon its face, an epitaph bears honorable testimony to his usefulness, his genius, the manly excellence of his character, and the perfect purity of his practice. For the encouragement of the living, and to show what great and good qualities death confers upon ordinary mortals; how it makes the timorous brave, the weak wise, and the selfish generous; I subjoin the inscription which his fellow-citizens, at the public expense, engraved upon the tomb of their deceased and venerated chief burgess:

' TRAVELLER!
Tread lightly on this sod,
For underneath rests all that was mortal of

THOMAS SNEAK SMALLHEAD, ESQUIRE,

A soldier of the Revolution,
For many years a Justice of the Peace in and for the County of
BURLINGTON,
Member of the Legislature, and first Chief Burgess of
BORDENTOWN.
Richly endowed with Heaven's gift of mind and heart,
Equally admired, esteemed, and beloved,
He charmed the social circle, and blest the domestic sphere:
In him were combined, in rare union, the virtues of a

CHRISTIAN AND A PATRIOT.

In her hour of need, his blood was given to his country;
In her hour of triumph,
She delighted to honor her patriot son.
On the 20th of January, 1816,
His fellow-citizens mourned in his, the departure of

GENIUS, VALOR, AND VIRTUE.

' Traveller, make bare thy feet!
Thou tread'st on holy ground:
Freedom keeps her vigils here,
And breathes her spirit round.

That sod, 't was moistened once
With freemen's blood; * yon mound,
'T is a hero's monument —
Thou tread'st on holy ground!'

S O N N E T

TO A NORTHERN LAKE ON A SUMMER'S DAY AT NOON.

How calm! No breath disturbs the sleeping air:
'Tis as if storms were not, and winds had died.
Yet from each point the evaporating tide
Unseen, unceasingly ascends to where,
In huge black clouds resolved, the mists prepare
Their tempest doings; on the whirlwind ride;
Or with the liquid levin-bolt launch wide
The dire commanded ruin. Thus, though fair,
Serene, and calm, the unbeliever long
May smooth his outward life, yet treacherously
Th' unseen, unceasing streams of thought ascend
Up to high Heaven; thence, in their foul dark throng
Engendered, shall God's wrath avenging fly,
And whelm his barren soul in woes that never end.

---

* Videlicet SCIPIO!

SONG.

I.

WHILE, o'er western mountains flying,
Evening fades to calm repose,
O'er the Day, serenely dying,
Night her starry mantle throws;
Beaming o'er the hills afar,
See the glowing Vesper Star!
And, as darker grows the night,
Still brighter shines her cheering light.

II.

When our day of Life is ending,
When our trials all are o'er,
When our sad remains are blending
With their parent earth once more;
Through the fearful night of gloom
That surrounds the silent tomb,
Faith, our Star, shall lead the way
To realms of Glory's endless Day.

II.

LIFE IN HAYTI.

NUMBER TWO.

THE earliest stirrers in the streets were children going to the river for water. They were generally black, though here and there a pair of yellow legs showed that the population was not *all* African. Pantaloons among this small fry were a scarce article. Shirts were more common; the wearers of this garment being about in equal proportion with others who were ' *in puris naturalibus.*'

They all bore a large calabash, or a five-gallon demijohn, on their heads, and some drove an ass, having a pair of kegs slung in a rude saddle across his back; and as the hungry little beast stooped to pick up the cane-parings or the mango-stones, the air resounded with the hard blows applied to his sides with a large stick, of which however he seemed as insensible as if he had been made of iron. An ancient philosopher is said to have died of laughter on seeing an ass eat thistles. I can believe it, for 'they have a way with them' which is irresistibly ludicrous, particularly when they *laugh*. This they do, like Leather-stocking, very silently, only sticking their noses up in the air, and turning their lips, upper and nether, inside out as it were, showing both ranges of teeth to their full extent. They seem to enjoy the grin exceedingly. They often laugh just before 'turning to' upon a nice bundle of fresh grass.

Occasionally an urchin would undertake to mount his donkey ' *en croupe ;* ' and if the latter chanced to be young and frisky, some capital sport ensued. The boy begins with a sort of Indian grunt, to urge his beast ; the latter answered by stopping short in the road : then the thick blows rain about his ears. But the donkey is in for a frolic. Down goes his nose to the ground, and up fly his heels into the air ; so straight that he seems for a moment to be standing on his head. Of course no cavalier could keep his seat under such *peculiar* circumstances, and accordingly the rider is soon sprawling in the gutter. Away goes the victor, delighted with his feat, and his hard trot soon shakes the kegs out of the slings, and they are scattered along the road. His saddle follows next; and having now shaken off all incumbrances, he stops, and suffers himself to be caught, looking as demure and innocent as a young calf. Young Jehu, having picked himself up, and gathered together his dispersed tackle, comes slowly along, scolding with great volubility; and while he is refitting his rigging, vows that his jack ' do n't know who he is dealing with, and that he 'll show him.' Saying this, he mounts again, but only to turn another somerset over the head of his Bucephalus; and thus they go, until they arrive at the river, where a curious scene is presented.

Here and there the four-footed servants are standing in the water, their kegs floating on the surface, while a drove of youngsters are sporting in the cool element, kicking up their heels, splashing about, and carrying on in the most amphibious manner, and all this within a hundred feet of the river's mouth, where its downward current meets the ocean waves, which come thundering in with terrific violence. But the little ebonies care neither for the strong current, nor its depth, nor for the waves of the ocean, nor yet for the sharks which are prowling about just outside the break of the billows. There they are, morning and night, tumbling about till they are tired; when they fill up their loads, and after getting safe home with the big demijohn on their heads, they run a greater risk of a taste of the cow-hide than of a good meal of salt fish and plantains.

There was another class of early risers, being perhaps the water-boys' mammas, who were trudging along, also bound to the river side. These were washer-women, who bore upon their heads bundles of clothes big enough to fill a small horse-cart. Each one wielded a ' beater,' a circular piece of heavy wood, with a handle eight inches long. Their *modus operandi* was as follows : The article to be cleansed is duly soaped and soaked ; it is then made up into small compass, and pounded unmercifully upon the nearest stone with the beater. They are then spread upon the sand to dry. These women marching homeward at night-fall, with both arms a-kimbo, balancing their huge burdens by the motion of the head, are as singular a spectacle as is to be met with in a tropical country.

After getting a breakfast of *café au lait*, French bread and fresh butter, topped off with an omelet, (what an appetite one has after a voyage!) I went down to see the fashions and the natives below stairs. And there they were, of all colors ; for the arrival of a vessel had drawn out the shop-keepers, the majority of whom are women, and they welcomed us with great cordiality. There was the old Guinea negress whose master had been murdered by his slaves. Her wrinkled cheeks bore each four or five broad stripes, stamped probably by her tribe when a child. She was dressed in a seersucker-gown, and wore a handkerchief upon her head, which was surmounted by a straw hat three feet broad in the brim. From her ears hung gold rings as large round as a dollar, and she wore six or eight on her fingers. She made us a low reverence, and was very respectful in her deportment, though one of the largest shop-keepers in the place.

There too was the bright-eyed, beautiful quadroon, her clear olive brow encircled with raven tresses of astonishing luxuriance. She wore the bright-colored madrass as a head-dress, while her well-shaped feet were enclosed in silk stockings and kid shoes. She was the daughter of a planter whose estate had been tilled by five hundred slaves, and who had revelled in all the luxury which vast wealth could command. But for the Revolution, she might now have been mistress of that estate. Indeed she *is* mistress of it; but the slaves are now her equals, and the plantation is a desert. Such are the strange histories of almost every individual in that eventful Island.

Old Madelaine, whom I first named, has told me her story. She says she was born in a large city in the interior of Africa; that on arriving in St. Domingo in a slaver, she met her present husband, who was her townsman and whom she had known at home. He is a likely black, and though an old man, has another wife and half a dozen young children under his roof, of whom the step-mother is fond as if they were her own. It is generally supposed that this old couple are natives of Timbuctoo. As before observed, a more accurate historical knowledge would have been a great advantage in understanding the characters of these people. I knew only that a servile insurrection had terminated some five-and-twenty years before, in the separation of this rich colony from the crown of France; but I did not know how the struggle originated; that the cry of 'Liberty and Equality' raised in France and echoed through the globe found eager listeners in the colored population of St. Domingo; by 'colored' I mean the grades between white and black; that, seeing the aristocracy trodden under foot in the mother country, they thought the triumph of human rights would reach their case, and place them on a footing with the whites. I did not know that their demands to be recognized as citizens had been treated with neglect, and that in revenge they had roused up the blacks to action; the consequences of which were soon seen in the conflagration of all the estates in the neighborhood; of Cape François and of the rich city itself, which was at the time the most superb in the new world, and said by the French to be excelled only by Paris itself. Neither did I know much of the subsequent history of the Island; of the black slaves who rose by their prowess to be kings and emperors; one of whom, Toussaint L'Ouverture, has been recently held up to the world as possessing more virtues than were ever before bestowed on any human being. No wonder Miss Martineau is so enthusiastic in her love for the race, if she believes Toussaint to have been as she has painted him in ' the Hour and the Man.'

I did not know that while the black Emperor Christophe, born a slave in St. Kitts, swayed his bloody sceptre over the north, the people of the south, among whom I was staying, feared and hated him, and disputed his power '*vi et armis;*' and that a regiment of soldiers having been won over by him turned traitors to their fellow-citizens, took to the mountains, and kept this whole district in an uproar for many years, having been subdued only three or four years before my arrival among them. Had I possessed all this information, I could better have understood the murderous visages and tigerish looks which I saw every day; not that they were universal, for the town's-people were many of them worthy, peaceable citizens; and the most ferocious had doubtless been killed off in their sanguinary wars.

There were in the employ of the House some twenty American blacks, who formed part of a considerable emigration which came to the Island from Philadelphia and New-York in 1824. Those whom I saw came principally from Bucks County, (Penn.,) and were by far the best blacks I ever met with. They had in their number several preachers, as Bradford, Robinson, Legrow, etc., and were well-behaved, industrious men, many having large families. They had been induced to emigrate by specious stories of the lands they would receive, and the great crops of coffee and sugar they would raise : but they soon found their mistake. If they had been fairly treated by the Government, and kindly received by the natives, they would have proved a valuable acquisition. They soon found that they could get no title-deeds to land without living upon it a certain number of years, and they accepted it on such conditions; but instead of being cordially received by the country negroes, the latter seem to have entertained for them a downright hatred. They stole every thing they could lay their hands on, and the major part of their victims were driven into the towns to keep themselves from starving, where they now live as day-laborers. A few individuals have persevered in the country, but they have great difficulty in getting a title to their land, for which piece of imposition the Government should take shame and confusion of face to itself.

The bloody scenes of which the Island was the theatre for so long a period have destroyed all congeniality of feeling between the Haytien black and his American brethren; or it may be that they are from different stocks. Were the Africans of the French and Spanish colonies from the same districts with those of the English? I believe the fact to be, that they all went to the same marts indiscriminately, and that the slave who is picking coffee in Brazil may have had a brother in Carolina gathering rice, or in the cane-fields of Cuba or Jamaica, or cutting throats to-day and smothered in a sulphur ship to-morrow, in St. Domingo.

The triumph of the Haytien blacks over their masters has rendered them audacious; and their half-rustic half-military mode of life has produced a lawlessness of feeling and conduct, which is inconceivable to those who have only seen the African in a state of servitude or submission. They look upon our blacks with undisguised contempt; while the peaceable disposition of the latter only lays him open to every species of imposition. Several of them went upon the estate of a mulatto woman, the widow of a revolutionary general. She was notorious for her wicked character. They 'took the act' as it is called, or bound themselves to work the plantation on shares for a term of years. After suffering every kind of ill treatment, they broke their contract in a body, and moved into the town where they lived a year or two, the old woman using every inducement to prevail upon them to return to her lands, where they might raise produce for her, and be cheated themselves. They resolutely refused to go, until at last she got authority to send a guard of soldiers after them to escort them. I saw the soldiers when they arrested one of the number, an old man named Tilghman, from Philadelphia. 'Come!' said they, 'march!' 'Tell them,' said the old man 'that if they want to get me there again, they must carry me, for I will not go.' Without more ado, they threw him on the ground and dragged him along by the heels for several rods, his head and shoulders scraping the ground. Not a voice dared to cry 'Shame!' but they dropped him at last, and the persecution was given up ; and the emigrants were *not* compelled to go to the hated plantation, for the authorities were tired of them.

It was soon evident that the emigrants gave a faithful account of things to their friends at home ; for though many contrived to get back to the States, they received no additions to their number. Among those who returned, was the young woman who was murdered in Broadway, a year or two since, by her husband. If these emigrants had gone to Liberia, they would have had land of their own without difficulty, and would now be living under their own vines and fig-trees, and probably not a larger proportion would have died than have perished in Hayti. There they would have had companions and countrymen, sympathizing in their joys and sorrows, and speaking the same language ; they would have had their churches and their schools, where their children could be taught. If rumors of wars, and standing armies ever die away in Hayti, it is to be hoped that the people will settle down into more sober and regular habits, and that industrious cultivators will be seen, instead of a rude and dissolute soldiery. Under such a change, this noble island will offer a happy home to millions of blacks, if so many are without an asylum : but at present it is difficult to imagine a country which presents less inducements to the emigrants ; for of what service is a fertile soil that must be cultivated in the midst of an inhospitable people? Be it observed that I am now speaking of the emigrant's reception. Whites generally have little cause to complain ; and I cheerfully bear testimony to the kindness experienced in a long residence. This is the more gratefully acknowledged, as the citizen of the United States is the only individual who is there entirely unprotected by his government. English, French, Danish, Swedes, Germans, etc., have their consuls and vice-consuls ; but not even a commercial agent of the United States is to be found in the whole island, though our vessels and our seamen frequent these parts more than all the rest.

In 1837, a planter from Florida purchased lands in the vicinity of Port-au-Plat, at the eastern end of the island, and removed thither with all his slaves. They of course became free, as he anticipated ; but what arrangement he has made with them, I am not aware. They must either labor for wages or on shares. As that quarter of the island has been comparatively quiet, the negroes are probably more civil; but if he made this move as a speculation, he has probably had cause to repent ere this. If undertaken with the benevolent design of improving the condition of his slaves, every one will *wish* him success, however problematical the result may be.

Taking a walk through the principal streets, I found that every house was a shop. 'Where,' said I, 'do you find purchasers where every one seems to have goods to sell?' 'Oh, you will see in a day or two.' Accordingly, on Saturday morning the mystery was solved. As soon as it was light, the occupants were out, parading the dry goods on empty crates and boxes and on lines under the balconies, in most showy style. Bright red and yellow handkerchiefs and dresses, white cotton and linen goods, piles of crockery, pins, needles, and other useful articles, were exposed for sale. The provision dealers had their tables spread out with a tempting display of salted pork, cut into various sized pieces; salt beef, soap in bars, red herrings, cheese, salt fish, salt mackerel, and a variety of other 'salaisons,' on which the people for the most part live; for though they have fresh pork and beef, yet by far the larger portion of their animal food is of the above articles. By eight o'clock the whole street looked like one great shop a mile long or more; every thing inside apparently being brought out of doors; though a closer inspection showed the shelves still garnished with demijohns of tafia, (a cheap rum,) poor French claret, olive oil, strings of garlic, etc. But they are ready none too early. The town is soon swarming with country people, bearing baskets on their heads and arms, and driving or leading mules and asses, also loaded with the products of the country; plantains, bananas, yams, fowls, oranges, tomatoes, cucumbers, beans, peas, and fruits of various kinds. These were all wending their way to the market-place, selling however on the road to whomsoever chose to buy. Such a spectacle as a West-India town presents at such a period, is worth a voyage to see. The shop-keepers hailing their rustic acquaintances: 'Here Jeannette, I have some *mouchoirs,* which will suit you to a charm.' 'Well, I'll call when I go back.' 'Samson, come and see these splendid manchets; horn handles; will last your life time.' 'Ma'amselle, with the red gown there! bring your bananas this way! How do you sell them? The bunches are very small.' A loud voice in the rear calls out: 'Clear the road there! Don't you see my jack has walked six leagues without taking his load off? Let me get along.' 'Ah, *vous mentez,* Jean Pierre, you black nigger; you know you stopped at Compere Bean Soleil's last night, and you and your beast had as much as you could eat, and a good night's rest to boot!' And here ensues a guffaw from shop-folks, countrymen, and every body else, Jean Pierre's being the loudest. Every one now wants to say something witty, but nobody listens. A jackass runs foul of a table and overturns it; the owner rushes out to make him or his owner pay damages; and such a shouting, shrieking, yelling takes place, as if Bedlam were let loose; for they laugh at nothing, quarrel at nothing, drink too much tafia, spend their money, and by three o'clock the town is deserted, the goods folded up and put away. Thus passes Saturday, and Sunday sees a repetition of the same scenes; with the addition of a parade of soldiery; and as many of these come in from the country, the day is more noisy if possible than the preceding. The shop-keepers find their account in all this; some of them bringing in three hundred dollars every fortnight.

A great proportion of the soil is rich, though but a small part is yielding its fruitfulness for the benefit of man, vast tracts being entirely desert and uncultivated. After the expulsion of the French, their lands fell into the possession of the local government, who gave away the best plantations to the most distinguished patriots, whether black or of mixed blood. Thus many who had been writhing under the task-master's whip, found themselves possessors of estates which had produced princely incomes. But though they became owners, they were far from being recipients of the same advantages as their white predecessors. The land was there, and the coffee-trees were still bearing luxuriant crops; but where were the gangs of slaves to gather and prepare them for market? In the first place, half of them had been slain in the war, and in the next place every one who was left received one half of all he assisted in cultivating. Under the ' *ancient regime,*' every estate was in perfect order; the slave receiving nothing but food to give him strength. Under the new state of things, every thing like order had vanished: the ci-devant slave was now the free ' cultivateur;' and ' liberty' did not mean labor. He was to be seen oftener with his musket and military coat than with his hoe and frock; oftener basking in the sun, or dancing to the sound of the tamboo, than digging in the cane-field or trimming the coffee trees; oftener, in short, construing liberty as uncontrolled licentiousness, than stooping to work, which made him think of the lash of the overseer.   St. Croix.

SONNET

ON A STEAMBOAT ASCENDING HUDSON-RIVER.

BY T. BRETT PIERSON.

Against the current strong, a power unseen
Hurries us onward. The revolving wheel,
Obedient to that power within, doth feel
No wish to linger near this lovely scene;
Though by the river-side the fields are green,
And cool the deep shade of the wooded hill;
Though down steep mountains leaps the laughing rill,
And sunny vales inviting smile between.
Thus in our hearts the love of God should work
Against the world's strong downward-rolling tide;
Undallying, unregretting then, we flee
The charms that on its banks alluring lurk,
Nor rest until our souls at anchor ride,
Safe in that haven blest where we would be.

New-York, October, 1841.

THE WESTERN FORESTS.

BY L. MCLELLAN, JR.

' THERE is a grandeur and solemnity in some of our spacious forests of the West, that awaken in me the same feeling that I have experienced in those vast and venerable piles, among the stained windows and clustering columns of a Gothic cathedral: and the sound of the wind sweeping through them, supplies occasionally the deep breathings of the organ.'   WASHINGTON IRVING.

WIDE, wide the dim primeval wood
  In mighty grandeur spreads around,
Casting its shadows heavily
  O'er all the moist untrodden ground :
Above, a solid roof it weaves
  In many a verdant arch and dome,
Far through whose thick expanding leaves
  The struggling sunbeams faintly come ;
And many a tall and knotted trunk
  Sustains the old majestic pile,
And many a shooting spray and branch
  Bend o'er to shape the vaulted aisle ;
And many a tempest-twisted tree
Forms chancel, nave, and sacristy,
Whose trunks the ivy and the grape
With waving festoons thickly drape.

Spreads the old forest dim and deep,
  Like some renowned baronial hold,
Some gray monastic edifice,
  Some vast cathedral, stained and old.
As now amid its alleys green
  You ramble on with solemn pace,
Pillar and aisle and architrave
  In the o'erleaning grove you trace ;
The curving arch, the fluted shaft,
  The cornice quaint, and sculptured frieze ;
Dark buttress, statue-covered wall,
  Your eye along the fabric sees.
The chapel opes its dusky room,
Now sun-lit, now profound in gloom ;
The altar from some turfy mound
Rears its green masses from the ground.

An all-pervading tinge of awe
  Into the inmost spirit flows,
As up the long-drawn aisle the foot
  Across the grassy carpet goes.
When slow the dimly-falling Eve
  The lonely place with darkness steeps,
And through each glimmering grot and dell
  With wooded form mysterious creeps,
The gazer in each swinging bough
  And in each lonesome shadowy nook,
May fancy the dull-vestured form
  Of aged priest with cross and crook :

Or dark monk telling o'er his beads ;
Or meek nun in her convent weeds,
Or mitred prelate at midnight
Muttering the doleful funeral rite.

In the uncertain sombre gloom
  Imagination rules at will ;
And spectral shapes the depths around
  In scarce-seen long procession fill.
The pale moon from her azure throne,
  As cold her silvery beams she sheds,
Reveals to Fancy's mystic gaze
  Groups gliding on with soundless tread ;
Some bridal throng in silks and gold ;
  Some mourning forms in garb of wo ;
Warriors with banners brave unrolled
  Marching with stately step and slow ;
The steel-clad baron on his steed,
The knight upon his barb of speed,
With gleaming casques and glancing brand,
Forth mustering for the Holy Land.

As slow that martial group departs,
  Amid the deepening shadows lost,
A train of weeping maidens come,
  With hands upon their bosom cross'd,
Each with a snowy wreath of flowers,
  Upon her marble temple bound ;
And slow they bare some lifeless form
  With sighs and sobbings to the ground.
Methinks that on the breeze of night
  That whispers through the leafy boughs,
I catch their lowly-muttered prayers,
  Their plaintive hymns, their convent vows ;
For the departed soul they raise
A requiem sad, a psalm of praise :
Then laying the pale dead in dust,
Their wailings in one final burst
Of sorrow trembles on the ear,
And in the gloom they disappear.

Sweet sounds, sad sounds amid those glades
  Forever ringing on are heard ;
In every tangled thicket peals
  The blithe, gay carol of the bird :
The lark from her green home up springs
  And pours her mellow gush of song ;
And the wild jay and purple dove
  Repeat their mellow descant long.
With many a plaintive note the breeze
  Along the murmuring forest moves,
Harp-like among the trembling leaves,
  Waking the music of the groves.
And when the winter's storm descends,
And the tall grove beneath it bends,
The deep-toned organ of the blast
Rolls grandly its full volume past.

Boston, October, 1841.

STRAY LEAVES.

FROM THE PORT-FOLIO OF A GEORGIA LAWYER.

It has been the fashion for many ages to consider courts as 'places where justice is judicially (and judiciously) administered.' Ask a young gentleman who has just worked his way into the intricacies, windings, and coils of the profession, what are the uses of law and lawyers, and he will forthwith launch into an eloquent and glowing discourse and argument, as to the propriety of sheltering the weak from the strong; the needy from the avaricious; the poor from the rich; the oppressed from the oppressor; and with a grave countenance, and possibly with a sincere heart, add, that law and lawyers accomplish all these desirable objects. The truth of the matter is, however, that such assertions have, under the present system of things, about as much foundation as Mahomet's coffin. I say under the present system, because if the suggestions I am about to offer shall be adopted by the law-givers of the country, law and lawyers may be made not only tolerable, but perhaps useful to the community at large. All great discoveries, and all great men have been ridiculed when their theories were first announced; and I am content to bear the fate of the celebrated astronomers, the eminent discoverers, and the scientific persons who have preceded me. That is modest, I am sure.

Now bear with me, gentle reader, and I will prove both my assertions. Let us look first to things as they are, and then to matters as they should be, and as I would make them. The great error of the present system consists, in preventing the same lawyer *from taking a fee on both sides of the case!* Start not, but reason; 'strike, but hear!' Let me state an example to you.

In the secluded village of ——, there dwell two members of the legal profession; one of them, whom we will call Mr. A——, is shrewd, learned, intelligent, and from his talents, learning, and character, possessing great influence with Court and Jury. The other, Mr. B——, is dull, ignorant, stupid, and tiresome, to all those whose ill fortune compels them to listen to him. C. and D. get involved in a legal difficulty; C. is clearly in the wrong, but he gets the start of D., and employs Mr. A—— as his advocate. No alternatives are left D. but to manage his own case, send to a distant part of the country, at a ruinous expense, for another lawyer, or confide his suit to stupid Mr. B——. His necessities drive him to the last horn of the dilemma. The case is called. D's counsel stutters and stammers, and tumbles through his statement of his client's wrongs; calls the wrong witness; presses him on the only weak point of his own case, and winds up with a tedious and unintelligible series of short convoluted sentences, leaving it a matter of no small doubt with the majority of his hearers on which side of the action he is employed.

He closes, and his adversary rises; states his case in a lucid, brief and happy manner; selects his witness judiciously, and interrogates him with great tact and courtesy, and concludes with a witty, brilliant, learned, and rapid commentary on the law and facts. What has become of thee, O Justice! while these unequally-matched followers of thine are conducting their contest? Who can doubt the issue of such a trial? And what becomes of the boasted protection which Right is said always to receive in the halls of judicature?

Now the remedy I propose to apply to this evil is to make it obligatory on the opposite party to employ *(and fee)* the same counsel his adversary has designated : then the same mind will be brought to bear upon the whole case; the same research and eloquence will be used on both sides. If the advocate be learned, both parties will equally have the advantage of his lore; if he be stupid, neither suitor will be prejudiced by the superior tact of an opposing counsel; the Judge will not be bothered; those 'good and lawful citizens of the State,' who are imprisoned in the jury-box, will not be confused; and (although I mention this latter effect as being only collateral and *inferior* to the other considerations,) the lawyers, poor fellows! will be better paid for the excitement, trouble, etc. etc., which they are compelled to undergo. What think you of my plan?

———

I AM fresh from the Circuit. Oh the delights of travelling on a Georgia road! Those picturesque gulleys; those corduroy cross-ways; those deep and muddy creeks, which you may swim or dive through as the humor takes you! And then the vehicle, which is called a stage (' all the world 's a stage ') for reasons which are deeper than my humble understanding can fathom! Let me give you a description of the one and its appurtenances, which conveyed my friend and myself to our last court. Imagine a box with two seats, with one large and one small wheel in rear, and the same quantity and dimensions in front, with more falls than springs in it. To this were yoked two tolerably good wheel-horses, and a third in what is technically called ' spider fashion,' that is, in front of the other two. A fourth horse, which had become a little lame, was tied by the throat to the rear of the vehicle.

Our coachman was a free and independent fellow-citizen, some six feet three inches, with yellow pantaloons, a ' wrap-rascal ' over-coat, and, as a matter of course, a white hat with a band of crape. Thus accoutred, and armed with a whip twice as long as himself, he prepared to mount.

'Hold on to that Scorpion filly!' said he to a score of half-grown negroes; ' grip her, Bill; clinch her, Jim.'

The Scorpion filly, surrounded and held by these adjuvant and sable subordinates of our Jehu, indulged herself in *cavorting;* which in Georgia parlance means a series of kicks and plunges, standing on the hind feet and then on the front, and all sorts of not-to-be-described actions and motions.

'Now let her go, boys!'

The filly, freed from the grasp of ' the boys,' and stopping but for one moment, that she might administer a kick to each of the unoffending wheel-horses, dashed off, and we followed, because like Gilpin we could not help ourselves. For a mile we were borne on tip-top speed over a ' cause-way,' or road made by putting large logs cross-wise. My bones will have the reminiscences of *that* mile to the last hour of my life ! Just as we were getting desperate with torture, the lame horse, who was tied to the rear, conceiving that this was a pace rather faster than he had bargained for, or than his infirmities would allow, gave a tremendous jerk, and brought us up all standing.

Then it was that the Scorpion filly showed herself to advantage. Inflicting, for reasons best known to herself, a multitude of kicks upon her quadruped companions, to whom she administered them with great energy and considerable impartiality, she at last paused for breath.

' Now 's *my* turn ! ' said our coachman.

Tying the reins to a post of the stage, he dismounted, and approaching the Scorpion cautiously, commenced the application of the lex (and the leg) talionis by many and furious kicks, which she attempted to return in kind. A considerable struggle in the rear made him stop.

' What 's that there horse a-doin', Mister ? ' asked he.

' Choking,' said I.

Whereupon he redoubled his kicks upon the filly, gratifying himself by a variety of epithets, which were more original than chaste. This the Scorpion seemed to think was adding insult to injury ; and so off she went again, at furious speed, dragging horses, vehicle, and passengers after her, and leaving Jehu to catch her as he could, which he never would have accomplished had not our safety-valve horse in the rear stopped us by a renewal of his Herculean jerk. When we came to a halt, we were hedged and hemmed in between two trees. ' *Jam* satis ! ' exclaimed I, and I got out. My friend followed my example, and we concluded we had had enough of spiders and scorpions, and would walk the rest of the way.

' Driver,' said my friend, who is pretty much of a wag, ' I have two requests to make of you. The first I prefer as a matter of conscience, and with the same feeling which induced the illustrious Emmet to ask to be shot, when he knew he must be hung ; I know I shall be refused. I ask you to knock the Scorpion filly in the head.'

' Can't and wo'n't ! ' was the pithy reply of the ' yellow blossom.'

' So I supposed,' resumed my companion ; ' I have one more to make. There 's a five-dollar bill. Take it.'

' Oh, I 'll do that,' eagerly answered the driver, suiting the action to the word.

' Yes, but *that 's* not the request. I want you to promise me on the word and honor of a stage-driver, that as soon as that brute meets her end, you will acquaint me with her death and all the particulars, by the first mail thereafter. Do you promise ? '

' I do,' was the grinning response ; and shouldering our carpet-bags we left him ; and as we cast a lingering though not a longing look behind, both the Spider and her master were furiously engaged in their old business of kicking.

The shades of twilight were deepening around us when we left our vehicle; and as we journeyed on, our path carried us by the side of a broad river. The waves rippled against the banks; the autumn wind moaned among the trees; and the 'diamonds of the sky' shone beautifully upon us. We walked on in silence. Oh, Night! beautiful Night! Thou wast given to us as well for reflection as repose. I love thee for the memories which thou ever bringest with thee; for the old familiar faces which glance at me through thy darkness; for the long-buried treasures and affections which thy dreams restore! Oh, Night! beautiful Night! If it were not for these restings in life's wilderness, who could abide the desolation of the day, 'when the hearts we loved are broken, and the forms we prized are cold!' Who could look upon the 'added stone' and the 'vacant chair?' Who could miss the cheerful laugh or the kind embrace that gladdened him once, and not droop and die beneath the remembrance and the loss? But oh, Night, beautiful Night! when thou puttest on thy 'starry robe,' and wooest us with thy soft attractions, Memory with her train rushes to the scene. The lost years return; the dead arise; crushed hopes are green and fresh again; youth renovates our withered frames; health lights up our faded cheeks; joy sparkles in our drooping eyes; and when the beam of the morning awakes us once more to sorrow and to pain, we bring consolation from the visions of the past to strengthen us through the bitterness of the present, and to make us happy and grateful for those hopes of the future which shall reünite us to the loved and cherished dead!

But I am wearying you: for a season, farewell!

LINES TO A SEA-SHELL.

There were, far in thy native ocean blue,
Deep grots, all sweet sea-sounds reëchoing;
Waves up the long smooth beach slow-travelling,
With solemn fall monotonously drew
Their rolling lengths along. Such sounds did through
Thy sinuous labyrinthine chambers ring;
And unforgetting, still they faintly sing
(After long years at unknown distance true,)
Their old accustomed song. Thus the old heart
Echoes its youth. The Bible-stories from
Our mother's lips, who taught us how to pray,
Our simple hymns, by chance remembered, start
Sometimes ev'n tears, that all unbidden come,
To think those innocent hours so very far away!

A LITERARY THIEF.

'Ox vient de me voler!' : 'Que je plains vos malheurs!'
'Tous mes vers manuscrits!' : 'Que je plains les voleurs!'

'The rascal has robbed me!' : 'I pity your grief:'
'All my manuscript verses!' : 'I pity the thief!'

THE 'INNER LIFE' OF THINGS

I.

TO AN OLD HORSE.

THY willing master, when thy years were young,
Proud of thy flying feet and flowing mane,
Upon thee clomb the hills or scoured the plain,
And round his prancing steed rich trappings hung.
Now thou art old. The echoing hills that rung
To thy loud neighings now are still; the hail
Pelts thy unsheltered head; nor doth remain
One friend of all that kindly round thee clung.
'T is thus with him who for his Master takes
The hard and heartless world. When young and strong,
It honors him; when old and gray, forsakes.
My MASTER, when old age makes dim mine eyes,
Will leave me dark and comfortless not long:
There is for me a *new* home — paradise!

II.

TO MY STOVE.

WHEN viewing oft the various fuel cast
Into thy dark devouring mouth, I've sighed
Over their former life in forest wide,
Where with tough roots rock-bound, they mocked the blast,
Or bent their leafy crests, fanned by the last
Faint lulling breath of evening. Their green pride
Thou, like the hungry grave, hast quite destroyed;
And, save a few gray ashes, all is past!
Thus wisely weigh, my Soul! thy worldly state.
Though like a green bay-tree thou flourishest,
By water-courses planted, and though great
Thy crowd of friends, and sweet thy present rest,
Remember thou thy certain end, and learn
Thou too must wither, and to ashes turn!

III.

TO A MUD-PUDDLE.

DOUBLE.

WHETHER from some smooth lake, by wooded height
Surrounded, or from mighty ocean's foam
At first updrawn, the pure sky was thy home:
There thou in clouds embosomed wast, whose bright
And burning lips have kissed the sun good-night,
Then donned sad mourning that his face was gone;
Or which, when weary wandering upon
Their wind-steeds, scattering shadows, would alight
To rest on fragrant mountains' piny tops;
Or, after some sweet shower, thy falling drops
With sun-beam tints mysteriously wove
The seven-infolded arch, emblem of love
And mercy. Now, fall'n from thy native clime,
Thou breed'st amphibious reptiles in thy slime!

—

THUS Man was first created pure. On high
His soul began his life, and heavenly grace

And beauty in his countenance did trace
Remembrances that here he still was nigh
His birth-place. Like a vapor passing by,
Yet with the glory of his Father's face
All glowing, shone his life. The glancing rays'
Of unveiled light in tints of love and joy
Did his pure soul reflect, far scattering
The varied radiance round. Now of his birth
How far forgetful ! From his high estate
How fallen ! Heavenly once, now ' of the earth,
Earthy ;,' with self-pollution foul ! A thing
Fiends gloat on, saints do mourn, and angels hate !

A R I O S T O .

' Our laughing climate and our air serene
Inspired our Ariosto. After war,
Our many long and cruel wars, he came
Like to a rainbow, varied and as bright
As that glad messenger of summer hours :
His light sweet gayety is like Nature's smile,
And not the irony of man.'

THE sight-weary traveller in Italy, when he wanders forth to view by
the soft twilight, the wonders of that storied land, where every stone
has its historical association, and the memory is more busy than the
eye ; where the violets of Pæstum and the laurel leaf of Vaucluse are
invested with a charm which no other land can give ; will be refreshed
and soothed by the sweet music which breaks upon his ear from every
quarter, in all the varied dialects of the many provinces : the sonnets of
Petrarch ; the gay baracoles of Boccacio ; the stately strophes of the
Gerusalemne Liberata, will wile away the evening hours.

Poetic and refined in their natures, the Italians have always delighted
in thus making themselves familiar with the great masters of poesy ;
and their musical voices and exquisite taste give them that natural
grace and appreciation, which it must be the *study* of the English or
the American to acquire. A foreign ear can scarce detect a false
emphasis or mispronounced word even in the lowest classes of Italian
speakers ; and yet Petrarch was so disgusted by hearing his verses in
the market-place marred by the common voice, that he would not write
in the 'lingua vulgare.' 'I feared the fate,' he said, ' which I see
attending others, who have written in Italian, Dante more particularly,
whose poems I have heard ruined in the lowest places of public resort,
and I had no hope that I could render my verses more flexible or of easier
pronunciation.' This custom then which the modern traveller finds in
Italy is proved to be a relic of olden time, and comes down consecrated
by the knowledge that Dante, Petrarch, and Ariosto listened with perchance a vexed ear to their own sweet stanzas, chanted by the gondo-
liers of Venice, the porters of Florence, or the carbonari of Naples.
In each quarter of the different cities was perhaps one more famous

than the rest among the humble inhabitants for power of voice who could gather by his door the loiterers of his neighborhood as he busily pursued his handicraft, and varied his monotonous work with snatches from the different poets.

———

In the gay city of Ferrara, which Tasso and Ariosto have so celebrated, dwelt a potter, whose busy hours were passed in moulding the dull clay into classic forms, for garden vases, fountains, water-pitchers, and the like. He had a good conception of the beautiful, as many a well-turned vase and graceful urn could testify ; and he prided himself not a little upon his superiority to his brother potters, not only in the excellence of his taste in the works of his hands, but upon his poetical genius, the melody of his voice, and the beauty of his recitations.

Many a dark-eyed daughter of Ferrara had sighed for the handsome young potter, who sang the praises of Laura and of Beatrice as well as Dante or Petrarch themselves could have done. Indeed it was often whispered that had the potter been Petrarch, or Petrarch been the potter, he would not have mourned the coldness of his lovely mistress.

A picturesque-looking establishment was the potter's studio, with its classic models and variously-moulded forms ; and many an idle citizen did he gather in early morning, or toward eventide, under his low walls, to listen to those melodies which printing was too rare an art to have placed in the hands of all the people.

One day quite a crowd had gathered about the potter, who was just putting the finishing touch to a beautiful vase which he had been making for the gardens of Ippolito, Cardinal d'Este. It was tall and delicate ; the model, of Grecian make, was before him. Animated by the success of his work, and gratified by the praises lavished upon it, he had chanted with more than usual spirit many of the thrilling scenes of the 'Inferno;' then gayly sung of Boccacio and his gardens of pleasure. As he paused for a few moments, the gathered crowd called upon him for some stanzas from Ariosto.

Ludovico or Lewis Ariosto had just begun to charm the people by the power of his muse, which, versatile and yet powerful, passed with the greatest ease from the terrible to the tender, from the soft to the sublime ; enchaining all hearts by the wonderful power of his language and the lightning flashes of his genius. The potter, yielding to the request of his attentive auditors, began the introduction to the ' Orlando Furioso,' and soon became so interested in it that he did not notice that one had drawn near the window of his establishment whose restlessness and grimaces indicated that he listened with no pleased ear to the charming poem. Once or twice he turned to leave, but an invisible spell kept him chained to the spot. Occasionally he raised his hand, as if in deprecation of some sentiment uttered by the unconscious reciter. Finally, as if moved by an irresistible impulse, he seized a large ewer which stood upon the window, and hurled it with great force at the potter. It dashed the beautiful vase he had just completed from his hand, and broke it into a thousand fragments ! Another and another quickly followed, and the poor potter could hardly escape being wounded by the creations of his own hand. The people rushed out from the shop to seize the madman as they deemed him, when what was their surprise to behold Ariosto himself. The potter began to expostulate: Ariosto exclaimed, 'Beware! I have not yet revenged myself!'

'What mean you?—what have I done to incur your displeasure?' said the poor man, who knowing Ariosto's connexion with the noblest family of Ferrara, dared not resist him.

'Villain!' said the enraged poet, 'I have only broken a few worthless pots; you have spoiled my most beautiful compositions to my face!'

———

In a quiet nook of one of the suburbs of Ferrara, was a sequestered cottage:

> 'Low and white yet scarcely seen
> Were its walls, for mantling green;
> Not a window let in light,
> But through wall-flowers, clustering bright;
> Not a glance might wander there,
> But it fell on something fair.'

This was the home of Ariosto—his pride and delight; humble but exquisitely beautiful; fit residence for such a poet. Amidst the green shades of his garden he found that repose which he needed, and derived new inspiration from its refreshing solitudes. One of his friends asked him one day how it chanced that he who could describe such stately castles and magnificent palaces should have built himself so lowly a tenement: 'Ah!' he replied, 'it costs much less money to build houses of verse than stone!'

This retreat was shared by one of long-tried love and truth, who on the day of Ariosto's encounter with the potter was seated in a recess of the room that opened out upon the lawn. She was copying in a clear and beautiful hand in a small book some poems which lay before her. Her lovely face, for lovely it was, though bereft of the first bloom of youth, was full of enthusiasm; and the words she wrote seemed rather her own inspiration than the writings of another. At her feet upon a soft mat and with a wreath of flowers he had been twining carelessly upon his head, was sleeping a boy whose rosy face upturned drew her frequent gaze; and ever and anon she fanned his cheek and fair young brow. This was Alessandra, the beloved of Ariosto, who won his affections by her beauty, and kept them by the charm of her manners, the cultivation of her mind, and her deep sympathy with his poetic tastes. Her influence was used to stimulate him to the exercise of his talent, and for the producing of those works which have brought his name down to posterity with those of the glorious triumvirate of the previous age.

Ariosto was indolent, and Alessandra was his amanuensis. Willingly had she relinquished her embroidery, (an art in which she was most skilful, and in which she was engaged when she first captivated the poet's fancy,) for the delightful task of copying Ariosto's poems; and her whole time was occupied in this, and in instructing her two boys, Virginio and Giovanni Battista, whom she wished to render worthy of their father.

She was now copying one of those playful comedies written for the amusement of the Duke of Ferrara. She had almost completed her work, when she was interrupted by the murmur of many voices approaching her quiet dwelling, mingled with sounds of lamentation and wailing. She hastily sprang to the window, and putting aside the embowering vines, saw as she thought her beloved Ariosto dead. He was upon a litter, his face covered with blood, and sadly disfigured. Alessandra uttered a heart-rending shriek, which rung through the house, startled the coming crowd, and aroused Ariosto himself, who feebly raised his head and asked what all this meant; but he soon relapsed into insensibility, and was carried into his own room. The best leech in Ferrara was summoned to attend him; and for many days his devoted and untiring companion watched over him without hope of his recovery.

Ariosto's constitution was exceedingly delicate, and he could not bear the violent excitement to which he had that morning subjected himself. While in the very fever of his rage, he had fallen, and striking his head heavily against the window, had nearly lost his life by the vehemence of his passion; and thus was the potter revenged for the injury done to his work, and the still greater wound inflicted upon his literary pride. The choleric temperament of the poet subjected him often to like scenes, though perhaps not quite as violent as this; and Alessandra was the only one who had power to soothe him when under their influence. Her lute, like the harp of David, charmed away the evil spirit; and when with her, he was gentle as a lamb.

During his illness, his house was besieged by all the noblest in Ferrara, who expressed the greatest interest in his fate. His genius was idolized by the Italians; and the people of Ferrara were proud that the mantle of Dante, Petrarch, and Boccacio had after so long a time fallen upon one of their own citizens, who would make their city a second Florence in literary fame. It was somewhat remarkable too that he walked in the steps of his great predecessors not only along the flowery hill of Parnassus, but in the more tortuous paths of diplomacy. While he was attached to the service of Ippolito, Cardinal d'Este, whose service was indeed a heavy bondage, but to whom he was bound by pecuniary obligation, he received an invitation from Alphonso, Duke of Ferrara, to undertake an embassy to the Pope Julius Second. The object of this mission was to avert the threatened vengeance of the Pontiff against Ferrara. He accepted the embassy, and was well received by his Holiness. He failed however in his object, yet gained much credit·for the tact with which he had conducted it; and he was afterward employed in many missions by both the Cardinal and the Duke. But Ariosto loved not these things. All he desired was, to live independently, and be able to follow his literary pursuits, free from the trammels of a courtier's life. But his limited means would not allow this, and he was compelled to sacrifice much of his time to public employments.

Soon after his recovery from the illness consequent upon his assault on the unlucky potter, he received from Alphonso the appointment of Governor of Garfagnana, a territory which had placed itself under the Duke's protection, and which, from being infested with a horde of banditti, required a vigilant magistrate.   In one of his own satires, Ariosto inquires why the appointment was given to him :

> ' He yields, and calls me to the post, but why?
> 'T were hard, I own, to give a clear reply ;
> From haste perchance, perchance from greater zeal
> To seek his servant's than his people's weal.'

But however this may be, he accepted the post, and fulfilled his part so well that the condition of the people was soon greatly improved.

Many romantic incidents are recorded of the observance and respect paid to him by the wild mountain robbers, whom no fear could tame, no power awe ; but who yielded to the genius of Ariosto what pontiff and lordly duke would have in vain sought from them.   Baretti relates a humorous incident :   ' Ariosto,' says he, ' took up his residence in a fortified castle, from which it was imprudent to venture without guards, as the whole neighborhood was filled with outlaws, smugglers, and banditti, who, after committing the most enormous excesses all around, retired for security against justice amidst the rocks and cliffs.   Ariosto one morning happened to take a walk without the castle in his nightgown, and in a fit of thought so far forgot himself, that step by step he found himself far from his habitation, and suddenly surrounded by a troop of these desperadoes, who certainly would have maltreated and murdered him, had not his face been known by one of the gang, who informing his comrades that this was Signior Ariosto, the chief of the banditti addressed him with great gallantry, and told him that since he was the author of the ' Orlando Furioso,' he might be sure none of the company would injure him, but on the contrary would see him safe back to the castle.   And so they did, entertaining him all the way with the various excellences they had admired in his poem, and bestowing upon it the most rapturous praises.   A rare proof of the irresistible power of poetry, and a noble comment on the fable of Orpheus and Amphion, who drew wild beasts and raised walls with the enchanting sound of their lyres ! '

These things were well suited to the romantic taste of Ariosto, and he greatly enjoyed his residence at Garfagnana, where he remained three years.   Alessandra and his sons were with him, and even in that wild place he gathered a few choice spirits with whom to hold literary companionship.

On Ariosto's return to Ferrara he again established himself in his dearly-loved cottage, and soon received an appointment from Alphonso, well adapted to his peculiar tastes.   The Duke was passionately fond of theatrical amusements.   He well knew Ariosto's talent for dramatic composition, and he therefore appointed him to superintend the regular theatre at his court.   No employment could have better suited the poet, and there was no one so well qualified to supply the stage with perfect dramas.   He it was who first introduced the practice of writing comedies in verse.   Under his supervision a superb theatre was erected, so convenient in its structure and magnificent in its embellishments that it was the admiration of all Italy.

But Ariosto was not long permitted to enjoy this new appointment. Extremely careless in his manner of eating, his digestive powers had become so weakened that he was seriously attacked with indigestion. The medicine which was employed to remove it acted too violently on his constitution, and his malady soon assumed the alarming form of consumption; and on the night of the 6th of June, 1533, he breathed his last, lamented not only by all Italy but by the whole of Europe, who had been charmed by the fascinating variety of his muse.

His funeral was honored by the presence of the noblest in Ferrara, and was rendered remarkable by the attendance of a large body of monks, who, contrary to the rule of their order, followed his body to the grave. He was laid in an humble tomb in the church of San Benedetto. Years after, Agostino Mosti, a gentleman of Ferrara, raised above it a noble mausoleum, worthy of the poet.

Ariosto's life was far more happy than that of any of the great poets who preceded him. Unlike Dante, his own country appreciated his services, and rewarded his zeal and political talent; unlike Petrarch, his life was gladdened by the devotion of the woman he loved, and the sweet ties of home and affection; and early dissipation did not pollute his mind, and make him, like Boccacio, the victim of unrelenting remorse; seeking peace, and finding none. His choleric temperament was his greatest misfortune; but that was incident to the peculiar constitution of his mind, which was like his own poetry, rapid in its changes, open to every feeling; now quick, impetuous, impulsive; anon gentle, tender, and soft, yielding to every emotion. He is the most beloved of all the poets among his own countrymen. Foreign nations give the crown to Tasso; but the Italians themselves place it upon the head of Ariosto.

He well understood the nature of his own mind when he refused the urgent solicitations of Cardinal Bembo, that he would write as Petrarch had done, in the Latin language. He knew that as a votary of the Latin muse he could only rank second; but he aspired to the first rank in Italian composition: in that walk he had none but Dante to compete with; and their minds were so entirely different, that it could scarce be called competition. What Ariosto wanted in sublimity, he atoned for by the greater smoothness and harmony of his style, and his fidelity to nature in his portraitures. His heroes are heroes indeed, but violent without rashness; his heroines are feminine and lovely; and nature itself is adorned, not distorted, by his art.

The plan of the 'Orlando Furioso' was suggested by the 'Orlando Inamorato,' a work written by Marteo Briardo, who was governor of Reggio at the time of Ariosto's birth. It was an unfinished poem in imitation of the Iliad, founded on the loves of Roland and Angelica, with the siege of Paris to represent that of Troy; and Briardo being possessed of good poetical powers, with a strong and lively imagination, it forms a fine introduction to the 'Orlando Furioso.'

The early life of Ariosto was almost a repetition of that of his brother

poets.   His genius displayed itself when he was very young, in the
composition of a play called Pyramus and Thisbe, which he taught his
brothers and sisters to perform; but his father, though pleased with
the poetical taste he discovered, dreaded its influence on his after life.
He had destined him for the study of the law, hoping he might rise by
the patronage of the noble house of Ferrara to a high station; and he
deemed the love of the Muses so entirely incompatible with a proper
attention to his legal studies, that he forbade him to write or read
poetry or any works of the imagination; and like the father of Ovid,
kept a jealous eye upon his poetic tastes.   This thraldom galled the
high spirit of the young poet, and he at times thought of throwing off
his father's protection, which was rendered so irksome by this restraint
upon his mind and tastes; but he was relieved from it, as Petrarch
had been before under the same circumstances, by the death of his
parent.   But to this succeeded new cares; the family were left without
the means of support; and Ariosto's pride and better feelings called
upon him to devote himself to providing for their necessary wants.
Day and night he labored for them; and he would not return to his
favorite pursuits and studies, till he was taken under the protection of
the Cardinal D'Este, and received from him a regular income.   In one
of his satires, he has left a description of his peculiar feelings and situation, at this period of his life :

> ' My father dies, thenceforth with care oppressed,
> New thoughts and feelings fill my harass'd breast;
> Homer gives way to lawyers and their deeds,
> And all a brother's love within me pleads;
> Fit suitors found, two sisters soon are wed,
> And to the altar without portions led.
> With all the wants and wishes of their age,
> My little brothers next my thoughts engage;
> And in their father's place I strive until'd
> To do whate'er that father's love inspired :
> Thus watching how their several wills incline,
> In courts, in study, or in arms to shine;
> No toil I shun their fair pursuits to aid,
> Still of the snares that strew their path afraid;
> Nor this alone, though press we quick to land,
> The bark 's not safe, till anchored in the strand.'

The duties thus described, Ariosto performed with the utmost care
and diligence.   He became indeed the father of his family.   His person has been described by his biographers as being large and well-
formed, except the shoulders, which were disproportioned, and gave
him an awkward appearance when he walked.   His complexion was
dark and his eyes penetrating; but his noble intellectual forehead
distinguished him from the common mortals by whom he was surrounded.   His voice was exquisitely melodious, like that of the angel
Israfel, which charmed all who listened to it.

The house where he lived in Ferrara is still preserved with the
utmost care, and shown as a sacred thing; and many a pilgrim has
bent thitherward his steps to offer his homage to the home of the poet;
and as he read the Latin inscription penned by himself which still
remains over the door, has almost fancied he could feel the presence of
the spirit which has hallowed the lowly tenement.   Ferrara, now lone

and deserted, is one of the saddest towns of Italy; and it would indeed be almost one of the has-beens, without name or place, had not Ariosto there warbled his sweet lays, and Tasso consecrated it by the sad seal of suffering genius.

THE MURDERER'S DEATH-BED.

BY R. M. CHARLTON.

'Twas a dark and drear autumnal night,
  And the wind rushed by with such fearful moan
That the cheek of the timid grew pale with affright,
And many a spectre rose up to the sight,
  As the lightning-flash through the darkness shone;
And the rain poured down in a ceaseless flood,
  And the thunder was rolling loud and near;
'T was a night and a time for a scene of blood,
  With no eye to see and no ear to hear!

In a chamber under an upper shed
  Was gathered a small and tearful band,
And one was stretched on a dying bed,
And many and fierce were the words he said,
  As he wildly gazed on his wasted hand;
As if there he saw the fatal stain
That had flowed from the blood of a brother's vein!

'How long,' he cried, with a frantic start,
'How long ere the life-blood shall leave my heart!'
This he said to one by his side
Who kissed his forehead, and then replied:
'Before the light of another day,
  Thy soul and thy life will have passed away;
Oh! calm, I pray thee, this fierce despair,
And lift thy heart to thy God in prayer;
Though that heart were as black as this fearful night,
There's a fount that can make it pure and bright.
It was for thee, it was for thee
That the Saviour died on the accursed tree:
Only deeply repent of the deed thou hast done,
And ask in His name, and salvation is won!'

'Alas, alas!' said the dying man,
'No fount nor prayer can remove this ban;
  Who was it said on the holy hill,
'Thou shalt not kill!—thou shalt not kill!'
I heard those words in my childhood's hour,
  And they startled me then, when I thought of their power;
  And those terrible words they haunt me still,
'Thou shalt not kill—thou shalt not kill!'
But my hand with my brother's blood is red,
And he sleeps, he sleeps with the murder'd dead!
And whenever I turn me round to pray,
He bars the entrance to Mercy's way;

I hear his shriek in this raging storm,
And I see his bloody and wasted form :
He stands there now ! Away, away !
I cannot, I will not, I dare not pray ! '

'T was a fearful sight I ween,
　　'T was a fearful sight,
　　At the dead of night,
To gaze on that sad scene !
The thunder rolled with a deaf'ning crash,
And bright as the day was the lightning's flash ;
And fierce and fast fell the drifting rain,
'Gainst the shingle roof and the window-pane ;
And there the wretched murderer lay,
With the tide of life fast ebbing away,
With no hope for mercy, no thought to pray !

Oh, 't is a terrible thing to die !
Though the sun be bright, and blue the sky ;
Though we think that the spirit will take its flight
To a fairer land and a region bright,
Yet 't is a terrible thing to leave
The hearts that for us will wildly grieve,
And to see no more around us press
The forms that delighted our lot to bless ;
And be laid in that dark, remorseless grave,
With the wretched felon and Guilt's vile slave,
And to rise no more from the loathsome sod
Till we stand at the bar of a righteous God !
'T is a terrible thing e'en thus to fly
From the gladsome earth and the clear blue sky ;
But when around the passing soul
The waves of eternal vengeance roll,
And the deadly gloom of unpardon'd sin
　　Brings fierce despair or fiercer doubt,
And the tempest of conscience howls within,
　　While the storm of the elements rages without ;
Oh ! stout and strong must the spirit be,
That can thus to its Maker's presence flee,
Nor leave behind with its latest breath,
Its frantic dread of such fearful death !

I may not wish and I dare not pray
For the manner my spirit shall pass away ;
To Him, to Him who my being gave,
I leave the choice of my death and grave ;
And whatever may be my future lot,
It matters not — it matters not !
For come he slow or come he fast,
On battle-field, or in tempest blast,
It is but Death that comes at last ;
So I meet my fate with unflinching eye,
So I look with faith to the cross on high,
It matters not how or when I die.
But I lift, O God ! my humble prayer
That my hand from my brother's blood be clear ;
Like the righteous man's let my spirit flee,
And like his, like his let my last end be !

Savannah, (Georgia,) October, 1841.　　　　　　　　　　　　R. M. C.

THE PARTISAN WARS OF STOKEVILLE.

FROM THE 'STOKEVILLE PAPERS.'

CHAPTER FIRST.

It was late in October, a few weeks previous to the elections, when as usual a great excitement broke out in Stokeville on political matters. About this time, Lawyer Brief and Lawyer Blank, Scribble, the young editor of the 'Rocket of Freedom,' and Managers Carbuncle and Brandy, were assembled in the evening at the office of Mr. Brief for the purpose of 'getting up a ticket' to be pressed through the county convention, which was to be holden on the following week.

Lawyer Brief opened the conference. He said it was known among themselves that he was anxious for the nomination of congressman, and Carbuncle was to run for sheriff. 'Now,' said he, 'we must manage this thing *right*. We must take the business into our own hands. To-morrow we have a meeting in this town to appoint delegates to the county convention. Now it is indispensable that the right kind of men are selected for this purpose; men who understand what we want, and who will be likely to play into our hands.'

'Oh certainly; by all means,' was responded from all sides. 'There is no trouble about managing this business,' continued Brief. 'There is policy to be observed in these matters as well as in all others.' He then proceeded, and cautiously unfolded the plan to be pursued when the town-meeting should have assembled; a plan which he assured them in conclusion 'could not fail.'

'Capital!' responded Blank, Carbuncle, and Brandy; 'capital!'

'Certainly; that is the way to manage,' resumed Brief; 'we thereby get the control of five delegates, to begin with.'

'But,' interposed Scribble, 'how are we to control the other forty-five?'

'Oh, without difficulty,' answered Brief carelessly; 'leave that to me and Blank.'

'Now Scribble,' said Brief, 'you must draw up a set of resolutions, expressive of the sense of the meeting, and carry them with you to the county convention, and we will make you chairman of the committee, and give you a chance to report them; and Blank and myself will prepare an address for the same occasion.'

'What!' exclaimed Scribble, with surprise; 'draw up resolutions for a meeting before it assembles!'

This remark of astonishment only excited laughter among Scribble's friends. They told him he was not 'initiated,' but thought he would learn after a while.

After the whole business was 'cut and dried,' to use a favorite phrase of Brief's; the delegates from the town of Stokeville nominated in advance to the county convention; the two candidates for congressman and sheriff, selected also in advance of the convention itself; a set of resolutions and an address concocted in advance; the clique adjourned to carry out their plot, by drawing in if possible the support of a majority of the nine remaining towns.

The next morning a large hand-bill made its appearance in Stokeville, 'got up' by Scribble, calling upon ' all the friends of the country to arouse and assert their rights,' by assembling in the afternoon at a place designated, for the purpose of nominating county and other officers. The hand-bill closed as follows : ' *The enemy is up and doing ! Our rights are in danger ! An awful crisis is at hand ! Let every man attend !* '

This hand-bill of course produced great agitation. The whole village was alarmed, and every man was waging a political war with his neighbor. At an early hour in the afternoon a crowded meeting assembled, and was organized by the appointment of a chairman and secretary. Every man had ' blood in his eye,' goaded as all were by a contemplation of the wrongs which were meditated against their rights. There was a spirit of resolute determination manifested, which was fearful to behold.

When order had been restored by the chairman, Mr. Blank rose and said that ' this was one of the most exciting contests which he had ever encountered. He did not rise to speak, but could not forbear making a few remarks. He repeated it, that since the American revolution, that revolution which cost so much blood and life and treasure, the blood and treasure of our forefathers, nothing had occurred which called so solemnly and imperatively upon us to turn out in defence of our rights, as the present contest. (Great clapping of hands.) ' The enemy is abroad ! ' said Mr. Blank. ' So he *is*, be Jasus ! ' interrupted an Irishman sitting by, ' for I seen him with my own eyes ! ' ' The enemy *is* abroad, as the gentleman says,' continued Mr. Blank ; ' and cheating, lying, bribery and deception will be resorted to for the purpose of winning the votes of a free and intelligent people. (Immense agitation.) There is nothing, gentlemen, too base for our opponents to resort to. They cannot stoop too low ! I do n't say, gentlemen, they would steal or murder ; I say I do n't *say* they would do these acts, but you can judge for yourselves. You have *seen* them, as well as myself, and understand them probably better. I see around me on every side, gentlemen, the hardy sons of toil — the bone and sinew of the country ; men who are the producers of all our wealth — the mechanic and the laborer ; and I am glad to find them where they will always be found ; on the side of their country and its free institutions.' (Great stamping of feet and clapping of hands, accompanied by cries, ' And where we always will be found.') ' Yes, gentlemen,' continued Mr. Blank, with greater emphasis, ' I am proud that I have the honor of acting with such men ; men who are influenced by no unworthy motive, and who like myself would be willing to pour out the last drop of their blood in the defence of their country ! (Terrible excitement, and some threats.) Can we ever submit, gentlemen, to see our liberties taken from us, and all our hopes as a free people blasted ? Can we ever suffer an unfeeling and purse-proud aristocracy to ride over us rough-shod ? (Never !

never!) Can we consent to become slaves? ('Not while we have breath!' was responded by a hundred voices.) Then let us arouse, fellow-citizens! Let us go into the contest with a determination to preserve our rights! Let us be vigilant! Let every man, regardless of self-interest, give himself up to the relief of his bleeding and suffering country!' (Great stamping, followed by nine cheers.)

Mr. Blank sat down, but pausing for a moment as if he had forgotten something, rose again amid profound silence.

'One word more,' said Mr. Blank. 'In the heat of my remarks, just closed, I forgot to advert to the business which called us together. We have met for the purpose of appointing delegates to a county convention, which county convention, as you all know, is to convene for the purpose of nominating county and other officers. We then choose, gentlemen, a congressman, an assemblyman, a sheriff, and some other officers. We want good men to represent our interests, and none other. Now gentlemen, I care not who are selected as delegates. There is not a man present who is not fit for the trust. For my own part, I am totally indifferent; and perhaps therefore some *other* gentleman would prefer making the nomination.'

Mr. Blank was about sitting down again, but loud cries were heard from all parts of the house, requesting *him* to nominate. Mr. Blank rose again. 'If it was the desire of the meeting,' he said, 'he would most cheerfully discharge the duty.' Then looking around upon the assemblage, as if in a state of indecision, he said slowly, 'I would nominate Mr. Blank, Mr. Brandy, Mr. Carbuncle and Mr. Scribble.'

Mr. Blank sat down. 'All you who are in favor of the nominations——'

The chairman was here cut short by Mr. Scribble, who popped up and proposed that 'Mr. Blank's name be added to the delegation,' making, he added, 'just the regular number.'

The amendment was accepted, and the chairman put the question to the meeting a second time, when the five candidates were nominated by unanimous consent; 'the Regency' as they were called, succeeding in nominating themselves, precisely in accordance with previous arrangements. Several inflammatory speeches were then delivered. Young men and old harangued the assembly. The whole room fairly blazed with eloquence. At last, a long string of resolutions was introduced by Scribble, and read with great applause; and then the meeting adjourned.

The next day another political caucus was held at the office of Brief, 'to adopt measures' to secure the delegations from other sections of the county, or at least a sufficient number of them to carry the nomination of Brief for congressman and Carbuncle for sheriff, in the approaching convention. Every member of the clique was present, and expressed himself highly delighted with the manner in which the caucus of the previous day 'went off.' Blank received great credit for his management, and his speech was highly lauded.

'Now,' said Brief, when the members were ready for business, 'we have secured five delegates for us, and there are fifty delegates to be chosen. 'Let me see,' he continued, in a tone of abstraction; 'fifty delegates; we must manage six towns, making thirty delegates, to give us a majority in open ballot. These delegations must be reached by us through leading-men in those towns. In Bungtown, there is Squire Great; in Applebury, Colonel Downs; in Chestnut-Hollow, Squire Dean; on Smoky Hill, Doctor Peck; and in the town of Four-Corners, Mr. Best. This number with our own makes six towns.

'Are you sure that these men are all 'true?'' inquired Blank, looking up to Brief for an answer.

'Just as true as the steelyards!' answered Brief.

'Did n't Squire Great, of Bungtown, split his ticket a couple of years since?' continued Blank; 'and did n't Best swear that he 'd 'bolt,' because he was n't nominated for constable last spring?'

'All those difficulties are settled long ago,' said Brief. 'But as I was saying, we must manage those five towns; and this is the policy: Beside the offices of congressman and sheriff, which Carbuncle and myself claim, there are the two offices of assemblyman and county clerk remaining. Now how can we dispose of these offices, to the best interests of the party, or in other words to further our own projects? That is the question. I have concluded that it is policy for Blank to visit all the gentlemen whose names we have mentioned, and arrange this business. We must pledge both to Squire Great and Mr. Best the support of the Stokeville delegation for their nomination to the assembly, provided they will insure to us the support of their two towns for the nomination of Carbuncle and myself. Colonel Downs and Doctor Peck must be similarly approached, with the promise of the office of county clerk; and Squire Dean must be put off with the promise of our support for assemblyman another year.

'But we can't pledge our delegation to support two men for the same office, can we?' exclaimed Scribble, with honest surprise.

'Can't *pledge?*' answered Blank; 'we can pledge our delegation for the support of fifty candidates; but to *fulfil* is another matter.'

'What!' exclaimed Scribble, 'play 'em false!'

'Scribble do n't understand political tactics, I see,' said Carbuncle, breaking into the conversation. 'He haint been in hand long enough. He do n't know how these things are done.'

Scribble confessed his ignorance, but hoped he should learn. 'Well, then, to resume the old subject,' said Blank, 'we are to pledge ourselves to Squire Great and Mr. Best for the assembly, and to Colonel Downs and Doctor Peck for county clerk. Now, which two out of the four shall we *cut* in convention?

'The one that commands the least votes, of course,' replied Brief.

'Certainly,' rejoined Brandy and Carbuncle.

'Squire Great is an old fool,' said Blank, 'but he would run well. His connexions would all vote for him. Best is a man of talent, but he can't carry strength with him; he is too obscure.'

'Yes,' continued Brief. 'Great has, beside a large connexion, a great many men in his employ, whom he would 'see to;' and his opponents can't say any thing against him; and he would moreover be 'willing to bleed freely in the cause,' by launching out his purse. Best is too poor; he can't stand a nomination: Great is our man.'

'Beside, 't wo'n't do to play Squire Great double,' said Brandy; 'if he should bolt he would carry others with him. He is not a man to be bamboozled with impunity.'

'Well then,' said Blank, 'we go for Great. Shall we support Peck or Downs for clerk?'

Peck was almost unanimously settled upon, because, as a physician, he was well known and popular. It was urged that he was capable of exercising a great political influence in his rides about the county. He might disseminate political information, it was said, and his mission would not be suspected. Beside, there was a large number of poor in the ranks of his opponents, whom he had visited gratis for years, 'and they would all go for him.' An objection was raised against Peck because he was rich and Downs was poor and needy, but it was immediately silenced as of no weight. 'If,' said Brief and Blank, 'Downs is poor, why there is no policy in giving the office to him; for as we have before said, we want a man who is willing to *bleed*. The more Great and Peck throw into the cause, so much the better is it for *us*. It all helps carry the ticket through. We are for victory, and a poor man will only be a clog upon us. No, no; Great and Peck are our men.'

'The next thing to be attended to,' said Brief, 'is to make provision for raising money. Let me see,' continued he, 'there are four candidates that we can tax; sheriff, congressman, county clerk, and assemblyman. Congressman must bleed five hundred; clerk and sheriff *two* apiece, and assemblyman one hundred. That makes a thousand dollars. That'll do very well, with what contributions we can raise.'

'Let us draw up a paper on the spot, that each of the candidates may pledge himself for his proportion at once,' said Blank.

All concurred in Blank's recommendation; they had been too often bit before, they said, to trust now to political promises. It was best to have it in black and white. A paper was drawn up promising 'to pay to Blank on demand, etc., the sums set opposite their respective names,' and signed by Brief, five hundred dollars, candidate for congress, and by Carbuncle, two hundred dollars, candidate for the assembly, and intrusted to Blank, who promised to see the other candidates, after the nominating convention. Scribble suggested to Brief and Carbuncle the precaution of not rendering themselves responsible before they made sure of their nomination, but he was only laughed at for his ridiculous ignorance.

The caucus then broke up. The next day Blank, in accordance with the arrangements of the preceding evening, 'put out' on the business which had been assigned him, viz.: To secure the delegations of five of the nine towns that were to be represented in the county convention for nominating candidates. He gave out that his business was 'to stir up the people.' All the 'leading men' who have been mentioned were seen and arrangements entered into; and nothing remained but the holding of the convention to carry them into effect. But that important and memorable gathering must not be described at the tail of a chapter; and we turn a new leaf to place it on record.

CHAPTER SECOND.

Scribble's paper, 'The Rocket of Freedom,' came out before the day of the convention. He was instructed and assisted by Brief in getting up an appeal to the party, not only to delegates but all others who felt interested in the cause, to attend. 'It is a time,' said the editor, 'when every man, be of what profession he may, is solemnly called upon, by all the ties which bind him to his country, to rush to the rescue! Let the farmer forget his crops; let the mechanic drop his tools; let the professional gentleman close his books; for a great crisis has arrived in our national affairs, and if we remain indifferent, our liberties are at end! We feel it our duty as a sentinel upon the watch-tower, to warn our countrymen. If the present opportunity is lost, it may be the last. Our opponents have left no means untried to make us slaves. They support measures which, if carried into effect, would blow this fair republic to atoms. We should have a king reigning over us, and *all* that our fathers fought for would forever be lost. Then farewell all our boasted hopes! farewell country! Then,' continued Scribble, 'if we wish to avert this evil, let us turn out, and show by our numbers that we will never tamely submit to such vassalage. Let us make a rally that will strike terror into the hearts of our adversaries; and finally, let us present such a front at the ballot-box, that our foes will slink away into their dens, and never show their faces again to an indignant and outraged people.'

An appeal like the above could not but rouse the patriotism of every man who had a single spark of political fire remaining in his bosom. It shot through the community like electricity. When the day for holding the convention came round, there was, to use the language of Scribble, 'a tremendous turn-out, such as was never before witnessed by the oldest inhabitant.' Wagons rolled in from every direction, loaded down with 'the hardy yeomanry of the land;' some singing, shouting and swearing; some tipsy and some sober. Previous to the organization of this important assemblage, Scribble, Blank, Brief, Brandy and Carbuncle might be seen, each with a knot of delegates about him, advising what course was best for the triumph of the party. It was carefully hinted by Scribble and Blank, that Brief would make an admirable member of congress, and would add great strength to the ticket; but they were 'afraid that he would never consent to the nomination.' They said he felt so delicate about it, that they were afraid the office could not be forced upon him. At the same time Brief and Brandy were advocating Carbuncle's claim to the office of sheriff. 'He had done so much for the party; was such an influential man; he commanded so many votes; and then he was such a true politician: 'always right,' said Brief; has his eye continually on the gun. The whole business of the convention was of course all settled before it convened; and this mock electioneering was only a kind of show-off, that the subsequent proceedings might not come wholly unsuspected, or smack too strongly of previous arrangement.

The convention was at length organized. Peter Snykes was appointed chairman, through the management of Brief, as it was understood he was 'fishing' for the office of sheriff in opposition to Carbuncle, and putting him in the chair would silence him at once, at least so far as pressing his claims in open convention was concerned. Another delegate from the south end of the county, who it had been hinted was anxious for the nomination of congressman, had his 'artillery spiked' by being made vice president. So far every thing moved on well. To use the words of Brief and Blank, it was 'all right,' and the result certain.

When the convention was called to order, Blank, who was the orator on all occasions, arose. He said that the convention had met for the discharge of an important duty — the nomination of county and other officers. It was incumbent upon the convention to nominate a congressman, a member of assembly, a sheriff, and a county clerk. For his part, he had no preference, provided a good man could be selected. He would support any man who should be designated by a majority of the delegates then present. He had not made up his mind who would be the proper man. He rather preferred to be governed by the voice of the convention. He really felt so very indifferent, that he had nothing to say on the subject, and should therefore sit down.

As soon as Blank closed, Brandy rose, and said he had an inquiry to make. He wished to know what plan was proposed for making the nomination? He was for the most democratic mode, and he presumed every member would concur with him. He was for an open ballot.

Brief rose on the instant, with the remark, 'that there certainly could be no objection to *such* a course.'

Several other members concurred, among whom may be mentioned Great, Peck, Best, etc., the expectants of the offices of county clerk and member of assembly.

The open ballot was finally agreed upon, and the nomination made the first business in order. It was resolved on motion of Blank, that the congressman and sheriff should be balloted for first. Tellers were appointed, and the tickets made and deposited; and when the canvass took place, it was declared that Brief and Carbuncle were nominated by a majority of just five votes over the president and vice president of the convention, their opponents. Every body said it was a fair ballot, and of course the matter was settled. The convention then proceeded to ballot for assemblyman and county clerk, and Peck and Best were declared by the tellers to have received a majority of the votes.

Some excitement was produced by the defeated applicants for these offices, when the result was known. Blank, Brandy, Carbuncle and Company insisted that they performed their promises in good faith; and there was no evidence to the contrary, every thing being effected under cover of a ballot; and so the matter passed off. The convention adjourned; a portion of the delegates who had been unsuccessful in the presentation of their favorite men were dissatisfied, and went snarling on their way home; and those who had been successful departed full of spirits and glee.

There was a great flourish in 'The Rocket of Freedom' the first week after the convention. The nominations were announced in staring capitals over the head of the paper, and a long editorial eulogy written for each of the candidates. In speaking of Brief, Scribble said that it was 'unnecessary to speak of him at all;' and were it not for the information of his political friends abroad, he should let him pass in silence. Where he was known, he was highly respected, and his unflinching devotion to the great cause was his best recommendation to strangers. The nomination had fallen upon him totally unexpected; yet he was not unconscious of the regards of a free people, nor of the high trust which they had seen fit to repose in him. If elected, he would show them that their confidence had not been misplaced. As to Carbuncle, he had always been an active politician; he was a man of sterling business qualifications; and as a servant of the people, *he* would never deceive them, etc., etc.

On the following week 'The Thunderer,' the opposition print of the village, appeared, arrayed in fire and brimstone, belching forth fury at every pore. The editor said it was as he had expected. 'Brief was nominated for congressman and Carbuncle for sheriff. Brief was a man,' he added, 'who did not possess one single qualification for that high and responsible office. He had violated every trust which ever had been committed to him. He had twice turned his coat; he was an aristocrat; he believed he had been indicted for a misdemeanor in another county, and obliged to flee from the pursuit of justice. He was in favor of levying a direct tax upon the poor to support the rich; and finally, he was a mere demagogue, who would at any time assist in blowing up this whole republic, if he could thereby further his own wicked and corrupt schemes. Carbuncle too was a man who had *no* character. The wonder was that a political party could be found which had the impudence to *nominate* him. His habits were such, (he would not say that he *drank*,) that no moral man could conscientiously cast his vote for him. Beside, he was incapable of discharging the duties of the high and responsible office to which he was nominated. His reputation for honesty was none too good; and the editor would take some future opportunity 'to show him up to the public in *that* respect.' His readers might expect more upon that theme.

Stokeville was in violent commotion. Every body was running around to get a sight of 'The Thunderer.' Such a scathing article it was thought must rouse the vengeance of Brief and Carbuncle; and the editor, it was predicted, would catch a raw-hiding before sun-set. Yet the editor of 'The Thunderer' had his friends, comprising the whole strength of the party to which he belonged. They all said their paper had not half told the truth, and that proof could be furnished to substantiate every charge which *had* been made. It was common report, they said, that Carbuncle was drunk every morning before breakfast, and totally unfit to discharge the office of hog-reeve, much less that of sheriff. And in regard to the other part of the charge, that he was 'incapable' and 'dishonest,' why every body knew it to be true. It was known that he could not add a column of figures or write his name; and as to his dishonesty, it was said he robbed his own brothers and sisters of the very property he was then holding, beside fleecing three or four widows and as many more poor orphan children out of the last penny they had in the world.

Brief met with a similar dissection at the hands of the friends of the editor of 'The Thunderer.' He had, they said, been charged with aristocracy. He was one of the rankest and most offensive aristocrats in the county, and it was high time the people visited him in their might. It was asserted that he was exclusive in his society; that he refused to drink with the people; that he wore a ruffle-shirt and overshoes; used wine after dinner, with other enormities too numerous to mention. They believed, as the editor of 'The Thunderer' had said, that he was in favor of levying a direct tax upon the poor to support the rich. He had no patriotism, and did n't care a copper for his country, except just so far as it administered to his own selfish purposes.

The 'Rocket of Freedom' of the following week came out in reply, hot with gall and bitterness; but instead of confining itself to the original issue, attacked with blood-thirsty ferocity the character of the editor of 'The Thunderer' himself. He called him a 'scoundrel' and a 'blackguard,' with other the like choice epithets; daubing him over with scurrilous language in every line; and concluding by invoking the ' just indignation of a virtuous public upon the head of so vile and abandoned a slanderer ! '

The editor of 'The Thunderer' replied in language equally chaste; and week after week this game of cut-and-thrust was followed up, to the infinite delight of all Stokeville. It is true some conscientious people might be found, who affected to frown down ' such coarse personalities,' as they termed them, but it was *only* affectation after all. Secretly, they devoured the articles of both editors with the appetite of an anaconda, and digested them with the stomach of an ostrich. The two candidates for assemblyman and county clerk were black-balled by the editor of 'The Thunderer' week after week, and almost every crime in the calendar was charged upon them. At length the day of election drew near; and arrangements must necessarily be entered into by the clique to carry matters through successfully. The plan of these arrangements and their result will be found in the following chapter.

CHAPTER THIRD.

THE clique were once more assembled at the office of Brief. In about a week the election was to be held, and the destiny of all office-expectants decided. It was then to be determined whether Brief should receive at the hands of the people the honor and dignity of a member of congress; be deputed to the great capital of the nation, to mix with ambassadors and senators; or whether he should have leave to remain at home, defeated and disgraced. Carbuncle too was all alive to *his* condition, and was anxious that every thing should be done which ingenuity could suggest to support the ticket, and carry it through triumphantly.

A poll-list of the votes of both political parties was presented by Scribble. It was carefully examined and revised. There was one column, however, under the head of 'doubtful' which contained a large array of names, and it was upon this class that the great impression was to be made. There was Tom Jones, Bob Bowles, Bill Smith, Pete Snykes, and ten or fifteen other vagabonds of a like kidney, whose votes always went to the highest bidder; Farmer Ploughtail, and Farmer Thrifty, with others, who were undecided; and two or three more who were eager for office, and whose suffrages might probably be secured by promising them promotion another year.

The next week on Monday the election was to open. It was arranged then, that Brandy was to invite the first-mentioned gentlemen to his tavern on the following Saturday, and ply them well with liquor and good cheer, and keep the 'steam up,' as it was called, until Monday morning, when they were to be marshalled and driven to the polls, like so many cattle, and their votes thus secured beyond any contingency. Brief was to use his influence with Farmers Thrifty, Ploughtail, etc., and Blank was to bargain with all office-expectants who might put in their claims.

Brandy was a gentleman perfectly qualified to discharge the mission which had been assigned to him. The next day he was busy about the village, penetrating every grog-hole and gambling-alley, looking up his 'troops' and insinuating himself into their good graces. He kept a smile on his face and a hearty shake in his hand for every one he met. His purse was continually open, and all drank freely, and called him a whole-souled fellow. He flattered them as 'hard-fisted' 'unflinching' politicians, who had stood the brunt of the battle for years, unwavering; though they had probably been bought and sold fifty times. He told them that it was upon *such* men the country relied in her hour of danger, and well she might rely upon them, for they were invincible. Arm in arm through the streets with his troops marched Manager Brandy, though perhaps he had not spoken to them before for months.

Saturday came round, and Brandy prepared a banquet for his friends. Scribble, Blank, Brief, and Carbuncle; Sam Jones, Bob Bowles, and Bill Smith, and twenty other 'gentlemen' were present. There was a great display of turkeys and pigs, and pastry of all sorts, with plenty of liquor to 'top off with.' All were hail fellows well met, and all were the 'cleverest souls in the world;' and every man who belonged to the opposite party was set down at once as the greatest villain that ever went unhung. There was not a man at the table, but declared himself ready to shed his blood for his party and its principles!

The 'row' wound up just as was anticipated. Every prospective 'freeman' fell under the table, and was taken up and put to bed; while Brief, Carbuncle and Company returned home to make farther arrangements for the coming contest. The next day, Brandy 'fired up' his troops early in the morning, and at regular intervals during the day; and the next night they retired in the same condition as the night previous. On election morning they were 'attended to' again, and as soon as the polls were opened, Brandy staggered them up, put tickets into their hands, and lifted them to the ballot-box, the tickets being taken and deposited amid the shouts and hurrahs of every party man in the room.

Blank managed his men by promising them, another year, any office they might ask for; and Brief, by financiering, secured Farmers Thrifty, Ploughtail, etc. But it is unnecessary to go through with a detailed history of the three days' election. All Stokeville was in commotion from the beginning to the end of the contest, produced by liquor and love of country. Some were singing, some were cursing, and some were fighting; and thus the war raged until four o'clock on the afternoon of the third day, when the polls were closed, and arrangements made for canvassing the votes.

After an hour had elapsed, it was announced that Brief was elected congressman, Carbuncle sheriff, and of course all the other candidates to the respective offices to which they had been nominated. The shouting was tremendous. Stokeville rang from centre to circumference. 'Three cheers for Brief! shouted one. 'Six cheers for Carbuncle!' shouted another; 'Nine cheers for the party!' yelled a third. The whole street was alive with boys hallooing to the top of their lungs; and it seemed as though the very houses shook with commotion.

The party which suffered a defeat began to dive and slink away, one by one, until it was impossible to find an opposition man in all Stokeville. Maddened and mortified, they had escaped from the triumphant shouts around them, and hid themselves beyond their reach. When night drew on, the fury increased. Brief, Blank, Carbuncle, Scribble, Brandy, and all the 'rank and file,' as they were called, got most gloriously drunk; annihilated decanters and wine-glasses; slashed out windows; stove the church-door, and rang the bell at midnight; broke into the houses of their political friends, and carried them, *sans* coat, vest and pantaloons, into the streets, amid songs and shouts; beside divers other matters, which shall not be mentioned. The boys fired guns and hurled blue lights and flaming balls through the air; and thus the fury was kept up, increasing in strength as the hours wore on, until the light in the east announced the approach of another day. Thus ended, for the time, the PARTISAN WARS OF STOKEVILLE. Perhaps they have their moral.

THE SUN.

THE daily sun, throned in the glowing dome,
Sheds universal blessings down. This round
Wide world, and all that it contains; the ground
Life-teeming, the dell where thick herds roam,
The busy mart, the still secluded home,
The *whole earth* were bleak chaos, but for thee!
All thriftily use thy light: none thankfully
Look upward whence their life-long blessings come.
Thou sendest, LORD! the glorious sun, to move
By thy command. Yet though no hour can fall
Unmarked by wondrous mercies of thy love,
How oft in our cold hearts thine eye doth find
Nor thankfulness nor passing thought, for all
The wonders that thou doest for mankind!

M O R N I N G .

'THE cock's shrill clarion' heralds in the day!
Now ope, from dream-land visions, myriad eyes,
And some to joy, many to sorrow rise:
The tuneful birds that throng the mountain gray
Sing joyously; and in the cottage pray
Tongues that sweet Slumber had in silence bound.
Thus, when th' archangel's trumpet-blast shall sound
Reëchoing through the universe, away
From worlds no longer tombs, shall we, on wing
Uprising, don our robes of glory!   All
The angelic harps and choirs shall then employ
New voices in their mighty song.   Then shall
The morning stars again together sing,
And all the sons of God shall shout for joy!

P O W E R S   T H E   S C U L P T O R .

TO THE EDITOR OF THE KNICKERBOCKER MAGAZINE.

SIR: I send you the translation of an article from the *Giornale Arcadico* of Rome, in relation to our countryman POWERS.   The author, Signor MIGLIARINI, is superintendent of the magnificent collection of ancient gems, coins, and medals, belonging to the Grand Duke of Tuscany, a post not only of high trust, but requiring the most extensive and intimate knowledge of art and antiquity.   To the profound learning and fine taste of Signor Migliarini, every one capable of appreciating them will bear witness, if they have had the pleasure of forming his acquaintance, or even of availing themselves of the special permission required to visit the inestimable cabinet intrusted to his charge.   Himself an artist in his youth, he was, while pursuing his studies at Rome, the companion of Coleridge and Allston, the latter of whom will doubtless hear with pleasure that his old associate inquires after him from every American with all the interest of early friendship.   Even the censure of such a man would be more valuable than the lavish and undistinguishing praise of shallow and unskilful observers, since he certainly would not condescend to criticise the works of any artist destitute of merit.   His warm and discriminating approbation of one beloved and admired for private worth as much as for professional excellence, must be hailed with honest exultation by every American, as a proof that our country is advancing in the arts that soothe, sweeten, and embellish life.   Placing it within the reach of those who do not read Italian, was therefore at once a duty of friendship and patriotism, the more imperative, since an attempt has been made to undervalue Powers as a sculptor.   Among us there is no need to stir the fires of avarice, ambition, or party-spirit; they burn with at least sufficient fierceness. But every spark of genius exhibited in the beautiful creations of the mind should be carefully fanned and cherished, that we may thus not only multiply the rational and innocent enjoyments of civilization, but leave something to posterity by which our age may be remembered.

If we fail in according to our artists due praise, it is often because our commendation is misdirected and excessive, the result of inexperience and national vanity, while any deficiency of patronage is to be attributed to the haste, impatience, and instability of our business-like existence, where every one is anticipating a future period of ease and affluence ; but for the present, so engrossing and so expensive are dress, equipage, and entertainments, has no time and no capital to spare. Yet our want of discrimination is at least as remarkable as any thing else. Thus, for example, our government have employed foreign artists of little reputation to the exclusion of our own, in reality far their superiors ; and the supposed advantage of cheap literature, but in truth the interest of a few publishers who live by literary piracy, is considered a sufficient objection to international copy-right.

Now so far as sculpture is concerned, it would seem clear that one of two courses should be adopted. If we design to ornament our capitol with the finest specimens money can command, we ought to go to masters of acknowledged excellence, to Thorwalsden for instance, and to Bartolini. In doing this however, we should give no proof of our own capacity as a people for the fine arts, and leave behind us no monuments of our progress in them. It would be evidence of nothing but that the American government having so much money to expend on statuary, had sense and taste enough to choose some one capable of executing their commission. But by employing the best native sculptors, even supposing them inferior to those already named, we should at least evince the possession of some original genius among ourselves, while every statue thus created by national patronage would become a land-mark in the history of art. Less than half the orders of congress have been given to our own Greenough, of whom we may justly be proud, and not one to Powers, Crawford, or Clevinger, whose works beside much intrinsic merit would possess imperishable historic interest. We are in the infancy of art. The men who now occupy the field can never be forgotten ; and in this view of the subject, as a citizen of the New World, not insensible to the wonders of the Old, I would rather see in our capitol statues from the chisel of any of the artists just mentioned, or from those of Dexter, Brown, or Brackett, with whose works I am less acquainted, and who are comparatively young in their profession, than those of any foreign master, however celebrated. Surely it is not creditable to us as a nation that we should employ third or fourth-rate foreign artists, while Greenough, by the unbiassed and unsolicited votes of his rivals, is elected professor of sculpture in the royal academy of Florence, and Powers extorts from the Italians his competitors the most sincere and enthusiastic admiration.

In relation to painting, congress has pursued a wiser course. The panels of the rotunda are to be filled by American painters. But in literature, on the other hand, while our press teems with republications of the flimsiest English productions ; books which look as if they had been written by contract at so much the thousand superficial feet, WASHINGTON IRVING it is understood has had lying by him for some time a most valuable MSS., whose publication is deferred because there is no adequate security for literary property; and Prescott's private fortune alone enabled him to put forth his admirable history in a becoming form. Yet no people vaunt more than we do of our distinguished men; few read more, newspapers included; and none assert higher claims to intelligence, or assume to be greater patrons of art and literature.

There is room to suspect that while we laud ourselves to the skies, it is generally without any very great reliance on our own opinions, and with a secret admiration of every thing foreign. Hence our prurient curiosity to hear all that is said of us by every itinerant book-maker, whose volume is purchased with an avidity proportioned to its dose of national and individual calumny.

Dealing too much in superlatives, we eulogize ourselves, our country, our institutions, our men, women and children; rail-roads, packet-ships, and steam-boats; every thing in short, except our servants, too much in the style of a Fourth-of-July oration. This is all a matter of course, and no one thinks of it an instant after it is uttered.

The criticism of a dispassionate and enlightened foreigner, therefore, upon any thing American, possesses double authority, on account of our habitual reverence for transatlantic opinions, and the distrust of our own self-sufficient and exaggerated praises. It often obtains greater credit than even the calm and sober approbation of those among us whose experience and cultivated taste entitle them to the highest respect, even Mr. EVERETT himself, for example; because there is a lurking, however unjust suspicion, that personal friendship or national pride may influence their judgment.

R. H. W.

HIRAM POWERS THE AMERICAN SCULPTOR.

FROM THE GIORNALE ARCADICO.

THE history of the fine arts expatiates over one of the most delightful regions of human knowledge, interesting us continually by a series of agreeable images, free for the most part from all that is revolting in every other kind of history. That portion of it which regards the early education of artists, directing them by the true path to the desired end, is of the utmost importance to studious youth, and has been the subject of attention from a very remote period. There is a peculiar charm in tracing the formation of some rare genius, who excites wonder and attains celebrity entirely unassisted by an able master. It is to an examination of this phenomenon I address myself, and in the plastic art exclusively.

Pliny on the authority of Duris tells us of Lysippus, that he became a great artist without having been the pupil of any one, noting however that Cicero held a different opinion.* If the passage of the Roman

---

* LYSIPPUM Sicyonium, Duris negat, Tullius fuisse discipulum affirmat. — PLIN., 34. 19, 6.

orator respecting Lysippus be that known to every one, there must have been some degree of prejudice in Pliny. It purports that Lysippus acknowledged the Lancer of Polycletes for his master.* But is it possible that the single statue of a young man could guide him in the great diversity of character which his numerous productions required? Beside, may we not suppose the existence of some other passage among the lost works of Cicero? It will not be useless therefore to review the few memorials left to us.† In the first place, we know of Lysippus that in his boyhood he was employed in the shop of a bronzist. It is natural therefore to believe, that guided by his inclination he began to exercise his talent in modelling. Uncertain in the choice of an instructer, he desired to take counsel from an experienced and unbiassed judge. Eupompus the painter merited this character, being already advanced in age, and having instructed Pamphylus, who at this period was the preceptor of the young Apelles. Eupompus must have known or divined the genius of Lysippus, for when the latter asked him what master he should follow, the former pointed to a crowd of men who were at hand, thus designing doubtless to teach him that he ought to imitate Nature in all her endless variety, and not any artist in his own peculiar manner. Whoever follows after another will never get before him, said Michael Angelo. It is therefore clearly forbidden to imitate any one, however celebrated, since we thus give up our birth-right as children of Nature, to become her grand-children only. From masters however, profiting by their experience, must be learned the means of imitating her by the best and shortest methods.

At present this precept deserves to be explained more at large than might be pleasing to those who recommend the imitation of Nature without selection or discrimination, not excluding even her defects. It has already been a thousand times repeated, how great is the diversity between the ancient Greeks and ourselves; between their customs and ours; how easy it was to obtain models then, and how difficult now. In our days these circumstances are studiously lost sight of. Let us proceed. Lysippus attained such celebrity that he was one of the three who were alone permitted to make likenesses of Alexander the Great.‡ He himself was wont to say that his predecessors had represented men as they are, and he as they ought to be; an assertion which remains uncontradicted.§ This is an evident indication that he sought the beau-ideal; that perfection of form of which Nature is too avaricious to bestow it by preference on any individual. I ask pardon for this digression, and return to my subject.

It is related of Silanion that he acquired fame without the aid of a master. On this topic Falconet sagaciously remarks: 'In order to make the fact surprising, it would be requisite to show that Silanion was born and had lived in a remote corner of the world where pictures

---

* POLYCLETI Doryphorum sibi Lysippus aiebat magistrum fuisse. — IN BRUT., 86.
† SED primo ærarium fabrum, audendi rationem cæpisse pictoris Eupompi responso. Eum enim interrogatum, quem sequeretur antecedentium, dixisse demonstrata hominum multitudine, naturam ipsam imitandam esse, non artificem. — PLIN., LOC. CIT.
‡ APELLES in painting, Lysippus in bronze, and Pyrgoteles in gems.
§ VULGOQUE dicebat, ab illis factos quales essent homines, a se quales viderentur esse. — PLIN., LOC. CIT.

and statues were unknown; but in the centre of Greece, amidst the master-pieces of art, in the age of Alexander, surrounded by the most celebrated artists, all astonishment vanishes.'

The instance I intend to produce includes all the conditions required by Falconet, may be regarded as unique, and therefore worthy of the greatest attention.

In the interior and agricultural portion of America, inhabited only by farmers, namely in the State of Vermont and village of Woodstock, HIRAM POWERS was born during the year 1805. He was removed while yet a child to Cincinnati, in Ohio, then a hamlet, now a city; but this, far from offering him any increased advantage, subjected him to a misfortune, the loss of his father. Necessity constrained him to support himself by his labor and ingenuity in mechanics. A secret consciousness of his genius however taught him for what he was destined. He imagined something like the plastic art while yet a stranger to its existence; and so vehement was the passion, that doubtless if he had not found, he would himself have created it. The first materials on which he employed himself, especially wax, did not entirely content him. In this state of restless desire he had approached his seventeenth year, when he saw for the first time a bust in plaster, which however destitute of merit strongly fixed his attention. After some time he found, even in Cincinnati, an amateur who attempted to model in clay the portrait of some celebrated personage. He saw the material and the mode of working it; in fine all he desired. To him this was a fortunate discovery, the realization of his dreams. To turn with avidity to the imitation of what he saw, to struggle eagerly first to equal, then to surpass it, to produce admirable likenesses, and such most assuredly as he himself had never seen, succeeded each other with such rapidity as scarcely left time to note the stages of his progress, so swift were the pinions of his happy genius.

If this artist, hurried forward by natural inspiration, had merely arrived at a servile, however faithful an imitation of nature, it would be no great wonder. But at the first glance he has formed for himself a just conception of the art of portraiture, uniting to the characteristic features the spirit and expression of the individual. He has dedicated himself to preserve the grandeur of the whole, at the same time that he represents the minutest details, and may be hailed as the DENNER of sculpture. He is careful that every head of his shall preserve, even in its smallest particulars, that type of unison, that mixture of variety and individuality coherent with themselves, which is the special attribute of nature, and totally escapes from the eyes of so many. Such a combination of rare qualities becomes marvellous in one who could not previously have had any idea of the works of ancient Greece, nor even of the sculpture of Donatello, Mino da Fiesole, and Gambarelli.

Continuing with increasing delight to model in clay, he had occasion to visit some of the principal cities of his country, whence at a favorable period, he directed his steps to Washington. Many of the distinguished men of the nation were assembled in congress, and Powers enjoyed the opportunity of multiplying portraits. Among the members of that respectable assemblage were to be found some who, having travelled among us, had acquired just notions of the fine arts. This is all one as saying, he encountered competent judges capable of appreciating the true merit of his labors.

Perceiving now that encouragement would not be wanting, Powers wisely resolved on a voyage to Italy, where he might finish what he had begun, and at the same time perfect himself in his art. Arrived at Florence, it was the same thing to find marble and direct all his energies to overcome its resistance; and when the instruments and mechanism in use were not sufficient to produce the results he sought, his own skill and ingenuity enabled him to fabricate others. He reproduced in the more obdurate material all that he had at first executed in the softer; and true and unprejudiced critics accorded him their admiration.

The fame of Apelles' portraits is known to every one. They were held so like the originals in every particular, that physiognomists founded their judgments upon them, in the same manner as if they had been living persons.*

Those who, with another name and end, occupy themselves with similar speculations, may find in the likenesses of Powers full scope for the exercise of their ingenuity, even though color be wanting. In fact, while engaged in examining some of them, another person present, who had perhaps a tincture of such knowledge, said to me with enthusiasm : ' Have you remarked that head ? What a penetrating character it has ! How expressive are all the features ! That is doubtless a new Demosthenes. That other must certainly be an upright arbiter of the laws. In that one yonder there is an energetic calmness which bespeaks the dictator,' etc., etc. Occupying myself only with the art, I listened carelessly, taking no interest in individuals unknown to me even by name, and little noting such observations, however plausibly supported. If what he said to me by conjecture was really well-founded, the truth of Pliny's sentence will be confirmed; that the admirable portion of this art consists in adding greater celebrity to men already celebrated.†

Such productions are rare in our day because many think it right to execute portrait in the heroic style, of which they have examples from the ancients, taking little pains to preserve an exact likeness. But though rare, some remarkable specimens have been produced in that line also. And among them it is impossible to pass over the magnificent and I may say colossal portrait of Pope Rezzonico in St. Peters at Rome, by the celebrated Canova.

In despite of those who detract from the merits of that great man, it cannot be denied that he has surpassed himself in the venerable image where devotion is embodied in the fine character of the head whose extensive surface enabled the artist to express the most minute details, consistently with general magnificence, so that the work seems less a statue than a picture from the pencil of Titian.

Let me anticipate, finally, the caution of some sophist who will possibly concede, what many excellent critics have already willingly con-

---

* IMAGINES adeo similitudinis indiscretæ pinxit, ut (incredibile dictu) Apion grammaticus scriptum reliquerit, quendam ex facie hominum addivinantem (quos metoposcopos vocant) ex iis dixisse aut futuræ mortis annos, aut præteritæ. — PLIN., 35, 36, 14.
† MIRUMQUE in hac arte est, quod nobiles viros nobiliores facit. — PLIN., 34, 19, 14.

ceded, the superiority of Powers in busts, but nevertheless hesitates to pronounce him a perfect sculptor, because he has not yet produced any thing in the more important branches of the art.

It should be remembered that his rapid and impetuous career in the one field has allowed him no time to labor in the other. But at present he is no longer the inhabitant of a remote region, a stranger to the arts, nor are ideas and examples wanting to his progress. He who has known how to reach so far without assistance, will in a better position easily attain all he requires.

It may be added, that he has already commenced the model of a statue, and we may reasonably promise ourselves he will carry it to the same perfection that marks every other work he has hitherto undertaken. Possessing as he does the gift of genius, joined to assiduity, a passionate love for his art, and the modesty necessary to be always capable of improvement, his success may be confidently predicted.

A. M. MIGLIARINI.

STANZAS.

STREAMLET! in thy placid face
Many an imaged form I trace ;
Bending o'er thy grassy side,
Childhood's grace and manhood's pride ;
And with feeble step and slow,
Mirrored there, the aged go.
Streamlet! as thou murmurest on
Tell of those who now are gone !

Say, who sat beneath the shade
That the willow-tree hath made ;
Drooping low thy banks above,
Whispering in its leaves, of love !
Here a mound of earth I see
Raised beneath the willow-tree :
Streamlet! as thou murmurest on,
Tell of those who now are gone !

When the moon-beam downward gave
Mournful light unto thy wave ;
When the stars together shone,
High, thy sparkling crest upon ;
When the flowers by Fancy drest
Hung in fragrance o'er thy breast :
Streamlet! as thou murmurest on,
Tell of those who now are gone !

Did some gushing eye with thee
Blend its tears of misery ?
Stooped some fevered brow to lave
In the coolness of thy wave ?
Whispered e'er a voice of love
Thy rich velvet banks above ?
Streamlet! as thou murmurest on,
Tell of those who now are gone !

Many a form hath o'er thee bent;
Many a laugh and low lament,
Many a joyous, mournful word
Hath thy rippling murmur heard.
Oft this tree, when flowers were dead,
O'er thy breast its leaves hath shed:
Streamlet! as thou murmurest on,
Tell of those who now are gone!

Came a pilgrim to thy brink,
Fast unloosing life's last link?
Gazed a child in mirthful glee,
Gentle streamlet! down on thee?
Sleep they all in Death's embrace?
Do I not their image trace?'
Streamlet! as thou murmurest on,
Tell of those who now are gone!

'One, but one to thee I name,
Often to my side that came;
First, in childhood's blooming hour,
Like a rose in summer bower,
Bent she o'er my tiny swell;
Her eyes' soft light like moonlight fell:
Ceaseless, as I murmur on,
Speak I now of CHILDHOOD gone!

'Next in maiden-pride she stood,
Bursting into womanhood;
Round her cheek dark tresses crept,
Where, half-seen, rose-blushes slept:
To a pale-browed youth she clung,
Like a leaf on aspen hung!
Like her form from off my wave,
Back her heart his image gave:
Ceaseless, as I murmur on,
Tell I now of LOVERS gone!

'She came again; the sun had set;
With drops of dew the flowers were wet:
Blent with dew and flowing wave,
Tears like glistening pearls she gave!
Pale her cheek; and lonely now
Leaned she o'er my grassy brow.
Ceaseless, as I murmur on,
Tell I now, THE LOVED had gone!

'When sad Autumn's breath had blown,
And the willow's leaves were strown,
I saw, with feeble step and slow,
That pale, life-weary mourner go!
Low beneath yon drooping shade
A fresh and lonely grave is made:
Ceaseless, as I murmur on,
Tell I now THAT MAIDEN gone!'

New-York University, Nov., 1841.   G. S. S.

THE QUOD CORRESPONDENCE.

The Attorney.

CHAPTER XI.

The opportunity which the attorney had been seeking for years was at length come. It was strange that one so notoriously infamous could have gained an ascendency over a man like Mr. Crawford, or kept on in a course of hypocrisy and deception for so long a time without detection. Often had he been placed in situations where he trembled lest his character should be unmasked and his schemes frustrated; but the devil aided him, and he did escape. The rumors in circulation against him were whispered in the old man's ear; but he shook his head, said that he knew him well; had seen nothing to give color to such tales; that they were vile slanders, and that he did not believe them.

In truth, to strong natural sense and great purity of character Mr. Crawford united a heart as guileless as that of a child. The very rumors that kept others off, drew him nearer to the attorney. His indignation was aroused at what he considered an unjust persecution, and strong in his own rectitude, he determined, as far as his influence would go, to let the world see that he was not biassed by it. His friends at last ceased to remonstrate, but shook their heads, and said he would pay for it some day.

There was one person however on whom these reports had their effect, and that was Mr. Crawford's daughter; but it was in vain that she urged her father to inquire about the man, to trace these tales to their source, and to ascertain their truth. He merely laughed; told her that she was a good girl; that he was sorry she did n't like the lawyer, and there the matter dropped; and thus it remained until his sudden and dangerous illness afforded an opportunity of which Bolton did not scruple to avail himself.

When the attorney made his appearance at his office on the morning after his interview with Higgs and Wilkins, he was so pale, his face so thin and ghastly, and his eye so black and bright, that it struck even his clerk, who was a young gentleman not ordinarily struck with any thing appertaining to the office.

During the whole of that long night his mind had been on the rack. His brain was teeming with cases similar to his own, with stories of those defrauded by designing relatives; of old men sent to mad-houses while they had their senses, and shut up with lunatics, gibbering idiots, and men stark raving mad; lying on straw in damp cells, while their relatives seized all they had and lived in luxury; of those stripped of their property by artful men whom they trusted, who wormed themselves into their confidence and then sent them into the world — beggars. Hundreds of tales of this sort sprang up in his memory, so fast and thick, that he wondered where he had heard them all. He recollected too that almost always the truth had worked out at last; those wronged had regained their own, and the wrong-doer met his meed. He had endeavored to sleep, but his slumber was but the continuation of his waking thoughts; and when he awoke it was still the same. He left his house and went to his office, and endeavored to attend to business; but he could not. Persons came to him seeking advice, or to inquire concerning law-suits which he had in his hands. Some he answered abruptly, so that they left his doors, never to enter them again; others, struck by his abstracted, anxious look, supposed that some heavy trouble had overtaken him, and went off; and many he refused to see. He remained several hours with the door locked, admitting none: then he suddenly started up, put on his hat, walked rapidly through the streets until exhausted, and returning to his office, locked the door and remained shut up until late in the day. But notwithstanding his bodily restlessness, there was no irresolution. His course was traced out clearly, decidedly, step by step. He formed plans to defend every part of his proceedings. Old musty law books had been drawn from their hiding places; the law of wills had been studied over with the most anxious care; its various changes and modifications had been noted, and books of reference, reports, old and modern, were examined. Yet the will was a clear one. It was a plain simple devise of his whole property, to his old *friend* Reuben Bolton, appointing him his sole executor, mentioning his daughter in terms of affection, but also speaking of her as illegitimate, and leaving her nothing. There was nothing in the will either abstruse or complex; nothing to hang a doubt upon; yet the attorney pored it over and over. He doubted on points of law, where he had never doubted before. He examined and reëxamined even the attestation clause; compared it with the statute; suggested difficulties and obstacles which were perfectly puerile, and which in any other state of mind he would never have dreamed of. There was scarcely a doubt that he had not raised, and was not prepared to meet. One thing only was wanting, and that was the death of Mr. Crawford. The lawyer haunted the house of the sick man like a spirit of evil. From morning till night, at all hours, he was there; sometimes in the drawing-room, sometimes stopping to inquire about him of the servants, and sometimes prowling at his very bed-side. The old man lingered for a long time, but he died at last.

It was a quaint, old-fashioned room in which he lay, unlike the rest of the house; with low ceilings, and filled with rich, luxurious, but antiquated furniture; for he had a curious taste in such matters. The walls were painted with grotesque and strange figures, engaged in some heathen ceremonial. Heavy curtains of a dark color hung from the bedstead, and down from the windows, sweeping the floor. Around the room were chairs of massive wood, elaborately carved, which he had collected with much trouble and expense; shelves, and book-cases too, with rare old volumes and dingy folios, whose writers had long since slept with the earth-worm. The whole house had been furnished to suit his daughter, with the exception of this single room; but here he had indulged his taste for the fantastic. Little by little he had collected these costly and rare articles. And now, in that dark old room, with all this mystic collection about him, the old man was passing away!

His daughter was watching at his bed-side. She knew that he must die. But hope is a still, pure spring, that wells from the bottom of the heart, and gushes up in spite of obstacles. She hoped that the filmy eye would again brighten; and that the deep labored breath would subside into the calm, regular respiration of natural sleep. How sad and dreary it was to sit there hour after hour, hearing nothing but that loud panting breath, with nothing to break the stillness except the low ticking of the watch which seemed to be whispering its warning in her ear; and the occasional far-off sound of the church-clock, which seemed like a solemn summons to the grave! How anxiously did that poor girl watch for one look of recognition, or some little mark of kindness from one who had loved her as none would ever love her again! How often did she press the hand that lay near her own, motionless and icy cold! But the pressure was not returned; and the face which once would have brightened at the slightest token of affection from her, remained rigid as if cut from stone.

It was late at night, and all was quiet, when the old man suddenly stretched out his hand, as if groping for something.

'Helen, my child!' he muttered.

The girl rose hastily, took his hand between her own, and bent over him.

'I want Helen,' muttered he, in the same indistinct tone, and looking in her face with a piteous expression, that made the tears gush from her eyes. 'I want my dear little girl, Helen.'

'I am here, father,' said she.

The old man looked long and earnestly at her; drew her closer to him; then shook his head, smiled vacantly, and laid his cheek on the pillow with an expression of patience and disappointment that made her very heart ache. He uttered something in a low tone, which she could not understand. At times he spoke of green fields; of boys in their play-grounds. She heard him murmuring the names of old gray-haired men who had gone to their graves long years before, and speaking to them as if they were children about him. Then he muttered on, sometimes of one thing sometimes of another; but always in a happy, cheerful vein; and sometimes he laughed; a gay, joyous, ringing laugh; one that might have burst from the lips of a young child; but oh! how sad from those of a dying old man! By degrees however the straggling rays of intellect seemed to concentrate; he spoke of more recent occurrences; then suddenly he raised himself in the bed, and pushed the hair back from his face.

'Helen,' said he, in a strong, clear voice, 'is that you?'

His daughter only pressed his hand.

'You're a good girl; God bless you! I'm going, Helen, and I've much to tell you.' He paused. The cloud which had for a moment been lifted, again obscured his mind, and he sank back on his pillow. The look of intelligence which had brightened his face disappeared and was succeeded by a blank, idiotic stare. Hour after hour his daughter continued to watch, until late in the night, when suddenly the respiration of the sick man became deeper and more labored; then came one long rattling gurgling breath. His daughter rose and bent over him; another deep, deep breath came; a pause; then one sharp convulsive quivering gasp; his head fell on one side; his jaw dropped; and all was over.

—

At about ten o'clock on the following morning, a short fat man, dressed in black, with a crape on his hat, walked gravely up the steps in front of the house, and rang the bell.

'I'm come to measure the old gentleman,' said he, in a sombre tone, as the red-eared servant opened the door.

'You're late in the day, my old feller,' replied the man, looking from behind the door; 'the old gentleman's off; he wo'n't wear clothes again.'

'But he will a coffin,' replied the man in black, 'and that's what I come for.'

'Oh!' exclaimed the servant, opening the door so as to admit him; 'you're the undertaker, are you?'

The man in black nodded, walked into the entry, took his hat off, brushed it with his sleeve, and laid it on a chair.

'Did he die easy?' inquired he, looking sadly at the man, who eyed him with respectful awe, and was at that moment engaged in calculating how many gentlemen that same undertaker had measured in the course of the last year. 'Did he die easy?'

'Oh! very easy, Sir, very easy,' replied the servant. 'He went off, a' most without knowing it his self.'

'That must be a great comfort to his friends, a very great comfort.'

'It was, Sir, a very great one. It makes 'em all feel uncommon comfortable.' As he spoke, he passed his hand gently over his stomach, as if something there also contributed in no small degree to his own state of complacency.

'They do n't all go off so, Sir,' said the undertaker solemnly. 'I've hee'rd tell of scenes that would curdle the blood, Sir; freeze the limbs, Sir; make the heart stand still, and all that sort o' thing, Sir. Them people always shrink; their spirits shrink before they go, and their bodies shrink arterwards. Most people stretches when they die, but *they* shrink. There was an elderly lady who I measured last week died in that very way. She went off desperate. She fit all her poor relations; tore down the bed-curtains, and finally expired in the act of biting off her own heel. Well, Sir, she was one of them that shrink. A ready-made coffin was ordered, and I measured her shortly arterwards. She was a five-foot-sixer. I went to the shop; no five-foot-sixers were ready. I returned and measured her again; she had shrunk so that she fitted in a five-foot-fourer, which we had on hand, as snug as a pea in its pod. There's evidence for you; the evidence of one's own senses!'

The red-eared servant drew in his breath solemnly.

'Gentlemen of our profession see strange sights, Sir,' continued the undertaker, growing mysterious, and sinking his voice. 'I'll tell you one. This is in confidence, you know,' said he, looking earnestly into the two opaque globes which appeared anxious to start from their owner's head into his own.

The servant nodded.

'Well, Sir, there was one man, an old man, a little fleshy, something like myself,' said he, looking with some complacency at his own little apple belly, 'but rich, Sir, rich as — as — as any body; a pious man too, Sir, quite pious; went to church reg'lar, sung loud, put money in the plate, Sir, and all that sort o' thing; but he had the blessedest long nose I ever did see. Well, he died on a suddent one day, and his nevvy, who was to get his cash, was desperate to get him under ground, for fear he would n't keep, *he* said; keep dead, *I* s'pected.' Here the undertaker paused, and looked darkly at the eyes of the servant. 'He ordered a coffin to be ready in twenty minutes. In twenty minutes I was there, and so was the coffin. We put him in it; but when we went to fasten on the lid, up stuck that nose, two inches above it. The nevvy clenched his teeth ———.'

'The lid wo'n't go on,' said I.

'It must!' said he.

'But it wo'n't; the nose wo'n't let it.'

'D — n the nose!' said he, shaking his fist at the old gentleman; 'flatten it.'

'It would be disrespectful to the departed,' said I.

'Then bore a hole in the lid and let it stick out; he *must* be buried to-day.'

'Well, Sir, we *did* bore a hole in the lid, and the nose *did* stick out; and he was buried in that way. Well, Sir,' continued he, looking cautiously about him, 'ten years arterwards I buried a young woman in that same vault, and I thought I'd look at the old gentleman's coffin. I did, Sir. The hole was there, but the nose was gone; GONE!' And the undertaker now looked horrified.

'They say bodies moulders in the tomb,' said the servant; 'perhaps noses moulders too.'

The undertaker cast a compassionate glance at the unsophisticated man before him, and then answered:

'No Sir, no Sir. He was buried alive, and as soon as he was left in that vault, and smelt its dampness, he pulled in his nose for fear he 'd catch cold. That was the way of it; and he must 'a died in fits, spasms, despair, horror, clenched teeth, and all that sort o' thing!'

'Perhaps he was smuddered there,' suggested the listener.

'It could n't 'a been,' replied the undertaker; 'that there hole was a wentilator.'

'Oh! it was, was it? Well, you know,' said the man half apologetically, 'I, not being in the coffin line, could n't know that.'

'Of course not, of course not.' The man in black then thrust his hand in his pocket and drew out a rule which he deliberately unfolded and put under his arm.

'Business brisk?' inquired the servant, apparently desirous of edging off from a subject in which he found himself beyond his depth.

'Mournfully brisk, Sir, mournfully brisk,' replied the undertaker, shaking his head, and again thrusting his hand in his pocket, from which, after a great jingling among keys and small coins, he drew out a pen-knife, and carefully passed its point under his finger-nails, which had lately been put in deep mourning. 'Scarlet fever is very prevalent among children, and there's a great demand for four-footers. But come, let's attend to the old gentleman.' So saying, he shut his knife, put it in his pocket, and motioned to the servant to lead the way. In a few minutes they returned. The undertaker took up his hat, contemplated the crape seriously, then opened the front door, and walked sadly toward his work-shop, meditating on the uncertainty of human life, and a sudden rise which had lately taken place in the price of mahogany.

The afternoon of the old man's funeral was a dreary one. The weather was wet and heavy. The rain came down in torrents. Sadness and silence brooded over the house where death had been busy. The cold unearthly chill of the grave had stolen from its home in the church vault, to claim the dead before its time. The servants moved about with stealthy steps. Conversations were carried on below the breath; all was subdued, still, dream-like. At last the undertaker came, and two or three men with him. He held whispered consultations with those who had charge of arranging the funeral. His was the only hurried step; for it was an every-day business with him; and he was only anxious that the dead should be so treated as to bring more custom to his shop. His manner broke the trance of the whole household. There began to be a slight bustle; his name was called loudly by those who wanted his opinion on different matters of funeral etiquette : a long consultation took place near the door of Miss Crawford's room; then there was a laugh suddenly cut short for fear it might reach her ear. Presently she heard heavy steps ascending the stairs, to the room over hers, where the corpse lay, and several voices speaking, and giving directions. The short, irregular, struggling tread, and abrupt, quick orders, told her that they were moving the body. Then followed a tramping of many feet, at the head of the stairs, and a rattling of the railings; then a thump against the wall.

'Take care, Bill!' said the undertaker; 'do n't let it slip! Gently now, gently; h'ist the feet over the railing; that's it. Can you and Ned hold it till I get under the head and support it ?'

'I think so,' responded a gruff voice; 'but be quick! He's devilish heavy.'

'Spry's the word,' replied the other; 'but do n't speak so loud; we're near the young lady's room, and she takes it hard, I'm told. There, come on; let it come. That's it.'

The steps now approached the room and passed the door, and in a few minutes the body was deposited in the passage. A dead silence ensued, broken only by the pattering of the rain on the window-panes. Presently a carriage drove up, then another and another, and persons were heard in the entry below, shaking their umbrellas, and stamping the wet from their feet. The coachmen in the street shouted and called to each other. One said something about a pleasant ride for the old gentleman; and then there was a loud laugh.

Helen heard all this, but it made no impression. The voices, the steps of the gathering friends all sounded in her ears with fearful distinctness, but every sense except that of hearing seemed lost.

At last all was silent. Then there was a heavy tramp in the room beneath, as of a moving multitude: the loud voice of the undertaker was heard calling to the hearse to drive on. Then came the cracking of whips and the noise of wheels; and the owner of that house had left it for ever.

CHAPTER XII.

At about dusk on the second evening after the death of Mr. Crawford, the attorney sat in his office with his arms folded, his feet thrust near the fire, and his eyes fixed on the ceiling. A single candle was burning on a table near him, with a dull heavy light, throwing all sorts of fantastic shadows and shapes on the wall. Light, it scarcely afforded; for in the remote parts of the room was an uncertain kind of mistness, through which every thing appeared strange and ghost-like. The very papers in the pigeon-holes seemed to nod and wink at each other; the high book-cases loomed out, like tall giants frowning across the room; the heavy folios which were piled along the floor, and under the desks and book-cases, wore the mysterious air of men secreting themselves; and a chair on which lay a hat, cloak and umbrella, looked like a portly man, wonderfully small in stature, but of ample dimensions, who stood up in one corner to be out of the way. The outer office was even more gloomy than the other; being a kind of receptacle for old coats, shelves filled with useless papers, book-cases tumbling to pieces, from age and neglect, and desks in various stages of decrepitude. It was full of odd angles and shadowy corners: the very place for dim figures to step suddenly out into the room; and with the sound of the wind, as it whispered and wailed through the loop-holes and crannies of the old house, it was enough to conjure up all sorts of dreary and mystic feelings.

Among this array of ruined and cast-off furniture, sat the attorney's clerk; a gaunt, thin-legged boy, with red hair, hollow eyes, large knee-joints, feet modelled after fire-shovels, and hands to match. He wore a round jacket of snuff-colored cloth extending a few inches below his arm-pits, and trousers of the same material, which reached a few inches above his hip-bones. The coat and trousers had once met, but the boy had lately taken it into his head to grow, and his shoulders, in increasing the distance between themselves and his hips, had carried the jacket with them. It is a matter of some doubt whether the boy's legs grew or not; if they did, it was downward; for they only increased the gap between the jacket and trousers; and had not a pair of stout suspenders connected his upper and lower extremities, it is not certain but that the shoulders might have sauntered off, leaving the legs altogether.

Various unaccountable impressions have always existed respecting the sympathy between a little boy's head and his hinder parts. Many think that his brain is best stimulated by the application of stimulants to the rear, and that the harder he sits the harder he studies. Nature is kind to small boys in making them tough in those aggrieved regions.

The attorney apparently labored under some of these impressions; for his clerk was perched at one of the cast-off desks, just mentioned, with Coke upon Littleton under his seat, and a volume of Blackstone, somewhat dog's-eared, under his nose. He was reading with intense earnestness; not that he had any peculiar relish for the writings of that learned gentleman; but being a little superstitious, he was at that particular moment under the firm conviction that a strange figure, with red eyes and green lips, was pleasantly peeping over his shoulder, and only waiting for him to look up to make some agreeable remark; and that from a small window with one pane, directly over the desk, and opening into a dark closet, a stout Irish lady, whom he had seen hung the week previous, was looking out, and superintending his studies with a maternal eye.

For a long time the attorney sat pondering in his back office. Over his head a solitary spider, who kept later hours than the most of his species, was straggling along the walls, with an uncertain, irresolute air, as if half asleep or out of his latitude. Bolton watched him until he was lost in the shadow of the room. Some chain of thought seemed snapped as he disappeared. The attorney unfolded his arms, rose to his feet, and muttered something to himself.

'No shrinking now; no, no! He's dead, stone dead; stiff in his coffin! *He* at least, can say nothing; and *she*,' said he, speaking aloud, 'let her do what she can! Tom!'

The long-legged boy started up and thrust his head in the door.

'Who's been here this afternoon?'

'Nobody but the old woman,' replied the boy, bluntly.

'She here again?' said the attorney, compressing his lips; 'she's always here, d — n her! What did she want?'

'Nothing now.'

'That's something strange,' said Bolton. 'What did she say?'

'She said,' continued the boy looking full in the face of the attorney, and watching the effect of his words, with a sort of malignant pleasure, 'that the last time she was here she told you her husband was dying by inches; that they had nothing to buy even bread with, and that if you let that deputy-sheriff seize his furniture under his very eyes, it would kill him outright.'

'I know it,' replied the attorney; 'something of that kind was said, but I did n't listen to her.'

'Well,' said the boy, 'the deputy *did* seize the furniture; and the man *did* die: and she came here to tell you; and to say that she hoped God would blight you in this world, and damn you hereafter. That's what she wanted; and when she said it, she shut the door, and hobbled through the entry, laughing loud enough to split her throat.'

Bolton compressed his lips, and turned deadly pale; but no further sign of emotion escaped him; and this too he mustered; for after a moment, he asked: 'Has any one else been here?'

The boy shook his head.

'Very well; shut the door; lock the outer one; and if any one knocks do n't answer.'

The boy jerked the door to, in pursuance of his instructions; and Bolton stood still until he heard the key turned in the outer door, and the boy seating himself at his desk.

'She *did* say so, and he *did* die!' muttered he. 'Well, that's *her* affair. Every thing was done according to law. Let her blame those who make laws, not those who enforce them. Now to my own affairs.'

As he spoke, he went to the drawer and took out a large brass key, with which he unlocked the iron safe, and after fumbling among other papers, finally drew out the forged will, laid it on the table, lighted another candle, and read it from beginning to end, without pausing until his eye rested on the names of the witnesses. 'George Wilkins, William Higgs,' muttered he; 'George Wilkins? George Wilkins? — ay, George Wilkins: God! how I wish you had your throat cut!' He folded up the paper, placed it in front of him, and resting his two elbows on the table, leaned his head between his hands, and seemed to read the endorsement. But other thoughts were in his mind.

'Yes he's dead; dead, in his coffin, in his vault, with the damp earth over him. He can't come back. *He* at least can't cross me. I wish one other was with him; I've got his name as a witness, and if he were dead, and I could prove it — the law is kind — it would let me do without him.' He rose, went to the safe, and feeling in one of the pigeon-holes, drew out a large Spanish knife. He held the blade to the light, and seemed in deep thought. He tried the point on the end of his finger. His teeth unconsciously became set, his nostril expanded, his dark eyes shone like jet, and he clenched the knife with a firm strong grasp. But almost at the same instant he relaxed his hand, and shook his head, muttering: 'No, no; it's too perilous.' Replacing the knife, he locked the safe and took out the key, as if to remove temptation.

'It wo'n't do; it wo'n't do!' said he, shutting his eyes, as if to keep out some fancy that *would* rise. 'Blood may come of it some day; but not now. But he has altered strangely. He's as wild and fierce as a tiger. He even begins to threaten. Let him look to himself! George Wilkins, I say look to yourself! I have you in my gripe; and go on you *shall*, step by step, until the law has separated you from the only one who stood between you and crime. Once rid of her, once where I will sink you, then betray me if you dare! Ha! ha! ha!'

Bolton laughed as he spoke; but God grant that such laughs may be few! It made even the long-legged clerk stop his ears and thrust his nose an inch nearer the dingy page in front of him; and it rang through the room so strangely, that it seemed to the attorney that another voice had taken it up, and was echoing it. He stopped and listened; but all was silent. Taking up the will, he thrust it in his pocket; and putting on his hat and cloak, went into the other office.

'You may go, Tom.'

Tom waited to hear no more. He darted from his desk; clutched up a small basket in which he usually brought his dinner; grabbed a ragged cap; blew out his candle, and dashed through the dark entry, as if fully persuaded that the devil was at his heels. As this was the ordinary manner in which that young gentleman took his departure, it excited no surprise in the attorney, who waited until the noise of his steps had died away, then returned to his own room, and bringing the light to the outer office, extinguished it and went out, shutting and locking the door after him.

He now directed his steps toward the upper part of the city. He followed a narrow street until he came to a great thoroughfare, where he joined the crowd which poured along it in the direction he wished to go. He was so intent on his plans, that he did not observe several persons who spoke to him, and who were so struck by his unusual air, that they turned to look after him when he had passed them. Had this not been the case, it is probable he would have remarked a man loitering slowly behind him, accelerating his pace when he quickened his; now stopping to gaze in a shop-window, now at the corner of a street, now lagging to read some illuminated sign; but always with his eye on him; and always preserving the same relative distance between them. Bolton at last turned into a side street, and before he had gone a hundred yards the man was at his side.

'A fine night, Sir,' said he.

Bolton looked at him, made some remark in reply, and slackened his pace to permit him to go by. The man however seemed to have no intention to quit him. The attorney then pushed on, but the stranger did the same. At length Bolton stopped and said:

'If you have any business with me, name it. If not, pursue your course and leave me to pursue mine. I will not be dogged in this manner.'

'For the matter of that,' replied the stranger, 'the street is free to every body; and if I happen to go in the same direction that you do, or to walk fast or slow, or to stop when you do, I suppose there is no law to regulate my pace or my pauses, or to prevent my walking in any direction I choose. You must know that. You are a lawyer I believe.'

'You have the devil's own coolness,' replied Bolton, with a sneer. 'I'll do you *that* justice.'

'Then I'm in luck; for I'm the first that ever got it at your hands,' replied the stranger.

Had there been light sufficient for the man who uttered this sarcasm to have seen the expression that passed over the attorney's face; the black eye lighten up till it seemed to glow with a red heat; the compressed lips, which trembled in spite of him; the clutched fingers; he would not have stood so carelessly without dreaming of harm, and might have wished his last words unsaid. 'Your name's Bolton,' continued he. 'You are a lawyer; and if you are nothing worse, I wrong you, that's all.'

'My name *is* Bolton,' said the other; 'well, what then?'

'You see that I knew you; and of course you suppose I had some object in following you.'

'Well, what is it? I can't spend the night in the street,' said the lawyer, sharply.

'You've made many others do so,' said the stranger, coldly. 'You should not turn up your nose at the broth which you have ladled out so often for them.'

Bolton made no reply, but stood stock still. The stranger, after hesitating a moment, demanded bluntly :

'Do you know one George Wilkins?'

'I do.'

'And are mixed up with most of his concerns?'

'What's that to you?' demanded Bolton. The other paid no attention to the question, but asked :

'Are you acquainted with his wife?'

'I never saw her.'

'And don't know that she's left him?'

'No.'

'Nor where she's gone to?—nor who she went with?'

'No,' said Bolton, sternly : 'I don't know the woman; never saw her. I suppose she went off because she found some one she liked better. Find *him*, and he'll tell you what you want to know. Women *will* do these things; and she I suppose is no better than the rest of them.'

The stranger clenched his fist; but before he had made up his mind what to do next, the attorney turned away and hurried along the street.

He kept on at a rapid pace until he came to the house lately occupied by Mr. Crawford. He walked past it once or twice, with a strange feeling of fear and irresolution. The whole house appeared deserted and the windows were closed, except one in the upper story, where a dim light was burning. The street was so quiet and lonely that it seemed to bring home to him a feeling of guilt which he had not experienced until then. He fancied that he saw the figure of the old man standing at his own door to guard it against him, and looking at him with such an expression of reproach and warning, that it made his heart sink. But he was not a man to give way to idle fancies. Walking hastily up the steps, he rang the bell. In a few moments the summons was answered by the red-eared man-servant, who in his usual manner opened the door just wide enough to permit his head to be seen from behind it, and in pursuance of the same usual custom looked at the person on the outside, and demanded who he was, and what he wanted. 'I wish to see Miss Crawford,' replied Bolton.

'You do, do you? Well you can't,' replied the servant positively. 'The old gentleman's just under ground; the young lady's 'most done up, and wo'n't see nobody; and none of the rest on us feels like entertainin' visiters.'

Bolton deliberated for a moment upon the expediency of kicking the man; but as the door was between him and that part of the servant's person which is usually the theatre of such performances, he merely bade him, in a sharp tone, to 'go to his mistress and to tell her that Mr. Bolton was there, and must speak to her on matters of business;' at the same time insinuating that if he did n't move rapidly he would help him. Although the servant was a fat man, and fat men are neither swift nor active, yet the idea of receiving the promised aid touched his pride; for he disappeared forthwith, and in a few moments returned and told the attorney that the young lady would see him.

The room into which he was conducted was large, and furnished in the most costly manner. Pier glasses, divans, and couches of rich silk ; tables, and ornaments of various kinds, showed that its former occupant had been lavish in all that could add to the comfort and beauty of his abode. It was with a mingled feeling of triumph and misgiving that the attorney muttered to himself, as these things flashed on his sight, 'Mine, mine; these are *mine!*' At the far end of the room, at a small table, sat Helen Crawford in deep mourning; and near her a girl of about her own age, engaged in sewing. The young lady half rose as he entered; but her companion went on sewing, and did not even raise her head from her work. Miss Crawford motioned to him to be seated, and without speaking, waited for him to open his business,. which he did in a very few words ; and after having explained the object of his visit, he said : ' Now, if you please, I will read the will.'

Miss Crawford merely bowed.

The attorney looked at her companion, who sat with her face averted, apparently without attending to the conversation.

' I have no secrets which this person may not hear,' said Miss Crawford, interpreting the look correctly.

The attorney merely bowed, and then slowly, as if nerving himself for his task, drew the will from his pocket and carefully spread it open.

' This is it,' said he, holding it to the light, and eyeing her steadily.

Miss Crawford said nothing; and the lawyer proceeded with a calm, slow voice to read the whole. As he went on, the color gradually left the cheek of the girl ; and when he had finished, she stood before him like a marble statue.

' Mr. Bolton,' said she, with a calmness that startled him, '*that* will was never made by my father. I pronounce it to be a forgery ; and I'll prove it so. The money and lands might all have gone ; but to sully the pure name of my mother, to brand my father, and stamp infamy on myself, is what I will never submit to. The proof of my mother's marriage and my own birth are too clear, and upon them I pronounce that will to be a forgery.'

' Miss Crawford,' replied the attorney, in a serious tone, ' I can make all allowance for disappointed expectations; but these are grave charges.'

' I know them to be such; and yet I repeat them,' said she; ' that paper I pronounce to be no will of my father's. It has either been altered or forged.'

' There's the signature,' replied Bolton, somewhat daunted at firmness and energy from a quarter where he expected none, and which made him desirous, if possible, of convincing her before he went away. ' You can tell whether it is your father's.' He reached the paper toward her. ' The will was executed on the tenth day of August last.'

The girl took it and scrutinized the signature; and so like was it, that she felt she might be wrong.

Slowly and half-unconsciously she read the formal attestation clause, until she came to the names of the witnesses, ' *William Higgs, George Wilkins.*'

As she pronounced these names, the girl who had first attracted the attention of the attorney started from her seat and threw a hurried glance at the paper. She was not observed however, by either; and the attorney continued :

'The will was executed on the tenth day of August last. These men, William Higgs and George Wilkins, were present at the time, and saw it, and will swear to it when it is necessary.'

The other girl now rose from her chair, went directly to the table and took the paper from the hand of the attorney. She did not look at the body of the will, but only at the signatures of the witnesses.

She placed it quietly on the table when she had done, and took her seat; but her face was like that of a corpse; and had the others been less interested in what was going on, they might have observed that though her head was bent over her work, she was doing nothing. Her hands were clasped together, and her features were convulsed as if with intense pain. She remained silent, and did not alter her position until the attorney had finished his business and was gone.

EVENING AND NIGHT.

A PAIR OF SONNETS.

' DAY unto day uttereth speech, and Night unto night showeth knowledge of Thee ! ' — PSALMS.

I.

As on a bank at eventide I lay,
The Sun o'er earth his golden splendor threw ;
He sank. Then twilight came with mellow hue,
And Nature's face grew dim in fading day :
Fast as their dazzling veil grew thin, each ray
From far peeped trembling; and as darker grew
The night, still brighter shone in the deep blue
The fixed eternal stars! My soul! thus may
It be with thee! Perchance the world's bright glare
May dazzle now ; yet when thy span of days
Begins to fade, and when earth, now so fair,
Grows dim, and death's long night draws on apace,
In Faith serene, O let thy steadfast eye
Rest on that Light that cometh from on high !

II.

WHEN heav'n is hid with many a folded cloud,
Black low'ring o'er the hills, how dark is Night !
And though the moon and stars, in glimmering white
Tip the green tree-tops, by the soft wind bowed,
And the smooth lake, where glancing ripples crowd
Their silver brothers shore-ward, yet is the sight
The dim reflection of a borrowed light.
Thus while the clouds of unbelief enshroud
The spiritual Heaven, how dark the Soul!
E'en when Heav'n-borrowed Faith shines in the skies,
'Tis darkness beautified, not chased away ;
Nor will the shade from our dim vision roll
Until the Sun of Righteousness shall rise
Upon our souls in Heaven's endless day.

H.

LITERARY NOTICES.

GERFAUT. By CHARLES DE BERNARD, author of 'The Gordian Knot,' etc. In two volumes. pp. 546. Brussels: Société Belge de Librairie: HAUMAN AND COMPANY.

BERNARD has been termed 'the BULWER of France;' and so far as we are enabled to judge, from the portions of his works which we have perused, we are inclined to consider the comparison a singularly striking and just one. 'Gerfaut' itself—for a MS. translation of which we are indebted to a friend who relieved the 'off hours' of the last season at Saratoga by rendering the original felicitously into English—abounds with the prominent characteristics of the author of 'Pelham;' his vivid portraitures of human passion; his eloquent episodes; his artistical contrasts; and his power of sustaining interest and stimulating curiosity. We hope soon to see 'Gerfaut' laid before the public; and in the mean time, to indicate a little the character of the 'venture,' for the benefit of some one of our enterprising publishers, as well as to afford the reader an insight into the conjugal relations of the French capital, we select one or two passages from the second volume, to diversify this department of our Magazine. To explain what immediately follows, it is only necessary to premise that Christian the Baron de Bergeinheim surprises Octave Gerfaut the hero in his young and beautiful wife's apartment, and overhears her declaration, in reply to the lover's ardent protestations, that she loves him! 'Hornlets or rudiments of horn' dance before the Baron's astonished eyes; the lady swoons and sinks to the floor; and straightway such a scene as this ensues:

"MADAME DE BERGEINHEIM longed to rise, but her strength failed her. She fell to her knees, and dropped at the feet of her lover. Without endeavoring to support her, he sprang from the divan, stepped over the body stretched before him, and drew his poignard.

"Christian stood at the threshold of the door, and remained immovable. There was a moment of grave and terrible silence. From without might be heard the moanings of the storm, (which seemed to redouble in violence, as if to take a part in the scene,) and a confused noise caused by the nervous rustling of the half-fainting young wife. She was extended on the floor, rumpling between her fingers the silk of the divan, and trying to lean upon it. Then in a moment all to her was hushed, except the noises without; for she had lost all consciousness, and slept in a stillness as of death. The eyes of the two men alone spake. Those of the husband fixed, threatening, revengeful; those of the lover glistening with a desperate despair.

"After an instant of this mutual fascination, the Baron made a movement as if to enter.

"'One step more, and you are a dead man!' said Gerfaut, in a hollow voice, and grasping firmly the handle of his dagger.

"Christian extended his hand, and made no other reply to this threat than a *look*; but *that* was so disdainful, the gesture so scornful, that a blade crossed over his would have appeared less formidable to the lover. Ashamed of his emotion in presence of such calmness, Octave returned his weapon to its scabbard, and emulated the threatening attitude of his antagonist.

"'Come! Monsieur,' said the latter, in a low tone; making a step backward.

"Instead of following his example, Gerfaut cast his eyes toward Clemence. She was plunged in a swoon so deep that he vainly sought to distinguish the murmur of her breath. He bent over her through an irresistible attraction of love and pity. But at the moment he had taken her in his arms to place her on the divan, and endeavored to restore her to consciousness, the hand of Bergeinheim arrested him. He scarcely felt upon his arm the pressure of those iron fingers which could have broken it in their vice-like pressure. The contact however was sufficient to recall him to the duty that honor imposed. In presence of the man whom he had insulted, the lightest sign of interest, the most distant mark of tenderness, became a new outrage; and there was a kind of cowardice in rendering himself still more culpable. If there is a being on earth to whom one owes respect, it is without doubt him whom your insult has made your enemy. Octave repressed the passionate feeling in his heart, and obedient to the beckoning which he had received, arose and said, with a grave and resigned look:

"'I wait your commands, Monsieur.'

"Christian motioned him to the door, inviting him to pass first; still maintaining, with extraordinary coolness, that politeness which a good education makes an indelible habit, but which at this moment had something in it more frightful than the most furious anger.

"Gerfaut again threw a glance of irresolution upon Clemence, and said as he advanced toward the door, in a tone almost supplicating:

"'You will not leave her without assistance? It will be too cruel to abandon her in such a state.'

"'It is not cruelty, but pity,' replied Bergeinheim, coldly; 'she will wake but too soon.'

"The heart of Octave smote him, but his countenance did not betray his emotion. He hesitated no longer, but passed out. The husband followed him without ever casting a look at the poor woman he had so pitilessly condemned; and she remained alone, stretched out in that beautiful boudoir, as if she had been in a tomb.

"The two men descended the stairs turning from the little cabinet, half-lighted by the feeble rays of the alabaster lamp. At the door of the library they found themselves in darkness. Christian opened a dark lantern with which he was provided, and which afforded sufficient light to guide their steps. To see passing in the middle of that night those two figures, their features illumined by the light of the lantern with a vacillating and yellowish reflection, one would have involuntarily foreseen some mournful drama in which each was to play an important part. Dante following Virgil through the burning paths of the doleful city walked not with a face more pale, a step more silent, than did Gerfaut, guided by his host through the long corridors of the chateau. It was with equal precaution the Baron preceded him. Fearing that the slightest noise would arouse some of the domestics, whose curiosity might be strangely excited by this nocturnal promenade, he held his breath and glided onward like a shadow; while he peered anxiously into the dark recesses of the passages they traversed.

"Without meeting any one, they at last arrived at the apartment of the Baron. With the same coolness which had hitherto characterized his conduct, Christian carefully closed the doors, lighted a candelabra upon the mantel, filled with candles, and turned toward his less calm companion. In circumstances which require quick decision; in the midst of those scenes, rare but solemn in life, where the shortest reflection is a dangerous delay; where voluntary action becomes imperious necessity; men of a poetical spirit have a singular disadvantage. The imagination, so vivid in meditative hours, in solitude, becomes their enemy, at times a fatal one. At each new idea it leaps forth to the encounter, in widely divergent flights, which encounter shades the most singular, ramifications the most imperceptible. But this promptness of comprehension, this excessive enlargement of the *pores of the soul*, impoverish their strength. They cause a kind of perspiration, fertile in conception, but slothful in action. The imagination then expands in such a manner before all things, that it penetrates none. It grows dull without piercing; it dazzles itself with its own light, and is lost in the infinity that it opens for itself, instead of arriving at the goal. It is a weapon which scatters, and whose cuts become more powerless as they cover a greater space.

"Since he had left the parlor, Gerfaut had been a prey to all these besettings of that strange torture. By an inexplicable physiological phenomena, his mind, instead of entering into the quick of that scene, so pressing, so imperious, was plunged like an eagle into the immeasurable spaces of the whole drama. In an instant he had devoured the past and the future of his passion; and he was almost entirely distracted from the present. His first interview with Clemence; the various incidents of that year, so full of remembrances; his success in her love, hour by hour; the thousand conquests, preludes of the last; and then the day so delightful changed into a night so horrible! The woman of his heart destroyed for him and by him!—the man to whom he must render a bloody account!—all these images flashed before his eyes like the dry leaves that a water-spout rolls up and scatters to the winds. Unconquerable emotion of regret, a pity full of despair, the foreboding of inevitable catastrophes, softened his heart by dazzling his mind. Then he saw under colors the most odious the egotism of his love, and the feeling which had imposed on him as a duty toward himself the completion of the triumph. That exigence so common of vanity appeared to him cowardice the most disgraceful. He detested himself. The last look of Clemence, as she fell fainting at his feet, that look of pardon and of love pierced his heart like a dagger. He had destroyed her!—the woman whom he loved!—the queen of his life! Hell was in the thought. For a few moments he could not conquer his distress; a dizziness seized him at the sight of the abyss hollowed out by his own hand, and into which he had cast the dearest part of his soul. It was like an emotion of frightful intoxication. The beating of his pulse, the convulsive twitching of his nerves, and an involuntary trembling, shook his whole frame. It was a horrid moment for him; for the violence of his emotions did not deprive him of perception, and he saw himself trembling, without being able like Bailey to say: 'It is with cold.'

"Near that pale face, on which a thousand passionate emotions fluttered like clouds in a storm, the face of Bergeinheim remained cold and sombre as a northern sky. It was a statue of marble whose contact is ice, by the side of a bronzed statue red from the furnace; or rather it was the knight about to grasp Don Juan with his sepulchral hand. At this moment the poet was beneath the soldier. His lofty intelligence found itself vanquished by a common mind. When Octave met Bergeinheim's glance, it was so full of implacable vengeance, it exhibited such a venomous hate, that he started as if stung by a viper. In the face of that outraged husband, so lofty in appearance and carriage, the poet felt the inferiority of his own position.

"A poignant emotion of anger and vanity came at length to his aid. Overcoming by a supernatural effort the irresistible powers to which he had yielded for an instant, he said to his nerves: 'Tremble no longer!' and his nerves became iron; to his heart, 'Calm thy beatings!' and his heart became stone. He stifled in his heart all the stings of conscience which might weaken its firmness, and resumed the disdainful countenance which was habitual to him. His eyes returned to those of his enemy, to their look of mortal defiance; and he began to speak like a man accustomed to conquer the events of his life.

" ' Before any explanation,' said he, ' I ought to declare on my honor that there is but one guilty, and that one is myself. The shadow of a reproach cast at Madame de Bergeinheim would be on your part the grossest injustice. I introduced myself unbidden and unauthorized into her apartment. I had just entered when you arrived. Necessity obliges me to confess a passion which is an insult to you! I am ready to repair it by any satisfaction in my power. But in placing myself at your discretion on this point, I must exculpate Madame de Bergeinheim from every thing that might cast a stain on her virtue or her reputation.'

" ' As to her reputation,' replied Christian, ' I will take care of that; as to her virtue ——— '

" He did not finish the sentence, but his countenance assumed an expression of incredulous irony.

" ' I swear to you, Monsieur,' replied Octave, with deep emotion, ' she is as innocent, as she should be free from insult: I swear to you ———. What oath shall I take, that will compel you to believe me? I swear to you that Madame de Bergeinheim has been false in none of her duties toward you; that I have never received from her the slightest encouragement; that she is as innocent of my folly as an angel in heaven!'

" Christian shook his head with a scornful smile.

" ' This day will be the most miserable of my life, if you do not believe me,' continued Gerfaut, with increased vehemence. 'I tell you Monsieur, that she is innocent — innocent! Do you hear? I have erred through an unworthy passion. I aimed to take advantage of you. You know that I had the key of the library. I made use of it, without her suspecting it. I would to heaven that you had been a witness of our whole interview! Can any one prevent a man from entering the apartment of a woman in spite of her, when he has succeeded in procuring the means himself? I repeat to you ——— '

" ' Enough, Monsieur,' replied the Baron, coldly. ' You now do all that any man could do in your situation — all that I could do myself. But this discussion is superfluous. Leave to her the task of exculpating herself. At this moment it should only be a question between you and me.'

" ' When I protest to you on my honor ——— '

" ' Monsieur, in an occurrence like this a false oath is not dishonorable. I have been a bachelor too, and I know that every outrage is permitted against a husband. Let us say no more about it, I pray you, and let us come to facts. I look upon myself as insulted by you, and you are bound to give me satisfaction for that insult.'

" Octave made a sign of acquiescence.

" ' One of us must die,' continued Bergeinheim, carelessly leaning against the mantel.

" The lover bowed his head a second time. ' I have offended you,' he said; ' it is for you to regulate the reparation that I owe you.'

" ' There is only one possible, Monsieur. Blood alone can wash out the stain. You know this as well as I. You have dishonored me; for that you owe me your life. If chance favors you, you will be rid of me, and I shall be wronged every way. There are some few arrangements to make. We will settle them immediately, if you have no objection.'

" He moved forward a chair which he offered to Gerfaut, and took another for himself. They sat down upon each side of a desk which was in the centre of the apartment, and with an apparently equal imperturbable coolness and haughty politeness prepared to discuss this deadly question.

" ' I need not repeat to you,' said Octave, ' that I agree now to all that you may decide upon; the weapons, place, witnesses.'

" ' Listen to me,' interrupted Bergeinheim. ' A moment ago, you spoke to me in favor of that young woman, in such a manner as to lead me to think that you do not wish to destroy her in the eyes of the world. I hope then that you will accede to the proposition that I am going to submit to you. An ordinary duel between us would arouse suspicions, and inevitably lead to a discovery of the truth. They would seek a plausible pretext; no matter what reason we should choose to give before witnesses. Between a young man who received into a house and a husband you know there can be but one motive for the duel, which is very obvious. In whatever manner ours shall end, the honor of that woman would be dead upon this earth, and it is that which I wish to avoid. She bears my name.'

" ' Explain your wish,' replied Octave, not seeing what his adversary wished to arrive at.

" ' You know, Monsieur,' replied Bergeinheim, ' that an article of the law gives me at this instant the right to slay you. I have not done it for two reasons; first, a gentleman should depend upon his sword and not his poignard, and then your dead body would embarrass me. Instead of using my right, I am going to risk my life against yours. The danger is the same for me, who have never insulted you, as for you, who have committed the greatest outrage against me with which a man can wither the existence of another. Thus the game is already unequal. But you understand that if there should be a person in the world who could suspect the cause of our duel, it will become a thousand times more so. You risk no more; while living or dead, I shall be publicly dishonored. I would willingly sacrifice my blood but not my honor.'

" ' If it is a duel without witnesses that you desire, I consent to it. I have entire confidence in your honor, and I hope you will concede the same sentiment to me.'

" Christian made a slight inclination of his head, and continued: ' It is more than a duel without witnesses, for the result must be regarded as an accident. It is the only means to prevent the scandal which I fear. This is what I have to propose to you. You know that to-morrow there is to be a boar-hunt in the forest of Mares. When the hunters have posted themselves, we two will take our stations at a place which I shall point out, where we shall be beyond the view of the other hunters. When the boars loup the enclosures, we will fire on each other at a signal agreed upon. In this manner the result, whatever it may be, will pass for one of those accidents of which the chase affords frequent examples.'

" ' I am a dead man!' thought Gerfaut, when he saw that the fusee was chosen by his adversary, and called to mind his extraordinary skill with that weapon, of which he had seen ample proofs. But far from betraying the least hesitation, his countenance assumed a still more arrogant expression.

" ' This kind of combat appears wisely chosen,' said he: ' I agree to it; for I desire as much as you that eternal oblivion should cover this unhappy affair.'

" ' Since we have no seconds,' replied Bergeinheim, ' we must arrange the lesser points, that nothing can betray us; it is inconceivable how circumstances the most trifling are often the most troublesome evidences! I was lately on a jury. We condemned a man to death upon the sole evidence of the wadding from a gun. Let us take care that nothing of the kind happens to us. I think that I have guarded against every thing. If you perceive I have forgotten any thing, will you be so kind as to mention it? The place of which I was speaking to you is a straight path, but open and in a right line. The ground is perfectly level, and runs from the south to north; so that at eight o'clock in the morning we shall have the sun obliquely. There will then be no advantage in position. Upon the skirt of the wood is an old elm tree; at about fifty paces in the path, is the stump of an oak, cut this year; these will be the two places where we meet. Is the distance agreeable to you?'

" 'Farther or nearer, it matters not. Nearer if you wish.'

" 'Nearer would be imprudent. In the hunt we are never stationed at a less distance from each other. Beside, fifty paces with a rifle is less than fifteen with a pistol. The first point is then arranged. We will remain covered, although it may not be the custom. A ball might strike the head where the cap covers it, and if it was not pierced through, that would give rise to suspicions; for in the chace the hunters never go with their heads bare.'

" Bergeinheim continued thus to enter into the multitude of details, attesting the singular precaution with which he had calculated the smallest incidents in an event of this kind. Octave could not repress a feeling of admiration at seeing this dispassionate zeal; playing with the preparations of death as a young girl with the flowers with which she is going to decorate her head on the night of a ball.

" 'It remains for us,' said Christian, 'to determine who shall have the first fire.'

" 'You, most certainly; you are the injured party.'

" 'You do not entirely grant that I am the injured party; it is therefore in dispute; and I cannot be judge and party at the same time. We must yield ourselves to chance.'

" 'I declare to you that I will not fire first,' interrupted Gerfaut.

" 'Reflect that it is a duel unto death, and that such delicacy is childish. Let us agree that he who gains the advantage of the fire will station himself at the skirt of the wood, and await the signal that the other shall give when the boars break the enclosure.'

" He took from his purse a piece of money, and threw it into the air.

" 'Head!' said the lover, forced to yield to the will of his adversary.

" The chance is yours,' replied Christian, carelessly looking at the crown; 'but remember, that if at the signal given by me you do not fire, or fire into the air, I will use my right. You know I rarely miss my aim.'

" These preliminaries settled, he took from a closet two rifles, loaded them with balls, measuring to see that they were of the same length and calibre. He put them back into the closet, turned the key, and offered it to Gerfaut.

" 'I would not so insult you,' said the latter.

" 'In fact, this precaution is useless. To-morrow you shall have the choice. Now that every thing is agreed upon,' continued he, in a serious tone, 'I have one request to ask of you, and I believe you have too much honor to refuse it. Swear to me that whatever may be the result, you will inviolably guard this secret. My honor is at your discretion this moment. As a gentleman to a gentleman, I require you to respect it.'

" 'If I have the sad fate to survive,' replied Gerfaut, not less seriously, 'I make the oath that you ask of me from the bottom of my soul. But I myself have a question to ask of you. Supposing the contrary event should occur? What are your intentions in regard to Madame de Bergeinheim?'

" Christian looked upon his adversary a moment, with a gaze that seemed to wish to read his most secret thoughts. 'My intentions!' said he, at length, in a tone of surprise and anger; 'this is a strange question. I do not recognize in you the right thus to question me.'

" 'My right is strange, in truth,' replied the lover, with a bitter smile; 'but whatever it may be, I shall use it. I have forever destroyed the happiness of that woman; if I cannot repair my fault, I ought at least, as far as it depends on me, to weaken its effects. Will you then answer me: if I fall to-morrow, what will be her fate?'

" Bergeinheim was silent, and bent his eyes with a sombre and pensive air upon the floor.

" 'Listen to me, Monsieur,' continued Gerfaut, with deep emotion; 'when I tell you she is not guilty, you do not believe me, and I despair of convincing you, for I understand your distrust. Nevertheless this will be the last word that will pass my lips, and you know that the words of a dying man are entitled to belief. If to-morrow you are revenged on me, I pray you let that atonement satisfy you. You see I do not blush to ask a favor of you. I implore you on my knees. Be kind to her! spare her! It is not her pardon I ask of you; it is pity for her innocence. Treat her kindly — honorably. Do not make her still more unhappy.' . . .

" He ceased, for his voice failed him, and he felt the tears in his eyes.

" 'I know my duty,' replied the Baron in a tone as harsh as that of Gerfaut had been pathetic: 'I am her husband, and I do not recognize the right in any person, and you the least of all others, to interpose between her and me.'

" 'I foresee the fate you have in reserve for her,' replied the lover with indignation. 'You will not spill her blood, for that would be imprudent; but you will kill her by degrees. You will make her die a new death, to satisfy your want of open vengeance. You are the man to plan each detail of her torture as coolly as you have just settled the preliminaries of our duel.'

" Instead of replying, Bergeinheim lighted a candle to put an end to the discussion.

" 'To-morrow, Monsieur,' said he.

" 'A moment,' cried Gerfaut, rising; 'you refuse me then a word which will quiet my fears as to the fate of the woman whom my love has destroyed?'

" 'I have nothing to answer you.'

" 'Then it is for me to protect her, and I will do it despite you and against you!' "

Desiring the reader to remark the peculiarly *French* character of the foregoing discussion, and the sanguinary preparations in which it results, we proceed to another extract, which finds the aggrieved husband returned to the apartment of his beautiful but as he fancies fallen wife. We have rarely encountered any thing more melo-dramatic.

"Recovering from her swoon, Madame de Bergeinheim remained for some time plunged into a torpot in which she scarcely knew her own thoughts. At first, she imperfectly saw the curtains of the bed on which she was lying, and believing herself suddenly awakened from her usual siesta, she tried to sleep again. By degrees, thought began to kindle up the shades of her mind. Half conscious of her misery, she opened her eyes, and saw that she had been sleeping full-dressed. At the same time her chamber appeared illumined by a light far more vivid than that of the lamp which was wont to burn in it during the night. Through the half-opened curtains, she beheld a large shadow reflected on the wall immediately opposite the bed. Raising herself up, she distinctly saw a man sitting in the angle of the chimney. Recognizing her husband, she fell back upon her pillow, frozen with terror. *Then* she remembered every thing; and the scene in the boudoir flashed through her mind, in all its awful details. She felt herself near swooning a second time, as she heard the steps of Christian advancing toward her; although he walked with great precaution. With a childish instinct she closed her eyes again, hoping that he would think her asleep; but her breathing betrayed her agitation and terror.

"The Baron gazed at her a moment in silence, and then opened the curtains.

"'You cannot pass the night thus,' said he; 'it is nearly three o'clock. You must go to bed as usual.'

"Clemence trembled at those words, though they had nothing very harsh in their tone. Without replying, she obeyed with a mechanical docility; but scarcely risen, she was compelled to lean against the bed, for her trembling limbs could not sustain her.

"'Do not be afraid of me,' said Bergeinheim, stepping back a few paces. 'My presence here has nothing in it which ought to alarm you. I wish only that it should be known I passed the night in your chamber; for it is possible that my return may arouse some suspicions. You know that our affection is only a comedy for the benefit of our domestics.'

"There was in the affected lightness of these expressions a sarcasm which the young wife felt, even to the inmost recesses of her soul. She had anticipated an explosion of fury, not quiet scorn. Her revolting pride brought courage to her.

"'I do not deserve such treatment from you,' said she; 'do not condemn me unheard!'

"'I have asked you nothing,' replied Christian, who had seated himself near the chimney; 'undress yourself, and sleep, if that be possible for you. It will be useless that Justine should make comments to-morrow on your night-dress or the alteration of your features.'

"Instead of obeying this time, she advanced toward him and endeavored to speak; but her emotion deprived her of the power. She was obliged to sit down.

"'You treat me *too* ill, Christian!' said she, when she had recovered her speech; 'I am not guilty; not so guilty as you suppose,' continued she, dropping her head.

"He looked at her a moment attentively, and then replied, without the slightest emotion:

"'You should know that my greatest wish is to be persuaded by you. I know appearances are often deceitful. Perhaps you can explain to me what passed here to-night. I am still disposed to believe you. Swear to me that you do not love M. de Gerfaut.'

"'I swear it!' said she, in a feeble voice, without raising her eyes.

"He took down a small silver crucifix which hung at the head of the bed.

"'Swear to me on this Christ,' said he, presenting it to his wife.

"She vainly tried to raise her hand; it seemed glued to the arm of the chair.

"'I swear it!' murmured she a second time, while her face became livid as death.

"A savage laugh, which sounded more like a groan, escaped the lips of Christian. Without adding a word, he put the Christ back in its place, and opening a secret panel between the windows, he placed a little cabinet on the table before his wife. At sight of this, she made a movement as if to seize it; but her strength failed her, and she leaned back to find a support.

"'Perjured before your husband and before your God!' said Bergenheim, slowly.

"Clemence remained for a long time unable to reply. Her respiration was so painful, that each breath seemed a suffocation. Her head, after swaying about the back of the chair without finding a position less painful, finally fell upon her breast, like an ear of corn broken by the rain.

"'If you have read these letters in my cabinet,' murmured she, when she had recovered strength to speak, 'you must see that I am not as unworthy as you think me. I am very culpable; but I have yet a right to pardon.'

"Bergenheim's features remained imprinted with the most desperate impassibility, while he listened to the words of justification which Clemence continued to utter, in a feeble and broken voice.

"'I know that I deserve your hate. . . . But if you knew what I suffer, you would pardon me! You left me in Paris, very young. . . . I ought to have contended more strongly. Nevertheless I used all my strength in the struggle. . . . You see that within a year I have become pale, and am much changed. I have grown old with a few years. I am not yet what the world calls a woman. . . . Lost! You ought to call him ——'

"'Without doubt,' replied Christian, with irony. 'Oh! you have a loyal chevalier!'

"'You do not believe me! you do not believe me!' replied she, wringing her hands in despair. 'But read those letters, read the last. See if it is thus one writes to a woman who is entirely guilty.'

"She longed to seize the package in the hands of her husband; but instead of giving it to her, he walked over to a candle, lighted it in the blaze, and threw it, all on fire, into the grate.

"Clemence uttered a shriek, and rushed to recover it; but the iron arm of Bergenheim seized her by the waist and thrust her back into her chair.

"'I understand why you cling to that correspondence!' said he, in a tone less calm than hitherto; 'but you are more tender than prudent. Suffer me to destroy the evidence which accuses you. Do you know that I have already slain a man on account of those letters?'

"'Slain!' cried Madame de Bergenheim, whom these words maddened, for she did not understand their true meaning, but applied them to her lover. 'Ah, slay me too, for I spoke false when I told you I repented. I do *not* repent! I *am* guilty. I have deceived you. I love him, and I abhor you! Yes, I *love* him! Slay me! I tell you I love him! Now slay ME!'

"She threw herself on her knees before him, and crept along the floor, which she struck with her small white hand, as if trying to break it. Christian raised her up, and re-seated her in a chair, despite all resistance. For a few moments it was difficult for him to hold her in it, so violent was the paroxysm which had seized her. She writhed in the arms of her husband; and the only accents which escaped her lips were the words repeated in a stifled voice, with the monotony of madness, 'I love him! Slay me! I love him! Slay me!'

"This grief was so horrible, that even Bergeinheim began to pity her.

.   .   .   .   .   .

"Presently she became immovable, and spoke no more. With a feeling of compassion, he left her and resumed his place. They remained for some time in silence, seated on each side of the chimney; he leaning his forehead against the marble; she bent in her chair, her face hidden in her hands; more distant from each other than if a whole world had separated them. The pendulum of the clock alone broke the solemn stillness, and rocked with its monotonous vibration the sad, sad reveries of the married pair.

"A noise against one of the windows interrupted this gloomy scene. Clemence sprang up as if revived by a galvanic shock. Her wandering eyes met those of her husband, interrupted in his mournful reflections by this unforeseen incident. He made an imperious gesture, to command silence, and both gazed at each other with mute attention and anxiety.

"The noise was heard a second time. A grazing against the window-blind was followed by a sound evidently produced by the throwing of something hard against the pane.

"'It is a signal,' said Christian, in a low voice, looking at his wife. 'You ought to know what it means.'

"'I do not, I swear to you,' replied Clemence, her heart palpitating with new emotion.

"'I am going to prove him: he is there, and has something to say to you. Arise and open the window!'

"'Open!' said she, with an air of terror.

"'Do what I bid you. Would you have him pass the night under your windows? Some of the servants may see him.'

"At this command, pronounced in a severe tone, Clemence arose, observing that the projection of their shadows on the ceiling might be perceived from without when the curtain was drawn. Bergeinheim changed the position of the candles, while his wife slowly directed her steps to the window whence the noise had proceeded. Scarcely had she opened it, when a purse fell on the floor.

"'Now close it again,' said the Baron. His wife obeyed with a passive docility which rendered her incapable of any effort of her own. He took up the purse, which was wrapped in worsted, and took from it the following billet:

'I HAVE destroyed you—you for whom I would willingly die. What avail now my regrets and my despair? All my blood will not wipe away one of your tears. Our position is so frightful, that I tremble to speak of it. I must tell you the truth, however terrible it may be. Do not curse me, Clemence! Do not blame me for that fatality which obliges me still to torture you. In a few hours I shall have expiated the wrongs of my love, or you, yes, you will be free! Free! Pardon me for the word. I feel how odious it is, but I am in too much anguish to find another. Whatever may happen, let me place at your disposition all the aid which it is possible for me to offer you; to give you at least a choice of miseries. If you never see me more, to live with him will perhaps be beyond your strength, for I know that you love me. In the contrary case — Here words fail me. I know no expression for my thoughts; and I dare address you in neither counsel nor prayer. All that I feel, is the desire to tell you that my existence wholly belongs to you; that I am yours till death! But I scarcely have the courage to throw at your feet the offering of a destiny already so sad, too soon perhaps bloody. . . . A fatal necessity at times imposes actions which opinion condemns, but which the heart absolves, for that alone can understand them. Hereafter you will feel the want of the freedom of suffering, so much will you find your palms unpitied by all who surround you. This right of grief I would secure to you. Do not blame me for what you are going to read. Never surely have words like these left a heart more desolate. During the whole day a post-chaise will await you behind the hill of Martigny. A fire lighted upon the rock, which you can see from your apartment, will give you notice of its presence. In a short time you can reach the Rhine. A faithful valet will be in waiting to conduct you to Munich, to the house of one of my relatives, whose character and position will guarantee to you an inviolable asylum. If your aunt or the other persons of your family cannot give you a sufficient protection, that which I present to you will at least secure you from all tyranny. There at least you will be permitted to weep. This is all that I can offer you. My heart is ready to break at this impotence of affection. When one crushes the scorpion upon the wound where he has infused his venom, he heals it. My death even will not repair the evil I have done you. It will be only one grief more. I did not know that suffering had a refinement so bitter. Do you comprehend this feeling of despair which I feel at this moment? To be loved by you has been for a long time the only wish of my heart; and now I must repent that I have seen it realised. In pity for you, let me ask that you will love me with a love that perishes only with thy life; that my memory will be peace to you, and that you will be able to sleep on my tomb. All this is so sad that I have not courage to continue. Adieu, Clemence! Once more, one last adieu! I should rejoice in my sorrow, to be able to say I love you. I dare no more. I feel myself unworthy to speak thus, for there is a ban upon my love. Is it not I who have destroyed you? The only language which seems still left for me is that which the assassin addresses to God, with his knees and face on the marble of the church: 'Pardon me!''

"Having read the billet, the Baron handed it to his wife, without saying a word, and resumed his sombre and pensive attitude.

"'You see what he asks of you,' said he, after a long interval, observing the lack-lustre glare with which the eyes of Madame de Bergeinheim ran over the paper.

"'My brain is so distracted,' replied she, 'that I do not know whether I understand or no. What says he of death?'

"The lips of Christian scornfully contracted. 'It does not concern you,' said he. 'No one slays women.'

"'They die without that,' replied Clemence, pausing, and looking wildly at her husband. 'You must then fight!' cried she at last, in a tone whose expression would not have been noticed in another tongue.

"'In truth you have guessed it,' replied he, with an ironical smile. You see, we all have a character to play. The woman deceives the husband; the husband fights with the lover; and the lover, to finish the comedy, proposes an elopement to the wife; for there is the bottom of his letter, in the midst of his oratorical precautions.'

"'You fight!' she said, rising up, with the energy of despair. 'You fight for me, unworthy and miserable as I am. . . . But it is I who ought to die. What have you done? And was he not free to love? I alone am guilty! I alone have offended you; and I alone deserve punishment. Do with me what you wish, Monsieur; shut me up in a convent, in a prison. Bring poison. I will drink it.'

"The Baron smiled scornfully.

" ' You are very much alarmed lest I may kill him,' said he, looking fixedly at her, his arms crossed over his chest.

" ' I fear for you — for us all. Do you think that I could live, after shedding your blood? If there *must* be a victim, take me ; or at least *commence* with me. In pity, say that you will not fight.'

" ' Think that you have the chance to become free, as he himself has told you.'

" ' Spare me ! ' she murmured, trembling with horror.

" ' It is a pity that it should require blood, is it not ? ' replied Bergenheim, with implacable mockery ; the adultery would be very sweet without that ! I am sure you must deem me brutal and unfeeling, thus to overlook your own estimate, and take your honor in earnest. Favor ! It is I who have a favor to ask of *you*. That astonishes you, perhaps. So long as I live, I will protect your reputation in spite of yourself ; but, if I die, try to keep a better guard over your passions. Be content that you have been false to me ; do not outrage my memory. I am rejoiced at this moment that we have no children ; for I should fear to intrust them to you, and should be compelled to deprive you of their guardianship. It is one sorrow the less. But as you bear my name, and I cannot deprive you of that, let me pray you not to trail it in the dust, when I shall be no longer here to guard it.'

" At these cruel words, the young woman became fixed on her chair, as if all the fibres of her body had been successively broken.

" ' You crush me to the earth ! ' said she, feebly.

" ' That is shocking to you,' continued the husband, whose vengeance seemed to revel in the most bitter taunts. ' You are young ; it is your first step ; and you have not yet finished your adventures. Quiet your fears. One gets accustomed to every thing. A lover always knows the sweetest phrases to console a widow, and conquer her repugnances. He has already commenced in his letter. If you become free, he will talk to you of Italy, of England, of America. He will tell you that one can live any where ; that if the crime — oh, he does not call it crime ! — he will call it ' passion,' ' oppressed love ' — that if your passion is proscribed in France, every where else it can ! —— '

" ' You kill me, Monsieur ! ' murmured she, falling almost unconsciously from her chair.

" Christian leaned toward her, and took her hand. ' Ponder over it much. If he kills me to-morrow, and asks you still to follow him, you will be infamous in obeying him. He is a man to make boast of you ; (do not writhe thus ;) that is frequently done. He is a man to lead you in his train, like a cour-tesan.'

" ' Some air ! · · · for pity ! · · · I am dying ! '

" Clemence closed her eyes, and feeble convulsions agitated her lips. The Baron at last felt the vindictive cruelty with which he had spoken begin to soften. After having pitilessly tortured the soul, he was shaken and almost disarmed by physical suffering. That inanimate woman whom he had just crushed with his scorn, had awakened in his bosom a sentiment approaching to remorse ; and it was with a kind of affection that he bestowed his care upon her. Without her having made a single movement, he undressed her and laid her on the bed. Seeing that there was nothing dangerous in her situation, and that it was only a general relaxation of the system caused by a succession of deep emo-tions, he left her side when he saw her eyes open again, and resumed his place in the angle of the chimney.

" The remainder of the night passed without any new incident. To have seen that unhappy man sitting in silence ; his forehead leaning upon his hand, and at a few paces distant that wretched woman lying in the pallor and immobility of death, one would have deemed it watching by the dead rather than a conjugal tête-à-tête. From time to time the crackling of the wainscotting, a distant sigh of the expiring storm, or a stifled groan from beneath the alcove, broke upon the silence. The noise of the parlor time-piece striking the hours, which were repeated by the great clock of the chateau, had itself the sound of a sepulchral knell. The candle, setting fire to their collerettes of paper, flick-ered in their sockets, and cast strange, unearthly shadows, like wax-tapers on a bier : yet Christian thought not of lighting others. Insensibly they subsided into darkness. Dim rays began to penetrate through the blinds. A piercing chill in the atmosphere announced that day was dawning. The morn-ing chaunt of the cock followed a moment after ; the barking of dogs in their kennels succeeded ; and at length the concert of birds, aroused from their sleep in the garden, was reëchoed by turns. The night had passed, and a new day had dawned, radiant for the world, but for a few, how full of threat-ening and alarm ! "

We are not averse, in these our days of servile imitation of foreign follies and vices, to place before American readers — as in the work before us, whose heroine is a married woman — an example of the kind toleration with which conjugal infi-delity is regarded in ' fashionable ' countries, par excellence, where a lady without her *cicisbeo* or *cavalier servente* is scarcely considered as belonging to legitimate ' society.' Long may it be before it shall be said of us, as it has been written by a shrewd observer of men and manners, of France and Italy, that there the social ' intercourse between the sexes begins where it usually ends in other countries ; by consummation ! ' But foreigners have admitted that we are improving under their tuition, and that by and by we may hope to acquire a very respectable reputa-tion for the neglect of moral duties. ' There is now a greater conjugal fidelity in New-York, than here,' said a French cavalier to our ' American in Paris ; ' ' but this is owing to facility of living, better assorted matches, and especially to a want of gallantry and address in the other sex. I tarried in New-York but two months, and I assure you I made quite a revolution among the women there. I do not say the New-Yorkers are naturally deficient of amiable qualities ; there are many who would fall in love, but have notes to pay in the bank ! '

The Glory and the Shame of England. By C. Edwards Lester. In two volumes. pp. 546. New-York: Harper and Brothers.

These volumes will excite attention, both at home and abroad. They are written in a style of spirited gossip, and with fearlessness, certainly, but as it seems to us, not always in good taste; nor are the descriptive portions in general very strikingly original. This we discovered, before reading thirty pages, in the *rifaciomento* of Mr. Dickens' eloquent reflections upon sleeping London, and Mr. Irving's emotions on approaching Westminster Abbey, 'with its towers rising in the blue haze above St. James' Park.' Yet Mr. Lester has one merit which above all others will insure success to his work. He is an enthusiastic observer and an earnest writer. He sees vividly and he enjoys deeply; and with these traits he could scarcely fail to carry his readers with him. We like his pictures of *men* better than his sketches of *things.* The account of his visit to Campbell, to Mr. Dickens, and other eminent authors and personages, forms the most attractive portion of the volumes; as is sufficiently evidenced indeed by their immediate translation to the journals of the day. Something in this kind is the interesting narrative of the last days of Byron, communicated to the author by an American gentleman who spent the winter of 1823, '24 in Greece, was intimately acquainted with the great poet, and was at Missolonghi when he died. The reader will perceive in the following a confirmation of the high opinion which Byron entertained of our country and countrymen, and which he manifests so often in his letters to his publisher, Murray; and especially, his gratification at the opinions of 'the American Irving,' touching his works, then in course of publication:

"In a few days I received another note from him, requesting me to call and bring with me Mr. Irving's Sketch Book, if I had it, or could get it for him. As that is a book I always carry with me, I took it in my hand and went once more to the illustrious author's residence. He rose from his couch when I entered, and pressing my hand warmly, said, 'Have you brought the Sketch Book?' I handed it to him, when, seizing it with enthusiasm, he turned to the 'Broken Heart.'

"'That,' said he, 'is one of the finest things ever written on earth, and I want to hear an American read it. But stay—do you know Irving?' I replied that I had never seen him. 'God bless him!' exclaimed Byron; 'he is a genius; and he has something better than genius—a heart! I wish I could see him; but I fear I never shall. Well, read—the Broken Heart—yes, the Broken Heart. What a word!'

"When I closed the first paragraph: 'Shall I confess it? I believe in broken hearts.' 'Yes,' exclaimed Byron, 'and so do I; and so does every body but philosophers and fools.' I waited, whenever he interrupted me, until he requested me to go on; for although the text is beautiful, yet I cared more for the commentary which came fresh from Byron's heart. While I was reading one of the most touching portions of that mournful piece, I observed that Byron wept. He turned his fine eyes upon me and said: 'You see me weep, Sir; Irving himself never wrote that story without weeping; nor can I hear it without tears. I have not wept much in this world, for trouble never brings tears to my eyes; but I always have tears for the Broken Heart.'

"When I read the last line of Moore's verses at the close of the piece, Byron said: 'What a being that Tom Moore is; and Irving, and Emmett, and his beautiful Love! What beings all! Sir, how many such men as Washington Irving are there in America? God do n't send many such spirits into this world. I want to go to America for five reasons. I want to see Irving; I want to see your stupendous scenery; I want to go to Washington's grave; I want to see the classic form of living freedom, and I want to get your government to recognize Greece as an independent nation. Poor Greece!! I have always been anxious to see Irving, and describe this scene to him. He does not need even Byron's praise, I know; still I think it would please him; but in this wish I have never been gratified.'"

The subjoined passage will be read with interest by thousands in America. It occurs in a pleasant account of a very pleasant visit to 'Boz:'

"I think Dickens incomparably the finest-looking man I ever saw. The portrait of him in the Philadelphia edition of his works is a good one; but no picture can do justice to his expression when he is engaged in an interesting conversation. There is something about his eyes at such times which cannot be copied. In person he is perhaps a little above the standard height; but his bearing is noble, and he appears taller than he really is. His figure is very graceful, neither too slight nor too stout. The face is handsome. His complexion is delicate—rather pale generally; but when his feelings are kindled his countenance is overspread with a rich glow. I presume he is somewhat vain of his hair, and he can be pardoned for it too. It reminded me of words in Sidney's Arcadia: 'His fair auburn hair, which he wore in great length, gave him at that time a most delightful show.' His forehead, a phrenologist would say (especially if he knew his character beforehand) indicates a clear and beautiful intellect, in which the organs of perception, mirthfulness, ideality and comparison, predominate. I should think his nose had once been almost determined to be Roman, but hesitated just long enough to settle into the classic Grecian outline.

"But the charm of his person is in his full, soft, beaming eyes, which catch an expression from every passing object; and you can always see wit half sleeping in ambush around them, when it is not shooting its wonted fires. Dickens has almost made us feel that

> 'Wit is the pupil of the soul's clear eye,
> And in man's world the only shining star.'

And yet I think his conversation, except in perfect *abandon* among his friends, presents but few striking exhibitions of wit. Still there is a rich vein of humor and good feeling in all he says. I passed two hours at his house, and when I left was more impressed than ever with the goodness of his heart. I should mention that during my visit I handed him Campbell's letter: it produced not the slightest change in his manner. I expressed, on leaving, the hope that little Nelly (in whose fate I confessed I felt a deeper interest than in that of most real characters) might, after all her wanderings, find a quiet and happy home. 'The same hope,' he replied, 'has been expressed to me by others; and I hardly know what to do. But if you ever hear of her death in a future number of the Clock, you shall say that she died as she lived.'

"Mr. Dickens is certainly one of the most lovely men I ever saw; and I wish that they who have formed the mistaken idea that his works are destitute of high moral sentiment, and written merely to amuse the vulgar, would only look into Oliver Twist or Nicholas Nickleby."

Mr. LESTER seems in writing of the 'Shame of England' to have been actuated by honest and good motives; but we think also that he must have been a little influenced by the idea hinted at in his preface, that he was describing 'a nation with whom at no distant day we may be brought into collision;' an event which for the well-being of both countries we say may GOD forbid! England *has* her deeds of shame, no doubt; as witness her career in India, and her late invasion of China; yet we must hope, if not believe — since there are many somewhat *too* remarkable incidents and coincidences in these volumes — that our author has been influenced by national predilections and private prejudices to dash in the *shadows* of his limnings with a rich brush.

THE POETS OF AMERICA: ILLUSTRATED BY ONE OF HER PAINTERS. Edited by JOHN KEESE. In one volume. pp. 320. New-York: SAMUEL COLMAN.

THIS beautiful volume will be an appropriate one for the benevolent designs of those who intend to 'practice kind deeds in ambush' during the forthcoming holidays. One could scarcely surprise a young friend with a prettier present. Mr. KEESE deserves great credit for continuing his series of American poets with so much discrimination; and the publisher should share the honors, since his own part is performed with kindred taste and abundant liberality. There are thirty-four illustrations, all well engraved and appropriate in design. Many of these are of such beauty as to demand especial admiration; but as we lack room to notice them in detail, we shall content ourselves with simply commending them to the reader's enjoyment. One hundred and twelve American writers, including among them the best of our poets, are represented in the volume, and for the most part well represented, by poems which have received the meed of public approval, and bear the stamp of the United States' Literary Mint, which pronounces them true gold. We are surprised to find that at least one half of the matter here gathered together has been penned by various writers for our own pages. The work, we may add, justifies in all respects the promise of its popular predecessor, and cannot fail to insure an increased demand for the third annual volume of the series.

EDITOR'S TABLE.

BOSTON AND ITS ENVIRONS. — We have not forgotten a remark which fell from the lips of J. FENIMORE COOPER, Esq., in a morning stroll upon the Battery not many months since. We had been speaking of American writers, scenery, manners, etc., in a desultory conversation, in the course of which the observant author of 'The Pioneers' took occasion, in substance, to say: 'We are in this country, Mr. C——, entirely too *provincial;* by which I mean, that in most of our Atlantic cities the great mass of society revolves in a circle. Every thing that is unlike the customs of their native city, or the metropolis in which they live, is with too many considered as out of the proper order; it is 'not the thing;' and how trifling soever the matter in which comparisons are instituted, this predetermined preference of one's own over his neighbor's situation or advantages often results in coldness and estrangement, not of individuals only but of communities.' There is far too much truth in these observations. In our own 'Commercial Emporium,' one of the most *cosmopolitan* cities in the world, scarcely excepting London, it has been said, both by our own citizens and by foreigners, that there is less of this spirit, owing to the heterogeneous character of our population, than in any other American metropolis. We are not so sure of this. At any rate we are confident that very many among us have been accustomed for example to regard Philadelphia, Boston, etc., as rather so many *contributary* towns, calculated rather to enhance the importance and prosperity of the 'City of the Empire State,' than as any thing very remarkable in themselves. These 'provincial' denizens of our goodly cities should exchange places oftener. They would find their mutual conceit lessened, their brotherly love enlarged, and their love of our common country greatly expanded.

These hastily-recorded thoughts have been suggested by a recent visit to the noble capital of Massachusetts. Led by partial encomiasts, we once accompanied a friend on a bleak and stormy March afternoon across the Sound and over the Boston and Providence rail-road, to the former city; arriving late in the morning, and departing homeward the same afternoon. It was on that memorable day that we learned to appreciate the definition of a *sirocco,* as given subsequently by Mr. COOPER; namely, 'a Boston east-wind *boiled!*' We had it *raw;* and what a saturating, soul-pervading element it was! And as we sat shivering down by the side of the three or four courses of granite that then slightly elevated the Bunker-Hill monument above the brow of the eminence on which it stands, and saw the cold mist sifting in from seaward in long, opaque, perpendicular streaks, hiding the city of hills from our sight, and shutting in the leaden waters that surrounded it, we 'wowed a wow,' as Herr Hernholz has it, that we would trust no man's praises of his native city again. But in the language of that self-marrying German, we have '*broked our swore,*' and rejoice that we have done so. We 'came again.' It was a mild autumnal morning, almost before day-dawn, when the cars swept over the long causeway that conducts the western traveller to the American Athens. Lurid fires from a cluster of iron-furnaces on the left flashed fitful flames against the gray morning sky as we entered the silent city, and took conveyance to the time-honored TREMONT. A gentleman with a thoughtful countenance, 'with beard severe, of solemn cut,' whom our companions termed 'THE DEACON'—he had however left the Church and taken to the Bar—received us with great courtesy, and waving his hand, we were straightway marshalled to our apartments.

Breakfast at the Tremont; a pleasant toilette; and an Indian-summer morning in the streets of Boston! There was nothing to detract from all these luxuries but the great Sun himself, who on a former occasion obstinately came up in the north and went down in the south; but who was now by way of variety doing us the honors of the city after quite another fashion. He had come up in the west and was making the best of his way to the east. But though 'aweary of the sun' and annoyed by his ridiculous behavior, we were not prevented from our invariable, aimless, hap-hazard ramble, when in a strange town. One moment saw us standing in State-street, (very like our own Wall-street,) gazing at the quaint and dusky old City-Hall, with its mystic telegraphic signals, and gay flags flouting the air, which arrests its farther progress; the next beheld us scanning the ponderous columns and huge granite-blocks of the new Custom-House, or strolling by the superb Market and Quincy Hall, and entering 'OLD FUNNEL,' with which latter it is connected by another funnel, or vast cylinder of lattice-work. What our reflections were in the old Cradle of Liberty, (the key is in No. 1,) 'it is n't best to mention;' though than that we would sooner have missed all else we encountered. To cross Charlestown bridge and ascend Bunker's Hill and the Monument was a natural transition from Fanueil Hall.

Behold us 'on our winding way' to the unfinished top of this immense column. Standing there, in the amber light of an Indian-summer day, what *can* surpass the grandeur, the beauty of the prospect? We have never seen its equal. Boston at your feet, sitting like Rome on its hills, and sending up its towers, domes, steeples, and turrets toward heaven; 'making a long arm' in all directions, and helping itself to villages almost as big as itself; the great ocean in the distance; the bay and harbor, with its gently-rounded islands; and far around, even to the verge of an almost limitless horizon, a noble amphitheatre of hills, with villages nestling at their feet, and white church-steeples gleaming through the smoky light; and beyond all, old Monadnock blending its pale blue summit with the sky! Such is the *coup d'œil* from the top of Bunker-Hill Monument.

The 'Literary Emporium' it is conceded may challenge comparison with any American metropolis for the quiet taste of its opulent citizens; for their love of literature and the arts; the patronage which they bestow upon books, pictures, statuary, etc., instead of those mere external ostentations which are only for the eye. But above all, Boston must claim the superiority over all her sister cities for the beauty of her environs. Surely nothing *need* exceed their attractions. In company with an attentive friend, who had himself a fine eye for the beautiful in nature, and who could pardon our enthusiasm, we passed one of the finest days of our most charming season in a ride among the rich and varied scenery that encircles the city for miles around and in nearly every direction. We pass for the present Cambridge, that charming *rus in urbe*, with its pretty white mansions, its gothic churches, and college buildings 'gray with a young antiquity;' and Mount Auburn, that matchless cemetery, which would require pages to do it justice. Ascending by a smooth road at a gradual elevation, and passing numerous country-seats, each upon its own gently-swelling eminence, and surrounded by ornamental forest-trees, we reached the estate and mansion of Mr. C——, of Watertown, which we propose to make the especial theme of a few remarks in a subsequent number; simply observing here, that the establishment of this gentlemen, in scope and in detail, is the only example which can be found in this country of that class of residences and their appurtenances which make the glory of an English nobleman's country-seat. From this 'Delectable Mountain' and this 'House Beautiful' we proceeded by fine gravel roads over a succession of similar hills, that now cradled a clear lake and now lifted amid the more garish foliage of broad-leafed forest trees a crest of solemn pines against the sky; each rounded eminence and swelling upland dotted with delightful country-seats; with ever and anon a 'pleasant vale scooped out, and villages between.'

But we are travelling over too much ground and must 'call a halt.' How greatly we enjoyed a morning call with our friend at the fine mansion of Mr. B——, with its marble statuary, 'Julius Cæsar, Nebuchadnezzar, and the rest of the Apostles,' 'standing out' as at Blarney Castle 'all naked in the could frosty air;' how we took our way townward through the beautiful suburban village of R——; how we wandered on that night, with the full autumn moon riding high in heaven, among the sinuous and time-worn streets and alleys of the 'North End;' here pausing to note a revolutionary cannon-ball imbedded in an old church, and there gazing at an antiquated edifice, like a half dozen ancient cocked-hats perched one upon the other, and towering upward; how we stood at midnight in the very midst of the grave-yard at Copp's Hill, where the 'stalwart Englishers' placed their deadly batteries, and saw the column that commemorates the day rising over the still water, with the silver moonlight sleeping upon its side; and how we were well nigh overcome with the solemnity, the historical holiness of the scene; all these things, as the Chinese have it, 'are on record;' and 'uniting these circumstances,' we may perhaps be warranted hereafter in troubling the reader with 'a prepared report.' Decidedly these are the intentions.

AN AMERICAN 'NEWBURY ESTABLISHMENT.' — GEOFFREY CRAYON tells us that among the early objects of interest which attracted his attention in his first wanderings about London, was the shop of the good Mr. NEWBURY, whose story-books for children had so often delighted him when a boy in his native country. Very similar we may suppose will be the emotions of our own country lads and lasses when they shall visit this great metropolis, and pause with eager curiosity by the windows of Messrs. APPLETON AND COMPANY, in Broadway, from whose teeming mart so many delightful little books have gone forth through the length and breadth of the land. We have at this moment before us a goodly number of these 'Tales for the People and their Children,' which are destined to take captive the hearts of thousands of our young friends, not less by the attraction of their varied contents than by the many pretty engravings with which they abound, and the neat and tasteful style of their external embellishments. Here we have three 'Tokens,' one of 'Remembrance,' another of 'Affection,' and a third of 'Friendship,' each containing short and well selected pieces of poetry of the heart and the affections, by good writers, numerous and various; 'Paul and Virginia,' so long beloved of juveniles; 'Mignionette, or the Graces of the Mind,' devoted to tales and poetry of a high moral and religious order; 'The Old Oak Tree,' a story of interest not only to the young but even to 'children of a larger growth' who are willing to be taught; 'Autumn and Winter, or Walks in the Country,' overflowing with engravings; and 'Pure Gold from the Rivers of Wisdom,' from the *twentieth* London edition. Such books for such readers were rare in our boyhood. Happy juveniles! — favored generation!

OUR YOUNG PAINTERS. — We have examined since our last, two or three small pictures by young American artists, to which we cannot resist the inclination briefly to advert. Mr. JOHN CARLIN, a young deaf and dumb person, educated at the Asylum in Philadelphia, and recently returned from a prolonged stay at Paris, where he has been assiduously engaged in studying his profession, has shown us several of his productions, which bespeak talent of a high order. His pen-and-ink drawings, illustrating MILTON, the 'Pilgrim's Progress,' and the 'Sketch-Book' of Mr. IRVING, are conceived in the true spirit, and have won the approbation of the best judges of art in the city, who have examined them, including the President of the Academy of Design, Mr. MORSE. Although it is no part of our object to make the KNICKERBOCKER dependent upon pictures for its attraction or popularity, yet it is not impossible that we may in a short time afford our readers an engraved transfer of one of Mr. CARLIN's paintings, which cannot fail to win their warm admiration. It is a scene from GEOFFREY CRAYON's story of '*Dolph Heyliger,*' and represents DOLPH's father introducing him into the awful sanctum of Dr. KARL VON KNIPPERHAUSEN. The scene is well chosen, and most effectively depicted; and if our subscribers are just to themselves and to us, they shall 'set eyes on it.' Otherwise, *otherwise,* perhaps.

Mr. LEWIS BRADLEY, of Utica, a young and retiring artist, need not shun publicity, if two sketches from his hand, now before us, may be taken as fair examples of his talent. One, in water-colors, represents the '*Frost-Rime on the Mohawk,*' a beautiful scene, requiring a true artist to do it justice, in its delicate details; and the other a view, in pencil, on the Bernese Alps. Both are exceedingly spirited; but the latter partakes of that vague and shadowy vastness which constitutes the 'sublime and beautiful.' To both these young artists we say, '*Macte virtute!*'

THE DECORATIVE ART, as applied to dwellings, is beginning to be understood and appreciated in our city. It is only remarkable, that with the wealth which abounds with so many in this metropolis, there should have been until within three or four years a comparative neglect of those rich and substantial embellishments of spacious apartments, which to an American eye are so often objects of admiration in England and France. It is not generally known perhaps that we have in New-York, in the establishment of Mr. GEORGE PLATT, at No. 12 Spruce-street, a dépôt for every description of internal decoration, and in the proprietor one of the most skilful and accomplished decorative artists in America, who with his father before him has embellished some of the most gorgeous houses and splendid palaces in Europe. In fact his establishment is altogether *unique.* We were surprised and delighted with the various styles with which his apartments are lined; here the oaken carving and tracery of the Elizabethan age; there the elaborate and florid manner of the era of Louis XIV. and Louis XVI. of France; on one side, the gorgeously painted wainscotting of gathered cerulean silk; and on another the more simple yet not less tasteful styles of a later day; the whole surrounded by fragments of the minor accessories of decoration, of exquisite matériel and workmanship. These embellishments will survive the lapse of years and generations, without losing either their fashion or their beauty. They are 'for all time,' like the higher orders of architecture; and it is the province of Mr. PLATT, when introducing them into the dwellings of our citizens, to make them harmonize with every thing around them: and what is an important consideration, moreover, we observed during a short call at his establishment that he possesses the faculty of being able to embody the designs of individual taste, which are often so peculiar as to be difficult of reduction to form. We hope to hear that many gloomy and naked-looking apartments in otherwise rich and handsome dwellings among us, (and elsewhere, since orders from a distance may be easily filled,) will be made to brighten under the plastic hand of our artist, who has already made himself most favorably known, not only by his decorative skill in the highest branches, but by the beautiful transparent muslin window-shades which he was here the first we believe to introduce to the public.

COUNTRY AND TOWN THEATRICALS. — We have been not a little amused by a series of articles in the ' *Spirit of the Times,*' under the head of ' Theatrical Adventures in the Country.' They exhibit a forcible picture of the ups and downs of a strolling player's life ; and must needs tend, one would think, to deter young men who may be ambitious of even limited histrionic distinction, from entering upon so thorny a profession. In one of the writer's professional excursions his manager finds himself in a woful predicament. His pieces will not 'draw' in the quiet New England village where he had temporarily set up shop ; he and his company are literally starving ; the men moodily pacing the stage ; the women, who had kept up their spirits to the last, sitting 'silent and sorrowful ; and the children, little sufferers ! actually crying for food.' ' I saw all this,' says the manager, ' and I began to feel suicidal. It was night, and I looked about for a rope : '

' At length I spied just what I wanted ; a rope dangled at the prompt-side, and near a steep flight of stairs, which led to a dressing-room. ' That 's it ! ' said I, with gloomy satisfaction ; ' I 'll mount those stairs, noose myself, and drop quietly off in the night : but let me see if it is firmly attached.' I accordingly approached, gave a pull at the rope ; when *whish !* I found I had set the rain a-going. And now a thought struck me. I leaped, danced, and shouted madly for joy. ' Where did you get your liquor ? ' growled some. ' He 's gone mad ! ' said Mrs. ——. ' Poor fellow ! hunger has made him a maniac ! Heaven shield us from a like a fate ! ' ' Hunger ! ' shouted I ; ' we shall be hungry no longer. Here 's food from heaven, manna in the wilderness, and all that sort of thing ! We 'll feed on rain ! ' I seized a hatchet, and mounting by a ladder, soon brought the rain-box tumbling to the ground. My meaning was now understood. An end of the box was pried off, and full a bushel of dried beans and peas were poured out, to the delight of all. Some were stewed immediately, and though *rather* hard, I never relished any thing better. But while the operation of cooking was going on below, we amused ourselves with parching some beans upon the sheet-iron — the thunder of the theatre — set over an old furnace, and heated by rosin from the lightning-bellows. Thus we fed upon rain, cooked by thunder and lightning ! '

The following incident, which occurred during the representation of ' Pizarro,' is an amusing exposition of the matériel of melodrama ; and to those who have never beheld the drama in the country, will be found to illustrate the remark of the poet, that

' Where ignorance is bliss, 't is folly to be wise : '

" The production of the piece was made a card of in the bills. The scene of the ' Temple of the Sun ' was ' got up at a enormous expense.' The altar alone cost (in the play-bills) fifty dollars. It was in reality a splendid affair. It was in fact the large box used for the transportation of the wardrobe, covered with canvass, upon which a sign-painter of the town, in consideration of a pass for himself and wife, had toiled laboriously for two days, producing for a result something strongly resembling a rainbow in a snarl. The sun was truly brilliant : it took nearly two sheets of pasteboard, upon which were lavished full three books of Dutch metal. A pan of spirits of turpentine was duly placed behind it, to be ignited by the descent upon a wire of a piece of lighted sponge, saturated with spirits. The arrangement, however, was unsatisfactory to Dan. He was sure the sponge would keep the *stage waiting,* and resolved to anticipate the possibility of a failure, by concealing himself behind the altar with a lighted candle, and touching off the sun himself. No one could dissuade him, and in his Pizarro dress (he was the best Pizarro in the country, by-the-by) behold him coiled up in the wardrobe box, with a bit of candle in his fingers, upon which the melted tallow streamed, causing him occasionally to utter a low whine. Dan was *very* mysterious on this occasion, and I looked forward with no little curiosity for the dénouement. At the change of scene, Dan became very much excited, so anxious was he to discharge his self-imposed duty faithfully. Sim stood upon a step-ladder at the wing, holding a candle, ready at the proper time to launch the heaven-born fire. Dan, who had crept partially from his box, ever and anon regarded Sim with a jealous eye. At length the cue was given ; the celestial flame slid down the wire as slick as grease ; the fire burned brightly upon the altar ; while Dan, raising himself suddenly, to bring his candle into play, struck with his head the top of the box, and with a crash over went the altar, over the altar went Dan, and over Dan went the pan of burning spirits ! The audience screamed, the actors stood aghast, and the omnipresent Sim rushing upon the stage, dashed a bucket of water upon the *sun-burnt* Spanish conqueror, the whole forming a tableau of the most startling effect.'

These are scenes from actual life, beyond peradventure ; as is evidently also the amusing account of the writer, of being brought with his fellows before the selectmen of a Connecticut manufacturing town, under the statute against ' strolling vagabonds.' But the sanctimonious worthies could prove nothing. ' Did you,' said the examiner to the first witness, 'see a man perform ' *Robin Roughhead*' at the play-house last night?' 'Guess I *did!*' was the reply; 'and darn'd well he *does* it, tew! Ha! ha! he! he!' And he almost exploded with laughter, in his recollection of the character. 'Was *this* the man?' asked the examiner. 'Bless ye, no!' said the witness; 'he had light, flaxy hair, a face as red as a beet, and the funniest lookin' mouth! Guy! how he *did* look, though!' And another guffaw rewarded his reminiscence. This difficulty of identity saved the whole *troupe*.

One of the prominent features of town theatricals, especially within the last five or six years, has been *Theatrical Benefits.* The public have been dosed with them *ad nauseam.* Beneficiaries, though not always worthy of the honor, are of course not averse to them; and actors greatly affect them, because on such occasions they choose their own parts; take those of each other, however foreign to their powers; and bent upon 'making a hit' in a new line, too often make themselves supremely ridiculous. A correspondent in the following programme of a Complimentary Benefit to a distinguished histrion, who though last is not *least*, has 'touched the matter to a fine issue: '

The Gann Benefit.

PARK THEATRE.

On Monday the 4th of June the above event will come off, on which occasion the front of the Theatre will be splendidly illuminated, exhibiting in the centre a transparency of the distinguished Beneficiary.

———

The performances will commence with the Tragedy of

Hamlet !

Hamlet by Mr. Gann, who will (by General Desire) introduce the song of ' *Meeta.*'

Claudius,	Mrs. Chippendale.	Laertes,	Mrs. Wheatley.
Grave-digger,	Miss C. Cushman.	Ophelia,	Mr. Richings.
Queen,	Mr. Nexsen, who has kindly volunteered his valuable services.	Ghost, (for this night only,) Mrs. Stickney, of the Bowery and Chatham Theatres.	

———

After which, an *Olio Entertainment*, consisting of Songs, Music, and Recitations, namely:

The Soldier's Dream, by Field Marshal Moonlight.
Recitation: Alexander's Feast, by Mr. Gann, accompanied on the Pedal Harp, by Mr. Barry.
Grand Concerto on the Flute, by Mr. Kyle, with Horn accompaniments.

———

Mr. Isherwood, having returned from the most successful tour ever known at the South, will appear in Collins' Ode on the Passions, in character: also, in Ground and Lofty Tumbling.

———

Glee: by Messrs. Simpson, Andrews, and Barry.
Recitation: 'Niblo's Garden, or the Expulsulated Cyprian,' .... W. Niblo.

———

In the second Act of Hamlet, a large silver watch will be presented to the Ghost in character, from the stage-box, by Gen. Morris, clad in martial uniform, who will recite a short poetical address, written by himself for the occasion.

———

Mr. Shales, the eminent Boston Tragedian, will rehearse the death-scene in Richard III., in which he was encored six times in one evening, in the principal theatre of his native city. The service of tin-plate presented him by the citizens of Boston, covered with pale green gauze, will be borne in during his terrific engagement with Richmond, by Mr. Simpson.

———

The Committee are rejoiced to be enabled to announce, that they have succeeded in persuading the proprietor of the Chatham Theatre in the most liberal manner to intercede with the celebrated MASTER DIAMOND to dance the well-known '*Pas Timbuctooian*,' or '*Jim-along-Josey*,' three times.

Mr. ISAAC EDGE, Dramatic Pyrotechnist, of Jersey-City, will appear in a *Tourbillon Spiral*, accompanied by a Congreve Rocket, with golden rain. During the shower, Mr. POVEY will (by particular desire) dance the *Cachuca*.

THE entertainments to conclude with the poetical and musical *pasticcio* of '*Jimmy get your Hoecake Done*,' by the whole company.

DOORS open at six; performances to commence at seven o'clock and close at two A. M. Tickets to be had of Mr. GANN at the door, and at the office of the 'New-York Mirror.'

'THE METHOD OF NATURE.'—We are bound to thank the author, Mr. RALPH WALDO EMERSON, for a copy of his Oration delivered before the Adelphi Society of Waterville college, (Maine,) in August last. It is the production of one who thinks much, often deeply, but who writes muddily; and this latter quality, we are sorry to be compelled to add, is the evident result of an imitation of the German-English style of THOMAS CARLYLE, which whoso handleth, not being expert therewith, useth an edged tool, and will assuredly be wounded thereby. There is *thought* enough in this production to furnish forth half a dozen of your modern college orators; but there is nevertheless not a thought in it, which is worth any thing, that would not have produced ten-fold more effect had it been left open to the hearer or reader's mind, instead of being covered with a grotesque garb of motley language. Now and then in a striking simile or felicitous illustration Mr. EMERSON approaches the visible and the natural; as in this passage, for example: 'The universal does not attract us until housed in an individual. Who heeds the waste abyss of possibility? The ocean is everywhere the same, but it has no character until seen with the shore or the ship. Who would value any number of miles of Atlantic brine bounded by lines of latitude and longitude? Confine it by granite rocks, let it wash a shore where wise men dwell, and it is filled with expression; and the point of greatest interest is where the land and water meet. So must we admire in man the form of the formless, the concentration of the vast, the house of reason, the cave of memory.' But he soon relapses into the vague and shadowy, and we lose sight of him in a Cimmerian fog. Mr. EMERSON, as he should know, has also *his* imitators; and we beg him to pause and reflect how much crude third-rate American transcendentalism he will be compelled to stand sponsor for, should he continue to perpetuate his peculiar style. We have seen essays from one or two of his inferior followers or pupils which would defy even himself to understand; essays in fact which remind us of nothing so much as the exordium of Monsieur BAISECUL's 'Speech before PANTAGRUEL and the Parlement of Paris,' which we render *ad lib.* from RABELAIS, and shall venture to quote 'in this connexion,' though it has little connexion of its own: 'Monsieur: I confess it is indisputably true, that as a woman of my family, a good old soul she is too, was carrying eggs to market to sell, she passed between the two tropics, six degrees toward the zenith and a trifle over; inasmuch as the Rhiphæan mountains in that year suffered from great scarcity of chances, notwithstanding a sedition of pastry diamonds excited among the toll-keepers and pedlers for the rebellion of the Swiss, who were assembled as numerous as the humming-birds that dress in skirts and bodices of calico; in the first season of the year that they slopped their cows with turtle-soup, and gave the girls the key of the coal-house to feed the dogs with oats, because all the night they did nothing but despatch messengers on foot and messengers on horseback to retain the syllogisms; but the physicians said that in his skim-milk they did not detect any evident signs of their having eaten crabs with mustard, if the gentry of the court had not issued a decree prohibiting the peripheries to molest the vestal virgins, because the green cheese had gracefully begun to dance the dead march with one foot in the fire and the head in the middle, as Cæsar says in his treatise on weasels in Lapland; but alas! Messieurs; God regulates every thing according to his will, and a carman lost his whip!'

MR. SPARKS' LECTURES ON AMERICAN HISTORY, before the New-York Historical Society, at the University, have won all suffrages. The spacious hall at the time we write this paragraph is crowded to overflowing by eager and attentive listeners to our eminent historian's matter-full themes; insomuch that over the sea of heads we could scarcely recognize the speaker's countenance. We place the fact on record; so that should the series be repeated, those who are now excluded may 'be there to see' and hear. The manner of the lecturer we learn is in fine keeping with the importance and dignity of his subject.

NEW-YORK IN THE OLDEN TIME. — Oh! for the primeval days of our vast over-grown city, when as yet New-Amsterdam was a mere pastoral town; 'shrouded in groves of sycamores and willows, and surrounded by forests and wide-spreading waters, that seemed to shut out all the cares and vanities of a wicked world!' those halcyon days, when there were no rattling cabs nor rumbling omnibusses, but when the peaceful burgomasters issued their potential edicts against 'goats and kine,' that they might not be permitted to trespass in the fields, orchards, and gardens, below the City Hall! Such were the aspirations which arose in our mind a few days since, while looking over the MS. pages of a volume recently translated into English from the original Dutch, by order of our worshipful Common Council: 'The Ordinances of the Director-General and the Burgomasters and Schepens of Nieuw-Nederlands, in 1653–4.' These 'ordinances' are replete with the very spirit of the time in which they were framed. We were at pains to transcribe several of them, as well as other legal records, partly for the entertainment of our readers, and partly to defend our renowned progenitor and namesake from the charge which has sometimes been brought against him of having caricatured our Dutch ancestors. Here, for example, is a case which clearly convinces us that the renowned decision of the sage WOUTER VAN TWILLER in the matter of WANDLE SCHOONHOVEN *vs.* BARENT BLEECKER was a legitimate judgment. It is the suit of HARMEN DE KUYPER against HANS JANSEN and HENDRICK VANTIESSEL, in company, defendants; 'a dispute concerning a sow with pigs.' The defendants appeared in court and offered to testify under oath that it was *their* sow with pigs, showing certain reasons for the same by them established; and they affirmed that they could produce no other proof. The parties on either side having been heard, it was ordered that the sow in dispute should be provisionally retained by Hans Jansen; 'and in the mean time inquiry shall be made respecting a sow that is running about the Hook; and in case no owner is found, Harmen de Kuyper may take possession of her as his own, and Hans Jansen and Hendrick Vantiessel may hold on to their sow with pigs!' In those days litigious plaintiffs could not carry up their cases to a half a dozen courts, one above the other. There were no lawyers to goad the parties on. In one of these records, SYMON JOOSLEN complains that 'NIEUWE JANSEN has again given him trouble about that pair of shoes.' The defendant comes into court and says it is not so, and that Symon can't prove it; and that he is willing to refrain from the subject of the shoes. In another, a slander-case is reported. ALLARD ANTONY told GODERIS VANDERGRIST that he was a 'hornbeest.' The parties came before the burgomasters, but the matter by their intervention was adjusted between themselves. Of a hundred cases that came before the burgomasters, 'time was given' the parties to adjust their difficulties, and it is rare that they appear again before them.

There were no breach-of-promise cases in those days. 'Would you know the reason why?' Read the following: 'Whereas a certain process has been moved before the court of the city of New-Amsterdam by PIETER KOCK, single man, a burger, and inhabitant of the said city, as plaintiff, at and against ANNA VAN VOORST, single maid, defendant, respecting a marriage contract or verbal promise of marriage between the said Pieter Kock and Anna Van Voorst, mutually entered into, and in confirmation thereof certain gifts and presents were made by the plaintiff to the aforesaid defendant. However, it appears by certain documents exhibited by the parties, that the defendant and bride of the said plaintiff, in consequence of certain misgivings, is in no way disposed to be married to the said Pieter Kock; and it was also proved by two witnesses on the 24th of December, 1653, testifying that

Pieter Kock had given her up, with the promise of a written acquittal. Therefore the Burgomasters and Schepens of this city having perused the documents exhibited by the parties, and having examined them, do by these presents decide, that as the promise of marriage has been made before the omniscient GOD, it shall remain in force; so that neither the plaintiff nor the defendant, without the knowledge and approbation of their lordships the Magistrates, and the other one of the registered parties, shall be permitted to enter into matrimony with any other person, whether single man or single woman. Provided however, that all the presents made in confirmation of the marriage contract shall remain in the possession of the defendant, while the parties remain together in good will and contentment with each other, or lawful marriage; or until with the consent of one another they shall be exempted from the contract. Furthermore, both the plaintiff and the defendant are condemned equally in the costs of this suit. Thus done and sentenced in the session of 18th December, 1654.'

There was great reverence in those good old times for the morals of the citizens, and especially for temperance and an orderly observance of the Sabbath. 'Having observed and remarked,' say the burgomasters, 'the insolence of some who are in the habit of getting drunk, quarrelling, fighting, and smiting each other, on the LORD's day, a penalty of six Carolus guilders is imposed upon any one who shall keep on tap, draw, or bring out on the Sabbath day, any wines, beers, or strong waters whatsoever;' and 'cakes and cracknels' are to be purchased on Saturday evening. Great care was taken of the city's defences. The owners of the hogs and goats that had been treading down the protections of Fort Amsterdam are forcibly warned: 'Horses, kine, and in an especial manner, goats and pigs, must be taken care of, or else they will be put in FISCAL VANDYCK's pound. Let every one take heed, and look out for costs!' Happy indeed, good DIEDRICH KNICKERBOCKER! would it have been, if the city of thine heart could always have existed in this state of lowly simplicity! 'But alas! the days of childhood are too sweet to last! Cities, like men, grow out of them in time, and are doomed alike to grow into the bustles and the cares, the miseries and the vices of the world!'

BOSWELLIANA. — Among the many entertaining articles in BLACKWOOD for October is a poetical and prose medley, in which we find a hit at the style of BOSWELL that is scarcely inferior to a similar satire which we quoted from an English work a few years since. BOSWELL, after taking several rebuffs from the 'leviathan,' proposes a glass of wine:

JOHN. — 'Yes, Sir, wine is the liquor of oblivion; it will enable me to forget you. Sir, you are superficial. Superficiality consists, not in the possession of space, but in the want of depth; not in the expansion of substance, but the shallowness of material. It is a negative idea.'

I was delighted with his eloquence. But I ventured an attempt to change the subject.

BOS. — 'Sir, I have heard in Scotland——' The lion was instantly roused. Shaking his brows majestically, he looked at me:

JOHN. — 'Sir, what can you have heard in Scotland? Sir, it requires some sense even to hear. To be sure,' he added with a solemn laugh, 'a man may be like an editor's box; formed to receive all the anonymous trash that fools or knaves pour into it; or he may be a moral poor-box, open to all the spurious coin of public credulity; or he may be like a pawnbroker's shop, meant only to retain the cast-off remnants of other men's property. But he may be no more fit to discuss the merits or demerits of a country, than a crow is fit to discuss the merits or demerits of London, because it may have perched accidentally upon St. Paul's. Sir, adhere to the Brighton sauce. Men are never ridiculous but when they aspire. No one objects to the ass for chewing the thistle.'

BOS. — 'Well, Sir, you do not deny that this syllabub has merit?'

JOHN. — 'No, Sir! It *has* merit. *That* you may discuss. But leave the substantialities of the table to others. Avoid pride. 'By that sin fell the angels.'

The manner of the greatest bore and best biographer of his time as the reader will perceive is felicitously conveyed even in these few passages.

A STORY FROM M. DE BALZAC. — Our readers will remember several interesting translations from the French of M. DE BALZAC, which were furnished to the KNICKERBOCKER by a valued correspondent, whom we hope soon again to encounter in its pages, and especially a masterly critique of COOPER's 'Pathfinder.' The following from the same eminent author has been translated by a friend, from whom we have received several papers of kindred interest, which are in store for our new volume. We have rarely perused a more striking and spirited sketch:

STORY OF THE CHEVALIER DE BEAUVOIR.

A SHORT time after the 18th Brumaire, there was a rising in Brittany and La Vendée. The First Consul, anxious to restore peace to France, entered into negotiations with the principal leaders. Adopting the most vigorous military measures, and combining every thing in his plans, he put into play the Machiavellian resources of the police, at that time intrusted to FOUCHÉ, and finally succeeded in quelling the disturbances of the West.

About this time a young man belonging to the family of Maille was sent by the royalists of La Vendée from Brittany to Saumur, to establish communications between certain persons of the city and its environs and the chiefs of the royalist insurrection. Informed of his design, the police of Paris despatched agents to arrest the young emissary on his arrival at Saumur. He was actually arrested the very day he landed, for he came in a batteau under the disguise of a master-mariner. But he was 'a man of deeds.' He had calculated all the chances of his enterprise, and his passport and papers were so well regulated that the agents sent to seize him were in utter doubt as to his identity.

The CHEVALIER DE BEAUVOIR had well conceived his character. He quoted his borrowed family, his false place of residence, and bore his examination so well, that he would at once have been set at liberty, had not the officers placed the most implicit confidence in their instructions. They were precise; in doubt, they preferred rather to commit an arbitrary act than suffer a man to escape, to whose capture the First Consul appeared to attach great importance. In those days of liberty the agents of the national power cared very little for what we call now-a-days '*legalité*.'

The chevalier was provisionally imprisoned, until the higher authorities should decide upon his case. The official sentence was soon ratified; and the police received orders to guard his person with the strictest vigilance, notwithstanding his continued declarations of innocence. He was now transferred, in conformity with the new orders, to the '*Escarpe*.' This name was well worthy the situation of the fortress. Perched upon very high rocks, with precipices for its fosses, its only approach was by a narrow and dangerous path, leading as is always the case to the principal gate, which was defended by a fosse, over which was thrown a draw-bridge.

The commandant of the prison, charmed to have in his keeping a man of distinction and of pleasing manners, and who seemed well informed, (qualities quite rare at that time,) received the Chevalier as a boon from Providence. He proposed to him the freedom of the '*Escarpe*' on his parole of honor, and that they should make common cause against the ennui of the place. Beauvoir asked nothing better. He was a noble gentleman; but he was unfortunately also a very handsome youth. He had an attractive face, bold air, engaging manners, and prodigious strength. He would have been an excellent chief for a party. The commandant assigned him the most commodious apartments of the chateau, and admitted him to his own table.

This commandant was a Corsican officer. He was married, and very jealous; perhaps because his pretty wife seemed to him difficult to watch. Beauvoir, it transpired, made advances to the lady. They were without doubt attracted to each other. Did they commit any imprudence? Did the feelings with which each inspired the other lead him beyond the bounds of that superficial gallantry which is almost our duty toward women? Beauvoir has never clearly explained this point in his story. At all events, the commandant thought himself warranted in exercising the strictest rigor over his prisoner. He was thrown into a cell situated immediately under the platform of the turret, and arched out of the solid rock. The walls were of desperate thickness; the turret was probably over a precipice. There was no chance for escape.

When Beauvoir became satisfied of the impossibility of gaining his liberty, he fell into one of those reveries which are the despair and consolation of prisoners. He occupied himself with those little nothings which grow into great things. He received the baptism of grief. He reflected himself, and only *remembered* there was a sun. After fifteen days he felt that terrible malady, the fever for liberty, which urges prisoners to desperate enterprises.

One morning the gaoler who brought food to Beauvoir, instead of leaving him, as was his custom as soon as he had set down his scanty pittance, stood with his arms folded, and gazed fixedly at him. Their conversation had never reached more than a few words, and the turnkey had never been the first to commence it.   You may well imagine the astonishment of the prisoner, when the man said to him :

' Monsieur, you have no doubt your own object in view in calling yourself Le Brun or Citizen Le Brun.   That is no business of mine.   It is nothing to me whether your name is Pierre or Paul ; but I know,' said he, twinkling his eye, ' that you are M. Charles-Felix Théodore, Chevalier de Beauvoir, and cousin to Madame la Duchesse de Maille.'

Knowing himself incarcerated in a strong prison, and inferring that his position could be made no worse by a confession of his real name, Beauvoir replied :

' Well, suppose I am the Chevalier de Beauvoir ? — what will you gain by it ? '

' Every thing,' replied the gaoler, in a whisper.   ' Listen.   I have received money to aid your escape. As I shall be shot if I am suspected of having had any thing to do with the affair, I will only assist you so far as to gain my money.   Look Monsieur ! ' — and he drew from his pocket a small file ; ' with this you can cut through one of the bars ; ' and he pointed to a narrow loop-hole with two bars across it, through which the light entered the cell.   ' Monsieur, you must cut through before you can pass out.'

' You may rest quiet.   I will pass.'

' You must leave the lower part of the bar to fasten your cord to.'

' Where is it ? '

' Here,' replied the turnkey, throwing him a knotted cord ; ' it is made of coarse linen, to lead to the belief that you made it yourself.   It is of sufficient strength ; and when you reach the last knot, step quietly to the ground.   The rest is your own affair.   You will probably find in the neighborhood a carriage and friends awaiting you.   Of that I wish to know nothing.   I have no need to tell you that there is a sentinel posted in the street.   You will risk perhaps a ball from his carbine ; but ———'

' Very well, very well,' said the Chevalier ; ' I will not rot here.'

' That might be best for you, after all,' sullenly replied the turnkey.

The hope of once more gaining his freedom produced in his mind such an excitement that he could spare no more time in discourse.   He immediately addressed himself to the work ; and the day was just sufficient for him to saw through the bar.   Fearing a visit from the commandant, he filled the crevice with crums of bread rolled in the filings, to give them the color of iron : he waited until he judged the garrison to be asleep, when he fastened his cord to the lower part of the bar, which he had left, agreeable to the instructions of the turnkey, and crept to the outer edge of the loop-hole, grasping with one hand the end of the bar which remained in the stone.   Here he awaited the darkest hour toward morning, when he judged the sentinels would be the least watchful.

Acquainted with all those details of his place of confinement, with which prisoners occupy themselves, even involuntarily, he awaited the moment when the sentinel who guarded his quarter of the building should have performed two-thirds of his duty, and retire to his box to avoid the fog.   Then he began to descend knot by knot ; suspended between heaven and earth, but grasping his cord with the strength of a giant.

Every thing went well.   He had reached the last knot, and was about to slip to the ground, when he bethought himself to try if he could reach the earth with his feet.   He found none!   His case was really embarrassing.   Covered with perspiration, fatigued, perplexed, he was in a situation in which it might truly be said his life hung upon a thread.   By a lucky accident his hat fell off.   He listened for the noise of its fall, but hearing nothing, he began to entertain some vague suspicions of a snare.   But whence the motive ?   A prey to conflicting doubts, he resolved to defer his escape until another night, or at least until the uncertain twilight of day-break, an hour which might not be unfavorable for his flight.   His great strength enabled him to clamber back toward the tower, but he was almost exhausted when he reached the outer edge of the loop-hole, where he remained watching like a cat on an eave-gutter.

Presently, by the feeble light of early dawn, he saw there was the trifling space of about one hundred feet between the end of the cord and the pointed rocks of a precipice !

' Thank you, Monsieur Commandant ! ' said he to himself, with the *sang froid* which characterized him.

After reflecting a moment on a fitting revenge, he judged it best to reënter his prison.   He threw all his little articles of dress on the bed, and left the the cord hanging without, to induce the belief that he had fallen ; and taking in his hand the iron bar which he had broken off, he stepped behind the door, and awaited the arrival of the perfidious gaoler.

The commandant did not fail to come, and earlier than usual, to gather up what had been left behind. He softly opened the door ; but as soon as he was sufficiently near, Beauvoir struck him a powerful blow over the head, and the traitor fell dead at his feet, without even uttering a cry. The bar had broken his skull.

The chevalier quickly disrobed the dead body; put on the clothes and imitated the walk of the gaoler; and, thanks to the early hour and the fancied security of the guards at the principal gate, made good his escape.

GOSSIP WITH READERS AND CORRESPONDENTS. — We have often admired the bearing of BAALAM'S ass on that interesting and solemn occasion when he was chosen to rebuke his master. The quiet manner of the beast is a lesson. His modest consciousness that he was nothing *but* an ass, after discharging his mission, is above all praise. 'Am not I thine ass, upon whom thou hast ridden these three years?' Our correspondent 'Crito,' who takes us to task for our remarks upon 'Criticism' in a subsection of a late 'Gossip,' has imitated the above-cited example in two particulars. He has thought like an ass and spoken like an ass. He has failed only to copy the ass's modesty. Now what we endorsed — and we abide by our position — was, that a merely adroit sentence-monger, by the help of a few notes from competent critics, a shallow display of borrowed authorities, and an affectation of learning, which a scholar could not fail to detect; that such a man, with very small *ideas* might succeed in playing off upon the public a large game of *words.* Such instances may be found in all large communities. The 'time gives it proof' continually. Mr. IRVING has finely satirized this class of critics, and their imposing assumption of superior acumen and the plural pronoun. The reader pictures to himself a learned man, deliberating gravely and scrupulously on the merits of a book; whereas the criticism is often the crude production of one who writes solemn common-places in short oracular sentences, in order to acquire a reputation for profundity which he assumes, thoughts which he borrows, and a style which he apes. No wonder that in view of these things GEOFFREY CRAYON should come to the conclusion that neither author nor reader is benefitted by what is now-a-days too often praised as criticism; and that if every one were to judge for himself, and maintain his opinion frankly and fearlessly, we should have more *true* literary judgments than at present. A correspondent, in a '*Modern Pattern Criticism,*' which we thought to have published, has hit off the critical manner to which we have alluded very felicitously. We give his opening merely, but *that* we think will 'be suffegance.' The reader will perceive that our contributor treats his author with great familiarity; omitting his titles of respect and dignity, and taking him patronizingly by the hand:

'WRITINGS OF BISHOP WHITE.

'MIND unopposed by mind fashions false opinions, and degenerates from its original rectitude. The stagnant pool resolves into putridity. It is the conflict of waters which keeps them pure. WHITE felt this, when he wrote the volume before us. It is replete with activity — the true life. His pen scatters pearls, but they shine not with a pale light. They do not flash; they burn. This is a great merit and a rare; and WHITE seldom fails to exhibit it. He has, it is true, neither HEBER'S smoothness, nor the pathos of SIR THOMAS BROWNE; neither the eloquence of ROBERT HALL, nor the grace of JEREMY TAYLOR, and several others of the old Fathers, EVELYN and the rest. But he has great cleverness. WHITE never offends. An author who has judgment enough to write well, should have judgment enough to prevent him from writing ill. This volume is composed with great plainness. WHITE never seeks to hide his mĕaning; never covets an obfuscate and obscure sight,' etc., etc.

But 'something too much of this,' says the reader; and we acquiesce in his judgment. Is the amiable and courteous 'Crito' satisfied? . . . We have substituted the lines of 'H. W. R.,' as requested, which 'bide their *time*' — the early spring-time; yet we cannot consent to destroy '*The Old Bridge,*' without preserving one or two of its 'timbers.' The two closing stanzas are very natural, and are evidently lines 'from under a bridge.'

'Amid the grass the green reeds shook
Along the water's edge,
And the gray field-rat to his nook
Scampered among the sedge,
While the still current, dark and slow,
All bright with bubbles, moved below.

'But now, alack! thou art waxed old,
And under thee no more
Are childhood's fairy legends told,
For my best days are o'er:
And they are passed away, who played
With me beneath thy grateful shade!'

We shall be well pleased to hear from 'STANNARD BARRET, the Second.' He is the '*Man in the Moon,*' and is to keep us advised of matters and things in that quarter. He says that that planet is the abode of the shades of bodies that every seven years, according to our philosophers, wear off from us poor humans, like the concentric rings of an onion. He has encountered the shapes of several of our living authors, and is to render us accounts of divers interviews with some of the most eminent among them. Our '*Max*' closes his epistle after the manner of a patriotic Moon'te: 'And now, illustrious Earthite! adieu till next you hear from me! Day begins to decline; and your globe, which never sets to us, will soon shed her pale earth-shine over the landscape. O how serene are these regions! Here are no hurricanes, nor clouds, nor vapors. Here in our great pits, poetically called valleys, I shall retire from all moonly cares, luxuriate in the coolness of the Conical Penumbra, and prepare to enlighten the benighted inhabitants of the shining patches of earth which we see with our glasses below us, and which constitute your little hemisphere. Farewell!' · · · We are indebted to an old and valued contributor for the ensuing Sonnet. The writer has many a time won the smiles and tears of our readers in his prose, but we were not before aware that he courted the Muses with success:

ARIADNE.

Sweet symphony! whose dying, dying strain
Is ne'er forgotten — hark! it comes again.
'T is sphere-like music — oh! 't is not of earth;
My soul declares it of celestial birth.
Watchful, I turn my eager eyes above,
To gaze with rapture on the Heaven of Love:
And there methinks I have discerned afar
The etherial lustre of my natal star.
Some love to gaze on Mars, with armor bright;
Some bask in Venus' more voluptuous light:
Not these though beautiful can numbered be
In the deep book of my astrology:
Star of the stars which glimmer on my sight,
And gem with glory all the vault of night,
O peerless star — O ARIADNE! rise,
And glow revealed to these delighted eyes!
'T is midnight in my soul; thy radiant crown
Shall scatter darkness where it beams adown;
Shine with a lustre purer than the day,
And be my star, my guiding-star, for aye!

G. S.

We have received several brief communications, taking the affirmative and negative of the questions started by our correspondent who placed '*Old Put.*' at the Bar' in a late issue, and citing proofs and examples in defence of the writer's positions; but we shall reserve these for a final summing up, when the promised rejoinder, which was not completed in season for the present number, shall have been laid before us. In the mean time we are glad to learn that our purpose to continue full faith in the 'wolf-story' is sanctioned by such authority as our correspondent below, who although eighty-five years of age, preserves his intellectual faculties unimpaired. Mr. PAINE, who addresses us the annexed note, is well known in Vermont, of which State he has been for forty years the United States' District Judge:

TO THE EDITOR OF THE KNICKERBOCKER.

SIR: I have seen in the KNICKERBOCKER for August, an article in relation to Gen. PUTNAM. I propose to make some remarks upon that article.

I am now more than eighty-four years old. My father, SETH PAINE, and Gen. ISRAEL PUTNAM were contemporaries and neighbors in Pomfret. I, from my earliest recollection until I was twenty-five years old, often heard my father tell the wolf story. It was exactly as follows:

'A wolf had made depredations on the sheep-folds in their neighborhood. At length General, then Mr. PUTNAM, my father, and one or two other neighbors, and a negro of Mr. PUTNAM's, with a large dog, went in pursuit of the wolf, and chased him into a horizontal cavern in a ledge of rocks.

'The dog was put into the mouth of the cavern, and the negro followed, to crowd him forward, but did not succeed. Mr. PUTNAM then, with a rope round his legs, crawled in on his hands and knees, and came in sight of the wolf, whose head and fierce eyes were toward him. Upon a signal agreed upon, he was drawn out by the rope. After he came out, he appeared furious, and determined to go in again with his gun. His companions remonstrated against this, as dangerous. The discharge of the gun might bring the rocks upon him and crush him. But he persisted; and the rope was again fastened to his legs.

'He went in, with his gun and a torch; and when near the wolf, he fired; and upon the report of the gun, he was drawn out again upon his belly. When he came out he was perfectly calm. He went in again with the rope round his legs, took the dead wolf by the ears, and in this manner was dragged out on his belly the third time, with the addition of the wolf.

'From my childhood until his death, I was well acquainted with PUTNAM. He was a modest, unassuming man, and had nothing of the braggadocio about him. I never heard him tell the wolf story, nor ever heard that he did. He was universally considered by all his neighbors a man of the strictest truth and veracity.'

The wolf story, as above related,—was universally believed in Pomfret. His courage was there always admitted ; and some of his early deeds, which were thought to discover a great degree of courage, were thought by many to amount to rashness.

I am aware that the credibility of this statement must depend upon the character of two persons for truth and veracity — my father and myself. My father has been dead nearly forty-eight years ; but there must yet be living in Pomfret and Brooklyn, and that vicinity, in Connecticut, persons who can vouch for his good character in this respect, as well as in all other respects.

There are persons in New-York who know me personally, and many more who know me by reputation.   ELIJAH PAINE.

Williamstown, (Vermont,) September 15, 1841.

If 'JR.' is to be believed, we of Gotham may claim the honor of being the '*Literary Emporium*' over our eastern sister, who now bears the title. We think our neighbors should concede it, after reading the annexed ; for the writer has wrought out by dint of evident hard labor several very difficult rhymes to establish his position :

THE GOTHAMITES A LITERARY PEOPLE.

As I was walking up Broadway,
And going to my dinner,
A strange thought popped into my head,
As sure as I 'm a sinner :
For just as it was four P. M.,
By the clock in St. Paul's steeple,
Thinks I within myself, ' We are
A literary people ! '

We 've Waverley House, and Waverley Place ;
(Shade of SIR WALTER, view them !)
And Waverley coaches have been made
To carry people to them :
And SHAKSPERE stands godfather to
Much more than I know well :
E. o. three eating-houses, and
One second-rate hotel.

Ere Gotham knew the wondrous things
That modern light has taught her,
Th' Rialto was supposed to be
A bridge built over water ;
But in such old wives' tales, belief
No longer can be found ;
Th' Rialto 's now an oyster-shop
In Broadway, under ground.

A basement linguist in Park-Row,
To prove our city are pat in
The ancient tongues of Greece and Rome,
Addresses us in Latin ;
Most classically tells us, that
Behind his painted lattice
Stewed oysters, steak, et cetera,
Are ' *Nusquam non paratus*.'

Nor while old lore is honored thus, is
The modern in disguise :
We 've Metamora omnibusses,
And KNICKERBOCKER ice :
The latter brings ' cold comfort ' when
The dog-days have begun,
And the former, like the tragedy,
Were meant to have a run.

On DIEDRICH, 'faith ! descends a stream
Of nomenclature popular,
As liquor runs from bottles, when
They best without a stopple are.
He 's first a ' KNICKERBOCKER House '
Four stories high, where are
Mint-juleps, punch, and all good drinks,
Aye furnished at the bar.

For riding out, he has a line
Of coaches of his own,
That for a shilling's fare will drive
Him all about the town :
And eke, to write his stories in,
A first-rate Magazine ! *
Was e'er to literary man
So kind a city seen ?

Sure any man, these manifest
Phenomena discerning,
Will own we Gothamites are deep
In literary learning :
A bumper then to Gotham town,
And at it take a deep pull ;
The toast : ' May we *forever* be
A LITERARY PEOPLE ! '   JR.

In reply to ' C. P. F.,' whose favor he tells us is ' not quite in his style,' he ' not being exactly in the vein,' we would say, as a friend observed in answer to the remark of a third, ' I am not *myself* to-day,' ' Well, whoever you are, you are a *gainer* by the change ! ' ' C. P. F.' will recognize the application. · · · The editor of the ' *Boston Morning Post*,' one of the most entertaining journals that reaches our table, speaking of our popular Magazine novel-series or continuous narratives, remarks, that among the high and the low, the intelligent and the ignorant, these periodical romances find their way. So prosperous, adds the editor, has been this system, that is now really hazardous to print a two-volume novel in a decent form ; and those which *do* make their appearance among us are not to be compared, in their externals of paper and printing, with the periodicals among which they are nearly overlooked. This is literally true. An 'American novel in two volumes' is now a somewhat rare article ; and three-quarters of those which have swarmed upon the public within the last six or seven years are seldom read or already forgotten. Our friend at *Pittsburgh* will find in the above a sufficient though not perhaps a satisfactory answer to his recent inquiry. · · · Many and many a time, we beg the writer of ' *Nature and Myself* ' to believe, have we felt what he describes (we are sorry to add) in language quite inadequate to the thoughts. The loss of a dear friend more than all is calculated thus to make us long to ' spurn the clay-cold bonds that round our being cling.' An autumnal eve ; the brave o'erhanging firmament at midnight ; the blue line of a distant mountain ; a bank of clouds above

---

* THE editor stepped out for a moment, just as a man withdraws from a convivial board when informed by a guest that he is to be toasted while absent, during which time a friend read the proof of this stanza, which would not otherwise have been suffered to remain. ' Oh ! by no means — certainly not ! ' This excuse ' it is hoped may please.'

the sinking sun; these and other sights of nature have often awakened in us the emotions of our friend — for such he is, although we know him not. At such periods one may say with BYRON:

'I live not in myself, but I become
Portion of that around me.
. . . I can see
Nothing to loathe in nature, save to be
A link reluctant in a fleshly chain,
Classed among creatures, when the soul can flee,
And with the sky, the peak, the heaving plain
Of ocean, or the stars, mingle, and not in vain.

'And when at length the mind shall be all free
From what it hates in this degraded form,
Reft of its carnal life, save what shall be
Existent happier in the fly and worm;
When elements to elements conform,
And dust is as it should be, shall I not
Feel all I see, less dazzling, but more warm?
The bodiless thought, the spirit of each spot?
Of which even now I share at times the immortal lot?'

'Are not the mountains, waves, and skies a part of me and of my soul, as I of them?' has been asked thousands of times by self-questioning thinkers; but the mystery can only be solved ' when this mortal shall have put on immortality!' . . . If '*A Friend to the Friendly*' has access to the 'London Quarterly,' he will find in the last number of that Review a far more pungent critique upon Mr. BUCK-INGHAM than any notice which has appeared in this country of that itinerant philanthropist's dull and labored volumes. It is exceedingly caustic and very just; and we commend it to the perusal of our correspondent. Mr. BUCKINGHAM, says the reviewer, seems to have lectured JONATHAN on three subjects; first, the personal history of Mr. BUCKINGHAM; secondly, that worthy gentleman's travels in the Holy Land; occasionally 'in the oriental costume;' thus enabling his auditors 'to transport themselves more easily in imagination to the scenes of sacred history; in fact placing before their eyes an express image, all but the beard, of the ancient patriarchs; nay, why may he not have had a beard in his box too, though he does not mention it?' — and thirdly, tee-totalism; in which latter no doubt ' the corporeal aspect of the lecturer was counted on for affording a lively attestation to the beautifying influences of Temperance.' Among the extracts from our public journals, re-quoted in the Review from BUCKINGHAM's Travels in America, is the beautiful description of the disinterment of the remains of WASHINGTON, from the *Philadelphia Gazette*, and the pen of its then editor, WILLIS GAYLORD CLARK. The reviewer singles it out for especial commendation, which the reader we think will admit is deserved. . . . '*A South-Street Merchant*' gives us authority to state that the novel of '*Lafitte, or the Pirate of the Gulf*,' purporting to be from the pen of Mr. J. H. INGRAHAM, was mainly written by another person, a modest and retiring graduate of Cambridge University, from whom the reputed author borrowed it in MS. He kept it for many months and finally, after repeated importunity, returned it to the writer, with the remark that ' it was very strange, but he had himself previously taken up the same subject, and in fact had written a novel upon it;' and he added that his ' friend would be *surprised* at the great similarity between the two stories.' And lo! when the said novel appeared, says our informant, he *was* surprised; for chapter after chapter, scene after scene, in short nearly the whole work, was found to have been taken bodily from the MS. in question! 'Curious, is n't it?' The original MS. we learn is still extant. Our correspondent's name will be furnished to Mr. INGRAHAM, (of whose address we are ignorant,) and our pages open to any explanation which he may give of a public report, which if false should be denied and disproved. . . . A passage in ' *Old Letters*,' (which, save an unimportant omission, will appear hereafter,) reminds us of a pleasant effusion of a popular correspondent, who though sitting now at the receipt of customs has not forgotten his old propensities nor his favorite literary medium. The commingled pseudo-affection and Jeremy-Diddlerism of the lover are irresistible:

AND must we part? — well, let it be!
'T is better thus, oh yes I believe me;
For though I still was true to thee,
Thou, faithless maiden! would'st deceive me.
Take back this written pledge of love!
No more I 'll to my bosom fold it;
The ring you gave, your faith to prove,
I can't return — because I 've sold it!

I will not ask thee to restore
Each *gage d'amour*, or lover's token,
Which I had given thee, before
The links between us had been broken.
They were not much; but oh, that brooch!
If for my sake thou'st d signed to save it,
For that at least I must encroach;
It was n't mine, although I gave it.

The gem that in my breast I wore,
That once belonged unto your mother,
Which when you gave to me, I swore
For life I 'd love you and no other;
Canst thou forget that cheerful morn,
When in my breast thou first didst stick it?
I can't restore it — it 's in pawn;
But, base deceiver! there 's the ticket!

Oh, take back all! — I cannot bear
These proofs of love — they seem to mock it;
There, false one! take your lock of hair —
Nay, do not ask me for the locket;
Insidious girl! that wily tear
In useless now, that all is ended;
There is thy curl — nay, do not sneer.
The locket 's — somewhere, being mended.

He goes on to say that he would have returned the beautiful dressing-case she had given him, but that his landlord had just visited him with a distress-warrant and ' positively cleared his lodgings!' . . . ' *England and China*' shall appear, if the writer will permit us to erase the second and third paragraphs, which were ill-judged as it seems to us when written, and especially so now, when the international vexed question, in one of its phases at least, has been satisfactorily disposed of. But in the main argument we are heartily with the writer. The war upon China and its peaceful inhabitants is ' unjust, unmanly, wicked and cruel, in all its aspects.' Well have the English earned the name of 'outside barbarians.' We have hitherto been amused with the 'special edicts' and vermilion proclamations of the Chinese; but in reading their official bulletin of the late attack on Canton, a feeling of pity predominates over every other emotion. After firing 'several tens of rounds' and 'smashing two great masts of the barbarian ships,' they were compelled to give way, and the 'red-bristling foreigners rushed to the plunder of the city,' entering at the large northern gate. 'Their rockets were thrown in masses; their balls bit the people's houses, and they caught on fire; all our own soldiers were hard pressed — they had not a place to stand on. Myriads of people were weeping and wailing; the number of those who invoked heaven and begged for peace, covered the roads. When I looked with mine own eyes upon this, my very bowels were torn asunder!' The war was for booty; and *money* purchased a suspension of these barbarous hostilities! Shame! · · · The writer of the following spirited sketch of a most picturesque and grand natural scene contents himself with 'doing well;' whereas would he but *cultivate* and more frequently exercise his fine poetical powers, and use the file a trifle more, he would not only 'do better,' but altogether excel many of his tuneful contemporaries, who have more fame but less merit than himself:

TRENTON FALLS, NEW YORK.

BY F. L. WADDELL.

THERE is a wild and danger-thrilling scene,
Where Terror sits enthroned; a deep ravine
Amid an amphitheatre of hills,
Whose tumbling stream the soul with wonder fills;
As Cayahoga rolls its fierce cascades,
'Neath frowning torrents dark with hemlock shades,
While ragged rocks uprear their moss-clad walls
O'er raging pools and tumbling waterfalls,
Loud booms from crag to crag the fitful surge,
Once youth and beauty's frolic-chant and dirge;
When, like a blue-bell on the torrent's edge,
Fair nymph! a zephyr dashed thee from the ledge;"
Caught by the enamored spirit of the wave,
The foam thy winding-sheet, the gulf thy grave!
There, as the shadows of retreating day
Fade o'er the sun-tipped cedar tops away,
With cautious heed along the beetling path,
Where darkly sweeps the leaping river's wrath,
Thick tasselled birch and maple hanging o'er,
'T is pure romance to thread the root-paved shore,
Watch the white mist curl o'er the wave-worn slide,
And mimic rainbows arch the arrowy tide;
As Memory, fluttering on her dusky wings,
Asks of the stream, where are the woodland kings?
There moose and beaver unmolested reigned,
Ere the rude saw-mill yon bold bank profaned,
And led the doe her spotted fawn to drink,
Where slopes the rural shed, the dizzy brink;
There the wise sachems, with an homage true,
Invoked from Nature's shrine the Manitou;
O'er clustered columns of their forest fane
Rose the wild music of the Indian strain;
Ere passed away the red lords of the chase,
Their mounds, memorials of their mighty race!
Far down the zig-zag dell, beside some pool,
The fresh breeze straying through the greenwood cool;
On a wild rose-bank, mid the fern enshrined,
Sweet meditation charms the musing mind,
As Mystery brings her sealed-up stores to light:

The salt sea Nautilus and Trilobite,
Hid mid that inland glen long years of time,
Since the vast deluge covered every clime;
By the great Architect of shells and skies,
Who made that gorgeous masonry arise,
Robes in its icy chains or summer dress
The glorious vale of quiet loveliness,
Displaying scenes Arcadia never knew,
Or poet's pen or artist's pencil drew;
There robins sing their evening serenade,
The blue-bird shakes his plumage in the glade;
On splintered tree-top caws the 'loafing' crow,
His comrades nestling in the limbs below;
While from the brow of overhanging hill
Gushes, all Horeb-like, a crystal rill,
As flirting near the amber-tinted spray,
A thousand butterflies chase the eve away;
With silky coat and buff-embroidered vest,
An emerald crown upon his freckled crest,
By berry-bearing bush, mid branches rude,
Rests the gay emperor of the solitude;
Around his peacock-colored subjects sport,
The lawless foresters of the tiny court;
While skims aloft with graceful, airy ease
The Taglioni of the dew-gemmed trees;
Her robe rich violet, trimmed with purple fringe,
And crimsoned bodice streaked with orange tinge;
Till melts the golden radiance from the west,
And flower-queens in their leafy couches rest;
While on the dogwood herald-moths encamp,
And flickering glow-worms in the logwood tramp;
When o'er the valley walks the full-orbed moon,
Lighting with splendor her rock-ribbed saloon;
Beyond the glitter of the sparkling sheet
Where o'er the falls the forests seem to meet,
Black stooping clouds reveal their lightning glance,
Sharp rumbling thunders through the gulf advance;
Beneath the shelving ridge with crouching form
I watch the grandeur of the midnight storm!

And now, not to speak it boastingly, we are *proud* of our 'file,' and not ashamed of our 'drawer.' Both are full. The following, in addition to articles named in our last, are among the papers in prose and verse which await insertion or examination: 'A Parallel between BONAPARTE and WELLINGTON;' 'The Country Doctor,' in continuation; 'Granada and the Alhambra;' 'A Pic-Nic,' by the 'American in Paris;' 'My Grandfather's Port Folio;' 'The Three Deacons,' and 'Flora B——;' 'Last Moments of TORRIJOS and his Companions;' 'Madness and Imprisonment of DANTE;' by Hon. R. H. WILDE;' 'The Taking of Basing-House,' by a new (and welcome) contributor; 'The Conscript,' a Tale; 'Life in Hayti;' 'The Quod Correspondence,' in continuation; 'The Storming of Stoney Point;' 'Some Thoughts upon Poetry and Poets;' 'The Polygon Papers,' No. Four; 'Song of the Winds;' 'A Tour in Virginia;' Articles on Gen. PUTNAM and his career; 'A Sketch of Alabama;' 'The Aristocracy of Stokeville;' 'The Night-Watch;' 'A Season in New-Orleans;' 'The Old Historian;' 'A Sick Bed;' 'The Bird of Paradise;' 'Verses to KATE;' 'The Little White Rabbit: a Tale;' 'A Bachelor's Choice;' 'The Sisters,' a Sonnet; 'November: a Leaf from my Journal;' 'The April Shower;' (in its season: it is very beautiful;) 'The Tableau Vivant, or Statue of Love;' with many others, which we lack the space to specify. Several notices of books, etc., are unavoidably crowded out of the present number.

---

* THE melancholy fate of Miss SUYDAM of New-York will long be remembered by visiters to Trenton Falls.

'Stop, Thieves!'—Rich people should never pilfer. They 'are without excuse' for the act. Our old friend and correspondent Capt. Marryat has been 'Raising the Wind' in his late story of that name, with a vengeance; for he has copied the tale of 'Desperation' from the Knickerbocker of February, 1835, in all its incidents, and most of its language. It was from the pen of Ollapod, and was widely admired. The 'Democratic Review' for September publishes as original the 'Lay of the Madman,' written for these pages in 1837, by Hon. Robert M. Charlton, of Savannah. And our excellent brother of the 'Southern Literary Messenger' has unwittingly suffered an impudent correspondent to address some beautiful 'original' 'Lines to Miss A. M. A——, of Richmond,' which were first printed in the Knickerbocker, from the ms. of Rev. Walter Colton, an old correspondent. Our contemporaries are too well endowed to need the aid of our old papers; and they will thank us we are sure for exposing their pseudo contributors.

LITERARY RECORD.

Appleton's 'Pictorial Library:' The 'Early English Church.'—There are no publishers in America who better deserve a liberal patronage at the hands of the reading public than Messrs. Appleton and Company of this city; and we are not surprised to learn that their publications are acquiring every where great popularity and rapid sales. In 'that first appeal which is to the eye' their issues are unsurpassed; and this is no indifferent merit. Their 'Pictorial Library of Standard Literature,' of which two volumes have just appeared, and others are in active preparation, will comprise upward of two thousand elegant engravings. 'The Vicar of Wakefield,' that matchless story of Goldsmith, accompanied by Aikin's memoir of the author, the whole crowded with appropriate illustrations, and printed in the most beautiful manner upon a large clear type and fine white paper, is before us, the first of the series, together with a copy of 'Robinson Crusoe,' to which the same praise in all respects will apply. These will be followed by a 'Life of Napoleon,' and 'Gems from Travellers,' the first of which, we are enabled to say from an examination of the sheets, will fully equal the two volumes to which we have alluded, in its numerous large engravings, from drawings by Horace Vernet, as well as in the beauty of its externals generally. All these works, considering their character and style, are of wonderful cheapness. A notice of 'The Early English Church,' reprinted by the Messrs. Appleton from the second London edition, and which should be in the hands of every well-informed churchman, is reserved for another number.

American Antiquities.—We had hoped to have been able to notice somewhat at large in the present number a very interesting volume by Mr. Alexander W. Bradford, upon 'American Antiquities and Researches into the Origin and History of the Red Race;' but we must limit our reference to a brief record of the main design of the work, which is to embody and collate the descriptions of the most remarkable of the ancient remains and ruins scattered over the continent; to compare the traditions, manners, customs, arts, language, civilization, and religion of its aboriginal inhabitants, internally, and with those of other nations; and thence to deduce the origin of the American race and its subsequent migration; or in other words, to attempt the determination of a portion of its unwritten history. It is not too much to say in praise of this beautiful volume that the author's design has been faithfully carried out. Messrs. Dayton and Saxton are the publishers.

'History of Scandinavia:' 'Democracy.'—Two important and very interesting volumes have just been added to Harpers' wide-spread Family Library, entitled 'Scandinavia, Ancient and Modern;' being a history of Denmark, Sweden, and Norway: comprehending a description of these countries; an account of the mythology, government, laws, manners, and institutions of the early inhabitants; and of the present state of society, religion, literature, arts, and commerce; with illustrations of their natural history. The foregoing is specific as to the nature of these volumes; and since the 'Northmen' and their countries have of late become themes of engrossing interest, we need add no more to insure a participation of the reader in our own high enjoyment than the fact that the authors of this work are Andrew Crichton, LL. D., author of 'The History of Arabia,' etc., and Henry Wheaton, LL.D., author of the 'History of the Northmen,' member of the Scandinavian and Icelandic Literary

Societies, and lately our Charge d'Affaires at Copenhagen; and that they are the first writers who have undertaken to embody the chronicles of these countries in a uniform and connected narrative, so as to exhibit under one view the state of government and society in ancient and modern times; the condition of the inhabitants and the productions of their soil; their institutions under the barbarous ages, and the progress they have now attained in literature, arts, and civilization. Numerous wood-cuts illustrate the work. To the succeeding number of the Family Library, 'Democracy,' by G. S. Camp, we shall take another occasion to advert, it being too elaborate and well-reasoned a work for a mere passing glance in this department.

The English Annuals for 1842. — Through the courtesy of Messrs. Appleton and Company, the English annuals for 1842, gleaming in blue and crimson, purple and gold, and garnished with all the splendors of the pictorial art, are lying before us. A running-glance over them, to indicate to our readers an outline of their various attractions, is all the justice we can at present render them.

The 'Book of the Boudoir,' or the Court of Queen Victoria, is a superb quarto, with portraits of twelve of the fair British nobility, countesses, viscountesses, ladies, etc., all from portraits of the life size; original paintings by eminent artists, and engraved under the superintendence of the eminent Finden. It is a charming volume.

The 'Picturesque Annual,' of lordly size, contains twenty-one engravings from original drawings by Allom, whose fine views of Constantinople attracted so much attention at the National Academy of Design the present season. The embellishments, which are truly superb, embrace the principal modern improvements and newly-erected monuments of the capital of France. The letter-press sketches are from the competent pen of Mrs. Gore, and the typographical execution and 'findings' are of the first order.

Fisher's Drawing Room Scrap-Book,' with poetical illustrations by Mary Howitt, is unquestionably more various and extensive in its five quarto embellishments than any of its contemporaries for 1842. The views are ransacked from all corners of the earth. Egypt, Palestine, Africa, Turkey, Greece, Germany, Switzerland, etc., have been laid under contribution for the work; beside which there are in its sixty-seven engravings, numerous pictures of a different description, including one or two from the old masters, and several portraits of distinguished persons. This annual will command a wide sale.

'Heath's Historical Annual' devotes its beautiful line embellishments to prominent events in the great Civil War, in the time of Charles the First and the Parliament, which history and romance have rendered memorable. There are fifteen engravings by Cattermole, scarcely one of which, well studied, but would repay the price of the splendid volume. The historical descriptions are by Rev. Richard Cattermole, B. D., who has with comprehensive brevity illustrated the illustrations of his illustrious relative, George the Artist.

'The Cabinet of Modern Art,' edited by Alaric A. Watts, formerly editor of the London Souvenir, has twenty-four line engravings, some of them of great excellence, the subjects of which have been selected from the finished works of the most distinguished painters of the day; pictures which have stood the test of public approbation in the several galleries in which they have been exhibited. Among others included in the volume, are the productions of Stothard, Howard, Collins, Newton, Martin, Chalon, Westall, Stephanoff, Parris, etc. Among the contributors are the late Miss Landon, that fine poet T. K. Hervey, William Howitt, and others equally well known to fame. In its externals 'The Cabinet' lacks the high finish of some of its brethren, but it is a very good annual nevertheless. 'The Gems of Art' is a volume similar in character and execution to the 'Cabinet,' and to which the same remarks will apply. The editor was assisted in his designs by the painters themselves who are represented in his works, as well as by many of the most distinguished collectors throughout England.

'The Forget-Me-Not,' although the smallest and least pretending of the whole English tribe of Christmas, New-year, and Birth-day presents, is by no means the least attractive. It has eleven engravings, four or five of them of exceeding beauty. We cannot say that the externals are of remarkable beauty. The contents however are good, and from various well-known pens. Mrs. Sigourney and Miss Hannah F. Gould we perceive are represented in its pages; the latter in one of the best things in the volume, which it opens; 'American Wild Flowers for Queen Victoria.' Messrs. Appleton and Company have the other English annuals for the coming year; as 'The Juvenile Scrap-Book,' by Mrs. Ellis, Heath's 'Book of Beauty,' 'Friendship's Offering,' and 'Keepsake;' but we have no room to record their various beauties. 'They must be seen to be appreciated.'

'INCIDENTS OF A WHALING VOYAGE.' — This is a volume from the pen, as we learn, of a son of Prof. OLMSTED of New-Haven, who was compelled by ill health to undertake a whaling voyage from the port of New-London, in 1839. He went as a passenger; and we must agree with the New-York Review, that 'we could not more precisely mark the difference between 'Two Years before the Mast' and those 'Incidents,' than by saying that the author of the one talks like a passenger, of the other like a sailor. Yet the latter is far from being an indifferent or dull book. It is liberally sprinkled with adventure and anecdote, and contains much valuable information upon the subject of whale-fisheries, as well as a very interesting description of the Sandwich Islands, and the effect of christianity upon their inhabitants. The volume is illustrated with several forcible engravings on stone, from original drawings by the author; and like all of the Messrs. APPLETON's publications, is well printed and bound.

MR. M'JILTON's ADDRESS. — There are many things in the recent Address delivered by Mr. J. N. M'JILTON before the Literary Societies of Lafayette college at its late commencement which we can heartily commend. Such are portions of the writer's comments upon American literature, and his earnest defence of the higher order of native talent. But when he talks of 'Barnaby Rudge' and 'Charles O'Malley' as productions 'calculated to vitiate the habits and corrupt the morals of American youth,' he exhibits a narrow mind, sheer ignorance, or a discreditable affectation of preëminent and adscititious virtue. Long say we may such works as 'Nicholas Nickleby' and 'Barnaby Rudge' occupy the place of indifferent literary productions, even though they be 'native American.' We ask no favor for our literary minores which shall prevent our full enjoyment of the labors of master-spirits of other countries.

CHILDE HAROLD: LOCKHART's SPANISH BALLADS. — Two more superbly-beautiful volumes than the illustrated and illuminated edition of LOCKHART's 'Spanish Ballads' and the embellished edition of BYRON's 'CHILDE HAROLD,' recently published in London by MURRAY, and just imported by APPLETON AND COMPANY, we have never had the good fortune to see. All that the art of engraving, printing, and coloring can do, has been bestowed upon these gorgeous books. They should be *seen*, not spoken of. Messrs. WILEY AND PUTNAM are about to issue an edition of the former, with important prose additions.

SCHOOL AND FAMILY DICTIONARY. — The sub-title of 'Illustrative Definer' characterizes the prominent merit of this book over other dictionaries. The author, Rev. Mr. GALLAUDET, of Hartford, (Conn.,) whom to name is a sufficient guaranty of his performance, has aimed at and attained great simplicity and clearness, and avoided the defect of defining one word by another often still more difficult, and the defining of the latter one by the very word which it had been used to define. Messrs. ROBINSON, PRATT AND COMPANY, Wall-street, are the publishers.

SCOTT's POEMS: MOORE's EPICUREAN. — Mr. C. S. FRANCIS, in continuation of the excellent and cheap edition of the complete works of SIR WALTER SCOTT, commenced by Mr. PARKER of Boston, has just published four handsome volumes, containing 'Rokeby,' 'Bridal of Triermain,' 'Lord of the Isles,' 'Waterloo,' etc. At the same low price and in the same neat form Mr. FRANCIS has also issued a revised and corrected edition of MOORE's 'EPICUREAN,' with notes.

GERMAN PROSE WRITERS. — Mrs. SARAH AUSTIN, favorably known in England and America for several literary performances of merit, is the compiler of a handsome volume which we find upon our table from the press of Messrs. APPLETON AND COMPANY, containing numerous fragments, various in kind but all of characteristic excellence, with biographical sketches of the several authors. The volume is a fair salmagundi of the German belles-lettre intellect, and is handsomely presented to the reader.

FRANCE, ETC. — Messrs. WILEY AND PUTNAM have issued a second edition of 'France, its King Court, and Government,' by our minister to France, Gov. CASS. It contains in addition the 'Three Hours at Saint Cloud,' written for these pages. We are glad to announce, on the authority of a letter just received from the author of this attractive volume, that our readers may anticipate a series of papers from the same eminent pen in the course of the ensuing volume.

NEW GREEK GRAMMAR. — Messrs. CROCKER AND BREWSTER, Boston, have published in a neat and convenient form, Part I. of a Grammar of the Greek Language, by Prof. CROSBY of Dartmouth College, containing the elements of general grammar, the rules of Greek grammar, so far as they apply to the Attic and common dialects, and a series of tables illustrative of Greek inflections. It purports to be literally a *practical* grammar, the author having aimed, not to present a theory of the language, but to exhibit in the plainest manner the forms and constructions which occur in the Greek classic writers. The volume bears evidence of having been prepared and printed with the most praiseworthy care.

'AMENITIES OF LITERATURE.' — This latest work of the elder D'ISRAELI will well reward perusal. A mind like our author's, full of all imaginable information connected with whatever theme he may have in hand, is incapable of producing a dull work. A more industrious bibliopolist scarcely ever put pen to paper. His facility of composition and the copiousness of his illustrations will often remind the reader of old BURTON. The present work treats of 'authors, scattered through all the ranks of society, among the governors and the governed; the objects of their pursuits, as usually carried on by their peculiar idiosyncrasy; and the secret connexion of the incidents of their lives with their intellectual habits.' He has developed that predisposition which is ever working in characters of native force; their faculties and their failures; the fortunes which they have shaped for themselves; the history in short of the mind of the individual, which cannot be found in biographical dictionaries, and which constitutes the psychology of genius. The work is in two volumes; and commends itself scarcely less by the neatness which marks its externals — a characteristic, let us add, of books from the press of the publishers, the Messrs. LANGLEY — than by the voluminousness and variety of its contents.

'THE UNITED STATES' LITERARY ADVERTISER AND PUBLISHERS' CIRCULAR' is the title of a neatly printed register of literature, the fine arts, etc., issued on the fifteenth of every month by the Messrs. LANGLEY, Chatham-street. It is devoted to the interests of American booksellers and publishers, and is designed as a medium of communication between the several members of the trade. It comprises not only the advertisements and announcements of the several publishing houses, but includes an unusual amount of literary intelligence respecting new works in preparation, American and foreign, together with other occasional information connected with literature, etc. Beside being indispensable to every bookseller, it will prove, it is believed, scarcely less acceptable to literary men, members of book societies, public libraries, etc., throughout the country.

BUNYAN'S 'HOLY WAR.' — The American Sunday School Union have judged wisely in the publication of this celebrated work, which next to the 'Pilgrim's Progress' is the most widely known of any production of its author. The interest which its records excites seems to be ever new; as those may prove, by reading the book now who have perused it years ago. The warfare waged between the powers of Good and Evil, 'for the regaining of the Metropolis of the World, or the losing and taking again of the town of Mansoul,' will repay a score of perusals, and the last shall scarcely be less interesting than the first. A large number of good engravings illustrate the text of the American edition, which is on sale in New-York at Mr. J. C MEEKS's, 152 Nassau-street.

EDUCATION. — Our thanks are due to JAMES BROWN, Esq., of Oswego, for a '*Lecture on Education,*' delivered before the Mechanics' and Manufacturers' Association of that flourishing town in July last, and now published by request. We must do the writer the justice to say that he treats a subject which ninety-nine times in a hundred is the theme of labored Dullness, in a manner the most comprehensive; in language simple yet always striking, and often eloquent; enforcing his positions by apposite comparisons and felicitous illustrations; and pursuing his theme with evident knowledge and reach of thought into its most important ramifications. We are glad to have taken up this not very enticing little pamphlet, for it has 'that within which passeth show' in the matter of paper and typography.

'FRENCH AND ENGLISH READING-BOOK.' — This is a little volume consisting of stories from real life, with marked idioms and translations, by Miss ORAM, with signs for reading applied to the French, by A. J. FRONTIN, a professor of modern languages. Idioms or peculiarities of expression do not come within the province of grammarians, and are only noticed singly in dictionaries. As they can only be taught by expression, in the use of language, this little book, especially prepared for the purpose, can scarcely fail to be of great use to the learner. It is a neat little volume, published by Mr. WILLIAM A. COLMAN, Broadway.

'THE RETROSPECT: or Review of Providential Mercies, with Anecdotes of Various Characters,' is the title of a volume of some two hundred and fifty pages, which we find on our table from the press of Mr. ROBERT CARTER, 58 Canal-street. It is from the pen of an English gentleman, formerly a lieutenant in the Royal Navy, and now a minister in the Established Church. When we mention that the American issue is from the *seventeenth* London edition, our readers will infer that it must be a work of some attraction; and in this method of judging they are equally privileged with ourselves; since arduous professional labors have left us no moment for its perusal.

NEW POEMS BY MRS. SIGOURNEY. — We receive in season to *notice* but not to review a handsome volume from the press of the Brothers HARPER, entitled 'Pocahontas, and other Poems,' by Mrs. L. H. SIGOURNEY. The mere announcement of a work from this lady's pen will secure the ready attention of her countrymen to its pages; but our distant readers may desire to know more of our old contributor's latest offering, and that desire it will be our aim hereafter to gratify.

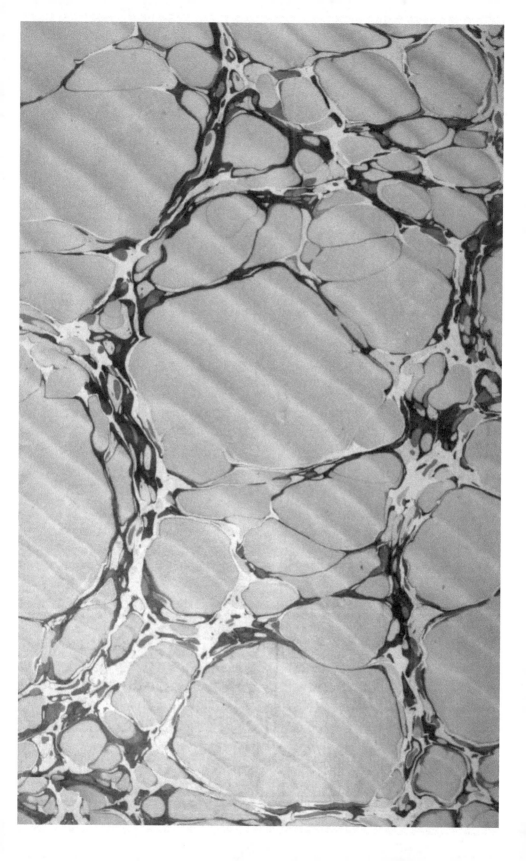

CPSIA information can be obtained
at www.ICGtesting.com
Printed in the USA
BVHW082345260819
556819BV00006B/958/P

9 781318 545940